FRENCH FOR MASTERY

Salut, les amis!

TEACHER'S EDITION

Jean-Paul Valette
Rebecca M. Valette

D. C. HEATH AND COMPANY
Lexington, Massachusetts   Toronto

Consultants
Charlotte Casgrain, Greenwich H.S., Greenwich, Connecticut
Karen Fritsche, Lincoln-Sudbury Regional H.S., Sudbury, Massachusetts
Natalie Goldschmidt, South Eugene H.S., Eugene, Oregon
Debra Griffin, Monnig Middle School, Fort Worth, Texas

Acknowledgments
In preparation for this revision, a survey was taken of teachers using the first edition of FRENCH
FOR MASTERY. The many questionnaires that were returned were very encouraging in their
positive evaluation of the program and very helpful in that they provided a direction for the
planning of the second edition. The authors would like to thank those who participated. We
also wish to thank the following teachers, who have used FRENCH FOR MASTERY, for
their special assistance in the project: Jane Carlin, Anne Craven, Pat McCann, Lillian
Scherban, and Maria Valis.

The authors would like to thank François Vergne for helping them assemble the realia which
appear in the text.

Project Editors	*Design and Production*
Roger Coulombe	Josephine McGrath, *Book Designer*
Valentia Dermer	Ann Rahimi-Assa, *Art Coordinator*
Anita Raducanu	Mel Dietmeier, *Illustrator*
Carol Shanahan	George Ulrich, *Map Illustrator*
Lawrence Lipson	Donna Lee Porter, *Production Coordinator*

D. C. Heath Consultants
Victoria Devlin
Teresa Carrera-Hanley

ii

The New Edition

We Listened to Teachers

During the preliminary planning of this completely new edition of FRENCH FOR MASTERY, teachers using the program were surveyed by mail and in personal interviews. The results of these surveys were both encouraging and helpful. They were encouraging in that the great majority of teachers of FRENCH FOR MASTERY reported that the program works for them in the classroom — its careful organization and pacing helps give students a real sense of satisfaction and success in learning about the language, and, more importantly, in learning how to use it. According to the teachers, the specific elements of the program that enhance its teachability are material of high-interest level to young learners; simple, straightforward grammar explanations; presentation of both "big-c" and "small-c" culture; and exercise material in situational contexts.

Also, the results of these surveys were extremely helpful in providing a direction for the planning of this new edition. Suggestions for changes most commonly requested by teachers included:

- an earlier introduction of high-utility vocabulary such as dates, time, numbers, weather expressions
- an earlier introduction of **-ir** and **-re** verbs
- an earlier introduction of the **passé composé**
- a more realistic first-year grammar load
- a greater variety of exercise material
- more cultural reading material
- more flexible ancillary material

In response to these suggestions, you will find in *Salut, les amis!*, the first book in the new FRENCH FOR MASTERY:

- *A new and greatly expanded Prélude.* Six short lessons now introduce and practice high utility vocabulary and expressions such as: greetings, introductions, expressions of time, weather expressions, numbers, and dates.

- *An earlier introduction of all present tense verb forms.* All regular present tense verb conjugations are now introduced by the end of Unit 4. In the previous edition, **-re** verbs were presented in Unit 6 and **-ir** verbs in Unit 7.
- *An earlier introduction of the passé composé.* The **passé composé** is now introduced in Unit 6, rather than in Unit 9.
- *A more realistic grammatical progression.* The presentation of double-object pronouns, the relative pronouns **qui** and **que**, and the future tense have been shifted to the second book. (Students can still talk about future events by using the near future, Unit 3.)
- *More challenging exercise material.* Sentence building exercises (*Un jeu*) have been added throughout *Salut, les amis!* to vary the exercise format and challenge the students.
- *Sections Magazines, expanded cultural reading material.* The *Images* sections have been completely redesigned and rewritten and are now called *Sections Magazines.* The *Sections Magazines* are graded cultural readers fully integrated into the vocabulary and structural progression of the text.
- *More useful and more flexible ancillary material.* For greater flexibility, the *Tests de contrôle* have been moved to the Workbook. Activity Masters have been added to the program to provide the teacher with duplicating masters containing answer forms for the tape exercises; the music and lyrics of the unit songs; games; reading activities; active vocabulary lists; and lists of useful expressions. And the program now includes a boxed set of Overhead Transparencies.

We think you and your students will enjoy using the new FRENCH FOR MASTERY. We listened.

Jean-Paul Valette
Rebecca M. Valette

iii

Introduction

The Teacher's Edition for FRENCH FOR MASTERY is an enlarged version of the Student Text. The front matter consists of four parts: a description of the characteristics and organization of the FRENCH FOR MASTERY program; suggestions about how to use the various components of the program; hints on how to supplement the basic materials; and a Reference Guide containing useful classroom expressions and a detailed listing of the contents of the program.

In the textbook itself, an overprint of small, blue type provides teachers with several kinds of information:

- Unit summaries of the main grammatical, vocabulary, and cultural objectives
- Supplementary questions on the *Presentation texts*
- Supplementary grammatical information
- Supplementary cultural information
- Supplementary vocabulary
- Suggestions for expanding and modifying exercises
- Suggested realia to enliven the presentation of culture
- Suggested optional activities
- Responses to all *Observations* questions
- Material designated as optional

It is important to note here that the term "optional" does not mean that the material should be left out. It simply designates material which can be adapted or omitted according to the specific objectives of the class, and/or which can be assigned as supplementary material for the better student or for the student who has a particular interest in the topic.

The following symbol is used in the overprint to designate material recorded on the Tape Program: ⊙━ .

The key **Str. A, B, C,** or **D** is used to cross-reference the *Observations* to the *Structure* section(s) to which they correspond.

Contents

v

Part One
Description of FRENCH FOR MASTERY

1. General Characteristics of the Program

A complete program for junior/senior high school students, FRENCH FOR MASTERY consists of three books, each accompanied by the following components:

- Teacher's Edition
- Workbook
- Tape Program (on cassettes as well as reels)
- Tapescript
- Testing Program

In addition, Books 1 and 2 are accompanied by Activity Masters. Book 1 is also accompanied by Overhead Transparencies. The core program is contained in the Student Text and the Teacher's Edition. The other components can be considered optional.

1.1 Objectives and Philosophy

The basic objectives of FRENCH FOR MASTERY are:

- to help each student attain proficiency in the four skills of listening, speaking, reading, and writing within a minimum period of time and in a way that makes language-learning seem effortless; and
- to present the language within the context of the contemporary French-speaking world and its culture.

In pursuing this goal, the authors have adopted a pragmatic approach and purposely have avoided relying on any one linguistic theory of language-learning. Their guiding principle has been that the material in itself should elicit a high level of student participation in the learning process. To this end, they have evaluated a variety of pedagogical techniques and have selected those that have produced the best results inside and outside the classroom situation. This interweaving and integration of techniques is at the heart of FRENCH FOR MASTERY. Teachers can adapt the program to their own teaching styles and to the needs of their own students.

1.2 Key Features

1.2.1 Broad cultural focus. In FRENCH FOR MASTERY, the cultural material is integrated into the learning process so that students attain an awareness of French culture as they read, study structures, and do the activities. In addition, there are segments of the program designed specifically to emphasize French culture:

1

- the *Note culturelle* of each lesson
- the four, full-color, illustrated sections in the text entitled *Section Magazine*
- the *Récréation culturelle* sections of the Workbook
- the photographs and realia presented throughout the text

From the beginning of the program, the students are exposed to the geographic, ethnic, and cultural variety of the French-speaking world, from Louisiana to the Ivory Coast, from Tahiti to Tunisia. For many students, this awareness will open a new dimension in their studies and stimulate their interest in learning French.

1.2.2 Accent on youth. An effective way of involving students in the learning of a foreign language is to make communication in the new language relevant to their own lives and subculture. The majority of the activities in this program have youth-related themes: hobbies, travel, schoolwork, dating, choice of career, relationships with parents, and attitudes toward love, friendship, money, success, and failure.

1.2.3 Adaptability of the program. FRENCH FOR MASTERY can be used in a variety of teaching situations:
- large or small classes
- slow or fast tracks
- audio-lingual or more traditional classes

The program is also adaptable to small-group teaching and lends itself to individualized and self-paced instruction. Part Two of this manual will suggest the various approaches available to the teacher in the presentation of the material.

1.2.4 Several approaches to grammar. Because there is no one way of teaching a foreign language, FRENCH FOR MASTERY incorporates several classroom-proven approaches to the presentation of French structures:

- *Guided discovery approach.* The new structures in each lesson are presented in key sentences in the *Presentation text* that begins each lesson. The *Conversation/ Observations* section that follows presents a limited number of short questions that pertain to the new structures. The questions are phrased in such a way that the students formulate their own generalizations about the new material.
- *Descriptive approach.* In the *Structure* sections the new material is explained in English and, where appropriate, presented graphically with examples and related exercises. These sections also serve as a grammar reference manual.
- *Modified contrastive approach.* When appropriate, new structures are compared and contrasted with previously learned French structures or with English equivalents. Areas of potential interference between French and English are mentioned explicitly: see, for example, Lesson 3.3, where in discussing the formation of the possessive, the difference in word order in French and in English is shown.
- *Analytic-synthetic approach.* More complex points of grammar are introduced across two or more lessons in minimal learning steps. Finally the entire pattern is summarized.

1.2.5 Variety in the learning material. Variety in presentation as well as in the content of the material is an essential element in fostering and maintaining student interest. Throughout FRENCH FOR MASTERY this feature has been given particular attention. For instance, instead of relying exclusively on dialogs, the lessons are also built around narratives, questionnaires, a datebook, or a scene from a play. Similarly, the exercises encompass a wide variety of formats, such as role-playing activities, *Questions personnelles*, open-ended sentences requiring a personal completion, and *Un jeu*, in which students match words to create sentences.

1.2.6 Focus on communication. To elicit the students' active participation in the learning process, all exercises of FRENCH FOR MASTERY, including those of the Tape Program and the Workbook, are set in situational contexts. The situations may be practical, such as planning a trip, answering an ad in the newspaper, or selecting items from a menu. Sometimes the situations are humorous; the students may be asked to play the role of an angel or a devil, or to react to a date being late. The purpose of these contextual exercises is to induce the students to use French in communication and self-expression rather than as a rote response to artificial drill stimuli.

1.2.7 Flexibility and efficiency in developing language skills. The language is presented and practiced through all four language skills. However, because of the variety of teaching materials included in FRENCH FOR MASTERY, the teacher may wish to focus on only one or two skills. For instance, if speaking is to be high-lighted, the teacher can stress the communication activities of the program: *Questions personnelles*, role-playing activities, the *Conversation* activity following each *Presentation*, and the oral *Entre nous* sections of the Student Text as well as the *Speaking* and *Conversation* activities of the Tape Program. The teacher could also use the *Récréation culturelle* sections in the Workbook to promote conversation.

Each skill is developed in its several aspects. For instance, for reading, many types of materials are presented: *Presentation texts*, *Notes culturelles, Entre nous* segments, and *Sections Magazines.* A similar scope of development characterizes the listening activities of the Tape Program, which involve active listening to recorded material from the Student Text, selective listening for grammatical signals such as verb tenses, gender, or number, and general listening comprehension of unfamiliar passages.

1.2.8 Logical organization. The learning pace is carefully programmed through a concise, measured grammatical progression. The presentation of the simpler and more frequently used structures precedes that of the more complex and less common ones. Each lesson in FRENCH FOR MASTERY concentrates on two to four aspects of grammar, and the amount of new vocabulary is carefully controlled. The introductory *Presentation text* of the lesson incorporates the new material into the context of previously mastered patterns and structures. Any unknown words are glossed in the margin or presented in the vocabulary section immediately following the *Presentation text.*

1.2.9 Systematic reentry of grammar and vocabulary. All vocabulary introduced in the *Vocabulaire pratique,* in the *Vocabulaire spécialisé,* and in the *Expressions pour la conversation / composition* is active, as are all the *Structures*; that is, the students should have control of this vocabulary in communicative situations. Lists of these words and expressions by unit appear in the Activity Masters. Passive vocabulary, for recognition only, is glossed when it appears and is also included in the French-English end vocabulary.

As the program progresses, the structures and vocabulary items are reentered in the exercises and reading materials. Suggestions for reviewing the structures and vocabulary are made in the overprint if the mastery of these elements is a requisite for learning the new material of the lesson.

All basic aspects of grammar and active vocabulary are incorporated in the *Tests de contrôle* that are found at the end of the Workbook. The teacher may use these tests informally for review if desired.

Book 2 of FRENCH FOR MASTERY, *Tous ensemble,* opens with a systematic review, in new contexts, of all important material presented in Book 1. Therefore, second-year students who have not completed Book 1 or who have used material other than FRENCH FOR MASTERY can confidently begin the second year with the material in Book 2.

1.2.10 Emphasis on French. FRENCH FOR MASTERY has been written in such a way that French may be used almost exclusively. The expanded *Prélude* section provides basic vocabulary and structure in context so that students can use French from the very first day. French names (pp. iv–v) and classroom expressions (see Part Four of this Teacher's Edition or the Activity Masters) should be introduced at the beginning of the course. The use of English in the book gradually diminishes. However, the *Observations* questions and the grammatical explanations in the *Structure* sections are in English throughout to prevent possible misunderstandings and to ensure that all students may use them for out-of-class reference and study.

1.2.11 Naturalness of the language. Language presented to beginning students must be simple, yet it must also be natural and idiomatic. The apparent conflict between simplicity and authenticity is resolved in FRENCH FOR MASTERY by the addition of *Expressions pour la conversation* and *Expressions pour la composition* in the *Entre nous* sections that end each lesson. In these sections, the students learn authentic, common expressions through dialog and composition practice. Expressions introduced in this way (e.g., **Eh bien!, Zut alors!, Tiens!, Dis donc!**) are then reentered in the *Presentation texts* of subsequent lessons.

2. Organization of FRENCH FOR MASTERY

The following pages describe *Salut, les amis!,* the first of the three books of FRENCH FOR MASTERY, 2nd edition.

2.1 The Student Text

The Student Text contains a preliminary unit (**Prélude**), eight basic units, and four illustrated cultural sections (**Section Magazine**). The book concludes with appendices, a complete French-English Vocabulary, and an active English-French Vocabulary.

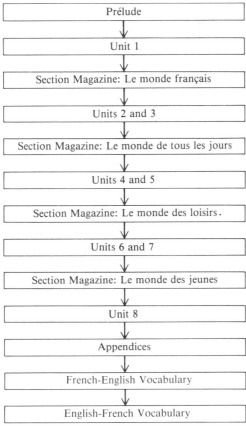

| Prélude |
| Unit 1 |
| Section Magazine: Le monde français |
| Units 2 and 3 |
| Section Magazine: Le monde de tous les jours |
| Units 4 and 5 |
| Section Magazine: Le monde des loisirs. |
| Units 6 and 7 |
| Section Magazine: Le monde des jeunes |
| Unit 8 |
| Appendices |
| French-English Vocabulary |
| English-French Vocabulary |

2.1.1 Organization of a unit. Each unit is built around a particular theme, such as hobbies, other leisure-time activities, shopping, and friendships. It is divided into five basic lessons that present the new structures and vocabulary of the unit.

2.1.2 Organization of a basic lesson. Each basic lesson consists of three parts: the presentation material, the instruction material, and the recombination material. The diagram shows the construction of a typical lesson.

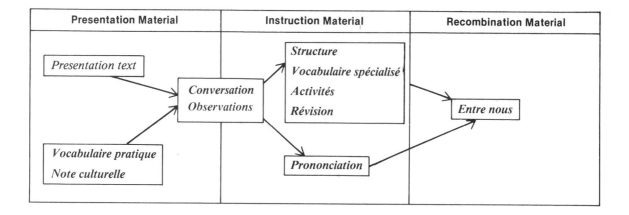

Presentation Material	Instruction Material	Recombination Material

Presentation text

Vocabulaire pratique
Note culturelle

Conversation
Observations

Structure
Vocabulaire spécialisé
Activités
Révision

Prononciation

Entre nous

- *The Presentation Material.* The function of the *Presentation text* is to introduce, in context, samples of the basic structures and vocabulary taught in the lesson. The context may assume a variety of formats:

  — A dialog (**Un garçon génial** — Lesson 7.2)

  — A conversation with the reader or a playlet (**En vacances** — Lesson 1.5)

  — A narrative (**Marie-Noëlle** — Lesson 3.2)

  — A personality questionnaire (**Êtes-vous sociable?** — Lesson 7.5)

The *Presentation text* is built on previously learned material plus the new structures and vocabulary of the lesson. Words that the students do not know are glossed or appear in the *Vocabulaire pratique/spécialisé* that immediately follows the *Presentation.*

The *Note culturelle* is a short reading passage about an aspect of French culture. It is derived from a reference in the *Presentation text.* For example, in Lesson 4.2, after a dialog with two girls looking at clothes, the *Note culturelle* describes French fashion and how teenagers dress.

The *Conversation/Observations* section links the *Presentation text* and the instruction material. Through the carefully sequenced *Observations* questions, the students are able to generalize about the new grammatical material of the lesson.

- *The Instruction Material.* In the *Structure* section, new grammar is explained in a simple, clear, and schematic manner. Immediately after the grammar explanations the rules are applied in situational exercises.

The exercises assume a variety of formats:

  — Situational activities, which require transformation skills
  — *Questions personnelles*, which are yes/no and open-ended questions about the student's life. These incorporate the new grammatical structures of the lesson while reviewing previously learned structures.

  — Open-ended sentences, which students complete with personal information

  — Given situations from which students draw conclusions

  — *Un jeu*, a recombination drill game in which the students are asked to derive as many logical sentences as they can from a given set of elements containing the new grammatical structures

All of these activities can be done either orally or in writing.

The vocabulary items in the *Vocabulaire spécialisé* are grouped thematically (sports, family, food, clothing) for ease in assimilation. Where feasible, the items are presented in a pictorial or sentence context.

The *Prononciation* sections, which are recorded in the Tape Program, introduce new sounds, intonation patterns, and spelling. As the course progresses, specific elements are reentered for practice or further explanation. For easy reference and to prepare students to use French-language dictionaries, the sounds are transcribed in the International Phonetic Alphabet.

• *The Recombination Material.* The *Entre nous* sections reinforce the new material of the lesson and help students further develop specific communication skills.

In the *Prélude*, in Units 1 through 5, and in Unit 7, the *Entre nous* sections contain *Mini-dialogues* and *L'art du dialogue* which reinforce conversation skills through dramatization and directed dialog.

The *Entre nous* sections of Units 6 and 8 reinforce writing skills through segments entitled *L'art de la composition, L'art de la correspondance,* and *À votre tour*.

All *Entre nous* sections contain a subsection, *Expressions pour la conversation/composition,* which provides the students with conversational fillers useful in developing natural communication skills.

2.1.3 Section Magazine. Four separate, full-color sections in the text, the *Sections Magazines* focus on the contemporary French-speaking world and specifically include material on young people and their interests. The students assimilate culture through exposure to illustrations, photographs, and varied readings in an exciting magazine format.

CONTENTS	
Section Magazine 1	**Le monde français**
Section Magazine 2	**Le monde de tous les jours**
Section Magazine 3	**Le monde des loisirs**
Section Magazine 4	**Le monde des jeunes**

Since the *Sections Magazines* are entirely in French, they serve as an aid in developing reading skills. The various illustrations, photographs, and realia also provide points of departure for conversation. The cultural projects at the end of each *Section Magazine* suggest further areas of study. In addition, the Activity Masters contain Reading Activities based on the *Section Magazine* material.

2.1.4 End matter. The end matter contains the following elements:

• Appendices
    Appendix 1 — Sound-spelling Correspondences
    Appendix 2 — Numbers
    Appendix 3 — Verbs
• French-English Vocabulary

This vocabulary lists all words in the text, except obvious passive cognates. Each word and expression considered "active" is followed by a reference number that provides the unit and lesson number where the word or expression first appeared actively in the text.

- English-French Vocabulary

This vocabulary lists only the active words and expressions: those from the *Vocabulaire pratique, Vocabulaire spécialisé, Expressions pour la conversation/ composition,* and *Structure* sections. Each entry in this vocabulary has a unit and lesson number referring the reader to the first active usage in the text.

2.2 The Tape Program

The Tape Program for FRENCH FOR MASTERY is designed to supplement the Student Text, providing additional practice in the development of audio-lingual skills.

2.2.1 General description. The Tape Program for FRENCH FOR MASTERY is available on dual-track 5-inch reels or on cassettes. The Tape Program for each lesson runs approximately 25 minutes. All the activities in the Tape Program, together with the correct oral and written responses, are printed in the Tapescript, a separate booklet available to the teacher.

2.2.2 Types of tape activities. The tape for each lesson contains a variety of activities. These are introduced in English so that all students may work independently with the Tape Program. The activities include the following categories:

- *Listening.* The students listen to an unpaused, dramatized reading of the *Presentation text* and to a reading of the *Note culturelle.*
- *Listening and Repeating.* (1) The speaker models words and sentences from the *Prononciation* sections of the Student Text. The students repeat these in the pauses provided. (2) The speaker models words from selected vocabulary, verb, and grammar charts of the Student Text. When the chart contains both words and sentences in which the words are used, the students repeat the words and listen to the sentences.
- *Listening for Signals.* The students hear a series of sentences and are asked to discriminate among sounds that signal grammatical information, such as singular or plural, masculine or feminine, past or present. Students mark their responses on the grids provided in the Activity Masters. When needed, or when a new activity format occurs, models are supplied. At the end the speaker gives the correct answers.
- *Listening Comprehension with Visual Cues.* The students see illustrations and hear several statements pertaining to them. They may be asked to match the statements with the illustrations, to indicate whether the statements are true based on the information in the visual, or to complete the illustrations based on the clues given in the sentences. For example, the students see detailed portraits, hear a corresponding number of descriptions, and decide which descriptions go with which persons. The students also indicate whether they understand specific words or expressions heard on the tape. This type of exercise is used chiefly to practice numbers and other specialized vocabulary.

• *Speaking.* (1) Directed activities: The students participate in situation drills similar, but not identical, to the activities in the Student Text. These provide variety in oral practice while helping to develop listening comprehension skills. In these activities each cue is followed by a pause for the student response. Then the speaker on the tape gives a confirmation of the appropriate response. (2) Open-ended activities: The speaker asks the students personal questions that incorporate the structures and vocabulary introduced in the lesson. Because the students give original answers, no corrective response is given on the tape.

• *Dictation.* The students listen to short sentences and write down what they hear. Write-on lines are provided in the Activity Masters.

• *French Songs.* Each unit features a traditional French song. The melody serves as a recurrent theme heard at the beginning of the tape and at selected intervals. At the end of each unit, the entire song is sung in French. Music and lyrics for student participation are printed in the Activity Masters.

2.3 The Workbook

The Workbook supplements the Student Text. In addition to providing written exercises to accompany the basic instructional material of the Student Text, each unit of the Workbook contains an illustrated cultural section entitled *Récréation culturelle.* The *Tests de côntrole* are also included in the Workbook.

2.3.1 Written exercises. For each basic lesson of the Student Text, the Workbook contains two to four pages of written exercises in situational contexts. Each lesson begins on a right-hand page so that students can tear out specific pages to hand in if the teacher so requests.

To avoid monotony and to stimulate the students' interest, all basic exercises are set in situational or game contexts. Most exercises require thoughtful rather than mechanical answers. Where appropriate, the activities are based on visual cues.

2.3.2 *Récréation culturelle.* Each Workbook unit ends with a section called *Récréation culturelle.* This section contains realia with related activities. The realia reinforce the cultural themes developed in the unit.

2.3.3 *Tests de contrôle. Tests de contrôle* are included in the Workbook. These tests consist of a series of situational review exercises. The students take these tests on their own and check their responses against the Answer Key at the back of the Workbook. The Answer Key contains an *Interpretation* section to help students evaluate their results and to refer them back to sections of the unit for further study if they get a prescribed number of wrong answers on any given point of structure. The *Tests de contrôle* sections were intentionally designed to be relatively simple in order to give students a feeling of achievement. These sections prepare them for the corresponding unit tests in the FRENCH FOR MASTERY Testing Program.

2.4 The Activity Masters

The FRENCH FOR MASTERY Activity Masters are a set of duplicating masters that include the following teaching aids:

- Tape Program Material
  - Tape Activity Sheets containing the answer grids and visual cues for the *Listening for Signals* and *Listening Comprehension* activities; write-on lines for the *Dictation* activities; the music and lyrics of the unit songs
- Non-Tape Program Material
  - Games for enjoyment and a change of pace
  - Reading Activities to accompany the *Sections Magazines*
  - Active Vocabulary Sheets by unit for reference and review
  - Useful Expressions, including Classroom Expressions and Expressions for the *Activités* (reprinted from the Teacher's Edition)

2.5 The Testing Program

The FRENCH FOR MASTERY Testing Program offers three types of testing materials: *Lesson Quizzes, Unit Tests,* and *Achievement Tests.* The tests are printed on duplicating masters (with overprinted answers for the teacher), and the listening portions are recorded on cassettes. A Test Guide accompanies the Testing Program.

2.5.1 Lesson Quizzes. The *Lesson Quiz*, designed to be administered in about 20 minutes, permits a quick and frequent evaluation of the students' mastery of the structures and vocabulary of a lesson. The test items are based on tape, visual, or printed-word cues, to allow for all possible learning styles. A Student Progress Chart (on a duplicating master) allows the teacher to keep track of each student's progress.

2.5.2 Unit Tests. The *Unit Test*, designed to be administered in about 45 minutes, focuses on the content of the unit and also evaluates communication skills. The test items, more varied than in the *Lesson Quizzes*, emphasize the elements of language.

2.5.3 Achievement Tests. The Testing Program provides two *Achievement Tests* (to follow Units 4 and 8), each designed to be administered over two 45-minute class periods. Broader in scope than the *Unit Tests,* the *Achievement Tests* go beyond the elements of language and focus on the listening, reading, and writing skills.

2.6 The Overhead Transparencies

The FRENCH FOR MASTERY program includes a boxed set of 39 Overhead Transparencies. Each transparency comes with a reverse-image master for making additional one-color transparencies. In this way, each teacher can have a set.

The Overhead Transparencies have been designed to teach and reinforce vocabulary; to practice essential verb forms; to introduce the students to the geography of the French-speaking world; to serve as a basis for oral compositions; and to help the teacher avoid the use of English in the classroom.

Part Two
Using FRENCH FOR MASTERY

3. Suggested Techniques

A basic characteristic of the FRENCH FOR MASTERY program is its flexibility. The classroom teacher can easily adapt the textbook and its related components to the needs and learning styles of the students. Each unit of FRENCH FOR MASTERY contains more activities than can be completed by the average class. The teacher should therefore select those that are most appropriate for specific classes and specific individuals. The purpose of this section is to help the teacher make these choices by showing how each of the components may be used. The suggestions are not exhaustive, but they form a base upon which the teacher may wish to build.

3.1 Using French in the Classroom

With the communicative tools and approach provided in FRENCH FOR MASTERY, students can use French in classroom interaction from the very beginning.

• The *Prélude,* the first six lessons of the text, provides basic French vocabulary that students are anxious to learn and that they need for basic communication: names, greetings, numbers, and information on telling time, giving the date, and talking about the weather.

• The teacher can copy the Classroom Expressions, found in this Teacher's Edition, and distribute the list to the class for communicating everyday classroom needs. This list is also in the Activity Masters, and teachers who have this component may run it off for easy distribution.

• The interrogative forms for yes/no questions and information questions are presented in Unit 1.

3.2 The First Day of Class

The goal of the first day of class should be to stimulate interest in French language and culture as well as to show that learning French is a profitable and not overwhelming task. The following suggestions can be used in whole or in part to plan the first day's lesson.

• Show the breadth and diversity of the French-speaking world. The map on pp. vi-vii is a good starting point.

• Explain that France played a role in the development of our country. (Check encyclopedias and American history textbooks for information about French people who influenced American history.)

11

• Explain that close to our country and even *within* our country there are large concentrations of French-speaking people—the province of Quebec in Canada, parts of Louisiana, and the northern New England states. (See *Note culturelle* on p. 43.)

• Show French influence in the names of American cities. (See *Section Magazine 1* p. 84.)

• Show the linguistic relationship between French and English. (*Section Magazine 1* pp. 80-89 includes a large number of French/English cognates.) Students will feel that they already know some French.

• Explain that knowing French can be an asset when looking for a job. (See *Section Magazine 1* pp. 86-87.)

3.3 Suggestions for Teaching the Basic Lessons

3.3.1 Using the Presentation text.
The *Presentation* is not intended for memorization, but rather for initial exposure to the basic structures of the lesson and as a point of departure for other activities. This material is available as an unpaused, dramatized recording in the Tape Program. The *Presentation text* can be used in the following ways:

• The students listen to an unpaused version either on the tape provided in the Tape Program or as read by the teacher.

— *With books open following the text.* In this way students see if they can understand the spoken word well enough to follow it in their texts. Students also hear the correct pronunciation as they are seeing the words.

— *With the books closed before having seen the text.* The teacher could pause or stop the tape at various intervals to ask questions. For a shorter presentation, the teacher could wait until the students have heard the entire text before stopping the tape or the reading.

• The teacher presents the *Vocabulaire pratique* or corresponding *Vocabulaire spécialisé* before the students hear the *Presentation* so that they will know the new vocabulary. Or, with faster groups, the teacher asks if the students can guess the new words from their contexts.

• The students perform various activities based on the *Presentation texts.*

— The students act out conversational *Presentation texts* by taking various parts.

— The students dramatize the text as the tape is being played.

— The students guess from illustrations what is going to happen and explain it in French as well as they can. They then listen to the tape and see what actually happens.

— The students use the illustrations to make up different stories.

— The students bring in visuals — posters, maps, original drawings — explain them and how they are related to the *Presentation,* and hang them on the bulletin board.

— Students prepare their own skits based on the situations of the *Presentations.*

— At the end of the lesson, the students reread, summarize, or enact the *Presentation* so that they can see how much they have learned.

3.3.2 Using the *Note culturelle.* The purpose of the *Note culturelle* is twofold: to awaken students to the culture of the French-speaking world, and to stimulate and reinforce the students' reading comprehension.

• If the cultural note relates to a topic that the teacher wishes to emphasize, the students may listen to the recording, learn the new vocabulary, read the note aloud, and summarize the information in French. A study of France would not be complete, for example, without a discussion of French cuisine. The cultural notes of Unit 4, Lesson 4 and Unit 8, Lesson 4 provide points of departure for such a discussion.

• The teacher and students could bring in photos or other materials relating to the topic of the cultural note. For example, the teacher might want to make a bulletin board display of French-speaking students and their schools. The *Note culturelle* on **Le lycée** in Unit 8, Lesson 1 would be a natural tie-in to such a display.

• Other notes may be used primarily for reading practice, for listening comprehension, or assigned as homework.

• When assigned as homework, the teacher may also ask the students to prepare true/false items or comprehension quizzes for other members of the class.

3.3.3 Using the *Conversation/Observations.* The questions of the *Conversation* allow the students to use some of the new structures of the lesson: they also serve as a springboard to the *Observations* segment, which in turn leads to the *Structure* sections.

In going over the *Observations* sections with the students, the teacher may ask them to open their textbooks to the appropriate page. In many lessons it is also possible, and sometimes preferable, to show the *Conversation* sentences on the chalkboard, on a chart, or on an overhead transparency. In this way, the teacher can more readily point to specific features of the sentences, drawing the students' attention to those points under discussion. If the sentences are reproduced on larger visuals, color or boxing may replace the boldface used in the text.

3.3.4 Teaching structure. In the *Structure* sections, each grammar point is presented with succinct explanations in English, with examples in French and, where appropriate, with illustrations. These descriptions, however, are intended to serve as reference sections, because in most classes the teacher will first introduce the grammar of the lesson orally. This oral introduction to the grammar may be done in one of the following ways:

• The teacher may introduce the structure in the context of the *Presentation text.*

• The teacher may prefer to begin with the *Conversation/Observations,* the inductive teaching tool that is already prepared for them.

• To increase student motivation, the teacher may begin by explaining why the students need to know the structure. For example, in Unit 3, Lesson 1, the teacher may explain to the student that someone may ask what she or he is going to do to-morrow. To answer in French, the student needs to know the construction **aller +** infinitive.

• For some students, it helps to present certain structures with props. For example, in order to teach **avoir** in Unit 2, Lesson 2, teachers might have items on their desks or in their pockets and ask the students questions about these items.

• When students learn a new structure, the teacher should have them practice with the *Listening for Signals* activities in the Tape Program until they can hear differences, in gender and in number, for example. Some students may need to play these tape activities repeatedly until they can recognize the new forms easily.

3.3.5 Using the *Activités*.
After the teacher presents the structure orally, the student must internalize it. It is at this point that differences in learning rate and learning mode become most apparent. In order to accommodate these differences, FRENCH FOR MASTERY provides many kinds of learning activities — more than any one teacher would be likely to use in a year. These cover a wide range, from simple to more challenging. They are also in a variety of formats so that students who need extra practice in a given structure will not be repeating the same kinds of activities. These learning activities are in the text, with variations suggested in the overprint of the Teacher's Edition, as well as in the Workbook and Tape Program.

Students learn new structures by practicing them in role-playing or situational exercises and by using the language for personal expression. In FRENCH FOR MASTERY, students are never given a series of unrelated sentences to transform; they always practice new structures in a situational context.

Types of Activities

Simple situational activities. The first activity after the oral presentation of a structure is usually a simple situational activity requiring a transformation. Students of all levels should do this first activity.

• The teacher could give the situation and cues while the students give responses with their books closed. It is better if the teacher gives the cue before mentioning the student's name so that everyone will pay attention.

• Students could break into pairs or small groups and cue each other for responses.

Questions personnelles and open-ended sentences. These are either yes/no questions, information questions, or open-ended sentences that require students to use French for personal expression.

• The teacher may ask these of several students individually in order to receive a variety of responses. Again, the question should be asked before calling on a student to answer it.

• Teachers should foster communication by encouraging students to listen to each other. When teachers ask questions, they should not repeat the students' responses but should check to see that other students are listening. For example: Teacher: **"Jean-Michel, à quelle heure dînez-vous?"** After Jean-Michel answers, the teacher calls on another student. Teacher: **"Anne, à quelle heure dîne Jean-Michel?"** If Anne cannot answer, the teacher tells her to ask Jean-Michel. In this type of activity, the students learn to listen to each other as they practice different personal pronouns, verb forms, structures, and vocabulary.

• The *Questions personnelles* also lend themselves to working in pairs. One student might ask another student a question and write the response. They could then switch roles.

• The teacher may prefer to assign these personal activities as written homework since the responses will be different. The teacher would then correct the papers individually and have the students rewrite the sentences that have errors.

• For an in-class writing activity, one student could give a response, which the other class members would write.

Un jeu. This activity requires a knowledge of the structure and basic vocabulary of the lesson. It is also challenging and fun for the students. In it they must use the words given in the three or four columns of the activity to create logical, grammatically correct sentences.

• As an oral activity, each student could be called upon to create a sentence. Other students could judge it for logic and correctness.

• As a special challenge, students may compete to see who can write the greatest number of logical, correct sentences within a given time frame, such as five or ten minutes.

3.3.6 Teaching vocabulary. One teacher may present vocabulary as it occurs in the *Presentation text* and the *Structure* sections. Another teacher may prefer to use the visuals of the unit to teach the words without reference to English. Still another teacher may rely more heavily on the groupings in the *Vocabulaire pratique, Vocabulaire spécialisé, Structure,* and *Expressions pour la conversation/composition.* These sections comprise all of the active vocabulary and use art, thematic grouping, and words in context to aid in vocabulary acquisition.

The vocabulary is reentered in activities and readings so that student progression through the text will reinforce its assimilation.

• Vocabulary learning is another place in which students could participate by the creation of collages. The *Vocabulaire spécialisé* on **Pays et nationalités** in Unit 2, Lesson 4 provides a wide range of possibilities for photos.

• There are numerous games that the teacher may play with the students in class to teach, build, and review vocabulary. For some possibilities, the teacher should see the game section in Part Three of this Teacher's Edition.

• The teacher may ask the students to write compositions or to prepare skits using new words. For example, when the class is studying the parts of the body (*Vocabulaire spécialisé* in Unit 6, Lesson 1), two students could play the roles of consulting doctors trying to obtain information from a patient, played by a third student.

• Visuals in the text are a source of variety in practicing vocabulary. The teacher could pick a line drawing or a photo from an earlier unit and have the students describe it. Or one student could describe a portion of the illustration as other students try to guess what the object is. The drawing of four people at the dinner table in Unit

5, Lesson 2 (p. 235) provides rich opportunities for vocabulary practice on food, utensils, and clothing. Students could also use this type of drawing to practice adverbs, adjectives, or prepositions of place.

• For the convenience of teachers in preparing additional materials, the active vocabulary is listed by unit in the Activity Masters.

3.3.7 Teaching pronunciation. Each lesson of the Student Text concludes with a *Prononciation* section that focuses on particular sounds, linkings, or intonation. However, it is very important that students understand that they cannot separate pronunciation from the rest of their study of French any more than they can separate structure or vocabulary. Students must hear and be encouraged to communicate in correct French whenever possible, hearing and imitating not only the sounds but the intonation patterns of French speakers.

The *Prélude* of the text is important in the teaching of pronunciation, not only because it represents the students' first exposure to the study of French, but also because it introduces the students to small but significant slices of the French language. As the teacher (or the tape) models the greetings, introductions, and sentences, the students must be encouraged to imitate as accurately as possible. At the outset of instruction the teacher should also insist on correct rhythm and stress patterns.

In the *Prononciation* sections, the sounds to be practiced are given in phonetic transcription. The teacher need not teach the International Phonetic Alphabet nor bring the students' attention to the complete alphabet in Appendix 1 unless the class expresses a definite interest. Even then it is unwise to present the entire alphabet at once; it is better to limit it to a few symbols, using some of the words the students know as examples.

Occasionally the *Prononciation* sections compare French sounds to related English sounds. You may wish to explain to students that French vowels and consonants are generally sharper and more tense than their English counterparts. All the *Prononciation* sections are recorded in the Tape Program so that the students may practice specific sounds by themselves.

3.3.8 Using the *Entre nous*. The *Entre nous* section, found at the end of each lesson, emphasizes a particular communication skill: conversation in the *Prélude* and Units 1, 2, 3, 4, 5, and 7; composition in Lessons 1-4 of Unit 6; and correspondence in Lesson 5 of Unit 6. Teachers may use these sections as they occur in the lessons or wait until the end of the unit and use these sections as part of a review.

• If the teacher uses these at the end of the unit, the class can be divided into five groups, giving each group an *Entre nous* activity to develop. Each group could then share its results with the rest of the class.

• Students may write new dialogs based on suggestions given in *L'art du dialogue* sections. For example, *L'art du dialogue* in Lesson 2 of Unit 5 suggests that students act out a new dialog keeping the same situation but changing the menu. The students would then be practicing food vocabulary and making other appropriate changes, as they gained confidence in pronunciation and sentence formation.

- For the guided compositions and letters, the students may write individually or in small groups using **je** or **nous** forms, as appropriate.
- The *Entre nous* sections may be used as practice for the faster learners while the teacher helps other students with problems they have in the unit.

3.4 Using the *Section Magazine*

The purpose of the *Sections Magazines* is, first and foremost, to interest and engage the students and encourage them to explore French culture and civilization. These sections also furnish additional reading practice and provide the basis for discussions and mini-speeches in French. They should be considered optional and supplementary to the units.

- At all stages of instruction, the *Sections Magazines* can be used to reinforce oral communication skills. In the beginning, simple questions can be asked about the passage and/or the illustrations, using vocabulary that the students already know. Towards the middle of the year, students can give mini-talks in which they describe one of the illustrations or ask the class simple questions about it.
- The teacher may assign a selection from a *Section Magazine* as homework. The students then prepare four statements that may be true or false, such as **"Le baseball est le sport le plus populaire chez les jeunes Français."** This obviously false statement is based on the reading **Vive le football!** in *Section Magazine 3.* In class, students form small groups and together prepare a list of the best true/false items. At a given signal, each group passes its list to the next group, which answers the questions. The first group to answer all ten items is the winner.
- Some teachers prefer to intersperse parts of the magazine sections with the normal classroom instruction and select a segment a week for a lesson in culture and reading practice. Because of the structure and vocabulary progression, however, these mini-treatments should not be undertaken before these sections occur in the text.
- Projects for student involvement are found in each *Section Magazine.* The teacher may assign these or have the students think up projects of their own. Students may also enjoy expanding the ideas of particular articles. For **Les secrets du visage,** in *Section Magazine 2,* the students could bring in photos of their favorite personalities and analyze them according to the perspective of the article.
- *Reading Activities* based on the four *Sections Magazines* are provided in the Activity Masters. These serve as a valuable supplement. The activities include questions on content, personal questions, exercises such as multiple choice, matching, fill-ins, sentence building, and sentence completion, and projects such as polls.
- The teacher and students may bring in posters, photographs, or other materials related to the *Section Magazine* being studied. In addition to the more obvious materials, such as photographs of places or of French-speaking youth, students could also bring in realia. For example, after reading **Parlez-vous français?** in *Section Magazine 1* students could expand the topic by bringing in place names from newspapers, labels from products, or foods from recipe books.

• The teacher may use the magazine sections as departure points for compositions in which students write their own magazine articles. Students could write about their favorite singers in the style of **Une idole** (*Section Magazine 3*), or late in the year they could pretend that one of these *Sections Magazines* has just come on the market as a new magazine. Their assignment is to write a review of this new magazine. **Les loisirs des jeunes Français** (*Section Magazine 3*) would be a good choice for this activity.

• The students will find that the photographs, realia, and art inspire discussion. They may discuss what is in a given piece, tell a story about it, or create a conversation among the people pictured. Students may also enjoy providing captions for various pictures. The more the students work with the visual material, the more they will internalize the cultural content.

3.5 Using the Workbook

Teachers will want to use this component in ways that best suit the needs of their particular classes.

3.5.1 Using the written exercises.
The Workbook contains numerous situational activities based on points of structure or vocabulary. Each Workbook activity is keyed to the text so teachers will know at what point they can assign a particular activity. Each lesson begins on a right-hand page so that teachers may request that students tear out specific lessons to hand in.

• The teacher may assign these activities as written homework for all students, only for students who need extra drill on specific items, or for students seeking extra credit.

• Part of the class could do the Workbook activities individually, while the teacher helped other students with concepts that were causing them difficulty.

• The teacher may assign all activities upon completion of a unit as a review.

• The students can use the Workbook for self-help by checking their answers with the Answer Key at the back. Those teachers who don't want their students to have access to the answers can tear out the Answer Key before distributing the Workbook.

3.5.2 Using the *Récréation culturelle.*
An original feature of the FRENCH FOR MASTERY Workbook is the *Récréation culturelle* section at the end of each unit. This section provides a change of pace between units. It contains games and realia that introduce students to authentic samples of the French language. The realia can provide a point of departure for oral communication activities. The various games may be done outside of class for homework, or in class as written activities in pairs or small groups.

3.5.3 Using the *Tests de contrôle.*
Tests de contrôle are found in the back of the Workbook. They provide a written review of the basic structures and vocabulary of each unit. The *Tests de contrôle* should precede any other unit test.

• The teacher may use these tests informally for review.

• The students may take these tests on their own and check their answers in the Answer Key of the Workbook. The Answer Key for these tests contains an *Interpretation* segments. This refers students to the structure, vocabulary section, or cultural note of their texts corresponding to areas with which they are having difficulties.

3.6 Using the Tape Program

The Tape Program introduces the student to spoken French through the voices of a number of French speakers, thus supplementing and complementing the model provided by the teacher. The tape activities are recorded at natural conversational speed to foster authentic listening comprehension. Students should be warned that they may not understand everything the first time they hear the tape. In some cases the teacher may wish to present a passage or exercise before playing the tape. At other times the teacher may stop the tape to have students repeat a sentence or phrase they have just heard. The more opportunity the students have to listen to the tape, the more readily they will grow to understand spoken French.

• *Listening to the Presentation text.* The teacher may wish to play the tape of the *Presentation text* as an introduction to the unit. The students can listen with their books closed, or follow the text with their books open, to get a general idea of what the text is about.

• *Listening for Signals.* These exercises are designed to test the students' ability to distinguish among sounds which signal grammatical information: noun markers, verb forms, etc.

• *Speaking.* The speaking exercises are similar to the situational textbook exercises. Since the students cannot read the cues, they are forced to listen carefully. Two types of activities form the basis of this section:

   — directed activities, in which there is only one correct response; and

   — open-ended activities, such as the simple personal questions which appear later on in the program.

• *Dictation.* Students hear short sentences read three times. The first time they listen; the second time each sentence is broken up into short phrases, which the students write down; the third time they check what they have written.

• *Listening Comprehension with Visual Cues.* This activity is based on an illustration in the Activity Masters. Students are actively involved, since the listening process is accompanied by "pencil work": they are asked to trace a path, to locate certain items by marking them with an *X,* to draw a picture, etc. Listening reinforced with a written activity causes the students to pay closer attention to what is being said, and the exercise becomes more meaningful to them.

• *Listening and Repeating.* Students hear a recorded version of the **Prononciation** sections, the **Vocabulaire spécialisé,** and the verb charts, and practice imitating the new sounds.

• *French Songs.* Each unit concludes with a song in French, the melody of which will have been heard at intervals throughout. Students can sing along with the tape, reading from the lyrics and music available on the Activity Masters. Songs feature simple lyrics, often with a familiar melody. For extra credit, musical students could learn and perform the songs on guitar for the class; whole class performances could become part of a larger festival.

3.7 Using the Testing Program

The FRENCH FOR MASTERY Testing Program includes five *Lesson Quizzes* and a *Unit Test* for each unit, and two *Achievement Tests*. The accompanying Test Guide also provides ideas for developing speaking tests and written composition tests.

3.7.1 Using the Lesson Quizzes.
The five *Lesson Quizzes* that accompany each unit are designed to be administered upon completion of each lesson. The *Quiz* items present a variety of formats, including fill-ins, short answers, multiple choice, statement completion, and full answers. The students should be able to complete each *Lesson Quiz* in about 20 minutes.

For slower learners, the teacher may wish to administer the *Lesson Quiz* as a series of short quizzes given upon completion of the individual sections of the lesson.

3.7.2 Using the Unit Tests.
The *Unit Tests* are designed to be administered upon completion of each unit. The students should be able to complete each *Test* in about 45 minutes. All the material of the unit is evaluated in discrete-point exercises.

For slower learners, the teacher may wish to administer each *Unit Test* over a two-day period. The listening portion could be given on the first day and the written portion on the second day.

3.7.3 Using the Achievement Tests.
The *Achievement Tests* are designed to be administered upon completion of the corresponding units (*Achievement Test 1: Prélude,* Units 1–4; *Achievement Test 2:* Units 5–8). The students should be able to complete each *Test* in two 45-minute class periods. The teacher may choose to administer the listening portion on the first day and the written portion on the second day.

For slower learners, the teacher may wish to include only selected items from each part of the *Test,* adjusting the scoring as necessary.

3.8 Using the Overhead Transparencies

3.8.1 When to use them.
The FRENCH FOR MASTERY Overhead Transparencies have been selected with particular attention to flexibility and multiple use. The transparencies may be used for (1) review (structures and vocabulary); (2) testing (especially vocabulary); (3) reentry and variety (previously learned vocabulary, and familiar transparencies in new contexts); (4) guided self-expression (conversation and composition); and (5) cultural awareness (maps).

3.8.2 How to use them.
There are several basic techniques for using the Overhead Transparencies. These are:

• *Transparency plus pointer.* The teacher projects the transparency and uses a pencil, a ruler, or a pointer to point to various images.

• *Transparency plus marker.* The teacher may write on the transparency with a water-soluble transparency marker and then easily wipe off these additions with a damp cloth or paper towel. Colored markers may be used to distinguish and reinforce various linguistic features.

• *Transparency plus overlay.* An overlay is a second transparency used to add visual material to an initial transparency. Besides the overlays provided in the box of visuals, teachers may use blank sheets of acetate to develop their own.

• *Transparency plus mask.* If the teacher wishes to project only a portion of the visual, a sheet of paper may be laid on the transparency as a mask.

• *Transparency plus moving elements.* It is possible to project both a still image (the original transparency) and a mobile image. Adding movable hands to a clockface is perhaps the most obvious example.

4. Lesson Plans

Lesson plans help the teacher visualize how a unit is going to be presented. By emphasizing certain aspects of the program and playing down others, the teacher can change the focus of a unit to meet student needs. Below are sample lesson plans showing how FRENCH FOR MASTERY can be used successfully in the junior and senior high school classroom. These are followed by suggestions for adapting material to slower and/or faster learners.

4.1 Sample Lesson Plans

The charts on pages 22–27 show, in abridged form, sample lesson plans for:
• a one-year sequence: Unit 3, Lessons 1–5: 45–50 minute 9th grade class
  Unit 6, Lessons 1–5: 45–50 minute 9th grade class
• a two-year sequence: Unit 3, Lessons 1–5: 45–50 minute 7th grade class

The charts are divided into five types of classroom activities: review, correction, presentation, oral activities, and written activities and/or assignments. Notes and suggestions regarding these follow the charts. The sequence of these activities during a given class period will depend on teacher preference and class needs. Probably, a class will not be able to do all the suggested activities; some will have to be shortened or omitted. For the teacher's convenience certain features, activities, and grammatical presentations are labeled "optional" in the overprint of the text.

The following abbreviations are used in the sample lesson plans: Vp — Vocabulaire pratique, Vs — Vocabulaire spécialisé, Str. — Structure(s), Act. — Activité(s).

Notes:
(1) Since lessons are of varying lengths, not all units will take the same number of days to complete.
(2) The Tape Program may be used effectively in schools with and without labs.
(3) The Unit Test may take less than a full period.
(4) The average school year allows time to work with the *Sections Magazines.*

4.1.1 Lesson Plans for Unit 3, Grade 9.

Day Unit/ Lesson	Review	Correction	Presentation	Oral Activities	Written Activities and/or Assignments
Day 1 3.1	Days of the week	Go over Unit Test 2	Presentation text and Vp Note culturelle Str. A: **Aller**	Act. 1, 2	Act. 1, 2 Learn **aller**
Day 2 3.1	**Aller**	Act. 1, 2	Vs p. 135 Str. B: **À** + l'article défini	Act. 3 Act. 4, 5, 6	Act. 3 Act. 4, 5, 6
Day 3 3.1	Questions using Vs p. 135	Act. 3 Act. 4, 5, 6	Conversation/Observations Str. C: **Aller** + l'infinitif Révision: **avoir** et **être**	Act. 7, 8 Act. de révision Un jeu	Act. 7, 8 Act. de révision Un jeu
Day 4 3.1	Questions to review structures: • **Où allez-vous (samedi)?** • **Aujourd'hui, est-ce que vous allez (nager)?**	Act. 7, 8 Act. de révision Un jeu	Prononciation Entre nous	Tape activities for Lesson 1	Workbook activities
Day 5 3.2	Questions from Day 4	Workbook activities	Presentation text and Vp Note culturelle Str. A: **Chez**	Act. 1, 2, 3	Quiz, Lesson 1 Act. 1, 2, 3
Day 6 3.2	Questions using **chez:** — **Où est P.?** — **Il est chez M.**	Go over Quiz, Lesson 1 Act. 1, 2, 3	Conversation/Observations Str. B: La possession avec **de**	Act. 4, 5, 6	Act. 4, 5, 6
Day 7 3.2	Questions using **de:** (teacher holds up someone's book) — **Est-ce que c'est le livre de P.?** — **Oui, c'est le livre de P. (Non, ce n'est pas le livre de P.)**	Act. 4, 5, 6	Str. C: **De** + l'article défini Str. D: **Jouer à** et **jouer de** Vs p. 145	Act. 7, 8 Act. 9 Un jeu	Act. 7, 8 Act. 9 Un jeu
Day 8 3.2	Vs p. 145 Question: • **Qui joue. . .?**	Act. 7, 8 Act. 9 Un jeu	Prononciation Entre nous	Tape activities for Lesson 2	Workbook activities
Day 9 3.3	Same as Days 7, 8	Workbook activities	Presentation text and Vp Conversation/Observations Str. A: **Mon, ma, mes; ton, ta, tes**	Act. 1, 2, 3	Quiz, Lesson 2 Act. 1, 2, 3
Day 10 3.3	Questions using **mon/ton** Review numbers	Go over Quiz, Lesson 2 Act. 1, 2, 3	Notes culturelles Vs pp. 152-153 Str. B: L'âge Str. C: Nom + **de** + nom	Act. 4, 5, 6 Un jeu	Act. 4, 5, 6 Un jeu

Day Unit/ Lesson	Review	Correction	Presentation	Oral Activities	Written Activities and/or Assignments
Day 11 3.3	Use **mon/ton** to describe family and their ages	Act. 4, 5, 6 Un jeu	Prononciation Entre nous	Tape activities for Lesson 3	Workbook activities
Day 12 3.4	Family	Workbook activities	Presentation text and Vs p. 157 Conversation/Observations Str. A: **Son, sa, ses**	Act. 1, 2, 3	Quiz, Lesson 3 Act. 1, 2, 3
Day 13 3.4	Review **mon/ton/ son** Family Animals	Go over Quiz, Lesson 3 Act. 1, 2, 3	Note culturelle Str. B: **Leur, leurs** Str. C: Les nombres ordinaux	Act. 4 Act. 5 Un jeu	Act. 4 Act. 5 Un jeu
Day 14 3.4	Review **mon/ton/ son/leur** Animals Numbers	Act. 4 Act. 5 Un jeu	Prononciation Entre nous	Tape activities for Lesson 4	Workbook activities
Day 15 3.5	Ordinal numbers: practice counting around room	Workbook activities	Presentation text and Vp Conversation/Observations Str. A: **Notre, nos; votre, vos** Str. B: Récapitulation: les adjectifs possessifs	Act. 1 Act. 2, 3	Quiz, Lesson 4 Act. 1 Act. 2, 3
Day 16 3.5	Review possessives Review stress pronouns	Go over Quiz, Lesson 4 Act. 1 Act. 2, 3	Note culturelle Str. C: **Être à**	Act. 4, 5 Un jeu	Act. 4, 5 Un jeu
Day 17 3.5	Str. A, B, C	Act. 4, 5 Un jeu	Prononciation Entre nous	Tape activities for Lesson 5	Workbook activities
Day 18 Unit 3	Review vocabulary and structures of Unit 3	Workbook activities		Récréation culturelle Learn unit song	Quiz, Lesson 5 Tests de contrôle
Day 19 Unit 3					Unit Test 3

4.1.2 Lesson Plans for Unit 6, Grade 9.

Day Unit/ Lesson	Review	Correction	Presentation	Oral Activities	Written Activities and/or Assignments
Day 1 6.1	Review commands by asking the students to act out various action verbs: • **Regardez Jean.** • **Faites du skate-board.**	Go over Unit Test 5	Presentation text and Vs p. 271 Note culturelle Str. A: Révision: **avoir** et **être**	Act. 1, 2	Act. 1, 2

Day Unit/ Lesson	Review	Correction	Presentation	Oral Activities	Written Activities and/or Assignments
Day 2 6.1	Questions using Vs p. 271: • **Avez-vous mal..?** • **Êtes-vous malade?** • **Avez-vous la grippe?** **Être** and **avoir**	Act. 1, 2	Conversation/Observations Str. B: Les questions avec inversion Str. C: L'article défini avec les parties du corps Vs p. 275	Act. 3, 4, 5 Act. 6, 7	Act. 3, 4, 5 Act. 6, 7
Day 3 6.1	Vs pp. 271 and 275 Str. A, B, C	Act. 3, 4, 5 Act. 6, 7	Prononciation Entre nous	Tape activities for Lesson 1	L'art de la composition Workbook activities
Day 4 6.2	Str. A, B, C	L'art de la composition Workbook activities	Presentation text and Vp Vs p. 280	Act. 1	Quiz, Lesson 1 Act. 1
Day 5 6.2	Vs p. 280 Review **avoir** and **-er** verbs	Go over Quiz, Lesson 1 Act. 1	Note culturelle Conversation/Observations Str. A: Le passé composé des verbes en **-er**	Act. 2, 3, 4	Act. 2, 3, 4
Day 6 6.2	Questions using passé composé: • **Est-ce que vous avez dansé hier?** • **Est-ce que vous avez travaillé beaucoup?**	Act. 2, 3, 4	Str. B: Le passé composé à la forme négative Str. C: Le participe passé du verbe **faire**	Act. 5, 6, 7, 8 Act. 9, 10	Act. 5, 6, 7, 8 Act. 9, 10
Day 7 6.2	Questions using passé composé of **faire:** • **Qu'est-ce que vous avez fait hier?** • **Vous avez fait du sport?**	Act. 5, 6, 7, 8 Act. 9, 10	Prononciation Entre nous	Tape activities for Lesson 2	L'art de la composition Workbook activities
Day 8 6.3	Str. A, B, C	L'art de la composition Workbook activities	Presentation text and Vp Note culturelle Vs p. 288	Act. 1	Quiz, Lesson 2 Act. 1
Day 9 6.3	Vs p. 288 Review passé composé	Go over Quiz, Lesson 2 Act. 1	Str. A: **Voir** Conversation/Observations Str. B: Le passé composé des verbes réguliers en **-re**	Act. 2, 3 Act. 4, 5, 6	Act. 2, 3 Act. 4, 5, 6
Day 10 6.3	**Voir** Passé composé of **-re** verbs	Act. 2, 3 Act. 4, 5, 6	Str. C: Les participes passés irréguliers en **-u** Str. D: Les questions au passé composé	Act. 7, 8, 9 Act. 10	Act. 7, 8, 9 Act. 10
Day 11 6.3	Review regular and irregular verbs in passé composé	Act. 7, 8, 9 Act. 10	Entre nous Prononciation	Tape activities for Lesson 3	L'art de la composition Workbook activities
Day 12 6.3	Str. A, B, C, D	L'art de la composition Workbook activities	Presentation text and Vp Str. A: **Mettre**	Act. 1, 2	Quiz, Lesson 3 Act. 1, 2

Day Unit/ Lesson	Review	Correction	Presentation	Oral Activities	Written Activities and/or Assignments
Day 13 6.4	**Mettre** Questions with **-ir** verbs: • **Est-ce que vous obéissez à vos parents?** • **Est-ce que vous réussissez à vos examens?**	Go over Quiz, Lesson 3 Act. 1, 2	Note culturelle Conversation/Observations Str. B: Le passé composé des verbes réguliers en **-ir** Str. C: Les participes passés irréguliers en **-is**	Act. 3, 4, 5 Act. 6, 7	Act. 3, 4, 5 Act. 6, 7
Day 14 6.4	Passé composé of **-ir** verbs	Act. 3, 4, 5 Act. 6, 7	Prononciation Entre nous	Tape activities for Lesson 4	L'art de la composition Workbook activities
Day 15 6.5	Passé composé of all verbs	L'art de la composition Workbook activities	Presentation text and Vp Note culturelle Str. A: **Sortir, partir, dormir**	Act. 1, 2	Quiz, Lesson 4 Act. 1, 2
Day 16 6.5	**Sortir, partir, dormir** Present of **être**	Go over Quiz, Lesson 4 Act. 1, 2	Conversation/Observations Str. B: Le passé composé avec **être** Vs p. 305	Act. 3, 4, 5 Act. 6, 7, 8, 9	Act. 3, 4, 5 Act. 6, 7, 8, 9
Day 17 6.5	Passé composé with **être**	Act. 3, 4, 5 Act. 6, 7, 8, 9	Prononciation Entre nous	Tape activities, Lesson 5	L'art de la correspondance Workbook activities
Day 18 Unit 6	Review vocabulary and structures of Unit 6	L'art de la correspondance Workbook activities		Récréation culturelle Learn unit song	Quiz, Lesson 5 Tests de contrôle
Day 19 Unit 6					Unit Test 6

4.1.3 Lesson Plans for Unit 3, Grade 7.

Day Unit/ Lesson	Review	Correction	Presentation	Oral Activities	Written Activities and/or Assignments
Day 1 3.1	Days of the week	Go over Unit Test 2	Presentation text and Vp Str. A: **Aller**	Act. 1, 2	Act. 1, 2 Learn **aller**
Day 2 3.1	Presentation text and Vp **Aller**	Act. 1, 2	Go over Presentation text Note culturelle Vs p. 135	Act. 3 Create sentences using **aller** and Vs	Act. 3 Write sentences using **aller** and Vs Prepare for Vocabulary Quiz
Day 3 3.1	Vs p. 135	Act. 3 Sentences	Str. B: **À** + l'article défini	Act. 4, 5, 6	Vocabulary Quiz Act. 4, 5, 6 Write 3 sentences saying where your friends want to go (à + definite article)
Day 4 3.1	**Aller**	Go over Vocabulary Quiz Act. 4, 5, 6 Sentences	Conversation/Observations Str. C: **Aller** + l'infinitif Révision: **avoir** et **être** Prononciation	Act. 7, 8 Act. de révision	Act. 7, 8 Act. de révision

Day Unit/ Lesson	Review	Correction	Presentation	Oral Activities	Written Activities and/or Assignments
Day 5 3.1	Questions to review structures: • **Où allez-vous (samedi)?** • **Aujourd'hui, est-ce que vous allez (nager)?**	Act. 7, 8 Act. de révision	Entre nous	Un jeu Entre nous in groups Workbook activities	Un jeu Workbook activities
Day 6 3.1	Str. A, B, C	Un jeu Workbook activities		Tape activities for Lesson 1	Study for Quiz, Lesson 1
Day 7 3.2	Questions using **aller** + infinitive and **à** + definite article		Presentation text and Vp Note culturelle		Quiz, Lesson 1 Copy Vp
Day 8 3.2	Presentation text and Vp	Go over Quiz, Lesson 1	Str. A: **Chez**	Act. 1, 2, 3	Act. 1, 2, 3
Day 9 3.2	Questions using **chez:** — **Où est P.?** — **Il est chez M.**	Act. 1, 2, 3	Conversation/Observations Str. B: La possession avec **de**	Act. 4, 5, 6	Act. 4, 5, 6
Day 10 3.2	Questions using **chez** Review **à** + definite article	Act. 4, 5, 6	Str. C: **De** + l'article défini	Act. 7, 8 Create sentences using **de** + definite article	Act. 7, 8 Write 3 sentences saying where a friend is coming from (**de** + definite article)
Day 11 3.2	Review **de** + definite article	Act. 7, 8 Sentences	Str. D: **Jouer à** et **jouer de** Vs p. 145	Act. 9 Un jeu	Copy Vs Act. 9 Un jeu Write 3 sentences saying who plays what (**jouer à, de**)
Day 12 3.2	Vs p. 145 Questions using **jouer à, de** • **Qui joue à, de...?**	Act. 9 Un jeu Sentences	Prononciation Entre nous	Entre nous in groups Workbook activities	Workbook activities Prepare for Vocabulary Quiz
Day 13 3.3	Vs p. 145 Str. A, B, C	Workbook activities	Presentation text and Vp	Tape activities for Lesson 2	Vocabulary Quiz Prepare for Quiz, Lesson 2
Day 14 3.3	Presentation text and Vp	Go over Vocabulary Quiz	Notes culturelles Conversation/Observations Str. A: **Mon, ma, mes; ton, ta, tes**	Act. 1, 2, 3	Quiz, Lesson 2 Copy Vp Act. 1, 2, 3
Day 15 3.3	Review numbers Questions using **mon/ton**	Go over Quiz, Lesson 2 Act. 1, 2, 3	Vs pp. 152-153 Str. B: L'âge	Act. 4, 5	Copy Vs Act. 4, 5
Day 16 3.3	Vs pp. 152-153 Numbers	Act. 4, 5	Str. C: Nom + **de** + nom	Use **mon/ton** to describe family and their ages Act. 6 Un jeu	Act. 6 Un jeu Prepare for Vocabulary Quiz

Day Unit/ Lesson	Review	Correction	Presentation	Oral Activities	Written Activities and/or Assignments
Day 17 3.3	Family and ages	Act. 6 Un jeu	Prononciation Entre nous	Entre nous in groups Workbook activities	Vocabulary Quiz Workbook activities
Day 18 3.3	Str. A, B, C	Go over Vocabulary Quiz Workbook activities		Tape activities for Lesson 3	Prepare for Quiz, Lesson 3
Day 19 3.4	Review **mon/ton**		Presentation text and Vs p. 157	Discuss animals using **mon, ma, mes**	Quiz, Lesson 3 Copy Vs
Day 20 3.4	Vs p. 157 Review numbers	Go over Quiz, Lesson 3	Conversation/Observations Str. A: **Son, sa, ses** Str. B: **Leur, leurs**	Act. 1, 2, 3 Act. 4	Act. 1, 2, 3 Act. 4
Day 21 3.4	Review **mon/ton/ son/leur** Animals Numbers	Act. 1, 2, 3 Act. 4	Str. C: Les nombres ordinaux	Act. 5 Un jeu Workbook activities	Act. 5 Un jeu Workbook activities
Day 22 3.4	Str. A, B, C	Act. 5 Un jeu Workbook activities	Prononciation Entre nous	Entre nous in groups Tape activities for Lesson 4	Prepare for Quiz, Lesson 4
Day 23 3.5	Ordinal numbers: practice counting around room		Presentation text and Vp Note culturelle		Quiz, Lesson 4 Copy Vp
Day 24 3.5	Presentation text and Vp	Go over Quiz, Lesson 4	Conversation/Observations Str. A: **Notre, nos; votre, vos** Str. B: Récapitulation: les adjectifs possessifs	Act. 1 Act. 2, 3	Act. 1 Act. 2, 3
Day 25 3.5	All possessives Stress pronouns	Act. 1 Act. 2, 3	Str. C: **Être à**	Act. 4, 5 Un jeu Workbook activities	Act. 4, 5 Un jeu Workbook activities
Day 26 3.5	Str. A, B, C	Act. 4, 5 Un jeu Workbook activities	Prononciation Entre nous	Tape activities for Lesson 5	Prepare for Quiz, Lesson 5
Day 27 3.5	Review all Presentation texts			Entre nous in groups Récréation culturelle	Quiz, Lesson 5
Day 28 Unit 3	Review vocabulary and structures of Unit 3	Go over Quiz, Lesson 5		Learn unit song	Tests de contrôle Prepare for Unit Test 3
Day 29 Unit 3					Unit Test 3

4.2 Notes and Suggestions Regarding the Five Classroom Activities

- *Review* (5–8 minutes)
  - Can be used at the beginning of class or following *Correction*.
  - Can include items from previous day's homework or classwork.
  - Should anticipate new material or review items whenever possible.
  - Should review or correct mistakes the teacher found while correcting previous day's tests or homework papers.
  - Could include conversational items, such as discussions of school or class events, weekends, weather, etc.
  - Should be in French as often as possible as this sets the tone for the rest of the class.
- *Correction* (5–10 minutes)
  - Should be in French whenever possible. Teach the alphabet, grammatical terms, accents, and punctuation early.
  - Could be first activity in teaching sequence.
  - Quizzes can occasionally be corrected immediately in class. This is especially good for teacher-prepared dictées and vocabulary quizzes.
  - Questions should be encouraged, concepts reviewed, and misunderstandings straightened out as this is really a teaching time.
  - Mistakes commonly made should be pointed out and any necessary reteaching should take place.
- *Presentation* (10–15 minutes)
  - New material can be presented first, or immediately following *Review*.
  - Tapes may be used when appropriate.
  - Comments and explanations should be in English only initially; on later days the material should be reexplained in French whenever possible.
  - The *Presentation text* at the beginning of each lesson should be referred back to and used as a model, since the various structure elements of a lesson are presented there.
- *Oral Activities* (10 minutes)
  - Presenting activities orally that will later be written reinforces what has been taught and minimizes the problem of students who might not understand the homework.
  - Dramatic presentation of dialogs and conversations, as well as creative material, can be used.
  - *Entre nous Mini-dialogues,* which are optional material, could be omitted and other material, such as the *Presentation text* of a lesson, substituted.
  - Other optional or enrichment material can be added here: *Section Magazine* or *Récréation culturelle.*
- *Written Activities and/or Assignments* (5–10 minutes)
  - Not all of every activity needs to be written out by every student. Faster learners might do only half, such as the even-numbered items.

— Some activities can be done in class, some outside of class as homework assignments. With a slower or beginning group, start each activity to be done for homework in class, so they know what to do.
— Testing might be best at the beginning of class on some occasions.
— Tests and Quizzes should be corrected immediately whenever possible, or at least by the next class meeting. They should be reviewed by the total group together, corrections made, questions asked. This makes testing a teaching time as well.
— Offer retakes on tests to those who want to prove they can do better.
— Individual vocabulary notebooks or flashcards are a good way to help review vocabulary.
— Corrected compositions or themes might also be recopied into a special notebook.
— A Vocabulary Quiz might be given in one of several ways:
  –labeling illustrations, such as a house, the body, or clothes
  –writing English meanings to given French words
  –writing French equivalents to given English words
  –spelling the French word correctly when it is said, then giving the English equivalent
  –matching two lists of French and English terms
  –writing a short sentence to show the meaning of a given French word
— Workbook Activities may be introduced along with each item of structure. In the lesson plans they have been used at the end of each lesson as a form of review and recapitulation.
— Print and hand out a syllabus of all written assignments for the lesson or the unit. Absent youngsters will know what to do next; there will be no confusion as to exact assignment; also helps to keep class progressing at good pace.

4.3 Adapting Material to Slower or Younger Learners

— Maximum repetition of material is needed, with as much student participation as possible.
— *Review* time should include the same or similar items for several days in a row.
— Teacher should stick to basic material from the text rather than introduce outside or extra material to enable students to master the essential concepts.
— Constant review is necessary.
— Required memorization and recitation over a period of several days by each class member helps all students to retain material: days, numbers, months, verbs, pronouns, etc.
— Flags, stickers, stars, seals, stamps, happy faces, and expressions such as "très bien," etc. really help when put on papers and tests.
— Have students make vocabulary notebooks or flashcards.
— Rewriting words/sentences correctly several times helps to avoid further mistakes.

— Sufficient variety in material and class activities helps to make drill less arduous.
— Do group work, board work, and have students check each other's work.
— Have students perform. They learn best when they say and do and are actively involved.
— Pictures, drawings, flashcards, charades, and objects help to make the material stick in their minds.
— Assign students to teach the rest of the class one word or phrase or verb from a vocabulary list; for example, several students each teach a different part of the body and drill the others until they know it.
— Invent games and use familiar ones to help drill and repeat work.

4.4 Adapting Material to Faster Learners

— French should be used as much as possible in class. Use the alphabet, grammar terms, etc.
— Students should write original compositions, résumés, or dialogs at least once a week. Perhaps a special notebook could be kept of these things.
— Students should not be required to write out every word of every drill. If they understand what is going on they should be allowed to do only half of an exercise, such as the odd- or even-numbered items.
— Assign additional reading material: readers, newspapers, etc.
— Use the optional or enrichment material.
— Good students can function as group leaders for a particular task.
— Assign students as tutors for other students.
— Discuss "other things" of importance to students in French: the weekend, the concert, the dance, the school lunch.
— Students should be encouraged to perform (perhaps write) scenes and skits and presentations for other classes, live or on videotape.
— Students can write letters in French to absent class members, etc.
— Students can take mini-sabbaticals (which exempt them from a night's assignment) to French events: movies, restaurant, art display, etc. with the idea they will report back to the class.
— If they have a chance to travel to another French-speaking country, students could be exempted from routine work but be expected to bring back a full report, realia, journal, personal stories, and photos to share with the class. The general outline should be worked out with the students before leaving.
— Students might want to work on an independent study project. Design a contract together stating what you want and what the students think can be covered, including various types of activities, oral work, and written assignments. This can also be used for a student who wants to move ahead rapidly in the program and is capable of such independence.

Part Three
How to Supplement FRENCH FOR MASTERY

5. Supplementary Material and Activities

Foreign language methodologists stress the importance of using realia and supplementary cultural activities for a number of reasons:

- They enliven the atmosphere of the class.
- They provide that needed change of pace.
- They allow for a more natural exchange between student and teacher.
- They permit the less linguistically oriented students to express themselves in other areas such as music, art, or cooking.
- They present students with a practical application of the skills learned in the classroom.
- They provide an interdisciplinary link to students' other studies.

5.1 Realia: Where to Find It and How to Use It

Realia, that is, authentic items relating to the contemporary French-speaking world, provide additional exposure to culture, a change of pace, and departure points for conversational activities. Students see how learning French will help them understand everyday items of interest to them. This section lists some sources of these materials and suggests how the teacher might use them. The listing is not exhaustive, but seeks to provide variety. Depending on the teacher's geographical area, some of these materials may be easier or more difficult to obtain. In addition, every teacher will have a personal preference as to what materials he or she will want to use or will feel most comfortable with.

5.1.1 The written language. Many of the following French-language magazines and newspapers may be purchased at shops that sell foreign language periodicals. Others are available by single copy or by subscription from the distributor.

Name	Country	Approx. Cost	Type	Useful contents	Distributor	Frequency
L'actualité	Canada	$1.00 per copy/ $9.00 per year	current events	ads, articles on travel, health, pastimes, current events	L'actualité 4059, rue Hochelaga Montréal, P.Q. H1W 9Z9	monthly
Elle	France	$2.50/$78	women's fashions	ads, trends, interior decorating, advice column, recipes, health	*	weekly

			events	ads	*	
Le Figaro	France	$1.00/$190	newspaper	current events, sports, entertainment, ads, weather	*	daily
Le Journal Français d'Amérique	U.S.	$.60/$13.50	newspaper	current events, sports	Journal Français d'Amérique 1051 Divisadero St. San Francisco, CA 94115	bi-monthly
Jours de France	France	$2.50/$64	fashion	ads, horoscope, cartoons	*	weekly
Le Monde	France	$1.00/$170	newspaper	games, hobbies, entertainment, weather, current events	*	daily
Ok âge tendre	France	$1.00/$48	youth	youth culture, teen fashions, ads	*	weekly
Une semaine de Paris – Pariscope	France	$1.25/$55	entertainment listings	movies, dance, music, theater, sports events	*	weekly
Paris-Match	France	$2.50/$70	current events	stories, sports, opinion polls, ads, TV programs	Paris-Match P.O. Box 8500 S. 4075 Philadelphia, PA 19178	weekly
Pilote	France	$1.25/$55	humor	comics, ads, cartoons	*	weekly
La Presse	Canada (Montréal)	$.50/$250	newspaper	current events, entertainment, ads	La Presse Ltée 7, rue Saint-Jacques Montréal, P.Q. H2Y 1K9	daily
Salut	France	$2.20/$56	youth	youth culture, ads	*	weekly
Sélections de Reader's Digest	Canada or France	$1.25/$13	general	jokes, ads, stories, articles	Reader's Digest OEM Pleasantville, NY 10570 (specify Canadian or Parisian edition)	monthly
Le Soleil	Canada (Québec)	$.50/$250	newspaper	current events, entertainment	Le Soleil C.P. 232382 Québec, P.Q. G14 7P5	daily
Télé 7 jours	France	$1.00/$41	TV guide	TV programs, articles, ads	*	weekly

* These periodicals can be purchased from any of the following distributors:

Larousse & Co., Inc.
572 Fifth Avenue
New York, NY 10036

French and European Publications, Inc.
115 Fifth Avenue
New York, NY 10020

French and European Publications, Inc.
652 Olive Street
Los Angeles, CA 90014

European Publishers Representatives, Inc.
11-03 46th Avenue
Long Island City, NY 11101

5.1.2 The spoken language. There are a number of radio stations in the United States that broadcast in French at some point during the day. Also, near the Canadian border it may be possible to receive some television programs in French. Channel 10 in New York City and Channel 6 in San Francisco televise a few hours a week in French. The teacher and students should check the newspapers for stations and times of French programs. The following is only a sampling of some of the radio stations with French broadcasts on their schedule.

City	State	Radio station call letters
Columbus	OH	WRFD
Ephrata	WA	KULE
Hartford	CT	WCCC-FM; WRTC-FM
Holyoke	MA	WREB
Honolulu	HI	KNDI
Levelland	TX	KLVT
Lewiston	ME	WCOU; WCOU-FM; WLAM
Moultrie	GA	WMGA
New Orleans	LA	WWNO-FM
Reidsville	NC	WFRC
San Francisco	CA	KQED-FM
Winnetka	IL	WNTH-FM

5.1.3 Other sources.

Brochures and posters: The sources for these are numerous; they are available both by mail and in the local community.

• Tourist offices.

— FRANCE
  French Government Tourist Office
  610 Fifth Avenue
  New York, New York 10020

  Commissariat Général du Tourisme
  127, av. des Champs-Élysées
  75008 Paris, France

  Mission interministérielle pour le tourisme
  17, rue de l'Ingénieur Robert Keller
  75740 Paris, France

— CANADA

Canadian Government Office of Tourism
235 Queen Street
Ottawa, Ontario, Canada K1AOH6

Gouvernement de Québec
Direction Générale du Tourisme
930, Chemin Sainte Foy
Québec, P.Q., Canada

— MARTINIQUE AND GUADELOUPE

Caribbean Tourism Association
20 East 46th Street
New York, New York 10017

— TAHITI

Tahiti Tourist Board
366 Madison Avenue
New York, New York 10017

— HAITI

Haiti Government Tourist Office
30 Rockefeller Plaza
New York, New York 10020

- ACTFL Materials Center
  2 Park Avenue
  New York, New York 10016
- Embassies and consulates of French-speaking countries.

The teacher or student may request information in French or in English on the country, its educational system, or any other aspect of life in that country.

One can also write for information and posters to the Services Culturels of the French consulates in Washington, New York, Chicago, San Francisco, Los Angeles, Houston, New Orleans, and Boston.

- American offices of transportation companies.

Students can write the United States offices of airline or shipping companies of French speaking countries requesting descriptive material in French or English, bilingual menus, bilingual brochures, or other realia. A local travel agency can furnish up-to-date addresses of companies such as Air France, Air Canada, Air Afrique, Swissair, KLM, and the French Line.

- Friends and relatives.

Students, friends, or parents who are traveling to a French-speaking country can be asked to bring back useful and interesting items, such as menus, city maps, train and bus schedules, TV and movie guides, programs of plays and concerts, records, games, tickets, candy wrappers, or anything else that might be of interest to the class.

- Food and Wines from France, Inc.
  Information Center for Food and Wine
  1350 Avenue of the Americas
  New York, New York 10019

Supplies posters on wine and cheese.

- Students themselves can collect objects that have French words or that come from French-speaking countries: food labels and packaging, stamps, games such as Mille Bornes.

Books: Students may use travel books to plan itineraries for imaginary trips. Books from the school library and encyclopedias provide photos of French-speaking countries, monuments, and works of art.

Pen pals: Students may enjoy corresponding with French-speaking students. To obtain pen pals, the teacher can write to the American Association of Teachers of French.

Bureau de Correspondance Scolaire
AATF
57 East Armory Avenue
Champaign, IL 61820

It might be possible to make an arrangement with a class in a French-speaking country whereby that class could send French realia and the English-speaking class could send English realia in exchange.

5.1.4 How to use the material. The teacher may want to use realia to enrich classroom activities and to help students make the transition from the classroom to the everyday French-speaking world.

- *Preparing realia for the students.* It is important for the teacher to prepare the realia for the students before exposing them to it. If it is too difficult or if there are too many unknown words and structures, the students may become discouraged. Teachers should be selective in the realia that they bring to class. In the beginning, the realia should have visuals that reinforce vocabulary and structures that the students have already learned. The teacher should edit the realia before showing it to the students. It would also be helpful to underline words or structures that students already know and prepare a brief glossary of items that they don't know. Students should not translate but try to understand what is being said from the context.

Radio and television programs are often difficult to understand. The teacher should tell students to concentrate on what they are able to understand. For example, news items may be easy for students to understand if they have heard some of the names on English broadcasts.

- *Useful materials.* Newspapers and magazines not only include feature articles but a number of items that focus on the world of today and that are easy to understand. TV guides, movie schedules, weather reports, ads for restaurants, food, or clothes provide useful teaching tools and are easy for students to understand. They can be used for:

— identification of vocabulary and structures already learned

— vocabulary building (new words, especially concrete nouns)

— culture expansion

— points of departure for conversation

Examples of types of realia to teach specific points are:

— wedding or birth announcements to illustrate French names

— weather reports to illustrate weather expressions and vocabulary

— ads about clothing sales or fashion magazines to illustrate clothing

— labels from the supermarket or grocery store ads to illustrate food

Many French periodicals contain ads for U.S. products and carry publicity (and even articles) patterned on U.S. models. This may give the impression that the French-speaking world tends to copy the American model. While "Americanization" is a very real phenomenon, you should make sure that your students understand that the French speakers have their own traditions and values. (Observant students will notice that some U.S. products are marketed with different types of ads in French, reflecting the French rather than the American value system.)

5.2 Games: Their Preparation and Use

Games are useful learning tools that are accessible to every teacher and that provide variety for the class. Used at the beginning of the class, games capture the students' attention. In the middle of the period, games may serve as a transition from one activity to the next. At the end of the class, they fill in the few minutes between the final activity on the lesson plan and the bell. The teacher can play these games with the entire class. Games also lend themselves to pair and small-group activity.

The main purpose of games is to further the linguistic aim of the lesson; they should not become the exclusive focus of the class. As a teaching aid, the Activity Masters feature a Games section based on the material in the Student Text. The following section provides sample games that the teacher can use or adapt.

5.2.1 Commercial games. There are many commercial games that are sold by companies handling foreign-language realia. Some games that are popular in English in the United States have French counterparts: French Scrabble, Scrabble pour Juniors, and Monopoly. Mille Bornes is a popular bilingual game in which players compete in a cross-country trip by car. Victoire! is a lotto game in French that can be played by beginners. In Word Master Mind, players try to duplicate each other's secret words.

5.2.2 Games created by the teacher. Many games that the students are familiar with in English may be played in French. Teacher-created games have a distinct advantage over commercial games; they can be "custom made" to fit the needs of a particular class or of a particular lesson.

(Oral games)

LE JEU DU PENDU, similar to HANGMAN

The teacher may suggest this game as a way to review the vocabulary of a given unit prior to the unit test. One student thinks of a word from a *Vocabulaire spécialisé* from one of the five lessons in the unit. This student then writes on the chalkboard a series of blanks corresponding to the number of letters in the word and draws a noose. When someone from the class guesses a letter that appears in the word, the student at the board enters that letter in all the spaces where it occurs in the word. When someone guesses a letter that is not in the word, the student leading the game adds a part of the body to the person in the noose. The object, of course, is to guess the word before being hanged. As the final activity, no matter who wins, a student should spell the complete word and supply the gender or identify the word as an adjective or verb, etc.

DEVINEZ LE MOT!

The teacher thinks of a familiar word and announces the number of letters it contains; for example, **lit** — **"trois lettres."** Students in the class volunteer possible three-letter words, and the teacher writes these possibilities on the board indicating how many letters in that word are the same as those in the key word.

	0	1	2	3
qui (une lettre)		*qui*		
son (zéro lettre)	*son*			
les (une lettre)		*les*		
ton (une lettre)		*ton*		
dit (deux lettres)			*dit*	

It is a good idea to ask the student to put the word in a sentence for clarity: **"Qu'est-ce qu'il *dit?*"** vs. *"Dis* **donc!"** The student who guesses the correct word goes to the board to lead the next round. The student should write the secret word on a piece of paper and share it with the teacher, who will then be able to help in confirming guesses if needed.

DEVINEZ L'OBJET!

In this game, one student thinks of an object, and the others take turns asking questions about it to find out what it is.

LA CHAÎNE

One student says a word: **tennis,** for example. The next student must give a word that begins with the last letter of that word, such as **sympathique.** The next student continues with a word beginning with the last letter of the preceding word. In this case, the third student might say **excellent.** This game may also be played in teams, in which each player has a turn coming up with an appropriate word in five seconds. If not, the team forfeits a point.

SIMON DIT

First the teacher goes through the motions of the game saying, for example, **"Simon dit: les mains sur la tête"** while touching his or her head. When the students understand, the teacher may lead the game without modeling the movements. Students learn to understand unfamiliar statements readily if they are asked to respond physically rather than orally.

ADIEU!

This game is similar to "Ghost" in English. Playing in groups of five or six, each student has a turn in saying a letter that contributes to the spelling of a French word. If in so doing, the student completes a word, he or she gets an **A**, the next time a **D,** and so on until they are out by having completed the word **Adieu.** The last person remaining in the game is the winner. If a student says a letter that the next person does not believe contributes toward the building of a word, the student who said it may be challenged. If the challenged student does not have a French word in mind, he or she receives a letter toward being eliminated from the game. However, if the challenged student does know a French word with that sequence of letters, the student who challenged receives one of the letters of **Adieu.**

(Written games)

JOYEUX NOËL ET BONNE ANNÉE

The teacher writes a phrase on the board. The students have a limited amount of time to see how many words they can form using the letters contained in the phrase. In the case of **Joyeux Noël et Bonne Année** some of the words the students might find are **je, eux, non, bon, an, aux, bel,** or **beau.** The title of a lesson or of a unit frequently makes a good phrase for this kind of activity.

JE L'AI!

After distributing sheets of paper divided into 16 squares, the teacher gives a category, such as food, clothing, or school life. The students then fill in the spaces with French words belonging to the category. One at a time, the teacher calls out words that belong in the category, and if the students have the words, they cross them off their sheets. The first one to get four in a row horizontally, vertically, or diagonally calls **"Je l'ai!"** and wins the game.

FIND THE WORDS

The teacher may create these puzzles as a test on unit vocabulary or as a break in the students' routine. The following sample uses some of the vocabulary from Unit 6. The teacher prepares the letter blocks with words hidden horizontally, vertically, or diagonally.

P	L	R	C	V	S	I	N	L	A
L	B	S	H	N	G	J	K	O	S
A	F	S	A	E	R	T	H	K	S
C	J	S	M	L	S	V	B	W	I
E	O	A	B	S	O	F	H	J	S
R	T	M	R	K	L	N	C	M	T
J	O	U	E	U	R	D	M	A	E
J	B	I	L	L	E	T	T	T	R
Z	X	M	N	V	P	I	E	C	E
U	O	P	T	R	G	D	L	H	G

JOUEUR
BILLET
PIECE
PLACE
CHAMBRE
MATCH
ASSISTER
SALON
SANS

CROSSWORD PUZZLES

Easy to prepare, crossword puzzles provide another method of checking vocabulary. The following puzzle, **Objets courants,** is based on the *Vocabulaire spécialisé* of Unit 2, Lesson 2.

									¹L
	²S	A	³C						I
	⁴V		A						V
⁵V	E	L	O	M	O	T	E	U	R
	L		E						E
	O		R						
		⁶R	A	D	I	O			

Horizontalement

2.

5.

6.

Verticalement

1.

3.

4.

LA POÉSIE SURRÉALISTE

Using a paper cutter, the teacher cuts typing paper lengthwise into 11-inch strips, one for each student. The teacher gives a specific instruction and each student writes a word or phrase beginning at the far left side of the strip of paper. They then fold back what they have written and pass their piece of paper to the next student. Then all students write a second word or phrase according to instructions, fold that back, and pass the paper on. This procedure continues until the sentences are completed. Students may read their sentences aloud or put them on the bulletin board.

Some sample instructions that the teacher may give are:

a. Write a possessive adjective, masculine singular.

b. Write a masculine singular adjective that precedes a noun.

c. Write a masculine singular noun.

d. Write a verb in the present tense, third-person singular (**il** form). Choose a verb that takes a direct object.

e. Write an expression of quantity.

f. Write a feminine plural noun.

g. Write a feminine plural adjective that follows a noun.

Possible sentences:

Mon grand sac mange beaucoup de dames furieuses.

Notre joli fromage choisit peu de trompettes rouges.

THÈMES ET CATÉGORIES

The teacher divides the class into several teams and assigns each team a section of the chalkboard. The first person of each team goes to the board and the teacher announces a category. The students at the board write as many words as they can think of in that category in ten seconds. After they return to their seats, a second student from each team goes to the board. The teacher announces a new category and the members of this group write as many words as they can think of in ten seconds. When every member of the team has been to the board, the class checks all the teams' entries and counts them. The team with the most correct words is the winner. If desired, the class can subtract the number of wrong words from the correct ones in calculating the team score. The teacher may use the themes of the *Vocabulaires spécialisés* as categories.

5.3 Poems and Songs

Poems and songs are a lively way to practice pronunciation, reinforce grammar, and teach French culture. It is helpful to present some background information on each poem or song before the students read or sing it. Songs with which the students are familiar and that emphasize repetition, such as **Alouette** and **Frère Jacques,** are best at the start. The unit songs recorded on the Tape Program (with music and lyrics printed in the Activity Masters) can serve to introduce songs into the classroom. Songs are a helpful and pleasant diversion, especially around the holiday season.

5.4 Cultural Activities

The opportunities for exposing students to French culture are numerous both in and outside the classroom.

5.4.1 Inside the classroom. For in-class activities, students could prepare an authentic French party with French pastries or prepare an authentic French meal. During Foreign Language Week celebrations, a class may organize and run a French café. The teacher can, of course, arrange for pen pals in a French-speaking country.

5.4.2 Outside the classroom. Cultural field trips are also a good way to provide an introduction to French culture. In order for these outside activities to be successful, to have an impact on the students, and to make them see and experience the relevance of French, they need to be carefully planned. Students could be given special assignments such as outside reading, research, etc. and could report to the class before the trip. Or, the assignment could be given to everyone for homework. Some possible ideas for trips are:

• *Going to a French restaurant.* The teacher could call the restaurant a few days before the trip and get copies of the menu for the students. Ideally a trip such as this would immediately follow a unit on food.

• *Visiting the French wing of an art museum.* Students will learn something of art and French history.

• *Going to French movies and plays.* Except in the case of dubbed or sub-titled movies, or plays translated into English, the teacher will have to thoroughly prepare the students for what they will be seeing.

• *Taking a vacation trip to a French-speaking country.* For those people living in the Northeast, such a trip may be very affordable. Long weekends in Montreal and Quebec will expose students to a neighboring French-speaking population.

Part Four
Reference Guide for FRENCH FOR MASTERY

This part of the Teacher's Edition contains reference materials for easy accessibility.

6. Useful Expressions

The teacher who wishes to conduct the class entirely in French may use the following vocabulary supplements.

6.1   Classroom Expressions

These classroom expressions may be duplicated and distributed to the students.

6.1.1 Vocabulaire

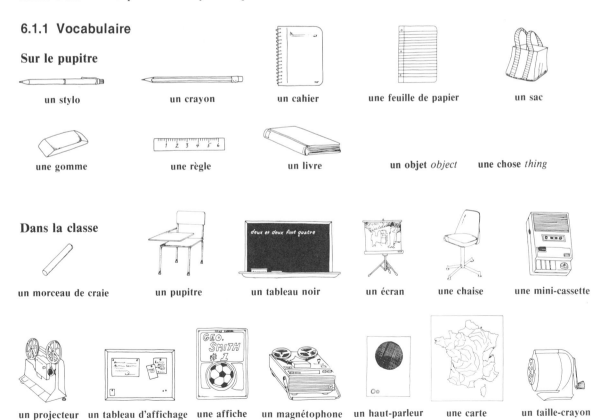

Sur le pupitre

un stylo   un crayon   un cahier   une feuille de papier   un sac

une gomme   une règle   un livre   **un objet** *object*   **une chose** *thing*

Dans la classe

un morceau de craie   un pupitre   un tableau noir   un écran   une chaise   une mini-cassette

un projecteur   un tableau d'affichage   une affiche   un magnétophone   un haut-parleur   une carte   un taille-crayon

6.1.2 Les matières

l'anglais	*English*
les maths (mathématiques)	*math*
l'algèbre	*algebra*
la géométrie	*geometry*
les sciences	*science*
la biologie	*biology*
la chimie	*chemistry*
la physique	*physics*
les sciences sociaux	*social science*
la géographie	*geography*
l'histoire	*history*
l'allemand	*German*
l'espagnol	*Spanish*
le français	*French*
l'italien	*Italian*
le latin	*Latin*
le dessin	*art*
la musique	*music*
les travaux manuels	*shop*
la gymnastique	*gym*
le sport	*sports*
la cuisine	*cooking*
la couture	*sewing*

6.1.3 Expressions pour la classe.

Écoutez (bien).	*Listen (carefully).*
Écoutez la bande.	*Listen to the tape.*
Répétez. (Ne répétez pas.)	*Repeat. (Don't repeat.)*
Parlez plus fort.	*Speak up. Speak louder.*
Écoutez la question.	*Listen to the question.*
Répondez. (Ne répondez pas.)	*Answer. (Don't answer.)*
Venez ici (devant la classe).	*Come here (in front of the class).*
Prenez le rôle de . . .	*Take the part of . . .*
Jouez le rôle de . . .	*Play the part of . . .*
Commencez.	*Begin.*
Merci.	*Thank you.*
Asseyez-vous.	*Sit down.*

Prenez votre livre (votre cahier).	*Take out your books (your notebooks).*
Ouvrez votre livre (votre cahier) à la page . . .	*Open your books (your notebooks) to page . . .*
Fermez votre livre (votre cahier).	*Close your books (your notebooks).*
Prenez un stylo (un crayon).	*Take out a pen (a pencil).*
Prenez du papier.	*Take out some paper.*
Lisez (à haute voix).	*Read (aloud).*
Continuez.	*Continue.*
Écrivez. (N'écrivez pas.)	*Write. (Don't write.)*
Levez-vous.	*Get up.*
Allez au tableau.	*Go to the board.*
Effacez.	*Erase.*
Regardez le tableau.	*Look at the board.*
Regardez-moi.	*Look at me.*
Faites attention.	*Pay attention.*
Silence.	*Silence.*
Taisez-vous.	*Quiet.*
Attention à la prononciation (l'orthographe).	*Careful with the pronunciation (spelling).*
Dites . . .	*Say . . .*
Tous ensemble.	*All together.*
Tout le monde.	*Everyone.*
Encore une fois.	*Once more.*
C'est bien.	*That's good.*
C'est très bien.	*That's very good.*
Ce n'est pas ça.	*That's not it.*
Essayez encore une fois.	*Try once more.*
Pour demain . . .	*For tomorrow . . .*
Pour la prochaine fois . . .	*For the next time . . .*
Préparez . . .	*Prepare . . .*
Faites l'exercice (les exercices) . . .	*Do the exercise (the exercises) . . .*
Je ne sais pas.	*I don't know.*
Je ne comprends pas.	*I don't understand.*
Répétez, s'il vous plaît.	*Please repeat.*
Que veut dire . . .?	*What does . . . mean?*
Comment dit-on . . .?	*How do you say . . .?*

6.2 Expressions for the *Activités*

Beginning with Unit 6, the direction lines for the activities and the pronunciation sections are in French. Although the students will be able to guess the meanings of most of the new terms from the context and previous experience with the exercises, the teacher may wish to copy and distribute the following vocabulary list for reference. This list may also be found as a duplicating master in the Activity Masters component.

NOMS:

un changement	*change*	**une chose**	*thing*
un mot	*word*	**une colonne**	*column*
un mot clé	*practice (key) word*	**une phrase**	*sentence*
un objet	*object*	**une réponse**	*answer*
un pronom	*pronoun*		
un son	*sound*		
un sujet	*subject*		

ADJECTIFS:

certain	*certain, some*	**suivant**	*following*
chaque	*each, every*		

PRONOMS:

ce que	*what*	**chacun(e)**	*each one, every one*
cela	*that*		

VERBES:

dire	*to say, tell*	**remplacer**	*to replace*
exprimer	*to express*	**utiliser**	*to use*

EXPRESSIONS:

affirmativement	*in the affirmative (saying "yes")*	**entre**	*between*
		entre parenthèses	*in parentheses*
attentivement	*carefully*	**lisez**	*read*
ces renseignements	*this information*	**négativement**	*in the negative (saying "no")*
d'après	*according to*		
décrivez	*describe*	**par**	*by*
dites	*say, tell*	**qui convient**	*(that is) appropriate*
en utilisant	*using*	**relisez**	*reread*
ensuite	*then, after(wards)*	**si oui ou non**	*whether or not*

7. Detailed Listing of the Contents

This section lists the contents of FRENCH FOR MASTERY in chart form. The teacher will find these charts useful in preparing course objectives, lesson plans, study guides, and tests. As the course progresses, the teacher may use the charts to recall where specific structures, vocabulary, sounds, or cultural topics were introduced. Lists have been established under the following headings: Structure, Vocabulary, Pronunciation, and Culture.

7.1 Structure

These charts list the grammar sections of the Student Text and cross-reference the related exercises.

Structure	Text Exercises	Workbook Exercises
Unit 1 Parlez-vous français?		
1.1 A. Les verbes en -er		
B. Le pronom sujet *je*	1	
C. L'élision	2, 3	C1
D. La négation avec *ne . . . pas*	4, 5, 6	D1, D2
1.2 A. Les pronoms sujets: *il, elle, ils, elles*	1, 2, 3, 4, 5, 6	A1, A2, A3
B. Questions à réponse affirmative ou négative	7, 8	B1, B2
1.3 A. Les pronoms sujets: *je, tu, nous, vous*	1, 2, 3	A1, A2, A3
B. Questions d'information	4, 5	B1, B2, B3
1.4 A. *Tu* ou *vous?*	1, 2	A1
B. Le présent des verbes réguliers en -er	3, 4, 5	B1
C. La construction: verbe + infinitif	6, 7, 8	C1, C2, C3
1.5 A. Le verbe *être*	1, 2	A1, A2
B. *Qui?*	3	B1
C. Expressions interrogatives avec *qui*	4	C1
D. L'interrogation avec inversion	5, 6, 7	D1
Unit 2 Salut, les amis!		
2.1 A. Noms masculins, noms féminins; l'article indéfini: *un/une*	1, 2	A1, A2
B. L'article défini: *le/la*	3, 4	B1
C. L'accord des adjectifs	5, 6	C1, C2
2.2 A. Le genre des noms: les objets	1, 2, 3, 4	A1, A2, A3
B. Le verbe *avoir*	5, 6	B1
C. L'article indéfini dans les phrases négatives	7, 8, 9	C1

	Structure	Text Exercises	Workbook Exercises
2.3	A. La place des adjectifs	1, 2, 3	A1, A2
	B. *Il est* ou *c'est?*	4, 5, 6	B1, B2, B3
2.4	A. L'article défini avec les noms géographiques	1, 2	A1
	B. Le pluriel: les noms et les articles	3, 4, 5, 6	B1
	C. Le pluriel: les adjectifs	7, 8	C1
	D. L'expression *il y a*	9	D1, D2
	E. Récapitulation: la forme des adjectifs	10	E1
2.5	A. Les expressions impersonnelles avec *c'est*	1, 2	A1
	B. Les pronoms accentués	3, 4, 5, 6	B1, B2, B3, B4
Unit 3	**Loisirs et vacances**		
3.1	A. Le verbe *aller*	1, 2	A1
	B. *À* + l'article défini	4, 5, 6	B1, B2, B3
	C. *Aller* + l'infinitif	7, 8	C1, C2
	Révision: *avoir* et *être*	AR	
3.2	A. *Chez*	1, 2, 3	A1, A2
	B. La possession avec *de*	4, 5, 6	B1
	C. *De* + l'article défini	7, 8	C1, C2
	D. *Jouer à* et *jouer de*	9	D1
3.3	A. Les adjectifs possessifs: *mon, ma, mes; ton, ta, tes*	1, 2, 3, 4	A1, A2
	B. L'âge	5	B1
	C. La construction: nom + *de* + nom	6	C1
3.4	A. L'adjectif possessif: *son, sa, ses*	1, 2, 3	A1
	B. L'adjectif possessif: *leur, leurs*	4	B1, B2
	C. Les nombres ordinaux	5	C1
3.5	A. Les adjectifs possessifs: *notre, nos; votre, vos*	1	A1
	B. Récapitulation: les adjectifs possessifs	2, 3	B1, B2
	C. *Être à*	4, 5	C1
Unit 4	**En ville**		
4.1	A. Les verbes réguliers en *-ir*	1, 2, 3	A1, A2
	B. L'expression interrogative *qu'est-ce que*	4	B1
	Révision: les nombres	AR	
	C. Les nombres de 60 à 100	5, 6, 7	C1, C2
	D. Les expressions interrogatives *combien* et *combien de*	8, 9	
4.2	A. *Acheter*	2	A1
	B. Les nombres de 100 à 1.000.000	3	
	C. L'adjectif interrogatif *quel?*	4, 5	C1
	D. L'adjectif démonstratif *ce*	6, 7, 8	D1, D2
4.3	A. Les adjectifs *vieux, nouveau* et *beau*	2, 3	A1
	B. La comparaison avec les adjectifs	4, 5, 6	B1, B2

	Structure	Text Exercises	Workbook Exercises
4.4	A. Expressions avec *avoir*	1, 2	A1, A2
	B. Les expressions *avoir envie de, avoir besoin de*	3, 4, 5	B1
	C. Le superlatif	6, 7	C1, C2
4.5	A. Les verbes réguliers en *-re*	1	A1
	B. Le pronom *on*	2, 3, 4	B1, B2
	C. Les prépositions avec les noms de pays	5	C1
Unit 5	**Au jour le jour**		
5.1	A. L'usage de l'article défini dans le sens général	1, 2	A1, A2
	B. Le verbe *espérer*	3, 4	B1
	C. L'article défini avec les jours de la semaine	5	C1
5.2	A. L'article partitif: *du, de la*	1, 2	A1, A2, A3
	B. L'article partitif dans les phrases négatives	3, 4	B1
	C. Le verbe *boire*	5, 7	C1
5.3	A. L'impératif: *tu* et *vous*	2, 3, 4	A1, A2
	B. Récapitulation: les articles (défini, indéfini, partitif)	5, 6	B1, B2
5.4	A. Le verbe *faire*	1, 2, 3	A1
	B. La construction: *faire du, faire de la*	4, 5, 6	B1
	C. Le verbe *venir*	7, 8	C1
	Révision: *être, avoir, aller, faire*	AR	AR
5.5	A. Le verbe *prendre*	1, 2, 3	A1
	B. L'impératif: *nous*	4, 5	B1
	C. La construction: *venir de* + infinitif	6, 7	C1, C2
Unit 6	**Un fana de football**		
6.1	A. Révision: le présent d'*être* et d'*avoir*	1, 2	A1
	B. Les questions avec inversion	3, 4, 5	B1
	C. L'usage de l'article défini avec les parties du corps	6, 7	C1, C2
6.2	A. Le passé composé des verbes en *-er*	2, 3, 4	A1
	B. Le passé composé à la forme négative	5, 6, 7, 8	B1
	C. Le participe passé du verbe *faire*	9, 10	C1
6.3	A. Le verbe *voir*	2, 3	A1
	B. Le passé composé des verbes réguliers en *-re*	4, 5, 6	B1
	C. Les participes passés irréguliers en *-u*	7, 8, 9	C1
	D. Les questions au passé composé	10	D1
6.4	A. Le verbe *mettre*	1, 2	A1
	B. Le passé composé des verbes réguliers en *-ir*	3, 4, 5	B1, B2
	C. Les participes passés irréguliers en *-is*	6, 7	C1
6.5	A. Les verbes *sortir, partir* et *dormir*	1, 2	A1
	B. Le passé composé avec *être*	3, 4, 5, 6, 7, 8, 9	B1, B2, B3, B4

Structure	Text Exercises	Workbook Exercises
Unit 7 Nous et les autres		
7.1 A. L'expression négative *ne . . . jamais*	1, 2	A1, A2
B. Les pronoms compléments *me, te, nous, vous*	3, 4, 5, 6	B1, B2
C. L'omission de l'article indéfini avec les professions	7	C1
7.2 A. Le verbe *connaître*	1, 2	A1
B. Les pronoms *le, la, les*	3, 4, 5, 6, 7, 8	B1, B2, B3
7.3 A. La construction: pronom + *voici, voilà*	1	
B. La place des pronoms à l'impératif	2, 3, 4	B1, B2
C. Le verbe *savoir*	5	C1
D. *Savoir* ou *connaître?*	6, 7	D1
7.4 A. Les expressions *quelqu'un, quelque chose* et leurs contraires	1, 2	A1, A2
B. Les pronoms *lui, leur*	3, 4, 5, 6	B1, B2
C. La place des pronoms compléments au passé composé	7, 8, 9	C1
7.5 A. Les verbes *dire, lire* et *écrire*	1, 2, 3, 4	A1, A2
B. La conjonction *que*	5	B1
C. Récapitulation: les pronoms compléments	6, 7, 8, 9	C1, C2
Unit 8 «La Leçon»		
8.1 A. Les verbes *pouvoir* et *vouloir*	1, 2, 3	A1
B. Le verbe *devoir*	4, 5	B1
C. La place des pronoms avec l'infinitif	6, 7	C1
8.2 A. Les adverbes en *-ment*	1, 2	A1
B. Les expressions de quantité avec les verbes	3, 4	B1
C. Les expressions de quantité avec les noms	5, 6	C1, C2
8.3 A. Le pronom *y*	1, 2, 3, 5	A1
B. Le pronom *en* remplaçant *de* + nom	6, 7	B1
8.4 A. Le verbe *ouvrir*	1	A1
B. Révision: *du, de la, des*	2, 3	B1
C. Le pronom *en* remplaçant *du, de la, des* + nom	4, 5, 6, 7, 8	C1, C2, C3
8.5 A. Le pronom *en* avec les expressions de quantité	2, 3	A1
B. Le pronom *en* avec *un, une* et les nombres	4, 5, 6, 7	B1, B2, B3

7.2 Vocabulary

The following tables summarize the contents of the *Vocabulaire spécialisé* sections.

Vocabulary Topic	Lesson	Page
Les nombres		
Les achats et les nombres de 0 à 10	P.3	16
Les nombres de 11 à 60	P.3	20
	Appendix 2	401
L'heure, la date et le temps		
L'heure	P.4	24
L'heure et les minutes	P.4	26
La date	P.5	30
Le temps et les saisons	P.6	36
Quand?	4.2	196
Le monde de tous les jours		
Salutations	P.1	4
Présentations	P.2	9
Objets courants	2.2	102
Ville et campagne	3.1	135
Les sports, les jeux et les passe-temps	3.2	145
Sports et passe-temps	5.3	237
Les sports	6.3	288
La famille	3.3	152
Les animaux domestiques	3.4	157
L'argent	4.1	187
Les vêtements	4.2	192
La mode	4.3	200
Les magasins et les commerçants	4.5	216
Les spectacles	5.1	223
Le théâtre	8.1	364
Les transports	5.5	253
Dans la maison	6.2	280
Les professions	7.1	315
On lit, on écrit, on dit	7.5	344

7.3 Pronunciation

The following list shows where specific phonemes (sounds), phonetic features, and sound-spelling correspondences are introduced for the first time and where they are reviewed. Some consonants which show only slight phonetic differences between French and English have not been given individual attention and practice. See also the Sound-spelling Correspondences chart, Appendix 1.

Phonemes	Introduced on page . . .	Reviewed on page . . .
Oral vowels		
/a/	49	375
/i/	49	
/u/	70	382
/y/	70	382
/o/	167	347
/ɔ/	113	299, 347
/e/	77	227, 397
/ɛ/	77	197, 227, 249, 375, 397
/ə/	197	256, 397
/ø/	155	331
/œ/	161	331
Nasal vowels		
/ã/	106	122, 375
/ɔ̃/	63	299
/ɛ̃/	99	122, 249
/œ̃/	122	241
Semi-vowels		
/w/	128	
/j/	211	249
/ɥ/	339	
Consonants		
/r/	56	307
/ʒ/	139	
/ʃ/	146	
/k/	189	
/t/	285	
/s/	316	
/ɲ/	325	
/p/	390	

Phonemes	Introduced on page . . .	Reviewed on page . . .
Special features		
Les lettres muettes	6	
L'alphabet	12	
Les signes orthographiques	12	
Les nombres de 1 à 10	18	
La liaison	24	204
Rythme et accent	32	
L'intonation	38	
Voyelles nasales	218	
Les lettres s et ss	234	
Les lettres ill et il	277	
Les lettres oi et oy	292	
Les terminaisons -tion et -sion	368	

7.4 Culture

The following list contains the cultural topic of each *Note culturelle* and *Section Magazine* reading selection. A specific cultural reading may be listed more than once if its topic fits different categories.

Topic	Section Magazine	Note culturelle
Le monde francophone		
Les Canadiens français		43
Qui parle français en Afrique?		59
Qui parle français en Europe?		65
Qui parle français dans le monde?		73
Bon voyage!	80	
Oui, ils parlent français!	87	
La carte du temps	88	

FRENCH FOR MASTERY

Second Edition

MASTERY

Salut, les amis!

Jean-Paul Valette
Rebecca M. Valette

D.C. HEATH AND COMPANY
Lexington, Massachusetts   Toronto
HEATH

Consultants
Charlotte Casgrain, Greenwich H.S., Greenwich, Connecticut
Karen Fritsche, Lincoln-Sudbury Regional H.S., Sudbury, Massachusetts
Natalie Goldschmidt, South Eugene H.S., Eugene, Oregon
Debra Griffin, Monnig Middle School, Fort Worth, Texas

Acknowledgments
In preparation for this revision, a survey was taken of teachers using the first edition of FRENCH FOR MASTERY. The many questionnaires that were returned were very encouraging in their positive evaluation of the program and very helpful in that they provided a direction for the planning of the second edition. The authors would like to thank those who participated. We also wish to thank the following teachers, who have used FRENCH FOR MASTERY, for their special assistance in the project: Jane Carlin, Anne Craven, Pat McCann, Lillian Scherban, and Maria Valis.

The authors would like to thank François Vergne for helping them assemble the realia which appear in the text.

Project Editors
Roger Coulombe
Valentia Dermer
Anita Raducanu
Carol Shanahan
Lawrence Lipson

D. C. Heath Consultants
Victoria Devlin
Teresa Carrera-Hanley

Design and Production
Josephine McGrath, *Book Designer*
Ann Rahimi-Assa, *Art Coordinator*
Mel Dietmeier, *Illustrator*
George Ulrich, *Map Illustrator*
Donna Lee Porter, *Production Coordinator*

Published simultaneously in Canada.

Printed in the United States of America.

International Standard Book Number: ~~0-669-02380-9~~ 0-669-02381-7

Library of Congress Catalog Card Number: 80-82107

Chers amis:

Before you begin your study of French, it might be worthwhile to review the many good reasons for learning this language — or for that matter any other modern language.

In today's world, French is a widely used language spoken daily by about 150 million people and understood by many millions more. French speakers represent a wide variety of ethnic and cultural backgrounds. They live not only in France and other parts of Europe, but also in North America, in Africa . . . in fact on all continents. French is the official language or <u>one of the official languages in</u> more than <u>30 countries</u> around the world. Knowing French can help you communicate with a large and diverse segment of the modern world.

French is also the language used by great philosophers, writers, and artists whose ideas have helped shape our own ways of thinking and feeling. The knowledge of French may help you better understand these ideas and, therefore, the world in which we live.

Another important reason to study French, or any other language, is that <u>language is a very important part of culture.</u> In learning a language you not only learn how other people express themselves but also how they live and what they think. This insight into another culture is important in a world where people of different backgrounds live in close contact. Your experience in learning French will also help you understand your own language and your own culture. It is often by comparing ourselves with others — by investigating how we differ and how we are similar — that we begin to learn who we really are.

Last but not least, French is an important world language <u>used in</u> <u>business and in the professions.</u> A knowledge of another language is important not only to translators and foreign language teachers but also to the many people — secretaries, sales representatives, accountants, lawyers — <u>who work in companies that do business with</u> <u>French-speaking countries</u> and to many employees in our government's foreign service.

As you can see, knowing French is not an end in itself, but a step toward several worthwhile objectives: communication with others, increased knowledge of the world in which we live, better understanding of ourselves . . . and maybe an extra advantage when you are looking for a job!

Now let's start . . .

En avant et bon courage!

Jean-Paul Valette   *Rebecca M. Valette*

Bonjour! Je m'appelle . . .

Alain	Henri	Nicolas
Albert	Hugues	Olivier
André	Jacques	Patrick
Antoine	Jean	Paul
Bernard	Jean-Claude	Philippe
Charles	Jean-François	Pierre
Christian	Jean-Louis	Raoul
Christophe	Jean-Paul	Raphaël
Claude	Jean-Philippe	Raymond
Daniel	Jean-Pierre	Richard
David	Jérôme	Robert
Denis	Joël	Roger
Édouard	Joseph	Samuel
Étienne	Laurent	Simon
François	Léon	Thomas
Geoffroy	Louis	Vincent
Georges	Luc	Yves
Gilbert	Marc	
Grégoire	Matthieu	
Guillaume	Michel	

Je m'appelle . . .

	Claire	Lucie	Sylvie
	Denise	Marguerite	Thérèse
	Diane	Marianne	Virginie
	Dominique	Marie	Viviane
	Éléonore	Marie-Anne	
Agnès	Élisabeth	Marie-Hélène	
Alice	Émilie	Marie-Louise	
Andrée	Ève	Marie-Thérèse	
Anne	Françoise	Marthe	
Anne-Marie	Geneviève	Michèle	
Annette	Hélène	Monique	
Barbara	Irène	Nathalie	
Béatrice	Isabelle	Nicole	
Brigitte	Janine	Patricia	
Caroline	Jeanne	Pauline	
Catherine	Joséphine	Rachel	
Cécile	Judith	Renée	
Chantal	Laure	Rose	
Charlotte	Lise	Sophie	
Christine	Louise	Suzanne	

Yves?
Guy?
Jean?
Henri?
Jacques?
Sébastien?
Jean-Paul?
Lucien?
Guillaume?
Philippe?
Charles?
Armand?
Gérard?
Pierre?
Jean-Pierre?
Eugène?
André?
Georges?
François?
Michel?
Paul?
Marc?
Luc?

Bonjour, le monde français!

Europe
1. (la) France
2. Monaco
3. (la) Belgique
4. (la) Suisse
5. (le) Luxembourg

Amérique du Nord
6. (le) Canada:
   (le) Québec
7. (les) États-Unis:
   (la) Louisiane
   (la) Nouvelle-Angleterre
8. Saint-Pierre-et-Miquelon

**Amérique Centrale,
Amérique du Sud**
9. (la) Guadeloupe
10. (la) Martinique
11. Haïti
12. (la) Guyane Française

Asie et Océanie
13. (le) Cambodge
14. (le) Laos
15. (le) Viêt-nam
16. (la) Nouvelle-Calédonie
17. (la) Polynésie Française:
    Tahiti

Afrique
18. (l')Algérie
19. (le) Bénin
20. (le) Burundi
21. (le) Cameroun
22. (la) Côte-d'Ivoire
23. (le) Gabon
24. (la) Guinée
25. (la) Haute-Volta
26. Madagascar
27. (le) Mali
28. (le) Maroc
29. (la) Mauritanie
30. (le) Niger
31. (la) République Centrafricaine
32. (la) République Populaire du Congo
33. (la) République Rwandaise
34. (la) Réunion
35. (le) Sénégal
36. (le) Tchad
37. (le) Togo
38. (la) Tunisie
39. (le) Zaïre

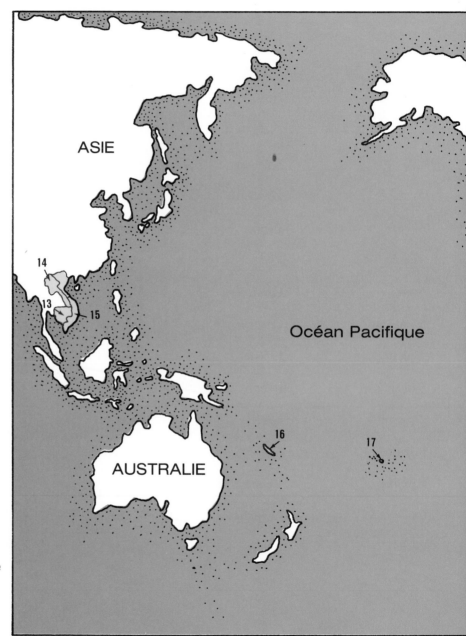

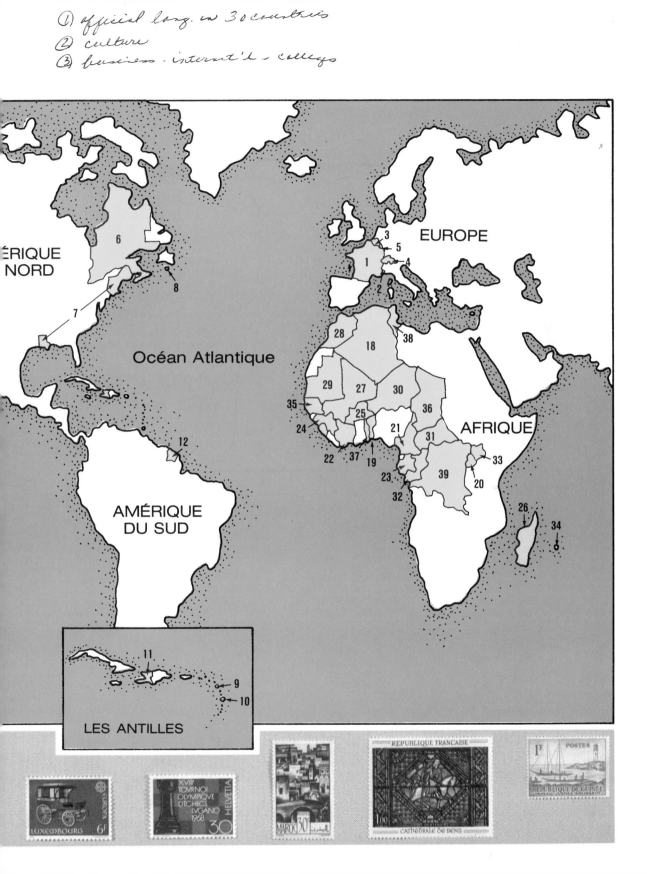

① official lang. in 30 countries
② culture
③ business · internat'l · colleges

ÉRIQUE
NORD

EUROPE

6

8

7

Océan Atlantique

3
5
1
4
2

38

28
18

29
27
30

35
25
24

36

22
37
19

21
31

AFRIQUE

23
32

33
39
20

26
34

AMÉRIQUE
DU SUD

11

9
10

LES ANTILLES

LUXEMBOURG 6f · EUROPA

XVIII TOURNOI OLYMPIQUE D'ÉCHECS LUGANO 1968 · 30 · HELVETIA

MAROC 30

RÉPUBLIQUE FRANÇAISE · 1.00 · CATHÉDRALE DE SENS

1F POSTES · RÉPUBLIQUE DE GUINÉE · TRAVAIL-JUSTICE-SOLIDARITÉ

Bonjour, la France!

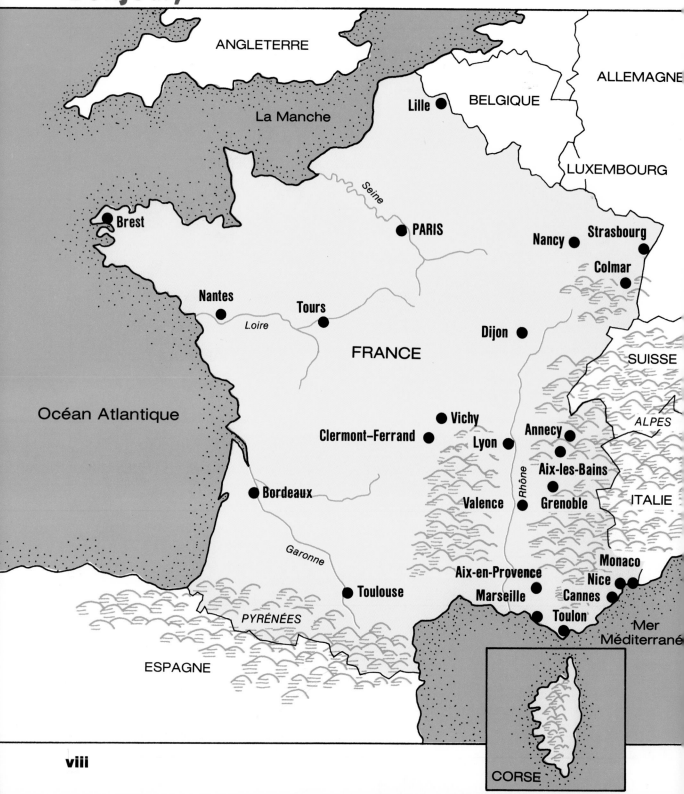

ANGLETERRE

La Manche

BELGIQUE

ALLEMAGNE

LUXEMBOURG

Lille

Seine

Brest

PARIS

Nancy

Strasbourg

Colmar

Nantes

Tours

Loire

FRANCE

Dijon

SUISSE

Océan Atlantique

ALPES

Vichy

Annecy

Clermont–Ferrand

Lyon

Aix-les-Bains

Rhône

Bordeaux

Valence

Grenoble

ITALIE

Garonne

Monaco

Aix-en-Provence

Nice

Toulouse

Marseille

Cannes

PYRÉNÉES

Toulon

Mer Méditerrané

ESPAGNE

CORSE

Contents

OBJECTIVES
The purpose of this preliminary unit is to introduce the students to the French language and French sounds through the presentation of a few stock phrases and other items that young people are generally eager to learn and will remember easily.

1. Greetings
2. Introductions
3. Numbers from 0 to 60
4. Time of day
5. Dates: days of the week and months of the year
6. Weather and the seasons

No formal grammar is presented in this unit. If you want to begin your teaching of French with formal grammar, you may want to start with Unité 1 which focuses on verbs. Then you may come back to these preliminary lessons as you progress through the book. Reentry points for the presentation or review of these materials are indicated in the text.

You may also wish to introduce the Classroom Expressions which are listed in the Teacher's Edition and in the Activity Masters.

PRÉLUDE
Bonjour, les Français!

PRÉLUDE
Leçon 1 Bonjour!

À Nice . . . le premier jour de classe
— Bonjour, Paul!
— Bonjour, Anne!

— Salut, Marc!
— Salut, Suzanne!

— Au revoir, Jacques!
— Au revoir, Monique!

— Qui est-ce?
— C'est Janine.

— Voici Philippe.
— Bonjour!

— Voilà Nathalie.
— Salut!

Paul

Anne

Marc

Suzanne

Janine

Philippe

Jacques

Monique

Nathalie

— Voici Monsieur Laval.
— Voici Madame Simonet.
— Voici Mademoiselle Rochette.

— Bonjour, Monsieur!
— Bonjour, Madame!
— Bonjour, Mademoiselle!

— Au revoir, Monsieur!
— Au revoir, Madame!
— Au revoir, Mademoiselle!

Monsieur Laval

Madame Simonet

Mademoiselle Rochette

Hello!

In Nice . . . the first day of school

Hello, Paul!
Hello, Anne!

Hi, Marc!
Hi, Suzanne!

Good-by, Jacques.
Good-by, Monique.

Who's that?
It's Janine.

Here's Philippe.
Hello!

There's Nathalie.
Hi!

Here's Mr. Laval.
Here's Mrs. Simonet.
Here's Miss Rochette.

Good morning, (Sir).
Good morning, (Ma'am).
Good morning, (Miss).

Good-by, (Sir).
Good-by, (Ma'am).
Good-by, (Miss).

NOTE CULTURELLE OPTIONAL

Nice You may refer the students to the map of France on p. viii.

Nice, a popular resort on the French Riviera (**la Côte d'Azur**),
is one of the oldest cities in France. (It was founded by the
Greeks about 400 B.C.) Today Nice is a prosperous and
modern city. Every year its famous Mardi Gras celebrations
(**le Carnaval de Nice**) attract thousands of visitors.

Nice was named by the Greeks in honor of Nike, the goddess of victory.

Vocabulaire spécialisé   Salutations *(Greetings)*

Bonjour!	*Hello!*	**Bonjour,** Jacques!
	Good morning! Good afternoon!	
Salut!	*Hi!*	**Salut,** Nathalie!
Au revoir!	*Good-by!*	**Au revoir,** Marc!
Voici . . .	*This is . . . Here's . . . Here comes . . .*	**Voici** Suzanne.
Voilà . . .	*That is . . . There's . . .*	**Voilà** Monsieur Laval.
Qui est-ce?	*Who's that? Who is it?*	**Qui est-ce?**
C'est . . .	*That's . . . It's . . .*	**C'est** Paul.
Monsieur	*Mr.* There is no French equivalent for the title "Ms."	**Voici Monsieur** Dumas.
Madame	*Mrs.*	**Voilà Madame** Pascal.
Mademoiselle	*Miss*	**Voilà Mademoiselle** Rochette.

You may point out that **voici** and **voilà** also correspond to *here are/come* and *there are.* **Voici Jacques et Nicole. Voilà Daniel et Suzanne.**

Marie-Laure Ducamp

Dîner

Vendredi 17 Novembre

Réponse avant le 10 novembre
45-47, Rue Pauline Borghèse
92200 Neuilly

. . . *écises*

FRANÇOIS F. VERGNE

256.12.49

85 RUE LA BOËTIE, 75008 PARIS.

monsieur et madame georges malassis
25, av. gabriel péri - 94170 le perreux
tél. 872.69.59

Note: **Monsieur, Madame,** and **Mademoiselle** are often abbreviated **M., Mme,** and **Mlle** in writing.

NOTES CULTURELLES

1. Bonjour! In many situations the Americans and the French behave and react in very similar ways. However, in certain situations their behavior is different. Every morning, for instance, French children greet their parents not only by saying **bonjour**, but also by kissing them. Whenever French people meet, they shake hands, even if they meet more than once during the day. Teenagers, especially boys, also shake hands. Girls often greet one another with a kiss on each cheek.

2. Bonjour, Monsieur! Bonjour, Madame! Bonjour, Mademoiselle! On the whole, the relationships between adults and teenagers are much more formal in France than in the United States. It is, for instance, perfectly proper for American students to greet their teacher with "Good morning" or "Hi." French students, however, do not greet their teachers with a simple **Bonjour** and would not think of using the informal **Salut.** To a teacher it is customary to say **Bonjour, Monsieur** (or **Bonjour, Madame** or **Bonjour, Mademoiselle**).

You may have noted that the French do not use the last name when greeting a person. They say **Bonjour, Madame,** whereas English-speaking people would say "Hello, Mrs. Jones" or "Hello, Mrs. Smith."

The Panthéon, located in the Quartier Latin in Paris, is the burial place of Voltaire, Rousseau, Hugo, Zola, and La Fayette.

Prononciation

Les lettres muettes *(The silent letters)*

Many letters in written French are not pronounced. These are called *silent letters.*

The **e** at the end of a word is silent.[1]

    Moniqu~e~   Ann~e~

The **s** at the end of a word is silent.

    Deni~s~   Jacque~s~   Other examples: Loui~s~, Charle~s~, Françoi~s~

The letter **h** is not pronounced.   However, as in English, the letters **ph** represent the sound /f/: Philippe. The letters **ch** represent the sound /ʃ/: Michel.

    T~h~omas   Nat~h~alie   Other examples: T~h~érèse, Élisabet~h~, Judit~h~

Usually a consonant at the end of a word is not pronounced. Exceptions: **c, f, l,** and sometimes **r** (the consonants of **careful**).

If necessary, review the difference between vowels and consonants.
vowels: a, e, i, o, u, y
consonants: all other letters

SILENT	PRONOUNCED
Bernar~d~	Mar<u>c</u>, Lu<u>c</u>
Rober~t~	Madam~e~ Resti<u>f</u>, Mad~e~moisell~e~ Lebeu<u>f</u>
Vincen~t~	Miche<u>l</u>, Danie<u>l</u>
Roge~r~	Bonjou<u>r</u>, Victo<u>r</u>!

Note: French is a relatively easy language to learn because it contains many words which are similar to English words. French, however, is *not* pronounced like English, and every letter is *not* pronounced as it is written. The **Prononciation** sections of your book will help you learn the French sound system. However, the best way to acquire a good French pronunciation is to listen to your teacher, listen to the tapes, and, whenever possible, listen to French people and French records.

ACTIVITÉ 1 Bonjour! Au revoir!

It is the first day of school. The following French boys and girls meet and say "hello." After classes they say "good-by." Play the roles of these students, using the words in parentheses. You may want to model the names for the students.

  → (bonjour)
    Paul / Louis   Paul: **Bonjour, Louis!**   Only the underlined final consonants are pronounced.
                  Louis: **Bonjour, Paul!**

(bonjour)	(salut)	(au revoir)
1. Annie / Philippe	6. Nathalie / Thomas	11. Lu<u>c</u> / Miche<u>l</u>
2. Isabelle / Monique	7. Janine / Charles	12. Paul / Victo<u>r</u>
3. Louise / Denise	8. Georges / Anne	13. Chantal / Catherine
4. Jacques / Nicolas	9. Yves / Élisabeth	14. Louis / Louise
5. Louis / Denis	10. Mar<u>c</u> / Sylvie	15. Denis / Denise

    [1]The slash line is used to remind you that a letter is not pronounced.

ACTIVITÉ 2 **Présentations** *(Introductions)*

Annie is a new student, and Pierre is introducing his friends to her. Annie says
"hello" to each one. Play the roles of Pierre and Annie according to the model.

→ Thomas   Pierre: **Voici Thomas.**   You should model the names. The final consonant of each name
               Annie: **Bonjour, Thomas!**   is silent.

1. Albert   3. Charles   5. Robert   7. Denis
2. Bernard   4. Édouard   6. Roger   8. Vincent

VARIATION: Pierre: Voilà Thomas.
                Annie: Salut, Thomas.

ACTIVITÉ 3 **Les professeurs**   OPTIONAL

Annie now asks Pierre who the teachers are. She greets them. Play the roles
according to the model.

→ Madame Dumas   Annie: **Qui est-ce?**   These family names are common not only in France, but also
                         Pierre: **C'est Madame Dumas.**   in French-speaking Canada and Louisiana. Be sure your
                         Annie: **Bonjour, Madame!**   students do not pronounce the final consonants. Remind them
                         that they should not use last names when greeting these people.

1. Madame Camus   4. Madame Michaud   7. Madame Brunet
2. Mademoiselle Ledoux   5. Monsieur Denis   8. Monsieur Lucas
3. Monsieur Simonet   6. Mademoiselle Dupont   VARIATION: Say good-by to each one.
                                                     Au revoir, Madame!

Entre nous

Expressions pour la conversation

The French often use the following expressions:

> **Je sais.**   *I know.*
> **Je ne sais pas.**   *I don't know.*

Mini-dialogues   OPTIONAL

Look at the first picture and the sample dialog; then create
new dialogs based on the pictures below.

NATHALIE: Qui est-ce?
 PHILIPPE: Je ne sais pas.
NATHALIE: Ah, je sais ... C'est Brigitte.

Brigitte

| **Bernard** | **Monique** | **Monsieur Simon** | **Madame Pascal** | **Mademoiselle Thomas** |

PRÉLUDE
Leçon 2 Une coïncidence

À Annecy ... à la Maison des Jeunes

Teenagers playing **le baby-foot.**

—Ça va, Jean-Paul?
—Ça va. Et toi?
—Ça va bien.

—Je m'appelle Hélène. Et toi?
—Je m'appelle Marie-Noëlle.

—Comment t'appelles-tu?
—Je m'appelle Jean-Michel.
—Moi aussi. Jean-Michel Vallée.
—Moi, je m'appelle Jean-Michel Valette.
—Quelle coïncidence!

NOTE CULTURELLE   OPTIONAL

Annecy
You may have the students locate Annecy on the map of France on p. viii.

Annecy, one of the most beautiful cities in France, is situated in the Alps on the shores of the **Lac d'Annecy.** Like many other French cities and towns, it has a modern youth center (**Maison des Jeunes**), which offers a wide variety of cultural and sports activities.

Avoid giving word-for-word translations of expressions such as **je m'appelle**. However, you may want to point out quickly that different languages have different ways of expressing the same idea. E.g. **Je m'appelle** literally means *I call myself* and not *My name is.*

Vocabulaire spécialisé **Présentations** *(Introductions)*

Je m'appelle . . .	*My name is . . .*
Comment t'appelles-tu?	*What's your name?*
Ça va?	*How are you? How's everything?*
Ça va.	*Fine. I'm OK. Everything's all right.*
Et toi?	*And you?*
Moi aussi.	*Me too.*

You may want to point out that literally **Ça va?** means *Are things going (all right)?*

Ça va . . .   **bien**   **très bien**

mal   **très mal**   **comme ci, comme ça**

A coincidence

In Annecy . . . at the Youth Center

How's everything, Jean-Paul?
Fine. And you?
Everything's fine (going well).

My name is Hélène. And yours?
My name is Marie-Noëlle.

What's your name?
My name is Jean-Michel.
Mine too. Jean-Michel Vallée.
My name is Jean-Michel Valette.
What a coincidence!

NOTE CULTURELLE

Niveaux de langue *(Levels of language)*

French teenagers are much more formal with adults than with their friends. This level of formality (or familiarity) is reflected in the way they speak. French students, for instance, use **Ça va?** when talking to their friends. When talking to their teachers, they would say **Comment allez-vous?** which is the more formal way of asking *How are you?* As you will learn later on, the French have two ways of addressing people: a *formal* form and a *familiar* form.

Although the names are fictitious, the following streets and avenues are real places. You may ask the students to point out the various cities on a map of France.

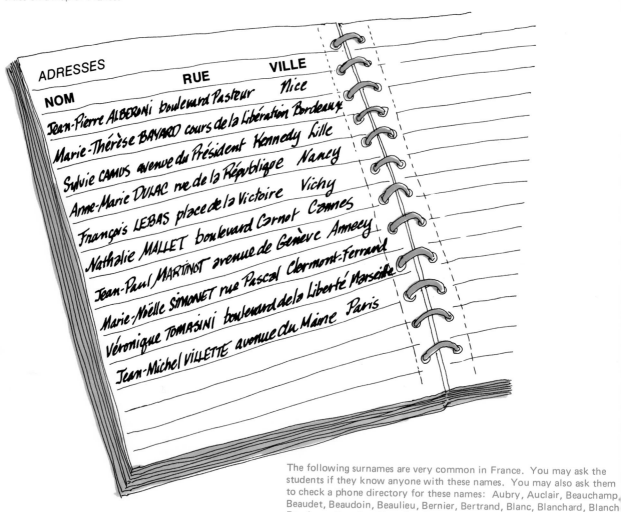

ADRESSES

NOM	RUE	VILLE
Jean-Pierre ALBERONI	boulevard Pasteur	Nice
Marie-Thérèse BAYARD	cours de la Libération	Bordeaux
Sylvie CAMUS	avenue du Président Kennedy	Lille
Anne-Marie DULAC	rue de la République	Nancy
François LEBAS	place de la Victoire	Vichy
Nathalie MALLET	boulevard Carnot	Cannes
Jean-Paul MARTINOT	avenue de Genève	Annecy
Marie-Noëlle SIMONET	rue Pascal	Clermont-Ferrand
Véronique TOMASINI	boulevard de la Liberté	Marseille
Jean-Michel VILLETTE	avenue du Maine	Paris

The following surnames are very common in France. You may ask the students if they know anyone with these names. You may also ask them to check a phone directory for these names: Aubry, Auclair, Beauchamp, Beaudet, Beaudoin, Beaulieu, Bernier, Bertrand, Blanc, Blanchard, Blanch Boudreau, Bouvier, Chevalier, Desmarais, Duchesne, Dumas, Dupont, Dup Dupuis, Duval, Gautier, Hamel, Joli, Joly, Lebeau, Leblanc, Leclair, Lecle Lejeune, Letendre, Marchand, Mercier, Meunier, Moreau, Pasquier, Prévos Renaud, Rousseau, Tessier, Tixier

NOTE CULTURELLE

Les noms français (French names)

Many French names have English equivalents:

Jean	*John*	**Jacques**	*James*	**Guillaume**	*William*	**François**	*Frank*
Hélène	*Helen*	**Suzanne**	*Susan*	**Monique**	*Monica*	**Marie**	*Mary*

It is not uncommon for French people to have two first names, usually beginning with **Jean** (for boys) or **Marie** (for girls). These names are hyphenated.

Jean-Pierre	**Jean-Marc**	**Jean-Paul**	**Jean-Michel**	**Jean-Philippe**
Marie-Hélène	**Marie-Laure**	**Marie-Claire**	**Marie-France**	**Marie-Louise**

Nicknames or shortened names are generally not used in France, except for young children.

Jojo (for **Georges**)	**Pierrot** (for **Pierre**)	**Dédé** (for **André**)
Mimi (for **Michèle**)	**Gigi** (for **Ginette**)	**Kiki** (for **Christine**)

You may assign French names to your students. If the American name doesn't have a French equivalent, you may use an approximatio For instance, Nancy may become Nathalie. See pp. iv–v for the list of names.

SUGGESTED REALIA:
1. Map of a French city
2. French phone directory
3. Guide Michelin with city maps

ACTIVITÉ 1 Je m'appelle . . .

Introduce yourself and ask the student next to you to do the same.

→ **Je m'appelle Nancy Martin.
Comment t'appelles-tu?**

ACTIVITÉ 2 À la Maison des Jeunes *(At the Youth Center)*   OPTIONAL

The following young people are introducing themselves. Play the roles of
each pair according to the model.

→ Paul / Sylvie   Paul: **Je m'appelle Paul. Et toi?**
                     Sylvie: **Je m'appelle Sylvie.**
                     Paul: **Ça va?**
                     Sylvie: **Ça va bien.**

The purpose of this exercise is to provide pronunciation practice. Be sure to model each name.

1. Jean / Marie
2. Thomas / Anne
3. Michel / Suzanne
4. Hélène / Philippe
5. Denis / Monique

6. François / Marie-Louise
7. Jean-Michel / Anne-Marie
8. Jean-Claude / Marie-Solange
9. Jean-Philippe / Marie-France
10. Jean-Louis / Mélanie

ACTIVITÉ 3 Ça va?   OPTIONAL

Sometimes we feel good, sometimes we don't. What would you say to a
French friend who asked you **Ça va?** in each of the situations described
below? Use an appropriate expression from the **Vocabulaire spécialisé.**

→ You have the flu.   **Ça va comme ci, comme ça.**

1. You received an A in French.
2. Your grandparents sent you a check.
3. Your best friend invited you to a party.
4. You lost your wallet.
5. You bent a wheel on your bicycle.
6. You won a prize in a photo contest.
7. You received a B on an English paper.
8. It is your birthday.

Prononciation

L'alphabet et les signes orthographiques *(spelling marks)*

1. L'alphabet

The alphabet is presented here to introduce the French sound system. By having the students repeat the letter, you may be able to identify those who have trouble hearing and repeating new sounds. These students may need extra practice with the Tape Program.

Repeat after the teacher:

A	a	H	hache	O	o	V	vé
B	bé	I	i	P	pé	W	double vé
C	cé	J	ji	Q	ku	X	ixe
D	dé	K	ka	R	erre	Y	i grec
E	e	L	elle	S	esse	Z	zède
F	effe	M	emme	T	té		
G	gé	N	enne	U	u		

Appendix 1 contains a reference list of Sound-spelling Correspondences.

2. Les signes orthographiques

Four spelling marks may appear on vowels:

(´)	l'accent aigu *(acute accent)*	**René**
(`)	l'accent grave *(grave accent)*	**Voilà Michèle.**
(^)	l'accent circonflexe *(circumflex accent)*	**Jérôme, dîner**
(¨)	le tréma *(diaeresis)*	**Noël, naïf**

Spelling marks, with the exception of the cedilla, are often omitted on capital letters. In this text, accents are used on capital letters to simplify the learning of spelling and pronunciation. Accents will, however, be missing from much of the realia. Explain that accents are often dropped in journalistic usage, especially on capital letters.

One spelling mark may appear under the letter **c**:

(¸)	la cédille *(cedilla)*	**Ça va, François?**

Note: These marks are part of the spelling of words. They cannot be left out.

ACTIVITÉ 4 **Au bureau des réservations** *(At the reservation desk)*

Imagine that you are an employee at the reservation desk of **Air France**, the French national airline. As you confirm the reservations of the following passengers, spell their last names in French.

→ Monsieur Marin **Monsieur Marin. M.A.R.I.N.** VARIATION: Have students spell their own names.

1. Mademoiselle Lucas
2. Monsieur Thomas
3. Mademoiselle Duval
4. Monsieur Marty
5. Madame Maubrey
6. Mademoiselle Aziza

Entre nous

Expressions pour la conversation

To ask about someone's health you would use one of the
following expressions:

(to a friend) **Comment vas-tu?** *How are you?*
(to an adult) **Comment allez-vous?** *How are you?*

You may explain that **Comment vas-tu?** is a little more formal than **Ça va?** Both expressions are
used when talking to friends. **Comment allez-vous?** is even more formal and is used with adults.

Mini-dialogues OPTIONAL

Create new dialogs by replacing the underlined words
with the words suggested in the pictures.

Madame Laval

PAUL: Bonjour, <u>Madame</u>.
MADAME LAVAL: Bonjour, Paul.
PAUL: <u>Comment allez-vous, Madame?</u>
MADAME LAVAL: <u>Très bien</u>. Et toi?

These expressions are given in the **Vocabulaire spécialisé** on p. 9.

| Janine | Monsieur Roland | Jean-Pierre | Mademoiselle Calmas |

PRÉLUDE
Leçon 3 Combien?

The objective of this lesson is to teach numbers. These are reentered in Prélude, Leçon 4 (teaching time) and P.5 (teaching dates). If you do not intend to teach students the minutes in P.4, you could simply introduce the numbers 1–10 at this time.

À Tours . . .

Dans une librairie

— Donnez-moi *Paris-Match*, s'il vous plaît.
— Voici, Mademoiselle.
— C'est combien?
— Cinq francs, Mademoiselle.
— Voilà cinq francs, Monsieur.
— Merci, Mademoiselle.

Dans un café

— Un Coca-Cola, s'il vous plaît!
— Oui, Mademoiselle. Et pour vous, Monsieur?
— Un café, s'il vous plaît . . . et un sandwich.
— Mais oui, Monsieur!

How much?

In Tours . . .

In a bookstore
Give me *Paris-Match*, please.
Here you are, (Miss).
How much is it?
Five francs, (Miss).
Here are five francs, (Sir).
Thank you, (Miss).

In a café
A Coca-Cola, please.
Yes, (Miss). And for you, (Sir)?
A cup of coffee, please . . . and a sandwich.
All right, (Sir).

The château Azay-le-Rideau in the Loire Valley.

NOTES CULTURELLES

1. Tours   The city of Tours is located on the Loire River in a region known for its castles, its gardens, and the purity of the French spoken there. It is an excellent starting point for bicycle trips.   You may have the students locate Tours on the map of France on p. viii.

2. Paris-Match   *Paris-Match* is one of the most popular French magazines.   If available, you may bring a copy of *Paris-Match* to class.

3. Le Coca-Cola   Coca-Cola is very popular among French teenagers. Although few young people have Coke with their meals, many order it at cafés. When ordering it, one may simply ask for **un coca**.

If available, you may show pictures of well-known "châteaux de la Loire": Chenonceaux, Amboise, Azay-le-Rideau, Villandry, Chambord, etc.

Leçon trois **15**

Vocabulaire spécialisé

Les achats et les nombres de 0 à 10
(Purchases and the numbers from 0 to 10)

0	**zéro**	4	**quatre**	8	**huit**
1	**un**	5	**cinq**	9	**neuf**
2	**deux**	6	**six**	10	**dix**
3	**trois**	7	**sept**		

Combien?	*How much?*
C'est combien?	*How much is it?*
C'est dix francs.	*It's ten francs.*
Oui	*Yes*
Non	*No*
Pardon.	*Excuse me.*
Merci.	*Thank you.*
s'il vous plaît	*please* (formal form)
s'il te plaît	*please* (familiar form)
Donnez-moi . . .	*Give me . . .* (formal form)
Donne-moi . . .	*Give me . . .* (familiar form)

Note: The French expressions corresponding to "please" and "give me" have both a *formal* and a *familiar* form. Be sure to use the formal form when speaking to your teacher or other adults, and the familiar form when speaking to your friends.

NOTE CULTURELLE OPTIONAL

L'argent français *(French money)*

The French franc (**le franc français**) is the monetary unit of France. The franc, which is worth somewhat less than a U.S. quarter, is divided into 100 **centimes.**

French money is issued as follows:

Pièces *(Coins)*

    **1 centime, 5 centimes, 10 centimes, 20 centimes, ½ franc (50 centimes),
    1 franc, 2 francs, 5 francs, 10 francs**

*Have the students note that the final **c** of franc is not pronounced. (This is an exception to the rule on p.6.)*

The 2-franc coin was introduced in the summer of 1979. The 5-franc bill has been withdrawn from circulation.

Billets *(Bills)*

    10 francs, 50 francs, 100 francs, 500 francs

Belgium and Switzerland, where French is one of the national languages, also use the franc as the monetary unit. The value of these currencies—**le franc belge** and **le franc suisse**—is different from that of the French franc.

*The approximate values of these currencies are:
1 franc belge = 3 cents
1 franc suisse = 50 cents*

Pictured on the bills are: 10 F: the composer Hector Berlioz (1803–1869); 50 F: the portrait painter Maurice Quentin de la Tour (1704–1788); 100 F: the painter Eugéne Delacroix (1798–1863); 500 F: the philosopher and mathematician Blaise Pascal (1623–1662).

SUGGESTED REALIA: French money; money from other French-speaking countries.

Prononciation

The distinction between vowel sound and consonant sound is an important one. For practice, give the students cognates and ask them to identify which words begin with a vowel sound and which begin with a consonant sound.

auto autobus hélicoptère hôtel harmonica américain chocolat café taxi bus radio restaurant télévision

Note: Students will encounter mainly the mute h; therefore, they should consider words beginning with h as beginning with a vowel sound, unless otherwise noted.

Les nombres de 1 à 10 *(The numbers from 1 to 10)*

Numbers are used alone, for instance in counting: 1, 2, 3, etc., or they are used with nouns: **1 centime, 2 francs, 3 dollars,** etc. Note how numbers are pronounced when they are used alone and when they are used with nouns.[1] Repeat after your teacher.

NUMBER ALONE	NUMBER + CONSONANT SOUND	NUMBER + VOWEL SOUND
1 un	un franc	un /n/ objet
2 deux	deux francs	deux /z/ objets
3 trois	trois francs	trois /z/ objets
4 quatre	quatre francs	quatre objets
5 cinq /k/	cinq francs	cinq /k/ objets
6 six /s/	six francs	six /z/ objets
7 sept /t/	sept francs	sept /t/ objets
8 huit /t/	huit francs	huit /t/ objets
9 neuf /f/	neuf francs	neuf /f/ objets
10 dix /s/	dix francs	dix /z/ objets

When numbers are used alone—
the final consonants of the numbers 5 to 10 are pronounced;
the **x** of **six** (6) and **dix** (10) is pronounced /s/.

When numbers are followed by nouns which begin with a consonant sound—
the final consonant of the number is *not* pronounced, except for the numbers **sept** (7) and **neuf** (9).

When numbers are followed by nouns which begin with a vowel sound, that is, **a, e, i, o, u, h,** and **y** + consonant—
the final consonant of the number is pronounced as if it were the first letter of the next word;
the **x** of **deux** (2), **six** (6), and **dix** (10) is pronounced /z/.

ACTIVITÉ 1 Séries

Continue the following series:

1. 1, 2, 3, . . .
2. 1, 3, 5, . . .
3. 2, 4, 6, . . .
4. 10, 9, 8, . . .
5. 10, 8, 6, . . .
6. 9, 7, 5, . . .

[1]Sounds are given between diagonal lines.

LOTO   TIRAGE N° 2
DU 9 JANVIER 1980

| 7 | 9 | 4 | 6 | 3 | 2 |

NUMERO COMPLEMENTAIRE   10

Have students practice numbers followed by nouns by having them count in chain exercises:
un taxi deux taxis trois taxis. . .
un hôtel deux hôtels trois hôtels. . .

ACTIVITÉ 2 La loterie *(The raffle)*

Imagine that you are attending a French school. The school has organized a raffle for the benefit of the choir, and you have been chosen to draw the winning numbers. Announce each one, beginning with **le** *(the)*.

→ 8 – 0 – 2 – 9   **le huit – zéro – deux – neuf**   VARIATION: Have the students close their books, and read the numbers aloud for them to write down.

1. 4 – 0 – 5 – 8
2. 9 – 4 – 8 – 1
3. 7 – 8 – 3 – 6
4. 3 – 1 – 0 – 2

5. 7 – 0 – 5 – 2
6. 1 – 3 – 5 – 6
7. 7 – 4 – 8 – 2
8. 3 – 6 – 7 – 9

ACTIVITÉ 3 Au café «Le Floride»

Imagine you are working in a large French café. Call out the following orders.

1. 8 cafés *(coffees)*
2. 3 chocolats
3. 5 thés *(teas)*
4. 6 sandwichs
5. 2 Coca-Colas
6. 10 chocolats
7. 5 cafés
8. 6 thés
9. 2 orangeades
10. 6 orangeades
11. 10 orangeades
12. 5 orangeades

Make sure that the students make the liaison with **orangeade.** (**Orangeade** is a type of orange soda.)

ACTIVITÉ 4 S'il te plaît, Papa . . .   OPTIONAL

Imagine that you want to do the following things, but you do not have any money. Estimate the price of each item in dollars, and ask your father for what you need. Follow the model.

→ to buy a record   **S'il te plaît, Papa, donne-moi cinq dollars.**

1. to buy two records
2. to buy a magazine
3. to buy a paperback
4. to go to the movies
5. to invite a friend to the movies

6. to invite two friends to the movies
7. to go out for pizza
8. to invite two friends to have ice cream
9. to buy a pair of sunglasses
10. to buy a cassette

This is a free-response exercise. Encourage several responses for each cue.

Vocabulaire spécialisé   Les nombres de 11 à 60 *(The numbers from 11 to 60)*

The numbers from 61 to infinity are presented on pp. 186 and 194.

11	onze	21	vingt et un	31	trente et un
12	douze	22	vingt-deux	32	trente-deux
13	treize	23	vingt-trois	33	trente-trois . . .
14	quatorze	24	vingt-quatre	40	quarante
15	quinze	25	vingt-cinq	41	quarante et un
16	seize	26	vingt-six	42	quarante-deux . . .
17	dix-sept	27	vingt-sept	50	cinquante
18	dix-huit	28	vingt-huit	51	cinquante et un
19	dix-neuf	29	vingt-neuf	52	cinquante-deux . . .
20	vingt	30	trente	60	soixante

You may have the students note the hyphen in compound numbers other than 21, 31, 41, etc.

Notes: 1. The word **et** *(and)* is used only with the numbers 21, 31, 41, 51.
2. You have seen that the numbers 1-10 are pronounced differently, depending on how they are used. The same changes in pronunciation also occur when these numbers are used in combination.

SUGGESTED REALIA: hotel or restaurant bills; other bills.

six /s/   six francs   six /z/ objets
trente-six /s/   trente-six francs   trente-six /z/ objets

As a class activity you may play "Loto" with cards bearing numbers from 1–60. ("Loto" is the French name for Bingo.)

✓ *ACTIVITÉ 5*   **Nouvelles séries** *(New series)*

Complete the following series:

1. 10, 20, . . . 60
2. 14, 16, . . . 40
3. 13, 15, . . . 41
4. 11, 21, . . . 51
5. 15, 25, . . . 55
6. 16, 26, . . . 56
7. 18, 22, 26, . . . 58
8. 19, 22, 25, . . . 58

VARIATION: Do each series as a chain exercise, choosing students at random.

✓ *ACTIVITÉ 6*   **Le standard** *(The switchboard)*

Imagine that you are working at the switchboard of IBM-France in Paris.
Ask for the following numbers:

→ 10.20.30 à Nice   **Donnez-moi le dix-vingt-trente à Nice, s'il vous plaît.**

1. 20.23.25 à Lille
2. 30.40.60 à Tours
3. 14.18.16 à Lyon
4. 42.32.52 à Nantes

5. 50.60.40 à Annecy
6. 23.33.53 à Cannes
7. 18.28.58 à Colmar
8. 41.51.11 à Marseille

VARIATION: You may dictate the numbers for recognition, omitting the names of the cities.

In France, except for Paris, telephone numbers are given as three sets of two-digit numbers. A two-digit number beginning with "0" would be read **zéro-un, zéro-deux,** etc.

ACTIVITÉ 7 S'il te plaît, Maman . . .   OPTIONAL

Imagine that you want to buy the following things, but you do not have any
money. This time ask your mother to give you what you need for your
purchases. Estimate the price of each item in dollars.   Keep prices under $60. Encourage
several responses for each cue.

→ a tennis racket   **S'il te plaît, Maman, donne-moi trente dollars.**

1. a used bicycle
2. a transistor radio
3. a pair of jeans
4. running shoes
5. a bathing suit
6. a record album

Entre nous

Expression pour la conversation

To express *surprise,* the French often say:

Oh là là!   *Oh dear! Wow! Whew!*

Mini-dialogues   OPTIONAL

Imagine that you are in a French café. Create new dialogs by replacing the
underlined words with the words suggested in the pictures.

CLAIRE: Un café, s'il vous plaît.
LE GARÇON (*waiter*): Oui, Mademoiselle.
CLAIRE: C'est combien?
LE GARÇON: Huit francs.
CLAIRE: Oh là là! C'est cher!
(*That's expensive!*)

SUGGESTED REALIA: café check.

un café

8 francs

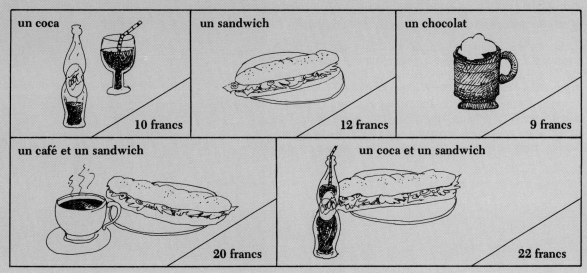

un coca — 10 francs

un sandwich — 12 francs

un chocolat — 9 francs

un café et un sandwich — 20 francs

un coca et un sandwich — 22 francs

Leçon 4

Conversations dans un café

This lesson is in two parts. The first part and the first conversation teach how to tell time using full hours. The second part and the second conversation teach the divisions of the hour. You may wish to skip the second part and come back to it at a later time.

À Dijon . . . dans un café

Conversation numéro 1: Hélène et Paul

HÉLÈNE: Quelle heure est-il?
PAUL: Il est une heure.
HÉLÈNE: Et à quelle heure est le concert?
PAUL: À deux heures!
HÉLÈNE: Ça va. Nous avons le temps!

The expression **ça va** was introduced in Leçon 2 with the meaning of *I'm fine.* In a more general sense **ça va** means *fine, good, that's okay.*

NOTES CULTURELLES OPTIONAL

1. Dijon   Dijon, in eastern France, is the capital of Burgundy **(la Bourgogne)**, a region famous for its wines.

2. Le café   The café plays an important role in French social life. From early in the morning until late at night, people can go there to have something to drink and a roll or sandwich to eat. Mainly the café is a place where people come together to talk and where an individual can sit quietly reading a newspaper, waiting for a friend, or watching the people go by. The café has two sections: **la terrasse**, where sidewalk tables are put out in fair weather, and **la salle**, which is always open.

You may have the students locate Dijon on the map of France on p.viii.

Conversation numéro 2: André et François

ANDRÉ: Quelle heure est-il?

FRANÇOIS: Il est deux heures.

ANDRÉ: Deux heures?

FRANÇOIS: Oui, deux heures. Pourquoi?

ANDRÉ: J'ai rendez-vous avec Michèle . . .

FRANÇOIS: À quelle heure?

ANDRÉ: À deux heures dix.

FRANÇOIS: Et Michèle est ponctuelle?

ANDRÉ: Oui, très ponctuelle . . . et très impatiente.

FRANÇOIS: Oh là là!

ANDRÉ: Au revoir, François!

FRANÇOIS: Au revoir, André!

Conversations in a café

In Dijon . . . in a café

Conversation number 1: Hélène and Paul

What time is it?
It's one o'clock.
And at what time is the concert?
At two.
Good. We have (the) time.

Conversation number 2: André and François

What time is it?
It's two o'clock.
Two o'clock?
Yes, two. Why?
I have a date with Michèle . . .
At what time?
At two ten. (At ten past two.)
And is Michèle on time?
Yes, (she is) very punctual . . . and very impatient.
Oh dear!
Good-by, François.
Good-by, André.

Vocabulaire spécialisé L'heure *(The time)*

Quelle heure est-il? *What time is it?*
Il est . . . *It is . . .*

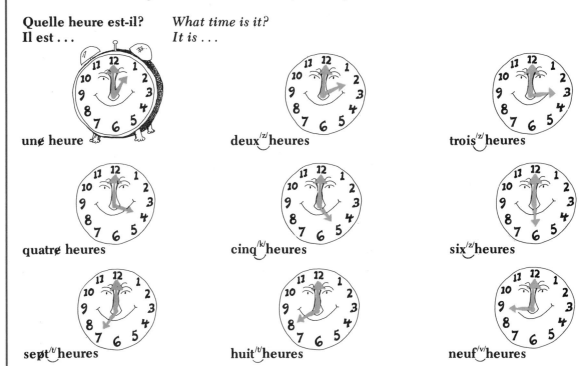

un¢ heure

deux/z/ heures

trois/z/ heures

quatr¢ heures

cinq/k/ heures

six/z/ heures

sept/t/ heures

huit/t/ heures

neuf/v/ heures

Prononciation

La liaison

Review what constitutes a vowel sound. Words beginning with **a, e, i, o, u,** and **y** + consonant begin with a vowel sound. Words beginning with mute **h** begin with a vowel sound. (The aspirate **h** will be introduced later.)

As you know, the final consonant of a word is usually silent in French. However, if the next word begins with a *vowel sound*, the final consonant is sometimes pronounced as if it were the first letter of this word. This is called **liaison.** Liaison means linking two words.

Liaison occurs only after *certain* words, such as numbers followed by nouns.

In written French, liaison is not marked by any sign. As a learning aid, new liaisons will be indicated with: ‿.

In liaison, a final **s** or **x** is pronounced /z/.

Il est trois/z/ heures.   Il est six/z/ heures.

In this book and in the Tape Program only required liaisons are presented. These are the only ones commonly encountered in conversational French.

Clock on the Strasbourg Cathedral.

dix /z/ heures

onze heures

midi   minuit

À quelle heure est le concert?
À onze heures.

At what time is the concert?
At eleven (o'clock).

Notes: 1. In English the expression *o'clock* may be left out. In French the word **heure(s)** may *not* be left out.
  2. The word **heure(s)** is abbreviated as **h.**
   Il est 3 h.
  3. To distinguish between A.M. and P.M., French speakers use the following expressions:

du matin *in the morning*	Il est trois heures **du matin.**
de l'après-midi *in the afternoon*	Il est deux heures **de l'après-midi.**
du soir *in the evening*	Il est dix heures **du soir.**

In telling time be sure to link the number to **heure(s).** Note the pronunciation of the number 9: **Il est neuf** /v/ **heures.**

✓ ACTIVITÉ 1   Quelle heure est-il?

Paul has a watch that does not work very well. He often asks Hélène what time it is. Play both roles according to the model.   Be sure students make the appropriate liaisons and link all words together.

→ 3 h.   Paul: **Quelle heure est-il?**
     Hélène: **Il est trois heures.**

1. 4 h.	3. 1 h.	5. 10 h.	7. 6 h.
2. 5 h.	4. 11 h.	6. 9 h.	8. 7 h.

VARIATION with **du matin, de l'après-midi, du soir.**

✓ ACTIVITÉ 2   À quelle heure?

Hélène is always well informed. This is why François asks her when certain activities take place. Play both roles according to the model.

→ le concert: 3 h.   François: **À quelle heure est le concert?**
      Hélène: **À trois heures.**
      François: **Merci.**

In this activity **le** and **la** are presented as anticipatory structures. You may model these nouns for the students.

1. la classe: 2 h.	4. le match *(game)* de tennis: 7 h.	7. le bus: 1 h. /bys/
2. le récital: 6 h.	5. le match de football: 5 h.	8. le train: 11 h.
3. le film *(movie)*: 8 h.	6. le programme de télévision: 9 h.	

You may introduce the notion of cognates and false cognates. Cognates have a similar spelling and meaning in both French and English (**classe, récital, programme**); false cognates have a similar spelling but different meaning (**football** is *soccer* in French). Stress the point that cognates are *never* pronounced the same way in French and English.

Vocabulaire spécialisé L'heure et les minutes *(The hour and the minutes)*

Il est . . .

une heure et quart   **deux heures et demie**   **dix heures moins le quart**

Exceptions: **midi et demi, minuit et demi.**

To indicate the half hour and the quarter hour, the following expressions are used:

 et quart

 et demie

moins le quart

Il est . . .

trois heures dix   **quatre heures moins vingt**

To indicate the minutes, the following are used:

 number (of minutes)

moins + number (of minutes)

With the growing popularity of digital clocks, there is an increasing tendency to use minutes after the hour: 10 h. 52
Il est dix heures cinquante-deux.

ACTIVITÉ 3 L'heure exacte

François checks the time with Caroline, who has a new watch. Play both
roles according to the model.

In this exercise all times fall between the hour and the half hour.

→ 1 h. 15   François: **Il est une heure et quart?**
                Caroline: **Oui, il est une heure et quart.**

1. 1 h. 30   4. 5 h. 30   7. 9 h. 26
2. 2 h. 15   5. 6 h. 20   8. 10 h. 14
3. 3 h. 30   6. 8 h. 25   9. 11 h. 12

ACTIVITÉ 4 À la gare *(At the train station)* OPTIONAL

Imagine that you are working at the information desk
of a French train station. Travellers ask you the
departure time of the trains listed below. Answer
them according to the schedule.

→ le train de Nice
  Le train de Nice est à six heures dix.

DÉPARTS			
Nice	6:10	Toulon	9:35
Lyon	7:15	Colmar	10:40
Cannes	7:30	Annecy	10:45
Tours	8:12	Marseille	10:50
Dijon	8:25	Paris	10:55

1. le train de Cannes 6. le train de Colmar
2. le train de Lyon 7. le train d'Annecy
3. le train de Tours 8. le train de Marseille
4. le train de Dijon 9. le train de Paris
5. le train de Toulon Note that in items 5–9, times fall between the half hour and the next hour so
  that students may practice the construction **moins** + number of minutes.

Entre nous

Expressions pour la conversation

To express their *disappointment* or their *displeasure*, French speakers use
the following expressions:

Zut!
Zut alors! *Darn (it)! Rats!*

Mini-dialogues OPTIONAL

Paul asks Anne what time it is. When she tells him, he realizes that he is
five minutes late. Read the model dialog carefully. Then create new dialogs
by replacing the underlined words, using the information contained in the
pictures. Make all necessary changes.

PAUL: Quelle heure est-il?

ANNE: Il est une heure cinq!

PAUL: Une heure cinq?

ANNE: Oui! Pourquoi? *(Why?)*

PAUL: Le film commence *(begins)* à une heure!

ANNE: Zut alors!

1:00 le film

4:30 la classe

9:50 le concert

10:20 l'opéra

2:20 le match

Il est cinq heures moins Il est dix heures moins cinq. Il est dix heures vingt-cinq. Il est deux heures vingt-cinq.
vingt-cinq.

Leçon 5

Le calendrier de Jacqueline

Voici Jacqueline.

Et voici le calendrier de Jacqueline.

l'anniversaire de Maman: le 3 octobre
l'anniversaire de Papa: le 10 septembre
l'anniversaire de Paul: le 21 décembre
l'anniversaire de Brigitte: le 4 janvier
l'anniversaire de Marie-Louise: le 22 juillet
la Saint Valentin: le 14 février
le premier jour de classe: le 15 septembre
le premier jour de vacances: le premier juillet
rendez-vous avec Marc: le 2 décembre
rendez-vous avec Michel: le 10 février

Shrove Tuesday is the last day before Lent, a period of 40 days of penance and fasting which precedes Easter. Traditionally Mardi Gras was the culmination of a period of celebration which ended abruptly on Ash Wednesday.

NOTE CULTURELLE

Les fêtes françaises *(The French holidays)*

Many French holidays are of Catholic origin. Here are some religious observances for which French students have one or more days of vacation:

la Toussaint	*All Saints' Day*	(November 1)
Noël	*Christmas*	(December 25)
Mardi Gras	*Shrove Tuesday*	(February or March)
Pâques	*Easter*	(March or April)

There are also other French holidays that are not of religious origin:

le 11 novembre	*Armistice Day*
le premier mai	*Labor Day*
le 14 juillet	*Bastille Day* (the French national holiday)

Heureux Noël et Bonne et Heureuse Année

Jacqueline's date book

Here's Jacqueline.

And here's Jacqueline's date book.

Mom's birthday	October 3
Dad's birthday	September 10
Paul's birthday	December 21
Brigitte's birthday	January 4
Marie-Louise's birthday	July 22
Valentine's Day	February 14
the first day of class	September 15
the first day of vacation	July 1
date with Marc	December 2
date with Michel	February 10

Vocabulaire spécialisé   La date

Les jours de la semaine *(The days of the week)*

lundi	*Monday*	aujourd'hui	*today*
mardi	*Tuesday*	demain	*tomorrow*
mercredi	*Wednesday*		
jeudi	*Thursday*		
vendredi	*Friday*		
samedi	*Saturday*		
dimanche	*Sunday*		

Point out that days of the week and months are not capitalized in French.

Citroën LN: la voiture qui simplifie la vie.

Les mois de l'année *(The months of the year)*

janvier	avril	juillet	octobre
février	mai	août	novembre
mars	juin	septembre	décembre

Review the numbers from 2–31 before teaching the dates.

La date

Quel jour est-ce?	*What day is it?*
C'est le 10 septembre.	*It's September 10th.*
Aujourd'hui, c'est le 3 octobre.	*Today is October 3rd.*
Noël est le 25 décembre.	*Christmas is December 25th.*
Mon anniversaire est le 2 mars.	*My birthday is March 2nd.*
L'anniversaire de Marc est le premier juin.	*Marc's birthday is June 1st.*
J'ai rendez-vous avec Paul le 4 juin.	*I have a date with Paul on June 4th.*

Notes: 1. To express a date, French speakers use the construction:

> **le** + number + month

> Exception: the *first* (of the month) is **le premier.**

2. When dates are abbreviated, the day is always given before the month:

> 2/8   le 2 août   1/10   le premier octobre

Communication activity: **Mon anniversaire est le...** (give your birthday) **Et toi?** (point to a student)
Robert: **Mon anniversaire est le...**
Then ask another student: **Quand** *(When)* **est-ce, l'anniversaire de Robert?**
Marie: **L'anniversaire de Robert est le...**

30   Prélude

ACTIVITÉ 1   Un jour de retard (A day behind)

François has trouble keeping up with the calendar. He is always one day
behind when thinking of the date. Sylvie corrects him. Play both roles.

→ samedi   François: **Aujourd'hui, c'est samedi.**
            Sylvie: **Non, c'est dimanche.**

1. lundi   mardi   3. jeudi   vendredi   5. dimanche   lundi
2. mardi   mercredi   4. vendredi   samedi   6. mercredi   jeudi

ACTIVITÉ 2   Un jour d'avance (A day ahead)

Philippe has the opposite problem. He is always one day ahead. Again
Sylvie corrects him. Play both roles.

→ 12 oct.   Philippe: **C'est le douze octobre.**
             Sylvie: **Non, c'est le onze octobre.**

1. 14 déc.   4. 8 avr.   7. 9 juin   10. 17 sep.
2. 24 jan.   5. 12 août   8. 6 juil.   11. 30 mars
3. 5 fév.   6. 21 oct.   9. 2 mai le premier mai   12. 1 nov.   le 31 octobre

ACTIVITÉ 3   Dates importantes   OPTIONAL

Give the following dates in French according to the model.

→ Noël (25/12)   **C'est le 25 décembre.**

1. la Saint Valentin (14/2)
2. la fête (holiday) nationale américaine (4/7)
3. le premier jour de l'année (1/1)
4. l'anniversaire de George Washington (22/2)
5. la fête de Christophe Colomb (12/10)
6. la fête nationale française (14/7)

In French the name Georges
is written with a final s.

Prononciation

Rythme et accent *(Rhythm and stress)*

The *rhythm* of French is very *regular*. Within a group of words all syllables are short and even. There is no pause or break between words. The *stress* or accent falls on the *last syllable* of a word or group of words, making that last syllable a little longer than the others.

(This is the opposite of English, where each word of two or more syllables has its own stress pattern and where the rhythm is irregular because of long [–] and short [∪] syllables.)

Contrast: *even rhythm and final stress*   *uneven rhythm*

Bŏnjŏur, Mădamȩ.   Gŏod mŏrnĭng, Ma'am.

Cŏmmĕnt t'appĕllȩs-tu?   What ĭs yŏur name?

ACTIVITÉ DE PRONONCIATION

TWO SYLLABLES	THREE SYLLABLES	FOUR SYLLABLES
Papa	Nathalie	Sylvie Dumas
Maman	Mélanie	Philippe Vallée
Madame	Mademoiselle	Madame Dulac
Jean-Paul	Jean-Michel	Je m'appelle Jean.
Bonjour	Bonjour, Paul.	Bonjour, Thomas.
Salut	Salut, Marc.	Salut, Suzanne.
Voici	Voici Lise.	Voici Michèle.
Voilà	Voilà Jacques.	Voilà Philippe.
Ça va.	Ça va mal.	Ça va très mal.
jeudi	un dollar	Il est midi.
mardi	deux dollars	Il est une heure.
demain	cinq dollars	Comme ci, comme ça.

Be sure students pronounce syllables evenly. This activity reviews basic material of earlier lessons.

FIVE SYLLABLES	SIX SYLLABLES
Voici Isabelle.	Voici Madame Lavoie.
Voilà Mélanie.	Voilà Sylvie Dumas.
C'est Monsieur Cardin.	C'est Mademoiselle Rochette.
Comment t'appelles-tu?	Je m'appelle Marc Rémi.
Je m'appelle Michèle.	Je m'appelle Jean-François.
Donne-moi un dollar.	Donne-moi vingt-cinq dollars.
Donnez-moi cinq francs.	Donnez-moi dix-huit francs.
le dix-sept avril	le vingt et un avril
C'est demain lundi.	C'est aujourd'hui dimanche.

Entre nous

Expression pour la conversation

To express *surprise*, you may say:

Vraiment?   *Really?*   — Demain c'est le quinze octobre. C'est mon anniversaire.
— **Vraiment?** C'est aussi *(also)* l'anniversaire de Maman.

Mini-dialogues OPTIONAL

Create new dialogs, using the suggestions in the pictures to replace the underlined words.

a) JACQUELINE: J'ai rendez-vous avec <u>Marc</u>.
CHARLOTTE: Vraiment? Quand? *(When?)*
JACQUELINE: <u>Le deux décembre</u>.

b) CAROLINE: Quand est-ce, l'anniversaire de <u>Marc</u>?
SUZANNE: C'est en <u>décembre</u>.
CAROLINE: Quel jour?
SUZANNE: Le <u>deux</u>.

Marc
le 2 décembre

Brigitte
le 4 janvier

Marie-Louise
le 22 juillet

Pierre
le 1 avril

Georges
le 16 août

Leçon 6 — La carte du temps

Aujourd'hui c'est le premier décembre.
Quel temps fait-il en France?
Ça dépend . . .

BORDEAUX

À Bordeaux:
Il fait bon.
Il fait dix degrés.

À Toulon:
Il fait douze degrés.
Il fait bon.
Il fait beau.
C'est magnifique!

À Paris:
Il fait beau à Paris en automne?
Aujourd'hui, non!
Il pleut.

À Grenoble:
Brrrr . . .
Il fait moins deux
   et il neige.
Oh là là! Il fait froid aujourd'hui!

The weather map	In Bordeaux:	In Paris:
Today is December first.	The weather is (It's) fine.	The weather is (It's) nice in Paris in the fall?
How's the weather in France?	It's ten degrees.	Not today!
It all depends . . .		It's raining.
	In Toulon:	**In Grenoble:**
	It's twelve degrees.	Brrr . . .
	The weather is (It's) fine.	It's minus two (two below zero)
	The weather is (It's) nice.	and it's snowing.
	It's great!	Oh dear! It's cold today.

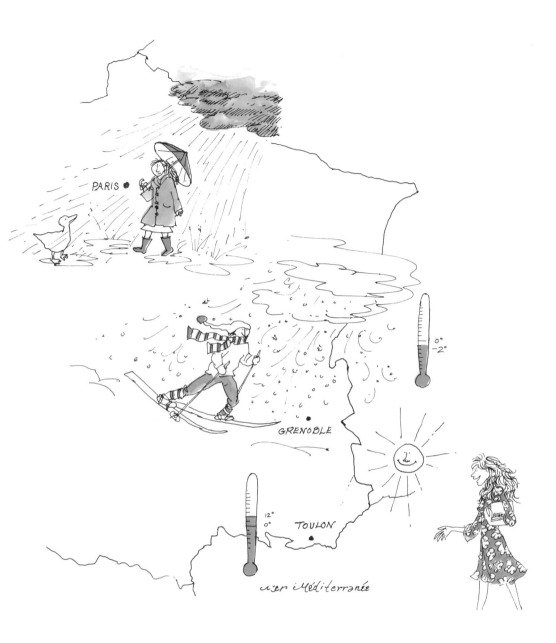

NOTE CULTURELLE OPTIONAL

Bonjour, la France!

Have you ever looked at a map of France? In size France is smaller than Texas, yet it is the largest country in Western Europe. It is also a land of many contrasts. It has plains, high mountains, and a long coastline. You can ski in the Alps, fish in the Atlantic, or relax on the beaches along the Mediterranean Sea. In this book you will learn more about France, its people, and the many other peoples of the world who also speak French.

Vocabulaire spécialisé Le temps et les saisons *(The weather and the seasons)*

Quel temps fait-il?   *How's the weather?*

	beau.	*It's nice.*	**en été** *in (the) summer*
	bon.	*It's fine (pleasant).*	**en automne** *in (the) fall*
Il fait	chaud.	*It's hot.*	**en hiver** *in (the) winter*
	frais.	*It's cool.*	**au printemps** *in (the) spring*
	froid.	*It's cold.*	
	mauvais.	*It's bad.*	

Il pleut.   *It's raining.*
Il neige.   *It's snowing.*

BULLETIN MÉTÉO

	Min. nuit	16 h.		Min. nuit	16 h.
Ajaccio	8	20	Nice	10	17
Biarritz	10	17	Paris	10	13
Bordeaux	0	15	Perpignan	11	18
Brest	12	14	Rennes	12	14
Dijon	3	12	Saint-Etienne	1	12
Lille	9	12	Strasbourg	2	12
Lyon	5	12	Toulouse	5	14
Marseille	8	16	Tours	11	13

Quelle température fait-il?   *What's the temperature?*

Il fait dix degrés.	10°	*It's ten degrees.*
Il fait zéro.	0°	*It's zero.*
Il fait moins cinq.	−5°	*It's five below.*

NOTE CULTURELLE   OPTIONAL

Le système métrique

Don't be surprised if a French person tells you that the weather is nice because the temperature outside has reached 15 degrees. The French use a Celsius thermometer. In fact, the French have been measuring distances in meters, liquids in liters, weights in grams, and temperatures in degrees Celsius for nearly two hundred years! They are the ones who invented the metric system!

You may want to introduce the following measurements: un mètre, un kilomètre; un gramme, un kilogramme, une tonne; un litre.

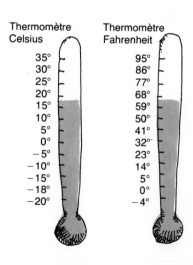

Thermomètre Celsius

35°
30°
25°
20°
15°
10°
5°
0°
−5°
−10°
−15°
−18°
−20°

Thermomètre Fahrenheit

95°
86°
77°
68°
59°
50°
41°
32°
23°
14°
5°
0°
−4°

ACTIVITÉ 1   Quel temps fait-il?

What we do often depends on the weather. We go skiing when there is
snow and swimming when the weather is warm. Read what the following
people are doing, and say what the weather is like.

→ Suzanne is putting on a sweater.   **Il fait froid. (Il fait frais.)**

1. Nathalie is going swimming.
2. Pierre is taking off his sweater.
3. Anne has her bathing suit on.
4. Caroline is shivering.

5. Pascal is trying to get a suntan.
6. Jacques does not want to go out.
7. Hélène is putting on her raincoat.
8. Sylvie will be able to go skiing.

ACTIVITÉ 2   La carte du temps *(The weather map)*

Imagine that you are the weather announcer for a French TV station. Study
the weather map and present the noon bulletin for each of the cities listed below.

→ À Bordeaux . . .   **À Bordeaux il fait six degrés. Il fait beau.**

1. À Lille . . .
2. À Lyon . . .
3. À Paris . . .
4. À Grenoble . . .
5. À Strasbourg . . .
6. À Toulon . . .
7. À Nice . . .
8. À Toulouse . . .
9. À Brest . . .

ACTIVITÉ 3   Votre ville *(Your town)*

Imagine that Christine, a French girl, is planning to spend a year in your
town as an exchange student. Tell her what the weather is like during the
months listed below.

→ En juillet . . .   **En juillet il fait chaud.**

1. En août . . .
2. En septembre . . .
3. En novembre . . .

4. En janvier . . .
5. En mars . . .
6. En mai . . .

ACTIVITÉ 4 Les quatre saisons *(The four seasons)* OPTIONAL

Describe the weather in the following cities for each of the four seasons.

en été   en automne   en hiver   au printemps

→ À Miami   **En été il fait chaud. En automne . . .**

1. À New York
2. À Chicago
3. À San Francisco
4. À Los Angeles
5. À Houston
6. À Denver

Prononciation

L'intonation

When you speak, your voice rises and falls. This is called *intonation*. In French, as in English, your voice goes down at the end of a statement. In the middle of a sentence your voice *rises* at the end of each group of words. (In English your voice levels off or drops at the end of each group of words.)

Voilà Nathalie.

L'anniversaire de Nathalie est en janvier.

L'anniversaire de Nathalie est le trente et un janvier.

Be sure that the students maintain an even rhythm and that they allow the stress to fall on the final syllable of each group of words.

ACTIVITÉ DE PRONONCIATION

Repeat after the teacher:

1. Voici Paul.
   Voici Philippe.
   Voici Marie-Hélène.
   Voici Jean-François Dumas.

2. Ça va.
   Ça va mal.
   Ça va très mal.
   Ça va comme ci, comme ça.

3. Je m'appelle Anne.
   Je m'appelle Anne-Marie.
   Je m'appelle Anne-Marie Dupont.

This activity reviews some of the expressions taught in this unit.

4. Il est deux heures.
   Il est deux heures dix.
   Il est deux heures et quart.
   Il est deux heures et quart du matin.

5. Il fait mauvais.
   Il fait mauvais en hiver.
   Il fait mauvais en hiver à Toulouse.

Entre nous

Expression pour la conversation

When French speakers pause or hesitate, they often say:

> **Euh ...**   *Er ... Uh ...*

Mini-dialogues   OPTIONAL

Nathalie asks Philippe to check the weather outside.
Read the sample dialog carefully, then create new dialogs by replacing the underlined words with the expressions suggested in the pictures.

NATHALIE: Quel temps fait-il aujourd'hui?
PHILIPPE: Il fait beau!
NATHALIE: Et quelle température fait-il?
PHILIPPE: Euh ... Il fait vingt degrés!

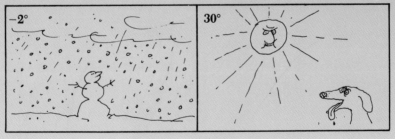

OBJECTIVES

To communicate and express themselves, students must have a good command of basic verb forms and verb constructions. For this reason, verbs are presented early in FRENCH FOR MASTERY. Unité 1 focuses on the following elements:

Language
  verbs
- concept of verb-subject agreement (Because of the importance of this concept, the various verb forms are presented progressively and then summarized at the end of the unit.)
- the present tense of -**er** verbs
- negative and interrogative constructions
- **être**

  pronouns
- subject pronouns

Vocabulary
- activities
- some useful words

Culture

In this unit the students are introduced to the French-speaking world, in its breadth and diversity.

UNITÉ 1
Parlez-vous français?

OPPOSITE: Mardi Gras celebration in Fort-de-France, Martinique.

Each *Presentation text* contains several examples of the structures introduced in the lesson. These STRUCTURES TO OBSERVE will be indicated at the beginning of each lesson.

UNITÉ 1

Leçon 1   Au Canada

STRUCTURES TO OBSERVE
• the pronoun **je** and the corresponding **-er** verb form
• the negative construction **ne. . .pas**

Bonjour!
Je m'appelle Suzanne Lavoie.
Je parle français.
Je parle anglais aussi.
C'est normal!
J'habite à Montréal!

Salut!
Je m'appelle Philippe Beliveau.
J'habite au Canada, mais je n'habite pas à Montréal.
J'habite à Québec.
Je parle anglais, mais je ne parle pas très bien.
Je parle français.
Vous aussi?
Magnifique!

In Canada
Hello!
My name is Suzanne Lavoie.
I speak French.
I also speak English.
That's logical (normal)!
I live in Montreal.

Hi!
My name is Philippe Beliveau.
I live in Canada, but I don't live in Montreal.
I live in Quebec City.
I speak English, but I don't speak very well.
I speak French.
You too?
Great!

CONVERSATION

Suzanne is talking about herself. Start a conversation with her by saying whether you do the same things (column A) or whether you don't (column B).

Suzanne:	A	B
Je **parle** anglais.	Je **parle** anglais.	Je ne **parle** pas anglais.
Je **parle** français.	Je **parle** français.	Je ne **parle** pas français.
En hiver, je **skie**.	En hiver, je **skie**.	En hiver, je ne **skie** pas.

OBSERVATIONS Str. B, D

Most sentences have a *subject* and a *verb*. The *subject* is the word (or group of words) which tells who is doing the action. The *verb* is the word (or group of words) which tells what action is going on.

In French the *ending* of the verb depends on the subject of the sentence. Reread the above sentences in which Suzanne speaks about herself. In these sentences and in your replies the subject is **je** *(I)*, and the verb is the word in heavy type.

• Which letter does the verb end in when the subject is **je**? -e

Now look at the suggested negative replies in column B.

• In a negative sentence, which word comes immediately *before* the verb? ne

• Which word comes immediately *after* the verb? pas

NOTE CULTURELLE OPTIONAL

Les Canadiens français

Did you know that Montreal is the second-largest French-speaking city in the world after Paris? Over one-third of the twenty-five million citizens of Canada are of French origin and speak French. The French Canadians are very much attached to their language and their culture. This may explain why the coat of arms of the city of Quebec still bears the motto «Je me souviens» *("I remember")*. The French Canadians remember their traditions.

Leçon un **43**

Structure

A. Les verbes en -er

When you look up a verb in the end vocabulary of this book, you will find it listed in the infinitive form: **parler** = *to speak*. The *infinitive* is the basic form of the verb. All other forms are derived from it. French verbs are grouped according to their *infinitive endings*. The most common infinitive ending is **-er**:

parler *to speak*   **skier** *to ski*

Verbs ending in **-er** are called **-er** *verbs*.

B. Le pronom sujet *je*

In a French sentence the ending of the verb depends on who the subject is.

parler	*to speak*	Je **parle** anglais.	*I speak English.*
skier	*to ski*	Je **skie.**	*I ski.*
visiter	*to visit*	Je **visite** Québec.	*I visit Quebec City.*

In a sentence where the subject is **je**, the verb is formed by replacing the **-er** ending of the infinitive with the ending -e .

Vocabulaire spécialisé

Activités   You may want to model the **je** form of these verbs.

parler   français   anglais   espagnol   italien
to speak, talk

jouer   au tennis   au football   au hockey
to play

Have the students observe that in French **football** means *soccer*.

In French, **volleyball** is abbreviated to **volley**. Similarly, **football** and **basketball** have become **foot** and **basket**.

ACTIVITÉ 1   Suzanne et Philippe

Suzanne tells Philippe what she does. Philippe tells her that he does different things. Play both roles according to the model.

→ parler anglais (français)

Suzanne: **Je parle anglais.**
Philippe: **Je parle français.**

1. parler espagnol (italien)
2. jouer au tennis (au hockey)
3. jouer au football (au volleyball)
4. téléphoner à Marc (à Denise)
5. dîner à six heures (à sept heures)
6. visiter Québec (Montréal)

Château Frontenac, Québec

skier
to ski

dîner
to have dinner

téléphoner   à Suzanne   à Paul
to call, phone

visiter   Paris
to visit

Leçon un   **45**

C. L'élision

In the sentences on the left, each verb begins with a consonant sound.
In the sentences on the right, each verb begins with a vowel sound.
Compare the form of the subject in each pair of sentences.

Je parle français.	**J'**habite à Québec.
Je téléphone à Paul.	**J'**invite Paul et Suzanne.
Je joue au hockey.	**J'**arrive de Montréal.

Je becomes **j'** before a vowel sound.

In French the final **e** of a few short words, such as **je,** is dropped when the
next word begins with a *vowel sound.* In written French the dropped **e** is
replaced by an *apostrophe* ('). This is called *elision.* (<u>El</u>ision means that the
final vowel is <u>el</u>iminated.)

New instances of elision will be indicated as they occur.

Vocabulaire spécialisé

Activités You may model the **je** form of
these verbs for the students.

habiter   à Québec   à New York
to live

arriver   de Montréal   de Paris   **inviter**   Paul et Marie
to arrive, come   *to invite*

ACTIVITÉ 2   La conférence des jeunes *(The youth conference)*

The following young people are attending the World Youth Conference.
After introducing themselves, they tell which language they speak and
where they live. Play the roles according to the model.

→   Suzanne (français / Québec)   **Je parle français.**   VARIATION: Je m'appelle Suzanne.
                                  J'habite à Québec.   J'arrive de Québec.

1. Paul (français / Paris)
2. Sylvie (français / Montréal)
3. Jacqueline (anglais / New York)
4. Thomas (anglais / Chicago)
5. Pietro (italien / Milan)
6. Maria (italien / Rome)
7. Teresa (espagnol / Mexico)
8. Paco (espagnol / Porto Rico)

ACTIVITÉ 3   Nathalie

Nathalie does many things. Complete her statements with **Je** or **J'**, as
appropriate.

→   — joue au tennis.   **Je joue au tennis.**
    — invite Pierre.   **J'invite Pierre.**

1. — skie en hiver.
2. — parle italien.
3. — téléphone à Paul.
4. — dîne à six heures.
5. — arrive de Paris.
6. — habite à Montréal.
7. — parle espagnol.
8. — invite Monique.

Vocabulaire spécialisé   Mots utiles *(Useful words)*

à	*at*	J'arrive **à** midi.
	in	J'habite **à** Montréal.
	to	Je parle **à** Pierre.
de	*from*	J'arrive **de** Québec.
	of, about	Je parle **de** Paris.
aussi	*also, too*	Je joue au tennis. Je joue au golf **aussi**.
bien	*well*	Je parle **bien** français.
mal	*poorly, badly*	Je parle **mal** espagnol.
très	*very*	Je joue **très** bien au football.
et	*and*	Voici Paul **et** voilà Sylvie.
ou	*or*	J'invite Suzanne **ou** Michèle.
mais	*but*	Je parle italien, **mais** je parle très mal.
avec	*with*	Je joue **avec** Suzanne.

Usually the adverbs **bien** and **mal**
come immediately after the verb.

Note: There is elision with **de** when the next word begins with a vowel sound:
         J'arrive **d'**Annecy.

D. La négation avec ne ... pas

Paul does not do what Sylvie does. Compare what each one says.

Sylvie:	Paul:	
Oui, je parle anglais.	Non, je **ne** parle **pas** anglais.	*I don't speak English.*
Oui, je joue au tennis.	Non, je **ne** joue **pas** au tennis.	*I don't play tennis.*
Oui, j'habite à Québec.	Non, je n'habite **pas** à Québec.	*I don't live in Quebec.*
Oui, j'invite Marc.	Non, je n'invite **pas** Marc.	*I don't invite Marc.*

To make a sentence negative, French speakers use the following construction:

> subject + **ne** + verb + **pas** + (rest of sentence)
> ↓
> **n'** (before a vowel sound)

√ *ACTIVITÉ 4* Hélas! *(Too bad!)*

Janine is a very active person. Her friend Thomas is not. Play both roles according to the model.

→ Je joue au tennis.   Janine: **Je joue au tennis.**
   Thomas: **Hélas, je ne joue pas au tennis!**

1. Je joue au volleyball.
2. Je joue avec Suzanne.
3. Je parle espagnol.
4. Je parle italien.

5. Je téléphone à Sylvie.
6. Je dîne avec Philippe.
7. Je visite Québec.
8. Je skie.

√ *ACTIVITÉ 5* Oui, mais ...

One cannot do everything. Philippe does certain things, but he does not do others. Play the role of Philippe according to the model.

→ J'invite Suzanne. (Monique)   Philippe: **J'invite Suzanne, mais je n'invite pas Monique.**

1. Je joue au tennis. (au hockey)
2. J'habite à Québec. (à Montréal)
3. Je parle à Paul. (à Marc)
4. J'invite Hélène. (Catherine)

5. Je téléphone à Jean-Paul. (à François)
6. Je joue avec Jacques. (avec Paul)
7. Je visite Paris. (Nice)
8. Je dîne avec Michèle. (Sylvie)

Make sure that students use n' in items 2 and 4.

ACTIVITÉ 6 Et toi?   OPTIONAL

Marie-Noëlle tells you what she does and asks whether you do the same things. Answer her according to the model.

→ Je danse très bien. Et toi?   **Je danse très bien aussi. (Non, je ne danse pas très bien.)**

1. Je parle espagnol. Et toi?
2. Je parle très bien français. Et toi?
3. J'habite au Canada. Et toi?
4. J'habite à Montréal. Et toi?

5. Je joue bien au tennis. Et toi?
6. Je joue mal au ping-pong. Et toi?
7. Je dîne à six heures et demie. Et toi?
8. Je skie en hiver. Et toi?

Prononciation

1. Le son *(The sound)* /i/[1]

Model word: Phi<u>li</u>ppe

Practice words: <u>i</u>l, M<u>imi</u>, S<u>y</u>lv<u>ie</u>, v<u>i</u>s<u>i</u>te, d<u>î</u>ne, <u>Y</u>ves, sk<u>ie</u>, h<u>i</u>ver

Practice sentences: Phi<u>li</u>ppe v<u>i</u>s<u>i</u>te l'<u>I</u>tal<u>ie</u>.
<u>Y</u>ves hab<u>i</u>te à N<u>i</u>ce.

The French sound /i/ as in **Mimi** is shorter than the English vowel *e* of *me*.

Comment écrire /i/ *(How to write /i/)*: **i, î, y**

2. Le son /a/

Model word: M<u>a</u>d<u>a</u>me

Practice words: <u>A</u>nnie, M<u>a</u>x, C<u>a</u>nnes, C<u>a</u>n<u>a</u>da, P<u>a</u>n<u>a</u>ma, ç<u>a</u> v<u>a</u>, J<u>a</u>cques

Practice sentences: M<u>a</u>d<u>a</u>me L<u>a</u>v<u>a</u>l h<u>a</u>bite <u>à</u> P<u>a</u>n<u>a</u>ma.
Ç<u>a</u> v<u>a</u>, N<u>a</u>th<u>a</u>lie?

The French sound /a/ is shorter and more precise than the English vowel *a* of *father*.

Comment écrire /a/: **a, à, â**

Entre nous

Expressions pour la conversation

To express their feelings about a situation French speakers often say:

Magnifique!	*Great!*
C'est magnifique!	*That's great!*
Dommage!	*Too bad!*
C'est dommage!	*That's too bad!*

Mini-dialogue   OPTIONAL

There are many things that Jacques cannot do very well.

JACQUES: Je joue au tennis.
MONIQUE: Magnifique!
JACQUES: Mais je ne joue pas bien!
MONIQUE: Dommage!

L'art du dialogue

a) Act out the dialog between Jacques and Monique.
b) Act out new dialogs where Jacques talks about his *playing volleyball*, his *speaking English*, his *speaking Spanish*. Replace **joue au tennis** and **ne joue pas** with the appropriate expressions.

[1]In this book French sounds are transcribed in phonetic symbols that you will find in many French dictionaries. One sound may have several different spellings. It may also happen that one letter or group of letters has several pronunciations. The sound-spelling correspondence table of the French language is listed on pages 399-400.

UNITÉ 1
Leçon 2 À la Martinique

STRUCTURES TO OBSERVE
* the subject pronouns **il, elle, ils, elles**
  and the corresponding **-er** verb forms
* yes/no questions

Voici Denis.
Il habite à Fort-de-France.
Est-ce qu'il parle français?
Oui, bien sûr!
Mais il parle créole aussi.

Voici Hélène.
Elle joue au tennis.
Est-ce qu'elle habite à
   Fort-de-France?
Non, elle habite à Saint-Pierre.

Voici Antoine et Jean-Philippe.
Ils jouent au football.
Est-ce qu'ils jouent bien?
Oui, ils jouent très bien.

Voici Marie et Sylvie.
Elles habitent à Sainte-Anne.
Est-ce qu'elles dansent bien?
Ah oui! Elles dansent très,
   très bien!

50 Unité un

Two of the favorite pastimes of Martinique young people are soccer
and dancing. Fort-de-France is the capital of Martinique. Saint-Pierre,
the former capital, was destroyed by a volcanic eruption in 1902.
Sainte-Anne is a small town on the southeastern tip of the island.

CONVERSATION

Are the following statements correct? If a statement is true, say **C'est vrai.**
If it is false, say **C'est faux.**

1. **Denis** parl**e** français. vrai
2. **Il** habit**e** à Fort-de-France. vrai
3. **Hélène** jou**e** au tennis. vrai
4. **Elle** habit**e** à Fort-de-France. faux
5. **Antoine et Jean-Philippe** jou**ent** au football. vrai
6. **Ils** jou**ent** mal. faux
7. **Marie et Sylvie** habit**ent** à Fort-de-France. faux
8. **Elles** dans**ent** bien. vrai

OBSERVATIONS   Str. A

Look at the even-numbered sentences. The names of the young people have been replaced by *pronouns.*

- Which pronoun is used to replace the following names:

  Denis? Hélène? Antoine et Jean-Philippe? Marie et Sylvie?
  il   elle   ils   elles

Sentences 1 to 4 tell what *one* person is doing. They have *singular* subjects.

- Which letter does each verb end in? -e
- Is this letter pronounced? no

Sentences 5 to 8 tell what *two* people are doing. They have *plural* subjects.

- Which three letters does each verb end in? -ent
- Are these letters pronounced? no

Départements are the administrative divisions of France. You may ask your students to locate Martinique on the map of the French-speaking world on pp.vi–vii.

NOTE CULTURELLE   OPTIONAL
La Martinique

Have you ever heard of Martinique? It is an island in the Caribbean Sea, south of Puerto Rico. The inhabitants of Martinique (**les Martiniquais**) are primarily of African origin. They speak French, as well as a language of their own, **créole.** Both Martinique and the nearby island of Guadeloupe are French **départements,** and the people who live there are French citizens. Did you realize that part of France is located so close to the United States?

In Martinique	
Here is Denis.	Here is Hélène.
He lives in Fort-de-France.	She plays tennis.
Does he speak French?	Does she live in Fort-de-France?
Yes, of course.	No, she lives in Saint-Pierre.
But he also speaks Creole.	
Here are Antoine and Jean-Philippe.	Here are Marie and Sylvie.
They play soccer.	They live in Sainte-Anne.
Do they play well?	Do they dance well?
Yes, they play very well.	Oh yes! They dance very, very well!

SUGGESTED REALIA: travel brochures.
SUPPLEMENTARY INFORMATION: In the Caribbean, French is also spoken in Haiti. A former French colony, Haiti gained its independence in 1804 and thus became the first independent black country. Today, many Haitians have immigrated to the U.S.

Structure

The negative construction is reviewed in column C. Make sure that the students understand it. If necessary, you may ask them to translate these negative sentences.

A. Les pronoms sujets: *il, elle, ils, elles*

In column A the subjects are *nouns*. In columns B and C these nouns have been replaced by *pronouns*. Note the forms of these pronouns and the corresponding verb endings.

A	B	C
Philippe téléphone.	**Il** téléphone à Anne.	**Il** ne téléphone pas à Sylvie.
Mélanie joue.	**Elle** joue au tennis.	**Elle** ne joue pas au volleyball.
Paul et Marc parlent.	**Ils** parlent français.	**Ils** ne parlent pas anglais.
Annie et Louise skient.	**Elles** skient bien.	**Elles** ne skient pas très bien.
Paul et Anne dansent.	**Ils** dansent mal.	**Ils** ne dansent pas bien.

To replace a noun subject, the French use the following subject pronouns:

	SINGULAR	PLURAL
Masculine	**il** *he*	**ils** *they*
Feminine	**elle** *she*	**elles** *they*

➔ The French have two pronouns which correspond to the English *they*.
Ils refers to a group of boys or a group including both boys and girls.
Elles refers to a group composed only of girls.

➔ There is liaison after **ils** and **elles** when the next word begins with a vowel sound.

NO LIAISON   LIAISON
Ils parlent français.   Ils habitent à la Martinique.
Elles téléphonent à Anne.   Elles invitent Anne.

The verb is formed by replacing the **-er** ending of the infinitive with the ending which corresponds to the subject.

When the subject is:		the ending is:
(singular)	**il, elle** (*one* person)	**-e**
(plural)	**ils, elles** (*two* or more people)	**-ent**

➔ The endings **-e** and **-ent** are both *silent* in spoken French. Therefore the singular and plural verb forms, like **joue (Anne joue)** and **jouent (Anne et Marie jouent)**, sound the same.

ACTIVITÉ 1 Paul? ou Marc et Sylvie?

Who is doing the following things? Look carefully at the ending of each verb
and complete the sentences with **Paul** or with **Marc et Sylvie,** as appropriate.

→ — joue au tennis.   **Paul joue au tennis.**

The purpose of this exercise is to make students aware of verb endings. Be sure they do not pronounce these endings.

1. — jouent au ping-pong.
2. — parle français.
3. — parlent créole.
4. — téléphonent à Denis.
5. — invite Antoine.
6. — dînent avec Jean-Philippe.
7. — habitent à la Martinique.
8. — habite à Québec.
9. — visite Montréal.
10. — dansent bien.

ACTIVITÉ 2 Aussi

Friends often share the same interests. Read what the following people are
doing and say that their friends (indicated in parentheses) do the same things.

→ Philippe parle créole. (Marc et Antoine)   **Marc et Antoine parlent créole aussi.**

1. Hélène joue au tennis. (Lucie et Annie)
2. Paul et Jacques parlent avec Suzanne. (Denis)
3. Antoine téléphone à Paul. (Isabelle et Claire)
4. Marc invite Suzanne. (Philippe)
5. Jacques et Denis habitent à Fort-de-France. (Paul)
6. Nicole arrive à une heure. (Monique et Lise)

VARIATION in the negative: The friends do not have the same interests. **Marc et Antoine ne parlent pas créole.** Be sure to use n' in items 4–6.

ACTIVITÉ 3 Français ou anglais?

The following students speak the language of the country where they live.
Say whether they speak French or English, using subject pronouns.

→ Paul habite à New York.   **Il parle anglais.**   VARIATION: They do not live in New York. **Ils n'habitent pas à New York.**

1. Caroline habite à Paris.
2. Jacques habite à Québec.
3. Antoine habite à Fort-de-France.
4. Sylvie habite à Chicago.
5. Denis et Charles habitent à **Miami.**
6. Hélène et Claire habitent à la **Martinique.**
7. Jacqueline et Robert habitent à **Dallas.**
8. Paul, Jacques et Anne habitent à **Annecy.**

ACTIVITÉ 4 Avec qui? *(With whom?)*

The following teenagers are doing things together with their friends.
Express this according to the model, using appropriate subject pronouns.

→ Hélène joue au tennis. (avec Mélanie)   **Elle joue au tennis avec Mélanie.**

1. Paul et Jean-Marc jouent au volleyball. (avec Isabelle)
2. Annette et Sylvie parlent français. (avec Antoine)
3. Philippe et Monique dînent. (avec Jean-Pierre)
4. Marc, Sylvie et Brigitte jouent au football. (avec Thomas)
5. Jean-Claude et François habitent à Paris. (avec Paul)
6. Thérèse et Monique habitent à Québec. (avec Lucie)
7. André et Jean-Paul arrivent à New York. (avec Jacques)
8. Monique et Albert arrivent à Boston. (avec Claire)

Be sure students use **ils** as the subject in items 3, 4, and 8. Be sure that they make the liaison after **ils** and **elles** in items 5–8.

ACTIVITÉ 5   Oui et non

Read what the following people are doing; then say that they are not doing something else. Use the expression in parentheses and the appropriate subject pronoun.

→ Monsieur Ballard téléphone à Paris. (à Québec)   **Il ne téléphone pas à Québec.**

1. Hélène parle à Paul. (à Jacques)
2. Monique et Sylvie skient en hiver. (au printemps)
3. Thomas et Jean-Luc jouent au tennis. (au ping-pong)
4. Jacqueline dîne avec Lucie. (Anne-Marie)
5. Paul et Marc invitent Mélanie. (Thérèse)

6. Madame Beliveau habite à Québec. (à Paris)
7. Monsieur et Madame Vallée habitent à Fort-de-France. (à Montréal)
8. Suzanne arrive de San Francisco. (de Chicago)

Be sure students use n'...pas in items 5–8.

Vocabulaire spécialisé   Activités

étudier (le français, l'anglais, la musique)
to study

danser
to dance

rentrer
*to come back,
go back, go home*

ACTIVITÉ 6   Les vacances sont finies. *(Vacation is over.)*

Read what the following students do during their vacation. Now that the vacation is over, they are studying and are not doing these things anymore. Express this according to the model.

→ Paul skie.   **Aujourd'hui il étudie.**
            Il ne skie pas.

   Marc et Anne dansent.   **Aujourd'hui ils étudient.**
                            Ils ne dansent pas.

1. Thérèse joue au tennis.
2. Henri dîne au restaurant.
3. Jean et Paul jouent au football.

4. Sylvie et Annie skient.
5. Catherine et Jacques dansent.
6. François et Robert visitent Paris.

54   Unité un

B. Questions à réponse affirmative ou négative *(Yes / no questions)*

The questions below ask for a *yes* or *no* answer. Such questions are called *yes/no questions*. Compare these questions with the statements on the right.

QUESTIONS	STATEMENTS
Est-ce que Denis habite à Fort-de-France?	Oui, Denis habite à Fort-de-France.
Est-ce qu'il parle français?	Oui, il parle français.
Est-ce que Marie joue au tennis?	Oui, Marie joue au tennis.
Est-ce qu'elle étudie avec Paul?	Oui, elle étudie avec Paul.

To transform a statement into a yes/no question, French speakers use the following construction:

> **est-ce que** + (rest of statement) ?
> ↓
> **est-ce qu'** (+ vowel sound)

→ Note the elision **est-ce qu'** when the next word begins with a vowel sound.

→ In informal questions you can change a statement into a yes/no question by simply letting your voice rise at the end of the sentence. This is like English.

QUESTIONS	STATEMENTS
Ça va?	Ça va.
Philippe parle français?	Philippe parle français.
Il parle bien?	Il parle bien.

✓ **ACTIVITÉ 7** Les étudiants français *(French students)*

Imagine that you are the president of the French Club. Your school is hosting the following French-speaking students for a month. Before welcoming them, you would like to know more about them. Ask questions according to the model.

VARIATION: Ask intonation questions.
Philippe parle anglais?

→ Philippe parle anglais. **Est-ce que Philippe parle anglais?**

1. Jeanne parle italien.
2. Marc joue au tennis.
3. Francine skie bien.
4. Claire étudie la musique.
5. Jacqueline habite à Paris.
6. Jean-Paul habite à Lyon.
7. Lucie et Charles jouent au volleyball.
8. Paul et Louis jouent au football.

There are no examples of elision in this exercise. To practice elision, substitute names beginning with a vowel sound: Anne, Annie, Antoine, Hélène, Isabelle, Olga, Yves. **Est-ce qu'Anne parle anglais?**

Leçon deux **55**

In French, **surprise-partie** means a *party,* not a surprise party.

ACTIVITÉ 8 À la surprise-partie *(At the party)* This activity reviews subject pronouns and practices elision with **est-ce qu'**.

The following teenagers are at a party. Ask whether they dance well. Use subject pronouns.

→ Philippe **Est-ce qu'il danse bien?**

1. Annie
2. Jean-Paul
3. Jacques et André
4. Nathalie et Suzanne
5. Robert et Sylvie
6. Louise et Mélanie
7. Henri
8. Lucie et Jean-Philippe

VARIATIONS: Est-ce qu'il parle bien anglais?
Est-ce qu'il étudie avec Paul? (Also, elision with **ils** and **elles**.)

Prononciation

Le son /r/

Model word: Paris

Practice words: Marc, Marie, Patrick, arrive, rentre, parle

Practice sentences: Marie arrive à Fort-de-France.
Marc parle créole.

The French /r/ is pronounced at the back of the throat. To pronounce a French /r/, say /ga/ and then clear your throat while keeping your tongue in the same position. The resulting sound is an /r/. Practice the French /r/ by pronouncing the French word **garage**.

Entre nous

Expressions pour la conversation

To attract a friend's attention you can say:

Tiens! *Look! Hey!* **Tiens,** voilà Marc!

There are many ways of saying *yes* or *no* in French:

Oui!	*Yes!*	**Oui,** Marc parle français.
Mais oui!	*Certainly!*	**Mais oui,** il parle français.
Bien sûr!	*Sure! Of course!*	**Bien sûr,** Marie parle français aussi.
Non!	*No!*	**Non,** Marc n'habite pas à Montréal.
Mais non!	*Of course not!*	**Mais non,** il n'habite pas à Québec.
Pas du tout!	*Not at all!*	**Pas du tout!** Il parle très bien français.
Au contraire!	*On the contrary!*	**Au contraire!** Il danse très bien.

Mini-dialogue OPTIONAL

Philippe and Annie are at a party at an international school. Annie knows
many of the guests.

PHILIPPE: Bonjour, Annie!
  ANNIE: Bonjour, Philippe! Ça va?
PHILIPPE: Ça va, merci!
  ANNIE: Tiens, voilà Jacqueline!
PHILIPPE: Est-ce qu'elle parle français?
  ANNIE: Bien sûr! Elle habite à Montréal!
PHILIPPE: Est-ce qu'elle parle avec un accent?
  ANNIE: Mais non! Au contraire, elle parle très bien!

L'art du dialogue

a) Act out the dialog between Annie and Philippe.
b) Now imagine that Patrick drops in. Patrick is from Fort-de-France. Act out the new dialog, replacing Jacqueline by **Patrick,** and Montréal by **Fort-de-France.** Make all necessary changes.
c) Now **Alice** and **Robert,** who are from **Québec,** show up. Act out the new dialog between Annie and Philippe, and make all necessary changes.

Leçon 3 Au club international

The International Club is having a big party.
Michèle meets several students from Africa there.

Michèle parle à Abdou.

MICHÈLE: Bonjour! Je m'appelle Michèle!
Et toi? Comment est-ce que tu t'appelles?
ABDOU: Je m'appelle Abdou.
MICHÈLE: Où est-ce que tu habites?
ABDOU: J'habite à Dakar.

Michèle parle à Adjoua et à Aya.

MICHÈLE: Est-ce que vous habitez à Dakar aussi?
ADJOUA: Non! Nous habitons à Abidjan.
MICHÈLE: Quand est-ce que vous rentrez à Abidjan?
AYA: Nous rentrons demain.
MICHÈLE: Pourquoi demain?
ADJOUA: Parce que les vacances sont finies.
MICHÈLE: Dommage!

At the International Club

Michèle is talking to Abdou.

Michèle: Hello! My name is Michèle!
And you? What's your name?
Abdou: My name is Abdou.
Michèle: Where do you live?
Abdou: I live in Dakar.

Michèle is talking to Adjoua and Aya.

Michèle: Do you live in Dakar also?
Adjoua: No! We live in Abidjan.
Michèle: When are you going back to Abidjan?
Aya: We are going back tomorrow.
Michèle: Why tomorrow?
Adjoua: Because vacation is over.
Michèle: Too bad!

CONVERSATION OPTIONAL

Michèle is asking you questions. Answer her by completing the sentences.

1. **Où** est-ce que **tu habites?** (à Philadelphie? à Akron? à . . .?)
   J'habite à . . .
2. **À quelle heure** est-ce que **tu dînes?** (à cinq heures et demie? à six
   heures? à . . .?)
   Je dîne à . . .
3. **Quand** est-ce que **tu joues** au tennis? (en été? en hiver? au printemps? . . .?)
   Je joue au tennis . . .

OBSERVATIONS Str. B   OPTIONAL

Reread Michèle's questions carefully.

• How does she say *you* in her questions?   tu
• Which two letters do the verbs end in when the subject is **tu**?   -es

In these questions Michèle is asking for information.   où   à quelle heure   quand
• Which interrogative expression does she use to say *where? at what time? when?*
• What expression does she use immediately after the interrogative expression?   est-ce que

SUPPLEMENTARY INFORMATION: Among other African countries
which use French as their official language are **le Zaïre** (the largest country
in Africa) and **Madagascar** (a large island off the east coast of Africa).

SUGGESTED REALIA: stamps from
French-speaking African countries.

NOTE CULTURELLE   OPTIONAL

Qui parle français en Afrique?

French is spoken in many countries of central and western
Africa. These countries are former French or Belgian colonies
which have maintained French as their official language.
Dakar is the capital of Senegal **(le Sénégal),** a country whose
inhabitants are predominantly Moslem. Abidjan is the capital
of the Ivory Coast **(la Côte-d'Ivoire),** one of the most prosperous and dynamic countries of western Africa.

Although not the official language, French is also spoken
by many people in the North African countries of Morocco **(le
Maroc),** Algeria **(l'Algérie),** and Tunisia **(la Tunisie).**

Abdou is a boy's name typical of Senegal. **Adjoua** and
Aya are girls' names typical of the Ivory Coast.

Turn to the map of the French-speaking world on pp. vi–vii.

Dakar, Sénégal

In the past, many African families used to give French names to their children. After these countries gained their independence
in the 1960's there was a return to African traditions and African names. In certain tribes, children are named after the day of
the week on which they are born, such as Adjoua (Tuesday) or Aya (Friday).

Structure

A. Les pronoms sujets: *je, tu, nous, vous*

In Lesson 2 of this Unit you learned four subject pronouns: **il, elle, ils, elles.**
The other four subject pronouns are: **je** (which you learned in Lesson 1), **tu,
nous,** and **vous.** Note the verb endings that correspond to these pronouns in
the sentences below.

SINGULAR		PLURAL		
je *I* ↓ **j'** (+ vowel sound)	Je parle français. J'habite à Paris.	**nous** *we*	Nous parlons français. Nous habitons à Dakar.
tu *you*	Tu parles français. Tu habites à Dakar.	**vous** *you*	Vous parlez français. Vous habitez à Québec.

→ In French there are two pronouns which correspond to the English *you:*

  tu   when speaking to *one* person
  vous   when speaking to *two* or more people

→ There is liaison after **nous** and **vous** when the next word begins with a vowel sound.

→ The following **-er** verb endings are used with the above subject pronouns:

  (je) **-e**   (tu) **-es**   (nous) **-ons**   (vous) **-ez**

  The **je** and **tu** endings are silent. The **nous** and **vous** endings are pronounced.

ACTIVITÉ 1   Tennis?

Imagine that you are looking for tennis partners at the Roland Garros tennis
club in Paris. Ask the following people if they play tennis, using **tu** or **vous,**
as appropriate.

→ Charles et Émilie   **Est-ce que vous jouez au tennis?**

1. Paul
2. Hélène
3. Jean-Paul et Marie-Anne
4. Claire
5. Sylvie et André
6. Suzanne, Édouard et Philippe

14.00 **TENNIS**
Coupe Davis
Tchécoslovaquie-France
EN DIRECT DE PRAGUE (sous réserve)

Vocabulaire spécialisé Mots utiles (Useful words)

beaucoup	*much, very much, a lot*	Nous étudions **beaucoup.**
un peu	*a little, a little bit*	Vous parlez **un peu** français.
maintenant	*now*	J'étudie **maintenant.** Maintenant often comes at the end of the sentence.
rarement	*rarely, seldom*	Tu joues **rarement** au tennis, Jacqueline?
souvent	*often*	Charles invite **souvent** Nathalie.
toujours	*always*	Nous skions **toujours** à Grenoble.

You may want to review the adverbs **bien** and **mal.**

Note: The above expressions usually come after the verb. They *never* come between the subject and the verb. Compare:

Nous <u>parlons</u> **toujours** français.   *We always <u>speak</u> French.*

Tu <u>ne joues pas</u> **souvent** au tennis.   *You <u>don't</u> often <u>play</u> tennis.*

Be sure the students do *not* say "très beaucoup." Stress that **beaucoup** means *very much.*

ACTIVITÉ 2   Dialogue

Be curious! Ask the person next to you if he or she does the following things. Use the pronoun **tu.** Your neighbor will answer you.

→ Il / elle étudie l'espagnol?   — **Est-ce que tu étudies l'espagnol?**
      — **Oui, j'étudie l'espagnol.**
      (Non, je n'étudie pas l'espagnol.)

1. Il / elle danse?
2. Il / elle danse souvent?
3. Il / elle étudie la musique?
4. Il / elle joue au tennis?
5. Il / elle téléphone beaucoup?
6. Il / elle étudie rarement?
7. Il / elle parle toujours français?
8. Il / elle parle un peu français?

ACTIVITÉ 3   En Amérique

A French journalist is writing an article about American high school students. Imagine he is asking questions about you and your friends. Answer him, using the pronoun **nous.**

→ Est-ce que vous étudiez beaucoup?
      Oui, en Amérique nous étudions beaucoup.
      (Non, en Amérique nous n'étudions pas beaucoup.)

1. Est-ce que vous jouez au baseball?
2. Est-ce que vous jouez au golf?
3. Est-ce que vous étudiez le français?
4. Est-ce que vous skiez en hiver?
5. Est-ce que vous dansez souvent?
6. Est-ce que vous téléphonez beaucoup?

B. Questions d'information

The questions in the chart below cannot be answered by *yes* or *no*. Since they ask for specific information, they are called *information questions*.

où?	*where?*	— Où est-ce que tu habites?	— À Dakar.
quand?	*when?*	— Quand est-ce qu'Aya rentre?	— Le 15 août.
à quelle heure?	*at what time?*	— À quelle heure est-ce que nous dînons?	— À six heures.
comment?	*how?*	— Comment est-ce que tu joues au tennis?	— Très bien!
pourquoi?	*why?*	— Pourquoi est-ce que tu invites Janine?	
parce que . . .	*because . . .*	— Parce que Janine danse très bien.	

There is usually liaison in the expression quand /t/ est-ce que. . . ?

To form an information question, French speakers often use the following construction:

interrogative expression + **est-ce que** + subject + verb + (rest of sentence) ?
↓
est-ce qu' (+ vowel sound)

→ The interrogative expression indicates what type of information is requested.

→ The expression **parce que** becomes **parce qu'** before a vowel sound.

J'invite Adjoua **parce qu'**elle danse bien.

où? quand? comment? qui? pourquoi?
il a réponse à tout
le petit Larousse en couleurs

LAROUSSE

Short questions with **où** are often formed as follows:

✓ ACTIVITÉ 4   Le club français | où + verb + subject | Où habite Aya?

The president of the French Club wants to know the addresses of some of the members. The secretary tells her where each one lives. Play both roles according to the model.

→ Sylvie (à Québec) La présidente: **Où est-ce que Sylvie habite?**
La secrétaire: **Elle habite à Québec.**

1. Jacques (à Montréal)   3. Aya et Adjoua (à Abidjan)   5. Jacqueline (à Paris)
2. Abdou (à Dakar)   4. Suzanne et Michèle (à Nice)   6. Louis et Antoine (à Toulouse)

✓ ACTIVITÉ 5   Curiosité

Annie says that her friends are doing certain things. Philippe wants more information. Play both roles according to the model.

→ Jacques arrive à Paris. (quand?)   Annie: **Jacques arrive à Paris.**
Philippe: **Quand est-ce qu'il arrive à Paris?**

1. Aya rentre à Abidjan. (quand?)   5. Thomas joue au tennis. (comment?)
2. Sylvie visite Abidjan. (quand?)   6. Hélène parle anglais. (comment?)
3. Louise dîne au restaurant. (à quelle heure?)   7. François étudie l'espagnol. (pourquoi?)
4. Paul téléphone à Marie. (à quelle heure?)   8. Isabelle parle avec Henri. (pourquoi?)

Prononciation

Le son /ɔ̃/

Model word: n<u>on</u>

Practice words: <u>on</u>ze, Sim<u>on</u>, dîn<u>on</u>s, visit<u>on</u>s, b<u>on</u>jour, b<u>om</u>be

Practice sentences: B<u>on</u>jour, Sim<u>on</u>!

Nous jou<u>on</u>s avec Yv<u>on</u>.

The sound /ɔ̃/ is a nasal vowel. When you pronounce a nasal vowel, air passes through your nasal passages. Be sure not to pronounce an /n/ or /m/ after a nasal vowel.

Comment écrire /ɔ̃/: **on** (**om** before **b** or **p**)

Entre nous

Expression pour la conversation

In addition to using **est-ce que** or letting your voice rise at the end of a sentence, there is another way to make a yes/no question in French, especially when you expect the other person to agree with you. You simply add **n'est-ce pas?** to the end of the sentence.

Aya habite à Abidjan, **n'est-ce pas?**	*Aya lives in Abidjan, doesn't she?*
Vous parlez français, **n'est-ce pas?**	*You speak French, don't you?*

Mini-dialogue OPTIONAL

The evening before Aya's departure for Abidjan, Philippe invites her to a restaurant. Madame Leblanc, Philippe's mother, asks her son about his plans.

MME LEBLANC:	Tu dînes avec *nous,* n'est-ce pas?	*us*
PHILIPPE:	Non, Maman. *Ce soir* je dîne *en ville.*	*Tonight; in town*
MME LEBLANC:	Avec *qui* est-ce que tu dînes?	*whom*
PHILIPPE:	Je dîne avec Aya. Elle rentre demain à Abidjan.	
MME LEBLANC:	Où est-ce que vous dînez?	
PHILIPPE:	Nous dînons «Chez Simone».	
MME LEBLANC:	Quand est-ce que tu rentres?	
PHILIPPE:	À onze heures.	
MME LEBLANC:	Au revoir. Et *amusez-vous bien.*	*have a good time*

L'art du dialogue

a) Act out the dialog between Madame Leblanc and Philippe.

b) Imagine that Madame Leblanc is talking to her two sons, **Philippe** and **Pascal**. Act out the new dialog.

Leçon 4   À Bruxelles

STRUCTURES TO OBSERVE
- the choice between **tu** and **vous**
- the infinitive construction after verbs such as **aimer**

Marc, un étudiant belge, parle avec Irène Arnold, une étudiante suisse.
Marc parle aussi avec Monsieur Arnold, le père d'Irène.
Monsieur Arnold travaille pour une compagnie internationale.

Marc et Irène

MARC: Irène, tu parles bien français.
IRÈNE: Je parle souvent français.
En famille nous parlons toujours français.
MARC: Tu aimes voyager?
IRÈNE: J'adore voyager. Mais hélas, je voyage rarement.

Marc et Monsieur Arnold

MARC: Monsieur Arnold, pourquoi est-ce que vous habitez à Bruxelles?
M. ARNOLD: Parce que je travaille pour une compagnie internationale.
MARC: Alors, vous voyagez souvent?
M. ARNOLD: Hélas oui. Je voyage souvent. Je déteste voyager.

Est-ce qu'Irène parle français? Est-ce qu'elle aime voyager? Est-ce qu'elle voyage souvent? Où est-ce que Monsieur Arnold habite? Pourquoi est-ce qu'il habite à Bruxelles? Est-ce qu'il voyage souvent? Est-ce qu'il aime voyager?

CONVERSATION

Imagine that Marc, an exchange student from Belgium, is talking to you. Answer his questions.

1. Est-ce que **tu** parles français?
2. Est-ce que **tu** skies?
3. Est-ce que **tu** joues au tennis?
4. Est-ce que **tu** étudies la musique?

Now imagine that Mademoiselle Pascal, a teacher from Belgium, is talking to you. Answer her.

5. Est-ce que **vous** parlez français?
6. Est-ce que **vous** skiez?
7. Est-ce que **vous** jouez au tennis?
8. Est-ce que **vous** étudiez la musique?

OBSERVATIONS Str. A

Marc, the student, and Mademoiselle Pascal, the teacher, ask you the same questions, but in different ways.

Marc, like you, is a student. He talks to you in an *informal* way.

• Which pronoun does he use? tu

Mademoiselle Pascal talks to you in a more *formal* way.

• Which pronoun does she use? vous

You may ask your students to locate these countries on the map of the French-speaking world on pp. vi–vii.

NOTE CULTURELLE

Qui parle français en Europe?

Have you heard of Brussels? Geneva? Luxemburg? Monaco? These are all cities outside France where the inhabitants speak French. Brussels **(Bruxelles)** is the capital of Belgium **(la Belgique)**, a country with two national languages: French and Flemish. Since many European organizations have their offices there, Brussels is considered one of the capitals of Europe.

Geneva **(Genève)** is the second largest city in Switzerland **(la Suisse).** It is the seat of the International Red Cross and of many United Nations agencies.

In spite of its small size, Luxemburg **(le Luxembourg)** is a very prosperous and dynamic country. It is also an important international center. **Monaco** is a popular resort, located on the French Riviera. It is known for its Grand Prix car race and its casino.

SUGGESTED REALIA: stamps from these countries.

Helvetia, the Latin name for Switzerland, appears on Swiss coins and stamps.

In Brussels

Marc, a Belgian student, is talking with Irène Arnold, a Swiss student.
Marc is also talking with Mr. Arnold, Irène's father.
Mr. Arnold works for an international company.

Marc: Irène, you speak French well.
Irène: I often speak French.
At home we always speak French.
Marc: Do you like to travel?
Irène: I adore traveling. But unfortunately (alas), I rarely travel.

Marc: Mr. Arnold, why do you live in Brussels?
M. Arnold: Because I work for an international company.
Marc: So you travel often?
M. Arnold: Unfortunately (alas), yes. I travel often. I hate to travel.

Structure

A. *Tu* ou *vous*?

In the Prélude, students learned that French speakers address one another with different degrees of formality. You may wish to review the notes on pp.5, 9, 16 before beginning this section.

Compare the pronouns which Marc uses when he speaks to his classmate Anne and when he speaks to Madame Robert, his English teacher.

Marc parle à Anne:
Tu parles bien anglais!
Où est-ce que **tu** habites?

Marc parle à Madame Robert:
Vous parlez bien anglais!   *You speak English well!*
Où est-ce que **vous** habitez?   *Where do you live?*

When talking to one person, French speakers sometimes say **tu** and sometimes **vous**.

> **Tu** is used to address a child, a member of the family, a close friend, or a classmate. **Tu** is called the *familiar* form of address.
>
> **Vous** is used to address everyone else. **Vous** is called the *formal* form of address.

→ **Vous** is also the plural of both the familiar and the formal forms:

FAMILIAR
Salut, Paul! Salut, Suzanne!
Est-ce que **vous** parlez espagnol?

FORMAL
Bonjour, Monsieur! Bonjour, Madame!
Est-ce que **vous** parlez anglais?

→ In the **Questions personnelles** and in most **Conversation** sections you will be addressed as **vous**. You should use **vous** when talking to your teacher. However, when talking to your classmates, you should use **tu**.
You may address your students as **tu**, since this form of address is being used more and more frequently by teachers in France.

ACTIVITÉ 1   À qui est-ce qu'il parle? *(To whom is he speaking?)*

François is spending his vacation in the home of his friend Marc. Note the form of address he uses in the following questions and decide whether he is speaking to Marc or to Madame Rémi, Marc's mother.

→ Est-ce que vous jouez très bien au tennis?   **François parle à Madame Rémi.**

1. À quelle heure est-ce que tu téléphones?
2. Est-ce que vous dînez souvent au restaurant?
3. Quand est-ce que tu rentres?
4. Est-ce que vous parlez espagnol?
5. Quand est-ce que vous rentrez à Paris?
6. Pourquoi est-ce que tu étudies aujourd'hui?

√ ACTIVITÉ 2   Une enquête *(A survey)*

Imagine that a French magazine has asked you to make a survey of how widely French is spoken in this country. Ask the following people if they speak French, using the familiar or formal form of address, as appropriate.

→ your cousin   **Est-ce que tu parles français?**

1. your math teacher
2. the principal
3. your best friend
4. your best friend's mother
5. your uncle
6. your neighbor's little boy
7. the student seated next to you
8. that student's father

B. Le présent des verbes réguliers en -er

You may practice the -er verb conjugation by asking the students to conjugate other verbs: je chante, tu chantes. . . ; je joue, tu joues. . .

Forms

Most verbs in **-er** form their present tense like **parler.**

Infinitive	parler	INFINITIVE STEM	ENDINGS
Present	je **parle**		**-e**
	tu **parles**		**-es**
	il/elle **parle**	(infinitive minus **-er**)	**-e**
		parl- +	
	nous **parlons**		**-ons**
	vous **parlez**		**-ez**
	ils/elles **parlent**		**-ent**

The present tense forms of **parler** consist of two parts:

(1) a part which does not change: the *stem* (which is the infinitive minus **-er**)
(2) a part which changes to agree with the subject: the *ending*

Verbs conjugated like **parler** are called *regular* **-er** verbs because their forms can be predicted.

At this point you may want to prepare a list of all the -er verbs already taught. This activity may be set up as a game. Ask each student to take a sheet of paper and write from memory as many verbs as he/she can remember. The student with the longest correct list is the winner.

Uses

Note the English equivalents of the French verbs in the present tense:

Irène **parle** français.
{ *Irène speaks French.*
Irène does speak French.
Irène is speaking French.

Irène **ne parle pas** anglais.
{ *Irène does not speak English.*
Irène is not speaking English.

Est-ce qu'Irène **parle** italien?
{ *Does Irène speak Italian?*
Is Irène speaking Italian?

→ In French the present tense consists of *one* word. It is used to describe what people *do* (regularly) or *are doing* (at the moment).

ACTIVITÉ 3   Voyage en France *(A trip to France)*

The purpose of this exercise is to review the **il/elles/je/ nous** forms of the **-er** verbs. Make sure that your students make the appropriate elisions and liaisons.

A group of American students are on a tour of France. During the trip they
do the following things:

arriver à Paris / téléphoner à Paul / visiter la tour Eiffel / inviter Sylvie /
parler français / arriver à Annecy / skier / visiter Toulouse / rentrer à New York

Describe the trips of the following people.

1. Paul   (begin with: **Il arrive à Paris. ...**)
2. Hélène et Louise   (begin with: **Elles arrivent à Paris. ...**)
3. you   (begin with: **J'arrive à Paris. ...**)
4. you and your best friend   (begin with: **Nous arrivons à Paris. ...**)

VARIATION: This activity may be used to review the **tu/vous** forms, as well as the negative and interrogative
constructions. Paul has missed the plane. (**Il n'arrive pas à Paris...**) A friend asks the members of the group
when they are doing each thing. (**Quand est-ce que vous arrivez à Paris?...**)

Vocabulaire spécialisé   Activités

chanter
to sing

écouter (la radio)
to listen to (the radio)

regarder (la télé)
to watch (TV)

regarder (Paul)
to look at

nager
to swim

travailler
to work

voyager
to travel

Note: **Regarder** has two meanings: *to look at* and *to watch.*
    Paul **regarde** Sylvie.   Sylvie **regarde** la télé.

La télé is the abbreviation which is commonly used to refer to télévision.
Make sure that your students *never* use à after écouter and regarder.
The verbs nager and voyager are regular in spoken French. In their written forms, the nous ending is -eons. This
nous form is not activated until Unité 5.2.

Activités 4 and 5 focus on two uses of the present tense in French. I play
tennis (in general); and, I am playing tennis (right now).

√ *ACTIVITÉ 4*   **Activités**

Ask your classmates whether they do the following things.

→ jouer au tennis   — **Est-ce que tu joues au tennis?**
                       — **Bien sûr, je joue au tennis.**
                          (Mais non, je ne joue pas au tennis.)

1. danser   5. voyager   9. parler français
2. skier   6. regarder la télé   10. parler anglais
3. nager   7. écouter la radio   11. travailler
4. étudier   8. jouer au football 12. chanter

ACTIVITÉ 5   **Et maintenant?**

Ask your classmates whether they are doing the things in **Activité 4** right
now.

→ jouer au tennis   — **Et maintenant, est-ce que tu joues au tennis?**
                       — **Non! Maintenant je ne joue pas au tennis.**

C. La construction verbe + infinitif

For preliminary practice of this construction,
you may have students conjugate the sentence:
Je n'aime pas travailler. Tu n'aimes pas travailler.

Note the use of the infinitive in the sentences of the chart below:

adorer	*to love, adore*	**J'adore nager.**
aimer	*to like*	**J'aime voyager.**
désirer	*to wish, want*	**Nous désirons visiter Bruxelles.**
détester	*to dislike, hate*	**Vous détestez regarder la télé.**

In French the infinitive is used after verbs like those listed above. Note the English
equivalents of the French infinitive.

Nous détestons **voyager.** { *We hate to travel.*
                              { *We hate travelling.*

→ In the negative the expression **ne . . . pas** goes around the first verb.

Je n'aime pas travailler.   *I don't like to work.*

√ *ACTIVITÉ 6*   **Expression personnelle**

Do you have plans for the future? Say whether or not you wish to do the
following things.

→ visiter Paris   **Je désire visiter Paris.**
                   (Je ne désire pas visiter Paris.)

1. visiter Québec   Dakar   4. travailler à Bruxelles   à Paris
2. habiter en France   en Russie   5. étudier l'italien   l'espagnol
3. voyager en Chine   en Afrique   6. visiter le Japon   l'Italie

ACTIVITÉ 7 Dialogue

Ask your classmates whether or not they like to do the following things.
Your friends will answer.

→ skier — **Est-ce que tu aimes skier?**
— **Oui, j'aime skier. (Oui, j'adore skier.)**
(Non, je n'aime pas skier.) (Non, je déteste skier.)

1. nager
2. chanter
3. écouter la radio
4. regarder la télé

5. travailler
6. voyager
7. étudier
8. parler anglais

9. parler français en classe
10. jouer au tennis
11. téléphoner
12. danser

ACTIVITÉ 8 Une excellente raison *(An excellent reason)* OPTIONAL

Say that the following people are doing certain things because they like to do them.

→ Aya voyage. **Aya voyage parce qu'elle aime voyager.**

1. Monique chante.
2. Charles étudie la musique.
3. Henri téléphone.
4. Isabelle chante.
5. Marc et Sylvie nagent.
6. Annie et Paul dansent.

7. Suzanne et Claire jouent au tennis.
8. Jacques et Philippe écoutent la radio.
9. Nous travaillons.
10. Nous parlons espagnol.
11. Vous regardez la télé.
12. Vous voyagez.

Be sure students make the liaison with
aimer in items 5–12.

VARIATION in the negative: Aya ne parle pas français
parce qu'elle n'aime pas parler français.

Prononciation

1. Le son /u/

Model word: v<u>ou</u>s
Practice words: <u>où</u>, n<u>ou</u>s, d<u>ou</u>ze, Abd<u>ou</u>, Adj<u>ou</u>a, j<u>ou</u>e, t<u>ou</u>jours, s<u>ou</u>vent
Practice sentences: Min<u>ou</u> habite à T<u>ou</u>l<u>ou</u>se.
Abd<u>ou</u> j<u>ou</u>e avec n<u>ou</u>s.

The French sound /u/ is similar to but shorter than the vowel in the English word *do.*
Comment écrire /u/: **ou, où**

2. Le son /y/

Model word: t<u>u</u>

Practice words: sal<u>u</u>t, aven<u>u</u>e, ét<u>u</u>die, min<u>u</u>te, L<u>u</u>cie, S<u>u</u>zanne, s<u>û</u>r

Practice sentences: S<u>u</u>zanne et <u>U</u>rs<u>u</u>le ét<u>u</u>dient.
Sal<u>u</u>t, L<u>u</u>cie. Comment vas-t<u>u</u>?
L<u>u</u>c habite aven<u>u</u>e d<u>u</u> Maine.

The sound /y/ has no English equivalent. To produce this new sound, try to
say the sound /i/ while keeping your lips rounded as if to whistle.

Comment écrire /y/: **u, û**

Entre nous

Expressions pour la conversation

To get someone's attention, you can say:

Eh!	*Hey!*	**Eh,** Paul! Quand est-ce que tu rentres?
Dis! **Dis donc!**	*Say! Hey!* (**tu** form)	**Dis donc,** Nathalie, est-ce que tu aimes voyager?
Dites! **Dites donc!**	*Say! Hey!* (**vous** form)	**Dites,** Marc et Irène, pourquoi est-ce que vous travaillez?

Mini-dialogue   OPTIONAL

Sometimes Nicole is a bit too enthusiastic.

MARC: Dis, Nicole, est-ce que tu aimes les *surprises-parties?*   *parties*

NICOLE: Bien sûr! J'adore les surprises-parties. J'adore danser!

MARC: Est-ce que tu danses bien?

NICOLE: Je danse très, très bien.

MARC: Et Sylvie, est-ce qu'elle aime danser?

NICOLE: Oh, Sylvie *aime bien* danser, mais elle ne danse pas bien.   *really likes*

MARC: *Dans ce cas,* c'est Sylvie *que* j'invite à la surprise-partie.   *In that case; whom*

NICOLE: Pourquoi Sylvie? *Pourquoi pas moi?*   *Why not me?*

MARC: Parce que je ne danse pas très bien. Je préfère inviter une fille qui ne danse pas bien. C'est normal, non?

L'art du dialogue

a) Act out the dialog between Marc and Nicole.

b) Imagine that Marc is thinking of playing tennis. Act out a new dialog, replacing **les surprises-parties** by **le tennis,** and **danser** by **jouer.** Leave out **à la surprise-partie.**

Leçon 5 En vacances

 Hélène est suisse. Elle vous parle. Écoutez.

Vous êtes étudiants, n'est-ce pas?
Moi, je ne suis pas étudiante.
Je suis interprète.
Je travaille pour Swissair.
D'habitude je suis à Genève.
Mais aujourd'hui, je ne suis pas à Genève.
Je suis à Tahiti.
Oui! À Tahiti!
Pourquoi?
Parce que je suis en vacances.
Et vous? Êtes-vous en vacances?
Non?
Où êtes-vous alors?
En classe?
Dommage!

Genève is located in the French-speaking part of Switzerland. It is the seat of many international organizations (Red Cross, UN agencies, etc.).

Pour qui est-ce qu'Hélène travaille? Où est-ce qu'elle est d'habitude?
Où est-ce qu'elle est aujourd'hui? Pourquoi est-ce qu'elle est à Tahiti?

CONVERSATION OPTIONAL

Hélène, the young person from Switzerland, is going to ask you a few questions about your summer activities. Answer her.

1. Voyagez-vous?
2. Nagez-vous?
3. Jouez-vous au tennis?

4. Travaillez-vous?
5. Étudiez-vous?

OBSERVATIONS   Str. D   OPTIONAL

Est-ce que vous voyagez? and **Voyagez-vous?** are two ways of asking the same question: *Do you travel?*

• In these two questions, which word is the *subject?* which word is the *verb?* . voyagez   vous

Reread Hélène's questions carefully.

• Which word comes first — the subject or the verb? the verb
• Which word comes second? the subject
• What connects the verb and the subject?   a hyphen

NOTE CULTURELLE   OPTIONAL

Qui parle français dans le monde?
(Who speaks French in the world?)

How many people in the world speak French? Maybe 100 million, maybe more. French is spoken in France, of course, but it is spoken and understood on every continent of the earth. It is spoken by many Europeans and Africans, and it is also spoken by people in Vietnam, in the Middle East, and in the Caribbean. It is spoken as far away as Tahiti, in the South Pacific, and as close as the eastern provinces of Canada. In fact, within the United States it is spoken by many families in New England and Louisiana.

Yes, French is truly an international language!

On vacation
Hélène is Swiss. She is speaking to you. Listen.
You are students, aren't you?
I'm not a student.
I'm an interpreter.
I work for Swissair.
Usually I am in Geneva.
But today I am not in Geneva.
I am in Tahiti.
Yes! In Tahiti!
Why?
Because I am on vacation.
And you? Are you on vacation?
No?
Where are you then?
In class?
Too bad!

You may want to refer students to the map of the French-speaking world on pp. vi–vii.

Leçon cinq **73**

Structure

A. Le verbe être

Note the forms of **être** *(to be)* in the present tense.

être		to be		
je	**suis**	*I am*	Je **suis** à Paris.	Je ne **suis** pas à Genève.
tu	**es**	*you are*	Tu **es** là?	Tu n'**es** pas à la maison?
il/elle	**est**	*he/she is*	Il **est** avec Hélène.	Il n'**est** pas avec Lucie.
nous	**sommes**	*we are*	Nous **sommes** en classe.	Nous ne **sommes** pas en ville.
vous	**êtes**	*you are*	Vous **êtes** ici.	Vous n'**êtes** pas là-bas.
ils/elles	**sont**	*they are*	Ils **sont** avec Jean.	Ils ne **sont** pas avec Yves.

→ The verb **être** does not follow a predictable pattern as do the regular **-er** verbs. **Être** is called an *irregular* verb.

→ Liaison is required in the form **vous êtes.**

→ Liaison is frequently heard after **est** and **sont,** and sometimes after other forms of **être.**

ACTIVITÉ 1   En vacances!

It is vacation time. Say where the following students are. Say also that they are not in class.

→ Paul (à Toulon)   **Paul est à Toulon. Il n'est pas en classe.**

1. Suzanne (à Nice)
2. Abdou (à Dakar)
3. tu (à la Martinique)
4. je (à Montréal)
5. Pierre et Jean-Marc (à Québec)
6. nous (à Genève)
7. Aya et Adjoua (à Abidjan)
8. vous (à Tahiti)
9. Philippe et André (à Annecy)
10. Jacques (à Lyon)

Vocabulaire spécialisé   Où?

ici	*here*	François travaille **ici.**
là	*there*	Pierre n'est pas **là.**
là-bas	*over there*	Qui est-ce, **là-bas?**
à la maison	*at home, home*	Nous regardons la télé **à la maison.**
au restaurant	*at the restaurant*	Vous dînez **au restaurant?**
en classe	*in class*	**En classe** nous parlons toujours français.
en vacances	*on vacation*	Jacques est **en vacances** à Tahiti.
en ville	*downtown, in town*	Je suis **en ville** avec Mélanie.

✓ACTIVITÉ 2   Où sont-ils?

What we do often depends on where we are. Express this, using the appropriate form of **être** and one of the following expressions:

en classe   en ville   en vacances   à la maison   au restaurant

→ Paul nage.   **Il est en vacances.**

In some instances more than one response may be appropriate. Encourage students to use their imagination.

1. Caroline regarde la télé.
2. Nous écoutons la radio.
3. Vous dînez avec Anne et Michèle.
4. Je joue au tennis.
5. Tu voyages beaucoup.

6. Philippe visite Genève.
7. Suzanne et Marc parlent avec le professeur.
8. Nous étudions.
9. Louis et Mathieu skient.
10. Vous nagez.

B. Qui?

The following questions begin with **qui?** *(who?)*. Note the word order.

Qui travaille?	Jean-Pierre travaille.
Qui joue au tennis?	Suzanne et Henri jouent au tennis.
Qui aime voyager?	Nous aimons voyager.

To ask who is doing something, French speakers generally use the following construction:

In **qui**-questions with **être**, the verb agrees with the subject which follows the verb: **Qui êtes-vous? Qui sont les filles là-bas?**

> **qui   +   verb   +   . . . (rest of sentence)   ?**

→ In **qui** questions the verb is singular, even if the expected answer is plural.

In the above constructions, **qui** is the subject of the sentence. When **qui** is the direct object, the regular interrogative constructions (with **est-ce que** or with inversion) are used. **Qui est-ce que tu invites? Qui invites-tu?**

✓ACTIVITÉ 3   Un sondage d'opinion *(An opinion poll)*

Imagine that you are taking a class survey about the leisure activities of young Americans. Ask who does the following things.

→ écouter la radio   **Qui écoute la radio?**

You may have a student at the board count how many in the class answer "yes" to each question.

1. voyager
2. voyager souvent
3. aimer chanter
4. danser
5. aimer danser

6. regarder la télé
7. détester regarder la télé
8. jouer au tennis
9. jouer au bridge
10. skier

C. Expressions interrogatives avec *qui*

Note the interrogative expressions in the questions below:

à qui	*to whom*	**À qui** est-ce que tu téléphones?
avec qui	*with whom*	**Avec qui** est-ce que vous voyagez?
de qui	*of (about) whom*	**De qui** est-ce que Pierre parle?
pour qui	*for whom*	**Pour qui** est-ce que Michèle travaille?

You may indicate that in conversational English the preposition often comes at the end of the sentence. This is *never* done in French.

Qui *(who, whom)* may be used with prepositions such as **à**, **avec**, **de**, and **pour** *(for)*, to form interrogative expressions.

➜ Information questions of this kind must *always begin with the preposition.*

✓ ACTIVITÉ 4 Curiosité

Hélène is telling Georges what she does. Georges wants more details. Play both roles according to the model.

➜ visiter Tahiti (avec)   Hélène: **Je visite Tahiti.**
Georges: **Avec qui est-ce que tu visites Tahiti?**

1. aimer danser (avec)
2. téléphoner souvent (à)
3. voyager (avec)
4. rentrer (avec)
5. travailler (pour)
6. regarder la télé (avec)
7. chanter (pour)
8. parler beaucoup (de)
9. parler français (à)

D. L'interrogation avec inversion   OPTIONAL

You may indicate that students have already encountered several questions with inversion: Qui est-ce? Quel temps fait-il? Quelle heure est-il?

Look at the two sets of questions below. They both ask the same thing. Compare the positions of the subject pronouns in each pair of questions.

Est-ce que **vous** parlez anglais?	Parlez-**vous** anglais?
Où est-ce que **tu** habites?	Où habites-**tu**?
À quelle heure est-ce que **nous** dînons?	À quelle heure dînons-**nous**?
Quand est-ce qu'**il** est en vacances?	Quand est-**il** en vacances?

This may be presented for recognition only. Inverted questions will be reviewed on p.273 when the addition of the letter t (parle-t-il?) is introduced.

In conversational French, questions are frequently formed with **est-ce que**. However, when the subject of the sentence is a pronoun, French speakers often prefer using the following construction:

interrogative expression (if any) + verb + subject pronoun + (rest of sentence) ?

➜ This is called *inversion,* since the subject and verb have been inverted, or turned around. Note that the verb and subject pronoun are connected with a hyphen.   Inversion is usually not used with je.

➜ There is liaison before **il/elle** and **ils/elles** in inversion.

ACTIVITÉ 5 Questions personnelles

1. Êtes-vous en vacances maintenant?
2. Aimez-vous chanter?
3. Jouez-vous bien au tennis?
4. Nagez-vous souvent en été?
5. Pourquoi regardez-vous la télé?   parce que j'aime/je déteste regarder...
6. Avec qui étudiez-vous?
7. Où habitez-vous?
8. À quelle heure arrivez-vous en classe?

VARIATION: Students may ask classmates the same questions using the **tu** form.

ACTIVITÉ 6 Le club des sports   OPTIONAL

Imagine that you are the president of a sports club. Ask the new members (indicated in parentheses) if they can do the following. Use **tu** or **vous**, as appropriate.

→ (Pierre) nager bien   **Nages-tu bien?**
    (Anne et Suzanne) jouer au ping-pong?   **Jouez-vous au ping-pong?**

1. (Caroline) nager?
2. (André et Pierre) nager le crawl?
3. (Hélène) skier?
4. (Albert et Thomas) skier bien?
5. (Marie-Thérèse) jouer au football?
6. (Jacques et Paul) jouer au tennis?

ACTIVITÉ 7 Interview   OPTIONAL

Olivier interviewed Charlotte, but forgot to write down his questions. Ask the questions again, using inversion and the interrogative expression in parentheses.

→ J'habite *à Tours*. (où?)   **Où habites-tu?**

1. Je travaille *à Paris*. (où?)
2. Je travaille *avec Madame Charron*. (avec qui?)
3. Je rentre à Tours *le 2 octobre*. (quand?)
4. Je voyage *en train*. (comment?)
5. J'arrive à Tours *à minuit*. (à quelle heure?)
6. J'habite à Tours *parce que j'aime Tours*. (pourquoi?)

Prononciation

1. Le son /e/

Model word: <u>e</u>t

Practice words: L<u>é</u>a, M<u>é</u>lanie, <u>É</u>dith, t<u>é</u>léphon<u>er</u>, écout<u>ez</u>, Qu<u>é</u>bec, t<u>é</u>l<u>é</u>, m<u>ai</u>

Practice sentences: L<u>é</u>a t<u>é</u>l<u>é</u>phone à <u>É</u>dith.
                    D<u>é</u>d<u>é</u> d<u>é</u>teste la t<u>é</u>l<u>é</u>.

The French vowel sound /e/ is much more tense than the English vowel sound in *day*. Smile when you say /e/. Keep your lips tight.

Comment écrire /e/: **é; et, ez, er** (final); **ai** (final)

2. Le son /ɛ/

Model word: <u>e</u>lle

Practice words: s<u>e</u>pt, <u>È</u>ve, Ann<u>e</u>tte, <u>E</u>stelle, <u>ai</u>me, dét<u>e</u>ste, Mich<u>e</u>l, Mich<u>è</u>le, <u>ê</u>tre

Practice sentences: Mich<u>e</u>l <u>ai</u>me <u>E</u>stelle.
                    Mich<u>è</u>le dét<u>e</u>ste <u>ê</u>tre av<u>e</u>c Ann<u>e</u>tte à Québ<u>e</u>c.

The French vowel sound /ɛ/ is pronounced with the mouth somewhat more open than for /e/. It is more tense than the English vowel sound in *get*.

Comment écrire /ɛ/: **è, ê; e** (+ pronounced final consonant); **e** (+ two consonants);
                    ai (+ pronounced final consonant)

Entre nous

Expressions pour la conversation

The French often begin or end sentences with:

alors	*then, well then, so*	—Sylvie n'est pas en ville.
		—**Alors,** où est-elle?
et alors?	*so what?*	—Sylvie est avec Michel.
		—**Et alors?**

Mini-dialogue   OPTIONAL

Marc is frantically looking for his girlfriend Sylvie. He calls Sylvie's friend Annie.

MARC: Allô, Annie?

ANNIE: Oui! Allô, Marc. Ça va?

MARC: Ça va! Dis, Annie, je *cherche* Sylvie.   *am looking for*
Est-ce qu'elle est en ville?

ANNIE: Non, elle n'est pas en ville.

MARC: Est-ce qu'elle est en classe, alors?

ANNIE: Non, elle n'est pas en classe.

MARC: Alors, elle est avec Michel?

ANNIE: Mais non, elle n'est pas avec Michel.

MARC: Tu es sûre?

ANNIE: Mais oui, elle n'est pas avec Michel.

MARC: Alors, où est-elle?

ANNIE: C'est simple. Elle est ici avec *moi*.   *me*

L'art du dialogue

a) Act out the phone conversation between Annie and Marc.
b) Act out a new phone conversation in which Marc is looking for his brother **Henri.**
c) Now imagine that Marc is looking for two girls: **Sylvie** and **Nathalie.** Act out the new conversation, making all the necessary changes.

OPPOSITE: Place de la Concorde and the Obélisque de Louxor, with the Église de la Madeleine in the background.

SECTION
MAGAZINE

1

VILLE DE PARIS

Accès aux avions
To planes

NOM : Surname VERGNE —
Prénoms : Christian names François Frédéric
Né le Date of birth 20 Juillet 1957
à Place of birth Paris 14°
Nationalité française
Profession : Etudiant
Domicile : Address 85 Rue La Boétie Paris 8°
N° 75-1670710
Ce passeport contient 32 pages
This passport contains 32 pages

AIR AFRIQUE
une grande compagnie dans un grand continent

AIR CANADA

AIR FRANCE

VOYAGE!

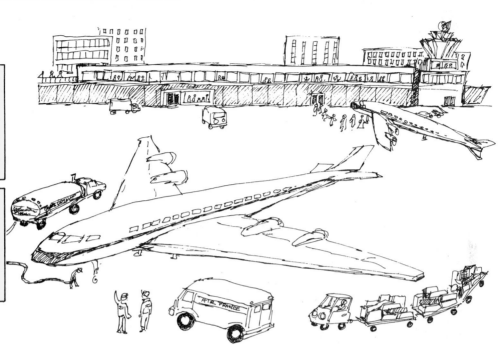

DÉPARTS	
Bruxelles	9h.10
Genève	9h.25
Dakar	9h.35
Tunis	9h.55
Alger	10h.20

ARRIVÉES	
Montréal	9h.22
Abidjan	9h.32
Casablanca	9h.41
Luxembourg	9h.57
Fort-de-France	10h.08

BDG. STN. / LIEU EMB!

FLIGHT/DATE   VOL/DATE

DESTINATION

SEAT   PLACE

BOS

680/20

HZ

V. COULD UP TO CONFIRMED JUSQU'À

3E

3E

INF. BÉBÉ

BOARDING PASS   AIR CANADA   CARTE D'EMBARQUEMENT

VALIDATION

VALIDATION

STAND-BY   EN ATTENTE

00A(6-78)

AGENT

GATE PORTE   TIME HEURE

2   845 A.

swissair +

Départs Departures

Départs Departures

16 58

81

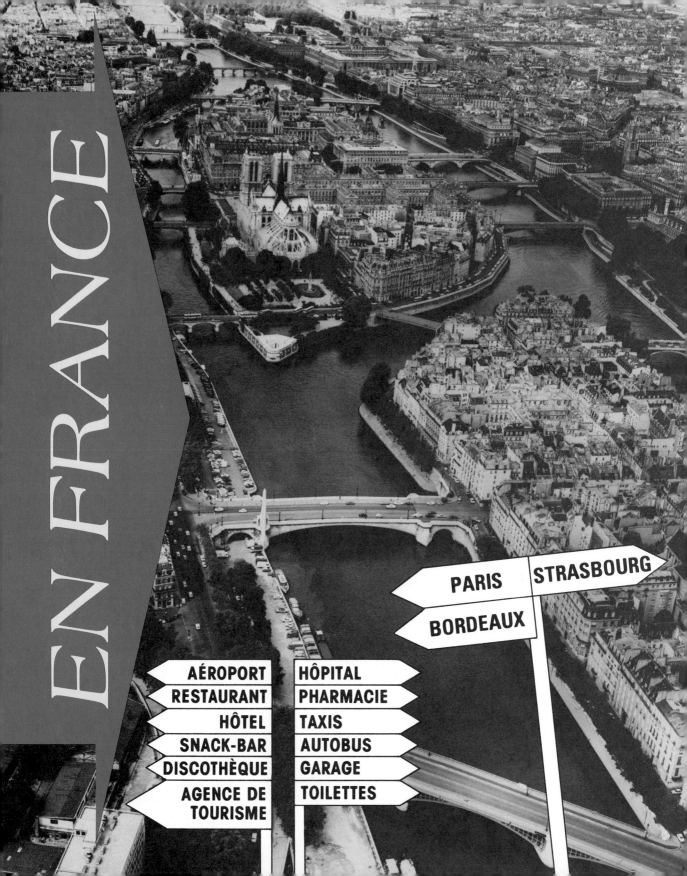

EN FRANCE

PARIS
STRASBOURG
BORDEAUX

AÉROPORT
RESTAURANT
HÔTEL
SNACK-BAR
DISCOTHÈQUE
AGENCE DE TOURISME

HÔPITAL
PHARMACIE
TAXIS
AUTOBUS
GARAGE
TOILETTES

CAFÉ	2 francs
THÉ	3 francs
CHOCOLAT	4 francs
COCA-COLA	4 francs
SANDWICH	5 francs

AVENUE DU PRÉSIDENT WILSON

RUE FRANKLIN

16ᵉ ARR

AVENUE DU PRÉSIDENT KENNEDY

DANGER

STOP

SILENCE

ATTENTION

PARIS

HOTEL DE TOURISME ★★ N.N. *Le Lisita*
2. Boulevard des Arènes — 30000 NIMES
(Face aux Arènes) — Téléphone : 67.66.20 — PARKING

CAFE RESTAURANT BRASSERIE *Les Fleurs* « PIZZERIA »
Cuisine soignée
Spécialités du Chef
18, Avenue Feuchères - NIMES - Téléphone : 67.22.39
(A côté de la Gare)
JARDIN D'ETE

Parlez-vous français?

Est-ce que vous parlez français?
Mais oui, vous parlez français. Tous les jours!° Tous les jours vous utilisez° des° expressions d'origine française.° Voici des exemples:

Domaine	Expressions
Unités de mesure	mètre, kilomètre, gramme, kilogramme
Automobile	auto, limousine, chauffeur
Cuisine	restaurant, café, chef, hors-d'œuvre, entrée, margarine, mayonnaise, bouillon, salade, purée, mousse, sauté, sauce, casserole
Mode°	chic, élégance, boutique, eau de cologne, eau de toilette
Art	théâtre, musique, sculpture, concert; flûte, clarinette; crayon, collage, papier-mâché
Danse	ballet, plié, tour-jeté, pirouette

Combien de ces° expressions connaissez-vous?°

Et connaissez-vous les villes suivantes° aux États-Unis? °

Bâton Rouge, la Nouvelle-Orléans, Louisville, Beaumont, Montpelier, Détroit, Terre Haute, Prairie du Chien, Des Moines, Pierre, Butte

Formidable! *Great!* **Tous les jours!** *Every day!* **utilisez** *use* **des** *some* **d'origine française** *of French origin* **Mode** *Fashion* **Combien de ces** *How many of these* **connaissez-vous** *do you know* **les villes suivantes** *the following cities* **aux États-Unis** *in the United States*

84

Bonjour, Christine!

Bonjour les amis!°
Je m'appelle Christine Descroix.
J'ai seize ans° et je suis une Sagittaire.
J'habite à Toulon avec mes° parents.
J'étudie l'anglais et l'espagnol
parce que je veux° travailler
dans une agence de voyages°.
J'aime voyager.
En juillet, je vais° visiter la Grèce°
avec ma° famille.
J'aime aussi danser.
J'aime le jazz et la musique pop.
Mes musiciens préférés° sont les Bee Gees.
Et vous?

Christine

les amis *friends* J'ai seize ans *I'm sixteen* mes *my* veux
want dans une agence de voyages *in a travel agency* vais
am going la Grèce *Greece* ma *my* préférés *favorite*

BOÎTE AUX LETTRES°

JANINE LEVASSEUR
PÉDIATRE
Docteur en Médecine

JEAN-PIERRE ALQUIER
DENTISTE

RAYMOND CICCOLI
INGÉNIEUR

FRANÇOISE SIMONET
PROFESSEUR DE PIANO

OLIVIER MUELLER
ARCHITECTE

SYLVIE LAMBERT
JOURNALISTE

JACQUELINE MALLET
PHARMACIENNE

ALBERT DUCLOS
PHOTOGRAPHE

SYLVIE LONGCHAMP
PROGRAMMATRICE IBM

ROBERT PECOUL
OPTICIEN

Mademoiselle Dupuis est canadienne. Elle habite à Québec et elle travaille dans une agence de voyages.° Elle parle français et anglais.

Monsieur Lamy est français. Il habite à Fort-de-France, la capitale de la Martinique. Il est professeur d'éducation physique.

boîte aux lettres *mailbox* **dans une agence de voyages** *in a travel agency* **allemand** *German* **médecin** *doctor* **belge** *Belgian*

Madame Kubler est suisse. Elle habite à Genève. Elle est pharmacienne. Elle parle français et allemand.°

Monsieur Teritaau habite à Tahiti. Il travaille pour le gouvernement français. Il parle tahitien et français.

Oui, ils parlent français!

Madame Kouadio habite à Dakar, la capitale du Sénégal. Elle est médecin.°

Monsieur Belkora est tunisien, mais il n'habite pas en Tunisie. Il habite à New York. Il est économiste et il travaille pour les Nations Unies. Il parle français, anglais et arabe.

Monsieur Pons est belge.° Il habite à Bruxelles. Il est ingénieur et il travaille pour une compagnie d'électronique. Il parle français.

87

LA CARTE DU TEMPS°

PARIS

Température¹: 5°   Temps: pluie

GENÈVE

Température: 1°   Temps: nuages

DAKAR

Température: 15°   Temps: soleil

ABIDJAN

Température: 24°   Temps: soleil

QUÉBEC

Température: −12° Temps: neige

Le premier janvier dans le monde francophone.°

MONTRÉAL

Température: −8°   Temps: neige

FORT-DE-FRANCE

Température: 22°   Temps: soleil

PORT-AU-PRINCE

Température: 16°   Temps: nuages

PAPEETE

Température: 25°   Temps: soleil

¹**Température** = degrés centigrades

la carte du temps the weather map
dans le monde francophone in the French-speaking world

Ils parlent français!

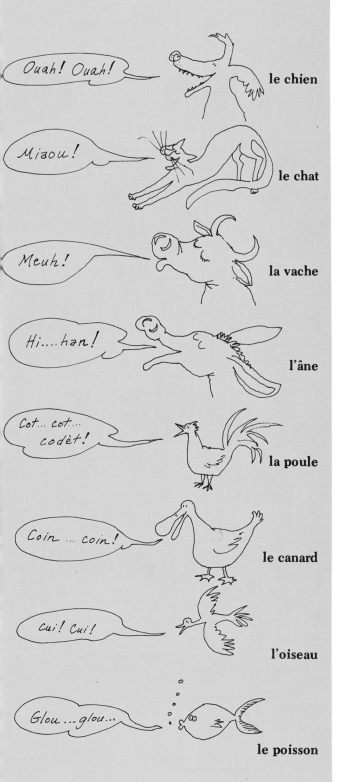

Ouah! Ouah! — le chien

Miaou! — le chat

Meuh! — la vache

Hi....han! — l'âne

Cot... cot... codèt! — la poule

Coin ... coin! — le canard

Cui! Cui! — l'oiseau

Glou...glou... — le poisson

PROJETS CULTURELS

Projets individuels

1. Select a French-speaking country or area and make a poster advertising it. (Source of pictures: travel brochures, travel magazines, the travel section of the Sunday paper)
2. Prepare a chart listing eight countries which use French as their official language. For each country, give the following information: population, size, capital, unit of currency, principal products. (Source: almanac)

Projets de classe

1. Imagine that your class is going to take a trip around the world. On this trip, you will stop in six French-speaking countries or areas (including islands). On a world map, draw the route which you will take. For each stop, prepare a display of travel brochures and plan a list of things you would like to do there. (Source: travel agencies, travel magazines, tour books)
2. Prepare a bulletin board exhibit of stamps from French-speaking countries. You may use a world map as a background. For each country, select stamps representing famous people and places, typical animals, flowers, plants, etc. (Source: actual stamps, reproductions of stamps from catalogs and stamp magazines)

OBJECTIVES
In this unit the students learn to describe themselves and to describe their environment:
people and things. To help them achieve this objective, the following elements are
presented:

Language
- avoir
- nouns and articles: gender and number
- descriptive adjectives: forms and uses, the noun-adjective agreement
- stress pronouns
- c'est vs. il est

Vocabulary
- people
- adjectives of description (physical aspect, personality, nationality)
- daily life objects
- countries

Culture
This unit focuses on French youth and interpersonal relationships, especially the concept
of friendship.

UNITÉ 2
Salut, les amis!

91

UNITÉ 2
Leçon 1   Invitations

STRUCTURES TO OBSERVE
• the indefinite article **un/une**
• the concept of gender: masculine vs. feminine
• the concept of agreement: article and noun; noun and adjective

Suzanne and Michèle are organizing a party with their brothers, Marc and Alain. Whom are they going to invite? Suzanne and Marc each have special guests in mind.

Suzanne et Michèle

SUZANNE: Est-ce que nous invitons Claude Dumas?
MICHÈLE: Claude Dumas? Qui est-ce? Un *garçon* ou une *fille?*   *boy; girl*
SUZANNE: Un garçon!
MICHÈLE: Un *ami?*   *friend*
SUZANNE: *Plus ou moins.* C'est le garçon avec qui je joue au tennis.   *More or less.*
MICHÈLE: *Comment est-il?*   *What's he like?*
SUZANNE: Il est *grand* et blond . . .   *tall*
MICHÈLE: Et bien sûr, il est très *beau* . . .   *good-looking*
SUZANNE: Euh . . . non. Mais il est *amusant* et très *sympathique.*   *amusing; nice*
MICHÈLE: Alors, d'accord! Nous invitons Claude à la surprise-partie.

Avec qui est-ce que Suzanne joue au tennis? Est-ce que Claude Dumas est blond?
Est-ce que Suzanne et Michèle invitent Claude Dumas?

NOTES CULTURELLES

1. Claude et Dominique Claude and Dominique are names that can be given either to boys or girls. There are other names that may also be given to boys or girls, but although they sound the same, they are spelled differently:

boys: **Michel   Daniel   Joël   Noël   René**
girls: **Michèle   Danièle   Joëlle   Noëlle   Renée**

OPTIONAL
2. Une surprise-partie The term **surprise-partie** is a word which French has borrowed from English. It is not a surprise party, in the American sense, but rather an informal party, usually with music and dancing. You will discover that modern French has borrowed quite a few words and expressions from English. Sometimes meanings change somewhat as a word is transferred from one language to another.

Other terms that French teenagers use to refer to parties are **une surboum** and **une boum**.

Marc et Alain

MARC: Est-ce que tu invites Dominique Laroche?

ALAIN: Dominique Laroche? Qui est-ce? Un garçon ou une fille?

MARC: Une fille.

ALAIN: Une amie?

MARC: Oui!

ALAIN: Est-ce que c'est la fille à qui tu téléphones *tout le temps*?   *all the time*

MARC: C'est ça!

ALAIN: Elle est grande et blonde, n'est-ce pas?

MARC: Elle est blonde, mais elle n'est pas très grande.

ALAIN: Et bien sûr elle est très belle . . .

MARC: *Pas spécialement!* Mais elle est très amusante et très   *Not especially!*
      sympathique! *C'est l'essentiel*, n'est-ce pas?   *That's the important thing*

ALAIN: D'accord! J'invite Dominique!

A qui est-ce que Marc téléphone souvent? Est-ce que Dominique est blonde?
Est-ce qu'Alain invite Dominique?

Vocabulaire pratique

NOM:	**une surprise-partie**	*(informal) party*	
EXPRESSIONS:	**c'est ça!**	*that's it! that's right!*	Tu arrives demain? Oui, **c'est ça!**
	d'accord?	*okay? all right?*	J'invite Paul. **D'accord?**
	d'accord!	*okay! fine!*	Oui, **d'accord!**
	être d'accord	*to agree*	Tu **es d'accord?**

CONVERSATION

1. Qui est Claude? **Un** <u>garçon</u> ou **une** <u>fille</u>?

2. Qui est Dominique? **Un** <u>garçon</u> ou **une** <u>fille</u>?

3. Qui êtes-vous? **Un** <u>garçon</u> ou **une** <u>fille</u>?

4. Qui enseigne (*teaches*) le français? **Un** <u>monsieur</u> (*man*) ou **une** <u>dame</u> (*woman*)?

OBSERVATIONS   Str. A

The underlined words above are *nouns*. In French, nouns are often introduced by *articles*. The words in heavy type are called *indefinite articles*.

- Does **garçon** refer to a male or female? Which article is used to introduce it? What about **monsieur**?   un

  un   male

- Does **fille** refer to a male or female? Which article is used to introduce it?   une
  What about **dame**?   female
  une

Structure

A. Noms masculins, noms féminins; l'article indéfini: *un*/*une*

All French nouns have a *gender*. They are either *masculine* or *feminine*.
Note the following masculine and feminine nouns:

MASCULINE		FEMININE	
 **un** garçon — *a boy*		**une** fille — *a girl*	
un ami — *a friend* (male)		**une** amie — *a friend* (female)	
un artiste — *an artist* (male)		**une** artiste — *an artist* (female)	

Nouns referring to men and boys are usually masculine.
Nouns referring to women and girls are usually feminine.

Nouns are often introduced by *indefinite articles*:

    un (*a, an*) introduces *masculine* nouns
    une (*a, an*) introduces *feminine* nouns

As a listening comprehension activity, you may use the following cognate nouns and ask your students if they refer to men or women: **un/une dentiste, un/une artiste, un/une journaliste, un/une photographe, un acteur/une actrice.**

→ There is liaison after **un** when the next word begins with a vowel sound.

→ You can often determine the gender of a noun from the form of the word that introduces it. For instance:

    If someone says: "Je téléphone à **un ami**," you know that person is calling a boy.
    If someone says: "Je téléphone à **une amie**," you know that person is calling a girl.

    This is because **un** signals that a noun is masculine, and **une** signals that a noun is feminine.

ACTIVITÉ 1 Qui est-ce?

Can you tell which of the two people (indicated in parentheses) is being introduced? (Your clue is **un** or **une**.) Respond according to the model.

→ Voici un ami. (Philippe, Jacqueline)   **Voici Philippe.**

1. Voici une amie. (Jean-Paul, Thérèse)
2. Voici un pianiste. (Marc, Suzanne)
3. Voici une artiste. (Pierre, Stéphanie)
4. Voici un touriste. (Monsieur Smith, Madame Jones)
5. Voici une journaliste. (Walter Cronkite, Barbara Walters)

Note the pronunciations: **femme** /fam/, **fille** /fij/, **monsieur** /məsjø/

Vocabulaire spécialisé   Personnes

un ami	*(close) friend*	**une amie**	*(close) friend*
un camarade	*classmate, school friend*	**une camarade**	*classmate, school friend*
un élève	*(high school) student*	**une élève**	*(high school) student*
un étudiant	*(college) student*	**une étudiante**	*(college) student, coed*
un garçon	*boy*	**une fille**	*girl*
un homme	*man*	**une femme**	*woman*
un monsieur	*gentleman, man (polite term)*	**une dame**	*lady, woman (polite term)*
un professeur	*teacher*	**une personne**	*person*

Comment s'appelle . . .?	*What's . . .'s name?*		
Comment s'appelle-t-il?	*What's his name?*	**Comment s'appelle-t-elle?**	*What's her name?*

Notes: 1. The noun **un professeur** is always masculine, whether it refers to a man or a woman. The noun **une personne** is always feminine, whether it refers to a male or female.

   Voici **Monsieur** Brun.   Qui est-ce? C'est **un** professeur.
   Voici **Madame** Lamblet.   Qui est-ce? C'est **un** professeur.

   2. To help you remember genders, the *masculine* nouns in the vocabulary sections are listed in the *left* column; the *feminine* nouns in the *right* column.

Literally, **un élève** means *pupil*. Although the term **étudiant** used to refer only to college students, its usage is now extending to high school students as well. Another term for high school student is **un lycéen/une lycéene**.

ACTIVITÉ 2 À l'école *(At school)*

Imagine that you are an exchange student in a French school. Introduce the following classmates according to the model, using the suggested noun.

→ Catherine (amie)   **Catherine est une amie.**   VARIATION: They are students.
Catherine est une étudiante.

(ami/amie)	(camarade)	(élève)
1. Jean-Paul	5. Marie-Noëlle	9. Suzanne
2. Antoine	6. Pierre	10. Philippe
3. Sylvie	7. Jean-Marc	11. Isabelle
4. Nathalie	8. Christine	12. Thomas

Be sure students use the appropriate article **un/une**, and use liaison with **ami** and **élève**.

B. L'article défini: le/la

Compare the words which introduce the nouns in each pair of sentences.

Voici **un** garçon.	Qui est **le** garçon?
Voici **une** fille.	Qui est **la** fille?
Voici **un** ami.	Qui est **l'**ami?
Voici **une** amie.	Qui est **l'**amie?

If students have problems with the meaning of the article, you may want to translate the sentences.

Nouns can also be introduced by *definite articles:*

le *(the)*   introduces *masculine* nouns
la *(the)*   introduces *feminine* nouns

→ **Le** and **la** become **l'** when the next word begins with a vowel sound.

The definite article **le / la** usually corresponds to the English *the.*

→ However, French speakers also use **le / la** with nouns in a general sense, while English usually leaves *the* out.

L'homme aime **la liberté.**   *Man loves liberty.*
La femme aussi!   *Woman too!*

The use of the definite article in the general sense is presented here for recognition. It is formally introduced in Unité 5.1.

√ **ACTIVITÉ 3   Au café**

Paul is looking at the people who come into the café. Express this according to the model.

VARIATIONS with cognates: un/une artiste, un/une touriste, un/une journaliste, un/une photographe, un/une Américain(e)

→ une fille   **Paul regarde la fille.**

1. un garçon
2. une dame
3. un professeur
4. une personne
5. un monsieur
6. une femme

7. un étudiant
8. une étudiante
9. un élève
10. une élève
11. une camarade
12. un homme

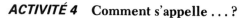

Items 7, 8, 9, 10, and 12 require l'.

√ **ACTIVITÉ 4   Comment s'appelle . . . ?**

Paul and Hélène are meeting after class. As Paul points out people, Hélène wants to know their names. Play both roles according to the model.

→ garçon   Paul: **Voici un garçon.**
       Hélène: **Comment s'appelle le garçon?**

VARIATION: Hélène asks Comment s'appelle-t-il/elle?

1. fille
2. monsieur
3. dame

4. professeur
5. personne
6. femme

7. étudiant
8. étudiante
9. homme

The purpose of this activity is to have students provide the proper articles without looking at the **Vocabulaire** for gender. Note that items 7–9 begin with a vowel sound.

C. L'accord des adjectifs *(Adjective agreement)*

Adjectives are used to describe nouns and pronouns. In the sentences below, the words in heavy type are adjectives. Compare the forms of the adjectives used to describe Marc and Suzanne.

> Marc est **blond**.   Suzanne est **blonde**.
> Il est **grand**.   Elle est **grande**.
> Il est **intelligent**. Elle est **intelligente**.

You may vary the examples with the following cognate adjectives: indépendant, tolérant, patient.

An *adjective* modifying a *masculine* noun or pronoun must be in the *masculine* form. An *adjective* modifying a *feminine* noun or pronoun must be in the *feminine* form. This is called *noun-adjective agreement*.

In written French, feminine adjectives are usually formed as follows:

> masculine adjective + **e** → feminine adjective

➡ If the masculine adjective already ends in **-e,** the feminine form is the same as the masculine form.

You may vary the examples with the following cognate adjectives: **optimiste, idéaliste, dynamique** timide.

  Marc est **sincère**.   Suzanne est **sincère**.

➡ Adjectives which follow the above pattern are called *regular* adjectives. Those which do not are *irregular* adjectives.

  Marc est **beau**.   Suzanne est **belle**.

The vocabulary lists all adjectives in their masculine form. However, if an adjective is irregular, the feminine form is given in parentheses.

Notes de prononciation

1. If the masculine adjective in the written form ends in a *vowel,* the feminine and masculine adjectives sound the same:
  sincère; bleu, bleue *(blue)*

2. If the masculine adjective in the written form ends in a *pronounced consonant,* the masculine and feminine adjectives sound the same:
  noir, noire *(black)*

3. If the masculine adjective in the written form ends in a *silent consonant,* that silent consonant is pronounced in the feminine form:
  grand, grande; intelligent, intelligente[1]

As a listening comprehension activity, you may ask your students to determine whether the following adjectives refer to men or women: élégant(e), patient(e), impatient(e), tolérant(e), indépendant(e).

[1] If the silent consonant in the masculine form is an **n,** the masculine adjective ends in a nasal vowel. In the corresponding feminine form, which ends in **-ne**, the final vowel is not nasal, and the adjective ends in the sound /n/: **brun, brune.**

Comment est-il? (literally, *How is he?*) is the equivalent of *What's he like?*

Vocabulaire spécialisé La description

Voici Alain.
Comment est-il?

Voici Suzanne.
Comment est-elle?

ADJECTIFS:

beau (belle)	*good-looking, beautiful*	Il est assez **beau**.	Elle est **belle**.
brun	*dark-haired*	Il est **brun**.	Elle n'est pas **brune**.
blond	*blond*	Il n'est pas **blond**.	Elle est **blonde**.
grand	*tall, big*	Il est assez **grand**.	Elle est **grande**.
petit	*short, little*	Il n'est pas **petit**.	Elle n'est pas **petite**.
amusant	*amusing*	Il est **amusant**.	Elle est **amusante**.
intelligent	*intelligent*	Il est **intelligent**.	Elle est **intelligente**.
intéressant	*interesting*	Il est **intéressant**.	Elle est **intéressante**.
sincère	*sincere*	Il est **sincère**.	Elle est très **sincère**.
sympathique	*nice, pleasant*	Il est **sympathique**.	Elle est **sympathique**.

ADVERBES:

assez	*rather*	Tu es **assez** intelligent.
très	*very*	Je suis **très** sincère.

VOCABULARY EXPANSION: **timide, optimiste, idéaliste, dynamique, indépendant, patient, poli** *(polite),* **réservé**

See also the **Vocabulaire** on pp.110–111.

Adverbs are invariable. Make sure that students do not try to make agreements with adverbs.

ACTIVITÉ 5 Les jumeaux *(The twins)*

The following pairs of twins have the same characteristics. Describe the girl in each pair.

VARIATIONS with cognates: **romantique, loyal, tolérant, indépendant, optimiste, pessimiste.**

→ Louis est brun. (Louise) **Louise est brune aussi.**

1. Daniel est petit. (Danièle)
2. Michel est grand. (Michèle)
3. Denis est blond. (Denise)
4. André est beau. (Andrée)
5. René est sincère. (Renée)
6. Charles est sympathique. (Charlotte)
7. François est amusant. (Françoise)
8. Martin est intelligent. (Martine)

ACTIVITÉ 6 Personnes célèbres *(Famous people)* OPTIONAL

Select four of the following well-known people. Describe each one in three affirmative or negative sentences.

→ Woody Allen **Il est assez petit. Il n'est pas très beau. Il est très amusant.**

1. John Travolta
2. Muhammad Ali
3. Raquel Welch
4. Barbra Streisand
5. Carol Burnett
6. Burt Reynolds
7. Jane Fonda
8. Robert Redford
9. Mickey Mouse
10. Dracula
11. King Kong
12. Superman

VARIATION: Individual students can read their descriptions aloud, and the others can guess which person has been described. **Qui est-ce? C'est Woody Allen.**

Prononciation

Le son /ɛ̃/

Model word: Al<u>ain</u>

Practice words: c<u>in</u>q, <u>in</u>vite, b<u>ien</u>, s<u>ym</u>pathique, <u>in</u>telligent, cous<u>in</u>

Practice sentences: Al<u>ain</u> <u>in</u>vite Juli<u>en</u> Dup<u>in</u>.

Mart<u>in</u> est un cous<u>in</u> améric<u>ain</u>.

The nasal vowel /ɛ̃/ sounds somewhat like the vowel sound in the American word *bank*, but it is shorter. Be sure not to pronounce an /n/ or /m/ after /ɛ̃/.

Comment écrire /ɛ̃/: **in** (**im** before **b** or **p**); **yn** (**ym** before **b** or **p**); **ain** (**aim** before **b** or **p**); **en** (in the letter combination **ien**)

Entre nous

Expressions pour la conversation

To express surprise, the French use:

Ah!   **Ah!** Voici Christophe.   **Oh!**   **Oh!** Dis donc! Il est grand!

To express doubt (or to show that they have not quite understood), the French use:

Comment?   *What?* (polite form)   **Comment?** Tu n'es pas à la surprise-partie?
Quoi?   *What?* (less polite)   **Quoi?** Tu n'invites pas Claude?

Mini-dialogue   OPTIONAL

Irène is talking to Christophe about someone she has just met.

IRÈNE: Dis! *J'ai fait la connaissance d'*un garçon . . .   *I met*
CHRISTOPHE: Ah? Comment est-il?
IRÈNE: Il est très beau!
CHRISTOPHE: Oh?
IRÈNE: Et très sympathique!
CHRISTOPHE: Brun ou blond?
IRÈNE: Très brun.
CHRISTOPHE: Grand ou petit?
IRÈNE: Assez grand.
CHRISTOPHE: Comment s'appelle-t-il?
IRÈNE: Claude Masson.
CHRISTOPHE: *Eh bien, tu perds ton temps.*   *Well, you're wasting your time.*
IRÈNE: Comment?
CHRISTOPHE: C'est *mon cousin.* Il est *idiot!*   *my cousin; stupid*

L'art du dialogue

a) Act out the dialog.
b) Imagine that Claude Masson is a girl. Reverse the roles of Irène and Christophe and make the necessary changes. Note: **Comment s'appelle-t-il?** becomes **Comment s'appelle-t-elle?** **un garçon** becomes **une fille; mon cousin** becomes **ma cousine; idiot** becomes **idiote.**

STRUCTURES TO OBSERVE
• avoir
• gender of nouns designating objects
• the use of **de** (instead of **un/une**) after **pas**

UNITÉ 2
Leçon 2   Le vélomoteur de Sylvie

Jean-Paul has been invited to a picnic, but he has trouble finding transportation.

Jean-Paul et Philippe

JEAN-PAUL:	Est-ce que tu as une bicyclette?
PHILIPPE:	Non, je n'ai pas de bicyclette,	
	mais j'ai un *vélomoteur*!	*motorbike*
JEAN-PAUL:	Un vélomoteur? *Formidable!*	*Great!*
	Où est-ce qu'il est?	
PHILIPPE:	Il n'est pas *là*...	*here*
	Il est à la maison et...	
JEAN-PAUL:	Et quoi?	
PHILIPPE:	*Il ne marche pas!*	*It doesn't work!*
JEAN-PAUL:	Zut alors!	
PHILIPPE:	*Écoute!* Téléphone à Sylvie.	*Listen!*
	Elle a un vélomoteur *qui* marche.	*that*

Jean-Paul et Sylvie

JEAN-PAUL:	Dis, Sylvie! Tu as un vélomoteur, n'est-ce pas?
SYLVIE:	Oui, bien sûr! J'ai un vélomoteur. Pourquoi?	
JEAN-PAUL:	Écoute... Je suis *invité* à un pique-nique,	*invited*
	et je n'ai pas de...	
SYLVIE:	Un moment! Est-ce que tu as un *permis?*	*license*
JEAN-PAUL:	Euh... non! Je n'ai pas de permis!	
SYLVIE:	*Pas de* permis, pas de vélomoteur!	*No*
JEAN-PAUL:	Et pas de pique-nique!	
SYLVIE:	*C'est la vie!*	*That's life!*

Est-ce que Philippe a une bicyclette?   À qui est-ce que Jean-Paul téléphone?
Est-ce que Sylvie a un vélomoteur?

CONVERSATION

In the questions below you are asked whether you have certain things.
Answer *yes* or *no*.

1. Avez-vous une radio?
   Oui, j'ai une radio.
   (Non, je n'ai pas **de** radio.)
2. Avez-vous une guitare?
3. Avez-vous un piano?
4. Avez-vous une raquette?
5. Avez-vous un téléviseur *(TV set)*?

OBSERVATIONS   Str. A, C

In the above questions, **radio, guitare, piano, raquette,** and **téléviseur** are
nouns referring to *things*.   piano, téléviseur

• Which of these nouns are *masculine?* Which are *feminine?*   radio, guitare, raquette

Reread the negative sentence in the model.

• What word is used instead of **un / une** after the negative word **pas?** de

NOTE CULTURELLE   OPTIONAL

Le vélomoteur

Very few French teenagers have cars, but many have a
moped or motorbike **(un vélomoteur).** In a country where
people are quite conscious of energy problems, the
motorbike has the advantage of being very economical . . .
and easy to handle through traffic jams. In order to drive a
motorbike, one must have a license **(un permis)** and wear a
crash helmet.

Refer students to Section Magazine p.174.
SUGGESTED REALIA: ads or brochures for French motorbikes, mopeds, and bicycles (Mobylette, Motobécane, Peugeot).

Structure

A. Le genre des noms: les objets

All French nouns, those referring to *things* as well as those referring to *people*, are either *masculine* or *feminine*. In the sentences below, note how the gender of the underlined noun is reflected in the words in heavy type.

MASCULINE	FEMININE	
Voici **un** <u>vélomoteur.</u>	Voici **une** <u>bicyclette.</u>	*Here is a motorbike/bicycle.*
Paul regarde **le** vélomoteur.	Paul regarde **la** bicyclette.	*Paul looks at the motorbike/ bicycle.*
Il marche bien.	**Elle** marche bien.	*It works well.*
Est-ce qu'**il** est **grand**?	Est-ce qu'**elle** est **grande**?	*Is it big?*
Non, **il** est **petit**.	Non, **elle** est **petite**.	*No, it is small.*

A *masculine* noun is introduced by a *masculine article* (**un, le,** or **l'**) and is modified by *masculine adjectives*. It can often be replaced by the *subject pronoun* **il**.

A *feminine* noun is introduced by a *feminine article* (**une, la,** or **l'**) and is modified by *feminine adjectives*. It can often be replaced by the *subject pronoun* **elle**.

→ When you learn a new noun, learn it together with the article that indicates its gender. Think of **un transistor, une bicyclette** (rather than just **transistor, bicyclette**).

Remind students that in the **Vocabulaire** sections, masculine nouns are on the left and feminine nouns are on the right.

voiture = auto   vélo = bicyclette

Vocabulaire spécialisé   Objets courants (Everyday things)

NOMS:

un appareil-photo

un livre

un transistor

un disque

un sac

un vélo

un électrophone

un téléviseur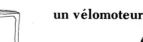

un vélomoteur

VERBE: **marcher**   *to work*   Est-ce que le téléviseur **marche** bien?

Note: When the subject is a person, **marcher** means *to walk*.

Contrast: Philippe **marche** rapidement.   *Philippe **walks** quickly.*
La voiture ne **marche** pas.   *The car doesn't **work**.*

Un téléviseur (or un poste de télévision) is a *TV set;* la télévision is *TV (programming).*

Also for *record player:* **un tourne-disque, une chaîne-stéréo.**

ACTIVITÉ 1 Où?

Alain wonders where certain things are. Michèle tells him. Play both roles according to the model.

→ un sac / ici   Alain: **Où est le sac?**
                   Michèle: **Il est ici.**

1. un disque / ici
2. une guitare / là
3. une cassette / là-bas

4. une raquette / ici
5. un livre / là
6. un électrophone / là-bas

7. un vélo / à la maison
8. une voiture / à la maison
9. un vélomoteur / là-bas

ACTIVITÉ 2 Tout marche bien. *(Everything is working well.)*

Alain shows Michèle various things he owns. Michèle asks whether these things are working well, and Alain says they are. Play both roles according to the model.

→ une radio   Alain: **Voici une radio.**
                Michèle: **Est-ce qu'elle marche bien?**
                Alain: **Oui, elle marche très bien.**

1. un appareil-photo
2. un électrophone

3. une mini-cassette
4. une montre

5. un transistor
6. un téléviseur

7. une auto
8. une moto

Another term for **mini-cassette** is **un magnétophone à cassettes.**
Make sure that students differentiate between **caméra** and **appareil-photo.**

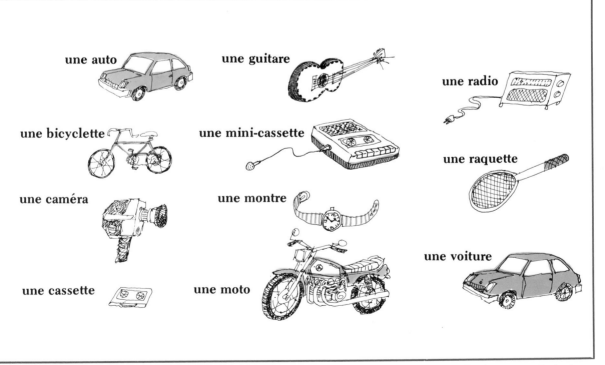

une auto   une guitare   une radio

une bicyclette   une mini-cassette   une raquette

une caméra   une montre

une cassette   une moto   une voiture

VOCABULARY EXPANSION: **un crayon, un stylo, un cahier, une gomme, une bande, un magnétophone, une calculatrice**
At this point you may wish to introduce the classroom vocabulary listed in the Teacher's Edition.

ACTIVITÉ 3 En ville

Alain and Michèle are window-shopping. Whenever Michèle points out something, Alain gives his opinion. Play both roles according to the model. Be sure to use the appropriate form of the adjective in parentheses.

→ une guitare (beau)   Michèle: **Regarde la guitare!**
                          Alain: **Elle est belle!**

1. un sac (grand)
2. un livre (amusant)
3. une radio (petit)

4. une montre (petit)
5. un téléviseur (grand)
6. une caméra (petit)

7. une raquette (beau)
8. un électrophone (petit)
9. un appareil-photo (beau)

Vocabulaire spécialisé Les couleurs

blanc (blanche)
gris
bleu
noir
rouge
vert
jaune

de quelle couleur? *what color?* —**De quelle couleur** est la radio?
—Elle est blanche et noire.

ACTIVITÉ 4 De quelle couleur...?

Give the colors of the following items which you have at home or in class. Be sure to make the necessary agreements.

→ la radio   **Elle est bleue (blanche, verte ...).**

(à la maison)   (en classe)   Additional cues: **le crayon, le stylo, le cahier**

1. le téléviseur
2. la voiture
3. le téléphone

4. la table
5. la lampe
6. le livre de français

VOCABULARY EXPANSION: **brun** *(red-brown)*, **violet/violette** *(purple)*, **orange, rose** *(pink)*. For recognition only: **bleu pâle** *(light blue)*, **bleu foncé** *(dark blue)*. Note that colors expressed with **pâle** and **foncé** are invariable. They do not agree with the nouns they modify.

B. Le verbe *avoir*

The verb **avoir** *(to have, own)* is irregular. Note the forms of this verb in the present tense.

avoir	to have	
j' **ai**	*I have*	**J'ai** un ami à Québec.
tu **as**	*you have*	**As-tu** une guitare?
il/elle **a**	*he/she has*	Est-ce que Philippe **a** une radio?
nous **avons**	*we have*	Nous **avons** un électrophone.
vous **avez**	*you have*	**Avez-vous** une montre?
ils/elles **ont**	*they have*	Ils n'**ont** pas la caméra.

➔ There is liaison in the forms **nous avons, vous avez, ils ont, elles ont.**

✓ *ACTIVITÉ 5*   **Qui a une guitare?**

Jean-Paul wants to borrow a guitar. Tell him that each of the following people has one.

➔ Roger   **Roger a une guitare.**   VARIATION: Est-ce que Roger a un transistor?

1. Lucie   3. nous   5. Isabelle   7. je
2. Marc et François   4. vous   6. Denise et Sylvie   8. tu

✓ *ACTIVITÉ 6*   **Qui a le téléphone?**   Avoir *le* téléphone is the French expression which corresponds to *to have a phone.*

Marc is trying to reach his friends, but they don't all have a telephone. Tell him who has a phone and who does not.

➔ François / non   **François n'a pas le téléphone.**

1. Sylvie / oui   3. Anne et Suzanne / oui   5. nous / oui   7. je / oui
2. André / non   4. Jean et Louis / non   6. vous / non   8. tu / non

C. L'article indéfini dans les phrases négatives

Note the form of the indefinite article in negative sentences:

pas un pas une } becomes	pas de ↓ pas d' (+ vowel sound)	(un sac?) (une radio?) (un électro- phone?)	Tu n'as **pas de** sac. Il n'a **pas de** radio. Je n'ai **pas d'**électro- phone.

Exception: After **être, pas un** and **pas une** do not change.

   Dominique n'est **pas un** garçon. Dominique est une fille!

ACTIVITÉ 7   Dialogue

Ask your classmates if they own the following things (1-4) or have the following pets at home (5-8).

→ une caméra — **Est-ce que tu as une caméra?**
— **Oui, j'ai une caméra. (Non, je n'ai pas de caméra.)**

1. un appareil-photo
2. un hélicoptère
3. une Mercédès
4. une trompette
5. un boa
6. un cobra
7. un éléphant
8. un canari

ACTIVITÉ 8   Oui et non

Anne owns the following things. Pierre does not. Express this according to the model.

→ un sac   **Anne a un sac. Pierre n'a pas de sac.**

1. un vélo
2. une radio
3. un électrophone
4. une guitare
5. une caméra
6. un vélomoteur
7. un appareil-photo
8. une raquette

ACTIVITÉ 9   Oui ou non?

We need certain objects to do certain things. Read what the following people are or are not doing. Then say whether or not they have the objects indicated in parentheses.   This exercise offers practice in cognate recognition.

→ Paul ne joue pas au tennis. (une raquette?)   **Il n'a pas de raquette.**
Henri joue au ping-pong. (une raquette?)   **Il a une raquette.**

1. François étudie. (un livre?)
2. Sylvie n'étudie pas. (un livre?)
3. Suzanne écoute la symphonie. (une radio?)
4. Jacques n'écoute pas le concert. (un transistor?)
5. Albert regarde le film. (un téléviseur?)
6. Nathalie ne regarde pas la comédie. (un téléviseur?)
7. Jean-Pierre est ponctuel. (une montre?)
8. Jean-Paul n'est pas ponctuel. (une montre?)

Prononciation

Le son /ɑ̃/

Model word: qu<u>an</u>d

Practice words: gr<u>an</u>d, Fr<u>an</u>ce, d<u>an</u>ser, H<u>en</u>ri, <u>An</u>dré, l<u>am</u>pe

Practice sentences: <u>An</u>dré et Fr<u>an</u>cine d<u>an</u>sent.
<u>An</u>dré r<u>en</u>tre <u>en</u> Fr<u>an</u>ce <u>en</u> dé<u>cem</u>bre.

The sound /ɑ̃/ is a nasal vowel. Be sure not to pronounce an /n/ or /m/ after a nasal vowel.

Comment écrire /ɑ̃/: **an** (or **am** before **b** or **p**); **en** (or **em** before **b** or **p**)

Entre nous

Expressions pour la conversation

To express admiration or appreciation, the French use words like:

Fantastique!
Formidable! } *Great! Terrific!*   Tu as une voiture? **Formidable!**
Sensationnel!

Mini-dialogue   OPTIONAL

Christophe, who is in charge of the class picnic, thought that he had solved the transportation problem.

CHRISTOPHE: Dis, Albert, tu as un vélo?
ALBERT: Non, je n'ai pas de vélo, mais j'ai une voiture.
CHRISTOPHE: Formidable! Elle marche?
ALBERT: Oui, elle marche très bien.
CHRISTOPHE: Sensationnel! Dis, *tu peux l'amener au*   *can you bring it to the*
           pique-nique?
ALBERT: C'est impossible.
CHRISTOPHE: Impossible? Pourquoi?
ALBERT: Elle n'est pas ici.
CHRISTOPHE: Où est-elle?
ALBERT: Elle est *chez ma grand-mère* qui habite en   *at my grandmother's*
        Alaska.
CHRISTOPHE: Zut alors!

L'art du dialogue

a) Act out the dialog between Christophe and Albert.

b) Write out a new dialog in which you replace **un vélo** by **une moto,** and **une voiture** by **un vélomoteur.** Make all other necessary changes.

STRUCTURES TO OBSERVE
• the position of adjectives: before and after the noun
• the constructions **il est** and **c'est**

UNITÉ 2
Leçon 3 **Dans l'autobus**

The students of the Lycée Carnot are going on a bus trip. Everyone is looking out the window, except Jean-Pierre and Catherine, who are busy looking at the people in the bus.

Qui est le garçon là-bas?
Ah, c'est Antoine.
Il est beau.
Il est amusant.
C'est un garçon sympathique.
C'est un garçon formidable.
C'est aussi le *petit ami* de Claire. *boyfriend*
Dommage!

Est-ce qu'Antoine est sympathique?
Qui est Antoine?

Catherine

CONVERSATION

1. Êtes-vous une personne **intelligente**?
2. Êtes-vous une personne **sincère**?
3. Avez-vous un ami **sympathique**?
4. Avez-vous une amie **sympathique**?

OBSERVATIONS   Str. A

In the above questions, nouns are used with adjectives.
• Do the adjectives come *before* or *after* the nouns?   after
• Is this the same as in English?   No. In English they come before.

Où est Claire?
Ah, elle est là-bas.
Elle est très *jolie*.   *pretty*
Elle est *drôle*.   *funny*
C'est une fille sympathique.
C'est une fille extraordinaire . . .
    mais c'est la *petite amie* d'Antoine.   *girlfriend*
Zut alors!

Claire

Antoine

Est-ce que
Claire est jolie?
Qui est Claire?

Jean-Pierre

NOTES CULTURELLES

1. Les amis   Who is a friend? For French teenagers, **un ami** or **une amie** is much more than just an acquaintance. It is a close friend, a person with whom you enjoy spending time now and with whom you will keep in touch over the years.

Le meilleur ami *(best male friend)* or **la meilleure amie** *(best female friend)* is the person with whom you share your problems as well as your joys, the person who is always there when you need someone to talk to.

Le petit ami *(boyfriend)* or **la petite amie** *(girlfriend)* is the very special person whom you are dating exclusively.

A classmate or friend whom you see often is **un camarade** or **une camarade.**

2. Le lycée   The **lycée** is the equivalent of the American senior high school.
The school corresponding to the American junior high school is **le C.E.S. (Collège d'Enseignement Secondaire).** Most French lycées bear the names of famous people. Lycée Carnot is named after Lazare Carnot (1753-1823), a famous French revolutionary. For a more detailed explanation of the French lycée, see p.363.

Structure

A. La place des adjectifs

In French, descriptive adjectives generally come *after* the noun they modify.

> Suzanne est une fille **intelligente** et **sympathique**.
> Paul a une bicyclette **bleue** et une guitare **noire**.

Only *a few* adjectives come *before* the noun. Here are some of these adjectives:

beau (belle)	*beautiful, handsome*	Antoine est un **beau** garçon.	The special form
joli	*pretty*	Sylvie est une **jolie** fille.	**bel** is introduced
grand	*big, large*	J'ai un **grand** /t/ électrophone.	in Unité 4.3.
petit	*little, small*	J'ai un **petit** appareil-photo.	
bon (bonne)	*good*	Nous avons un **bon** électrophone.	
mauvais	*bad*	Vous avez un **mauvais** /z/ appareil-photo.	

→ There is liaison between **grand, petit, bon,** and **mauvais,** and the noun which follows. In liaison, **-d** is pronounced /t/, and **-s** is pronounced /z/. Also, in liaison, **bon** is pronounced like **bonne.**

→ Note the special meanings: **un petit ami** *(boyfriend),* **une petite amie** *(girlfriend).*

ACTIVITÉ 1 Photos

Paul is showing pictures of his friends and commenting on each one. Play the role of Paul according to the model. Use the nouns **garçon** and **fille,** as appropriate.

→ Jacques (drôle)   **Jacques est un garçon drôle.**
     Mélanie (intelligente)   **Mélanie est une fille intelligente.**

1. Marie-Noëlle (amusante)
2. Jacqueline (sympathique)
3. Jean-François (sincère)
4. Isabelle (intéressante)
5. Henri (optimiste)
6. Suzanne (indépendante)

VARIATIONS with **timide, idéaliste, pessimiste, dynamique, romantique.**

Vocabulaire spécialisé   La personnalité

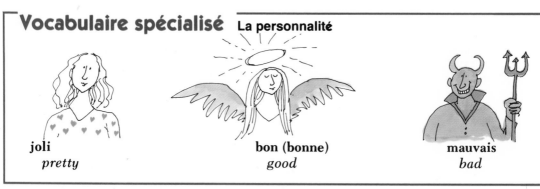

joli
pretty

bon (bonne)
good

mauvais
bad

Joli is used with girls; **beau** is used with boys.

ACTIVITÉ 2   Les amies

The following boys have girlfriends with similar characteristics.
Describe the girls.

→ Paul est sympathique.   **Il a une amie sympathique.**

1. Pierre est brun.
2. Charles est blond.
3. Philippe est amusant.

4. Jean-François est sincère.
5. Robert est intelligent.
6. Denis est élégant *(well-dressed).*

ACTIVITÉ 3   La course de vélos *(The bicycle race)*

A group of friends have organized a bicycle race. Describe the bicycle of
each participant, using the adjectives in parentheses and the noun **vélo.**

→ Mélanie (vert)   **Mélanie a un vélo vert.**
    Michel (mauvais)   **Michel a un mauvais vélo.**

1. François (rouge)
2. Caroline (petit)
3. Isabelle (beau)
4. Robert (bleu)
5. Claire (bon)

6. Philippe (blanc)
7. Catherine (grand)
8. Albert (jaune)
9. Sylvie (joli)
10. Sophie (mauvais)

drôle
funny

pénible
annoying

bête
silly, stupid

Another term for **pénible** is **embêtant.**
Another term for *stupid* is **idiot.**

B. Il est ou c'est?

The distinction between il est and c'est is an important but difficult concept. You may present it here for recognition only.

The sentences below describe **Paul** and **Anne.** Note the constructions in heavy type.

	Comment est-il/elle?	**Qui est-ce?**	
Paul	**Il est** amusant	**C'est** un ami.	**C'est** un ami amusant.
	Il est intelligent.	**C'est** un élève.	**C'est** un élève intelligent.
Anne	**Elle est** sympathique.	**C'est** une amie.	**C'est** une amie sympathique.
	Elle est intelligente.	**C'est** une élève.	**C'est** une élève intelligente.

In descriptions French speakers use **être** in the following constructions:

Il est ⎱ Elle est ⎰ + adjective	and	C'est + article + noun + adjective (if any)

→ The above constructions are used to describe things as well as people.

Voici un vélo.	**Il est** grand.	**C'est** un vélo français.
Voilà une voiture.	**Elle est** belle.	**C'est** une voiture américaine.

→ In negative sentences **c'est** becomes **ce n'est pas.**

Ce n'est pas Paul.   Ce n'est pas le professeur.

The adjective may also precede the noun: **C'est une belle voiture.**

→ **C'est** is also used with the names of people.

C'est Nicole!   **C'est** Madame Lamblet!

ACTIVITÉ 4   D'accord!

Alain and Suzanne are often of the same opinion when they discuss people they know. Play both roles according to the model.

→ Philippe est un ami sympathique.   Alain: **C'est un ami sympathique!**
Suzanne: **D'accord! Il est sympathique!**

1. Paul est un garçon intelligent.
2. Thérèse est une fille amusante.
3. Richard est un beau garçon.
4. Annie est une jolie fille.
5. Monsieur Rigolot est un professeur amusant.
6. Madame Chouette est une femme sympathique.
7. Mademoiselle Callet est une personne intelligente.
8. Monsieur Gentil est une personne sincère.

ACTIVITÉ 5   Descriptions

Complete the following descriptions with **Il/Elle est** or **C'est,** as appropriate.

A. Antoine
1. — grand.
2. — blond.
3. — un garçon sympathique.
4. — un mauvais élève.

B. Suzanne
5. — une fille blonde.
6. — une camarade sympathique.
7. — très amusante.
8. — assez petite.

C. La moto d'Antoine *(Antoine's motorcycle)*
9. — une moto confortable. ^cognate
10. — une bonne moto.
11. — rouge et jaune.
12. — très moderne. ^cognate

D. Le vélomoteur de Suzanne
13. — gris et bleu.
14. — très économique. ^cognate
15. — un joli petit vélomoteur.
16. — assez moderne.

ACTIVITÉ 6 **Le salon de la voiture** *(The car show)* OPTIONAL

Imagine that you are attending the annual car show as a reporter for an automobile magazine. You look at the following cars. First say that each one has the characteristic indicated in parentheses. Then give your opinion of each one, using **bonne** or **mauvaise** and the noun **voiture**.

→ Voici une Cadillac. (grande)   **Elle est grande. C'est une bonne (mauvaise) voiture.**

1. Voici une Renault. (petite)
2. Voici une Fiat. (jolie)
3. Voici une Toyota. (économique)

4. Voici une Rolls Royce. (élégante)
5. Voici une Citroën. (moderne)
6. Voici une Peugeot. (belle)

Prononciation

Le son /ɔ/

Model word: b<u>o</u>nne

Practice words: P<u>au</u>l, R<u>o</u>ger, téléph<u>o</u>ne, m<u>o</u>derne, électroph<u>o</u>ne

Practice sentences: Yv<u>o</u>nne est b<u>o</u>nne et j<u>o</u>lie.
                      À N<u>oë</u>l, Nic<u>o</u>le téléph<u>o</u>ne à C<u>o</u>lette.

The sound /ɔ/ is pronounced somewhat like the *o* in the English word *model*, but the French sound /ɔ/ is both shorter and more tense.

Comment écrire /ɔ/: **o**; (sometimes) **au**

Entre nous

Expression pour la conversation

To emphasize a statement or an answer, you may say:

Eh bien! *Well!* — **Eh bien,** François, est-ce que tu as un vélomoteur?
                         — **Eh bien,** non!

Mini-dialogue OPTIONAL

Suzanne is at the window describing someone she sees in the street.
Alain is trying to guess who it is.

SUZANNE: Tiens! Voilà un garçon. Il arrive *en* voiture.   *by*
ALAIN: Est-ce que c'est une grande voiture?
SUZANNE: Non, elle est petite.
ALAIN: Est-ce qu'elle est rouge?
SUZANNE: Non, elle est bleue.
ALAIN: Eh bien, c'est Robert. Il a une petite voiture bleue!
SUZANNE: Eh bien, non! Ce n'est pas Robert. C'est Paul.

L'art du dialogue

a) Act out the dialog between Alain and Suzanne.
b) Act out a new dialog in which Suzanne sees **Sophie** (and not **Thérèse**) coming on a small motorbike (**un vélomoteur**). Make the necessary changes.

STRUCTURES TO OBSERVE
• plural forms of nouns
• plural forms of definite and indefinite articles
• plural forms of adjectives

UNITÉ 2
Leçon 4

Le bal du Mardi Gras

For Mardi Gras the International Club has organized a costume party. Everyone is trying to identify the guests.

JEANNE: Regarde les clowns là-bas!
SOPHIE: Qui est-ce?
JEANNE: Paul et David!
SOPHIE: Des étudiants américains?
JEANNE: Non, des étudiants anglais!
SOPHIE: Ils sont très drôles!
JEANNE: Oui, mais . . . Ils sont un peu snobs!
SOPHIE: Dommage!

Est-ce que Paul et David sont français? Est-ce qu'ils sont américains? Est-ce qu'ils sont anglais?

ROBERT: Regarde les filles là-bas!
JULIEN: Les filles *en* rouge? Qui est-ce?
ROBERT: C'est Monique et Marie.
JULIEN: Elles sont américaines?
ROBERT: Non, ce sont des étudiantes françaises . . . de la Guadeloupe!
JULIEN: Elles sont très jolies!
ROBERT: . . . et très sympathiques aussi!
JULIEN: *Tant mieux!*

in

Est-ce que Monique et Marie sont américaines? Est-ce qu'elles sont françaises? Où est-ce qu'elles habitent?

So much the better!

CONVERSATION

Do you have many good friends? Of course you do! Answer the following questions in the affirmative.

1. Avez-vous **des amis sympathiques?**
2. Avez-vous **des amies sympathiques?**
3. Avez-vous **des amis intéressants?**
4. Avez-vous **des amies intéressantes?**

OBSERVATIONS   Str. B, C

Reread the above questions.

- What is the *plural* of **ami?** of **amie?**   amis/amies
  Which letter do plural nouns end in? Is this letter pronounced?   no
  s
- Which indefinite article comes before **amis?** before **amies?**   des/des
  What is the *plural* of **un?** of **une?**   des/des
- What is the *plural* of **sympathique?** of **intéressant?** of **intéressante?**   sympathiques/intéressants/
  Which letter do plural adjectives end in? Is this letter pronounced?   intéressantes
  s   no

NOTES CULTURELLES

1. Mardi Gras   When you see children in costumes going from door to door in the United States, you know it's Halloween. In France you will not see children out in costumes until February or March for the celebration of **Mardi Gras.** In some parts of the French-speaking world (New Orleans, Quebec, Haiti, Martinique, as well as Nice and Cannes in France) **Mardi Gras** or **Carnaval** is celebrated with a ten-day pageant, which has been prepared for many months. In other parts of France, **Mardi Gras** may simply be the occasion for a big costume party.

2. La Guadeloupe   Guadeloupe is a small Caribbean island close to Martinique. The inhabitants of Guadeloupe and Martinique are French citizens, primarily of African ancestry.
You may refer the students to the map of the French-speaking world on pp.vi–vii.

guadeloupe
martinique

Literally, **Mardi Gras** means "Fat Tuesday." It is the last day before le Carême *(Lent),* the traditional 40-day period of fasting before Easter in the Catholic religion.
SUGGESTED REALIA: Mardi Gras travel brochures.

Structure

You may want to have the students practice the pronunciation of the feminine and masculine forms of the following adjectives of nationality.

anglais /e/   anglaise /ɛz/   français, japonais
canadien /jɛ̃/   canadienne /jɛn/   italien, égyptien
américain /ɛ̃/   américaine /ɛn/   mexicain

A. L'article défini avec les noms géographiques

Note the use of the definite article in the following sentences:

Le Canada est un pays américain.   *Canada is an American country.*
La Californie est jolie.   *California is pretty.*

In French most *geographical* names are introduced by a definite article. It is used with *countries*, *rivers*, and *mountains*, but not with *cities*.

Paris est la capitale de **la France**.   *Paris is the capital of France.*

Exceptions: **Israël, Panama** (no articles); **la Nouvelle-Orléans, Le Havre**

Vocabulaire spécialisé   Pays et nationalités

un pays	country	une nationalité
l'Amérique	America	
le Canada	Canada	canadien (canadienne)
les États-Unis	United States	américain
le Mexique	Mexico	mexicain
l'Europe	Europe	
l'Allemagne	Germany	allemand
l'Angleterre	England	anglais
la Belgique	Belgium	belge
l'Espagne	Spain	espagnol
la France	France	français
l'Italie	Italy	italien (italienne)
la Suisse	Switzerland	suisse
l'Asie	Asia	
la Chine	China	chinois
le Japon	Japan	japonais
l'Afrique	Africa	
l'Égypte	Egypt	égyptien (égyptienne)

You may remind students that adjectives of nationality take the same endings as other adjectives.

l'Australie *Australia*

Notes: 1. Most countries whose names *end* in **-e** are feminine.

    la France   **la Suisse**   Exception: **le Mexique**

This applies to states also: le Colorado, le Texas, la Californie, la Virginie.

All other countries are masculine.

    le Japon   **le Canada**

2. Adjectives of nationality are not capitalized in French.

    J'ai un ami **français** et une amie **anglaise**.

However, when these adjectives are used as *nouns* to refer to people, they are capitalized.

    Paul parle avec un **Français** et   *Paul is talking with a Frenchman and*
    une **Anglaise**.   *an English woman.*

The names of languages are not capitalized: **l'anglais, l'allemand.**

In French, **l'Amérique** is considered as one continent. It is subdivided into **l'Amérique du Nord, l'Amérique centrale,** and **l'Amérique du Sud.**

  VOCABULARY EXPANSION: le Brésil/brésilien, le Portugal/portugais, la Norvège/norvégien, la Hollande/hollandais, la Suède/suédois, la Russie/russe, le Viêt-nam/vietnamien

ACTIVITÉ 1   Aimez-vous la géographie?

Give the continents where the following countries are located:

en Asie   en Amérique   en Europe   en Afrique

You may refer the students to a world map and ask them to locate these countries.

→   France   **La France est en Europe.**

1. Allemagne
2. Chine
3. Italie
4. Japon
5. Mexique
6. Angleterre
7. Espagne
8. Canada
9. Danemark
10. Sénégal
11. Viêt-nam
12. Portugal
13. Tunisie
14. Algérie
15. Côte-d'Ivoire (*Ivory Coast*)
16. Suisse

ACTIVITÉ 2   Une question de nationalité

The following people own things which were made in the countries where they live. Express this according to the model.

→   Luisa habite à Séville. (une guitare)
     Elle a une guitare espagnole.

1. François habite à Paris. (un téléviseur)
2. Nathalie habite à Québec. (un disque)
3. Michèle habite à New York. (une voiture)
4. Pietro habite à Rome. (une moto)
5. Birgit habite à Munich. (une caméra)
6. Tatsuo habite à Tokyo. (une auto)
7. Lin habite à Hong-Kong. (une bicyclette)
8. Pedro habite à Mexico. (une guitare)

VARIATION: Give each person's nationality.
            Luisa est espagnole.

B. Le pluriel: les noms et les articles

When referring to several objects, the French use the subject pronouns **ils/elles**. Voici des montres. Elles marchent bien.

Compare the *singular* and *plural* forms of the articles and nouns in the sentences below:

SINGULAR	PLURAL
Où est **le garçon?**	Où sont **les garçons?**
Qui est **la fille** là-bas?	Qui sont **les filles** là-bas?
J'invite **l'étudiant.**	J'invite **les étudiants.**
Je parle à **un garçon.**	Je parle à **des garçons.**
Nous invitons **une fille.**	Nous invitons **des filles.**
Paul est **un ami.**	Paul et Charles sont **des amis.**
C'est **une amie.**	Ce sont **des amies.**

Plural nouns

In written French the plural of most nouns is formed as follows:

$$\text{singular noun} \quad + \quad \text{s} \quad \rightarrow \quad \text{plural noun}$$

If the noun ends in **-s** in the singular, the singular and plural forms are the same.

> Voici **un Français.**   Voici **des Français.**

→ In spoken French the final **-s** of the plural is always *silent*. Therefore, singular and plural nouns sound the same. You can tell, however, if the noun is singular or plural by listening to the article which introduces it.

> Voici **une amie.**   Voici **des amies.**

In English, one usually listens to the noun in order to tell if it is singular or plural: the girl, the girls. However, in a few cases one must listen to the word which introduces the noun: this fish, these fish.

Plural articles

The forms of the plural articles are summarized in the chart below.

	SINGULAR	PLURAL	
Definite Article	**le (l')** **la (l')**	**les**	**les garçons** **les amis** **les filles** **les amies**
Indefinite Article	**un** **une**	**des**	**des** sacs **des** électrophones **des** montres **des** autos

→ There is liaison after **les** and **des** when the next word begins with a vowel sound.

Les Peugeot Diesel. D'abord des Peugeot.

In French, family names and proper nouns do not usually take an **-s**.

→ **Des** corresponds to the English article *some*. While *some* is often omitted in English, **des** *must* be expressed in French. Contrast:

Voici	des	livres.
Here are	*some*	*books.*

J'invite	des	amis.
I'm inviting	. . .	*friends.*

→ In *negative* sentences, except after **être**:

pas des	becomes	**pas de**		(**des** disques?)	Marc n'a **pas de** disques.
		↓			
		pas d'	(+ vowel sound)	(**des** amis?)	Tu n'as **pas d'**amis.

Note the construction with **être**: Vous n'êtes pas des étudiants.

→ The plural of **c'est** (**ce n'est pas**) is **ce sont** (**ce ne sont pas**).

C'est une amie.   **Ce sont** des amies.
Ce n'est pas (un) ami.   **Ce ne sont pas** des amis.

C'est is used instead of **ce sont** before names of people: C'est Henri et Pierre.
C'est Monsieur et Madame Dupont.

ACTIVITÉ 3 Présentations *(Introductions)*

Introduce the following young people as friends of yours. Use **un, une,** or **des.**

→ Jacqueline   **Jacqueline est une amie.**
   Paul et Marc   **Paul et Marc sont des amis.**

1. Caroline
2. Jean-Philippe
3. Suzanne et Hélène
4. Henri et Charles
5. Georges, Louis et Simon
6. Sylvie, Nicole et Michèle

ACTIVITÉ 4 Imitations

Say that Paul and Henri are doing the same things their cousin Philippe does. Follow the model, using *plural* forms.

→ Philippe parle à une amie.   **Paul et Henri parlent à des amies.**

1. Philippe invite une amie.
2. Il dîne avec un ami.
3. Il parle à un journaliste.
4. Il joue au tennis avec un garçon.
5. Il joue au tennis avec une fille.
6. Il invite un camarade.
7. Il parle à un professeur.
8. Il écoute un professeur.

ACTIVITÉ 5 Dans un grand magasin *(In a department store)*

Sylvie is in a department store. The salesperson tells her that the things she is looking for are over there. Play both roles.

→ une montre   Sylvie: **Je désire une montre.**
                              L'employé(e): **Les montres sont là-bas.**

1. une caméra
2. un téléviseur
3. une guitare
4. une raquette
5. un livre
6. un disque
7. un électrophone
8. un appareil-photo

Note the liaison in items 7 and 8. The plural of **appareil-photo** is **appareils-photo.**

✓ **ACTIVITÉ 6**   **Dans un petit magasin**

This time Sylvie is shopping in a small store. Whenever she asks for certain items, the salesperson says that they do not have them. Play both roles. (Note: **Je regrette** means *I am sorry.*)

→ une caméra   Sylvie: **Avez-vous des caméras?**
              L'employé(e): **Je regrette ...   Nous n'avons pas de caméras.**

1. un transistor
2. une cassette
3. une radio
4. une raquette
5. un appareil-photo
6. un électrophone

C. Le pluriel: les adjectifs

Note the *plural* forms of the adjectives in the sentences below.

Roger est **américain.**	Jim et Bob sont **américains.**
Anne est une amie **française.**	Louise et Claire sont des amies **françaises.**
Marc est un élève **français.**	Paul et Michel sont des élèves **français.**

In written French the plural of an adjective is formed as follows:

> singular adjective   +   s   →   plural adjective

If the adjective ends in **-s** in the singular, the singular and plural forms are the same.

→ In spoken French the final **-s** of plural adjectives is silent.

→ There is liaison when a plural adjective comes *before* a noun that begins with a vowel sound:

The plural forms of **beau** are taught in Unité 4.3.

les élèves   les bons élèves
les appareils-photo   les petits appareils-photo

Liaison is not required after a plural noun followed by an adjective beginning with a vowel sound: **les livres italiens** or **les livres italiens**

ACTIVITÉ 7   Le client

You are going shopping. Ask whether the store carries the items you are looking for.

→ un disque américain   **Avez-vous des disques américains?**

1. un disque français
2. un vélo anglais
3. une moto italienne
4. un livre canadien
5. un sac rouge
6. une montre suisse
7. un vélomoteur bleu
8. une cassette espagnole
9. une grande bicyclette
10. un petit électrophone
11. un bon appareil-photo
12. un petit téléviseur

The use of **de** instead of **des** before an adjective is not taught at this level. In conversational French it is common to use **des**. **Avez-vous des grands sacs? / Avez-vous de grands sacs?**

ACTIVITÉ 8   L'école internationale

Read where the following students at an international school normally live and say what their nationalities are.

→   Suzanne et Mélanie habitent à Paris.   **Elles sont françaises.**

1. Thomas et Daniel habitent à Bordeaux.
2. Marie et Anne habitent à Québec.
3. Paul et François habitent à Québec.
4. Jim et Bob habitent à Chicago.
5. Linda et Louise habitent à Boston.
6. Pietro et Mario habitent à Rome.
7. Rafael et Carlos habitent à Mexico.
8. Jane et Silvia habitent à Liverpool.

D. L'expression *il y a*

Note the use of **il y a** in the sentences below:

Dans la classe . . .
   il y a un professeur intéressant,
   il y a une fille française,
   il y a des élèves intelligents.

In the class . . .
   there is an interesting teacher,
   there is a French girl,
   there are intelligent students.

Il y a (*there is, there are*) has only one form. It is used with both *singular* and *plural* nouns.

→   Note the interrogative and negative constructions with **il y a:**

Est-ce qu'il y a un téléviseur ici?
Est-ce qu'il y a des disques?

Non, **il n'y a pas** de téléviseur ici.
Non, **il n'y a pas** de disques.

Remind students that **pas un/une/des** becomes **pas de (d')** after **il y a**.
The inverted form **y a-t-il** is not taught at this level.

ACTIVITÉ 9   Dans la classe

Ask your classmates if the following items (1-7) and people (8-14) are in the classroom. Your classmates will answer as appropriate.

→   un téléviseur   **—Est-ce qu'il y a un téléviseur?**
                  —Mais oui! Il y a un téléviseur.
                  (Mais non! Il n'y a pas de téléviseur.)

1. un électrophone
2. une mini-cassette
3. des disques
4. des cassettes
5. des livres
6. des livres français
7. un appareil-photo

8. des garçons
9. des filles
10. des garçons sympathiques
11. des filles sympathiques
12. des élèves français
13. des élèves canadiens
14. des élèves intelligents

If items 1, 7, 12-14 are answered in the negative, be sure **pas d'** is used.

Remember that liaison is required *before* the noun. It is optional after a plural noun, and never occurs after a singular noun. les élèves   les bons élèves   les élèves américains

E. Récapitulation: la forme des adjectifs

Here is a form chart for the endings of regular adjectives:

	SINGULAR	PLURAL		
Masculine	—	-s	un ami **intelligent**	des amis **intelligents**
Feminine	-e	-es	une amie **intelligente**	des amies **intelligentes**

√ *ACTIVITÉ 10*   **Similarités**   OPTIONAL

The children in Alain's family are all alike. Describe (a) his sister Suzanne,
(b) his brothers Pierre and Paul, (c) his older sisters Nicole and Yvonne.

→ Alain est grand.   (a) **Suzanne est grande.**

(b) **Pierre et Paul sont grands.**

(c) **Nicole et Yvonne sont grandes.**

This activity may be performed by
dividing the class into three parts: one
responds with (a), the other with (b),
and the third with (c).

1. Alain est brun.
2. Alain est intelligent.
3. Alain est français.
4. Alain est drôle.

5. Alain est sympathique.
6. Alain est intéressant.
7. Alain n'est pas embêtant *(annoying)*.
8. Alain n'est pas pénible.

Prononciation

Les lettres: voyelle + n (m)

The letter group "vowel+**n**" ("vowel+**m**") represents a nasal vowel, unless it
is followed by a vowel or another **n** (**m**).

Contrast the pronunciation of the nasal and non-nasal vowels in the following
words. (Be sure not to pronounce an /n/ after a nasal vowel.)

NASAL VOWELS

/ɑ̃/ Jean, Antoine, Christian
/ɛ̃/ Martin, cousin
     canadien, américain
/œ̃/ un, brun

NON-NASAL VOWELS

/an/ Jeanne, Anatole, Christiane
/in/ Martine, cousine
/ɛn/ canadienne, américaine
/yn/ une, brune

Entre nous

Expression pour la conversation

When you are not sure, or when you want to avoid saying yes or no, you can say:

peut-être *maybe, perhaps* —Tu as dix dollars?
—**Peut-être** . . . Pourquoi?

Mini-dialogue   OPTIONAL

Marc wonders why Sylvie is wearing glasses.

MARC:	Tiens, tu as des *lunettes?*	*glasses*
SYLVIE:	Bien sûr!	
MARC:	Est-ce que tu es *myope* maintenant?	*nearsighted*
SYLVIE:	Non, je ne suis pas myope.	
MARC:	Alors, pourquoi est-ce que tu as des lunettes?	
SYLVIE:	Parce que c'est la *mode,* idiot!	*style*
MARC:	Tu as des idées bizarres!	
SYLVIE:	Peut-être . . . Mais *toi,* tu n'as pas d'idées!	*you*

L'art du dialogue

Act out the dialog between Marc and Sylvie.

UNITÉ 2
Leçon 5 À la Maison des Jeunes

Un groupe d'amis arrive à la Maison des Jeunes.

Tennis

ANDRÉ: Tu aimes jouer au tennis?
ISABELLE: Bien sûr! C'est formidable, non?
ANDRÉ: Tu joues avec moi?
ISABELLE: Avec toi? D'accord!

Est-ce qu'Isabelle aime jouer au tennis?

Basketball

PIERRE: Qui joue au basket?
PHILIPPE: Moi!
CLAIRE: Moi aussi!
PIERRE: Et André? Il ne joue pas avec *nous*?   us
CLAIRE: Non. Il joue avec Isabelle!
PIERRE: Avec *elle*?   her
CLAIRE: Pourquoi pas? Elle joue très bien.
PIERRE: C'est vrai!

Avec qui est-ce qu'André joue au basketball?
Comment est-ce qu'Isabelle joue?

Monopoly

SYLVIE: Tiens! Voilà Marc et voilà Paul!
BÉATRICE: Nous jouons au Monopoly avec *eux*?   them
SYLVIE: Est-ce qu'ils jouent bien?
BÉATRICE: Euh, non . . . Marc joue mal . . .
SYLVIE: Et Paul?
BÉATRICE: *Lui, il triche!*   He cheats!
SYLVIE: Alors, je ne joue pas avec eux.
BÉATRICE: *Moi non plus!*   Me neither!

Est-ce que Marc joue bien au Monopoly? Est-ce que Paul joue bien?
Est-ce que Sylvie et Béatrice jouent avec Marc et Paul?

CONVERSATION

Let's talk about your best male friend: **votre meilleur ami.**

1. Est-ce que vous parlez français avec **lui**?
2. Est-ce que vous étudiez avec **lui**?
3. Est-ce que vous jouez au tennis avec **lui**?

Now let's talk about your best female friend: **votre meilleure amie.**

4. Est-ce que vous parlez français avec **elle**?
5. Est-ce que vous étudiez avec **elle**?
6. Est-ce que vous jouez au tennis avec **elle**?

OBSERVATIONS   Str. B

Reread the above questions, paying special attention to the pronouns that follow the word **avec.** These are called *stress pronouns.*

- Which stress pronoun is used to refer to your best *male* friend? ^lui
  Is this the same as the subject pronoun **il**? ^no
- Which stress pronoun is used to refer to your best *female* friend? ^elle
  Is this the same as the subject pronoun **elle**? ^yes

NOTES CULTURELLES   OPTIONAL

1. La Maison des Jeunes   Most French cities have a public youth center called **La Maison des Jeunes et de la Culture** or, simply, **La Maison des Jeunes.** There young people gather to practice their favorite sports, to play cards, to watch movies, to listen to folk music, to dance, and to have a good time together. They can also develop their artistic talents by participating in plays or by taking art or pottery lessons. Often **La Maison des Jeunes** also offers practical training for useful skills such as car repair, shop, typing, sewing . . . and English!

2. Le Monopoly   Monopoly is as popular in France as it is in the United States. The French **Monopoly** board uses Paris street names, and naturally millionaires are millionaires in French francs!

SUGGESTED REALIA: French Monopoly game.

MAISON DES JEUNES ET DE LA CULTURE
49 rue des martyrs
JOUÉ LES TOURS

Les spectacles
Modern'Jazz Danse

FEVRIER			
DANSE	Samedi 4	21 h.	Ballet de "Modern'Jazz". Direction S. ALZETTA.
DANSE	Samedi 4 Dimanche 5		Stage de danse - "Modern'Jazz" avec S. ALZETTA.
RENCONTRE	Mardi 7	21 h.	Conférence FRANCE - URSS
SEJOUR	Samedi 11	19 h.	Départ Séjour SKI

Structure

A. Les expressions impersonnelles avec c'est

Note the use of **c'est** in the sentences below:
(modification)

vrai	*true, right*	Tu parles italien? **C'est vrai?**
faux (fausse)	*false, wrong*	Non, **c'est faux!**
facile	*easy*	Je parle anglais. **C'est facile.**
difficile	*hard, difficult*	J'étudie le chinois. **C'est difficile.**

French speakers often use impersonal expressions formed as follows:

> **C'est**
> **Ce n'est pas** } + masculine adjective

➜ Impersonal expressions are sometimes formed with adverbs,
such as **bien** and **mal**.

C'est bien!	*That's good (fine).*	Tu étudies? **C'est bien!**
C'est mal!	*That's bad.*	Alain n'étudie pas. **C'est mal!**

ACTIVITÉ 1   Vrai ou faux?

Imagine your little cousin is making statements about geography. Tell him
whether his statements are right or wrong. Use: **Oui, c'est vrai!** or **Non, ce
n'est pas vrai!**

After **en** the definite article is not
used with names of countries.

➜ Paris est en France.   **Oui, c'est vrai!**

1. Miami est en Floride.
2. San Francisco est en Californie.
3. Berlin est en Italie.
4. Rome est en France.
5. La Tunisie est en Amérique.
6. Abidjan est en Afrique.
7. Fort-de-France est en Suisse.
8. Genève est en Suisse.

ACTIVITÉ 2   Expression personnelle   OPTIONAL

Say whether or not you like to do the following things and why. Use **C'est**
or **Ce n'est pas** with adjectives such as **amusant, intéressant, drôle, pénible,
facile, difficile.**

➜ nager   **J'aime nager parce que c'est amusant (ce n'est pas difficile).**
           Je n'aime pas nager parce que c'est pénible (ce n'est pas amusant).

1. téléphoner
2. parler français
3. parler français en classe
4. danser
5. voyager
6. regarder la télé
7. dîner en ville
8. jouer au golf
9. écouter la musique classique

B. Les pronoms accentués

Stress pronouns are sometimes called disjunctive pronouns.

In each sentence below, the first pronoun is a *stress pronoun,* and the second is a *subject pronoun.* Compare the two sets of pronouns.

	STRESS PRONOUN	SUBJECT PRONOUN	
Singular	Moi, Toi, Lui, Elle,	je tu il elle	parle français. étudies l'espagnol. a un vélomoteur. joue au tennis.
Plural	Nous, Vous, Eux, Elles,	nous vous ils elles	sommes américains. habitez en France. ont une petite voiture. dansent très bien.

Point out that four stress pronouns have the same forms as the corresponding subject pronouns: **elle, nous, vous, elles.** Four stress pronouns have different forms: **moi, toi, lui, eux.**

Stress pronouns occur frequently in French. They are used—

1. in short statements where there is no verb:

Qui danse bien?	**Moi!**	*Me! (I do!)*
Qui parle italien?	**Pas lui!**	*Not him! (He doesn't.)*

2. to reinforce a subject pronoun:

Moi, j'adore danser.   *I love to dance.*

3. after words like **avec** and **pour:**

Marie joue avec **lui.**   *Marie plays with him.*
Il travaille pour **nous.**   *He works for us.*

4. before and after **et** and **ou:**

Toi et moi, nous étudions beaucoup.   *You and I, we study a lot.*
Qui rentre maintenant? **Eux ou vous?**   *Who is going back now? They or you?*

5. After **c'est** and **ce n'est pas:**

C'est Pierre?   Oui, c'est **lui!**   *Is it Pierre? Yes, it's him (he).*
C'est Claire?   Non, ce n'est pas **elle!**   *Is it Claire? No, it's not her (she).*

ACTIVITÉ 3   Une enquête (*A survey*)

A French magazine is making a survey. Answer the questions affirmatively or negatively.

→ Qui parle français?   **Moi! (Pas moi!)**

1. Qui étudie le français?   l'espagnol
2. Qui a des amis français?   allemands
3. Qui a des amis en Californie?   en Floride
4. Qui a des disques?   cassettes
5. Qui aime nager?   marcher
6. Qui adore danser?   chanter

ACTIVITÉ 4   La photo

Alain and Suzanne are looking at a photograph of their kindergarten class. Alain tries to remember everyone's name. Suzanne lets him know if he is right or wrong. Play both roles.

→ Henri (oui)   Alain: **C'est Henri?**   Michèle (non)   **C'est Michèle?**
                     Suzanne: **Oui, c'est lui!**   **Non, ce n'est pas elle!**

1. Antoine (oui)   5. Louise et Claire (non)
2. Martine (oui)   6. Monsieur Duval (oui)
3. Jean-Pierre (non)   7. Madame Lemoine (non)
4. Marc et André (oui)   8. Mademoiselle Thomas (oui)

√ ACTIVITÉ 5   Non!   OPTIONAL

Answer the questions below in the negative, and then give the correct information (in parentheses). Reinforce your answers with stress pronouns.

→ Pierre habite à Abidjan? (à Dakar)   **Non! Lui, il habite à Dakar!**

1. Christine parle anglais? (espagnol)   5. Nous jouons bien? (vous / mal)
2. Charles chante mal? (bien)   6. Tu joues au tennis? (je / au golf)
3. Paul et Georges étudient souvent?   7. Vous habitez à Paris? (nous / à Dijon)
   (rarement)   8. J'étudie l'espagnol? (tu / l'anglais)
4. Alice et Michèle voyagent rarement?
   (souvent)

ACTIVITÉ 6   Pourquoi?

Suzanne wants to know why Paul does the following things. Play the role of Suzanne, using stress pronouns in your questions.

→ Je joue avec Pierre.   Suzanne: **Pourquoi est-ce que tu joues avec lui?**

1. Je rentre avec Pierre et Antoine.   4. Je travaille pour Monsieur Moreau.
2. J'étudie avec Paul.   5. Je travaille aussi pour Madame Lasalle.
3. Je dîne avec Jeannette et Isabelle.   6. Je danse avec Hélène.

Prononciation

Le son /wa/

Model word: t<u>oi</u>

Practice words: m<u>oi</u>, v<u>oi</u>ci, v<u>oy</u>age, Madem<u>oi</u>selle, v<u>oi</u>là

Practice sentences: Ben<u>oî</u>t v<u>oy</u>age avec m<u>oi</u>.
                    V<u>oi</u>là Mademoiselle Descr<u>oi</u>x.

Comment écrire /wa/: **oi, oî, oy**

Entre nous

Expressions pour la conversation

To introduce a mild reproach, you can say:

Écoute!	(tu form)	*Listen!*	**Écoute**, Alain! Tu es pénible aujourd'hui.
Écoutez!	(vous form)	*Listen!*	**Écoutez**, vous deux! Vous jouez mal!

Mini-dialogue OPTIONAL

Alain is at a party. He would like to invite Dominique to dance, but he has a problem.

ALAIN: Avec qui est-ce que tu danses maintenant?

DOMINIQUE: Avec Jacques.

ALAIN: Avec lui? Écoute, Jacques est sympathique, mais il n'est pas très drôle. Pourquoi est-ce que tu ne danses pas avec moi? Moi, *au moins* . . . *at least*

DOMINIQUE: C'est vrai! Jacques n'est pas *spécialement* drôle, mais il danse très bien! *especially*

ALAIN: Et moi?

DOMINIQUE: Toi?

ALAIN: Oui, moi!

DOMINIQUE: Écoute, Alain. Tu es sympathique, mais quand je danse avec toi, *tu me marches toujours sur* *you always step on my feet* *les pieds*. Alors . . .

L'art du dialogue

a) Act out the dialog between Alain and Dominique.

b) Now imagine that it is **Dominique** who would like to dance with **Alain**. Reverse the roles of Alain and Dominique. Replace Jacques with **Jacqueline** and make the necessary changes. Act out the new dialog.

c) Now imagine that **Alain** and **Paul** would like to dance with **Dominique** and **Sylvie**. Write a new dialog in which you replace Alain by **Alain et Paul**, Dominique by **Dominique et Sylvie**, Jacques by **Jacques et Thomas**, and **tu me marches** by **vous nous marchez**. Make all other necessary changes.

OBJECTIVES

In this unit the students will learn to talk about their recreational activities, especially sports and music, and to discuss their future plans. They will also learn to describe their family, their family relationships, and their personal belongings.

Language
- **aller**
- **aller** + *infinitive* and the near future
- contracted forms of the definite article with **à** and **de**; **jouer à** and **jouer de**
- **chez**
- various ways of describing ownership and relationship: **de, être à**, possessive adjectives

Vocabulary
- the family and relatives
- the city and places in the city
- recreational activities

Culture

This unit focuses on certain aspects of the life of young people in France, especially leisure-time activities and vacations.

UNITÉ 3
Loisirs et vacances

OPPOSITE: The Centre Pompidou (Beaubourg) in Paris.

UNITÉ 3
Leçon 1

Week-end à Paris

STRUCTURES TO OBSERVE
- aller
- the contraction au
- the future construction aller + infinitive

Aujourd'hui, c'est samedi.
Les élèves *ne vont pas* en classe.
Où est-ce qu'ils vont alors?
Ça dépend!

aren't going

It depends!

Voici Jean-Michel et voici Nathalie.
Jean-Michel va au concert.
Nathalie va au théâtre.

Voici Pierre.
Où est-ce qu'il va?
Est-ce qu'il va au concert?
Au théâtre?
Au cinéma?
Non! Il va au café.
Il a rendez-vous avec Élisabeth.

Voici Martine.
Elle a un grand sac et des lunettes de soleil.
Est-ce qu'elle va à un rendez-vous secret?
Non!
Elle va au Centre Pompidou.
Elle va regarder les acrobates.
Et *après*, elle va *aller* à la bibliothèque.

afterwards; to go

Voici Jean-Claude.
Est-ce qu'il va visiter le Centre Pompidou?
Est-ce qu'il va regarder les acrobates?
Est-ce qu'il va écouter un concert?
Est-ce qu'il va aller au cinéma?
Hélas, non!
Il va rester à la maison.
Pourquoi?
Parce qu'il est malade.
Pauvre Jean-Claude!
Il fait *si* beau *dehors!*

Alas

so; outside

CONVERSATION   OPTIONAL

Jean-Claude is asking you if you are going to do certain things next weekend.

1. Est-ce que vous allez étudier?
   Oui, **je vais** étudier.
   (Non, **je ne vais pas** étudier.)
2. Est-ce que vous allez travailler?

3. Est-ce que vous allez voyager?
4. Est-ce que vous allez skier?
5. Est-ce que vous allez rester à la maison?

OBSERVATIONS   Str. C

The above questions refer to next Saturday and Sunday.

- Do they concern *present* or *future* events?   future events
- What expression did you use to say *I am going* (to do something)?   je vais
  I am not going (to do something)?   je ne vais pas
- Are the verbs which follow these expressions in the *infinitive?*   yes

NOTE CULTURELLE   OPTIONAL

Le Centre Pompidou

What place in Paris attracts more visitors than the Eiffel Tower, the Louvre Museum, and Notre Dame Cathedral? It is **Le Centre Pompidou** (also known as **Beaubourg**), an immense cultural center, which is free and open to the public.

On the large modern plaza in front of the building one can be entertained by mimes, jugglers, and acrobats. From the glass-encased escalators one has a magnificent view of Paris. Special exhibits focus on modern art and architecture. But the most popular section by far is the library! It is the first large library in France to offer open access to books, slides, cassettes, and videotape materials, and to provide audio-visual rooms where visitors can work with television cameras.

The Centre Pompidou is named after Georges Pompidou, president of France from 1969–1974.

Vocabulaire pratique

NOMS:	**un rendez-vous**	*date, appointment*	**les lunettes de soleil** *sunglasses*
ADJECTIFS:	**malade**	*sick*	Vous n'êtes pas **malades!**
	riche ≠ **pauvre**	*rich ≠ poor*	**Pauvre** Alain! Il est très malade.
VERBE:	**rester**	*to stay*	Il déteste **rester** à la maison.
EXPRESSION:	**en classe**	*in class* *to class*	Aujourd'hui les élèves sont **en classe**. Quand les élèves sont malades, ils ne vont pas **en classe**.

You should stress that **rester** means *to stay,* and not "to rest." You may want to explain the concept of false cognates, using **rester** as an example.
One may say either **avoir rendez-vous** or **avoir** *un* **rendez-vous**.

Structure

A. Le verbe *aller*

Aller*(to go)* is the only *irregular* verb ending in **-er.** Note the forms of **aller** in the present tense.

Infinitive		**aller**	*to go*	J'aime **aller** en France.
Present	je	**vais**	*I go, I am going*	Je **vais** à la maison.
	tu	**vas**	*you go, you are going*	**Vas-**tu à Québec?
	il/elle	**va**	*he/she goes, he/she is going*	Paul **va** à Paris.
	nous	**allons**	*we go, we are going*	Nous **allons** en ville.
	vous	**allez**	*you go, you are going*	Est-ce que vous **allez** là-bas?
	ils/elles	**vont**	*they go, they are going*	Ils ne **vont** pas en classe.

The verb **aller** is usually accompanied by a word or phrase indicating a place. (After the verb *to go* in English, the place is often left out.)
Compare:

Quand est-ce que **tu vas à Paris?** *When are you going to Paris?*
Je vais à Paris en septembre. *I am going (to Paris) in September.*

ACTIVITÉ 1 Lundi et dimanche

On Monday the following students are going to class. On Sunday they are not going. Express this according to the model.

→ Charles **Lundi, Charles va en classe. Dimanche, il ne va pas en classe.**

1. Philippe
2. Suzanne
3. moi
4. toi

5. Michèle et Denise
6. les élèves
7. nous
8. vous

VARIATION: Mardi, Charles va en ville. Mercredi, il ne va pas en ville.

ACTIVITÉ 2 Les vacances

The following students at a Swiss boarding school are going home for vacation. To which of the following cities is each one going?

à Paris? à Québec? à Boston? à Tokyo?

→ Jean-Michel est canadien. **Jean-Michel va à Québec.**

1. Je suis français.
2. Charlotte est américaine.
3. Nous sommes japonais.
4. Tu es canadienne.

5. Vous êtes françaises.
6. Tatsuo est japonais.
7. Mike et Susan sont américains.
8. Vous êtes canadiens.

Vocabulaire spécialisé Ville et campagne

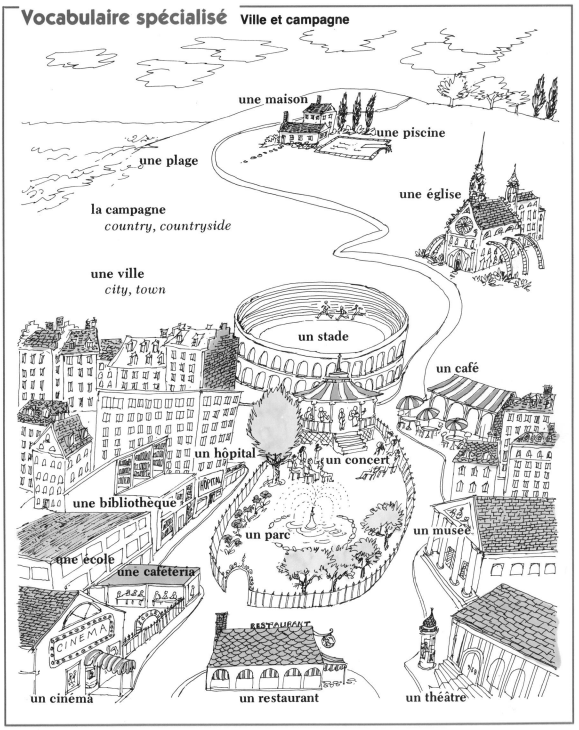

une maison

une piscine

une plage

une église

la campagne
country, countryside

une ville
city, town

un stade

un café

un hôpital

un concert

une bibliothèque

un parc

un musée

une école

une cafétéria

CINEMA

RESTAURANT

HÔPITAL

un cinéma

un restaurant

un théâtre

Review à la maison *(at home)*.
VOCABULARY EXPANSION: un hôtel, un magasin, une boutique; un temple (église protestante), une synagogue

Leçon un   **135**

ACTIVITÉ 3 Là où j'habite OPTIONAL

Indicate whether the following places are found in your neighborhood.

→ un cinéma   **Il y a un cinéma. (Il n'y a pas de cinéma.)**   You may remind the students that un/une becomes de (d') after pas.

1. un stade
2. une plage
3. un théâtre
4. un restaurant

5. une église
6. une piscine
7. un hôpital
8. une bibliothèque

9. un parc
10. une école
11. un musée
12. une cafétéria

You may wish to review the various meanings of à with these examples:

at   Nous sommes à la plage.
to   { Nous allons à la campagne.
      { Nous parlons à Paul.
in   Nous habitons à Paris.

B. À + l'article défini

The preposition **à** has several meanings: *in, at, to*.
Note the forms of **à** + *definite article* in the sentences below:

Voici le cinéma.	Paul est **au** cinéma.	Françoise va **au** cinéma.
Voici la piscine.	Sylvie est **à la** piscine.	Jacques va **à la** piscine.
Voici l'hôpital.	Henri est **à l'**hôpital.	Marie va **à l'**hôpital.
Voici les Champs-Élysées.	Anne est **aux** Champs-Élysées.	Lise va **aux** Champs-Élysées.

The preposition **à** contracts with **le** and **les**, but *not* with **la** and **l'**.

à + le → au	à + les → aux

→ There is liaison after **aux** when the next word begins with a vowel sound.
Le professeur parle **aux élèves.**

ACTIVITÉ 4 À Paris

The following students are visiting Paris. Say where each one is going.

→ Monique: le théâtre   **Monique va au théâtre.**   VARIATION: They are now at these places. Monique est au théâtre.

1. Paul: le café
2. Jacqueline: le cinéma
3. Nicole: le restaurant
4. Suzanne: le musée

5. Charles: le concert
6. Philippe: la bibliothèque
7. Louis: le Centre Pompidou
8. Anne: les Invalides[1]

9. Alain: le Louvre[2]
10. Marc: l'Arc de Triomphe
11. Sylvie: les Champs-Élysées
12. Étienne: la tour Eiffel

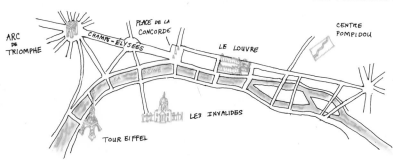

[1]Formerly a hospital for disabled veterans (**les invalides**); now housing a military museum and the tomb of Napoleon (1769-1821).
[2]Former royal palace begun in 1204 and finished under Louis XIV (1638-1715); now a national museum housing the "Mona Lisa" and the "Vénus de Milo."

ACTIVITÉ 5   Dialogue

Ask your classmates if they often go to the following places and events.

→ le restaurant   Élève 1: **Est-ce que tu vas souvent au restaurant?**
Élève 2: **Oui, je vais souvent au restaurant.**
(Non, je ne vais pas souvent au restaurant.)

VARIATION in the plural:
—Allez-vous. . . ?
—Oui, nous allons. . .

1. le théâtre	4. la campagne	7. l'église	10. le parc
2. la plage	5. le stade	8. la bibliothèque	11. le cinéma
3. la piscine	6. le musée	9. l'hôpital	12. le concert

ACTIVITÉ 6   Le bon endroit *(The right place)*   OPTIONAL

Can you tell where the following people are? Read the first sentence. Then complete the second sentence with an appropriate place.

→ Paul regarde un film. Il est . . .   **Il est au cinéma.**

1. Janine dîne. Elle est . . .
2. Hélène nage. Elle est . . .
3. Charles joue au football. Il est . . .
4. Jean regarde les sculptures modernes. Il est . . .
5. Annie étudie. Elle est . . .
6. Robert est très malade. Il est . . .

VARIATION: Have a student name a place. E.g. **Je suis à l'école.** Have other students suggest what that classmate might be doing. **Tu étudies. Tu écoutes le professeur. Tu regardes les filles/les garçons,** etc.

C. *Aller* + l'infinitif

The following sentences describe *future* events. Note the words in heavy type.

Nathalie **va nager.**   *Nathalie **is going to swim.***
Paul et Marc **vont jouer** au tennis.   *Paul and Marc **are going to play** tennis.*
Nous **allons rester** à la maison.   *We **are going to stay** at home.*

To express the near future, the French use the following construction:

> present of **aller** + infinitive

This construction corresponds to the English construction: *to be going* (to do something).
Note the interrogative and negative forms:

Est-ce que tu vas visiter Paris?   *Are you going to visit Paris?*
Non, **je ne vais pas** visiter Paris. *No, **I'm not going** to visit Paris.*

→ In negative sentences the word **ne** comes before the verb **aller,** and the word **pas** comes between **aller** and the infinitive.

✓ ACTIVITÉ 7   Tourisme

Say where the following people are going this summer and what they are going to visit.   À is used with names of cities; en is used with feminine countries or states.

→ Monique (à Paris / la tour Eiffel)   **Monique va à Paris. Elle va visiter la tour Eiffel.**

The French Quarter.

1. Alice (à New York / la statue de la Liberté)
2. nous (en Égypte / les pyramides)
3. vous (à Rome / le Vatican)
4. toi (à la Nouvelle-Orléans / le Vieux Carré)
5. moi (à San Francisco / Alcatraz)
6. les élèves (en Floride / le Cap Canaveral)

ACTIVITÉ 8 Dialogue

Ask your classmates if they are going to do the following things this weekend.

→ étudier
Élève 1: **Est-ce que tu vas étudier?**
Élève 2: **Oui, je vais étudier. (Non, je ne vais pas étudier.)**

1. travailler
2. écouter la radio
3. regarder la télé
4. visiter un musée

5. jouer au volleyball
6. nager
7. inviter des amis
8. danser

9. aller à la campagne
10. aller à la bibliothèque
11. jouer au tennis
12. rester à la maison

RÉVISION: *avoir* et *être* OPTIONAL

être: je suis, tu es, il est, nous sommes, vous êtes, ils sont
avoir: j'ai, tu as, il a, nous avons, vous avez, ils ont

ACTIVITÉ DE RÉVISION Vacances à Paris OPTIONAL

Say that the following people are on vacation, that they have a car, are going
to Paris, and are going to visit **le Centre Pompidou.**

→ Charles
Élève 1: **Charles est en vacances.**
Élève 2: **Il a une voiture.**
Élève 3: **Il va à Paris.**
Élève 4: **Il va visiter le Centre Pompidou.**

1. vous
2. moi

3. Hélène
4. Monsieur Rémi

5. Colette et Marie
6. Paul et Robert

7. toi
8. nous

UN JEU *(A game)* OPTIONAL

Activities entitled *UN JEU* can be challenge activities. The winner
is the student with the most logical and grammatically correct
sentences. These activities can also be given as written assignments.

How many logical sentences can you make in five minutes, using elements
of columns A, B, and C? Be sure to use the appropriate forms of **aller,** as
shown in the models below.

A	B	C
je	le restaurant	nager
tu	le café	marcher
Philippe	la cafétéria	dîner
nous	la plage	jouer au volleyball
vous	la piscine	jouer au football
Michèle et Sophie	le musée	regarder les garçons et les filles
	le parc	danser
	la campagne	parler avec des amis
	le stade	écouter un concert
	la discothèque	visiter une exposition (*exhibit*)

→ **Tu vas au café. Tu vas parler avec des amis.**
→ **Michèle et Sophie vont à la piscine. Elles vont nager.**

Prononciation

Le son /ʒ/

Model word: <u>j</u>e

Practice words: <u>J</u>ean, <u>J</u>acques, <u>G</u>i<u>g</u>i, <u>G</u>eorges, <u>G</u>ilbert, jaune, rou<u>g</u>e

Practice sentences: <u>G</u>i<u>g</u>i joue avec <u>G</u>eorges et <u>G</u>ilbert.

<u>J</u>eudi, <u>J</u>ean-<u>J</u>acques va voya<u>g</u>er.

The sound /ʒ/ is pronounced like the **g** of **rouge.** The sound /ʒ/ is almost never introduced by the sound /d/ as in the English name *John.*

Comment écrire /ʒ/: **j**; **g** (before **e, i, y**); **ge** (before **a, o**)

Entre nous

Expressions pour la conversation

The following expressions are often used in conversation:

Allons!	*Let's go!*
Allons . . !	*Let's go (somewhere)!*
Ça n'a pas d'importance.	*It doesn't matter.*

Mini-dialogue   OPTIONAL

Bill is spending the summer vacation with a French family. It is Sunday and his friends are discussing where to go that afternoon.

MICHÈLE: Où est-ce que nous allons aujourd'hui?

JACQUES: Allons au cinéma! Il y a un très bon film.

ANDRÉ: Au cinéma? C'est *ridicule!*   ridiculous
Il fait très beau aujourd'hui. Allons à la plage.

BRIGITTE: Moi, je préfère aller au café.

MICHÈLE: Et toi, Bill, où est-ce que tu préfères aller? Au cinéma, à la plage ou au café?

BILL: Ça n'a pas d'importance.

JACQUES: Pourquoi est-ce que ça n'a pas d'importance?

BILL: Parce qu'en France, il y a des jolies filles
partout!   everywhere

L'art du dialogue

a) Act out the dialog between Bill and his friends.
b) Imagine that the scene takes place in Paris. André wants to go to **les Champs-Élysées,** and Brigitte wants to go to **le Centre Pompidou.** Act out the new dialog, making all the necessary changes.

Leçon 2 Marie-Noëlle

STRUCTURES TO OBSERVE
• possession with **de**
• the contraction **du**
• constructions with **chez**

Marie-Noëlle est une fille sympathique, mais . . .
   elle a une mauvaise *habitude*.
Elle emprunte toujours tout.

habit

Elle a la montre de Jacqueline,
         le skate-board de Philippe,
         les disques de Pierre . . .

Elle va à la plage avec le transistor d'Antoine,
                  le sac de Françoise,
                  le bikini de Nathalie.

Et quand elle joue au tennis,
         elle emprunte le short de Sylvie,
                  le tee-shirt de la cousine de Sylvie,
                  la raquette du cousin de Sylvie.

Où est Marie-Noëlle aujourd'hui?
Est-ce qu'elle est *chez elle?*
Non, elle est *chez Thérèse!*
Est-ce parce que Thérèse a un *nouveau* vélomoteur?
Non, c'est parce que Thérèse a un frère très intelligent,
   très beau et très sympathique!
C'est *plus* important *que* le vélomoteur, non?

at home
over Thérèse's
new

more . . . than

Quelle est la mauvaise habitude de Marie-Noëlle? Où est Marie-Noëlle aujourd'hui?
Pourquoi est-ce qu'elle est chez Thérèse?

Imagine that someone is asking you who has the following objects.
Answer that Marie-Noëlle has them.

1. Qui a **la montre de Jacqueline?**
   Marie-Noëlle a la montre de Jacqueline.
2. Qui a les disques de Pierre?
3. Qui a le sac de Françoise?
4. Qui a le short de Sylvie?
5. Qui a le skate-board de Philippe?

OBSERVATIONS   Str. B   OPTIONAL

Reread the first question.

• How do you say *Jacqueline's watch* in French?
• Which noun comes *first?* **la montre** or **Jacqueline?**
  Which noun comes *second?*
  Which little word comes between the two nouns?

la montre de Jacqueline/la montre/Jacqueline/de

NOTE CULTURELLE   OPTIONAL

L'américanisation

In many ways French teenagers have adopted an American life style. They drink Coca-Cola, wear T-shirts and jeans, and play basketball and volleyball.

Just as people borrow customs from one another, so languages borrow words. Most French sports terms are of English origin: **le volleyball, le football, le basketball, le golf,** etc. Recently many other new words have been borrowed by the French: **le short, le tee-shirt, le skate-board,** etc. Often the French shorten these borrowed words. They talk of **le volley, le foot, le basket, le skate,** and they give these words a French pronunciation.

Of course, English has also borrowed many words from French: **boutique, restaurant, rendez-vous, chic, . . .** you can probably extend this list without difficulty!

Vocabulaire pratique

NOMS:	**un cousin** *cousin* (male)	**une cousine** *cousin* (female)
	un frère *brother*	**une sœur** *sister*
VERBE:	**emprunter** *to borrow*	**J'emprunte** des livres à la bibliothèque.
EXPRESSION:	**tout** *all, everything*	**Tout** est intéressant.

Structure

Chez is used only with nouns or pronouns referring to people.
In Unité 4.5 students will learn to differentiate between:
Je vais chez le docteur.   *I am going to the doctor's.*
Je vais à l'hôpital.   *I am going to the hospital.*

A. *Chez*

Note the English equivalents of **chez** in the following sentences:

Je suis **chez moi**.	*I am (at) home (at my house).*
Tu es **chez Marie-Noëlle**.	*You are at Marie-Noëlle's (house).*
Paul va **chez lui**.	*Paul is going home (to his house).*
Henri va **chez Jacques**.	*Henri is going to Jacques' (house).*
Annette va **chez une amie**.	*Annette is going to a friend's (house).*

Students may have already seen **chez** in the names of restaurants: **Chez Pierre.**

Chez cannot stand alone. It must be followed by a *noun*, a *stress pronoun*, or **qui**.
Note the word order in questions:

Chez qui vas-tu? { *To whose house are you going?*
                       Whose house are you going to?

→ There is liaison after **chez** when the next word begins with a vowel sound.

Marie-Noëlle n'est pas chez elle. Elle est chez une amie.

There is never liaison between **chez** and a proper name: chez Alice.

ACTIVITÉ 1   Les visites de Marie-Noëlle

Before leaving for a summer in the United States, Marie-Noëlle visits her friends to say good-by. Say where she is going.

→ Charles   **Marie-Noëlle va chez Charles.**

1. Françoise
2. Thérèse
3. Paul et André
4. un ami suisse
5. une amie canadienne
6. des amis américains
7. le professeur
8. Madame Dupont

ACTIVITÉ 2   Le championnat de football

The soccer championship is on TV tonight, and everyone is staying home to watch it. Express this, using **rester chez** and the appropriate stress pronoun.

→ Paul   **Paul reste chez lui.**   Review the stress pronouns if necessary.

1. Marie-Noëlle
2. Monsieur Duroc
3. le professeur
4. Pierre et Jean
5. Anne et Julie
6. Ève et moi   Ève et moi, nous restons chez nous.
7. nous
8. vous
9. toi
10. moi

VARIATIONS: Everyone is home. **Paul est chez lui.** Everyone is going home. **Paul va chez lui.**
Everyone is going back home: **Paul rentre chez lui.**

142 Unité trois

ACTIVITÉ 3 Où sont-ils? OPTIONAL

There are things we do when we are at home, and other things we do some place else.
Read the following sentences and say whether the people are at home or not.

→ Paul nage. **Il n'est pas chez lui.** You may encourage different responses
Anne étudie. **Elle est chez elle.** Paul est chez lui. Il a une piscine.

1. André skie.
2. Tu voyages.
3. Caroline regarde la télévision.
4. Jean et Louis écoutent des disques.
5. Je téléphone.
6. Lise et Annie jouent au tennis.
7. Vous dînez au restaurant.
8. Nous empruntons un livre à la bibliothèque.

B. La possession avec *de*   Remind students that the French do not use ' or 's
to indicate possession or relationship.

To indicate possession or relationship, French speakers use the construction:

noun + **de** + noun	**la guitare de Paul** *Paul's guitar*
↓	
d' (+ vowel sound)	**les amies d'Anne** *Anne's friends*

→ To remember the word order, think of **de** as meaning *of* or *which belongs to.*

✓ ACTIVITÉ 4 Un tapeur *(A leech)*   If more than one person is indicated as the owner, the word **de**
must be repeated. **Voici la voiture de Michel et de Jean.**

Jacques borrows everything from his friends. Indicate who owns the things he has.

→ la caméra (Pierre) **Il a la caméra de Pierre.**

1. l'électrophone (Paul)
2. la radio (Marc)
3. la moto (Albert)
4. les lunettes de soleil (Alain)
5. les disques (Robert)
6. les cassettes (Julien)

ACTIVITÉ 5 Les objets trouvés *(Lost and found)*

The following things have been turned into the lost and found office.
Identify their owners.

→ le livre (Antoine) **C'est le livre d'Antoine.**

1. le sac (Sylvie)
2. la raquette (Sophie)
3. la mini-cassette (René)
4. l'électrophone (Olivier)
5. les lunettes (Isabelle) Be sure students use
6. les livres (Philippe) ce sont in items 5 and 6.

ACTIVITÉ 6 Présentations *(Introductions)*

Imagine you are hosting a French party. Introduce the following people.

→ Isabelle (cousine / Marc) **Isabelle est la cousine de Marc.** Make sure students use appropriate articles.

1. Jacques (cousin / Sylvie)
2. Marc (ami / Caroline)
3. Pauline (amie / Pierre)
4. Philippe (camarade / Charles)
5. Suzanne (petite amie / Paul)
6. Robert (frère / Marc)
7. Thomas (frère / Christine)
8. Jeannette (sœur / Pascal)

C. *De* + l'article défini

The preposition **de** has several meanings: *of, from, about.*
Note the forms of **de** + *definite article* in the sentences below:

le concert	Nous arrivons **du** concert.	Nous parlons **du** concert.
la tour Eiffel	Nous arrivons **de la** tour Eiffel.	Nous parlons **de la** tour Eiffel.
l'opéra	Nous arrivons **de l'**opéra.	Nous parlons **de l'**opéra.
les Champs-Élysées	Nous arrivons **des** Champs-Élysées.	Nous parlons **des** Champs-Élysées.

The preposition **de** contracts with **le** and **les**, but *not* with **la** and **l'**.

de + le → du	**de + les → des**

→ There is liaison after **des** when the next word begins with a vowel sound.

Où sont les livres des‿élèves?

MOZART
"Don Giovanni"
Chœurs et Orchestre du Théâtre National de l'Opéra de Paris
Dir. : Lorin Maazel
Coffret 3 disques ou 3 cassettes CBS 79321

ACTIVITÉ 7   Rendez-vous

After visiting Paris, the following students are meeting in a café. Say from which place each one is coming.

→ Jacques: l'Arc de Triomphe   **Jacques arrive de l'Arc de Triomphe.**

1. Sylvie: la tour Eiffel
2. Isabelle: le théâtre
3. Jean-Paul: le Centre Pompidou
4. François: le Quartier Latin
5. Nicole: l'Opéra
6. Marc: le Louvre
7. André: les Champs-Élysées
8. Pierre: les Invalides

ACTIVITÉ 8   Non!

Paul is accused of having borrowed the following items from the people indicated in parentheses. He insists that he does not have them. Play the role of Paul.

→ la guitare (le cousin de Marc)   **Non! Je n'ai pas la guitare du cousin de Marc.**

1. le vélo (le cousin de Suzanne)
2. les disques (la cousine de Charles)
3. la caméra (l'élève américain)
4. l'appareil-photo (l'élève américaine)
5. le livre (le professeur)
6. la raquette (l'amie de Denise)

D. *Jouer à* et *jouer de*

Note the constructions with **jouer** in the sentences below:

Chantal **joue au** tennis.   *Chantal **plays** tennis.*
Elle **joue de la** guitare.   *She **plays the** guitar.*

French speakers use the following constructions with **jouer:**

> **jouer à** + definite article + sport, game

> **jouer de** + definite article + instrument

In conversational French, words are often shortened. **J'aime jouer au volley. Martine joue du saxo.**
l'appareil-photo → l'appareil photographique   la moto → la motocyclette   l'auto → l'automobile

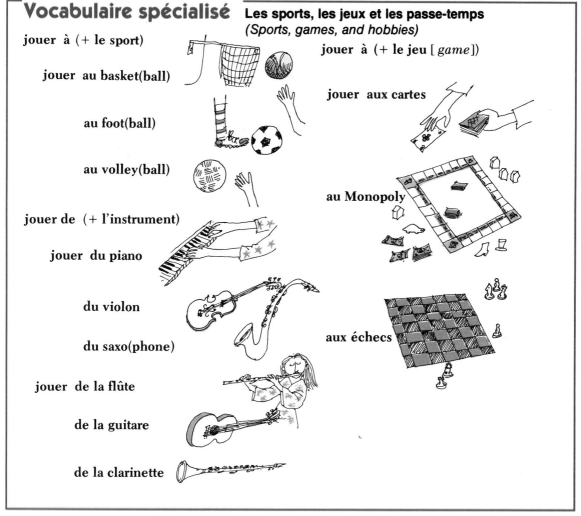

Vocabulaire spécialisé

Les sports, les jeux et les passe-temps
(Sports, games, and hobbies)

jouer à (+ **le sport**)

   jouer au basket(ball)

     au foot(ball)

     au volley(ball)

jouer à (+ **le jeu** [*game*])

   jouer aux cartes

   au Monopoly

jouer de (+ **l'instrument**)

   jouer du piano

     du violon

     du saxo(phone)

   aux échecs

jouer de la flûte

   de la guitare

   de la clarinette

VOCABULARY EXPANSION: sports: jouer au hockey, au baseball, au squash, au golf
                jeux: jouer aux dames *(checkers)*, au trictrac or jacquet *(backgammon)*, au bridge
                instruments: jouer du violoncelle *(cello)*, du hautbois *(oboe)*, de la
                   trompette, du tuba, de la batterie *(drums, drum set)*

ACTIVITÉ 9   Dialogue

Ask your classmates if they play the following instruments and games.

→ le ping-pong   Élève 1: **Est-ce que tu joues au ping-pong?**
                    Élève 2: **Oui, je joue au ping-pong.**
                            (Non, je ne joue pas au ping-pong.)

VARIATION in the plural:
—Est-ce que vous jouez. . .?
—Oui, nous jouons. . .

   le piano   Élève 1: **Est-ce que tu joues du piano?**
                    Élève 2: **Oui, je joue du piano.**
                            (Non, je ne joue pas du piano.)

1. le volley   4. la clarinette   7. le Monopoly   10. la trompette
2. le basket   5. le saxo   8. les cartes   11. le banjo
3. le football   6. la flûte   9. les échecs   12. le violon

UN JEU

The people in column A are talking to friends and relatives of the people in column C. Using the expression **parler à**, form sentences similar to the models below. How many sentences can you make in five minutes?

A	B	C
Adèle	le cousin	Charles
Jean-Pierre	la cousine	Jacqueline
Jacques et Pierre	le frère	le garçon italien
Hélène et Béatrice	la sœur	la fille espagnole
	le meilleur (*best*) ami	les étudiants canadiens
	la meilleure amie	

→ **Jean-Pierre parle au frère du garçon italien.**

→ **Hélène et Béatrice parlent à la cousine des étudiants canadiens.**

Prononciation

Le son /ʃ/

Model word: <u>ch</u>ez

Practice words: <u>Ch</u>arles, Mi<u>ch</u>el, Ra<u>ch</u>el

Practice sentences: <u>Ch</u>arles a une moto blan<u>ch</u>e.
                    Ra<u>ch</u>el et Mi<u>ch</u>èle dînent <u>ch</u>ez <u>Ch</u>arlotte.

The sound /ʃ/ is pronounced like the *ch* of the English word *machine*.
Do not pronounce a /t/ before /ʃ/, unless the **t** appears in the French word.

Contrast: /ʃ/ ma**ch**ine   /tʃ/ ma**t**<u>ch</u>

   Comment écrire /ʃ/: **ch**

Entre nous

Expression pour la conversation

au moins   *at least*   Pierre a **au moins** cinquante disques de musique classique.

Mini-dialogue   OPTIONAL

PIERRE: Où vas-tu?
ANDRÉ: Je vais chez Jacques.
PIERRE: Pourquoi chez lui? Pourquoi pas chez moi?
ANDRÉ: Parce que lui, au moins, il a une sœur sympathique.
PIERRE: Eh bien, j'ai une mauvaise *nouvelle* pour toi!   *piece of news*
       Sa sœur n'est pas là. Elle est à Montréal où elle   *His*
       va *passer* les vacances chez des amis.   *to spend*

L'art du dialogue

a) Act out the dialog between Pierre and André.
b) Imagine that **Pierre** and his brother **Paul** meet André. In Pierre's lines replace **je** and **moi** by **nous** and make the necessary changes.
c) Write and act out a new dialog between **Colette** and **Marie.** Marie wants to visit **Chantal,** who has a good-looking brother (**frère; son frère).**

STRUCTURES TO OBSERVE
• the possessive adjectives
  mon, ma, mes and **ton, ta, tes**
• how to state someone's age

Leçon 3

Christine a un petit ami.

Christine a deux passions: le ski et la *photo*.
En hiver elle va en vacances à La Plagne, une *station de ski*
dans les Alpes. Et, bien sûr, elle *prend* beaucoup de photos.

photography
ski resort
takes

Un jour Hélène regarde l'album de photos de Christine.

HÉLÈNE: Qui est la fille *en* bleu? Est-ce que c'est *ta* sœur?   *in; your*

CHRISTINE: Non. C'est *ma* cousine Suzanne.   *my*

HÉLÈNE: Et les garçons dans la voiture de sport? Ce sont tes frères?

CHRISTINE: Non! Ce sont mes cousins.

HÉLÈNE: *Quel âge ont-ils?*   *How old are they?*

CHRISTINE: Jean-François *a vingt et un ans* et Gérard a dix-neuf ans.   *is 21*
Ils sont très sympathiques.

HÉLÈNE: Ah . . . Et le garçon en jaune? Il *a l'air* sympathique aussi!   *seems*
Qui est-ce?

CHRISTINE: Écoute, Hélène! Tu es trop *curieuse!*   *curious*

HÉLÈNE: Ah, ah! C'est ton petit ami, *je parie!*   *I bet*

stages
chamois

ÉCOLE DE SKI été

hiver

LA PLAGNE

E.S.F. LA PLAGNE
E.S.F. PLAGNE-VILLAGES
73210 LA PLAGNE

Tél. (79) 09 00 40
(79) 09 04 40

Où va Christine en hiver? Où est La Plagne? Comment s'appelle la cousine de Christine?
Comment s'appellent les cousins de Christine? Qui est le garçon en jaune?

Let's be on very friendly terms. In the following questions you will be addressed as **tu**. The questions are about people you know.

1. Comment s'appelle **ton** père (*your father*)?　　Il s'appelle . . .
2. Comment s'appelle **ta** mère (*your mother*)?　　Elle s'appelle . . .
3. Comment s'appelle **ton** meilleur ami?　　Il . . .
4. Comment s'appelle **ta** meilleure amie?　　Elle . . .
5. Comment s'appellent **tes** cousins?　　Ils . . .
6. Comment s'appellent **tes** cousines?　　Elles . . .

OBSERVATIONS　Str. A　　OPTIONAL

Reread the above questions. The words in heavy type all mean *your*.
They are called *possessive adjectives*.

• Which possessive adjective is used before a *masculine singular* noun (**père**)?　ton
before a *feminine singular* noun (**mère**)?　ta
before a *masculine plural* noun (**cousins**)?　tes
before a *feminine plural* noun (**cousines**)?　tes

NOTES CULTURELLES　OPTIONAL

1. Le ski en France　How far do you live from a ski area?
In France skiing is a very popular sport, and many teenagers
spend Christmas and February vacations on the slopes.
Some schools have organized special **classes de neige,**
where entire school groups go to a ski area and combine
classes in the morning with skiing in the afternoon.

The most popular ski resorts are located in the Alps and the
Pyrenees. **La Plagne,** at an altitude of about 6,000 feet, is
one of the highest and most modern ski areas in the Alps.

2. La photo (la photographie)　The art of photography
was discovered by two Frenchmen: **Nicéphore Niepce** and
Jacques Daguerre. In fact, the first photographs were called
"daguerreotypes" (1839). Today photography is a favorite
pastime of many French young people.

SUGGESTED REALIA: travel brochures advertising ski areas in France or Switzerland. You may obtain these brochures at
your local travel agency and bring them to class. Some popular French ski resorts are Val d'Isère, Chamonix, and Courchevel.

Vocabulaire pratique

NOMS:	**un album**	*album*	**une photo**	*photograph, picture*
			les vacances	*vacation*
	un petit ami	*boyfriend*	**une petite amie**	*girlfriend*
	un meilleur ami	*best friend* (male)	**une meilleure amie**	*best friend* (female)
EXPRESSIONS:	**dans**	*in*	La photo est **dans** l'album.	
	trop	*too, too much*	Tu parles **trop.** Tu es **trop** curieux.	

Structure

A. Les adjectifs possessifs: *mon, ma, mes; ton, ta, tes*

One way of indicating possession and relationship is to use *possessive adjectives*.
Note the forms of the possessive adjectives **mon** *(my)* and **ton** *(your)*
in the chart below:

	SINGULAR	PLURAL	
Masculine	mon	mes	mon cousin · mes cousins mon̮ ami · mes̮ amis
Feminine	ma ↓ mon (+ vowel sound)	mes	ma cousine · mes cousines mon̮ amie · mes̮ amies
Masculine	ton	tes	ton disque · tes disques ton̮ album · tes̮ albums
Feminine	ta ↓ ton (+ vowel sound)	tes	ta sœur · tes sœurs ton̮ amie · tes̮ amies

Possessive adjectives agree with the nouns they introduce.

→ French speakers use **ton, ta, tes** with people whom they address as **tu**.
   Paul, tu as **tes** livres avec toi?

→ **Ma** and **ta** become **mon** and **ton** when the next word begins with a vowel sound.
   Hélène est **mon** amie.   Où est **ton** auto?

→ There is liaison after **mon, ton, mes, tes** when the next word begins with a vowel sound.

ACTIVITÉ 1 Le tour de l'école *(Around school)*

Marc is showing his school to his cousin Michèle. Play the role of Marc.

→ l'école   **Voici mon école.**

1. le camarade
2. la camarade
3. l'ami Charles
4. l'amie Élisabeth
5. la classe
6. les livres
7. les professeurs
8. les amis

ACTIVITÉ 2   Départ *(Departure)*

Pierre is packing his suitcase and cannot find the things listed below. His sister Annie tells him that she does not have them. Play both roles.

→ la raquette   Pierre: **Où est ma raquette?**
　　　　　　　　Annie: **Je n'ai pas ta raquette.**

1. le short
2. la caméra
3. l'appareil-photo
4. la guitare

5. les lunettes de soleil   où sont
6. le transistor
7. les disques   où sont
8. le tee-shirt

ACTIVITÉ 3   Expression personnelle   OPTIONAL

Say what your favorites are, according to the model. (Note: **préféré** means *favorite*.)

→ la ville préférée   **Ma ville préférée est San Francisco (Boston, Atlanta, . . .)**

1. le disque préféré
2. le livre préféré
3. le film préféré
4. le programme de télé préféré
5. le jour préféré
6. le mois préféré
7. la saison préférée
8. le restaurant préféré

Additional cues: **la couleur préférée, l'acteur préféré, l'actrice préférée, le musée préféré, l'instrument préféré**

Vocabulaire spécialisé   La famille

NOMS: **La famille proche** (*Immediate family*)

un père	*father*	**une mère**	*mother*	**les parents**	*parents*
un grand-père	*grandfather*	**une grand-mère**	*grandmother*	**les grands-parents**	*grandparents*
un fils /fis/	*son*	**une fille**	*daughter*	**les enfants**	*children*
un frère	*brother*	**une sœur**	*sister*		

✓ ***ACTIVITÉ 4***   **La famille de Christine**

Hélène is looking at Christine's photograph album. Hélène asks whether the people in the pictures are members of her family, and Christine says that they are. Play the two roles.

→ la cousine Lucie   Hélène: **C'est ta cousine Lucie?**
                 Christine: **Oui, c'est ma cousine Lucie.**

1. le père
2. la tante
3. le grand-père
4. l'oncle André
5. la grand-mère
6. la mère
7. les cousins
8. les cousines

NOMS: **La famille éloignée** *(Distant family)*

un oncle *uncle*	**une tante** *aunt*	**les parents** *relatives*
un cousin *cousin* (male)	**une cousine** *cousin* (female)	

ADJECTIFS: **jeune** ≠ **âgé** *young* ≠ *old*

Note: **Les parents** may mean either *parents* or *relatives*.

B. L'âge

To ask someone's age, the French say:

Quel âge avez-vous? or **Quel âge as-tu?**

To state how old someone (or something) is, the French use the following expression:

avoir . . . ans	Mon père **a 42 ans.**	*My father is 42 (years old).*
	Mes cousines **ont 16 ans.**	*My cousins are 16 (years old).*

➔ Although the words *years old* may be left out in an English expression of age, the equivalent French sentence can *never* omit the word **ans**.

ACTIVITÉ 5 Expression personnelle

Say how old the following people are by completing the sentences below. If you do not know for sure, make a guess!

1. Moi, j'ai . . .
2. Mon père . . .
3. Ma mère . . .
4. Mon meilleur ami . . .
5. Ma meilleure amie . . .
6. Mon oncle préféré . . .
7. Ma cousine préférée . . .
8. Le professeur . . .

C. La construction: nom + *de* + nom

Compare the word order in French and English.

J'ai une raquette.	C'est une **raquette de tennis.**	*It's a tennis racket.*
Paul a une voiture.	C'est une **voiture de sport.**	*It's a sports car.*
Tu as une classe.	C'est une **classe d'anglais.**	*It's an English class.*
Qui est le professeur?	C'est le **professeur de musique.**	*He's the music teacher.*

When a noun modifies another noun, French speakers frequently use the construction:

> main noun + **de** + modifying noun
> ↓
> **d'** (+ vowel sound)

➜ In French the *main noun* comes *first*. In English the main noun comes second.

➜ There is no article after **de.**

ACTIVITÉ 6   Complétez...

Complete the following sentences with an expression made up of **de** + underlined noun.

➜ J'aime le <u>sport</u>. J'ai une voiture . . .   **J'ai une voiture de sport.**

1. Claire aime le <u>ping-pong</u>. Elle a une raquette . . .
2. Nous adorons le <u>jazz</u>. Nous écoutons un concert . . .
3. Jacques aime la <u>musique classique</u>. Il écoute un programme . . .
4. Vous étudiez l'<u>anglais</u>. Vous avez un livre . . .
5. Tu étudies le <u>piano</u>. Aujourd'hui tu as une leçon . . .
6. Thomas et Paul aiment l'<u>espagnol</u>. Ils ont un bon professeur . . .
7. Je regarde mes <u>photos</u>. J'ai un album . . .

UN JEU   OPTIONAL

Form logical sentences similar to the models below, using elements of columns A, B, C, and D. How many sentences can you make in five minutes or less?

A	B	C	D	
je	avoir	des disques	tennis	volley
Paul	écouter	un concert	musique disco	ping-pong
Christine	regarder	un programme	musique classique	sport
nous		un match (*game*)	piano	français
		une classe	basket	
		une raquette		

➜ **Nous regardons un match de volley.**
➜ **J'ai une raquette de ping-pong.**

Prononciation

Le son /ø/

Model word: d<u>eu</u>x

Practice words: <u>eu</u>x, bl<u>eu</u>, pl<u>eu</u>t, curi<u>eu</u>se, <u>Eu</u>gène, j<u>eu</u>, j<u>eu</u>di

Practice sentences: <u>Eu</u>génie est trop curi<u>eu</u>se.

Ils ont d<u>eu</u>x livres bl<u>eu</u>s avec <u>eu</u>x.

The sound /ø/ is pronounced with the lips rounded and tense. The tip of the tongue touches the lower front teeth.

Comment écrire /ø/: **eu**

Entre nous

Expression pour la conversation

To say that someone (or something) is attractive (or interesting), the French often use the following expression:

pas mal —Cette fille est jolie, n'est-ce pas?
—Oui, elle est **pas mal**.

> Pas mal is invariable. In conversational style, the negative ne is often omitted before the verb, although pas mal is a negative expression.

Mini-dialogue OPTIONAL

Henri regarde les photos de Monique. Il *trouve que* la cousine de Monique est très jolie, mais . . .

     HENRI: Qui est-ce, *cette* fille? C'est ta sœur?

MONIQUE: Non, c'est ma cousine.

     HENRI: Elle est pas mal. Quel âge est-ce qu'elle a?

MONIQUE: Elle a seize ans.

     HENRI: Dis, Monique . . .

MONIQUE: Oui?

     HENRI: Quel est le numéro de téléphone de ta cousine?

MONIQUE: C'est le 70-22 . . . à Tahiti![1]

thinks that

that

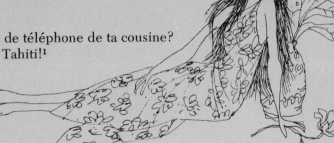

L'art du dialogue

a) Act out the dialog between Monique and Henri.
b) Now the roles are reversed. It is **Monique** who is asking about **Henri**'s cousin. Act out the new dialog, replacing **cette fille** by **ce garçon**, **sœur** by **frère**, and **cousine** by **cousin**. Make the necessary changes.

[1]Tahiti is a French island in the South Pacific.

Leçon 4

Vive les grandes vacances!

Bonjour!
Je m'appelle Olivier Pécoul.
Nous habitons à Paris, mais en été nous allons en vacances
  à La Grande-Motte.
Voici l'*immeuble* où nous habitons là-bas.

apartment house

Monsieur Moreau habite au premier *étage*
  avec *sa femme* et sa fille.

floor
his wife

Mademoiselle Lamblet habite au
  deuxième étage avec son père et sa
  mère.

Paul, mon meilleur ami, habite au
  troisième étage avec sa sœur et ses
  parents.

Comment s'appelle le meilleur
ami d'Olivier? Où est-ce qu'il
habite?

Mademoiselle Imbert habite au quatrième
  étage avec son chien Malice, ses deux
  chats Neptune et Pompon, son
  perroquet Coco et son canari Froufrou.
  (Je *pense que* c'est une personne très
  intéressante, mais mon père pense
  qu'elle est un peu bizarre.)

parrot
think that

Pourquoi est-ce que le père
d'Olivier pense que Mademoiselle
Imbert est bizarre?

Monsieur et Madame Martinot habitent au
  cinquième étage avec *leur* fils et leurs
  deux filles.

their

Et au sixième étage habite un garçon
  super-intelligent et très sympathique!
  Et *ce* garçon . . . c'est moi!

À quel étage habite Olivier?

that

On a detailed map of France, you may want to locate the following popular beach resorts:
On the Atlantic: La Baule, Trouville, Deauville, Les Sables-d'Olonne, Bayonne, Biarritz, Saint-Jean-de-Luz
On the Mediterranean: Cannes, Nice, Saint-Tropez

CONVERSATION

How well do you know the families of your best friends. Let's see.
(If you are not sure of an answer, use your imagination!)

A. Qui est ton meilleur ami?

1. Comment s'appelle **son** père?
2. Comment s'appelle **sa** mère?
3. Comment s'appellent **ses** frères
(ou **ses** sœurs)?

B. Qui est ta meilleure amie?

4. Comment s'appelle **son** père?
5. Comment s'appelle **sa** mère?
6. Comment s'appellent **ses** frères
(ou **ses** sœurs)?

OBSERVATIONS   Str. A

Reread the questions above. Compare the possessive adjectives in heavy type used in parts A and B. son père   son père

- How do you say *his* father? *her* father?   sa mère
- How do you say *his* mother? *her* mother?   sa mère
- How do you say *his* brothers? *her* brothers?

  ses frères   ses frères

NOTE CULTURELLE   OPTIONAL

Les grandes vacances

Do you go away for summer vacation (**les grandes vacances**)? Or do you stay at home and look for a job? In France very few teenagers work during the summer, for vacation time is devoted strictly to relaxation. Most young people spend their vacations with their families away from home. Many go to the country or to the mountains, but the favorite vacation spots are the beaches along the Atlantic (**l'Atlantique**) and the Mediterranean (**la Méditerranée**). **La Grande-Motte** is a new summer resort in southern France.

Vocabulaire spécialisé   Les animaux domestiques

un animal	animal
un chat	cat
un chien	dog
un cheval	horse
un oiseau	bird
un poisson	fish
un poisson rouge	goldfish

Note: Nouns which end in **-al** form their plural in **-aux: des animaux, des chevaux.**
Nouns which end in **-eau** form their plural in **-eaux: des oiseaux.**

VOCABULARY EXPANSION: **un canari, un perroquet** *(parrot),* **une perruche** *(parakeet),* **un serpent,** **un cochon d'Inde** *(guinea pig),* **un hamster** (no liaison), **une souris blanche** *(white mouse)*

Structure

A. L'adjectif possessif: *son, sa, ses*

Note the forms of the possessive adjective **son** (*his, her, its*):

	SINGULAR	PLURAL		
Masculine	son	ses	son vélo son͜ ami	ses disques ses͜ amis
Feminine	sa ↓ son (+ vowel sound)	ses	sa radio son͜ amie	ses photos ses͜ amies

→ **Sa** becomes **son** before a vowel sound.

→ There is liaison after **son** and **ses** when the next word begins with a vowel sound.

Note the uses of the possessive adjective:

le vélo de Marc:	**son** vélo	***his*** *bicycle*	It is possible to distinguish
le vélo de Christine:	**son** vélo	***her*** *bicycle*	between *his* and *her* by adding
la radio de Marc:	**sa** radio	***his*** *radio*	à lui or à elle after the noun.
la radio de Christine:	**sa** radio	***her*** *radio*	
les photos de Marc:	**ses** photos	***his*** *pictures*	
les photos de Christine:	**ses** photos	***her*** *pictures*	

→ The choice between **son, sa, ses** depends on the *gender* (masculine or feminine) and the *number* (singular or plural) of the *following* noun. It does *not* depend on the gender of the owner.

The same pattern holds true for things:

la radio de la voiture	sa radio	*its radio*
les photos du livre	ses photos	*its pictures*

ACTIVITÉ 1   Chez Marc

Paul wants to know whether the following things belong to Marc. Olivier answers *yes*. Play the two roles.

→ le vélo   Paul: **Est-ce que c'est le vélo de Marc?**
              Olivier: **Oui, c'est son vélo.**

1. la guitare
2. les disques
3. l'électrophone
4. les livres
5. le téléviseur
6. les posters
7. l'album de photos
8. la photo
9. la caméra
10. les lunettes de soleil
11. l'appareil-photo
12. la moto

Use **ce sont** with items 2, 4, 6, 10.

VOUS AVEZ UNE AUTOMOBILE

AVEZ-VOUS UN VÉLO?

LE VÉLO, C'EST LA SANTE

ACTIVITÉ 2   Chez Marie et Christophe

The animals or things in part A belong to **Marie.** Those in part B belong to
her brother **Christophe.** Point them out, as in the models.

	A: Marie		B: Christophe
→ le vélo	**C'est son vélo.**	→ le disque	**C'est son disque.**

A: Marie		B: Christophe	
1. la radio	5. le poisson rouge	9. la guitare	13. les livres
2. le sac	6. la guitare	10. l'électrophone	14. les oiseaux
3. le chien	7. les disques	11. le chat	15. les photos
4. l'album	8. les cassettes	12. le cheval	16. les disques

Be sure students use **ce sont** with plural items.

ACTIVITÉ 3   Invitations

The following people are each inviting a friend or relative to the school
dance. Express this according to the model.

→ Michel: la petite amie   **Michel invite sa petite amie.**

1. André: la cousine	4. Pascal: l'amie Sophie	7. Guillaume: l'amie Janine
2. Jean-Claude: la sœur	5. Monique: le cousin	8. Paul: l'amie Thérèse
3. Marie-Noëlle: le frère	6. Nathalie: l'ami Antoine	

B. L'adjectif possessif: *leur, leurs*

The possessive adjective **leur** *(their)* has the following forms:

	SINGULAR	PLURAL	
Masculine	leur	leurs	**leur** cousin **leurs** livres **leur** album **leurs** amis
Feminine	leur	leurs	**leur** cousine **leurs** photos **leur** école **leurs** amies

→ There is liaison after **leurs** before a vowel sound.

→ The use of **leur** or **leurs** depends on whether the noun introduced is *singular* or *plural*.

le chien de Paul et de Philippe: **leur** chien   *their dog*
les chats de Paul et de Philippe: **leurs** chats   *their cats*

ACTIVITÉ 4   Les millionnaires

Monsieur and Madame Richard are millionaires. Imagine you are showing
their estate to a friend. Point out the items below.

→ la maison   **Voici leur maison.**

1. la piscine	3. la Rolls Royce	5. les chiens	7. l'hélicoptère
2. la Mercédès	4. le parc	6. les chevaux	8. le court de tennis

Cognates are sometimes introduced into the activities so that students learn to recognize and handle them.
These words are not considered active vocabulary.

The x of **deuxième, sixième, dixième,** etc. is pronounced /z/.
There is no liaison before **huitième** and **onzième: un huitième (onzième) étage.**
With numbers ending in **un,** the regular pattern is followed: **le vingt et unième président.**

C. Les nombres ordinaux   This may be presented for recognition only.

Numbers like *first, second,* and *third* are used to rank persons or things, to put them in a given order. They are called *ordinal numbers.* Compare the ordinal numbers with the regular numbers.

(2)	**deux**	**deuxième**	Février est le **deuxième** mois de l'année.
(3)	**trois**	**troisième**	Mercredi est le **troisième** jour de la semaine.
(4)	**quatre**	**quatrième**	J'habite au **quatrième** étage *(floor).*
(12)	**douze**	**douzième**	Qui habite au **douzième** étage?

To form ordinal numbers, the French use the following pattern:

> **number   (minus final e, if any)   +   ième**

For extra practice with ordinals you may have students rank:

Exceptions: un (une)   →   **premier (première)**
                       cinq   →   **cinquième**
                       neuf   →   **neuvième**

—the days of the week: **Mardi est le deuxième jour.**
—the months of the year: **Mars est le troisième mois.**
—the US presidents: **Lincoln est le seizième président.**
—team standings: **Les Red Sox sont la première équipe** *(team).*

→ Ordinal numbers are adjectives and come *before* the noun.

✓ **ACTIVITÉ 5**   **La course de bicyclettes** *(The bicycle race)*

Give the order of arrival of the following participants in the bicycle race.

→ Jacques (6)   **Jacques est sixième.**

1. Catherine (4)
2. Henri (7)
3. Paul (8)
4. Marie-Françoise (2)
5. Thomas (1)
6. Jacqueline (10)
7. Isabelle (11)
8. Marc (12)

UN JEU

The people in column A cannot do the things in column B, because they do not have the things in column C. Express this in logical sentences, as in the models below. How many different sentences can you make in five minutes?

A	B	C
Paul	jouer au ping-pong	le téléviseur
Suzanne	jouer au tennis	la radio
Charles et Henri	regarder le match	l'électrophone
Annie et Pauline	écouter le concert	la voiture
mes cousins	voyager	la raquette
mes amies	danser	les disques
mon meilleur ami	aller à la campagne	la moto
ma sœur	écouter la musique	

→ **Annie et Pauline ne vont pas à la campagne parce qu'elles n'ont pas leur voiture.**
→ **Ma sœur ne joue pas au ping-pong parce qu'elle n'a pas sa raquette.**

Prononciation

Le son /œ/

Model word: h<u>eu</u>re

Practice words: n<u>eu</u>f, l<u>eu</u>r, s<u>œu</u>r, act<u>eu</u>r, profess<u>eu</u>r, j<u>eu</u>ne

Practice sentence: L<u>eu</u>r s<u>œu</u>r arrive à n<u>eu</u>f h<u>eu</u>res.

Comment écrire /œ/: usually **eu;** sometimes **œu**

Note: The letters **eu** are usually pronounced /œ/ before a final pronounced
consonant other than /z/ (as in the ending **-euse**).

Contrast: /œ/ l**eu**r   /ø/ curi**eu**se

Entre nous

Expression pour la conversation

To show that you understand, or agree with a statement, you can say:

Ah bon! *All right!*   **Ah bon!** Je comprends (*understand*) maintenant.

Mini-dialogue   OPTIONAL

SUZANNE: Où est Philippe?

CLAIRE: Il est avec son oncle, dans son *bateau.*   boat

SUZANNE: Dans son bateau? Philippe a un bateau
maintenant? Formidable!

CLAIRE: Mais non, c'est son oncle qui a le bateau.

SUZANNE: Ah bon! Je comprends maintenant.

L'art du dialogue

a) Act out the dialog between Suzanne and Claire.
b) Now imagine that Philippe is with his aunt. Replace **oncle** by **tante**, and make all
necessary changes.

UNITÉ 3

Leçon 5   L'album de timbres

STRUCTURES TO OBSERVE
• the construction **être à** to indicate possession
• the possessive adjectives **notre, nos** and **votre, vos**

Scène 1

Un jour, Pierre va dans le *grenier* et trouve un album de timbres.   *attic*
«À *qui est-il?*» demande Pierre à ses cousins.   *"To whom does it belong?"*
Il y a beaucoup de candidats pour *cet* album.   *this*

PIERRE:	À qui est l'album?
BERNARD:	Je pense qu'il est à mon frère.
JACQUES:	Non, il n'est pas à lui. Il est à moi.
PHILIPPE:	Non, il n'est pas à toi. Il est à moi.
PAUL ET HENRI:	Ce n'est pas vrai! Il est à nous!
	Regardez! Il y a *nos* initiales sur la *couverture*.
PIERRE:	S'il y a *vos* initiales, il est à vous!
	Tenez! Voilà votre album!

our; cover
your
Look!

Scène 2

Paul et Henri regardent l'album et *découvrent* . . . qu'il est *vide*.   *discover; empty*

PAUL:	Eh Pierre! Ce n'est pas notre album de timbres.
	Il n'est pas à nous. Est-ce qu'il est à toi, Jacques?
JACQUES:	Non, il est au frère de Bernard!
BERNARD:	Non, il n'est pas à lui! Il est à toi, Philippe.
PHILIPPE:	Il n'est pas à moi!
PIERRE:	Alors, à qui est-il?
HENRI:	Eh bien, *il n'est à personne!*

it doesn't belong to anyone

Où est-ce que Pierre trouve un album de timbres? Qui sont les candidats pour l'album? Est-ce qu'il y a beaucoup de timbres dans l'album?

In the following questions you are asked if you have certain things
with you now.

1. Avez-vous **votre** livre de français avec vous?
2. Avez-vous **votre** radio avec vous?
3. Avez-vous **vos** disques?
4. Avez-vous **vos** photos?

OBSERVATIONS   Str. A   OPTIONAL

In the above questions the words in heavy type are the possessive
adjectives which correspond to **vous**.

• What is the form of this possessive adjective before a *singular* noun?   votre
• What form is used before a *plural* noun?   vos

NOTE CULTURELLE   OPTIONAL

Les timbres français

Do you collect stamps? For many French people, young and
old, stamp collecting is a favorite hobby. Indeed, French post-
age stamps are very beautiful. Many of them have an educational value: they depict famous persons, monuments,
buildings, landscapes, and works of art. Special issues com-
memorate historical and scientific events. A study of French
stamps is, in fact, an excellent introduction to French culture.

SUGGESTED REALIA: French stamps.

Vocabulaire pratique

NOM:	**un timbre**	*stamp*	
VERBES:	**demander à**	*to ask*	Paul **demande:** Où est l'album?
	penser	*to think*	Je **pense** que c'est l'album de Philippe.
	trouver	*to find*	Nous ne **trouvons** pas ton album.
EXPRESSIONS:	**que**	*that*	Paul pense **que** c'est son album.
	si	*if*	Je ne sais pas **si** Jean va téléphoner.
	sur	*on*	Les initiales sont **sur** l'album.

Note: **Si** becomes **s'** before **il** and **ils**. However, no elision occurs with **elle** or **elles**.
Contrast:
Je demande à Paul **s'**il a mon album.
Je demande à Marie **si** elle a mon livre de français.

Structure

A. Les adjectifs possessifs: *notre, nos; votre, vos*

The possessive adjectives **notre** *(our)* and **votre** *(your)* have the following forms:

	SINGULAR	PLURAL		
Masculine/ Feminine	**notre**	**nos**	**notre** cousin **notre** amie	**nos** cousins **nos** amies
Masculine/ Feminine	**votre**	**vos**	**votre** album **votre** sœur	**vos** albums **vos** sœurs

➔ There is liaison after **nos** and **vos** before a vowel sound.

➔ The French use **votre** and **vos** when speaking to —

several people: (aux élèves) { Voici **votre** école.
Voici **vos** livres.

one person whom they address as **vous**: (au professeur) { Voici **votre** école.
Voici **vos** livres.

Be sure students pronounce the **o** in **notre** and **votre** like the **o** in **bonne**.
Note: When **notre** and **votre** come before a vowel sound, the **e** is dropped.
This is similar to the pronunciation of **quatre heures**.

ACTIVITÉ 1 Là-bas

In a big department store a customer is looking for various things. The person at the information desk points out where they are to be found. Play both roles.

➔ les disques

Le client (La cliente): **Où sont vos disques?**
L'employé (L'employée): **Nos disques sont là-bas.**

1. les livres
2. les posters
3. les radios
4. les cassettes
5. le restaurant
6. la cafétéria
7. les albums de timbres
8. les caméras

MAISON-LOISIRS
verrerie, vaisselle,
électroménager - 3ᵉ ét.
radio - t.v. - photo : r.-c.
ameublement, éclair. : 3ᵉ ét.
tapis : 4ᵉ ét.
sport, loisirs, jardin : 4ᵉ ét.
centre de bricolage : 4ᵉ ét.
HOME-LEISURE
glassware, table-ware,
household appliances 3rd f.
radio, TV, photo. : g.-f.
furniture, light fittings
3rd floor
carpeting - 4th floor
sport, leisure, garder. 4th f.
Do-it-yourself centre : 4th f.

CADEAUX
souvenirs et articles de
Nice, parfums, bijoux,
disques, livres et articles
de fumeurs :
rez-de-chaussée
orfèvrerie : 3ᵉ étage
GIFTS
souvenirs of Nice,
perfumes, jewelry,
records, books
and gifts for the smoker
ground floor
golds and silverware :
3rd floor

Galeries Lafayette

B. Récapitulation: les adjectifs possessifs

Review the possessive adjectives in the chart below:

THE OWNER	THE POSSESSIVE ADJECTIVE			ENGLISH EQUIVALENT
	before a singular noun		before a plural noun	
	Masculine	*Feminine*		
je tu il, elle	mon ton son	ma (mon +vowel) ta (ton +vowel) sa (son +vowel)	mes tes ses	*my* *your* *his, her, its*
nous vous ils, elles	notre votre leur		nos vos leurs	*our* *your* *their*

→ The gender and the number of a possessive adjective are determined only by the *noun it introduces*.

Voici Monique et **sa** collection. *Here is Monique and **her** collection.*
Voici Robert et **sa** collection. *Here is Robert and **his** collection.*

ACTIVITÉ 2 Au revoir!

The following people are taking a trip to Canada, and their friends and family are seeing them off. Say with whom each person is arriving at the airport.

→ Monique (le petit ami et les cousines)
Monique arrive avec son petit ami et ses cousines.

1. Jacques (le père et la mère)
2. Pauline (la sœur et le frère)
3. Henri (l'oncle et la tante)
4. Isabelle (les cousins et les cousines)
5. Pierre (les parents et la grand-mère)
6. Monsieur Dumas (la fille et les fils)
7. moi (les amis et la sœur)
8. toi (les amies et le frère)
9. Louis et André (le père et la tante)
10. Hélène et Sylvie (la mère et l'oncle)
11. vous (les amis et la cousine)
12. nous (les amies et le cousin)

ACTIVITÉ 3 La surprise-partie OPTIONAL

Say what everyone is bringing to the party. Use the appropriate possessive adjectives.

→ vous (un électrophone et des disques)
Vous arrivez avec votre électrophone et vos disques.

1. moi (une guitare)
2. toi (un livre et des disques)
3. nous (une voiture)
4. vous (des cassettes et un banjo)
5. Paul (une clarinette)
6. Michèle (des photos)
7. Jacqueline et Anne (des disques)
8. Marc et Philippe (un appareil-photo)

C. Être à

Review the contractions au and aux. Le livre est au professeur.
Il n'est pas aux élèves.

To indicate possession the French also use the expression **être à** *(to belong to).*

être à + { noun / stress / pronoun

La caméra **est à Marie.**	*The movie camera **belongs to Marie.***
Les timbres **sont à Pierre.**	*The stamps **belong to Pierre.***
L'album n'est pas **à lui.**	*The album does not **belong to him.***
Les photos **sont à moi.**	*The pictures **belong to me.***

Note the use of **être à** in questions:

À qui est le livre? { *To whom does the book **belong**? / **Whose** book **is** it?*

À qui sont les timbres? { *To whom do the stamps **belong**? / **Whose** stamps **are** they?*

Remind the students that in questions the preposition *always* comes at the beginning of the sentence:
À qui est la montre?
To whom does the watch belong?
(Whom does the watch belong to?)

√ *ACTIVITÉ 4* **Rendez à César . . .** *(Render unto Caesar . . .)*

Give back the things listed below to their rightful owners.
(Remember: **à + le → au; à + les → aux**)

→ les timbres (Pierre) **Les timbres sont à Pierre.**

1. l'appareil-photo (Jacques)
2. les photos (Sylvie)
3. la raquette (Philippe)
4. le chien (la fille)
5. le chat (le garçon)
6. les livres (le professeur)
7. la caméra (les cousins de Denise)
8. les cartes (les amis de Chantal)

ACTIVITÉ 5 **Une guitare**

Monique has found a guitar. She asks Marc if it belongs to the following people. Marc says *no*. Play both roles, using a stress pronoun in Marc's answers.

→ Paul   Monique: **Est-ce qu'elle est à Paul?**   VARIATION with les timbres: Est-ce qu'ils sont à Paul?
Marc: **Non, elle n'est pas à lui.**

1. Philippe
2. Élisabeth
3. Hélène
4. Georges
5. Paul et Jacques
6. Lucie et Charlotte
7. toi
8. vous

Tell what the people in column A are doing, selecting activities from column B. Then decide which objects of column C might belong to them. Be sure to use the expression **être à** according to the models below. How many sets of sentences can you make in five minutes?

A	B	C
je	skier	les livres
tu	voyager	les disques
Anne-Marie	écouter un concert	l'album
mon cousin	regarder un match	la radio
mes amis	jouer au tennis	le téléviseur
Louise et Anne	jouer au football	la voiture
nous	jouer au volleyball	le ballon (*ball*) de foot
vous	étudier	le ballon de volley
	collectionner les timbres	la raquette
		les skis

→ **Tu étudies. Les livres sont à toi.**

→ **Anne-Marie joue au volleyball. Le ballon de volley est à elle.**

Prononciation

Le son /o/

Model word: au

Practice words: beau, jaune, piano, radio, faux, vélo, drôle, hôtel, nos, vos

Practice sentences: Margot a un beau piano.

Voici vos vélos jaunes.

The sound /o/ is pronounced somewhat like the *o* in the English word *noble*, although it is shorter and more tense.

   Comment écrire /o/: **o, ô; au, eau**

Note de Prononciation: The letter **o** is pronounced:
/o/ at the end of a word, before a final silent consonant, and in the ending **-ose**; /ɔ/ otherwise.
Contrast: /o/ idiot, vélo, piano, nos, vos
              /ɔ/ idiote, école, Noël, notre, votre

Entre nous

Expression pour la conversation

To disagree with a request, you may say:

Pas question! *Nothing doing!* *No way!*

Mini-dialogue   OPTIONAL

La générosité d'Henri a des limites.

MONIQUE: Où est ton frère, Henri?

HENRI: Il n'est pas *là*. Il est en vacances.   *here*

MONIQUE: Dis, *est-ce que je peux* emprunter son   *may I*
électrophone?

HENRI: Bien sûr.

MONIQUE: Et ses disques?

HENRI: Ses disques aussi!

MONIQUE: Et ses cassettes?

HENRI: Bien sûr.

MONIQUE: Et sa guitare?

HENRI: Sa guitare! Mais mon frère n'a pas de guitare.

MONIQUE: Et la guitare là-bas?

HENRI: Ah *ça*, pas question! Elle n'est pas à lui.   *that*
Elle est à moi!

L'art du dialogue

a) Act out the dialog between Monique and Henri.

b) Now imagine that instead of looking for Henri's brother, Monique is looking for his sister. Replace **ton frère** by **ta sœur** and make the necessary changes. Act out the new dialog.

c) Imagine that Henri has two brothers and that Monique is looking for them. Replace **ton frère** by **tes frères** and make the necessary changes. Act out the new dialog.

d) Suppose that Monique is interested in Henri's banjo rather than his guitar. Act out the new dialog, replacing **sa guitare** by **son banjo**. Make the necessary changes.

SECTION MAGAZINE 2

Le langage des COULEURS

Est-ce que les couleurs parlent?
Bien sûr!
Chaque° couleur a une signification.
Voici le langage des couleurs:

ROUGE	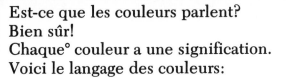	Courage. Passion.
ORANGE		Courage. Initiative.
JAUNE		Dynamisme.
VERT		Patience.
BLEU		Calme. Optimisme.
VIOLET		Mélancolie.
BLANC		Idéalisme. Sincérité.
NOIR		Romantisme. Mystère.

Est-ce que vous avez une couleur préférée?°
Est-ce que votre couleur préférée correspond à votre personnalité?

Chaque *Each*   **préférée** *favorite*

Petit catalogue des compliments . . . et des insultes

Les noms à la mode°

Comment est-ce que vous vous appelez?°
Jim, Bob ou Carl? Linda, Annie ou Sylvia?
Est-ce que votre nom est un nom à la mode?
En France, il y a des noms à la mode . . . et les modes° changent.

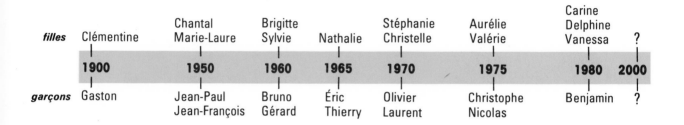

filles	Clémentine	Chantal Marie-Laure	Brigitte Sylvie	Nathalie	Stéphanie Christelle	Aurélie Valérie	Carine Delphine Vanessa	?
	1900	**1950**	**1960**	**1965**	**1970**	**1975**	**1980**	**2000**
garçons	Gaston	Jean-Paul Jean-François	Bruno Gérard	Éric Thierry	Olivier Laurent	Christophe Nicolas	Benjamin	?

Nicole et Jean-Pierre

sont heureux de vous annoncer la naissance de

Fabrice

le 28 Juin 1972

Monsieur
2, Ru

Le Docteur et Madame VALETTE,

Olivier et Charlotte,

sont heureux de vous annoncer la

naissance de

Renaud

Le 27 Mars 1976

135, rue de l'Ermitage   37100 Tours

naissances

Mme LHÉRITIER
de CHEZELLE
son arrière-grand-mère, laisse à
Delphine PRADEL
la joie d'annoncer la naissance
de son frère
Camille
Lyon, 19 octobre 1979

Mr. Nicholas RATUT
et Mme, née Patricia Willemetz,
partagent avec Alexandre la joie
d'annoncer la naissance de

Vanessa

Neuilly, le 1er septembre 1979.

Les noms à la mode *Popular names*   **Comment est-ce que vous vous appelez?** *What's your name?*
les modes *fashions*   ILLUSTRATIONS: **heureux** *happy*   **naissance** *birth*

Les secrets du VISAGE°

Regardez-vous° dans la glace!°
Regardez la forme de votre visage!
Avez-vous un visage ovale? rond? carré?°
C'est une question importante.

Certaines° personnes disent° en effet
que la forme de votre visage détermine
votre personnalité.

Vous avez un visage ovale . . .

Vous êtes très romantique . . .
Comme° les personnes ro-
mantiques, vous êtes
généreux,° mais vous êtes
aussi impressionnable.
Vous êtes un peu timide et
vous n'êtes pas toujours très
patient.
Vous aimez la musique et
vous aimez danser. Vous
adorez voyager.

Vous avez un visage rond . . .

Vous avez beaucoup de sens
pratique.
Vous êtes sérieux et vous
aimez l'action. Mais vous
n'êtes pas très tolérant.
Vous aimez les sports.

Vous avez un visage triangulaire . . .

Vous êtes une personne intellectuelle et vous
avez aussi un tempérament d'artiste.
Vous aimez exprimer° vos opinions et vous
aimez discuter° avec vos amis.

Vous avez un visage carré . . .

Vous êtes réaliste . . .
Vous avez aussi une grande
curiosité intellectuelle.
Vous avez un sens pratique
très développé.
En général, vous aimez
commander . . . mais vous
n'aimez pas être commandé.

Vous avez beaucoup
d'imagination, mais vous
n'êtes pas très organisé. Vous
êtes aussi assez superstitieux.
Vous avez beaucoup d'amis,
mais vous n'êtes pas toujours
très patient avec eux.
Vous détestez l'ordre et la
discipline.

Et maintenant analysez la personnalité de ces° Français célèbres.°

Napoléon, *empereur*

Brigitte Bardot, *actrice*

Jacques Cousteau, *explorateur*

---

visage *face*   **Regardez-vous** *Look at yourself*   **glace** *mirror*   **carré** *square*   **Certaines** *Some*   **disent** *say*
Comme *Like*   **généreux** *generous*   **exprimer** *to express*   **discuter** *to argue*   **ces** *these*   **célèbres** *famous*

Vive le vélomoteur!

Quel est le véhicule qui° a un moteur, deux roues,° et deux pédales? Le vélomoteur, bien sûr!

Le vélomoteur est très populaire en France. Chaque° jour des milliers° de jeunes Français utilisent° leur vélomoteur pour aller à l'école . . . En été, ils utilisent leur vélomoteur pour aller à la plage ou à la campagne.

Le vélomoteur a beaucoup d'avantages:
  Il est très pratique.
  Il est très économique.
  Et il n'est pas dangereux . . .
    si vous êtes prudent!

Vive le vélomoteur!

qui *that*   roues *wheels*   **Chaque** *Every*   des milliers *thousands*   utilisent *use*
ILLUSTRATION: **Stationnement: ne payez plus le droit de vous arrêter** *Parking: stop paying for the right to stop*

L'ART DES CADEAUX°

Choisir° un cadeau est souvent un problème.
Qu'est-ce que° vous allez choisir pour l'anniversaire d'un ami? pour
l'anniversaire d'une amie?
Ça dépend de° leur personnalité.
Voici des suggestions:

Pour un garçon	Pour une fille

Si le garçon est . . .

 élégant
un pull,°
une cravate°

 sportif
un tee-shirt

 intellectuel
un livre

 musicien
un disque

 romantique
une plante

bon avec les animaux
un chien

 votre meilleur ami
votre photo

Si la fille est . . .

 élégante
un pull,
un foulard°

 sportive
un tee-shirt

intellectuelle
un livre

 musicienne
deux billets° d'opéra
(un pour elle et un
pour vous)

 romantique
une plante, des fleurs°

 votre meilleure amie
votre photo

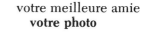

L'art des cadeaux *The art of gift-giving*   **Choisir** *To choose*   **Qu'est-ce que** *What*   **Ça dépend**
de *That depends on*   **pull** *pullover*   **cravate** *tie*   **foulard** *scarf*   **billets** *tickets*   **fleurs** *flowers*

L'album de photos de Brigitte

Bonjour! Je m'appelle Brigitte Martinot.
J'ai dix-sept ans et j'habite à Annecy.
Je vais au lycée° Berthollet où je suis élève de première.°
Voici quelques° photos de famille:

La fille avec le vélo, c'est moi. Je vais souvent à la campagne à vélo.

Voici mon père. Il est dentiste. Il a des lunettes drôles, n'est-ce pas?

Voici Maman. Elle aussi, elle travaille. Elle est chef° du personnel dans une banque. Elle a beaucoup de responsabilités.

Voici ma soeur Annie sur son vélomoteur.

Voici Pierre, mon frère. Il aime skier, mais ce n'est pas un champion...

Qui est-ce? Non, ce n'est pas mon cousin. C'est... mon petit ami! Comment s'appelle-t-il? Ah ça,° c'est un secret!

176

lycée *high school*   de première *11th grade*
quelques *some*   chef *head*   ça *that*

Avez-vous une bicyclette?   une radio?   un appareil-photo?

Voici la proportion de jeunes Français qui ont ces° objets:

radio   80%   appareil-photo   60%   électrophone   55%

bicyclette   65%   vélomoteur   18%

possessions *belongings*   **ces** *these*   ILLUSTRATION: **foire** *market*   **jouets** *toys*   **177**

Nos meilleurs amis

Quel est le meilleur ami de l'homme?
C'est le chien, naturellement!
Voici le portrait de quatre chiens
populaires en France.

Le terrier   Il y a de nombreuses espèces° de terriers: les fox-terriers, les terriers irlandais,° les terriers écossais,° les bull-terriers. Les terriers sont des chiens de chasse.° Ils sont de couleur blanche et noire ou blanche et jaune. Ils ont beaucoup de personnalité. Ce sont des chiens très intelligents . . . et souvent capricieux!

Le Saint-Bernard   Le Saint-Bernard est un chien très grand, très fort° et très musclé. Son courage est légendaire.

Le caniche   Il y a des caniches noirs, des caniches blancs, des caniches gris et des caniches bruns.° Le caniche est un chien extrêmement° intelligent et très loyal.

Le basset   Il s'appelle «basset» parce que c'est un chien bas sur pattes.° Le basset est un chien petit et très musclé. Il a la réputation d'être très courageux.

178   **de nombreuses espèces** *many kinds*   **irlandais** *Irish*   **écossais** *Scottish*   **de chasse** *hunting*
bruns *brown*   **extrêmement** *extremely*   **fort** *strong*   **bas sur pattes** *short-legged*

VIVE L'ÉCOLE!

À l'âge de onze ans, les jeunes Français entrent au collège, ou plus exactement° au C.E.S. (Collège d'Enseignement Secondaire). À l'âge de dix-sept ou dix-huit ans, ils passent° le « bac » (ou baccalauréat). En France, le baccalauréat représente la fin° des études° secondaires.

Voici la correspondance approximative entre° les études secondaires en France et aux États-Unis.

EN FRANCE			AUX ÉTATS-UNIS	
Âge	École	Classe	École	Classe
11 ans		sixième	elementary school	6th
12 ans	C.E.S.	cinquième		7th
13 ans		quatrième	junior high school	8th
14 ans		troisième		9th
15 ans		seconde		10th
16 ans	lycée	première	high school	11th
17 ans		terminale		12th

PROJETS CULTURELS

Projets individuels

1. *Get a French newspaper (Le Figaro, France-Soir) and look at the birth and wedding announcements. Make a list of the first names which are popular now (birth announcements) and those which were popular about twenty years ago (wedding announcements).*

2. *Using pictures of people in French magazines and newspapers, describe their personalities according to the shapes of their faces. Use the texts in* Les secrets du visage *as models.*

Projets de classe

1. *Prepare a bulletin board exhibit about French cars. Use advertisements from French and American magazines, newspaper clippings, and (if you wish) model cars.*

2. *Using pictures from French magazines (Paris-Match, Jours de France, etc.), make a display which shows French people at work and at play. Write a short caption (in French) for each picture.*

---

plus exactement *more exactly*   **passent** *take*   **fin** *end*   **études** *studies*   **entre** *between*
ILLUSTRATIONS: **langue vivante** *modern language*   **renforcé** *intensive*   **TP = travaux pratiques** *lab*
SN =sciences naturelles

OBJECTIVES

In this unit the students will learn to express themselves in simple shopping situations. They will learn how to use French money and how to make comparisons concerning people and things.

Language
- **acheter**
- **-ir** and **-re** verbs
- demonstrative and interrogative pronouns
- the comparative and the superlative forms
- expressions with **avoir**
- the impersonal subject pronoun **on**

Vocabulary
- clothing
- shops and shopping
- money

Culture

This unit introduces shopping customs, especially with respect to clothing, and stresses the importance of personal appearance.

UNITÉ 4
En ville

UNITÉ 4
Leçon 1   Au Bon Marché

STRUCTURES TO OBSERVE
- regular verbs in **-ir**
- the expression **qu'est-ce que?**
- numbers

Dans deux mois les vacances *commencent*!   *begin*
Aujourd'hui, Brigitte et Michèle vont en ville.
Elles vont dans un grand magasin *qui* s'appelle « Au Bon Marché ».   *which*
Pourquoi? *Pour regarder* les bikinis, bien sûr!   *To look at*

Scène 1. Brigitte, Michèle

BRIGITTE: Alors, Michèle, *qu'est-ce que tu choisis?*   *what are you choosing*
           le bikini jaune ou le bikini bleu?
MICHÈLE: Le bikini rouge! Regarde, il est *mignon!*   *cute*
BRIGITTE: Peut-être, . . . mais il est trop petit pour toi!
MICHÈLE: Ça n'a pas d'importance!
BRIGITTE: Comment! Ça n'a pas d'importance?
MICHÈLE: Je suis au régime . . . Je vais *maigrir!*   *to lose weight*

Scène 2. Brigitte, Michèle, une employée

L'EMPLOYÉE: Vous choisissez le bikini rouge?
MICHÈLE: Oui, Madame! Combien est-ce qu'il *coûte?*   *cost*
L'EMPLOYÉE: Il coûte *cent* francs, Mademoiselle.   *one hundred*
MICHÈLE: Euh . . . Et le bikini bleu?
L'EMPLOYÉE: *Quatre-vingts* francs.   *eighty*
BRIGITTE *(à Michèle)*:   Et *combien d'argent* as-tu?   *how much money*
MICHÈLE: Euh . . . Quatre-vingts francs . . .
           (à l'employée) Excusez-moi, Madame. Je ne choisis
           pas le bikini rouge . . . Je choisis le bikini bleu.
BRIGITTE: Dommage, le bikini rouge est vraiment très joli!
MICHÈLE: *Voyons,* Brigitte! Il est trop petit pour moi!   *Come on*

Où vont Brigitte et Michèle? Comment s'appelle le magasin où elles vont? Quel bikini est-ce que Michèle choisit dans la scène 1? Pourquoi? Quel bikini est-ce que Michèle choisit dans la scène 2? Pourquoi?

How good are you at arithmetic? Do you remember the numbers in French?
Let's see.

1. How much is *four times twenty* in English?
2. How do you say *four* in French? How do you say *twenty*? quatre/vingt
3. What do you think the number **quatre-vingts** means? eighty
4. How much is *eighty* plus *ten* in English?
5. What do you think the number **quatre-vingt-dix** means? ninety
6. How much is *eighty* plus *fifteen*?
7. What do you think the number **quatre-vingt-quinze** means? ninety-five

NOTE CULTURELLE   OPTIONAL

Le grand magasin

Where would you buy a tennis racket? a pair of shoes? a bicycle? a camera? Probably in a department store. To buy these items, many French people go to the **grand magasin.** One of the oldest and most famous **grands magasins** in Paris is **Au Bon Marché**. It was founded in the nineteenth century by a man who wanted to give everyone a chance to buy good but inexpensive items. **Bon marché** means *inexpensive.*

Vocabulaire pratique

NOMS:	**un magasin**	*store, shop*
	un grand magasin	*department store*
	un régime	*diet*
EXPRESSION:	**être au régime**	*to be on a diet* Je ne **suis** pas **au régime.**

Structure

If your students find that **choisir** is too much of a tongue twister, you may practice the forms of -ir verbs with **finir: Je finis à midi,** etc. You may also want to use a clock and review times: **Tu finis à trois heures,** etc.

A. Les verbes réguliers en -ir

Many French verbs end in **-ir.** Most of these verbs are conjugated like **choisir** *(to choose).* Note the forms of this verb in the present tense, paying special attention to the *endings.*

Infinitive	**choisir**		STEM	ENDINGS
Present	je **choisis**	un livre		**-is**
	tu **choisis**	des disques		**-is**
	il/elle **choisit**	des photos	(infinitive minus **-ir**) **chois-**+	**-it**
	nous **choisissons**	un vélo		**-issons**
	vous **choisissez**	une voiture		**-issez**
	ils/elles **choisissent**	une caméra		**-issent**

Note that all final consonants are silent.

bien choisir, c'est choisir la (S)amaritaine

Vocabulaire spécialisé   Verbes réguliers en *-ir*

choisir	*to choose*	Est-ce que tu **choisis** le bikini bleu?
finir	*to finish*	Les classes **finissent** à midi.
grossir	*to get fat, gain weight*	Marc **grossit** parce qu'il n'est pas au régime.
maigrir	*to get thin, lose weight*	Je **maigris** parce que je suis au régime.
réussir	*to succeed, pass* (a test)	Nous **réussissons** parce que nous étudions.
ne réussir pas	*to fail, flunk* (a test)	Vous **ne réussissez pas** parce que vous n'étudiez pas.

The negative form of the infinitive is **ne pas réussir.** The form **ne réussir pas** is given here so as not to confuse students at this point.

ACTIVITÉ 1   L'examen

Some students finish the exam and pass the course. Others do not finish and fail. Express this according to the models.

→ Paul finit.   **Il réussit.**

Catherine ne finit pas.   **Elle ne réussit pas.**

1. Je finis.
2. Tu ne finis pas.
3. Mes amis finissent.
4. Les mauvais élèves ne finissent pas.
5. Nous finissons.
6. Vous ne finissez pas.
7. Philippe ne finit pas.
8. Michèle finit.
9. Mes amies ne finissent pas.
10. Ils finissent.

ACTIVITÉ 2   Le régime

Some of Michèle's friends have decided to go on a diet and are losing weight.
The others are not on a diet and are gaining weight. Describe what is
happening to each of the people mentioned below according to the models.

→ Monique est au régime.   **Elle maigrit. Elle ne grossit pas.**
   André n'est pas au régime.   **Il grossit. Il ne maigrit pas.**

1. Nous sommes au régime.
2. Vous n'êtes pas au régime.
3. Danièle et Nicole sont au régime.
4. Paul et Jacques ne sont pas au régime.
5. Je suis au régime.
6. Tu n'es pas au régime.
7. Albert est au régime.
8. Sylvie n'est pas au régime.

ACTIVITÉ 3   Questions personnelles

1. À quelle heure finissent les classes aujourd'hui?
2. À quelle heure finit la classe de français?
3. Quand finit l'école cette année (*this year*)?
4. Quand vous allez au restaurant avec vos amis, est-ce que vous choisissez
   un restaurant cher (*expensive*)?
5. Quand vous êtes au restaurant avec votre famille, qui choisit le menu?

B. L'expression interrogative *qu'est-ce que*

Note the use of the interrogative expression **qu'est-ce que** (*what*) in the
sentences below.

Qu'est-ce que Michèle choisit?   Elle choisit un bikini.
Qu'est-ce qu'André regarde?   Il regarde un film.

To ask *what* people are doing, etc., the French use the following construction:

Qu'est-ce que   +   subject   +   verb   +   (rest of sentence)   ?
↓
Qu'est-ce qu' (+ vowel sound)

→ Note also the expression: **Qu'est-ce que c'est?**   *What is it? What's this?*
   Qu'est-ce que c'est?   C'est une Renault. C'est une voiture française.

With inverted questions only **que** is used: **Que choisit-elle? Que regardez-vous?**

ACTIVITÉ 4   Le transistor de Georges

Because Georges is always listening to his radio, he has trouble hearing
what Sophie tells him. He asks her to repeat what she said. Play both roles.

→ Je finis . . . (la leçon)   Georges: **Qu'est-ce que tu finis?**
                                Sophie: **Je finis la leçon.**

1. Je choisis . . . (des cassettes)
2. Je choisis . . . (un short)
3. Je regarde . . . (un match de tennis)
4. Je regarde . . . (un western)
5. J'écoute . . . (un concert)
6. Je visite . . . (un musée)
7. J'étudie . . . (le piano)
8. J'ai . . . (une guitare)

RÉVISION: les nombres

Review the numbers from 0 to 60 in Appendix 2.A on page 401.

ACTIVITÉ DE RÉVISION   **Problèmes de maths**   OPTIONAL

Do the following multiplications out loud. (**Fois** means *times*.)

→ 2 × 2   **deux fois deux, quatre**   You may want to use **font** for this exercise: **deux fois deux font quatre.**

1. 3 × 6	4. 6 × 10	7. 3 × 7	10. 15 × 3	13. 2 × 14
2. 2 × 11	5. 7 × 7	8. 3 × 13	11. 12 × 3	14. 5 × 11
3. 4 × 8	6. 8 × 7	9. 2 × 8	12. 3 × 17	15. 6 × 9

C. Les nombres de 60 à 100
You may practice these numbers by having the students count in sequence around the classroom: 60, 61, 62...; 60, 62, 64...; 60, 63, 66...

Read the numbers from 60 to 100, paying special attention to the way the French express the numbers 70, 80, and 90.

The ending **s** in **quatre-vingts** occurs only with the number 80.

60 **soixante**	80 **quatre-vingts**
61 **soixante et un**	81 **quatre-vingt-un**
62 **soixante-deux**	82 **quatre-vingt-deux**
63 **soixante-trois**	83 **quatre-vingt-trois**
64 **soixante-quatre**	84 **quatre-vingt-quatre**
65 **soixante-cinq**	85 **quatre-vingt-cinq**
66 **soixante-six**	86 **quatre-vingt-six**
67 **soixante-sept**	87 **quatre-vingt-sept**
68 **soixante-huit**	88 **quatre-vingt-huit**
69 **soixante-neuf**	89 **quatre-vingt-neuf**
70 **soixante-dix**[1]	90 **quatre-vingt-dix**
71 **soixante et onze**	91 **quatre-vingt-onze**
72 **soixante-douze**	92 **quatre-vingt-douze**
73 **soixante-treize**	93 **quatre-vingt-treize**
74 **soixante-quatorze**	94 **quatre-vingt-quatorze**
75 **soixante-quinze**	95 **quatre-vingt-quinze**
76 **soixante-seize**	96 **quatre-vingt-seize**
77 **soixante-dix-sept**	97 **quatre-vingt-dix-sept**
78 **soixante-dix-huit**	98 **quatre-vingt-dix-huit**
79 **soixante-dix-neuf**	99 **quatre-vingt-dix-neuf**
	100 **cent**

$4 \times 20 = 80$

$60 + 10 = 70$

$4 \times 20 + 10 = 90$

To practice listening comprehension, you may play "Loto" (Bingo).

ACTIVITÉ 5   **Week-end**

The following students are spending the weekend in the country. Say how much money each one has.

→ Philippe (60 F)   **Philippe a soixante francs.**

1. Michèle (65 F)	3. Marc (80 F)	5. Annette (85 F)	7. Alain (73 F)
2. Sylvie (75 F)	4. Antoine (95 F)	6. Robert (100 F)	8. Isabelle (91 F)

[1]In Switzerland, numbers from 70 to 99 follow the pattern from 20 to 69: 70 is **septante** (71 is **septante et un**, 72 is **septante-deux**, etc.), 80 is **octante**, and 90 is **nonante**.

ACTIVITÉ 6 Les bikinis OPTIONAL

Several bikinis are for sale. Each girl buys the most expensive one she can afford.

bikini bleu = 80 F	bikini jaune = 90 F	bikini rouge = 95 F

→ Suzanne (93 F) **Suzanne a quatre-vingt-treize francs.**
   Elle choisit le bikini jaune.

1. vous (87 F)   3. tu (100 F)   5. Marie (83 F)
2. elles (98 F)   4. Paulette (92 F)   6. Yvette (99 F)

Vocabulaire spécialisé L'argent

NOMS:	**l'argent**	*money*	**une pièce** *coin*	
	un billet	*bill, bank note*	You may introduce **la monnaie** *(change)*.	
ADJECTIFS:	**cher (chère)**	*expensive*	La raquette est **chère**.	
	bon marché	*inexpensive*	Les disques sont **bon marché**.	
VERBES:	**coûter**	*to cost*	Les cassettes **coûtent** vingt francs.	
	dépenser	*to spend*	Je n'aime pas **dépenser** mon argent.	

Note: The expression **bon marché** is invariable. It never takes endings to agree with the noun it modifies.

Bon marché is invariable because it is really a noun which means *good market*.

LOTO
c'est pas cher,
SIMPLE

ACTIVITÉ 7 Leur argent OPTIONAL

Help the following people count their money.

→ Albert a un billet de 50 francs et 3 pièces de 5 francs.
   Albert a soixante-cinq francs.

1. Sylvie a 2 billets de 50 francs.
2. Charles a 8 billets de 10 francs.
3. Michèle a 9 billets de 10 francs.
4. Marc a 8 billets de 10 francs et 2 pièces de 1 franc.
5. Annie a 8 billets de 10 francs et 11 pièces de 1 franc.
6. Paul a 9 billets de 10 francs et 1 pièce de 5 francs.

D. Les expressions interrogatives *combien* et *combien de*

Note the use of **combien** and **combien de** in the following sentences:

combien + verb   For simplicity the questions below use inversion. It is also possible to use **est-ce que**:
Combien est-ce que les disques coûtent? Combien de timbres est-ce que tu as?

    how much   **Combien** coûte le livre?   *How much does the book cost?*
                            Combien coûtent les disques?   *How much do the records cost?*

combien de + noun

    how much   **Combien d'**argent dépenses-tu?   *How much money are you*
                                                 spending?

    how many   **Combien de** timbres as-tu?   *How many stamps do you have?*

→ **Combien de** becomes **combien d'** before a vowel sound.

The construction **Combien est-ce que tu as de disques?** is not presented here.
Expressions of quantity are introduced in Unité 8.2.

ACTIVITÉ 8   Questions personnelles

1. Combien de frères avez-vous? combien de sœurs?
2. Combien de cassettes avez-vous? combien de disques?
3. Combien de garçons est-ce qu'il y a dans la classe? combien de filles?

Be sure students repeat the noun in their answers: **J'ai 20 cassettes.**

ACTIVITÉ 9   Les collections de Jean-Louis

Jean-Louis collects the following things. Sylvie asks him how many items
he has in each collection and how much they cost. Play both roles.

→ des disques   Jean-Louis: **J'ai des disques.**
                        Sylvie: **Combien de disques as-tu?**
                                Combien coûtent tes disques?

1. des posters   3. des pièces américaines   5. des disques de jazz
2. des timbres   4. des disques de musique disco   6. des photos

UN JEU   OPTIONAL

The people in column A are spending the amounts of money indicated in
parentheses. Say how many items from column B they are choosing. Many
combinations are possible. How many sentences similar to the models
below can you make in five minutes?

A	B
moi (75 francs)	un magazine (5 francs)
toi (60 francs)	un livre (15 francs)
Nicole (55 francs)	un disque (30 francs)
nous (100 francs)	une cassette (25 francs)
vous (95 francs)	
Pierre et Alain (90 francs)	

→ **Nous dépensons 100 francs. Nous choisissons trois disques et deux magazines.**

→ **Je dépense 75 francs. Je choisis deux disques et un livre.**

Prononciation

Le son /k/

Model word: <u>qu</u>'est-ce <u>qu</u>e

Practice words: <u>C</u>olette, <u>qu</u>and, <u>Qu</u>ébec, cin<u>q</u>, <u>qu</u>inze

Practice sentences: <u>Qu</u>'est-ce <u>qu</u>e <u>C</u>atherine choisit?

<u>C</u>laude a <u>qu</u>atre-vingt-<u>qu</u>atorze francs.

Hold a piece of paper in front of your mouth and pronounce the English words *cat* and *scat*. The paper moves when you say *cat* because you produce a puff of air as you pronounce the sound / k/. The paper does not move when you say *scat*. The French / k/ is always pronounced like the *k*-sound in *scat*, without a puff of air.

Comment écrire /k/: **c** (before **a, o, u**); **k, qu,** final **q**

Note: The letters **qu** practically always represent the sound / k/: **qui.**

Entre nous

Expression pour la conversation

Ça dépend! *It depends!* —Tu choisis le vélo vert ou le vélo blanc?

—Je ne sais pas . . . **Ça dépend!**

Mini-dialogue OPTIONAL

Les *échanges* d'Henri ne sont pas toujours très *équitables.* *trades; fair*

HENRI: Dis, Monique, combien de disques de jazz as-tu?

MONIQUE: Soixante-quinze!

HENRI: Très bien. *Je te propose* un échange. *I propose to you*

MONIQUE: Qu'est-ce que tu désires *échanger*? *to trade*

HENRI: Ta collection de disques de jazz *contre* ma collection de *against*
musique pop. Es-tu d'accord? *(in exchange for)*

MONIQUE: Ça dépend! Combien de disques de musique pop as-tu?

HENRI: Cinq ou six.

L'art du dialogue

a) Act out the dialog between Henri and Monique.

b) Henri proposes another trade: his French stamps (**les timbres français**) against Monique's American stamps (**les timbres américains**). Act out the new dialog, making the appropriate changes.

Leçon 2

Rien n'est parfait!

Cet après-midi, François et André sont dans un magasin de *vêtements. Ce* magasin s'appelle «Tout pour les jeunes».

This afternoon
clothing; This

Scène 1.

FRANÇOIS: Je vais *acheter* un *pull.*   *to buy; sweater*
ANDRÉ: Quel pull est-ce que tu achètes? Ce pull noir?
FRANÇOIS: Non, ce pull bleu.
ANDRÉ: Il est très chaud.
FRANÇOIS: . . . et très chic!
ANDRÉ *(qui regarde le prix):* Il est aussi très cher.
FRANÇOIS: Combien est-ce qu'il coûte?
ANDRÉ: Trois cents francs!
FRANÇOIS: *Oh mon Dieu! Quelle horreur!*   *My goodness!*
How awful!

Scène 2.

ANDRÉ: *Comment trouves-tu* cette *veste?*   *What do you think of;*
jacket
FRANÇOIS: Quelle veste? Cette veste-ci?
ANDRÉ: Non. Cette veste-là!
FRANÇOIS: Elle est très chic!
ANDRÉ: . . . et elle n'est pas chère!
FRANÇOIS: Mais elle est trop grande!
ANDRÉ: *Rien n'*est parfait!   *Nothing*

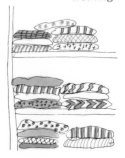

    Qu'est-ce que François va acheter? Combien coûte le pull? Est-ce qu'il est cher? Qu'est-ce que François pense de la veste? Est-ce que la veste est chère? Pourquoi est-ce que la veste n'est pas parfaite?

Let's discuss what you think about this class. Answer affirmatively or negatively.

1. Est-ce que vous aimez **ce** livre?
2. Est-ce que vous aimez **cette** classe?
3. Est-ce que vous aimez **ces** illustrations?

OBSERVATIONS   Str. D   OPTIONAL

In the above questions, the words in heavy type are used to point out specific things. They are called *demonstrative adjectives* and correspond to *this (these)* and *that (those)* in English.

• What is the form of the demonstrative adjective before a masculine singular noun (**livre**)? ce

before a feminine singular noun (**classe**)? cette

before a plural noun (**illustrations**)? ces

NOTE CULTURELLE   OPTIONAL

L'élégance française

Have you heard of **Pierre Cardin, Yves Saint-Laurent, Chanel?** These French designers have made French fashions known all over the world. French people, in general, tend to be rather fashion-conscious and pay careful attention to their personal appearance. For a French teenager, being well-dressed does not mean wearing expensive clothes, but wearing clothes that are well cut and colors that do not clash. It also means dressing to fit the occasion. Shorts and sneakers are fine for the beach, but not for going shopping or going out to eat. As for jeans, they are the uniform of French youth . . . as long as they fit well and are clean!

Vocabulaire pratique

NOMS:	**les jeunes**	*young people*
	le prix	*price*
ADJECTIVES:	**chaud**	*warm, hot*
	chic	*elegant, in style*
	parfait	*perfect*

You may want to teach **froid** *(cold).*

Note: The adjective **chic** is invariable: **un pull chic, une veste chic.**

SUGGESTED REALIA: fashion magazines *(Elle, Marie-Claire),* ads for French designer products (Cardin, Yves Saint-Laurent, Dior, etc.).

Other clothing items are presented on p.200.

Vocabulaire spécialisé
(modification)

Les vêtements *(Clothing)*   Les vêtements is active vocabulary.

Pour la campagne . . .

un anorak

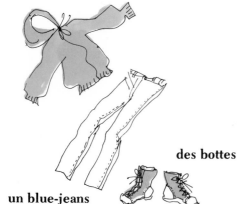

des bottes

un blue-jeans

Pour la ville . . .

un pull(-over)

des lunettes

un pantalon

des chaussures

une veste

Pour le sport . . .

un tee-shirt

un short

des chaussettes

Pour la plage . . .

un maillot de bain

des lunettes de soleil

des sandales

VERBE: **porter**   *to wear*   Qu'est-ce que vous **portez** aujourd'hui?

ACTIVITÉ 1 Expression personnelle: De quelle couleur?

Describe what you wear at the following times. Give the color of each item.

1. Quand je vais au stade, je porte . . .   You may want to review weather expressions on p.36.
2. Quand je joue au tennis, je porte . . .
3. Quand je vais à la plage, je porte . . .
4. Quand je vais à la montagne, je porte . . .
5. Quand il fait froid, je porte . . .
6. Quand il fait chaud, je porte . . .

Structure

A. Acheter

Note the forms of the verb **acheter** *(to buy)* in the present tense, paying special attention to the **e** of the stem.

Infinitive	acheter			
Present	j' **achète** une veste tu **achètes** un pull il/elle **achète** un anorak		nous **achetons** des sandales vous **achetez** des bottes ils/elles **achètent** des lunettes de soleil	

Many verbs which end in **e** + consonant + **er** have the following stem change:

> **e** → **è** in the **je, tu, il,** and **ils** forms of the present

Point out that the endings are regular. You may also point out that the stem change occurs only when the e is accented: **il ach**è**te** *but* **nous ach**e**tons.** The contrast between /ε/ and /ə/ is reviewed in the **Prononciation** section.

ACTIVITÉ 2 Achats *(Purchases)*

The following people all received money for Christmas. Say what each one is buying.

→ Pierre (des skis)   **Pierre achète des skis.**

1. Monique (un bikini)
2. Jacqueline et Denise (des sandales)
3. moi (un appareil-photo)
4. Jean-Claude (un anorak)
5. nous (un chien)
6. vous (des poissons rouges)
7. Henri et moi (des bottes) nous. . .
8. Hélène et toi (des lunettes de soleil) vous. . .

VARIATION in the negative: **Pierre n'achète pas de skis.**
For additional practice, introduce **amener** *(to bring).*
These people are bringing a friend to a picnic. **Pierre amène un ami.**

Mille is always invariable. Multiples of cent only take an s when cent
is the last word of the number: trois cents but trois cent dix.

B. Les nombres de 100 à 1.000.000

100 cent	200 deux cents	1.000 mille
101 cent un	201 deux cent un	2.000 deux mille
102 cent deux	202 deux cent deux	10.000 dix mille
103 cent trois	203 deux cent trois	100.000 cent mille
110 cent dix	900 neuf cents	1.000.000 un million

In writing numbers the French use periods where the Americans use commas,
and vice versa.

Stress that 100 is cent (and not, un cent); 101 is cent un (and not, cent et un), etc.

ACTIVITÉ 3   À la banque (At the bank)   OPTIONAL

As a warm-up, practice numbers in chain
activities: 100, 200, 300, etc.; 110, 120,
130, etc.; 125, 150, 175, etc.

Help the bank teller add the following amounts of money.

→ 100 F + 10 F   Cent francs plus dix francs égalent (equal) cent dix francs.

1. 100 F + 50 F
2. 100 F + 100 F
3. 100 F + 150 F

4. 100 F + 500 F
5. 100 F + 225 F
6. 500 F + 400 F

7. 500 F + 500 F
8. 1.000 F + 9.000 F

For additional practice, read a page number from this book. (E.g. p.275) When students have found
the page, hold your book open to that page so they can check if they are right.

C. L'adjectif interrogatif quel?

The interrogative adjective quel (what? which?) is used in questions. It
agrees with the noun it introduces and has the following forms:

	SINGULAR	PLURAL		
Masculine	quel	quels	Quel garçon?	Quels‿amis invites-tu?
Feminine	quelle	quelles	Quelle fille?	Quelles‿amies invites-tu?

→ There is liaison after quels and quelles when the next word begins with
a vowel sound.

Except in liaison, the four forms of quel sound the same.

You may remind students that they have already seen quel in
expressions such as: Quelle heure est-il? Quel temps fait-il?

ACTIVITÉ 4   Achats (Purchases)

André is shopping for the following items before going on a summer trip to
France. Françoise asks him which ones he is buying. Play both roles.

→ un maillot de bain   André: J'achète un maillot de bain.
     Françoise: Quel maillot de bain est-ce que tu achètes?

1. un short
2. des chaussettes

3. une guitare
4. un pantalon

5. des sandales
6. des lunettes de soleil

VARIATIONS: a) with choisir: Je choisis un maillot de bain.
b) with inversion: Quel maillot de bain achètes-tu?

ACTIVITÉ 5   Questions personnelles

1. Quelle ville habitez-vous?
2. À quelle école allez-vous?
3. À quel cinéma allez-vous?
4. À quelle plage allez-vous?

5. Dans quel magasin achetez-vous vos vêtements?
6. Dans quel magasin achetez-vous vos chaussures?
7. Quels programmes regardez-vous à la télé?
8. Quelles langues (languages) parlez-vous?

D. L'adjectif démonstratif ce

The demonstrative adjective **ce** *(this, that)* agrees with the noun it introduces.
It has the following forms:

	SINGULAR *(this, that)*	PLURAL *(these, those)*		
Masculine	ce ↓ cet (+ vowel sound)	ces	**ce** pantalon **cet** anorak	**ces** pantalons **ces** anoraks
Feminine	cette	ces	**cette** guitare **cette** auto	**ces** guitares **ces** autos

→ There is liaison after **cet** and **ces** when the next word begins with a vowel sound.

→ To distinguish between a person or an object which is close by and one which is further away, the French sometimes use **-ci** or **-là** after the noun.

André achète **ces** chaussures-**ci**.   *André is buying **these** shoes (over here).*
Françoise achète **ces** chaussures-**là**.   *Françoise is buying **those** shoes (over there).*

You may point out that -ci and -là stand for ici *(here)* and là *(there)*.

ACTIVITÉ 6   Combien?

Imagine that you are shopping in a French department store and are interested in buying the following objects. Ask the prices.

→ le maillot de bain   **Combien coûte ce maillot de bain?** VARIATION: Another student provides a price.

1. les chaussures
2. le tee-shirt
3. la cassette
4. les sandales
5. le short
6. les lunettes de soleil
7. la guitare
8. l'anorak cet
9. l'appareil-photo cet
10. l'électrophone cet

ACTIVITÉ 7   Différences d'opinion

Whenever they go shopping together, Paul and Brigitte cannot agree on what they like. Play both roles according to the model.

→ un short   Paul: **J'aime ce short-ci.**
Brigitte: **Eh bien, moi, j'aime ce short-là.**

1. une chemise
2. un pantalon
3. des chaussures
4. des sandales
5. une cassette
6. des disques
7. une bicyclette
8. un anorak

Vocabulaire spécialisé Quand?

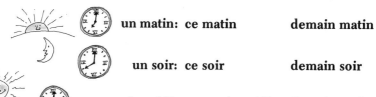

un matin:	ce matin	demain matin
un soir:	ce soir	demain soir
un après-midi:	cet après-midi	demain après-midi
une nuit *(night):*	cette nuit	

ce week-end, cette semaine, ce mois-ci, cette année
cet été, cet automne, cet hiver, ce printemps

ACTIVITÉ 8 **Projets** *(Plans)* OPTIONAL   This activity may be assigned as written homework.

Describe your plans — real or imaginary — by completing the sentences
below.

1. Demain matin, je vais...
2. Demain après-midi, je vais...
3. Ce soir, je vais...
4. Ce week-end, je vais...

5. Ce mois-ci, je vais...
6. Cet hiver, je vais...
7. Cet été, je vais...
8. Cette année, je vais...

UN JEU OPTIONAL

When you see what people are wearing, you can often tell what they are
going to do. How many different logical sentences can you make in five
minutes? Follow the models below:

A	B	C
André	un maillot de bain	nager
Françoise	des lunettes de soleil	skier
Sylvie	un short	aller à la plage
Henri	des chaussettes blanches	aller à un concert
Michèle	des chaussures de ski *(ski boots)*	jouer au tennis
	un anorak	jouer au football
	un pantalon très chic	aller à la campagne
	des chaussures noires	
	des bottes	

→ **Sylvie porte un short. Elle va jouer au football.**
→ **Françoise porte un anorak. Elle va skier.**

CONVERSATION   OPTIONAL

Let's make some comparisons.

Comment s'appelle votre meilleur ami?

1. Êtes-vous **plus grand (grande) que** cet ami?
2. Êtes-vous **plus généreux (généreuse) que** lui?
3. Êtes-vous **plus drôle que** lui?

OBSERVATIONS   Str. B   OPTIONAL

In the above questions you are asked to *compare yourself* to your best friend.

• How do you say *taller than* in French?   plus grand(e) que
  How do you say *more generous than?*   plus généreux (généreuse) que

• In all the above comparisons, which word comes *before* the adjective?   plus
  Which word comes *after* the adjective?   que

In questions 2 and 3 **cet ami** has been replaced by a pronoun.

• Is this pronoun a *subject* pronoun or a *stress* pronoun?   stress

SUGGESTED REALIA: ads for clothes, mail-order catalogues.

NOTE CULTURELLE   OPTIONAL

L'achat des vêtements *(Buying clothes)*

Do you buy your own clothes? For a French teenager shopping for clothes may be a problem . . . especially when mother comes along. In general, French young people do not receive enough allowance to buy their own clothes. Since clothes are fairly expensive, they have to rely on their parents' generosity, and also on their tastes, which may not be the same as their own.

chaussures ASTER hommes
Paris - Tel. 373.02.37.

Vocabulaire pratique

ADJECTIFS:	**conservateur (conservatrice)**	*conservative*
	généreux (généreuse)	*generous*
EXPRESSIONS:	**plus ≠ moins**	*more ≠ less*

Vocabulaire spécialisé La mode

(nouns only)

le style
élégant   *elegant*
court ≠ long (longue)   *short ≠ long*
nouveau (nouvelle) ≠ vieux (vieille) *new ≠ old*

la mode *fashion*
être à la mode   *to be in fashion*   Cette robe n'**est** pas **à la mode!**
                     to be fashionable   Brigitte **est** toujours **à la mode.**

Note: Words which end in **-eau** form their plural in **-eaux**.

    un chapeau   des chapeaux   **un manteau   des manteaux**

VOCABULARY EXPANSION: **un bonnet** *(wool hat),* **une casquette** *(cap),* **des gants** *(gloves),* **un foulard** *(scarf),* **un mouchoir** *(handkerchief),* **un imperméable** *(raincoat),* **des collants** *(tights),* **une ceinture** *(belt)*
les accessoires: une bague *(ring),* **un collier** *(necklace),* **une boucle d'oreille** *(earring)*

ACTIVITÉ 1   Questions personnelles

1. Qu'est-ce que vous portez aujourd'hui?
2. Qu'est-ce que vous portez quand vous allez à un concert?
3. Qu'est-ce que vous portez quand vous allez à une surprise-partie?
4. Qu'est-ce que le professeur porte aujourd'hui? et l'élève à côté de *(next to)* vous?

Structure

A. Les adjectifs *vieux, nouveau* et *beau*

Note the position and forms of the irregular adjectives **vieux** *(old)*, **nouveau** *(new)*, and **beau** *(beautiful, good-looking)*.

	BEFORE A CONSONANT SOUND	BEFORE A VOWEL SOUND
Masculine Singular	un **vieux** manteau un **nouveau** manteau un **beau** manteau	un **vieil** /j/ anorak un **nouvel** anorak un **bel** anorak
Feminine Singular	une **vieille** robe une **nouvelle** robe une **belle** robe	une **vieille** auto une **nouvelle** auto une **belle** auto
Masculine Plural	des **vieux** manteaux des **nouveaux** manteaux des **beaux** manteaux	des **vieux** /z/ anoraks des **nouveaux** /z/ anoraks des **beaux** /z/ anoraks
Feminine Plural	des **vieilles** robes des **nouvelles** robes des **belles** robes	des **vieilles** /z/ autos des **nouvelles** /z/ autos des **belles** /z/ autos

The adjectives **vieux, nouveau,** and **beau** usually come before the noun.
When this occurs, there is liaison between the adjective and the noun if the noun begins with a vowel sound.

Remind students of other adjectives which come before the noun: **grand, petit, bon, mauvais, joli.**

ACTIVITÉ 2 Les soldes de printemps *(Spring sales)*

The following people are taking advantage of the big spring sale at "Au Bon Marché" to replace their old things with new ones. Express this according to the model.

→ Jacqueline (une jupe) **Jacqueline a une vieille jupe.** VARIATION: Jacqueline trouve une belle jupe.
Elle achète une nouvelle jupe.

1. Henri (un costume)
2. Brigitte (un manteau)
3. Paul (une cravate)
4. Sylvie (des bas)
5. Michèle (un chemisier)

6. Philippe (des chemises)
7. Jean-Claude (un chapeau)
8. Georges (un anorak) vieil/nouvel
9. Catherine (un électrophone) vieil/nouvel
10. Vincent (un appareil-photo) vieil/nouvel

In formal French, **des** becomes **de** when the adjective precedes the noun. This form is not presented at this level: **des manteaux rouges/de beaux manteaux.**

ACTIVITÉ 3 Différences d'opinion

Paul shows Sylvie the new things he bought. Sylvie says she likes the old ones better. (Note: **mieux** means *better.)*

→ un maillot de bain

Paul: **Regarde mon nouveau maillot de bain.
Il est beau, n'est-ce pas?**
Sylvie: **Moi, j'aime mieux ton vieux maillot de bain.**

1. une veste
2. un pantalon
3. une chemise

4. une cravate
5. un anorak
6. un short

7. des tee-shirts
8. des chaussures
9. des lunettes de soleil

B. La comparaison avec les adjectifs

Note how *comparisons* are expressed in French.

Cette robe est **plus élégante que** ce manteau.   *more elegant than*
Ce pull est **plus joli que** cette chemise.   *prettier than*

Paul est **moins intelligent que** Richard.   *less intelligent than*
Il est **moins amusant que** lui.   *less amusing than*

Je suis **aussi sympathique que** mes amis.   *as nice as*
Je ne suis **pas aussi riche qu'**eux.   *(not) as rich as*

To make comparisons, French speakers use the following constructions:

more . . . than *. . . -er than* (+) **plus** *less . . . than* (−) **moins** *as . . . as* (=) **aussi**	+ adjective	(if expressed) + **que** + { noun stress pronoun **qu'** + (a vowel sound) }

→ There is liaison after **plus** and **moins** when the next word begins with a vowel sound.

→ In comparisons the adjective always agrees with the noun or pronoun it modifies.

Le chemisier est plus **cher** que la jupe.

Les vestes sont moins **chères** que les manteaux.

→ After **que**, *stress pronouns* must be used.

Note the following irregular comparative form:

> The comparative of **bon (bonne)** is **meilleur (meilleure).**

Brigitte est **meilleure** en tennis que Paul.
but: En classe, elle est **moins bonne** en anglais que lui.

The irregular comparative **pire** is not taught, since this form is used less and less frequently.

202 Unité quatre

ACTIVITÉ 4 Comparaisons

How much do you think the following items cost? Give your opinion, saying whether you think the first one is more expensive, less expensive, or as expensive as the second one.

→ une guitare / une raquette **Une guitare est plus (moins, aussi) chère qu'une raquette.**

1. un vélo / une auto
2. un transistor / une caméra
3. un électrophone / un appareil-photo
4. un anorak / un manteau
5. une veste / un pantalon

6. un costume / une robe
7. un blue-jeans / un maillot de bain
8. des chaussettes / des bas
9. une voiture / une maison
10. des bottes / des sandales

ACTIVITÉ 5 Expression personnelle

Compare the following by using the adjectives suggested. Give your personal opinion.

→ les hommes (généreux) les femmes
Les hommes sont plus (moins, aussi) généreux que les femmes.

1. le tennis (intéressant) le ping-pong
2. le français (difficile) l'espagnol
3. le livre de français (bon) le livre de maths
4. la classe de musique (amusante) la classe d'anglais
5. New York (beau) Chicago
6. la Floride (belle) le Texas
7. la Nouvelle Angleterre (jolie) la Californie
8. les Français (intelligents) les Américains
9. les Françaises (élégantes) les Américaines
10. les garçons (sympathiques) les filles

ACTIVITÉ 6 Questions personnelles

Use the appropriate stress pronouns in answering the questions below.

→ Êtes-vous plus grand(e) que votre meilleur ami?

Oui, je suis plus grand(e) que lui.
Non, je suis moins grand(e) que lui.
Je suis aussi grand(e) que lui.

1. Êtes-vous plus grand(e) que votre meilleure amie?
2. Êtes-vous plus riche que votre frère (si vous avez un frère)?
3. Êtes-vous plus riche que votre sœur (si vous avez une sœur)?
4. Êtes-vous plus généreux (généreuse) que vos amis?
5. Êtes-vous plus conservateur (conservatrice) que vos parents?
6. Êtes-vous meilleur(e) en français que vos camarades?
7. Êtes-vous meilleur(e) en maths que vos camarades?
8. Êtes-vous meilleur(e) en sport que vos amis?

COSTUMES
CHEMISES
PULLS
en
trois
longueurs

✳

CRAVATTERIA
Yves St Laurent
Givenchy
Pucci
Dior

✳

❦ELYSÉES❦
SOIERIES
CHEMISIER HABILLEUR
65, Champs-Elysées - Paris 8ᵉ

If Pierre is taller than Nathalie, then she is shorter than he is. Make as many sets of logical sentences as you can in five minutes. Use the appropriate stress pronouns as in the models below.

A	**B**	**C**	**D**
je	grand	Robert	mauvais
tu	riche	Jacqueline	bête
Alain	libéral (libéraux)	mes cousins	conservateur
Hélène	intelligent	mes amies	pauvre
mes amis	amusant	Nathalie	petit
mes cousines	bon en sport		pénible
Pierre	bon en anglais		

→ **Je suis plus libéral que mes amies. Elles sont plus conservatrices que moi.**

→ **Tu es meilleur en anglais que mes cousins. Ils sont plus mauvais que toi.**

Prononciation

Révision: la liaison

There is liaison between a word introducing a noun and the noun, if it begins with a vowel sound.

les, des, ces	les élèves, des écoles, ces églises, les Anglais, ces Américains
mes, tes, ses	mes amis, tes amies, ses enfants, ses élèves
nos, vos	nos amis, nos amies, vos élèves, vos enfants
leurs	leurs élèves, leurs écoles, leurs oncles, leurs enfants

There is liaison between an adjective that comes before a noun and the noun, if the noun begins with a vowel sound.

bon, mauvais	un bon ami, un mauvais élève, les meilleurs amis
vieux, nouveau	nos vieux amis, les nouveaux appareils-photo, les nouvelles élèves
beau, joli	les beaux anoraks, les jolis enfants, les belles autos
grand, petit	un grand électrophone, un petit anorak, les grandes autos

There is liaison between **plus** and **moins** and the adjective which follows, if it begins with a vowel sound.

plus	plus intéressant, plus intelligent, plus amusant, plus indépendant
moins	moins intéressant, moins intelligent, moins amusant, moins indépendant

In the questions below you will be asked who in your family is *the youngest,*
the tallest, the funniest, and *the most generous.*

1. Qui est la personne **la plus** jeune de votre famille?
2. Qui est la personne **la plus** grande?
3. Qui est la personne **la plus** drôle?
4. Qui est la personne **la plus** généreuse?

OBSERVATIONS Str. C OPTIONAL

In the above questions you are comparing one person to the
others in a group (your family).

• Which words come before the adjective? la plus

• Is an article used before the adjective? yes

• Is this article the same as the one which introduces the noun?
yes

NOTE CULTURELLE OPTIONAL

Les croissants et la cuisine française

Have you ever eaten a **croissant** or an **éclair? Croissants**
are delicious pastries, shaped like crescents, which the
French order with coffee when they go out for breakfast. **Éclairs** are long cream puffs with vanilla filling and
chocolate frosting. The French are famous for their cuisine,
which many people consider as the best in the world. It is
therefore not surprising that the English language has borrowed many words from the French to designate food. Do you
know the following: **hors-d'œuvre, filet mignon, mousse,
crêpe, bouillon, soufflé, omelette?**

SUGGESTED REALIA: bilingual French-English menu.

instructions

1° mettez les pièces
demandées
· attendez la chute

Vocabulaire pratique

NOMS:	**un gâteau** *(pl.* **gâteaux)**	*cake*	**une idée** *idea*
	un problème	*problem*	**une pâtisserie** *pastry; pastry shop*
ADJECTIFS:	**cher (chère)**	*dear*	
	✓**fatigué**	*tired*	
	gros (grosse) ≠ **mince**	*fat ≠ slim, slender, thin*	
VERBE:	**payer** *to pay, pay for*	Est-ce que tu **paies** les pâtisseries?	
EXPRESSION:	**comme** *like, as*	Mais oui, **comme** toujours!	

Note: Verbs which end in **-yer,** like **payer,** have the following stem change:
y → i in the **je, tu, il,** and **ils** forms: **je paie** *but:* **nous payons**

You may want to present the complete conjugation of **payer.**
Another verb conjugated like **payer** is **envoyer** *(to send).*

Structure

A. Expressions avec *avoir*

Note the use of **avoir** in the following sentences:

Paul **a faim**.	*Paul is hungry.*
Brigitte **a chaud**.	*Brigitte is hot.*

Before teaching these expressions, you may want to review the forms of **avoir**: Quel âge avez-vous? Paul, quel âge a Betty?

French speakers use **avoir** in many expressions where English speakers use the verb *to be*.

Vocabulaire spécialisé Expressions avec *avoir*

avoir chaud	*to be (feel) warm*	Quand j'**ai chaud** en été, je vais à la plage.
avoir froid	*to be (feel) cold*	**As-tu froid** maintenant? Voici ton pull.
avoir faim	*to be hungry*	Il est midi. Nous **avons faim.**
avoir soif	*to be thirsty*	Mes amis vont au café quand ils **ont soif.**
avoir raison	*to be right*	Est-ce que vous **avez** toujours **raison?**
avoir tort	*to be wrong*	Paul n'étudie pas. Il **a tort!**
avoir de la chance	*to be lucky*	J'**ai de la chance.** J'ai des parents généreux.

You may want to review **il fait froid/chaud**, and contrast these expressions with **avoir froid/chaud**.

ACTIVITÉ 1 L'examen de géographie

Imagine you are teaching geography in France. Listen to the following statements made by your students and tell them if they are *right* or *wrong*.

→ New York est la capitale des États-Unis.   **Vous avez tort.**

1. Washington est la capitale des États-Unis.
2. Ottawa est la capitale du Canada.
3. La Nouvelle-Orléans est une ville de Louisiane.
4. Québec est une ville en France.
5. En Floride, il fait chaud.
6. En Alaska, il fait froid en hiver.
7. À Chicago, il fait chaud en hiver.
8. Les Mexicains parlent espagnol.

ACTIVITÉ 2 Pourquoi?

Explain why the people mentioned below are doing what they are doing. Complete each sentence with **parce que** and the appropriate form of one of the following expressions: **avoir faim, avoir soif, avoir chaud, avoir froid.**

→ Georges achète un gâteau . . .   **Georges achète un gâteau parce qu'il a faim.**

1. Nous achetons un Coca-Cola . . .
2. Tu achètes un manteau . . .
3. Jacqueline va à la piscine . . .
4. Mes amis achètent des sandwichs . . .
5. Philippe va au café . . .
6. J'achète une pizza . . .
7. Vous nagez . . .
8. Mes cousins achètent un Pepsi . . .

B. Les expressions *avoir envie de, avoir besoin de*

Note how the expressions **avoir envie de** *(to want, feel like)* and **avoir besoin de** *(to need)* are used in the sentences below.

avoir envie de

+ noun	J'ai envie d'une pizza.	*I want (feel like having) a pizza.*
+ infinitive	J'ai envie de nager.	*I want to swim (feel like swimming).*

avoir besoin de

+ noun	J'ai besoin de 5 dollars.	*I need 5 dollars.*
+ infinitive	J'ai besoin d'étudier.	*I need to study.*

➜ Note the interrogative and negative constructions with these expressions:

Est-ce que vous avez envie de travailler?   **Est-ce que vous avez besoin d'**argent?
Nous n'avons pas envie de travailler.   **Nous n'avons pas besoin d'**argent.

votre machine
a besoin
de calgon !

ACTIVITÉ 3   Dialogue

Ask your classmates if they feel like doing the following things.

➜ voyager   Élève 1: **Est-ce que tu as envie de voyager?**
                    Élève 2: **Oui, j'ai envie de voyager.**
                               (Non, je n'ai pas envie de voyager.)

1. visiter Paris
2. visiter Québec
3. travailler en France
4. aller au cinéma ce soir
5. aller à la piscine aujourd'hui
6. étudier cet après-midi
7. parler français
8. acheter une voiture de sport

VARIATION with the plural: —Avez-vous envie de voyager?
                                   —Oui, nous avons envie de voyager.

ACTIVITÉ 4   Combien?   OPTIONAL

The following students are shopping for certain things. Say how much money you think each one needs.   Elicit several responses with different prices.

➜ Hélène achète un blue-jeans.   **Elle a besoin de dix-sept (quinze, vingt) dollars.**

1. Sylvie achète des chaussures.
2. Paul achète un gâteau.
3. Nous achetons un album de timbres.
4. Vous achetez un maillot de bain.
5. J'achète un anorak.
6. Tu achètes un pantalon.
7. Jacqueline achète une raquette.
8. Mon cousin achète une veste.

VARIATION: The people are in France. Give approximate prices in francs: $1≅4 francs.

ACTIVITÉ 5   Questions personnelles

1. Maintenant avez-vous chaud? Avez-vous froid?
2. Maintenant avez vous faim? Avez-vous soif?
3. En général, avez-vous de la chance?
4. En général, avez-vous besoin d'argent?
5. Avez-vous besoin d'amis?
6. Avez-vous besoin de compliments?
7. Avez-vous besoin d'étudier beaucoup?
8. Avez-vous envie d'être professeur?
9. Avez-vous envie de voyager?

C. Le superlatif

To compare somebody or something to a larger group, the *superlative construction* is used. Note this construction in the following sentences:

Paul est le garçon **le plus intelligent** de la classe. *the most intelligent boy in the class*
Louise est la fille **la moins dynamique**. *the least energetic girl*

Où est le restaurant **le plus cher** de la ville? *the most expensive restaurant in town*
Où sont les magasins **les moins chers**? *the least expensive stores*

In French the superlative is expressed as follows:

			(if expressed)
the most / *the least*	le, la, les +	{ plus / moins } + adjective	+ **de** + name of reference group

The position of the superlative adjective is the same as that of the simple adjective. **Paul est le plus jeune garçon de la famille.**

→ There is liaison after **plus** and **moins** before a vowel sound.

→ The superlative form of **bon (bonne)** is **le meilleur (la meilleure)**.

En français, Jeanne est **la meilleure** élève de la classe.
En anglais, Paul est **le meilleur**.

ACTIVITÉ 6 À Montréal

Paul and Brigitte are visiting Montréal. Paul wants to go to the most expensive places, and Brigitte to the least expensive. Play both roles.

→ le café   Paul: **Où est le café le plus cher?**
            Brigitte: **Où est le café le moins cher?**

1. le restaurant
2. les magasins Où sont
3. la boutique
4. l'hôtel
5. le cinéma
6. la cafétéria

VARIATION: Où est le meilleur café?

ACTIVITÉ 7 Un sondage *(An opinion poll)*   OPTIONAL

Name the best person, place, or thing in each category. Follow the model.

→ le comédien: drôle   **Le comédien le plus drôle est (Woody Allen).**

1. la comédienne: amusante
2. l'acteur: beau
3. l'actrice *(actress)*: intelligente
4. les musiciens: bons
5. le programme de télé: drôle
6. l'équipe *(team)* de football: bonne
7. la voiture: confortable
8. la voiture: bonne
9. la ville: belle
10. la couleur: jolie

As a class activity, you may want to tabulate the results of the students' votes, and perhaps compare them with other French classes.

In order to do certain things we need other things. Express this in logical sentences, using elements from columns A, B, and C. How many different sentences can you make in five minutes? Be sure to use the expressions **avoir envie de** and **avoir besoin de,** as in the models below.

A	B		C	
je	écouter le concert	danser	un dollar	une voiture
tu	acheter un vélo	nager	cinq dollars	un maillot de bain
Pierre	aller à la campagne	skier	cent dollars	un transistor
nous	acheter un sandwich	voyager	un passeport	un électrophone
vous	acheter un disque		un anorak	un ballon *(ball)*
mes amis	jouer au volley			

→ **Nous avons envie d'acheter un disque. Nous avons besoin de cinq dollars.**
→ **Pierre a envie de voyager. Il a besoin d'un passeport.**

Prononciation

Le son /j/

Model word: p<u>i</u>ano
Practice words: P<u>i</u>erre, v<u>i</u>olon, étud<u>i</u>er, janv<u>i</u>er, f<u>ill</u>e, fam<u>ill</u>e, trava<u>ill</u>er
Practice sentences: Dan<u>i</u>el est canad<u>i</u>en. Il joue du p<u>i</u>ano.
Cette f<u>ill</u>e ital<u>i</u>enne trava<u>ill</u>e en janv<u>i</u>er.

The French sound /j/ is similar to the *y*-sound in the word *yes.* It is very short and tense.
Comment écrire /j/: **i**+vowel; **ill**

Entre nous

Expression pour la conversation

To show that you heard what someone has said, but do not want to answer, you can say:

Hm!

Mini-dialogue   OPTIONAL

Pourquoi *est-ce que Pierre flatte* Nathalie?   *is Pierre flattering*

PIERRE: Tu es la fille la plus sympathique de la classe.
NATHALIE: Hm!
PIERRE: Tu es aussi la fille la plus jolie ...
NATHALIE: Hm, Hm!
PIERRE: Et la plus généreuse! Tiens, *prête-moi* dix francs!   *lend me*
NATHALIE: Alors, là, mon cher Pierre, tu as tort! Je suis la fille la moins généreuse
... et toi, tu es le garçon le plus *innocent!* Au revoir, Pierre!   *naive*

L'art du dialogue

a) Act out the dialog between Pierre and Nathalie.
b) Imagine that the roles are reversed. **Nathalie** is flattering **Pierre.** Act out the new dialog.

UNITÉ 4
Leçon 5   Ici, on n'est pas en Amérique.

STRUCTURES TO OBSERVE
• verbs in -re (vendre)
• the impersonal pronoun on

Jim passe l'été en France chez ses amis Brigitte et Philippe.
Est-ce qu'il aime sa nouvelle existence? Oui, bien sûr! Mais
de temps en temps, il a un petit problème d'adaptation.   *from time to time*
Aujourd'hui, *par exemple . . .*   *for instance*

BRIGITTE: Où vas-tu, Jim?
    JIM: Je vais à la pharmacie.
PHILIPPE: À la pharmacie? Tu es malade?
    JIM: Mais non, je ne suis pas malade! Je vais acheter le
           journal et des bonbons!
BRIGITTE: Voyons, Jim! *On ne vend pas* le journal à la   *One doesn't sell*
           pharmacie!
PHILIPPE: Et on ne vend pas de bonbons *non plus!*   *neither*
BRIGITTE: En France, *on* achète le journal *chez le marchand*   *people; at the*
           de journaux.   *newsstand*
PHILIPPE: Et on achète les bonbons *chez l'épicier!*   *at the grocer's*
    JIM: Mais en Amérique, on . . .
BRIGITTE: Écoute Jim! Ici, *on* n'est pas en Amérique!   *you*
    JIM: Oh là là! *La vie* est compliquée!   *Life*

CONVERSATION

Let's talk about the kinds of things *one* can buy in an American drugstore.

1. Est-ce qu'**on achète** le journal à la pharmacie?
    Oui, **on achète** . . . (Non, on n'achète pas . . .)
2. Est-ce qu'**on achète** des magazines?
3. Est-ce qu'**on achète** l'aspirine?
4. Est-ce qu'**on achète** les médicaments *(medicine)?*

OBSERVATIONS   Str. B   on achète

• How do you say *one buys* in French? Which pronoun corresponds to *one?*   on

• Is this pronoun followed by a *singular* or *plural* verb?   singular

Où est-ce que Jim passe l'été? Où est-ce qu'il va? Pourquoi est-ce qu'il veut *(want)* aller à la pharmacie?
Où est-ce qu'on achète le journal en France? Où est-ce qu'on achète les bonbons?

Le **shopping** is an example of an Anglicism that is more and more used in France. You may present the expression **les courses.**

NOTE CULTURELLE

Le shopping et les petits commerçants
(Shopping and shopkeepers)

Where do you go to buy the newspaper? Probably to a newsstand or to the neighborhood drugstore. In France you would go to the newsstand **(chez le marchand de journaux)** or to the tobacco shop **(le bureau de tabac)** which, in addition to cigarettes, often carries magazines, newspapers, matches, and stamps. You would certainly not go to the pharmacy, which sells only medicine.

Shopping habits change from country to country. Thus, in France many people go to different stores to buy individual food items. Imagine, for instance, that you are shopping for today's meal. You would go to the butcher's **(chez le boucher)** for the meat, to the baker's **(chez le boulanger)** for the bread, to the grocer's **(chez l'épicier)** for the soft drinks, to the dairy **(chez le crémier)** for the milk, to the fruit stand **(chez le marchand de fruits)** for the fruits. Of course, if you had a car, you could also go to the supermarket **(le supermarché)** or to a huge shopping center (called **l'hypermarché**) and buy everything on your list there. Many people in France still prefer the friendly atmosphere of the small individual shops, and also the quality of their products. Thus, to have fresh bread, some people still go to the local baker three times a day: before breakfast, before lunch, and before dinner.

Vocabulaire pratique

NOMS:	**des bonbons**	*candy*
	un journal (*pl.* **journaux**)	*newspaper*
ADJECTIFS:	**compliqué ≠ simple**	*complicated ≠ simple*
VERBE:	**passer** (+ time)	*to spend* (time)

Structure

A. Les verbes réguliers en -re

Many French verbs end in **-re.** Most of these are conjugated like **vendre** *(to sell).*
Note the forms of this verb in the present tense, paying special attention to the endings.

Infinitive	vendre		STEM	ENDINGS
Present	je **vends** ma raquette			**-s**
	tu **vends** tes disques			**-s**
	il/elle **vend** son violon		(infinitive minus **-re**)	—
	nous **vendons** nos livres		**vend-**	**-ons**
	vous **vendez** vos cassettes			**-ez**
	ils/elles **vendent** leurs vélos			**-ent**

➡ The **d** of the stem is silent in the singular forms, but it is pronounced in
the plural forms.

Vocabulaire spécialisé   Verbes réguliers en -re

attendre	*to wait, wait for*	Yvette **attend** Michèle au café.
entendre	*to hear*	Est-ce que vous **entendez** la radio?
perdre	*to lose, waste*	Je n'ai pas envie de **perdre** mon argent.
vendre	*to sell*	**Vendez**-vous votre vélomoteur?

Répondre, another -re verb, is introduced on p. 287.

Be sure students understand that **attendre** means *to wait for;*
pour is never used with **attendre.**

ACTIVITÉ 1   Rendez-vous

The following people are waiting for their dates at a café. Express this,
using the appropriate form of **attendre.**

➡ Jim (Michèle)   **Jim attend Michèle.**

1. nous (nos amis)
2. vous (vos cousines)
3. moi (Paul)
4. toi (Brigitte)
5. Louis et Éric (Claire et Sylvie)
6. les étudiants (les étudiantes)
7. Jacques et moi (Louise et Hélène)
8. Annette et toi (François)

Jacques et moi, nous. . .
Annette et toi, vous. . .

B. Le pronom *on*

The subject pronoun **on** is often used in French. Note its English
equivalents in the sentences below.

On achète l'aspirine à la pharmacie.	*One buys (**You** buy) aspirin at the drugstore.*
On vend des magazines au bureau de tabac.	*One sells (**They** sell) magazines at the tobacco shop.*
En France, **on** parle français.	*In France* **people (you, they)** *speak French.*

The impersonal pronoun **on** does not refer to a specific person. It corresponds
to the English pronouns *one, you* (in general), *they* (in general), or *people* (in general).

→ The pronoun **on** is always used with the **il/elle** form of the verb.

→ There is liaison after **on** when the next word begins with a vowel sound.

→ In conversation, **on** is often used instead of **nous**:

Est-ce qu'**on** regarde la télé ce soir?
*Are **we** watching TV tonight?*

Sometimes a construction with **on** is used in French where English would use the passive.
On parle français ici. *French is spoken here.*

On est bien
dans la laine.
On est bien
dans un pull
Starcot.

ACTIVITÉ 2   En hiver ou en été?

Do the following happen mainly in winter or in summer?

→ aller à la piscine   **On va à la piscine en été.**

1. nager
2. skier
3. jouer au tennis
4. jouer au football
5. aller à la plage
6. porter des lunettes de soleil

7. porter un manteau
8. organiser des pique-niques
9. être en vacances
10. avoir chaud
11. avoir froid
12. avoir la grippe *(the flu)*

ACTIVITÉ 3   En France et en Amérique

French customs are sometimes different from American customs. First
describe the French custom. Then describe the American custom, using the
expression in parentheses. Use **on** in both sentences.

→ Les Français parlent français. (anglais)   **En France, on parle français.**
                                                En Amérique, on parle anglais.

1. Les Français jouent au football. (au baseball)
2. Les Français jouent au rugby. (au basketball)
3. Les Français ont des petites voitures. (des grandes voitures)
4. Les Français dînent à huit heures. (à six heures)
5. Les Français achètent les magazines au bureau de
   tabac *(tobacco shop).* (à la pharmacie)
6. Les Français ont un mois de vacances. (deux semaines)

Vocabulaire spécialisé

Les magasins et les commerçants
(Shops and shopkeepers)

une épicerie
une pâtisserie
une librairie
une pharmacie
l'épicier
l'épicière
le pâtissier
la pâtissière
le libraire
la libraire
le pharmacien
la pharmacienne
un magasin de chaussures
un magasin de disques
un magasin de vêtements
le marchand de vêtements
la marchande de chaussures
le marchand de disques

Note: **Chez** is used with names of shopkeepers, whereas **à** is used with names of shops.
Contrast:

Je vais **chez le pharmacien**.   *I am going to the pharmacist's.*
Je vais **à la pharmacie**.   *I am going to the pharmacy.*

VOCABULARY EXPANSION: boucherie: boucher/bouchère
boulangerie: boulanger/boulangère
charcuterie: charcutier/charcutière
You may want to present these nouns with the corresponding foods on p.229.

ACTIVITÉ 4   Le shopping

Imagine that you are living in Paris, and an American friend is visiting you. This friend wants to buy the following things. Tell him/her in whose shop these items are sold according to the model. Use the nouns given in the **Vocabulaire spécialisé.**

→ des disques   **On vend des disques chez le marchand de disques.**

1. des livres
2. des cassettes
3. des bonbons
4. des cachets (*tablets*) d'aspirine
5. des chemises
6. des journaux
7. des blue-jeans
8. des sandales
9. des tee-shirts
10. des gâteaux
11. des éclairs
12. des médicaments (*medicine*)

C. Les prépositions avec les noms de pays   Review names of countries on p.116

Note the *prepositions* used with names of countries in the sentences below.

le Canada	Pierre habite **au** Canada.	Jacqueline va **au** Canada.
la France	Nous sommes **en** France.	Nous allons **en** France.
les États-Unis	Vous habitez **aux** États-Unis.	Quand vas-tu **aux** États-Unis?

To express location *in* or movement *to* a country, French speakers use:

au   if the name of the country is *masculine singular*   au Canada
en   if the name of the country is *feminine singular*   en France
aux if the name of the country is *plural*   aux États-Unis

Have the students note the liaison: aux /z/ États-Unis.

ACTIVITÉ 5   Langues internationales (*International languages*)

Say which of the following languages is spoken in each of the countries listed below.

anglais   français   espagnol

Remember: countries with names that end in **-e** are feminine.

→ l'Angleterre   **En Angleterre, on parle anglais.**

1. l'Australie
2. le Pérou
3. le Canada
4. les États-Unis
5. la France
6. le Sénégal
7. la Belgique
8. le Guatemala

What we wear often depends on what we are doing or how we feel. Express this in logical sentences similar to the models, using elements of columns A and B. How many different sentences can you make in five minutes?

A	B
nager	un pull
skier	des vêtements élégants
jouer au tennis	un anorak
jouer au football américain	un maillot de bain
aller à la plage	un short
aller dans un restaurant élégant	des sandales
avoir froid	un casque *(helmet)*
avoir chaud	

→ **Quand on a froid, on porte un pull.**

→ **Quand on joue au tennis, on porte un short.**

Prononciation

Voyelles nasales

When you say a nasal vowel followed by a consonant sound, be sure not to pronounce an /n /.

Practice the following words:

/ã/   v<u>en</u>d, att<u>en</u>d, <u>en</u>t<u>en</u>d

/ãd/   v<u>en</u>dent, att<u>en</u>dent, <u>en</u>t<u>en</u>dent

Entre nous

Expression pour la conversation

To ask someone how to say something, you use the expression:

Comment dit-on . . .? *How do you say . . .?*   **Comment dit-on** « snack bar »
en français?

Mini-dialogue OPTIONAL

Jim visite Paris avec son ami Philippe. Il *découvre* que le   *discovers*
français n'est pas trop difficile.

JIM: J'ai faim!
PHILIPPE: Moi aussi.
JIM: Alors, allons dans un . . . Dis, comment dit-on «snack bar» en français?
PHILIPPE: On dit «snack-bar».
JIM: Et comment dit-on «hot dog»?
PHILIPPE: On dit «hot-dog».
Le français est une *langue* très simple, n'est-ce pas?   *language*

L'art du dialogue

a) Act out the dialog between Jim and Philippe.
b) Imagine that the conversation is taking place in the United States, and the roles are reversed. Philippe wants to know how to say **restaurant** and **omelette** (*omelet*). Replace **français** with **anglais**.

OBJECTIVES

In this unit the students will learn to discuss three important aspects of daily life: food (meals, shopping, going to a restaurant), leisure activities (especially sports and creative activities), and how to stay in shape.

Language
- **préférer**
- the use of the definite article in the general sense
- forms and uses of the partitive article; comparison of partitive and other articles
- the imperative
- **prendre**
- **faire** and expressions with **faire**
- **venir** and the recent past with **venir de**

Vocabulary
- food
- sports and recreational activities
- transportation

Culture

This unit focuses on leisure-time activities, vacations, and certain aspects of school life.

UNITÉ 5
Au jour le jour

Leçon 1

STRUCTURES TO OBSERVE
• use of the definite article in the general sense
• use of the definite article with days of the week (**dimanche** vs. **le dimanche**)
• **préférer**

Il n'y a pas de démocratie!

Aujourd'hui c'est dimanche.
Le dimanche, la famille Brunet va en général au cinéma.   *On Sundays*
Quels films est-ce qu'ils aiment? Quand il y a quatre enfants
dans une famille, il y a souvent quatre opinions différentes.
Aujourd'hui, *par exemple*...   *for example*

MME BRUNET:	Jacques, qu'est-ce que tu préfères *voir* aujourd'hui?	*to see*
JACQUES:	Une comédie! Il y a une excellente comédie américaine au Quartier Latin.	
GUILLAUME:	Je déteste les comédies, *surtout* les comédies américaines. Il y a un très bon film policier aux Champs-Élysées.	*especially*
MONIQUE:	Ah non! Je déteste la violence! Je déteste les films policiers! J'ai envie de voir une comédie musicale.	
NICOLE:	Une comédie musicale, une comédie musicale ... Mais les comédies musicales, c'est bon pour les filles de ton âge! Moi, je préfère les films d'aventures.	
MME BRUNET:	Un moment! *Qui est-ce qui paie les billets?*	*Who is paying for the tickets?*
JACQUES:	C'est Papa, *j'espère!*	*I hope*
MME BRUNET:	Alors, c'est lui qui décide.	
GUILLAUME:	Ce n'est pas *juste!*	*fair*
MME BRUNET:	Paul, quel film préfères-tu voir aujourd'hui?	
M. BRUNET:	Un western avec John Wayne.	
MONIQUE:	Je n'aime pas John Wayne.	
GUILLAUME:	Je déteste les westerns.	
NICOLE:	J'aime les westerns, mais je déteste les westerns avec John Wayne.	
MME BRUNET:	Écoutez. Vous avez le *choix!* Aller au cinéma ou rester à la maison.	*choice*
JACQUES:	Bon, on va au cinéma, mais ...	
MONIQUE:	DANS CETTE FAMILLE ...	
GUILLAUME:	IL N'Y A PAS ...	
NICOLE:	DE DÉMOCRATIE!	

CONVERSATION

Let's talk about your likes and dislikes.

1. Aimez-vous **le** sport?
2. Aimez-vous **la** télé?
3. Aimez-vous **les** westerns?
4. Aimez-vous **la** musique classique?

OBSERVATIONS   Str. A

In the above questions you were asked whether, *generally speaking*, you liked certain things. Reread the names of these things.

- Which words introduce these names? Are these words *articles*? What type of articles?   le, la, les   yes   definite
- If you were asking the same questions in English, would you use a definite article?   no

Beginning with this unit, the **Notes culturelles** are in French.

NOTE CULTURELLE   For reading and listening practice.

Les jeunes Français et le cinéma

Allez-vous souvent au cinéma? Ou préférez-vous regarder les films à la télévision? Le cinéma est une distraction° très populaire en France. Les jeunes Français aiment surtout les comédies, les films d'aventures, les films de science-fiction . . . et les westerns.

En général, les films américains ont beaucoup de succès en France. Ces films sont souvent «doublés».° Cela signifie° que dans la version française, John Wayne, Robert Redford, Raquel Welch et Jane Fonda parlent . . . français! Voici le titre° de certains° films américains:

    Le pont° de la rivière Kwaï (1957)
    Le jour le plus long (1962)
    2001: L'odyssée de l'espace (1968)
    La fièvre° du samedi soir (1978)

distraction *leisure activity* **doublés** *dubbed* **Cela signifie** *That means* **titre** *title* **certains** *some* **pont** *bridge* **fièvre** *fever*

The newest French and foreign films are usually shown in the movie theaters on the Champs-Élysées. The theaters in the Quartier Latin are smaller and often present film classics, retrospectives, and art films.

**LA BANDE DES QUATRE
(BREAKING AWAY)**

20th Century-Fox Présente/Presents A PETER YATES FILM "LA BANDE DES QUATRE/
BREAKING AWAY"
DENNIS CHRISTOPHER   DENNIS QUAID   DANIEL STERN et/and JACKIE EARLE HALEY
avec/also starring BARBARA BARRIE   PAUL DOOLEY
Pour la Première fois à l'écran/introducing ROBYN DOUGLASS
Réalisé et Mise en Scène de/Produced and Directed by PETER YATES
Scenario de/Written by STEVE TESICH
Arrangements Musicaux/Music adapted by PATRICK WILLIAMS
Dirigé par/Conducted by LIONEL NEWMAN
Color by DeLuxe

READ THE WARNER BOOK

PG/Parental Guidance Suggested
Some Material May Not Be Suitable For Children

DURÉE: 100 MINUTES   **RUNNING TIME: 100 MINUTES**

Vocabulaire spécialisé   Les spectacles (*Shows*)

le cinéma	*movies*		
un dessin animé	*cartoon*	une comédie	*comedy*
un film	*movie*	une comédie musicale	*musical comedy*
un film d'aventures	*adventure movie*		
un film policier	*detective movie*		
le théâtre	*theater*		
un drame	*drama*	une pièce de théâtre	*play*
un acteur	*actor*	une actrice	*actress*

SUGGESTED REALIA: movie sections from French daily newspapers (*Le Figaro, Le Monde*).

Structure

A. L'usage de l'article défini dans le sens général

Note the use of the definite article (**le, la, l', les**) in the sentences below.

Paul aime **les comédies**.	*Paul likes comedies (in general).*
Brigitte aime **le cinéma**, mais elle n'aime pas **les westerns**.	*(Generally speaking) Brigitte likes movies, but she does not like westerns.*
Est-ce que **les Américains** aiment **la musique classique**?	*(In general) do Americans like classical music?*
Le tennis est un sport formidable.	*(Generally speaking) tennis is a fantastic sport.*

In French, the *definite article* precedes nouns used in a *general* or *collective* sense.

This is not the case in English. You may point out that in French most nouns are introduced by a determiner: a definite or indefinite article, a possessive, demonstrative, or interrogative adjective, a number, etc.

ACTIVITÉ 1   Expression personnelle

Say whether or not you like the following entertainment. Begin your sentences with **J'adore, J'aime beaucoup, Je n'aime pas**, or **Je déteste**.

→ les westerns   **J'aime beaucoup les westerns. (Je déteste les westerns.)**

1. les dessins animés
2. la musique classique
3. les comédies
4. les comédies musicales
5. les films policiers
6. les films de science-fiction
7. les pièces de théâtre
8. les drames
9. les films d'aventures

ACTIVITÉ 2   Questions personnelles

1. Étudiez-vous la musique? la danse? le théâtre? le piano? l'espagnol?
2. Aimez-vous la musique classique? le jazz? la musique disco?
3. À la télé, regardez-vous les films? les comédies? les matchs de baseball? les matchs de football américain? les jeux *(games)*?
4. À la radio, écoutez-vous la musique pop? l'opéra? les drames policiers?
5. Détestez-vous la pollution? la violence? l'injustice?
6. Aimez-vous l'école? les examens? les vacances?

The plural of **match** has two spellings: **matchs** and **matches**.

B. Le verbe *espérer*

Note the forms of the verb **espérer** *(to hope)*. Pay careful attention to the **é** of the stem.   You may want to review the present tense of **acheter**, which has a similar stem change.

Infinitive	espérer	
Present	j' espère	nous espérons
	tu espères	vous espérez
	il/elle espère	ils/elles espèrent

Verbs like **espérer** which end in **é** + consonant + **er** have regular endings and the following stem change:

> **é ⟶ è**   in the **je, tu, il,** and **ils** forms of the present

➜ **Préférer** *(to prefer)* is conjugated like **espérer**.

   Qu'est-ce que tu **préfères?** les comédies ou les westerns?

ACTIVITÉ 3   Ce week-end

There is a flu epidemic, but the following people are planning to have a busy weekend and hope not to get sick. Say whether or not they hope to do the following things.

➜   Paul (aller en ville)   **Paul espère aller en ville.**

   Denise (aller chez le docteur)   **Denise n'espère pas aller chez le docteur.**

1. René et Brigitte (acheter des disques)
2. nous (inviter des amis)
3. toi (être malade)
4. moi (être fatigué)
5. Philippe (dîner au restaurant)
6. nous (rester à la maison)
7. vous (jouer au football)
8. Martine (avoir la grippe [*flu*])

ACTIVITÉ 4   Dialogue

Ask your classmates which of the following entertainments they prefer. Use the appropriate definite articles. (Note: Feminine nouns are marked with an asterisk.)

➜   cinéma ou télé*?   Élève 1: **Préfères-tu le cinéma ou la télé?**
   Élève 2: **Je préfère le cinéma (la télé).**

   comédies* ou drames?   Élève 1: **Préfères-tu les comédies ou les drames?**
   Élève 2: **Je préfère les comédies (les drames).**

1. cinéma ou théâtre?
2. jazz ou musique* pop?
3. musique* disco ou musique* classique?
4. ballet classique ou danse* moderne?
5. sport ou musique*?
6. piano ou guitare*?
7. pièces* de théâtre ou films?
8. films d'aventures ou dessins animés?
9. films d'horreur ou comédies* musicales?
10. films policiers ou westerns?

VARIATION in the plural: use **nous** and **vous.**

C. L'article défini avec les jours de la semaine

Note the use of the definite article in the following sentences:

Le samedi, nous n'allons pas en classe.	*On Saturdays we do not go to class.*
Le dimanche, je vais au cinéma.	*On Sundays I go to the movies.*

The definite article is used with *days of the week* to indicate *repeated* or *habitual* events.

➜ When an event happens only once, no article is used:

Jeudi, je vais aller au théâtre.	*On Thursday* (i.e., *this Thursday*) *I am going to the theater.*

RÉVISION: les jours de la semaine

lundi, mardi, mercredi, jeudi, vendredi, samedi, dimanche

You may want to review the date on p.30.

ACTIVITÉ 5   Questions personnelles

1. Quels jours avez-vous une classe de français? une classe d'anglais?
2. Quels jours est-ce que vous n'allez pas à l'école?
3. Quels jours regardez-vous la télé?
4. Où allez-vous le samedi matin? le samedi après-midi? le samedi soir?
5. Où allez-vous le dimanche matin? le dimanche après-midi? le dimanche soir?

UN JEU   OPTIONAL

Match the nouns in column A with those in column B and write complete sentences similar to the models below. (Note: Feminine nouns are marked with an asterisk.)

A	B
banane*	science*
aluminium	fruit
automne	langue* *(language)*
physique*	métal
léopard	art
cinéma	spectacle *(show)*
sculpture*	animal
français	saison*
tennis	sport

➜ **Le tennis est un sport.**
➜ **Le léopard est un animal.**

Prononciation

Révision: les sons /e/ **et** /ɛ/

Contrast: /e/ espérer, comédie, dessin animé, cinéma, théâtre
        Préférez-vous aller au cinéma ou regarder la télé?

    /ɛ/ j'espère, tu préfères, pièce, il achète, chère
        Ma chère Michèle, j'espère que tu vas aimer la pièce.

Entre nous

Expression pour la conversation

après tout   *after all*   **Après tout,** il aime aussi les comédies.

Mini-dialogue   OPTIONAL

Jean-François a un *défaut:* il est un peu snob.   shortcoming

HÉLÈNE: J'aime beaucoup le football.
JEAN-FRANÇOIS: Eh bien, moi, je préfère le tennis et le
            polo . . .
HÉLÈNE: J'adore le cinéma.
JEAN-FRANÇOIS: Moi, je préfère le théâtre.
HÉLÈNE: J'aime la musique pop.
JEAN-FRANÇOIS: Moi, j'aime *uniquement* l'opéra et la   only
            musique classique.
HÉLÈNE: Dommage! J'ai deux *billets* pour le concert   tickets
            des Bee-Gees. Je vais inviter ton frère.
JEAN-FRANÇOIS: Euh . . . *attends!* Après tout, j'aime aussi la   wait
            musique pop.
HÉLÈNE: Eh bien, moi, je n'aime pas les garçons
            qui changent toujours d'idée . . . Et je déteste   who always change their mind
            les snobs!

L'art du dialogue

a) Act out the dialog between Hélène and Jean-François.
b) Act out a new dialog where **Hélène** and **Suzanne** are talking to **Jean-François** and **Alain.**
   Use **nous** instead of **je,** and divide the roles among four people. Replace **deux** by **quatre, ton
   frère** by **vos cousins,** and make the necessary changes.

UNITÉ 5
Leçon 2

Une minute . . . J'arrive!

 Il est midi et demi. Jean-Paul et Sylvie vont à la *cantine*.
Sylvie regarde le menu.

school cafeteria

JEAN-PAUL: Qu'est-ce qu'il y a aujourd'hui?

SYLVIE: Il y a du poisson!

JEAN-PAUL: Du poisson?

SYLVIE: Oui, du poisson!

JEAN-PAUL: *Quelle horreur!* Bon, aujourd'hui, je ne mange pas!

How awful!

SYLVIE: Il y a aussi du gâteau.

JEAN-PAUL: Du gâteau! Hm . . .

SYLVIE: Et de la glace!

JEAN-PAUL: Une minute . . . J'arrive! *Arriver means to come in the sense of arriving at a specific place.*

Quelle heure est-il? Où sont Jean-Paul et Sylvie? Qu'est-ce qu'il y a au menu? Est-ce que Jean-Paul aime le poisson?
Est-ce qu'il aime la glace?

NOTE CULTURELLE

For reading and listening practice.

La cantine

Êtes-vous externe° ou êtes-vous demi-pensionnaire?°

Dans une école française, les externes vont chez eux pour le déjeuner.° Les demi-pensionnaires restent à l'école et vont à la cantine. À la cantine, le menu est simple et le choix° est limité. Un menu particulier° correspond à chaque° jour de la semaine. Par exemple,° spaghetti le lundi, bifteck° le mardi, omelette le mercredi, etc. . . . En général, on sert° du poisson le vendredi.

externe *day student* **demi-pensionnaire** *day student who eats lunch at school* **déjeuner** *lunch* **choix** *choice* **particulier* *special* **chaque** *each* **Par exemple** *For example* **bifteck** *steak* **sert** *serves*

You may explain that fish on Friday used to be traditional in France when it was the Catholic custom. This tradition is still observed although it has lost its religious significance.

CONVERSATION

Imagine that Jean-Paul is asking you what there is in the refrigerator of the typical American family. Answer each question affirmatively.

1. Est-ce qu'il y a **du** Coca-Cola?
2. Est-ce qu'il y a **du** ketchup?
3. Est-ce qu'il y **de la** mayonnaise?
4. Est-ce qu'il y a **de la** margarine?

OBSERVATIONS Str. A

In the above questions, you are asked if there is *a certain quantity* (rather than a specific amount, such as one pound, two pints, etc.) of Coke, ketchup, mayonnaise, and margarine in the average American refrigerator. The French use a special article — the *partitive article*—to express the idea of *a certain quantity of* or *a certain amount of.*

- What is the form of the partitive article before a masculine singular noun (like **Coca-Cola** or **ketchup**)? du
- What is the form of the partitive article before a feminine singular noun (like **mayonnaise** or **margarine**)? de la

Other food items are presented on p.388.

Vocabulaire spécialisé Le menu

la soupe
l'omelette (*f.*)
le poisson

la viande:
l'agneau (*m.*)
le rosbif
le poulet
le jambon

la salade
le pain
le fromage

le dessert:
le gâteau   la glace

VERBES: **commander** *to order*   Je vais **commander** de la glace et du gâteau!
        manger *to eat*   Est-ce que tu **manges** du pain français?

Note: Verbs ending in -**ger**, like **manger, nager,** and **voyager,** add an **e** in the **nous** form of the present:

        nous mangeons   nous nageons   nous voyageons

The **e** is needed to maintain the /ʒ/ sound of the stem. This spelling change is presented at this level for recognition only and does not appear on tests.

Structure

For simplicity, only the singular forms of the partitive article are presented. The plural form **des** has been introduced as the plural of the indefinite article: **une orange/des oranges.**

A. L'article partitif: *du, de la*

In the sentences below, people are talking about *certain quantities* of food. Note the words in heavy type.

Voici **du** rosbif.	*Here is (some) roast beef.*
Avez-vous **du** jambon?	*Do you have (any) ham?*
Est-ce qu'il y a **de la** soupe?	*Is there (any) soup?*
Il y a **de la** salade.	*There is (some) salad.*
Nous commandons **de l'**agneau.	*We are ordering (some) lamb.*
Antoine mange **de l'**omelette.	*Antoine is eating (some) omelet.*

To express *a certain quantity*, French speakers use the partitive article. The partitive article has the following forms:

Masculine Singular	**du** **de l'** (+ vowel sound)	**du** rosbif, **du** jambon **de l'**agneau
Feminine Singular	**de la** **de l'** (+ vowel sound)	**de la** soupe, **de la** salade **de l'**omelette

→ The English equivalent of the partitive article is *some* or *any*. Often English uses *no* article. However, in French, the partitive article may not be left out.

Il y a	**du**	poulet et	**de la**	salade aujourd'hui.
There is	. . .	*chicken and*	. . .	*salad today.*

ACTIVITÉ 1 Le dîner *(Dinner)*

Imagine that you have organized a dinner for the French Club. Tell a friend what there is on the menu.

→ le rosbif   **Il y a du rosbif.**

1. la soupe	3. le poisson	5. le pain	7. le gâteau
2. l'omelette	4. la salade	6. le fromage	8. la glace

ACTIVITÉ 2 Au restaurant

A lady is ordering food in a French restaurant. She tells the waiter (**le garçon**) what she likes and asks whether they have those items. The waiter says yes. Play both roles according to the model.

This activity practices cognate recognition and reenters the use of le/la in the general sense.

→ le poisson   La dame: **J'aime le poisson. Avez-vous du poisson?**
　　　　　　　　　　Le garçon: **Bien sûr, nous avons du poisson.**

1. le caviar	3. le melon	5. le poulet	7. l'agneau
2. le céleri	4. le jambon	6. la moutarde *(mustard)*	8. la margarine

VARIATIONS with la sole, la mayonnaise, l'omelette, le camembert.

B. L'article partitif dans les phrases négatives

Compare the forms of the partitive article in affirmative and negative sentences:

Manges-tu **du** dessert?	Non, je **ne** mange **pas de** dessert.	*I'm **not** eating (**any**) dessert.*
Avez-vous **de la** viande?	Non, nous n'avons **pas de** viande.	*We have **no** meat.*
Est-ce qu'il y a **de l'**omelette?	Non, il **n'**y a **pas d'**omelette.	*There isn't **any** omelet.*

> In negative sentences **du, de la,** and **de l'** become **de** and **d'.**

Exception: After **Ce n'est pas,** the regular partitive article is used.

C'est de l'agneau. **Ce n'est pas du** rosbif!

ACTIVITÉ 3 Au régime

Charles is on a diet. He may eat everything except fish and meat. Say what foods he orders and what foods he does not order.

→ le jambon **Il ne commande pas de jambon.**
   la glace **Il commande de la glace.**

1. l'agneau
2. l'omelette
3. le dessert
4. la soupe
5. la salade
6. le rosbif
7. le poulet
8. le gâteau
9. le poisson
10. le pain
11. le fromage
12. la viande

On mange encore de la bonne viande à Paris.

Hippopotamus.
3 restaurants de viande à Paris.

ACTIVITÉ 4 Dialogue

Ask your classmates whether or not they often eat the following foods.

→ du poisson Élève 1: **Manges-tu souvent du poisson?**
               Élève 2: **Oui, je mange souvent du poisson.**
                            (Non, je ne mange pas souvent de poisson.)

1. de la glace
2. du pain
3. du pain français
4. du fromage américain

5. du fromage français
6. de l'agneau
7. de la soupe
8. de l'omelette

VARIATION in the plural: —Mangez-vous...
                               —Oui, nous mangeons...
Note that in spoken French, **nous mangeons** is a regular form.

C. Le verbe *boire*

Note the forms of the irregular verb **boire** *(to drink)* in the present tense.

Infinitive		boire	Qu'est-ce que vous désirez **boire**?
Present	je	**bois**	Je **bois** toujours du café.
	tu	**bois**	Tu **bois** du thé.
	il/elle	**boit**	Isabelle **boit** de la limonade.
	nous	**buvons**	Nous **buvons** de l'eau minérale.
	vous	**buvez**	Vous ne **buvez** pas de bière?
	ils/elles	**boivent**	Les enfants **boivent** du lait.

Vocabulaire spécialisé   Les boissons *(Beverages)*

le café

le Coca-Cola (le coca)

le jus d'orange

le lait

le thé

le vin

ACTIVITÉ 5   À la fête internationale *(At the international party)*

At the international party the guests are drinking their typical national beverages. Express this according to the model.

→ **Pietro est italien. (du vin rouge)   Pietro boit du vin rouge.**

1. Nous sommes américains. (du coca)
2. Vous êtes anglais. (du thé)
3. Je suis français. (du vin)
4. Maria est brésilienne *(Brazilian).* (du café)
5. Mes amis sont chinois. (du thé)
6. Karl est allemand. (de la bière)
7. Tu es turc. (du café)
8. Vous êtes américains. (du jus d'orange)

ACTIVITÉ 6   Le réfrigérateur   OPTIONAL

Say whether or not the following items are in your refrigerator at home.

→ le coca   **Oui, il y a du coca. (Non, il n'y a pas de coca.)**

1. le vin blanc
2. le vin rouge
3. l'eau
4. l'eau minérale
5. le thé
6. la bière
7. le jus d'orange
8. la limonade
9. le lait
10. la glace
11. le jambon
12. le fromage

la boisson   *drink, beverage*

l'eau

la bière

l'eau minérale

la limonade

La limonade is like ginger ale. To order lemonade, one asks for un citron pressé.

ACTIVITÉ 7 Expression personnelle

Complete the sentences below with foods and beverages listed in the vocabulary sections of this lesson. Use the appropriate partitive articles.

→ Chez moi je bois . . .   **Chez moi je bois du lait.**

Elicit various responses from different students. You may ask the class to repeat certain answers. Qu'est-ce que Nancy boit le matin? Que boivent les parents de Dick?

1. Le matin (*In the morning*) je bois . . .
2. Mes parents boivent . . .
3. Nous ne buvons pas . . .
4. À la cantine (*school cafeteria*) nous buvons . . .
5. À la cantine nous ne buvons pas . . .
6. À la cantine je mange . . .
7. J'aime manger . . .
8. Ce soir, j'espère manger . . .
9. À la maison nous mangeons souvent . . .
10. À la maison nous ne mangeons pas souvent . . .

UN JEU OPTIONAL

Prepare menus for the following people. Each menu must have three foods and a beverage. (See the vocabulary sections of this lesson.)

→ une personne qui aime manger

Pour la personne qui aime manger il y a du rosbif, de l'agneau, de la glace et du vin.

1. une personne malade
2. une personne qui est au régime
3. un végétarien
4. un athlète
5. un Français
6. un Anglais

Prononciation

Les lettres s et ss

Between vowels the letter **s** represents the sound /z/:

angla<u>i</u><u>s</u>e, mayonna<u>i</u><u>s</u>e, ma<u>i</u><u>s</u>on, frança<u>i</u><u>s</u>e

Between vowels the letters **ss** represent the sound /s/:

boi<u>ss</u>on, sui<u>ss</u>e, réu<u>ss</u>ir, fini<u>ss</u>ez, maigri<u>ss</u>ez, gro<u>ss</u>ir

Contrast:

poi<u>ss</u>on—poi<u>s</u>on; de<u>ss</u>ert—dé<u>s</u>ert; chau<u>ss</u>ettes—chemi<u>s</u>e; choi<u>s</u>i<u>ss</u>ez

Entre nous

Expressions pour la conversation

To contradict a *negative* question, French speakers do not say **oui**.
Instead they say:

> **si** *yes* —Tu n'as pas faim ce soir?
>   —**Si**, j'ai très faim!

To refuse politely something which has been offered, you may say:

> **(Non,) merci.** *No, thank you.*   —Vous ne buvez pas de thé?
>   —**(Non,) merci**, je n'ai pas soif.

Mini-dialogue   OPTIONAL

Pourquoi est-ce qu'Isabelle
ne mange pas?

MME MERCIER:	Tu ne manges pas de salade, Isabelle?	
ISABELLE:	Non, merci . . .	
MME MERCIER:	Alors, tu vas manger du fromage, et *puis* de la glace.	*then*
ISABELLE:	Merci, Maman. Vraiment.	
MME MERCIER:	Comment? Tu n'as pas d'appétit aujourd'hui?	
ISABELLE:	Si Maman, j'ai de l'appétit, mais . . .	
MME MERCIER:	Mais quoi?	
ISABELLE:	Ce soir je suis *invitée* à une *surboum* chez Charles.	*invited; party*
MME MERCIER:	Et tu réserves ton appétit pour le buffet, je suppose?	
ISABELLE:	Euh oui . . . La mère de Charles fait des sandwichs *absolument* extraordinaires!	*absolutely*

Like match, sandwich has two plural forms: sandwichs and sandwiches.

L'art du dialogue

a) Act out the dialog between Madame Mercier and Isabelle.
b) Imagine that the menu has been changed but that the situation remains the same. Madame Mercier proposes **(la) soupe** (instead of **salade**), **(la) salade** (instead of **fromage**), and **(le) gâteau** (instead of **glace**). Act out the new dialog after making the appropriate changes.

Leçon 3 L'ABC de la santé

Vous êtes en excellente *forme* physique et morale, n'est-ce pas?   *shape*
Et vous désirez rester en forme?
C'est simple! Observez ces dix recommandations:

1. Mangez des fruits et de la salade!
2. Ne mangez pas de viande *à chaque*   *at every meal*
   repas!
3. Buvez de l'eau minérale ou du jus de
   fruits!
4. Ne buvez pas de bière!
5. Allez à l'école *à pied* ou *utilisez* votre   *on foot; use*
   bicyclette!
6. Pratiquez un sport: jouez au tennis, au
   basket ou au volley!
7. Nagez en été et skiez en hiver!
8. Choisissez un *passe-temps* intéressant: *hobby*
   la *photo*, la musique, la *poterie*,   *photography; pottery*
   par exemple!   *for example*
9. Ne restez pas *constamment devant* la   *constantly; in front of*
   télé.
10. Ne perdez pas votre *temps!*   *time*

CONVERSATION

You may do this activity with a show of hands. How many of you have parents who tell you to study? How many don't tell you to study?

If your parents are typical parents, they often tell you what to do and what not to do.
Do they give you the following advice? Answer **oui** or **non** for each item.

1. **Étudie!**
2. **Travaille!**
3. **Mange** plus!
4. **Mange** moins!
5. Ne **regarde** pas la télé!
6. Ne **dépense** pas ton argent!

OBSERVATIONS Str. A

To make *suggestions* or to *give advice*, one uses a verb form called the *imperative*.
In the above suggestions, the **tu** form of the imperative is used.

• Which letters do the infinitives of the above verbs end in? -er

• Which letter does the **tu** form of the imperative end in? -e

• Is the **tu** form of the *imperative* different from the **tu** form of the *present*? How?
yes   There is no final **s.**

NOTE CULTURELLE

For reading and listening practice.

La marche°

Comment rester en forme? À l'école, les jeunes Français pratiquent leur sport favori:° le volley, le basket ou le football (le football français, bien sûr!). En hiver ils vont skier, et en été ils vont nager.

Mais il y a aussi un autre° sport qu'on pratique toute l'année en France: la marche. En semaine,° les jeunes Français marchent pour aller° à l'école. Le week-end, ils marchent pour aller au cinéma, à la plage, ou chez leurs amis. En moyenne,° les Français marchent huit kilomètres par° jour.

Et vous, est-ce que vous marchez huit kilomètres par jour? Non? Alors, qu'est-ce que vous faites° pour rester en forme?

La marche Walking **favori** favorite **un autre** another
En semaine During the week **pour aller** to go
En moyenne On the average **par** per **qu'est-ce que
vous faites** what do you do

VOCABULARY EXPANSION: **un patin** (skate), **un patin à roulettes** (roller skate), **un patin à glace** (ice skate), **le ski de fond** (cross-country skiing), **le ski nautique** (water-skiing), **le camping**

Vocabulaire spécialisé   Sports et passe-temps (Sports and hobbies)

NOMS:			
le dessin	art, drawing	**la cuisine**	cooking
le footing	} jogging	**la danse**	dancing
le jogging		**la gymnastique**	gymnastics
le patinage	skating	**la natation**	swimming
le ski	skiing	**la photo**	photography
le vélo	bicycling	**la poterie**	pottery
		la voile	sailing

ADJECTIFS:	
dangereux (dangereuse)	dangerous
difficile	hard, difficult
excellent	excellent
facile	easy
intéressant	interesting
passionnant	exciting
violent	violent

Le jogging is a relatively new word in French.
In French, ballet is referred to as **la danse classique.**

ACTIVITÉ 1   Opinions

Give your opinions about the following sports and pastimes according to the model. Use adjectives from the **Vocabulaire spécialisé.**

→ le ski   **Le ski est un sport passionnant (dangereux, . . .)**

la poterie   **La poterie est un passe-temps facile (intéressant, . . .)**

les sports
1. le patinage
2. le vélo
3. la gymnastique
4. la voile
5. la natation

les passe-temps
6. la sculpture
7. la danse
8. la photo
9. la cuisine
10. le dessin

Structure

A. L'impératif: *tu* et *vous*

Note the forms of the *imperative* in the sentences below, and compare them with the corresponding **tu** and **vous** forms of the *present*.

	PRESENT TENSE	AFFIRMATIVE IMPERATIVE	NEGATIVE IMPERATIVE
-er verbs	(tu manges)	**Mange** de la salade.	**Ne mange pas** de pain.
	(vous mangez)	**Mangez** du fromage.	**Ne mangez pas** de rosbif.
-ir verbs	(tu choisis)	**Choisis** cette veste.	**Ne choisis pas** ce pantalon.
	(vous choisissez)	**Choisissez** ce disque.	**Ne choisissez pas** ce livre.
-re verbs	(tu vends)	**Vends** ton ballon *(ball)*.	**Ne vends pas** ta raquette.
	(vous vendez)	**Vendez** votre voiture.	**Ne vendez pas** votre vélo.

The *imperative* is used to give orders, advice, and suggestions. The **tu** and **vous** forms of the imperative of **-ir** verbs and **-re** verbs are the same as the corresponding forms of the present tense.

Note: The **tu** form of the imperative of **-er** verbs = the **tu** form of the present minus **-s**.

→ As in English, subject pronouns are not used in the imperative.

→ The above pattern also applies to most irregular verbs.

(aller)	tu vas	**Va** à la maison.	vous allez	**Allez** chez vous.
(boire)	tu bois	**Bois** du jus de fruits.	vous buvez	**Buvez** du lait.

ACTIVITÉ 2 Baby-sitting

Le baby-sitting is another example of an English word which has recently entered the French language.

Imagine that you are baby-sitting for Christophe, a seven-year-old French boy. Tell him to do the following things.

→ dîner   **Dîne, Christophe.**

1. manger du pain
2. finir ta soupe
3. regarder la télé
4. choisir un programme intéressant
5. jouer du piano
6. aller dans ta chambre *(room)*

VARIATION: You are caring for Christophe and Lise. **Dînez, Christophe et Lise.**

ACTIVITÉ 3 Chez le docteur

Imagine that you are working in the office of a French doctor. One of your patients, Monsieur Dupont, is allowed to eat everything, with the exception of meats. He should drink only nonalcoholic beverages. Give him his instructions, using **manger** for items 1–8 and **boire** for items 9–16.

→ de la viande   **Ne mangez pas de viande.**   Be sure students use **de (d')** in negative sentences.

du lait   **Buvez du lait.**

1. du jambon
2. de la salade
3. du poulet
4. de la soupe
5. de l'agneau
6. du gâteau
7. du rosbif
8. du poisson
9. de l'eau minérale
10. de la limonade
11. du jus d'orange
12. du whisky
13. de l'eau
14. du vin
15. du thé
16. de la bière

The following irregular imperatives are not taught at this level.

être	Sois généreux.	Soyez patients.
avoir	Aies du courage.	Ayez de la patience.

ACTIVITÉ 4 **L'ange et le démon** *(The angel and the devil)*   OPTIONAL

Christine is thinking whether she should do certain things. The angel gives
her good advice. The devil gives her bad advice. Play the roles of the angel
and the devil.

→ préparer l'examen   L'ange: **Prépare l'examen.**
                        Le démon: **Ne prépare pas l'examen.**

1. étudier les verbes
2. téléphoner à ta grand-mère
3. inviter les amis
4. aller à l'école
5. respecter tes professeurs

6. finir la leçon
7. penser à l'avenir *(future)*
8. boire du lait
9. perdre ton temps *(time)*
10. vendre les disques de ton frère

B. Récapitulation: les articles (défini, indéfini, partitif)

Articles are used much more frequently in French than in English. The choice
of a *definite*, *indefinite*, or *partitive* article depends on what is being described.

Use:	to describe:	
the *definite* article **le, la, l', les**	a noun used in the *general* sense	J'aime **le gâteau.** *(As a rule) I like cake.*
	a *specific* thing	Voici **le gâteau.** *Here is the cake (I baked).*
the *indefinite* article **un, une, des**	one (or several) *whole* item(s)	Voici **un gâteau.** *Here is a (whole) cake (not divided).*
the *partitive* article **du, de la, de l'**	*some, a portion of, a certain amount of* something	Voici **du gâteau.** *Here is some (a serving, a piece of) cake.*

You may want to review these uses with other examples: **la (une, de la) glace; le (un, du) poulet; le (un, du) fromage.**

→ The definite article is used after the following verbs:

With these verbs, other articles may also be used: **Avez-vous** le pain? J'ai un pain. etc.

adorer	Charles **adore le** dessert.	**détester**	Nous **détestons** l'eau minérale.
aimer	Mes amis **aiment la** glace.	**préférer**	**Préférez-vous la** viande ou **le** poisson?

→ The partitive article is often used after the following verbs and expressions:

avoir	**Avez**-vous **du** pain?	**manger**	Tu **manges du** poulet.
boire	Claire **boit de la** limonade.		
commander	Nous **commandons du** jambon.	**il y a**	**Il y a du** thé pour vous.

→ The French do *not* use the partitive article with a noun that is the subject of the sentence.

Il y a **du** rosbif et **de la** glace dans le réfrigérateur.
but: **Le** rosbif et **la** glace sont dans le réfrigérateur.

→ The partitive article may also be used with nouns other than foods.

Avez-vous **de** l'argent?	*Do you have (any, a certain amount of) money?*
Michèle a **du** talent!	*Michèle has (some, a certain amount of) talent!*

ACTIVITÉ 5   Cocktail

Monsieur and Madame Moreau have invited friends to a cocktail party. Say which drinks the following people like and what they are having.

→ Monsieur Mercier (le vin blanc)
Monsieur Mercier aime le vin blanc. Il boit du vin blanc.

1. Madame Mercier (l'eau minérale)
2. Monsieur Charron (le whisky)
3. Madame Charron (le jus d'orange)
4. Monsieur Lavie (la bière)
5. Mademoiselle Masson (le champagne)
6. Madame Arnaud (la limonade)

ACTIVITÉ 6   Expression personnelle

Give your opinions about the following items. In the first sentence use the first verb and the *definite* article. In the second sentence use the second verb and the *partitive* article.

→ le lait (aimer / boire)   **J'aime le lait. Je bois du lait.**
(Je n'aime pas le lait. Je ne bois pas de lait.)

1. la glace (aimer / manger)
2. le poisson (aimer / manger)
3. l'eau minérale (aimer / boire)
4. le chewing-gum (aimer / acheter)
5. l'argent (aimer / dépenser)
6. le courage (admirer / avoir)
7. le talent artistique (respecter / avoir)
8. l'ambition (admirer / avoir)

Prononciation

Le son /œ̃/

Model word: <u>un</u>

Practice words: br<u>un</u>, <u>un</u> café, <u>un</u> fromage, <u>un</u> homme

Practice sentences: J'ai <u>un</u> frère qui est br<u>un</u>.

Tu as <u>un</u> ami qui a <u>un</u> vélo?

The sound /œ̃/ is a nasal vowel. Be sure not to pronounce an /n/ after the nasal vowel unless liaison is required.

Comment écrire /œ̃/: **un** (or **um** before **b** or **p**)

Entre nous

Expression pour la conversation

To agree with a statement or with a question, the French often use the following expression:

C'est ça! *That's it! That's right!* —Vous habitez à Paris?

—**C'est ça!**

Mini-dialogue OPTIONAL

Jean-Paul a rendez-vous dans un café avec Lynn, une amie américaine.

JEAN-PAUL: Alors, Lynn! Qu'est-ce que tu vas commander?

LYNN: Un sandwich!

JEAN-PAUL: Et qu'est-ce que tu vas boire avec ton sandwich?

LYNN: Du lait!

JEAN-PAUL: Du lait? Mais voyons, Lynn, tu es en France ici! Commande du vin rouge ou du vin blanc!

LYNN: Mais je n'aime pas le vin!

JEAN-PAUL: Alors, commande de la bière!

LYNN: C'est ça! *(au garçon)* Garçon, s'il vous plaît! Un *sandwich au fromage!* Avec une bière . . . et un grand *verre* de lait!

Waiter

cheese sandwich

glass

L'art du dialogue

a) Act out the dialog between Jean-Paul and Lynn.

b) Now imagine that Lynn wants to drink orange juice (**le jus d'orange**). Jean-Paul suggests mineral water (**l'eau minérale**) and coffee (**le café**). Create the new dialog and act it out.

Leçon 4 **Tout s'explique!**

 Jacques *rencontre* ses amis Antoine et Marie-Claude.

meets

JACQUES:	Salut, Antoine! Salut, Marie-Claude!
	Qu'est-ce que vous faites aujourd'hui?
ANTOINE:	Moi, je vais au stade.
JACQUES:	Qu'est-ce que tu fais là-bas?
ANTOINE:	Je vais *faire un match* de foot avec des *copains*.
JACQUES:	Et toi aussi, Marie-Claude, tu vas faire du sport?
MARIE-CLAUDE:	Moi, non. Je ne vais pas au stade . . .
JACQUES:	Bon, alors *viens* au cinéma avec moi. Il y a un bon film!
MARIE-CLAUDE:	Impossible. J'ai une classe à trois heures.
JACQUES:	Comment? Mais *nous sommes* samedi! Il n'y a pas classe aujourd'hui!
MARIE-CLAUDE:	Le samedi je fais de l'anglais dans une école *privée*.
JACQUES:	Tiens! Tu fais de l'anglais maintenant? Est-ce qu'il y a un bon *laboratoire de langues* à cette école?
MARIE-CLAUDE:	Euh, non. Mais . . .
ANTOINE:	. . . mais il y a un jeune professeur américain, très beau et très sympathique!
JACQUES:	*Tout s'explique* maintenant!

What are you doing

to play a game; friends

come

= c'est

private

language lab

Everything is clear

Où va Antoine? Qu'est-ce qu'il fait là-bas? Où va Marie-Claude? Quelle langue est-ce qu'elle étudie? Pourquoi est-ce qu'elle aime étudier l'anglais?

CONVERSATION OPTIONAL

Let's talk about what you do in school.

1. Est-ce que vous **faites de** l'anglais?
   Oui, je **fais de** l'anglais. (Non, je ne **fais** pas d'anglais.)
2. Est-ce que vous **faites du** français?
3. Est-ce que vous **faites de** l'italien?
4. Est-ce que vous **faites du** sport?
5. Est-ce que vous **faites de la** musique?

OBSERVATIONS Str. B   OPTIONAL

The questions above use a new verb: **faire** *(to do, make).*

• Which *article* is used to introduce the names of the activities? a partitive article

NOTE CULTURELLE   For reading and listening practice.

L'étude° de l'anglais

Pourquoi étudiez-vous le français? Parce qu'un jour vous espérez aller en France ou au Canada? ou parce que c'est obligatoire° dans votre école?

   En France, l'étude des langues° est obligatoire à l'école secondaire. Soixante-quinze pour cent (75%) des jeunes Français choisissent l'anglais. Ensuite° viennent° l'allemand (quinze pour cent), l'espagnol (huit pour cent) et l'italien (deux pour cent). Pourquoi est-ce que l'anglais est si° populaire en France? Parce que c'est une langue très utile° quand on voyage. Et dans un grand nombre de professions, c'est une langue indispensable.°

étude *study* **obligatoire** *required* **langues** *languages*
Ensuite *Then* **viennent** *come* **si** *so* **utile** *useful*
indispensable *necessary*

Structure

A. Le verbe *faire*

Be sure students pronounce the ai of **faisons** as /ə/.

Note the forms of the verb **faire** *(to do, make)* in the present tense:

Infinitive		faire	Qu'est-ce que vous avez envie de **faire** aujourd'hui?
Present	je	**fais**	Je **fais** des exercices.
	tu	**fais**	Tu **fais** des progrès.
	il/elle	**fait**	Jacques **fait** des projets de vacances.
	nous	**faisons**	Nous **faisons** un voyage.
	vous	**faites**	Qu'est-ce que vous **faites**?
	ils/elles	**font**	Lise et Paul **font** un match de tennis.

Faire is one of the most useful verbs in French. Its principal meaning is *to do, make.*

Qu'est-ce que vous **faites** ce soir?	*What are you doing tonight?*
Paul **fait** des progrès en anglais.	*Paul is making progress in English.*
Nous **faisons** des projets pour demain.	*We are making plans for tomorrow.*

Faire is also used in many expressions:

Juliette **fait un match** de volley.	*Juliette is playing a game of volleyball.*
Paul **fait un voyage.**	*Paul is taking a trip.*

Other familiar expressions with **faire:** Quel temps fait-il? Il fait beau . . .

Vocabulaire spécialisé   Expressions avec *faire*

faire attention	*to pay attention, be careful*	Pierre ne **fait** pas **attention** en classe. Il y a une voiture! **Faites attention!**
faire des progrès	*to make progress*	Nous **faisons des progrès** en français.
faire des projets	*to make plans*	**Fais-tu des projets** pour les vacances?
faire les courses	*to go shopping*	Nous **faisons les courses** le vendredi.
faire un match	*to play a game (match)*	Lise et Paul **font un match** de tennis.
faire un voyage	*to take a trip*	Cet été, je vais **faire un voyage** en France.

VOCABULARY EXPANSION: faire la cuisine, faire une excursion, faire le tour du monde; faire l'idiot/l'innocent . . . (to act stupid, innocent . . .)

ACTIVITÉ 1   Auto-école *(Driving school)*

The following students are learning to drive. Say who is paying attention to the instructor and who is not.

→ Jacques (non)   **Jacques ne fait pas attention.**

1. Catherine (oui)
2. nous (oui)
3. Pierre et Antoine (non)
4. toi (non)
5. moi (oui)
6. Jacqueline (non)
7. mes amies (oui)
8. Sylvie et moi (oui) nous . . .
9. François et toi (non) vous . . .

VARIATION: Those who pay attention are making progress. **Jacques ne fait pas de progrès.**

ACTIVITÉ 2   Vive les vacances!

The following students are taking trips abroad. Say where they are going.

→ Paul (au Canada)   **Paul fait un voyage au Canada.**

1. Jacqueline (en Chine)
2. nous (en Afrique)
3. mes cousines (au Japon)
4. moi (au Sénégal)
5. toi (au Portugal)
6. vous (en Égypte)

VARIATIONS: a) Say they are making interesting plans. **Paul fait des projets intéressants.**
b) Ask what they are going to do in these countries. **Qu'est-ce que Paul va faire au Canada?**

ACTIVITÉ 3   Questions personnelles

1. Est-ce que vous faites attention quand le professeur parle? quand vos parents parlent? quand vous étudiez?
2. Est-ce que vous faites des progrès en français? en anglais? en maths? en sciences?
3. Est-ce que vous faites souvent les courses? Qu'est-ce que vous achetez quand vous faites les courses? Qui fait aussi les courses chez vous, votre père ou votre mère?
4. Aimez-vous faire des voyages? Faites-vous souvent des voyages? Est-ce que vous allez faire un voyage cet été? où? avec qui?
5. Est-ce que vous faites souvent des choses (*things*) intéressantes? quelles choses?
6. Aimez-vous faire des projets? Faites-vous des projets pour le week-end? pour les vacances? pour l'avenir (*future*)?

B. La construction: *faire du, faire de la*

Note the use of **faire** in the following sentences:

Est-ce que tu **fais de l'espagnol?**	*Do you study (Are you learning) Spanish?*
Non, je **fais du latin.**	*No, I study Latin.*
Paul **fait du ski.**	*Paul skis.*
Hélène **fait de la natation.**	*Hélène swims.*
Nous **faisons de la poterie.**	*We do pottery.*
Est-ce que vous **faites du théâtre?**	*Are you active in theater?*
Mes amis **font de la guitare.**	*My friends play (are learning to play) the guitar.*

Faire is often used in the following constructions:

faire du, de la, de l', des $\begin{cases} + & \text{sport} & \textit{to play, participate actively in} \\ + & \text{school subject} & \textit{to study, learn} \\ + & \text{instrument} & \textit{to play, learn to play} \\ + & \text{pastime} & \textit{to do, be active in} \end{cases}$

→ In negative sentences, **faire de (d')** is used.

Faites-vous **des** maths?   Non, nous ne faisons pas **de** maths.

This is a special use of the partitive article. **Faire du sport** means *to do a certain amount of sport.*
VOCABULARY EXPANSION: *school subjects:* **faire des maths, de la biologie, de l'histoire, des sciences, du latin, du dessin**

ACTIVITÉ 4 À la Maison des Jeunes *(At the Youth Center)*

Say that the following people are doing what they like to do.

→ Christine aime la danse classique. **Elle fait de la danse classique.**

1. Anne aime la danse moderne.
2. Robert aime le ping-pong.
3. Tu aimes la guitare.
4. Vous aimez la gymnastique.

5. Nous aimons le sport.
6. Henri et Jacques aiment la photo.
7. J'aime la poterie.
8. Claire et Marie aiment le théâtre.

ACTIVITÉ 5 Dialogue OPTIONAL

Ask your classmates if they participate in the following activities.

→ le sport Élève 1: **Est-ce que tu fais du sport?**
　　　　　 Élève 2: **Oui, je fais du sport.**
　　　　　　　　　 (Non, je ne fais pas de sport.)

1. la photo
2. la natation
3. le ping-pong
4. le skate-board
5. le vélo
6. la voile
7. la poterie
8. le dessin
9. le judo
10. le volley
11. le ski
12. la gymnastique
13. le piano
14. la guitare
15. la planche à voile
　　(wind-surfing)

ACTIVITÉ 6 Questions personnelles

1. Vous faites du français, n'est-ce pas? Aimez-vous le français?
2. Faites-vous de l'espagnol aussi? de l'allemand?
3. Faites-vous de l'anglais? Est-ce que la classe d'anglais est difficile?
4. Qu'est-ce que vous préférez? l'histoire ou la géographie? le dessin ou les maths? le français ou les sciences?
5. Qu'est-ce que vous avez envie de faire à l'université? du français? des maths? de l'histoire? des sciences?

C. Le verbe *venir*

Note the forms of the irregular verb **venir** *(to come)* in the present tense.

Infinitive		venir	Nous allons **venir** avec des amis.
Present	je	**viens**	Je **viens** avec toi.
	tu	**viens**	Est-ce que tu **viens** au cinéma?
	il/elle	**vient**	Jacqueline ne **vient** pas avec nous.
	nous	**venons**	Nous **venons** à cinq heures.
	vous	**venez**	Quand **venez**-vous?
	ils/elles	**viennent**	Ils **viennent** de Paris, n'est-ce pas?

➜ **Revenir** *(to come back)* is conjugated like **venir**.

ACTIVITÉ 7 Oui ou non?

Pierre has asked his friends to go to the movies with him. Say who is
coming and who is not.

VARIATIONS: Philippe ne vient pas demain.
Philippe ne vient pas au pique-nique.

➜ Philippe (non) **Philippe ne vient pas.**

1. Sylvie (non)
2. nous (oui)
3. toi (non)
4. Henri et Claude (oui)
5. mes cousines (non)
6. moi (oui)
7. vous (non)
8. Hélène et moi (oui) nous. . .
9. Charles et toi (non) vous. . .
10. Isabelle (oui)

ACTIVITÉ 8 La convention des jeunes OPTIONAL

The following people are participating in the International Youth
Convention. Say where each one comes from.

➜ Jean-Philippe est français. (Paris) **Il vient de Paris.**

1. Henri est suisse. (Genève)
2. Je suis sénégalais. (Dakar)
3. Vous êtes français. (Nice)
4. Nous sommes tunisiens. (Tunis)
5. Jim est américain. (la Nouvelle-Orléans)
6. Janet et Gail sont anglaises. (Liverpool)
7. Tu es canadienne. (Montréal)
8. Jean et Jacques sont haïtiens. (Port-au-Prince)

VARIATION: Say they are all returning from the jamboree which was in Brussels. Il revient de Bruxelles.

RÉVISION: *être, avoir, aller, faire*   OPTIONAL

These are the four most frequently used verbs in French. Review their forms.

être:	je suis, tu es, il est, nous sommes, vous êtes, ils sont
avoir:	j'ai, tu as, il a, nous avons, vous avez, ils ont
aller:	je vais, tu vas, il va, nous allons, vous allez, ils vont
faire:	je fais, tu fais, il fait, nous faisons, vous faites, ils font

ACTIVITÉ DE RÉVISION: Tourisme

The following people are travelling this summer. Give each one's nationality and say where they are going. Then say that they are studying a second language and that they have the corresponding textbook.
(Languages: **français, anglais, espagnol**)

→ Jim (américain /à Québec)   **Jim est américain.**
Il va à Québec.
Il fait du français.
Il a un livre de français.

1. Luisa et Clara (mexicaines /à Boston)
2. nous (américains /à Acapulco)
3. toi (canadien /à Madrid)

4. vous (anglais /à Paris)
5. Sylvie (française /à Chicago)
6. moi (américain /à Nice)

VARIATION: Add a review of **revenir.** Each one returns. **Jim revient de Québec.**

UN JEU   OPTIONAL

If we are carrying a tennis racket, it is probably because we are going to the tennis courts to play tennis. How many logical sentences can you make in five minutes using the verbs **avoir, aller,** and **faire** with elements of columns A, B, C, and D? See the models below.

A	B	C	D
moi	un kimono	en ville	le ski
toi	des skis	dans les Alpes	le volleyball
Catherine	un ballon *(ball)*	à la Maison des Jeunes	le judo
nous	un dictionnaire	*(Youth Center)*	le karaté
vous	un appareil-photo	à la plage	la photo
mes camarades	un sac	à l'école	le français
		au stade	le basketball
			les courses

→ **Catherine a un kimono. Elle va à la Maison des Jeunes. Elle fait du judo.**
→ **J'ai des skis. Je vais dans les Alpes. Je fais du ski.**

Prononciation

Les sons /jɛ̃/ et /jɛn/

Contrast: /jɛ̃/   b<u>ien</u>, v<u>iens</u>, canad<u>ien</u>, ital<u>ien</u>

Jul<u>ien</u> v<u>ien</u>t avec Luc<u>ien</u>.

       /jɛn/   v<u>ienn</u>ent, canad<u>ienn</u>e, ital<u>ienn</u>e

Les deux Canad<u>ienn</u>es ne v<u>ienn</u>ent pas.

Entre nous

Expressions pour la conversation

To ask someone to wait for you, you may say:

Une seconde!	*Just a second!*
Une minute!	*Just a minute!*

Mini-dialogue   OPTIONAL

Marc n'est pas un garçon très *sportif*, mais il y a des occasions spéciales . . .   *athletic*

MARC: Qu'est-ce que tu fais cet après-midi?

HÉLÈNE: Je vais au stade avec Vincent.

MARC: Qu'est-ce que vous allez faire?

HÉLÈNE: Du footing! Tu viens?

MARC: Euh, non . . . Je n'ai pas mes chaussures.

HÉLÈNE: Dommage!

MARC: Pourquoi «dommage»?

HÉLÈNE: Parce qu'après le footing, Vincent va inviter ses amis au cinéma.

MARC: Une seconde . . .! Je viens avec toi!

HÉLÈNE: Et tes chaussures?

MARC: Elles sont *là* dans mon sac!   *here*

L'art du dialogue

a) Act out the dialog between Marc and Hélène.

b) Prepare a new dialog where Hélène is going to the pool (**la piscine**) to swim (**faire de la natation**), and where Marc says he doesn't have his swimsuit (**le maillot de bain**). Make all necessary changes.

c) Write and act out a new dialog where Hélène is talking to **Marc** and **Florence**. Divide Marc's role into two parts and make all necessary changes.

UNITÉ 5

Leçon 5

STRUCTURES TO OBSERVE
• the **nous** form of the imperative
• **prendre**
• the construction **venir de** + infinitive

Week-end en Normandie

Aujourd'hui, nous sommes le 5 juillet. C'est un dimanche.
Dehors il fait très beau. Quels sont les projets de Nicole et
de son frère Pierre?

Outside

NICOLE: Dis, Pierre! Qu'est-ce qu'on fait aujourd'hui?

PIERRE: *Restons* à la maison . . . et regardons la télévision.

Let's stay

NICOLE: Ah non! Il fait trop beau pour rester à la maison
aujourd'hui! Allons à la plage!

PIERRE: Oui, mais comment?

NICOLE: *Prenons* ta moto!

Let's take

PIERRE: Elle ne marche pas.

NICOLE: Alors, prenons le bus.

PIERRE: C'est dimanche! Il n'y a pas de bus aujourd'hui!

NICOLE: Alors, prenons un taxi.

PIERRE: Je n'ai pas d'argent.

NICOLE: *Moi non plus.* Alors, téléphonons à Georges. Il a
une voiture.

Me neither.

PIERRE: Je *viens de téléphoner.* Il n'est pas chez lui.

just called

NICOLE: Il n'y a pas de solution!

PIERRE: Mais si, il y a toujours une solution . . .

NICOLE: Quelle solution?

PIERRE: Allons à la plage *à pied.*

on foot

NICOLE: Dix kilomètres à pied??! Non, mais tu n'es pas *fou,*
par hasard! Il fait trop chaud pour marcher. Et
puis . . . je suis fatiguée, moi!

crazy
by any chance
besides

PIERRE: Alors, qu'est-ce qu'on fait?

NICOLE: Restons à la maison . . . et regardons la télévision.

Quel jour est-ce? Qu'est-ce que Pierre désire faire aujourd'hui? Est-ce que Nicole est d'accord? Qu'est-ce qu'elle désire
faire? Pourquoi est-ce que Pierre ne prend pas sa moto? Pourquoi est-ce que Nicole et Pierre ne prennent pas le bus?
Alors, qu'est-ce qu'ils font?

Let's talk about things you have done within the past hour.
Have you just . . .?

1. **Venez**-vous **de** parler avec le professeur?
   Oui, **je viens de** parler avec le professeur.
   (Non, **je** ne **viens** pas **de** parler avec le professeur.)
2. **Venez**-vous **de** parler avec vos amis?
3. **Venez**-vous **de** regarder le livre?
4. **Venez**-vous **de** manger un sandwich?
5. **Venez**-vous **de** boire un coca?

OBSERVATIONS   Str. C   OPTIONAL

Look at the *affirmative* answer in the model.

• How do you say *I have just?* je viens de

• Is the verb which follows this expression an *infinitive?* yes

SUGGESTED REALIA: map and travel brochures of Normandy, ads for vacation clubs (Club Méditerranée).

NOTES CULTURELLES For reading and listening practice.

1. La Normandie   La Normandie est une région située° à l'ouest° de la France, sur la côte° Atlantique. En été, des millions de touristes viennent passer leurs vacances sur ses plages de sable fin.°

2. À la plage   Allez-vous souvent à la plage en été? Et qu'est-ce que vous faites quand vous êtes là-bas? Probablement vous nagez ou vous prenez° des bains de soleil° . . . ou vous regardez les gens° qui passent! En France, la plage est le centre d'activités diverses. Certains° jouent aux boules.° D'autres° font du ski nautique° ou de la planche à voile.° D'autres jouent au volley. Parfois° un club sportif° organise un championnat° . . . Et la plage est toujours un excellent endroit° pour se faire° de nouveaux amis.

située *situated*   **ouest** west   **côte** *coast*   **sable fin** *fine sand*
prenez *take*   **bains de soleil** *sunbaths*   **gens** *people*
Certains *Some people*   **jouent aux boules** *bowl*   **D'autres** *Others*
ski nautique *water-skiing*   **planche à voile** *wind-surfing*
Parfois *Sometimes*   **sportif** *athletic*   **championnat** *championship*
endroit *place*   **pour se faire** *to make*

ICI COMMENCE LA NORMANDIE

Le Mont-Saint-Michel, one of the most visited spots in France, is located in Normandy. So is the famous beach of Deauville. On June 6, 1944 the American troops led by General Eisenhower landed at various points along the Normandy coast, thus beginning the liberation of France from the German occupation.

Structure

A. Le verbe *prendre*

Note the forms of the irregular verb **prendre** *(to take)* in the present tense.

Infinitive		prendre	Je vais **prendre** mon vélo.
Present	je	**prends**	Je **prends** un taxi.
	tu	**prends**	**Prends**-tu ta guitare?
	il/elle	**prend**	Isabelle **prend** son appareil-photo.
	nous	**prenons**	Nous **prenons** des photos.
	vous	**prenez**	Vous **prenez** votre voiture?
	ils/elles	**prennent**	Nicole et Pierre ne **prennent** pas le bus.

Distinguish between the /ə/ in **prenons** and **prenez**, and the /ɛ/ of **prennent**.

→ The *singular* forms of **prendre** follow the pattern of regular -**re** verbs. The *plural* forms are *irregular*.

→ When used with names of foods and beverages, **prendre** means *to have.*

Prenez-vous du café ou du thé?   *Are you having coffee or tea?*

Vocabulaire spécialisé   Verbes conjugués comme *prendre*

apprendre	*to learn*	Nous **apprenons** le français.
apprendre à + infinitive	*to learn how to*	Ils **apprennent** à parler anglais.
comprendre	*to understand*	Est-ce que vous **comprenez** tout?

ACTIVITÉ 1   Le banquet

For the 25th reunion there is an alumni banquet. Say what everyone is having.

→ moi (du caviar)   **Je prends du caviar.**

1. Hélène (du vin blanc)
2. Sylvie et Marc (du champagne)
3. toi (du gâteau au chocolat)
4. moi (du rosbif)
5. vous (de l'agneau)
6. nous (de la bière)
7. Michèle (de la glace)
8. mes amis (de la salade)

ACTIVITÉ 6 Pourquoi sont-ils fatigués?

The following students are falling asleep in class. Explain why they are so tired.

→ Paul (jouer au volley) **Paul vient de jouer au volley.**

1. Sylvie (jouer au basket)
2. Josette (faire du sport)
3. Catherine (faire un match de tennis)
4. moi (faire du judo)

5. toi (nager)
6. nous (marcher dix kilomètres)
7. vous (faire un match de foot)
8. mes amis (faire du footing)

Profitez de la ville. Prenez le bus.

ACTIVITÉ 7 Avant le week-end *(Before the weekend)* OPTIONAL

Madame Dumas is asking Pierre and Nicole to do certain things before the weekend. Pierre says he has just done them. Nicole says that she is going to do them. Play all three roles.

→ étudier Madame Dumas: **Étudiez!**
      Pierre: **Je viens d'étudier.**
      Nicole: **Je vais étudier.**

1. finir les leçons
2. jouer du piano
3. faire les courses

4. apprendre le vocabulaire
5. téléphoner à grand-mère
6. aller chez le dentiste

UN JEU OPTIONAL

If you are happy, it may be because of something you have just done, or something you are going to do. Form logical affirmative or negative sentences like those in the models below. How many sentences can you make in five minutes, using elements from columns A, B, C, and D.

A	B	C	D
moi	avoir faim	aller	jouer au foot
toi	avoir soif	venir de	faire un match de tennis
Pierre	être fatigué		avoir rendez-vous avec un ami
Nicole	être content *(happy)*		avoir une dispute avec un ami
nous			perdre un match de basket
vous			aller au restaurant
mes amis			aller au café
			manger du rosbif
			dîner en ville
			prendre un Coca-Cola

→ **Pierre a faim. Il va aller au restaurant.**
→ **Nicole n'a pas faim. Elle vient de dîner en ville.**

Prononciation

Révision: le son /ə/

In spoken French the /ə/ is frequently dropped: a) when it is not in the first syllable of a word (**revénir**) b) when it is preceded and followed by one consonant sound only (**vénons, démander**).

In the middle of a word, the letter **e** followed by a single consonant represents the sound /ə/. The **e** of short words like **de, ne, te, je** is also pronounced /ə/.

venir, venons, venez, revenir, revenons, revenez, comprenons, prenez

Nous venons de demander à René de revenir.

Entre nous

Expressions pour la conversation

For emphasis, you may use expressions like:

| certainement | *certainly* | Elle est **certainement** très sympathique. |
| sûrement | *surely* | Il est **sûrement** très intelligent. |

Mini-dialogue   OPTIONAL

Est-ce qu'une nouvelle voiture *apporte le bonheur?*   *bring happiness*

ANNE-MARIE: Je viens de téléphoner à mon cousin Raymond.
CHRISTINE: Eh bien?
ANNE-MARIE: Il vient d'acheter une nouvelle voiture.
CHRISTINE: Il est certainement très content!
ANNE-MARIE: Au contraire! Il est *furieux!*   *furious*
CHRISTINE: Furieux? Pourquoi?
ANNE-MARIE: Parce que cet après-midi il vient d'avoir un accident!
CHRISTINE: Zut alors!

L'art du dialogue

a) Act out the dialog between Anne-Marie and Christine.
b) Prepare a new dialog where Anne-Marie has just phoned her cousin **Claire,** who has just bought a new motorbike (**un vélomoteur**). Make all necessary changes. (The feminine of **furieux** is **furieuse.**)
c) Now prepare a dialog where Anne-Marie has just called her cousins **Paul** and **André.** They have just bought a new motorcycle (**une moto**).

OPPOSITE: Medieval dancing at the Pont Neuf Festival, Paris.

SECTION
MAGAZINE 3

Les loisirs° des jeunes Français

Qu'est-ce que vous faites quand vous avez une soirée de libre?° Voici comment des jeunes Français âgés de 16 à 20 ans ont répondu à° cette question.

	garçons	filles
Je regarde la télévision.	24%	20%
Je sors° avec mes amis.	20%	18%
Je vais au cinéma.	16%	14%
Je lis.°	14%	20%
Je vais au concert ou au théâtre.	10%	12%
Je vais danser.	8%	10%
Je fais du sport.	6%	4%
Je bricole.°	2%	2%

THEATRE
DES CHAMPS-ELYSEES

RÉTROSPECTIVE 1947-1974
CRÉATIONS 1975

MARCEL MARCEAU

avec
PIERRE VERRY

4 PROGRAMMES DIF...
LOCATION AU THEATRE : 225.44...

Le LIVRE de POCHE

TELE 7 JOURS

····MERCREDI····

chaîne 1

16.30
THEATRE
TARTUFFE
de Molière

20.35
OPÉRETTE
GIPSY
de Francis Lopez
avec
José Todaro

chaîne COULEUR 2

21.25
DRAMATIQUE
LA REINE GALANTE
d'André Castelot

23.40
CINEMA
CASINO ROYALE
de John Huston
avec
Ursula Andress

HOCKEY SUR GLACE

FINALE
de la COUPE de FRANCE
Palais des Sports de TOURS
C.P.M. CROIX LILLE
contre
A.S.G. TOURS

mammouth

disco·thèques

loisirs *leisure activities*   soirée de libre *free evening*   ont répondu à *answered*   sors *go out*
lis *read*   bricole *build and fix things*   ILLUSTRATIONS: contre *against*   chaîne *channel*

Une idole

Joe Dassin n'est pas jeune.
Il a trente ans ... ou plus.
Il n'est pas français. Il est américain.
Et cependant° aujourd'hui, Joe Dassin est
  l'un des chanteurs° les plus populaires en
  France. C'est une «idole des jeunes».
Joe Dassin est né° à New York.
Il va à l'université de Michigan, où il étudie
  la sociologie.
C'est un étudiant brillant. Ses parents
  pensent qu'il va être professeur. Ses
  professeurs pensent qu'il va être un
  sociologue célèbre.°
Mais Joe Dassin préfère chanter.
Un jour il quitte° l'université et il arrive en
  France.
Il chante en anglais, puis° en français.
Ses chansons° deviennent° immédiatement
  très populaires. Son grand succès° s'appelle
  «Les Champs-Élysées». Quand ce disque
  passe à° la radio, des milliers° de jeunes
  Français et de jeunes Françaises écoutent
  leur idole avec ferveur.

cependant *nevertheless*   chanteurs *singers*
est né *was born*   célèbre *famous*   quitte *leaves*
puis *then*   chansons *songs*   deviennent *become*
succès *hit*   passe à *is played on*
des milliers *thousands*

CONNAISSEZ-VOUS CES FILMS?

Allez-vous souvent au cinéma?
Quels sont vos films préférés?°
Les films d'aventures? les comédies? les westerns? les
drames psychologiques? . . . ou les dessins animés?

Le cinéma est l'une des distractions° préférées des jeunes
Français. Les films américains sont spécialement° populaires.
Voici une liste de films qui ont connu un grand succès° en France.
Est-ce que vous reconnaissez° ces films? Lisez° les titres° français
de ces films. Faites correspondre° le nom° de ces films avec leur
équivalent anglais.

Titres français	Titres américains
1. Superman	a. Star Wars
2. L'exorciste	b. Snow White and the Seven Dwarfs
3. Butch Cassidy et le Kid	c. Jaws
4. Blanche-Neige	d. The Exorcist
5. Le crime de l'Orient Express	e. The Bridge on the River Kwai
6. Le pont de la rivière Kwaï	f. Superman
7. Certains l'aiment chaud	g. Some Like It Hot
8. Les dents de la mer	h. 2001: A Space Odyssey
9. Autant en emporte le vent	i. Close Encounters of the Third Kind
10. La guerre des étoiles	j. Murder on the Orient Express
11. Rencontres du troisième type	k. Butch Cassidy and the Sundance Kid
12. 2001: L'odyssée de l'espace	l. Gone with the Wind
13. La fièvre du samedi soir	m. Alice in Wonderland
14. Alice au pays des merveilles	n. Saturday Night Fever

RÉPONSES:

1-f, 2-d, 3-k, 4-b, 5-j, 6-e, 7-g, 8-c, 9-l, 10-a, 11-i, 12-h, 13-n, 14-m

Connaissez-vous *Do you know*   **préférés** *favorite*   **distractions** *pastimes*   **spécialement** *especially*   **qui ont connu un grand succès** *that were very successful*   **reconnaissez** *recognize*   **Lisez** *Read*   **titres** *titles*   **Faites correspondre** *Match*   **nom** *name*

LES HÉROS
DE PAPIER

Qui est votre héros préféré?°

Un acteur? un athlète? un inventeur?
Un musicien? un artiste? un homme illustre° . . . ou une femme?

Beaucoup de jeunes Français ont leur héros favori. Mais ce héros
n'est pas nécessairement° une personne réelle.° C'est souvent un
héros de papier, c'est-à-dire° un personnage de bandes dessinées.°

Voici quelques° personnages très populaires en France:

From TINTIN AU TIBET, by Hergé.
© by Éditions Casterman, Paris

©DARGAUD EDITEUR PARIS 1971 d'après
GOSCINNY ET MORRIS

Tintin et Milou

Tintin est un jeune détective. Avec
son chien Milou, Tintin résout° les
énigmes° les plus difficiles.

Lucky Luke

Lucky Luke est un cow-boy
intrépide° qui représente la justice
au Far West. Avec son cheval, Jolly
Jumper, il poursuit° les frères Dal-
ton, quatre bandits très dangereux.

Astérix

Astérix est un homme très petit mais
très courageux. Avec ses amis il
attaque les Romains, ennemis des
Français, ou plus exactement° des
Gaulois.

préféré *favorite*   **illustre** *well-known*   **nécessairement** *necessarily*   **réelle** *real*   **c'est-à-dire**
that is to say   **personnage de bandes dessinées** *comic strip character*   **quelques** *some*   **résout** *solves*
énigmes *mysteries*   **intrépide** *fearless*   **poursuit** *pursues*   **exactement** *exactly*

Vive le football!

Quel est le sport le plus populaire chez les jeunes Français? Le football, naturellement. Aujourd'hui 500.000 jeunes Français de 12 à 16 ans sont inscrits° à la Fédération Française du Football.

Le coût° du football

Le football est un sport simple . . . mais il n'est pas gratuit.° Quand on désire bien jouer au football, on doit° avoir un équipement adéquat.

Voilà le coût de cet équipement:

ligne de but

90 à 120 mètres

ligne de touche

45 à 90 mètres

ailier gauche

ailier droit

avant centre

inter gauche

inter droit

demi gauche

demi droit

arrière central

arrière gauche

arrière droit

gardien de but → but

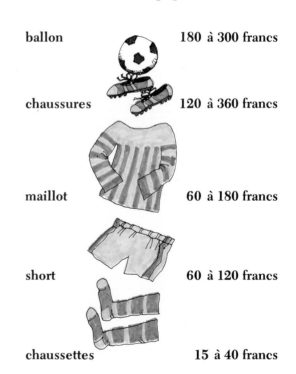

ballon	180 à 300 francs
chaussures	120 à 360 francs
maillot	60 à 180 francs
short	60 à 120 francs
chaussettes	15 à 40 francs

TOTAL: 435 à 1.000 francs

inscrits *registered* coût *cost* **gratuit** *free* **doit** *must*

GALERIE de CHAMPIONS

Ces champions sont très différents, mais ils ont quelque chose° en commun. Ils parlent français ou ils sont d'origine française. Est-ce que vous les connaissez?°

NOM:	**René Lacoste**	**Jacqueline Gareau**
SPORT:	tennis	athlétisme°
NATIONALITÉ:	française	canadienne
REMARQUE:	membre de l'équipe° française victorieuse en Coupe Davis (1927); père de la fameuse° «Chemise Lacoste»	vainqueur° du marathon de Boston (1980)—division féminine; vainqueur du marathon de Montréal (1979)

NOM:	**Jean-Claude Killy**	**Guy Lafleur**	**Ron Guidry**
SPORT:	ski	hockey	baseball
NATIONALITÉ:	française	canadienne	américaine
REMARQUE:	vainqueur de 3 médailles d'or° (slalom spécial, slalom géant, descente°) aux Jeux Olympiques de Grenoble (1968)	joue pour les Canadiens de Montréal; vainqueur du trophée individuel pour le Joueur le plus utile° à son club (1977, 1978)	joue pour les Yankees; vainqueur du trophée «Cy Young» (1978); sa famille est d'origine acadienne

quelque chose *something*   les connaissez *know them*   équipe *team*   fameuse *famous*   athlétisme *track and field*
vainqueur *winner*   médailles d'or *gold medals*   descente *downhill*   Joueur le plus utile *Most Valuable Player*

UN JEU:
Où sommes-nous?

Imaginez que vous voyagez en France. Vous entendez les expressions suivantes.° Où êtes-vous?

Lisez° attentivement la liste d'expressions. Faites correspondre° chaque° expression avec l'endroit° où vous entendez cette expression.

1. «Un coca, un thé et deux jus de fruits!»
2. «Deux billets° pour le match France-Italie!»
3. «Deux gâteaux au chocolat et une glace à la vanille!»
4. «*Paris-Match* et *Elle,* s'il vous plaît!»
5. «Donnez-moi la soupe, le poulet, le fromage et le yogourt, s'il vous plaît.»
6. «Avez-vous des places° pour le dessin animé?»

a. chez le pâtissi
b. au café
c. au restaurant
d. chez le march de journaux
e. au cinéma
f. au stade

RÉPONSES:
1-b, 2-f, 3-a, 4-d, 5-c, 6-e

suivantes *following* Lisez *Read* Faites correspondre *Match* chaque *each* endroit *place*
billets *tickets* places *seats*

Les animaux et le langage

On dit° . . .

1. avoir un caractère de chien
2. avoir une tête° de cochon
3. avoir un appétit d'oiseau
4. avoir une faim° de loup
5. avoir un estomac d'autruche
6. avoir une fièvre° de cheval
7. avoir une langue° de vipère
8. verser des larmes° de crocodile

Cela signifie° . . .

avoir un mauvais caractère
être très obstiné
avoir un petit appétit
avoir très faim°
manger beaucoup
être très malade
parler mal de ses° amis
être hypocrite

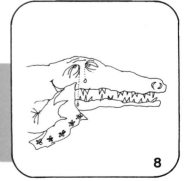

On dit *People say*   **Cela signifie** *That means*   **tête** *head*   **faim** *hunger*   **fièvre** *fever*   **langue** *tongue*   **ses** *one's*   **verser des larmes** *to cry tears*

UN TEST: La mode et vous

Êtes-vous à la mode?
Est-ce que la mode influence vos décisions?
Est-ce que vous faites attention à l'apparence
  des personnes ou des choses?°
Voici un test simple.
Pour chaque° question, choisissez l'une des
  options: A, B ou C.

1. Quand vous choisissez une paire de
   chaussures, quel est l'élément qui°
   détermine votre choix?°
   A. la couleur
   B. le style
   C. le confort
2. Quand vous achetez des vêtements, quel
   est l'élément qui a le plus d'influence sur
   votre décision?
   A. l'opinion de vos amis
   B. la publicité
   C. le prix
3. Est-ce que vous allez acheter un nouveau
   maillot de bain cet été?
   A. Oui, parce que je veux° être à la
      mode.
   B. Oui, parce que je n'ai pas de
      maillot de bain.
   C. Non, je vais porter mon maillot de
      bain de l'année dernière.°
4. Qui est Pierre Cardin?
   A. un artiste français
   B. un couturier° français
   C. un champion français
5. «Chanel N° 5» est un produit° français.
   Quel est ce produit?
   A. un parfum
   B. une liqueur
   C. un shampooing
6. Quand vous achetez le journal de
   dimanche, est-ce que vous regardez la
   page de la mode?
   A. Oui, toujours.
   B. Oui, de temps en temps.°
   C. Non, jamais.°
7. Imaginez que vous êtes invité(e) à une
   surprise-partie très élégante.
   L'ami(e) avec qui vous allez à cette
   surprise-partie n'est pas très bien
   habillé(e).° Quelle est votre réaction?
   A. Vous êtes furieux (furieuse).
   B. Vous êtes mal à l'aise.°
   C. Ça n'a pas d'importance.
8. Vous êtes invité(e) à l'opéra. Quels
   vêtements est-ce que vous allez porter?
   A. Des vêtements que vous allez
      acheter spécialement° pour cette
      occasion.
   B. Des vêtements assez élégants.
   C. Un blue-jeans et un tee-shirt.

266

Combien est-ce que ça coûte?

Le junior sport
3 vitesses

- Cadre de 48 cm. Entrejambe 71 à 79 cm.
- Plateau acier 40 dents.
- Roue libre : 16x19x22 dents.
- Pour les 10 à 18 ans.
Cadre vert blanchi
02-0383-2 .... 698.00
Cadre orange
02-0383-5 .... 698.00

SUR LE CHEMIN DU LYCÉE, DU COLLÈGE...

INTERPRÉTATION

Marquez 1 point pour les réponses suivantes:°
1-A ou 1-B, 2-A ou 2-B, 3-A, 4-B, 5-A, 6-A, 7-A ou 7-B, 8-A. Combien de points avez-vous?

7-8 points	Vous êtes l'esclave° de la mode.
5-6 points	Vous êtes conscient(e)° de la mode. Pour vous, l'élégance et l'apparence sont des choses importantes.
2-4 points	Vous êtes réaliste. Vous ne jugez° pas les personnes et les choses uniquement° sur leur apparence.
0-1 point	Vous êtes un(e) individualiste, mais vous n'êtes pas très sensible au monde extérieur.°

choses *things* **chaque** *each* **qui** *that* **choix** *choice*
veux *want* **dernière** *last* **couturier** *fashion designer*
produit *product* **de temps en temps** *once in a while*
jamais *never* **habillé(e)** *dressed* **mal à l'aise** *uncomfortable*
(ill at ease) **spécialement** *especially* **suivantes** *following*
esclave *slave* **conscient(e)** *conscious* **jugez** *judge*
uniquement *only* **sensible au monde extérieur** *aware of the world around you*
ILLUSTRATIONS: **soldes** *clearance sale* **souliers** *shoes*

PROJETS CULTURELS

Projets individuels

1. Make a list of ten players of the National Hockey League who have French names. (*Source: almanac*)
2. Get a French newspaper (*Le Figaro, Le Monde, France-Soir*) and look at the movie section. Make a list of ten American movies which you can identify and give their English and French titles.

Projets de classe

1. Prepare a bulletin board display showing the differences between *le football* (soccer) and *le football américain. Indicate the size of the playing field, the team size, equipment, and scoring.*
2. Prepare a bulletin board display of French foods. You may wish to choose one or two categories, such as wine and cheese, and use actual labels from imported products. These labels may be arranged against an outline map of France to show their region of origin. (*Source: food and wine stores, French magazines*)

OBJECTIVES

In this unit the students will learn to talk about their body and their health. They will also learn how to talk about past events. As an introduction to the passé composé, the affirmative, negative, and interrogative forms of être and avoir are reviewed.

Language
- the passé composé with avoir and être
- the negative and interrogative forms of the passé composé
- regular and irregular past participles
- the verbs voir, mettre, sortir, partir, dormir

Vocabulary
- parts of the body
- health terms
- verbs conjugated with être in the passé composé

Culture

This unit focuses on certain aspects of a teenager's life (parent-child relationships, use of the phone) and on two sports popular in France, soccer and tennis.

UNITÉ 6
Un fana de football
(une histoire en 5 épisodes)

6.1 Première journée: Jean-Marc est malade.

6.2 Deuxième journée: Jean-Marc a de la chance.

6.3 Troisième journée: Une invitation ratée

6.4 Quatrième journée: Jean-Marc désobéit.

6.5 Cinquième journée: Jean-Marc a décidé d'obéir.

This unit is built around a continuous story in five episodes. The main character is Jean-Marc, a French student who is an avid soccer fan. Unfortunately he gets sick a few days before an important professional game which is being played in the city where he lives. The other characters in the story are: **le docteur Brunet:** the family doctor; **Florence:** a friend; **Madame Lambert:** Jean-Marc's mother; **Philippe:** Doctor Brunet's son and a friend of Jean-Marc.

UNITÉ 6

Leçon 1

Première journée: Jean-Marc est malade.

STRUCTURES TO OBSERVE
- **être** and **avoir** (review)
- inverted questions
- the use of the definite article with parts of the body

Mercredi matin

Jean-Marc n'est pas bien. Il a de la fièvre. Il a mal à la tête.
Il a mal à la gorge. Il a mal au ventre. Il a mal *partout* . . .
Aujourd'hui Jean-Marc ne va pas en classe. Il va chez le docteur Brunet.

everywhere

JEAN-MARC: Docteur, je suis malade.
LE DOCTEUR BRUNET: Où avez-vous mal?
JEAN-MARC: J'ai mal à la tête!
LE DOCTEUR BRUNET: Avez-vous mal à la gorge?
JEAN-MARC: J'ai très mal à la gorge!
LE DOCTEUR BRUNET: Avez-vous mal au ventre?
JEAN-MARC: J'ai mal au ventre aussi.
LE DOCTEUR BRUNET: Vous avez une mauvaise grippe!
Rentrez chez vous. Prenez de l'aspirine . . . et restez
au lit!   *in bed*
JEAN-MARC: Rester au lit? Pendant combien de temps?
LE DOCTEUR BRUNET: Pendant une semaine!
JEAN-MARC: Une semaine, c'est long! . . . Et dimanche, il y a un
très bon match de foot au stade! Est-ce que je . . .
LE DOCTEUR BRUNET *(impatient):* Vous n'avez pas envie d'être plus
malade? Alors, il n'y a pas de match de foot pour
vous dimanche!
JEAN-MARC: Mais Docteur . . .
LE DOCTEUR BRUNET *(très impatient):* Il n'y a pas de «mais» . . . !
Rentrez chez vous! Immédiatement!

Pourquoi est-ce que Jean-Marc ne va pas en classe? Où est-ce qu'il va? Où est-ce qu'il a mal? Quelle maladie *(sickness)*
est-ce qu'il a? Est-ce qu'il va aller au match de football dimanche?

CONVERSATION
OPTIONAL

Questions sur le texte:

1. Est-ce que Jean-Marc a de la fièvre?
2. Est-il malade?
3. A-t-il mal à la tête?
4. Va-t-il en classe?
5. Chez qui va-t-il?

DOCTEUR RAYMOND RENAULT
43, BOULEVARD BÉRANGER
37000 TOURS

OBSERVATIONS Str. B

The subject of the first question is a *noun:* Jean-Marc.
- Does it come *before* or *after* the verb? before

In questions 2 to 5, the noun has been replaced by a *pronoun.*
- Which pronoun? il

- Does the pronoun come *before* or *after* the verb? after

- Is **est-ce que** used in these questions? no

Questions 2 to 5 are called *inverted questions* because the subject and the verb have been switched around, or *inverted.*

NOTE CULTURELLE
For reading and listening practice.

Le médecin

Allez-vous chez le médecin quand vous êtes malade? En France, quand vous êtes très malade, c'est souvent le médecin qui vient chez vous. C'est vrai surtout° dans les petites villes et à la campagne. Quand on est malade, on voit° d'abord° un médecin généraliste. Ensuite,° si c'est nécessaire, on voit un spécialiste.

Voici quelques° spécialistes: **le pédiatre** (pour les enfants), **le cardiologue** (pour les malades du cœur°), **le chirurgien**° (pour les opérations comme l'opération de l'appendicite).

surtout *especially* **voit** *sees* **d'abord** *first* **Ensuite** *Then*
quelques *some* **malades du cœur** *people with heart disease* **chirurgien** *surgeon*

With **avoir l'air,** the adjective may agree either with **air** *(m.)* or with the subject. **Les étudiantes ont l'air fatigué** *or* **fatiguées.**

Vocabulaire spécialisé La santé *(Health)*

NOMS:	le médecin	*doctor*	Jean-Marc va chez le médecin.
	la fièvre	*fever, temperature*	Il a de la fièvre.
	la grippe	*flu*	Il a la grippe.
ADJECTIFS:	fatigué	*tired*	Quand je travaille beaucoup, je suis fatigué.
	malade	*sick*	Anne est fatiguée, mais elle n'est pas malade.
	triste	*sad*	Pourquoi es-tu triste?
VERBES:	avoir l'air	*to look, seem*	Tu as l'air triste.
	avoir mal	*to be in pain*	As-tu mal?
	avoir mal	*to have*	
	à la tête,	*a headache,*	J'ai mal à la tête.
	à la gorge,	*a sore throat,*	J'ai mal à la gorge.
	au ventre	*a stomachache*	Mais je n'ai pas mal au ventre.
	être bien	*to be well, feel good*	Tu n'es pas bien.
EXPRESSIONS:	pendant combien de temps?	*for how long?*	Pendant combien de temps vas-tu rester à la maison?
	pendant	*for* (+ time), *during*	Pendant une semaine.

Note: In French, a *doctor* is usually referred to as **un médecin,** and addressed as **docteur.**
Mon médecin s'appelle **le docteur** Brunet.   Bonjour, **Docteur!**

VOCABULARY EXPANSION: **une maladie** *(disease, sickness),* **les oreillons** *(mumps),* **la rougeole** *(measles),* **la varicelle** *(chicken pox),* **un rhume** *(cold),* **un médicament** *(medicine),* **un(e) malade** *(patient, sick person)*

Structure

A. Révision: le présent d'être et d'avoir

The purpose of this review is to practice the affirmative and negative forms of être and avoir as an introduction to the passé composé. Be sure that the students have mastered these verbs.

Être and avoir are the most frequently used verbs of the French language. Review the forms of these verbs in the sentences below.

Je **suis** intelligent.   J'**ai** des idées formidables.
Tu n'**es** pas français.   Tu n'**as** pas de passeport français.
Jean-Marc **est** malade.   Il **a** de la fièvre.
Nous ne **sommes** pas riches.   Nous n'**avons** pas d'argent.
Vous **êtes** malade.   Vous **avez** la grippe.
Mes amis ne **sont** pas ici.   Ils **ont** rendez-vous en ville.

In negative sentences the verb construction is:

subject + **ne** + verb + **pas** + rest of sentence

From this point on, all direction lines are in French. A reference list of the recurring words used in the exercises appears in the Teacher's Edition and in the Activity Masters.

ACTIVITÉ 1   Où sont-ils?

Décrivez les personnes suivantes. Pour cela, utilisez le verbe **avoir** et l'expression entre parenthèses. Utilisez cette description pour dire où sont ces personnes. Pour cela, utilisez le verbe **être** et l'une des expressions suivantes:

   en classe   à la plage   à la maison

→ Robert (la grippe)   **Robert a la grippe. Il est à la maison.**

1. Jacqueline (son livre d'anglais)
2. Louis et Paul (très mal à la tête)
3. moi (mon maillot de bain)
4. vous (un examen important)
5. toi (tes lunettes de soleil)
6. nous (une discussion avec le professeur)
7. vous (très mal au ventre)
8. mes cousins (leurs livres de maths)

ACTIVITÉ 2   Comment sont-ils?

Décrivez les personnes suivantes en utilisant le verbe **avoir** et la première expression entre parenthèses. Complétez cette description en utilisant le verbe **être** et la seconde expression dans des phrases affirmatives ou négatives. Étudiez attentivement les modèles.

→ Jacqueline (de la fièvre / malade)   **Jacqueline a de la fièvre. Elle est malade.**
   moi (des idées extraordinaires / stupide)   **J'ai des idées extraordinaires. Je ne suis pas stupide.**

1. Madame Fric (une Rolls Royce / pauvre)
2. nous (un «A» à l'examen / bons en français)
3. Philippe (un passeport français / américain)
4. mon grand-père (soixante ans / jeune)
5. Nathalie (une belle robe / élégante)
6. vous (de la fièvre / bien)
7. mes cousins (de l'argent / riches)
8. toi (beaucoup d'énergie / fatigué)
9. moi (un «F» à l'examen / triste)

B. Les questions avec inversion

Inverted questions with **avoir** and **être** are important because they are often used in interrogative sentences in the passé composé. Be sure students master these forms.

When the subject of the sentence is a pronoun, questions may be formed by *inverting*, that is, reversing the order of the subject and the verb. Note the word order in the following inverted questions.

être	avoir
Suis-je malade?	**Ai-je** la grippe?
Es-tu chez toi?	**As-tu** des disques?
Est-il (Est-elle) sympathique?	**A-t-il (A-t-elle)** beaucoup d'amis?
Sommes-nous intelligents?	**Avons-nous** des idées intéressantes?
Êtes-vous français?	**Avez-vous** des amis à Paris?
Sont-ils (Sont-elles) au stade?	**Ont-ils (Ont-elles)** leurs ballons de volley?

Inversion with **je** is not common. The **est-ce que** construction is preferred.

The word order in inverted questions is:

Yes / No Questions	verb + subject pronoun + (rest of sentence) ?	Es-tu malade?
Information Questions	interrogative expression + verb + subject pronoun + (rest of sentence) ?	Où es-tu maintenant?

→ When the subject is **il, elle, on, ils,** or **elles,** liaison is required between the verb and the pronoun. The liaison consonant is always /t/.

→ If the **il / elle** form of the verb ends in a vowel, the letter **-t-** is inserted in the written form. Compare:

Est-elle en France?	A-t-elle son passeport?
Prend-il /t/ de l'aspirine?	Va-t-il à l'hôpital?
Quel pull choisit-elle?	Quelle robe achète-t-elle?

In inversion, the letter **d** is pronounced /t/.

ACTIVITÉ 3 Pique-nique

Imaginez que vous organisez un pique-nique à la plage. Demandez si les personnes suivantes ont les choses entre parenthèses. Dans chaque phrase utilisez un pronom sujet et l'inversion.

→ Isabelle (des boissons)   **A-t-elle des boissons?**

1. Jacques (un sac)
2. Paul et Henri (une voiture)
3. Nathalie (une guitare)
4. Sylvie et Louise (une radio)
5. le cousin de Paul (un ballon de volley)
6. la cousine d'Henri (un ballon de foot)

ACTIVITÉ 4   L'épidémie

Imaginez qu'il y a une épidémie de grippe. Demandez si les personnes suivantes ont la grippe. Demandez aussi où sont ces personnes d'après le modèle.

→ Suzanne et Claire (chez elles)   **Ont-elles la grippe? Sont-elles chez elles?**

1. Isabelle (en classe)
2. toi (à la maison)
3. Charles (chez le médecin)
4. Paul et Antoine (à l'hôpital)
5. vous (à l'école)
6. tes frères (chez eux)
7. tes cousines (à la maison)
8. le professeur (chez lui)

ACTIVITÉ 5   Curiosité   OPTIONAL

Jean-Marc dit ce qu'il fait (phrases 1-6) et ce qu'il fait avec ses amis (7-12). Posez-lui *(Ask him)* des questions sur *(about)* ses activités. Pour cela, utilisez les expressions interrogatives entre parenthèses et l'inversion.

→ Je travaille. (pourquoi)   **Pourquoi travailles-tu?**

Nous travaillons. (quand)   **Quand travaillez-vous?**

1. Je dîne en ville. (avec qui)
2. Je parle français. (quand)
3. J'étudie. (pourquoi)
4. Je joue au tennis. (avec qui)
5. Je parle anglais. (où)
6. Je regarde la télé. (quand)

7. Nous dansons. (avec qui)
8. Nous dînons en ville. (pourquoi)
9. Nous jouons au basketball. (avec qui)
10. Nous écoutons la radio. (quand)
11. Nous regardons la télé. (où)
12. Nous parlons espagnol. (pourquoi)

C. L'usage de l'article défini avec les parties du corps

Note the use of the definite article in the following sentences:

Qu'est-ce que tu as dans **la** main?	*What do you have in **your** hand?*
J'ai **les** cheveux noirs.	*I have black hair. (**My hair is black**.)*
Vous avez **les** yeux bleus.	*You have blue eyes. (**Your eyes are blue**.)*
Il a mal à **la** tête.	*He has a headache. (**His head hurts**.)*

In general, the French use the *definite article* with parts of the body.   English often uses the possessive adjective.

Note: The expression **avoir mal à** (+ definite article + part of the body) has several English equivalents.

Avez-vous **mal?**	*Are you in pain?*	*Does it hurt?*
J'ai **mal à la** gorge.	*My throat hurts.*	*I have a sore throat.*
J'ai **mal au** ventre.	*My stomach aches.*	*I have a stomachache.*

Avoir mal au cœur means *to feel nauseated*. Avoir une crise cardiaque means *to have a heart attack*.

Vocabulaire spécialisé   Les parties du corps *(The parts of the body)*

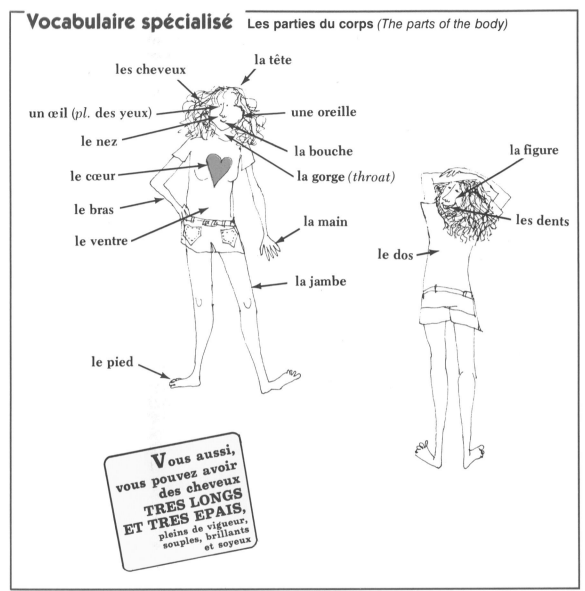

les cheveux

la tête

un œil *(pl.* des yeux)

une oreille

le nez

la bouche

le cœur

la gorge *(throat)*

le bras

la main

le ventre

la jambe

le pied

la figure

les dents

le dos

Vous aussi, vous pouvez avoir des cheveux **TRES LONGS ET TRES EPAIS,** pleins de vigueur, souples, brillants et soyeux

VOCABULARY EXPANSION: **le front** *(forehead),* **le menton** *(chin),* **le cou** *(neck),* **l'épaule** *(shoulder),* **le coude** *(elbow),* **le doigt** *(finger),* **le genou** *(knee),* **le doigt de pied** *(toe),* **l'estomac** *(stomach)*

ACTIVITÉ 6   Questions personnelles

1. Avez-vous les yeux bleus ou noirs?
2. Avez-vous les cheveux longs ou courts?
3. Pour un garçon, préférez-vous les cheveux longs ou courts?
   Et pour une fille?
4. Avez-vous mal à la tête quand vous étudiez le français?
5. Avez-vous souvent mal aux dents? mal au dos? mal au ventre?

You may point out that **figure** is a false cognate which means *face.* You may also point out the relationship between **dent** and *dentist.* You should stress the fact that **cheveux** is usually plural in French: **J'ai les cheveux noirs.** **Un cheveu** is used to refer to a single hair: **Il y a un cheveu dans ma soupe.**

Quand on commet un excès *(overdoes things)*, on est souvent indisposé ensuite. Décrivez ces malaises. Pour cela, utilisez l'expression **avoir mal à** + l'article défini + la partie du corps *(part of the body)* qui convient.

→   Pauline danse trop.   **Elle a mal aux pieds.**   Remind students that à + le → au
                                                          à + les → aux

1. Albert mange trop.
2. Je regarde trop la télé.
3. Vous écoutez trop vos disques.
4. Nous étudions trop.
5. Vous faites trop de jogging.

6. Paul nage trop.
7. Marc et Henri jouent trop au foot.
8. Suzanne mange un kilo de bonbons.
9. Lise et Marie écoutent la musique pop pendant cinq heures.

Entre nous

Expression pour la composition

ensemble *together; at the same time*

Je vais au cinéma avec François. Nous allons toujours au cinéma **ensemble.**

Le langage du corps   OPTIONAL   *Body language*

Dans la conversation les Français *utilisent* souvent les expressions avec des   *use*
parties du corps. Voici quatre de ces expressions amusantes.   *parts of the body*

mettre les pieds dans le plat   *to put; dish*

Une personne qui met les pieds dans le
plat n'est pas très diplomate. Elle fait des
erreurs de tact.

Par exemple: Pierre organise une surprise-partie. Il invite Sylvie et Jean-
Marc, le petit ami de Sylvie. Il invite aussi Philippe. Philippe est l'*ancien*   *former*
petit ami de Sylvie. C'est aussi l'ennemi de Jean-Marc. Pierre met les pieds
dans le plat parce qu'il invite Jean-Marc et Philippe ensemble.

avoir un poil dans la main   *hair*

Une personne qui a un poil dans la main
est une personne *paresseuse*.   *lazy*

Par exemple: Demain Albert a un examen très important. Est-ce qu'il
prépare l'examen? Non! Albert écoute la radio, il regarde la télévision et
après le dîner il va au *lit*. Albert n'étudie pas. Il déteste étudier. Il a un poil   *bed*
dans la main!

Prononciation

Les lettres *ill* et *il*

Mot clé: travaille

Répétez les mots: œil, oreille, appareil, soleil, maillot

Répétez les phrases: Anne travaille à Marseille.
　　　　　　　　　　Mireille a mal à l'œil.

After a vowel, the letters **ill** and **il** often represent the sound /j/.

After a consonant, the letters **ill** are sometimes pronounced:
/ij/ fille famille brillant billet
/il/ ville village mille million

avoir les yeux plus gros que le ventre

Une personne qui a les yeux plus gros que
le ventre est une personne qui mange trop
et qui perd son appétit.

Par exemple: Jacqueline est invitée à dîner chez des amis. *Avant* le dîner,　　　*Before*
Jacqueline mange une glace. Elle mange des bonbons. Elle va chez le
pâtissier et achète un gâteau . . . Et quand elle arrive chez ses amis, elle
n'a plus faim. Jacqueline a les yeux plus gros que le ventre.　　　*is no longer hungry*

être un casse-pieds

casser *to break*

Un casse-pieds est une personne qui est
très pénible.

Par exemple: Jean-Pierre *veut* aller au cinéma quand ses amis veulent aller　　*wants*
au concert. Il veut regarder un match de football quand son frère veut
regarder un film. Il veut écouter de la musique disco quand sa sœur
veut écouter de la musique classique. Jean-Pierre est un casse-pieds!

L'art de la composition

Choisissez l'une des personnes suivantes: Pierre, Albert, Jacqueline, Jean-Pierre.
Composez un petit dialogue (de 6 à 10 lignes) entre cette personne et un(e)
ami(e) ou une personne de sa famille. Dans ce dialogue, la personne doit agir
selon (*must act according to*) sa personnalité. Si possible, utilisez le mot
ensemble dans le dialogue.

Exemple: Jean-Pierre et sa sœur Isabelle

　　Isabelle: Tu viens au concert avec moi?
Jean-Pierre: Je déteste les concerts.
　　Isabelle: Et ce week-end, tu fais un pique-nique avec nos amis?
Jean-Pierre: Je déteste aller à la campagne.
　　　　　etc.

Leçon 2

Deuxième journée: Jean-Marc a de la chance.

Jeudi soir

Jean-Marc *a passé* la *journée au lit.* Le soir, son amie Florence *a téléphoné.*
Jean-Marc et Florence *ont comparé* leurs occupations de la journée.

*spent; = jour;
in bed; called
compared*

FLORENCE: *Qu'est-ce que tu as fait* aujourd'hui?

JEAN-MARC: *J'ai regardé* la télé ... J'ai écouté mes disques ...
J'ai joué aux cartes avec ma mère ... J'ai ...

FLORENCE: Comment? Tu n'as pas étudié? Tu n'as pas préparé
l'examen de la semaine prochaine?

JEAN-MARC: Bien sûr que non, je n'ai pas étudié!
Je suis malade, non?

FLORENCE: Tu as de la chance!

JEAN-MARC: Pourquoi?

FLORENCE: Parce que nous en classe, nous avons travaillé
comme des brutes ... Dis, Jean-Marc ...

JEAN-MARC: Oui?

FLORENCE: Comment est-ce qu'on fait pour avoir la grippe?

*What did you do
I watched*

= beaucoup

CONVERSATION

Did Jean-Marc do the following things yesterday? Answer simply with **oui** or **non.**

1. Est-ce que Jean-Marc **a étudié?**
2. Est-ce qu'il **a regardé** la télé?
3. Est-ce qu'il **a écouté** ses disques?
4. Est-ce que son amie Florence **a téléphoné?**

OBSERVATIONS   Str. A

The above questions refer to what Jean-Marc *did yesterday.*

- Do these questions refer to *present* or *past* events?   past

- Are the verbs in heavy type in the *present?*   no

The verbs in heavy type are in a *past* tense: the **passé composé.** Look carefully at these verbs.

- Do they consist of *one* or *two* words? The first word is a form of which *verb?*   two / avoir
  In which letter does the second word end?   -é

NOTE CULTURELLE
Le téléphone

For reading and listening practice.

Avez-vous le téléphone? Combien de téléphones avez-vous chez vous? Un, deux, . . . peut-être trois? Téléphonez-vous souvent à vos amis? En général, les jeunes Américains utilisent° souvent le téléphone pour parler avec leurs amis.

Les jeunes Français, eux, utilisent rarement le téléphone. Pourquoi? D'abord,° parce que cinquante pour cent (50%) seulement° des maisons françaises ont le téléphone. Ensuite,° parce que le téléphone coûte cher.° L'usage du téléphone est un privilège, souvent réservé pour des occasions exceptionnelles.

utilisent *use*   **D'abord** *First*   **seulement** *only*   **Ensuite** *Then*
coûte cher = **est cher**

Lambert Dumas 8 r Anselme Payen 15ᵉ	306.21.06
Lambert E 23 r Auguste Vitu 15ᵉ	578.01.08
Lambert E 13 r Cinq Diamants 13ᵉ	580.52.22
Lambert E 20 r Émile Duployé 18ᵉ	254.62.63
Lambert E 2 r Gauguin 17ᵉ	754.76.75
Lambert E 1 r Marcel Sembat 18ᵉ	255.73.66
Lambert E 9 av Porte de Vanves 14ᵉ	541.63.01
Lambert E 13 r Quatre Frères Peignot 15ᵉ	577.87.63
Lambert E 4 r Roger 14ᵉ	322.13.10

⌐ Vocabulaire pratique

ADJECTIFS:	**dernier (dernière)**	*last*	Samedi **dernier,** j'ai joué *(I played)* au tennis.
	prochain	*next*	Où vas-tu le week-end **prochain?**
EXPRESSIONS:	**comme**	*like, as*	Je parle français **comme** un Français.
	hier	*yesterday*	**Hier,** je n'ai pas joué au rugby.
	pour + infinitive	*to, in order to*	J'étudie le français **pour** aller en France.

Vocabulaire spécialisé   Dans la maison

un meuble	*piece of furniture*	**une pièce**	*room*
les meubles	*furniture*		

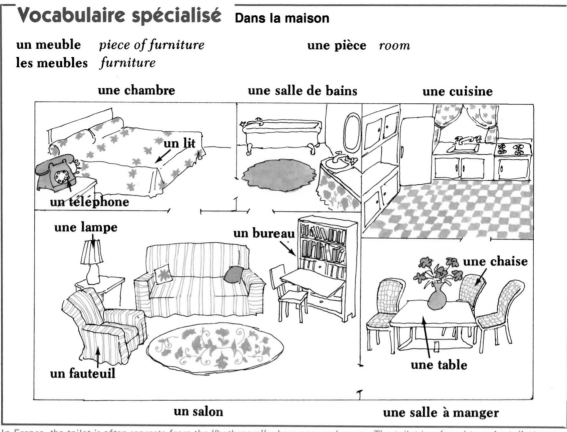

In France, the toilet is often separate from the "bathroom" where one washes up. The toilet is referred to as **les toilettes** or **les WC** (/dublavese/ or simply /vese/).

ACTIVITÉ 1   **Votre maison**

Décrivez les meubles de votre maison. Pour cela, complétez les phrases suivantes.

1. Dans ma chambre, il y a un lit, . . .
2. Dans la chambre de mes parents, il y a . . .
3. Dans la salle à manger, il y a . . .
4. Dans le salon, il y a . . .
5. Dans la cuisine, il y a . . .

Structure

A. Le passé composé des verbes en -*er*

Florence talks about what she and her friends did yesterday. She describes past events and uses a *past tense*, the **passé composé**.

Note the forms and uses of the **passé composé** in the sentences.

Hier, j'**ai téléphoné** à Jean-Paul.	*Yesterday I called Jean-Paul.*
Nous **avons joué** au tennis.	*We played tennis.*
Mes amis **ont acheté** des disques.	*My friends bought some records.*

The **passé composé** is used to describe past events. It is composed of two words.
Note the forms of the **passé composé** of **travailler**.

You may point out that the passé composé is so named because it is "composed" of two words.

Infinitive	travailler			
Passé composé	j' ai travaillé		nous avons travaillé	
	tu as travaillé		vous avez travaillé	
	il/elle a travaillé		ils/elles ont travaillé	

The **passé composé** of most verbs is formed as follows:

> present of **avoir** + past participle

→ For all **-er** verbs, the past participle is formed by replacing the **-er** of the infinitive by **-é.**

jouer	→	joué	Nous **avons joué** au volley.
parler	→	parlé	Jacques **a parlé** à Antoinette.
téléphoner	→	téléphoné	Vous **avez téléphoné** à Jean-Marc.

→ The past participle of **être** is **été.**

Nous **avons été** en ville aujourd'hui.   *We have been in town today.*

The **passé composé** has several English equivalents:

il **a travaillé** { *he worked*
{ *he has worked*
{ *he did work*

ACTIVITÉ 2   Au téléphone

Les personnes suivantes ont téléphoné à Jean-Marc hier, parce qu'il est malade.
Dites qui a téléphoné. Pour cela, utilisez le passé composé de **téléphoner.**

→ Florence   **Florence a téléphoné hier.**

1. Jacques
2. Denise
3. ses cousins
4. nous
5. toi
6. moi
7. vous
8. André et Georges

ACTIVITÉ 3   Les soldes *(Sales)*

«Au Printemps», un grand magasin parisien, a des soldes de meubles. Dites
ce que les personnes suivantes ont acheté et combien elles ont payé. Pour
cela, utilisez le passé composé des verbes **acheter** et **payer.**

→ Madame Duval (un lit / 300 francs)   **Madame Duval a acheté un lit.**
                                           Elle a payé trois cents francs.

1. mes parents (une table / 100 francs)
2. Monsieur Vallée (un bureau / 500 francs)
3. ma mère (un fauteuil / 200 francs)
4. moi (une lampe / 100 francs)
5. toi (un bureau / 400 francs)
6. nous (deux fauteuils / 300 francs)
7. vous (une chaise / 100 francs)
8. ma cousine (deux chaises / 200 francs)

You may want to do this activity in two steps: with **acheter** first, then with **payer.** You may want to review the numbers in Appendix 2, p. 401.

ACTIVITÉ 4 La surprise-partie

Florence et Philippe organisent une surprise-partie. Florence demande à Philippe s'il a fait *(did)* les choses suivantes. Il répond *(answers)* que oui. Jouez les deux rôles.

→ acheter du coca? **Florence: Tu as acheté du coca?**
   Philippe: Oui, j'ai acheté du coca.

1. acheter du jus d'orange?
2. inviter Carole?
3. parler à Denise?
4. trouver l'électrophone?

5. préparer les sandwichs?
6. écouter les cassettes?
7. téléphoner à Suzanne?
8. emprunter les disques?

You may first want to review the negative of **avoir** by having the class conjugate a sentence like: **Je n'ai pas 5 dollars. Tu n'as pas. . .** Then do a similar exercise with a sentence in the passé composé: **Je n'ai pas travaillé hier. Tu n'as pas travaillé. . .**

B. Le passé composé à la forme négative

(modification)

In the answers to the questions below, the verbs are in the negative.

Jean-Marc a étudié?	Non, il **n'**a **pas** étudié.
Vous avez regardé la télé?	Non, nous **n'**avons **pas** regardé la télé.
Tes amis ont téléphoné?	Non, ils **n'**ont **pas** téléphoné.
Tu as acheté le journal?	Non, je **n'**ai **pas** acheté le journal.

For negative sentences in the **passé composé**, the word order is:

subject	+	n'	+	present of **avoir**	+	**pas**	+	past participle	+	(rest of sentence)

ACTIVITÉ 5 Florence et Jean-Marc

Le week-end dernier, Florence a fait *(did)* les choses suivantes. Jean-Marc, qui est malade, n'a pas fait ces choses. Exprimez cela d'après le modèle.

→ nager **Florence a nagé. Jean-Marc n'a pas nagé.**

1. jouer au volley
2. dîner au restaurant
3. acheter des disques
4. visiter le musée

5. inviter ses amis
6. jouer au basket
7. être en ville
8. être au cinéma

ACTIVITÉ 6 Et vous?

Dites si oui ou non vous avez fait *(did)* les choses suivantes le week-end dernier.

→ nager **J'ai nagé le week-end dernier. (Je n'ai pas nagé le week-end dernier.)**

1. jouer au tennis
2. étudier
3. travailler
4. regarder la télé
5. organiser une surprise-partie

6. danser
7. dîner en ville
8. voyager
9. être au cinéma
10. être au concert

ACTIVITÉ 7 Le jeu des erreurs historiques   OPTIONAL

Les paragraphes suivants contiennent *(contain)* plusieurs *(several)* erreurs
historiques. Rectifiez *(Correct)* ces erreurs. Pour cela, mettez *(put)* les
phrases incorrectes à la forme négative. Puis *(Then)* relisez le paragraphe.

→ George Washington . . .
  a été le premier président
  américain.
  a parlé avec Abraham Lincoln.
  a habité à Paris.

**George Washington a été le premier
président américain.
Il n'a pas parlé avec Abraham Lincoln.
Il n'a pas habité à Paris.**

1. Benjamin Franklin . . .
   a habité à Philadelphie.
   a été président des États-Unis.
   a inventé la photographie.
   a visité San Francisco.

2. Abraham Lincoln . . .
   a été président des États-Unis.
   a libéré les esclaves *(slaves)*.
   a voyagé en France.

3. Les frères Wright . . .
   ont inventé le télégraphe.
   ont inventé le téléphone.
   ont inventé l'avion.
   ont exploré la lune *(moon)*.

4. Les astronautes américains . . .
   ont été sur la lune.
   ont trouvé des hommes sur la lune.
   ont exploré la planète Mars.

ACTIVITÉ 8 Voyages   OPTIONAL

Les étudiants français de la colonne A ont visité les États-Unis l'été
dernier. Dites où chaque étudiant a été. Pour cela, choisissez une ville de
la colonne B. Ensuite, dites ce que cet étudiant a fait dans cette ville et ce
qu'il n'a pas fait. Pour cela, utilisez les expressions de la colonne C dans
une phrase affirmative et une phrase négative. Étudiez attentivement le
modèle et soyez logique *(be logical)*!

A	B	C
moi	San Francisco	visiter l'Empire State Building
toi	Miami	nager dans l'océan Atlantique
nous	Los Angeles	admirer les Red Sox
vous	Washington	visiter la Maison Blanche
Pierre et Thérèse	Houston	parler espagnol
Jean-Claude	Boston	nager dans l'océan Pacifique
	New York	dîner à Chinatown
		visiter l'Astrodome

→ **Nous avons été à New York.**

  Nous avons visité l'Empire State Building.

  Nous n'avons pas nagé dans l'océan Pacifique.

C. Le participe passé du verbe *faire*

Note the past participle of **faire** in the following sentences:

Qu'est-ce que tu **as fait** cet été? — *What did you do this summer?*
J'**ai fait** un voyage en France. — *I took a trip to France.*

Vous **avez fait** des projets? — *Did you make plans?*
Non, nous n'**avons** pas **fait** de projets. — *No, we did not make any plans.*

The past participle of **faire** is **fait.**

➜ Remember that after a negative verb, **un, une, des, du,** and **de la** become **de.**

ACTIVITÉ 9   À la Maison des Jeunes *(At the Youth Center)*

Aujourd'hui, les amis de Florence ont été à la Maison des Jeunes. Dites ce que chacun a fait.

➜ Florence (de la danse)   **Florence a fait de la danse.**

1. Sylvie (du judo)
2. moi (de la photo)
3. toi (du ping-pong)
4. nous (du volley)
5. vous (du jogging)
6. mes sœurs (de la gymnastique)
7. Charles et Antoine (de la poterie)
8. Isabelle (du piano)

VARIATION: Because it was raining they did not go to the Youth Center. **Florence n'a pas fait de danse.**

ACTIVITÉ 10   Vive les vacances!

Dites où les personnes suivantes ont été pendant les vacances. Dites aussi si oui ou non elles ont fait les choses entre parenthèses. Soyez logique! *(Be logical!)*

➜ Paul: à la piscine (étudier / nager)
   Paul a été à la piscine. Il n'a pas étudié. Il a nagé.

1. Sylvie: à la plage (nager / faire du ski nautique [*water-ski*])
2. nous: à la campagne (visiter des monuments / faire du camping)
3. vous: en France (visiter Paris / parler italien)
4. moi: à la piscine (jouer au volley / travailler)
5. Pierre et Denis: à Miami (nager / faire du ski)
6. toi: à Québec (parler français / faire des progrès en français)
7. mes amis: en Espagne (voyager en avion / faire un voyage intéressant)

Prononciation

Le son /t/

Mot clé: <u>t</u>oi

Répétez les mots: <u>t</u>able, <u>t</u>éléphone, <u>t</u>ê<u>t</u>e, <u>t</u>ris<u>t</u>e, <u>th</u>é, <u>t</u>rès, <u>t</u>an<u>t</u>e, <u>th</u>éâ<u>t</u>re

Répétez les phrases: <u>Th</u>érèse est <u>t</u>rès <u>t</u>ris<u>t</u>e.

Ma <u>t</u>an<u>t</u>e regarde <u>t</u>oujours la <u>t</u>élé.

The French sound /t/, like the sound /k/, is pronounced without releasing a puff of air.

Comment écrire /t/: **t, th**

Entre nous

Expression pour la composition

ensuite   *then, after*   J'ai téléphoné à Pierre. **Ensuite** j'ai téléphoné à Paul.

Le journal de Nathalie   OPTIONAL

Nathalie a un *journal.* Dans ce journal elle parle des *événements* de la *journée.*   *diary; events;*
= jour

Samedi 15 juin

Aujourd'hui je n'ai pas été au lycée parce que nous n'avons pas classe le samedi. Ce matin j'ai aidé ma mère à la maison. Ensuite, nous avons fait les courses. J'ai été à la pâtisserie où j'ai acheté un gâteau pour dimanche. Cet après-midi j'ai téléphoné à Jean-Claude. Nous avons été à la piscine. Nous avons nagé et nous avons joué au volley. Après le dîner, j'ai étudié un peu. J'ai préparé l'examen de lundi. Ensuite, j'ai regardé la télé. J'ai fait beaucoup de choses aujourd'hui.

I helped

things

✳ L'art de la composition

Maintenant commencez votre journal. Décrivez la journée de samedi dernier. Faites des phrases où vous utilisez le passé composé des verbes suivants (dans des phrases affirmatives ou négatives):

• jouer, étudier, travailler, acheter, inviter, téléphoner, regarder, écouter

• être

• faire (les courses, les devoirs [*homework*], une promenade, un match, du sport, du jogging, du français . . .)

Beginning now, you may ask students to keep a diary for every day of the week. At first you may guide your students by assigning them only a few verbs to use.

Leçon 3

Troisième journée: Une invitation ratée

STRUCTURES TO OBSERVE
• the passé composé of regular **-re** verbs
• irregular past participles in **-u**
• **voir**

Vendredi après-midi

Jean-Marc commence à trouver le temps long.
Ce matin il a invité Florence mais . . .

Voici, les événements de vendredi:

Et voici comment Jean-Marc raconte ces événements, vendredi soir:

Ce matin, Jean-Marc invite
  Florence pour cet après-midi.
Cet après-midi, il attend Florence.

« Ce matin, j'ai invité Florence pour
  cet après-midi.
 Cet après-midi, j'ai attendu Florence.

Il attend longtemps.
Il perd patience.
Il entend le téléphone.
Il répond . . .

J'ai attendu longtemps.
J'ai perdu patience.
J'ai entendu le téléphone.
J'ai répondu . . .

Il entend la *voix* de Florence.
Elle a une mauvaise nouvelle pour
  lui . . . mais une bonne nouvelle
  pour elle!
Elle est malade! Elle a la grippe!

J'ai entendu la voix de Florence.
Elle a eu une mauvaise nouvelle
  pour moi . . . mais une bonne
  nouvelle pour elle!
Elle est malade! Elle a la grippe!

voice

Alors . . . il boit du thé.
Il *voit* un match de tennis à la télé.
Après, il voit un film intéressant.
Il ne perd pas son temps!

Alors . . . j'ai bu du thé.
J'*ai vu* un match de tennis à la télé.
Après, j'ai vu un film intéressant.
Ah non, je n'ai pas perdu mon temps! »

sees; saw

CONVERSATION

Questions sur le texte:

1. Qui est-ce que Jean-Marc **a attendu**?
2. Qu'est-ce qu'il **a entendu**?
3. Est-ce qu'il **a perdu** son temps?
4. Qu'est-ce qu'il **a bu**?

OBSERVATIONS   Str. B, C

The above questions concern past events.

- Which tense are they in? passé composé
- Which letter do the past participles end in? -u
- Can you identify the infinitives of the verbs in the first *three* sentences? attendre, entendre, perdre
  Do these verbs have *regular* present tense forms? yes
- Can you identify the infinitive of the verb in the *last* sentence? boire
  Is this verb regular in the present tense? no

NOTE CULTURELLE   For reading and listening practice.

Vive le tennis!

D'après vous,° qui est le meilleur joueur° de tennis? Bjorn Borg, peut-être, ou Jimmy Connors ou John McEnroe? Aujourd'hui il n'y a pas de très grands° joueurs de tennis français, mais dans les années 1920 et 1930, la France a eu° de très grands champions comme René Lacoste qui a gagné plusieurs° matchs en Coupe Davis° (et qui est aussi le père de la fameuse chemise Lacoste!).   A cause de° cette tradition, le tennis a toujours été un sport populaire en France. Aujourd'hui des millions de jeunes Français jouent au tennis.

Et vous, jouez-vous au tennis? Ou préférez-vous regarder les matchs à la télévision?

D'après vous *According to you*   **joueur** *player*   **grands** *great*
a eu *had*   **plusieurs** *several*   **Coupe Davis** *Davis Cup*
À cause de *Because of*

Vocabulaire pratique

NOMS:	**un événement** *event*	**une chose** *thing*	
		une nouvelle *(piece of) news*	

VERBES: en **-er**

commencer	*to begin, start*	À quelle heure **commence** le film?
raconter	*to tell (about)*	Vous **racontez** des choses stupides.
trouver le temps long	*to be bored*	**Trouvez**-vous **le temps long** quand vous êtes en vacances?

en **-re**

perdre son temps	*to waste one's time*	Je n'aime pas **perdre mon temps**.
répondre (à)	*to answer*	**Répondez au** professeur!

EXPRESSION: **longtemps**   *for a long time*   Il déteste attendre **longtemps**.

Note: The **nous** form of **commencer** is written with ç: Nous **commençons** demain.

Vocabulaire spécialisé Les sports

NOMS: **un joueur** *player*   **une joueuse** *player*
un match *game, match*   **une équipe** *team*

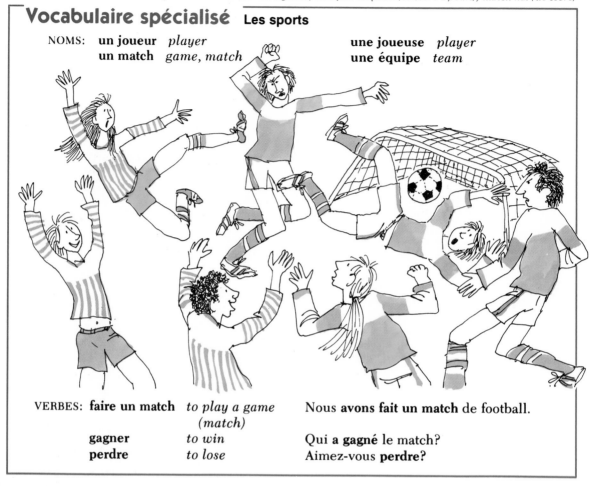

VERBES:	**faire un match**	*to play a game (match)*	Nous **avons fait un match** de football.
	gagner	*to win*	Qui **a gagné** le match?
	perdre	*to lose*	Aimez-vous **perdre**?

ACTIVITÉ 1 Questions personnelles

1. Jouez-vous au tennis? Êtes-vous un bon joueur (une bonne joueuse)? En général, est-ce que vous gagnez ou est-ce que vous perdez?
2. Est-ce que votre école a une équipe de football américain? une équipe de basket? une équipe de football? Est-ce que ces équipes sont bonnes ou mauvaises? Est-ce qu'elles gagnent souvent?
3. Regardez-vous les matchs de baseball à la télé? le matchs de football américain? les matchs de tennis?
4. D'après vous *(According to you),* qui est le meilleur joueur de tennis? la meilleure joueuse?
5. Quelle est votre équipe de baseball favorite? votre équipe de football favorite?
6. Quelle équipe a gagné les World Series l'année dernière? Quelle équipe a perdu?

Structure

To help the students remember the meaning of **voir**, you may ask them to give the meanings of the following related English words: *view, vision, clairvoyant.*

A. Le verbe *voir*

Note the forms of the irregular verb **voir** *(to see)* in the present tense.

Infinitive	**voir**		Est-ce que vous allez **voir** un bon film ce week-end?
Present	je	**vois**	Je ne **vois** pas Philippe. Où est-il?
	tu	**vois**	Est-ce que tu **vois** souvent tes amis?
	il/elle	**voit**	Hélène **voit** souvent Paul.
	nous	**voyons**	Nous **voyons** un match de football à la télé.
	vous	**voyez**	Est-ce que vous **voyez** bien avec vos lunettes?
	ils/elles	**voient**	Mes amis **voient** souvent leurs grands-parents.

Croire *(to believe)* is conjugated like **voir**. You may ask your students to conjugate it.

ACTIVITÉ 2   Vue d'avion *(View from the plane)*

Les étudiants suivants vont en France en avion. Dites ce que chacun voit de l'avion.

→ Hélène (un village)   **Hélène voit un village.**

1. Jacques (un stade)
2. moi (la campagne)
3. mes cousins (une église)
4. Denis et Alain (des voitures)
5. toi (une piscine)
6. vous (un train)
7. Louise (une ville)
8. nous (des maisons)

The village of Gordes, near Avignon.

ACTIVITÉ 3   Questions personnelles

1. Voyez-vous bien? Avez-vous des lunettes?
2. Est-ce que vous voyez vos amis pendant les vacances? Est-ce que vous voyez vos professeurs?
3. Est-ce que vous voyez souvent vos cousins? Est-ce que vous voyez vos cousins pendant les vacances? à Noël *(Christmas)*?
4. Qu'est-ce que vous préférez voir à la télé? un match de football ou un match de baseball?
5. Quand vous allez au cinéma, quels films aimez-vous voir? les comédies? les films d'aventures? les films policiers?

B. Le passé composé des verbes réguliers en -re

In the following sentences, the verbs in the **passé composé** form are regular -re verbs. Note the final vowel of the past participles.

attendre	*to wait for*	Paul **a attendu** le bus.
entendre	*to hear*	J'**ai entendu** le concert à la radio.
perdre	*to lose*	Nous **avons perdu** le match.
répondre	*to answer*	Mes cousins n'**ont** pas **répondu** à ma lettre.
vendre	*to sell*	J'**ai vendu** ma vieille bicyclette.

For regular -re verbs, the past participle is formed by replacing **-re** by **-u.**

ACTIVITÉ 4 **Au marché aux puces** *(At the flea market)*

«Le marché aux puces» est l'endroit *(place)* idéal pour acheter et vendre des choses d'occasion *(secondhand)*. Dites ce que les personnes suivantes ont acheté et vendu. Pour cela, utilisez le passé composé d'**acheter** avec la première chose entre parenthèses et le passé composé de **vendre** avec la deuxième chose.

The purpose of this activity is to have students practice the passé composé of both -er and -re verbs.

→ Jean-Marc (une guitare / son transistor)
   Jean-Marc a acheté une guitare. Il a vendu son transistor.

1. Anne (une robe / des disques)
2. toi (une flûte / des magazines)
3. moi (un fauteuil / deux chaises)
4. nous (un poisson rouge / la radio de ma grand-mère)
5. vous (un appareil-photo / le vélo de votre grand-père)
6. Anne et Claude (des sandales / des photos)

ACTIVITÉ 5 **La panne** *(The breakdown)*

Ce matin, le bus de l'école a eu une panne. Les élèves patients ont attendu. Les élèves impatients n'ont pas attendu. Exprimez cela en utilisant le passé composé d'**attendre.**

→ Pierre n'est pas patient.   **Il n'a pas attendu.**

1. Jacqueline est patiente.
2. Nous sommes patients.
3. Tu n'es pas patient.
4. Louis et Henri ne sont pas patients.
5. Janine est patiente.
6. Je ne suis pas patient.
7. Mes amis ne sont pas patients.
8. Vous êtes très impatients.

ACTIVITÉ 6 **Routine**

Hier, les personnes suivantes ont fait ce qu'elles font aujourd'hui. Dites ce qu'elles ont fait hier.

→ Le professeur perd patience.   **Hier aussi, il a perdu patience.**

1. Notre équipe perd le match.
2. Mon père attend le bus.
3. Jacques attend sa petite amie.
4. Le boulanger *(baker)* vend du pain.
5. Madame Brunet répond au téléphone.
6. Le secrétaire répond à une lettre.
7. Les vendeurs *(salespeople)* vendent des disques.
8. J'entends la clarinette de mon frère.

C. Les participes passés irréguliers en -u

A few verbs have irregular past participles which end in **-u**.
Study each one carefully.

avoir	*to have*	**eu**	J'ai **eu** une bonne note *(grade)* en français.
boire	*to drink*	**bu**	Qui a **bu** mon coca?
voir	*to see*	**vu**	Hier j'**ai vu** un film de Woody Allen.

Vous avez vu France Soir en ce moment?

ACTIVITÉ 7 Joyeux anniversaire! *(Happy Birthday!)*

Pour leur anniversaire, les personnes suivantes ont eu un cadeau *(gift)* correspondant *(that corresponds)* à leurs préférences personnelles. Lisez les préférences de chaque personne. Utilisez ces renseignements pour dire quel cadeau chacun a eu. Pour cela, utilisez le passé composé d'**avoir** et l'un des cadeaux suivants:

une raquette, une calculatrice, un électrophone, un ballon de volley, un chien, une caméra, des skis

→ Jean-Marc aime les animaux.   **Il a eu un chien.**

1. Nous aimons la musique.
2. Vous aimez le ski.
3. Mes cousins aiment le volley.
4. Tu aimes les maths.
5. J'aime le tennis.
6. Hélène aime la photo.

ACTIVITÉ 8 Et vous?

Dites si oui ou non vous avez fait les choses suivantes la semaine dernière.

→ boire du café   **Oui, j'ai bu du café.**
    (Non, je n'ai pas bu de café.)

1. avoir une bonne surprise
2. avoir un accident
3. avoir un « A » en français
4. boire de l'eau minérale
5. boire du champagne
6. voir un bon film à la télé
7. voir un film policier
8. voir une comédie de Woody Allen

ACTIVITÉ 9 Accusations

Florence a passé l'après-midi au cinéma. Pendant son absence, ses amis ont été chez elle. Quand elle rentre, Florence trouve son appartement en désordre. Elle demande qui a fait les choses suivantes. Jouez le rôle de Florence. (Attention: certains verbes ont un participe passé en **-é**; les autres *(others)* ont un participe passé en **-u**.)

→ boire mon coca?   **Qui a bu mon coca?**

1. boire mon pepsi?
2. manger mon sandwich?
3. regarder mes photos?
4. perdre mes disques?
5. emprunter mon électrophone?
6. vendre mes posters?
7. jouer avec ma caméra?
8. insulter mon poisson rouge?

D. Les questions au passé composé

You may want to review the formation of questions on pp.55, 62, 76, 273.

In the **passé composé**, as in the present tense, there are several ways of asking questions:

Tu as parlé à Jean-Marc?
Est-ce que tu as parlé à Jean-Marc? } *Did you speak to Jean-Marc?*
As-tu parlé à Jean-Marc?

Quand **est-ce que tu as vu** ce film? } *When did you see that movie?*
Quand **as-tu vu** ce film?

A yes/no question may be formed by using intonation alone, **est-ce que**, or inversion. An information question may be formed by using **est-ce que** or inversion.

➜ In the **passé composé** inverted questions are formed as follows:

> (interrogative expression) + present of **avoir** + subject pronoun + past participle

Remind students that in the il/elle form, a -t- is inserted between the verb and the subject pronoun.

Jean-Marc a vu un film.   Quel film a-t-il vu?
Florence a téléphoné.   A-t-elle téléphoné à Jean-Marc?

ACTIVITÉ 10   Dialogue

Demandez à vos amis si oui ou non ils ont déjà fait *(have ever done)* les choses suivantes. Faites attention à la forme du participe!

➜ voyager en avion?   —**Est-ce que tu as voyagé en avion?**
    —**Oui, j'ai voyagé en avion.**
    (Non, je n'ai pas voyagé en avion.)

1. voyager en train?
2. jouer au football européen?
3. jouer dans l'équipe de football de l'école?
4. nager un kilomètre?
5. dîner dans un restaurant français?
6. visiter Québec?
7. faire du ski?
8. faire du ski nautique *(water-ski)*?
9. boire du champagne?
10. boire du vin français?
11. voir un film français?
12. voir Paris?

VARIATION with inversion: **As-tu voyagé en avion?**

Prononciation

Les lettres *oi* et *oy*

The letters **oi** represent the sound /wa/.

m<u>oi</u>, t<u>oi</u>, s<u>oi</u>r, v<u>oi</u>r, pourqu<u>oi</u>, v<u>oi</u>ci, b<u>oi</u>re, b<u>oi</u>sson
Je ne v<u>oi</u>s pas pourqu<u>oi</u> tu restes chez t<u>oi</u> ce s<u>oi</u>r.

The letters **oy** + *vowel* represent the sound /waj/.

v<u>oy</u>ons, v<u>oy</u>ez, v<u>oy</u>age, v<u>oy</u>elle
V<u>oy</u>ez-vous souvent Mademoiselle Tr<u>oy</u>at?

Entre nous

Expressions pour la composition

enfin	*finally, at last*	Vous êtes là! **Enfin!**
finalement	*finally*	Nous avons bien joué, mais **finalement** nous avons perdu le match.
Quel (+ nom)!	*What a . . . !*	Jacques a téléphoné. **Quelle** bonne surprise!

Quelle journée! OPTIONAL

journée = jour

Aujourd'hui Jean-Pierre et ses amis ont eu une journée difficile. Voilà comment Jean-Pierre *décrit* cette journée dans son *journal*. *describes; diary*

Ce matin, j'ai eu une dispute avec mon frère. *quarrel*
Cet après-midi, j'ai eu une autre dispute avec Jacqueline, ma meilleure amie. *another*
J'ai perdu mon livre de maths dans l'autobus.
Mon père a perdu les clés de la voiture. *keys*
Ma mère a perdu les clés de la maison.
L'équipe de football de notre école a joué un match très important... et nous avons perdu!
Mon ami Raphaël a eu une mauvaise note en maths. *grade*
Après la classe, j'ai mangé trois glaces et j'ai bu trois cocas... et j'ai eu mal au ventre le reste de la journée!
Mon ami François a emprunté la voiture de son père... et il a eu un accident.
Finalement quand j'ai regardé le calendrier ce soir, j'ai vu que nous sommes... le vendredi 13.
Mon Dieu, quelle journée! *My goodness (Wow)*

L'art de la composition

De temps en temps *(From time to time)* nous avons une mauvaise journée comme la journée de Jean-Pierre. Décrivez une journée semblable *(similar)*. Si possible, utilisez les verbes ci-dessus *(above)*.

Leçon 4

Quatrième journée: Jean-Marc désobéit.

STRUCTURES TO OBSERVE
- passé composé of regular verbs in -ir
- irregular past participles in -is
- mettre

Samedi

Maintenant Jean-Marc trouve le temps très, très long.
Il pense aussi au grand match de foot de demain. Il décide
d'assister à ce match avec . . . ou sans *autorisation!*　　　　　*permission*

Samedi matin

JEAN-MARC: Dis, Maman. Qu'est-ce que tu fais cet après-midi?

MME LAMBERT: Je vais au cinéma avec ton père.

JEAN-MARC: Et demain?

MME LAMBERT: Je vais au concert avec une amie, et ton père va jouer
aux cartes chez ses amis.

JEAN-MARC: *Est-ce que je peux* aller au match de foot?　　　　*May I*

MME LAMBERT: Pas question! Le docteur Brunet *a dit* de rester une semaine au lit!　　*said*

JEAN-MARC: Mais, Maman . . .

MME LAMBERT: Il a dit aussi: «Il n'y a pas de MAIS!»

Samedi après-midi

Les parents de Jean-Marc sont au cinéma.
Jean-Marc *a promis* à sa mère de rester à la maison.　　　　*promised*
Mais il n'a pas obéi.
Il *a mis* un pull. Il a mis son manteau.　　　　*put on*
Il *a pris* le bus pour aller au stade.　　　　*took*
Là, il a pris un billet pour le match de demain.
Il a choisi la meilleure place!

CONVERSATION

Questions sur le texte:

1. Est-ce que Jean-Marc a obéi à sa mère?
2. Est-ce qu'il a pris un taxi pour aller au stade?
3. Qu'est-ce qu'il a pris au stade?
4. Est-ce qu'il a choisi une bonne place?

OBSERVATIONS   Str. B, C

The verbs in the above questions are in the **passé composé.**

- Which letter do the past participles of the verbs in questions 1 and 4 end in?   -i
  What is the infinitive of each of these verbs? Are these verbs *regular*? yes

obéir, choisir
- Which two letters do the past participles of the verbs in questions 2 and 3 end in? -is
  Is the final **s** pronounced? What is the infinitive of this verb? prendre

no

NOTE CULTURELLE   For reading and listening practice.

Vive le football!

Quel est votre sport favori°? le baseball? le football américain? le basket? Et qu'est-ce que vous pensez du football européen? Ce sport est très populaire en France et dans tous° les pays où l'on parle français. En semaine° les jeunes Français jouent au « foot » à l'école. Le week-end, ils regardent les matchs professionnels à la télévision. Les grands événements de l'année sont la Coupe° de France qui oppose° les meilleures équipes françaises, et les matchs internationaux qui opposent les meilleures équipes européennes.

favori *favorite*   **tous** *all*   **En semaine** *During the week*   **Coupe** *Cup*   **oppose** *matches up*   Instead of **on** after a vowel sound, **l'on** is often used: où **l'on** parle français.

SAMEDI
7 JUIN

19.55
FOOTBALL
FINALE DE LA
COUPE DE
FRANCE
En direct
du Parc des Princes

Vocabulaire pratique

| NOMS: | **un billet** *ticket* | **une place** *seat* |

VERBES: en **-er**		
assister (à)	*to attend, be present at, go to*	Ce soir je vais **assister** à un concert.
décider (de)	*to decide*	Nous avons **décidé** d'aller à Paris cet été.
en **-ir**		
obéir (à)	*to obey*	Est-ce que vous **obéissez** à vos parents?
désobéir (à)	*to disobey*	Jean-Marc **désobéit** à sa mère.
EXPRESSION: **sans**	*without*	Pourquoi allez-vous au cinéma **sans** moi?

Note: After **sans**, the indefinite article **un, une, des** is usually omitted.

On ne voyage pas **sans passeport.** *One does not travel without a passport.*

Be sure that students use à after **obéir** and **désobéir.** You may also want to review the conjugation of -ir verbs.

Structure

A. Le verbe *mettre*

The verb **mettre** *(to put)* is irregular. Here is the form chart for the present tense.

Infinitive	mettre			
Present	je	mets	nous	mettons
	tu	mets	vous	mettez
	il/elle	met	ils/elles	mettent

→ In the singular forms, the **t** of the stem is silent. The **t** is pronounced in the plural forms.

→ The verb **mettre** has several English equivalents:

to place	**Mettez** le vase sur la table.	*Place the vase on the table.*
to put	**Mettez** votre sac ici.	*Put your bag here.*
to put on	Je **mets** ma veste.	*I'm putting on my jacket.*
to turn on	**Mets** la télé, s'il te plaît.	*Turn on the TV, please.*
to set	Je ne **mets** pas la table.	*I'm not setting the table.*
to take (time)	On **met** dix minutes pour aller en classe.	*It takes ten minutes to go (get) to class.*

→ **Promettre** *(to promise)* is conjugated like **mettre**.

Je **promets** de travailler.   **Promettez**-vous à vos parents d'obéir?

ACTIVITÉ 1   Élégance

Florence et ses amis vont à une surprise-partie. Dites quels vêtements chacun met pour cette occasion.

You may have the students review clothes on pp.192 and 200.

→ Florence (une jupe verte)   **Florence met une jupe verte.**

1. Nathalie (une jupe bleue)
2. Michel (un pull orange)
3. Suzanne (un manteau)
4. nous (nos pantalons gris)
5. vous (vos chaussures noires)
6. Jean et Pierre (leurs vestes beiges)
7. mes amies (des chemisiers jaunes)
8. moi (un blue-jeans)

ACTIVITÉ 2   Questions personnelles   OPTIONAL

1. Quels vêtements mettez-vous le dimanche?
2. Quels vêtements mettez-vous pour aller à l'école?
3. Combien de temps mettez-vous pour aller à l'école?
4. Est-ce que vous mettez votre argent à la banque *(bank)*?
5. Qui met la table chez vous?
6. Promettez-vous à vos parents d'obéir?
7. Promettez-vous à vos amis d'être patient(e) avec eux?

ATTENTION OU VOUS METTEZ LES PIEDS...
NE PAYEZ PAS LA GRIFFE
ACHETEZ SEULEMENT LA QUALITÉ ET L'ÉLÉGANCE
35 rue du Château-d'eau
75010 Paris - 208.72.68
38 rue de Berri
75008 Paris - 225.49.50
CHICHE

B. Le passé composé des verbes réguliers en -ir

In the following sentences, the verbs in the **passé composé** are regular **-ir** verbs. Note the final vowel of the past participles.

choisir	*to choose*	**J'ai choisi** une belle cravate pour mon père.
finir	*to finish*	**As-tu fini** la leçon?
grossir	*to gain weight*	Vous **avez grossi** pendant les vacances.
maigrir	*to lose weight*	Quand il a eu la grippe, Jean-Marc **a maigri.**
obéir	*to obey*	Les élèves n'**ont** pas **obéi.**
désobéir	*to disobey*	Pourquoi **avez**-vous **désobéi?**
réussir	*to succeed,*	Jacques n'**a** pas **réussi** à l'examen de français.
	be successful (with)	

> For regular **-ir** verbs, the past participle is formed by replacing **-ir** by **-i.**

ACTIVITÉ 3   Calories en plus ou en moins

Lisez ce que les personnes ont fait pendant les vacances. Utilisez ces renseignements pour dire si elles ont maigri ou non. Utilisez le passé composé de **maigrir** dans des phrases affirmatives ou négatives.

→ Nathalie a joué au tennis.   **Elle a maigri.**   VARIATION with grossir: Elle n'a pas grossi.

1. Henri a nagé.
2. Nous avons fait du sport.
3. J'ai mangé beaucoup de macaronis.
4. Sylvie a bu beaucoup de coca.
5. Tu as fait du sport.
6. Mes amis ont été malades.
7. Vous avez eu la grippe.
8. Je n'ai pas fait d'exercices.

ACTIVITÉ 4   Routine

Dites que les personnes suivantes ont fait hier ce qu'elles font aujourd'hui.

→ Pierre n'obéit pas.   **Hier aussi, il n'a pas obéi.**

1. Paul choisit un disque.
2. Jacqueline finit la leçon.
3. Thérèse réussit à l'examen.
4. Robert obéit à ses parents.
5. Catherine ne réussit pas le gâteau.
6. Isabelle ne finit pas le livre.

ACTIVITÉ 5   Chez le médecin   OPTIONAL

The purpose of this activity is to review the forms of the past participles of the three groups of regular verbs.

Le docteur Lasanté a fait certaines recommandations à un client qui désire maigrir. Un mois après *(after)*, il vérifie les progrès de ce client. Jouez le rôle du docteur Lasanté et de son client. Pour cela, utilisez le passé composé des verbes suivants d'après le modèle.   All the verbs below are regular. Be sure students use the correct form of the past participle.

→ manger des bonbons (non)   Le docteur: **Avez-vous mangé des bonbons?**
Le patient: **Non, je n'ai pas mangé de bonbons.**

1. vendre votre voiture (oui)
2. choisir un bon club de sport (oui)
3. acheter une bicyclette (oui)
4. nager (oui)
5. jouer au tennis (oui)
6. grossir (non)
7. maigrir (oui)
8. perdre 10 kilos (oui)

C. Les participes passés irréguliers en -is

A few verbs have irregular past participles in **-is**. Study these verbs
carefully.

mettre	*to put*	mis	Où **as-tu mis** mes livres?
promettre	*to promise*	promis	Jean-Marc **a promis** d'obéir.
apprendre	*to learn*	appris	Nous **avons appris** la leçon.
comprendre	*to understand*	compris	Thérèse n'a pas **compris** le professeur.
prendre	*to take*	pris	Est-ce que tu **as pris** ma bicyclette?

The final **s** of the above past participles is not pronounced.

ACTIVITÉ 6   Poisson d'avril *(April fools')*

Traditionnellement *(Traditionally)* le premier avril est un jour où les
jeunes Français jouent des tours *(tricks)* à leurs amis ou aux membres de
leur famille. Décrivez les tours joués par les personnes suivantes. Pour cela,
utilisez le passé composé de **mettre**.

→ Catherine (du vinaigre dans la soupe)   **Catherine a mis du vinaigre dans la soupe.**

1. Charles (l'aquarium dans le réfrigérateur)
2. mes cousins (les poissons rouges dans la piscine)
3. nous (du ketchup dans le yogourt)
4. toi (du ketchup sur la chaise de ta sœur)
5. Annie (du yogourt dans la veste de Paul)
6. vous (le chien dans le lit de vos parents)
7. moi (la bicyclette de mon frère dans la salle de bains)
8. les élèves (un chien dans la voiture du professeur)

ACTIVITÉ 7   Un jour à l'école

Michèle parle de ce qu'elle fait maintenant. Ce soir Michèle va téléphoner
à Florence. Elle va lui dire *(to tell her)* ce qu'elle a fait aujourd'hui. Jouez le
rôle de Michèle parlant *(talking)* à Florence. Pour cela, mettez les
expressions suivantes au passé composé.

→ Je prends mon sac.   **J'ai pris mon sac.**

1. Je mets mon pull.
2. Je mets mon manteau.
3. Je prends mes livres.
4. Je prends le bus.
5. Je mets mes livres sur la table.
6. Je n'apprends pas les verbes.
7. Je ne comprends pas la leçon.
8. Je ne comprends pas le problème de maths.
9. Je promets au professeur d'étudier plus.

Prononciation

Révision: les sons /ɔ̃/ et /ɔn/, /ɔm/

Contrastez: /ɔ̃/   b<u>on</u>   m<u>on</u>   compr<u>en</u>dre   c<u>on</u>bien   d<u>on</u>c   t<u>on</u>   s<u>on</u>

           /ɔn/, /ɔm/   b<u>onn</u>e   M<u>on</u>ique   c<u>om</u>mencer   c<u>om</u>me   d<u>onn</u>e   aut<u>om</u>ne   pers<u>onn</u>e

The letters **on (om)** represent the nasal vowel /ɔ̃/, unless they are followed by
a vowel or an **n** or **m**. When pronouncing /ɔ̃/, be sure not to pronounce an /n/
or /m/ after it.

Entre nous

Expressions pour la composition

tous les (+ plural masculine noun)		**Tous les mois**, je vais chez mon oncle.
toutes les (+ plural feminine noun)	*every*	Je téléphone à mes cousins **toutes les semaines.**

Bravo Nathalie! OPTIONAL

Tous les mois, Nathalie décide d'*accomplir* certains objectifs. Le mois   *to accomplish*
dernier elle a décidé de faire les choses *suivantes* et elle a réussi. Voici   *following*
comment Nathalie *décrit* ces objectifs.   *describes*

> J'ai maigri. J'ai perdu deux kilos.
> J'ai appris à jouer au bridge.
> J'ai appris à faire du <u>patin à roulettes</u>.   *to roller-skate*
> J'ai participé à un 5.000 mètres. Je n'ai
>   pas gagné, mais j'ai fini en 25 minutes!
> J'ai réussi à l'examen d'anglais parce que j'ai
>   appris les verbes irréguliers. J'ai eu un « A ».
> J'ai fini quatre livres.
> J'ai pris <u>quelques</u> bonnes résolutions.   *a few*
> J'ai promis à mon frère d'être plus patiente avec lui.
> J'ai promis à mes parents de travailler un peu plus.
> J'ai choisi un joli <u>cadeau</u> pour l'<u>anniversaire</u>   *gift; birthday*
>   de mon père.

L'art de la composition

Et vous, avez-vous accompli certaines choses le mois dernier? Décrivez ces choses. Si
possible, utilisez les **expressions ci-dessus** (*above*).

Leçon 5

STRUCTURE TO OBSERVE
• passé composé with **être**

Cinquième journée:
Jean-Marc a décidé d'obéir.

Dimanche . . .
Avant le match

Les parents de Jean-Marc *sont sortis* après le *déjeuner*.   *went out; lunch*

Monsieur Lambert est sorti à une heure et quart. Il *est allé* chez ses amis.   *went*

Madame Lambert est sortie à une heure et demie. Elle est allée au concert.

À deux heures, Jean-Marc est sorti aussi et il est allé *directement* au stade.   *directly*

Après le match

Après le match, Jean-Marc a rencontré Philippe . . . le fils du docteur Brunet.
C'est une très mauvaise surprise.

> PHILIPPE: Salut, Jean-Marc! Ça va?
>
> JEAN-MARC: Euh oui . . . plus ou moins. Dis, tu *es venu* seul?   *came*
>
> PHILIPPE: Non, je suis avec mes frères.
>
> JEAN-MARC: Et vos parents, est-ce qu'ils sont venus?
>
> PHILIPPE: Ma mère n'est pas venue, mais mon père est ici.
>
> JEAN-MARC: Où?
>
> PHILIPPE: Là-bas. Pourquoi?
>
> JEAN-MARC: *Pour rien.*   *No reason.*
>
> PHILIPPE: Dis donc, Jean-Marc, ça ne va pas? Tu as l'air malade. *Tu veux*   *Do you want*
> parler à mon père? Tiens, *justement, le voilà.*   *in fact, here*
> *he comes now*
>
> JEAN-MARC: Euh, non . . . Merci! Excuse-moi!

À la maison

Jean-Marc est rentré immédiatement chez lui.

Ses parents sont rentrés assez tard.

Ils ont trouvé leur fils très, très malade.

Madame Lambert a proposé d'amener Jean-Marc chez le docteur Brunet.

Jean-Marc a répondu à sa mère:

«Oh, non Maman. Le docteur *m'a dit* de rester une semaine au lit.   *told me*
Alors, j'obéis. Je vais rester au lit jusqu'à mercredi!»

CONVERSATION

Questions sur le texte:

1. Où est-ce que Monsieur Lambert **est allé?**
2. Où est-ce que Jean-Marc **est allé?**
3. Est-ce que Philippe **est allé** seul (*alone*) au stade?
4. Où est-ce que Jean-Marc **est allé** après le match?

OBSERVATIONS   Str. B

The verbs in heavy type are forms of the **passé composé** of **aller.**

• Is the **passé composé** of **aller** conjugated with **avoir?**   no

• Which verb is used to form the **passé composé** of **aller?**   être

For reading and listening practice.

NOTE CULTURELLE

La discipline familiale°

Est-ce que vos parents sont stricts ou tolérants? En général, la discipline familiale est plus stricte en France qu'aux États-Unis. Si un enfant désobéit à ses parents, il est souvent puni.° Voici quelques° exemples de punitions:° rester à la maison le samedi soir, ne pas regarder la télévision pendant une semaine, être privé d'argent de poche.°

familiale *family* **puni** *punished* **quelques** *some* **punitions** *punishments* **être privé d'argent de poche** *to be deprived of (not to be given) pocket money*

Vocabulaire pratique

ADJECTIF:	**seul**	*alone, by oneself*	Je vais aller **seul** au cinéma.
VERBES:	**amener**	*to bring, take along*	Qui **amènes**-tu à la surprise-partie?
	proposer	*to suggest, offer*	Je vais **proposer** à mes amis d'aller au match.
	rencontrer	*to meet*	Ce soir je vais **rencontrer** Pierre au café.
EXPRESSIONS:	**avant**	*before*	Qu'est-ce que tu fais **avant** le dîner?
	après	*after, afterwards*	Qu'est-ce que tu fais **après?**
	jusqu'à	*until*	Je vais étudier **jusqu'à** dix heures.
	tard	*late*	Il est minuit. Oh là là, il est **tard!**

Note: The verb **amener** is conjugated like **acheter.**

J'**amène** un ami à la surprise-partie. Et vous, qui **amenez**-vous?

There are two verbs which correspond to the English verb *to bring:*
apporter (used only with things)   J'apporte mes disques.
amener (used with people or things)   J'amène un ami. Il amène sa guitare.

Structure

A. Les verbes *sortir, partir* et *dormir*

The verbs **sortir** *(to go out, get out)*, **partir** *(to leave)*, and **dormir** *(to sleep)* are irregular. Here is the form chart of the present tense of these verbs.

Infinitive	sortir		partir		dormir	
Present	je	**sors**	je	**pars**	je	**dors**
	tu	**sors**	tu	**pars**	tu	**dors**
	il/elle	**sort**	il/elle	**part**	il/elle	**dort**
	nous	**sortons**	nous	**partons**	nous	**dormons**
	vous	**sortez**	vous	**partez**	vous	**dormez**
	ils/elles	**sortent**	ils/elles	**partent**	ils/elles	**dorment**

→ **Sortir** and **partir** have several meanings. Note the constructions with these verbs:

sortir	*to go out*	Le samedi, je **sors** avec mes amis.
sortir de	*to get out of (a place)*	Nous **sortons de** l'école à deux heures.
partir	*to leave*	Le bus **part** dans dix minutes.
partir de	*to leave (a place)*	Quand **partez-vous de** Paris?
partir à	*to leave for (a place)*	Quand **partez-vous à** la campagne?

ACTIVITÉ 1   Bonne nuit!

Lisez dans quelles conditions sont les personnes suivantes. D'après vous, est-ce que ces personnes dorment bien ou non? Exprimez votre opinion. Pour cela, utilisez l'expression **dormir bien** dans des phrases affirmatives ou négatives.

→ Alain est malade.   **Il ne dort pas bien.**

1. Mes cousins ont la grippe.
2. J'ai un examen demain.
3. Vous êtes seul dans une grande maison.
4. Jacqueline est très fatiguée.
5. Tu n'as pas de problèmes.
6. Nous ne sommes pas nerveux *(nervous)*.
7. Sylvie a fait beaucoup de sport.
8. Jean-Claude et Paul ont mal à la tête.

ACTIVITÉ 2   Questions personnelles

1. Est-ce que vous sortez le week-end?
2. En général dormez-vous bien ou mal?
3. Combien d'heures est-ce que vous dormez par *(per)* nuit?
4. Le matin *(In the morning)*, à quelle heure partez-vous de la maison?
5. Est-ce que vous prenez le bus? À quelle heure est-ce que le bus part?
6. Est-ce que vous allez partir en vacances cet été?

B. Le passé composé avec *être*

The **passé composé** of certain verbs, such as **aller**, is formed with **être** instead of **avoir**. The sentences below describe where certain boys and girls went during vacation. Note the forms of the **passé composé** of **aller**, paying special attention to the past participles.

Je **suis** **allé** à Paris.	Je **suis** **allée** à Québec.	*I went/have gone*
Tu **es** **allé** à Nice.	Tu **es** **allée** à Dakar.	*You went/have gone*
Il **est** **allé** à Toulon.	Elle **est** **allée** à Lyon.	*He/She went/has gone*

Nous **sommes** **allés** au Canada.	Nous **sommes** **allées** en Israël.	*We went/have gone*
Vous **êtes** **allés** au Japon.	Vous **êtes** **allées** à Tahiti.	*You went/have gone*
Ils **sont** **allés** en Italie.	Elles **sont** **allées** à Rome.	*They went/have gone*

The **passé composé** of many verbs of motion (such as **aller, arriver, sortir, partir,** etc.) is conjugated with **être**. These verbs are shown in the "**être** stadium" on page 305.

In negative and interrogative sentences, the word order in the **passé composé** is the same with **être** as with **avoir**.

avoir	être
Est-ce que tu as visité la France?	**Est-ce que tu es allé** en France?
As-tu visité la France?	**Es-tu allé** en France?
Je n'ai pas visité la France.	**Je ne suis pas allé** en France.
Paul n'a pas visité Paris.	**Paul n'est pas allé** à Paris.

When the **passé composé** of a verb is conjugated with **être** (and not with **avoir**), the past participle agrees in gender and number with the subject. Contrast:

avoir			être		
Jean-Paul	a visité	le Canada.	Il	est all**é**	à Québec.
Florence	a visité	le Canada.	Elle	est all**ée**	à Montréal.
Mes amis	ont visité	le Canada.	Ils	sont all**és**	à Toronto.
Mes amies	ont visité	le Canada.	Elles	sont all**ées**	à Vancouver.

→ Note that the four forms of **allé** have the same endings as regular adjectives. Note also that although they are spelled differently, they are pronounced the same.

You may remind the students that the pronoun **vous** may be masculine or feminine, singular or plural. Accordingly, the agreement of the past participle with **vous** depends on who **vous** is.
Monsieur Moreau, est-ce que vous êtes allé au Japon?
Louise et Marie, est-ce que vous êtes allées au Japon?

ACTIVITÉ 3   Êtes-vous bon détective?

Imaginez que vous avez trouvé un carnet *(notebook)* avec les observations suivantes. Notez que ces observations sont incomplètes et qu'elles sont écrites *(written)* au passé composé. Étudiez chaque observation attentivement. Pouvez-vous *(Can you)* dire si cette observation concerne une ou plusieurs *(several)* personnes et quel est le sexe de ces personnes? Observez la forme du participe passé et complétez chaque observation avec **un garçon, une fille, des garçons, des filles,** et **est** ou **sont.**

→ —— allées au cinéma.   **Des filles sont allées au cinéma.**

1. —— allé au restaurant.
2. —— allés à la plage.
3. —— allée à la piscine.
4. —— allées au concert.

5. —— allés à Nice.
6. —— allée au théâtre.
7. —— allé au stade.
8. —— allées en ville.

ACTIVITÉ 4   Vacances à l'étranger *(Vacations abroad)*

Dites où les personnes suivantes sont allées pendant les vacances. Dites aussi si elles ont parlé **français, anglais** ou **espagnol.**

→ Jacques (au Mexique)   **Jacques est allé au Mexique. Il a parlé espagnol.**

1. nous (au Chili)
2. Janine et Louise (à Chicago)
3. toi (à Genève)
4. moi (en Espagne)

5. Jean-Marc (à San Francisco)
6. vous (à Québec)
7. Pierre (en Bolivie)
8. mes amis (à Dakar)

ACTIVITÉ 5   L'école buissonnière *(Playing hooky)*

Aujourd'hui les étudiants ne sont pas allés en classe. Exprimez cela et dites aussi où ils sont allés.

→ Jean-Marc (au stade)   **Jean-Marc n'est pas allé en classe.
Il est allé au stade.**

1. Lise et Danièle (au cinéma)
2. moi (à la plage)
3. toi (à la piscine)
4. nous (au match de foot)
5. vous (en ville)
6. Jacqueline (acheter des chaussures)

Vocabulaire spécialisé Au stade

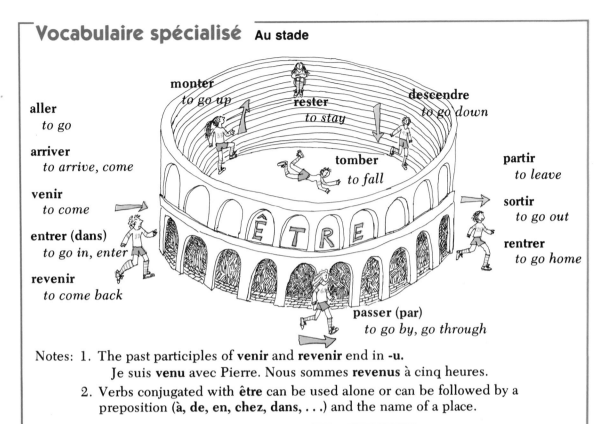

aller
to go

arriver
to arrive, come

venir
to come

entrer (dans)
to go in, enter

revenir
to come back

monter
to go up

rester
to stay

tomber
to fall

descendre
to go down

ÊTRE

partir
to leave

sortir
to go out

rentrer
to go home

passer (par)
to go by, go through

Notes: 1. The past participles of **venir** and **revenir** end in **-u.**
Je suis **venu** avec Pierre. Nous sommes **revenus** à cinq heures.

2. Verbs conjugated with **être** can be used alone or can be followed by a
preposition (**à, de, en, chez, dans, . . .**) and the name of a place.

Jean-Marc est entré	**dans**	le stade.
Jean-Marc entered	. . .	*the stadium.*

3. Other verbs conjugated with **être** are: These verbs have irregular
naître (né)   *to be born*   Je **suis né** en France.   present tense forms which are not taught here.
mourir (mort)   *to die*   Mon grand-père **est mort** l'année dernière.

These verbs cannot take a direct object. When used with direct objects,
monter and **descendre** are conjugated in the passé composé with **avoir**.
Je suis monté à la tour Eiffel. J'ai monté mes bagages.

ACTIVITÉ 6   Jim et Juliette

Jim et Juliette sont allés en France l'été dernier. Juliette a fait les mêmes
(same) choses que Jim. Jouez le rôle de Juliette décrivant *(describing)* le
voyage. Jouez aussi le rôle de Jim et de Juliette.

→ Jim est allé en France.   Juliette: **Je suis allée en France.**
            Jim et Juliette: **Nous sommes allés en France.**

1. Jim est arrivé à Paris.   5. Jim est descendu à Nice.
2. Jim est resté à l'hôtel.   6. Jim est parti à Nice en train.
3. Jim est monté à la tour Eiffel.   7. Jim est allé à Toulon.
4. Jim est sorti avec des amis français. 8. Jim est rentré à New York en septembre.

ACTIVITÉ 7 Le voyage de Jean Allidet

Imaginez que vous travaillez pour un magazine français. Vous racontez le voyage aux États-Unis de Jean Allidet, un acteur français très célèbre (*famous*). Voici vos notes. Faites la description du voyage de Jean Allidet en utilisant vos notes.

→ Jean Allidet arrive à New York.　**Jean Allidet est arrivé à New York.**

1. Il descend dans un hôtel.
2. Il monte à l'Empire State Building.
3. Il va à la Statue de la Liberté.
4. Il part en Floride.
5. Il reste à Miami.
6. Il vient à la Nouvelle-Orléans.
7. Il revient à New York.
8. Il passe par Philadelphie.
9. Il rentre à Paris.
10. Il rentre chez lui.

Here, **descendre** means *to stop*.

Partez avec Air Canada.
Paris-Montréal
aller et retour :

1800 F.
seulement.*

ACTIVITÉ 8 Lieux de naissance *(Birthplaces)*　OPTIONAL

Imaginez que vous allez en France avec les personnes suivantes. Au contrôle des passeports, un employé demande où chaque personne est née. Répondez en complétant *(by completing)* les phrases suivantes.

→ Ma mère . . .　**Ma mère est née à San Francisco.**

1. Mon père . . .
2. Mon meilleur ami . . .
3. Ma meilleure amie . . .
4. Je . . .

ACTIVITÉ 9 Dialogue　OPTIONAL

Demandez à vos amis ce qu'ils ont fait le week-end dernier. Pour cela, utilisez le passé composé des verbes suivants. (Attention: Certains verbes sont conjugués avec **être**, les autres *(others)* sont conjugués avec **avoir**.)

→ inviter (qui?)　　—**Qui as-tu invité?**
　　　　　　　　　—**J'ai invité un ami.**
　aller (où?)　　　—**Où es-tu allé?**
　　　　　　　　　—**Je suis allé au cinéma.**

1. sortir (avec qui?)
2. téléphoner (à qui?)
3. aller en ville (avec qui?)
4. rencontrer (qui?)
5. acheter (quelles choses?)
6. rentrer à la maison (à quelle heure?)
7. regarder (quel programme?)
8. aller au lit (à quelle heure?)

Prononciation

Révision: le son /r/

Répétez: Robert, rare, grand-père, préfère, dormir, sortir, rencontrer

Richard va partir à trois heures.

Claire reste à Paris chez son grand-père.

Marc rencontre Renée après le concert.

Remember, the French /r/ is not at all like the American *r*. The French /r/ is pronounced at the back of the throat. It is softer at the end of a word.

Entre nous

Expressions pour la correspondance

How do the French begin their letters? This depends on how well they know the people they are writing to. Here are the various forms of address:

	when writing to:
Monsieur, Madame, Mademoiselle	an adult you do not know or barely know
Cher Monsieur, Chère Madame, Chère Mademoiselle	an adult you know quite well
Cher Philippe, Chère Isabelle	a friend
Mon cher Philippe, Ma chère Isabelle	a close friend

The French often end personal letters to friends with expressions such as:

Amitiés	*Best regards*	(lit. **amitié** means *friendship*)
Amicalement	*Love*	(lit. **amical** means *friendly*)

Une carte postale   OPTIONAL

Martine est en vacances à Nice. Elle *écrit* une *carte postale* à Monique, une camarade de classe.

writes; postcard

> Ma chère Monique,
> Enfin les vacances! Nous sommes arrivés à Nice vendredi dernier. Samedi matin, je suis allée nager avec ma soeur. À la plage, nous avons rencontré des garçons très sympathiques. Nous sommes sorties avec eux hier soir... Nous sommes allées au cinéma. Ensuite, nous sommes allées danser dans une discothèque. Nous sommes rentrées chez nous à minuit! Quelle vie!
> Amicalement,
> Martine

life

L'art de la correspondance

Écrivez une carte postale où vous décrivez ce que vous avez fait le week-end dernier.

OBJECTIVES
In this unit the students learn to discuss personal relationships with friends, family, teachers, etc. To help them achieve this objective, the grammar of the unit focuses on object pronouns.
Language
  • **connaître**
  • **connaître** vs. **savoir**
  • direct and indirect object pronouns (forms, uses, and position in the present, imperative, and passé composé)
  • negative expressions
  • omission of the definite article with professions
  • **dire, lire, écrire**
  • the conjunction **que**
Vocabulary
  • professions
  • reading and writing
  • review and expansion of verbs according to which take direct and indirect objects
Culture
The cultural information presented in this unit focuses on various aspects of teenage social life: how to introduce someone, what compliments people make, the importance of good manners, pocket money, and love.

UNITÉ 7
Nous et les autres

OPPOSITE: The Jardin du Luxembourg, Paris.

Leçon 1 Chantage

STRUCTURES TO OBSERVE
• the negative construction **ne. . .jamais**
• the object pronouns **me** and **te** (forms and position)

Scène 1. Anne et Sylvie

ANNE: Tu m'invites à ta surprise-partie?

SYLVIE: Ça dépend! Je t'invite . . . si tu me *présentes* à ton cousin,
le journaliste.

ANNE: Et si je ne te présente pas?

SYLVIE: Pas d'invitation!

introduce

CONVERSATION

Let's talk about your relationships with your friends. Answer simply with
oui or **non.**

1. Est-ce que vos amis **vous** invitent souvent?
2. Est-ce qu'ils **vous** téléphonent?
3. Est-ce qu'ils **vous** présentent *(introduce)* à leurs amis?
4. Est-ce qu'ils **vous** prêtent *(lend)* leurs disques?

OBSERVATIONS   Str. B

Reread the first question.

• How do you say: *Do your friends invite you often?*   Est-ce que vos amis vous invitent souvent?

• What is the *subject* of that question? What is the *verb*?   vos amis/invitent

• In the same question, what is the French *pronoun* that corresponds to *you*?   vous

• In the above questions the pronouns in heavy type are the *objects* of the verb.
Do these object pronouns come *before* or *after* the verb? Is it the same in English?
before   no

Qu'est-ce que Marc veut *(want)* ? Qu'est-ce que Philippe veut en échange?

Scène 2. Marc et Philippe

MARC: Dis, Philippe! Tu me *prêtes* ta moto? *lend*

PHILIPPE: D'accord, si tu me prêtes vingt francs.

MARC: *Désolé*, mais je *ne* prête *jamais* d'argent. *Sorry; never*

PHILIPPE: Eh bien, moi, je ne prête jamais ma moto.

MARC: Bon. Voilà vingt francs . . . mais c'est du *chantage*! *blackmail*

NOTE CULTURELLE

For reading and listening practice.

Les présentations°

Êtes-vous une personne sociable? Quand vous êtes à une surprise-partie, ou à la plage, ou dans l'autobus, est-ce que vous parlez aux personnes que° vous ne connaissez° pas mais que vous trouvez sympathiques? En général, les Français sont plus réservés° que les Américains. Avant de parler° aux personnes qu'ils ne connaissent pas, ils attendent d'être présentés.°

Imaginez que vous êtes à une surprise-partie. Comment allez-vous présenter votre ami Patrick à votre amie Carole? C'est simple. Vous dites° à Carole: «Carole, je te présente Patrick.» Et Carole dit à Patrick: «Enchantée!»,° c'est-à-dire,° «Je suis enchantée de faire ta connaissance.»°

Les présentations *Introductions* **que** *whom* **connaissez** *know*
réservés *reserved* **Avant de parler** *Before speaking*
présentés *introduced* **dites** *say* **Enchantée** *Delighted*
c'est-à-dire *that is (to say)* **faire ta connaissance** *to meet you*

Structure

A. L'expression négative ne . . . jamais

Compare the following negative constructions.

Vous étudiez?	⌈Nous n'étudions **pas**.	We **don't** study.
	⌊Nous n'étudions **jamais**.	We **never** study.
Tu fais du footing?	⌈Je **ne** fais **pas** de footing.	I **don't** go jogging.
	⌊Je **ne** fais **jamais** de footing.	I **never** go jogging.

Like **ne . . . pas**, the negative expression **ne . . . jamais** consists of two parts:

ne (n')   which comes before the verb
jamais   which comes immediately after the verb

→ In the **passé composé**, the word **jamais** comes between **avoir** or **être** and the past participle.

Je n'ai **jamais** vu Paris.   *I **never** saw Paris. (I have **never** seen Paris.)*
Je **ne** suis **jamais** allé en France.   *I **never** went to France. (I have **never** gone to France.)*

You may indicate that after **jamais** (as with **pas**) **un, une, des, du, de la → de (d').**

ACTIVITÉ 1   Jamais le dimanche

Le dimanche, les personnes suivantes ne font jamais ce qu'elles font pendant la semaine. Exprimez cela d'après le modèle.

→ Charles achète le journal.   **Le dimanche, il n'achète jamais le journal.**

1. Anne étudie.
2. Philippe étudie les verbes.
3. Marc travaille.
4. Sylvie travaille dans un café.
5. Nous parlons français.
6. Vous allez à la cantine (*cafeteria*).
7. Les élèves prennent le bus.
8. Tu dînes au restaurant.
9. Mes amis jouent au foot.
10. J'achète du chocolat.
11. Vous regardez la télé.
12. Tu fais du sport.

ACTIVITÉ 2   Un philosophe

Monsieur Lermite, un philosophe célèbre (*famous*), a décidé d'habiter dans une île déserte (*desert island*) pour écrire (*to write*) son dernier livre. Dites que pendant cette retraite (*retreat*), il n'a jamais fait les choses suivantes.

→ regarder la télé   **Il n'a jamais regardé la télé.**

1. écouter les nouvelles
2. inviter des amis
3. dîner au restaurant
4. téléphoner
5. voir ses cousins
6. aller au concert
7. aller au théâtre
8. sortir

Be sure students use **être** in items 6, 7, 8.

To prepare for this activity and to review the passé composé with **avoir** and **être**, ask students if they have been to remote places:
—Avez-vous visité le Japon, l'Afrique, la Chine, l'Australie, l'Égypte?
—Je n'ai jamais visité . . .
—Êtes-vous allé(e) au Japon? en Afrique? en Chine? en Australie? en Égypte?
—Je ne suis jamais allé(e) . . .

B. Les pronoms compléments *me, te, nous, vous*

In the sentences below, the pronouns in heavy type are *objects* of the verb. Note the forms of these pronouns and compare their positions in French and English.

Tu **me** parles?	*Are you speaking **to me**?*
Oui, je **te** parle.	*Yes, I am speaking **to you**.*
Tu **m'**invites dimanche?	*Are you inviting **me** on Sunday?*
Bien sûr, je **t'**invite.	*Of course, I'm inviting **you**.*
Vos parents **vous** parlent souvent?	*Do your parents often speak **to you**?*
Est-ce qu'ils **vous** comprennent?	*Do they understand **you**?*
Oui, ils **nous** parlent souvent et ils **nous** comprennent.	*Yes, they often speak **to us**, and they understand **us**.*

The *object pronouns* which correspond to the subject pronouns **je, tu, nous, vous** are:

me ↓ m' (+ vowel sound) } *me, to me*	nous	*us, to us*
te ↓ t' (+ vowel sound) } *you, to you*	vous	*you, to you*

Object pronouns come *before* the verb.

→ In negative sentences, object pronouns come after **ne.**

Pierre ne **me** parle pas.	*Pierre does not speak **to me**.*
Il ne **nous** invite jamais.	*He never invites **us**.*

→ There is liaison after **nous** and **vous** when the next word begins with a vowel sound.

Vos amis **vous** écoutent? Mais oui, ils **nous** écoutent toujours.

ACTIVITÉ 3   Isabelle

Isabelle, une jeune étudiante française, vient d'arriver à votre école. Vous décidez de faire certaines choses pour elle. Proposez ces choses à Isabelle d'après le modèle.

→ téléphoner ce soir   **Je te téléphone ce soir, d'accord?**

1. téléphoner demain aussi
2. inviter demain soir
3. inviter à la surprise-partie
4. inviter ce week-end
5. acheter une glace
6. acheter un Coca-Cola
7. voir cet après-midi
8. voir après la classe
9. amener au cinéma

VARIATION: Isabelle and Pierre are new students. **Je vous téléphone...**

ACTIVITÉ 4   Sylvie et Charles

Sylvie est toujours aimable *(friendly)* avec ses amis. Charles n'est pas aimable. Décrivez l'attitude de Charles d'après le modèle.

VARIATION with **ne. . .jamais**:
Charles ne me parle jamais.

→ **Sylvie me parle.   Charles ne me parle pas.**

1. Sylvie nous parle.
2. Sylvie t'invite.
3. Sylvie vous invite.
4. Sylvie m'écoute.
5. Sylvie vous regarde.
6. Sylvie nous comprend.
7. Sylvie m'aime.
8. Sylvie nous attend.
9. Sylvie te trouve mignon *(cute).*

Vocabulaire spécialisé   Verbes

aider	*to help*	Mes amis m'**aident.**
chercher	*to look for*	Je **cherche** Paul. Où est-il?
	to pick up, get	Je te **cherche** chez toi à midi. D'accord?
donner	*to give*	Je te **donne** mes vieux disques.
présenter	*to introduce, present*	Sylvie **présente** Jean-Pierre à Christine.
prêter	*to lend, loan*	Je vous **prête** mon vélo si vous me **prêtez** 10 francs.

Note: **Chercher** can be used with both people and things.

Paul va à l'école. Il **cherche** Jacqueline.   André va à l'école. Il **cherche** ses livres.

ACTIVITÉ 5   Dialogue

Make sure that the students understand that **chercher** means *to look for* and that they do not use **pour** after **chercher**.

Demandez à vos camarades de faire les choses suivantes pour vous ce week-end. Vos camarades vont accepter ou refuser.

→ téléphoner samedi

Élève 1: **Tu me téléphones samedi?**
Élève 2: **Oui, je te téléphone samedi.**
   (Non, je ne te téléphone pas samedi.)

1. téléphoner dimanche
2. inviter au cinéma
3. présenter à ton cousin
4. présenter à ta cousine
5. prêter ton vélo
6. prêter ta radio
7. donner deux dollars
8. acheter un gâteau
9. aider avec le français
10. aider avec les maths
11. chercher chez moi
12. chercher au cinéma

ACTIVITÉ 6   Questions personnelles   OPTIONAL

1. Est-ce que vos amis vous téléphonent souvent? Est-ce qu'ils vous invitent? Est-ce qu'ils vous respectent? Est-ce qu'ils vous comprennent? Est-ce qu'ils vous parlent de leurs problèmes? Est-ce qu'ils vous prêtent leurs disques? Est-ce qu'ils vous aident?

2. Est-ce que vos professeurs vous comprennent? Est-ce qu'ils vous respectent? Est-ce qu'ils vous donnent des bonnes notes *(grades)?* Est-ce qu'ils vous donnent des mauvaises notes? Est-ce qu'ils vous donnent des examens? Est-ce qu'ils vous aident?

3. Est-ce que vos parents vous aident? Est-ce qu'ils vous comprennent? Est-ce qu'ils vous donnent des conseils *(advice)?* Est-ce qu'ils vous prêtent la voiture?

C. L'omission de l'article indéfini avec les professions

Note how professions are described in French.

Je suis **étudiant**.	*I am a student.*
Paul est **photographe**.	*Paul is a photographer.*
Ma mère est **professeur**.	*My mother is a teacher.*

After the verb **être**, French speakers do not use **un/une** before the names of professions, unless these nouns are modified by adjectives. Compare:

Madame Moreau est **dentiste**.   Madame Moreau est **une excellente dentiste**.

Vocabulaire spécialisé   Les professions

un avocat   **une avocate**
lawyer

un garçon   **une serveuse**
waiter   *waitress*

un ingénieur   **un ingénieur**
engineer

un interprète   **une interprète**
interpreter

un journaliste   **une journaliste**
journalist

un médecin   **un médecin**
doctor

un professeur   **un professeur**
teacher, professor

un vendeur   **une vendeuse**
salesperson

Note: Certain names of professions (like **ingénieur, professeur, médecin**) are always masculine.

Madame French est **mon** professeur de français.

VOCABULARY EXPANSION: un infirmier/une infirmière *(nurse)*, un/e chimiste *(chemist)*, un programmateur/une programmatrice or un programmeur/une programmeuse, un employé/ une employée, un ouvrier/une ouvrière *(laborer)*, un/e dentiste

Leçon un   **315**

ACTIVITÉ 7   Quelle est leur profession?

Lisez ce que font les personnes suivantes. Utilisez ces renseignements pour dire quelle est la profession de chaque personne.

→ Madame Carabin travaille dans un hôpital.   **Elle est médecin.**

1. Mademoiselle Bock travaille dans un café.
2. Madame Glotte parle anglais, espagnol et japonais.
3. Monsieur Lancette visite les malades *(sick people)*.
4. Monsieur Micro interviewe le président.
5. Madame Calcul travaille pour une compagnie d'électronique.
6. Monsieur Bouquin travaille à l'université.
7. Monsieur Barreau aide ses clients quand ils ont des problèmes avec la police.
8. Mademoiselle Chanel vend du parfum dans un grand magasin.

Pour Algérie et Ouest Africain

INGENIEURS

spécialisés en Agronomie, Zootechnie, Génie Rural, Céréaliculture, Agro-vulgarisation, Agro-économie, Agro-formation.
Expérience variable suivant les postes.
Ecrire avec curriculum vitæ Havas Contact 156 Bd Haussmann 75008 Paris sous réf. 54544 qui transmettra.

Prononciation

Le son /s/

Mot clé: <u>s</u>ac

Répétez les mots: <u>c</u>e, <u>ç</u>a, voi<u>c</u>i, <u>six</u>, François, <u>S</u>ylvie

Répétez les phrases: <u>C</u>e <u>s</u>oir, <u>S</u>ylvie <u>s</u>ort avec François.

<u>C</u>e garçon a <u>s</u>ept di<u>s</u>ques.

Di<u>x</u> et <u>six</u> font <u>s</u>eize.

Remind students that **s** between vowels is pronounced /z/: **musique.**

Comment écrire /s/:

  s   at the beginning of a word or next to a consonant: sort, reste
  ss between two vowels: poisson
  c   before **e, i, y:** ce, difficile, Nancy
  ç   before **a, o, u:** ça, garçon
  x   in the words: dix, six, soixante

You may have students practice the following French tongue twister:
Si six scies *(saws)* scient *(saw)* six saucisses, combien six cent six scies scient-elles de saucisses?

316 Unité sept

Entre nous

Expression pour la conversation

tout de suite *right away, right now*   Venez tout de suite!
Nous partons maintenant!

Mini-dialogue

Christine a des difficultés avec le problème de maths ... mais elle trouve une solution.

CHRISTINE: Dis, Nathalie, je ne comprends pas le problème de maths. Tu m'aides?
NATHALIE: Euh ... je n'ai pas le temps aujourd'hui.
CHRISTINE: Écoute, si tu m'aides, je t'invite chez moi ... et je te présente mon cousin.
NATHALIE: Il est sympa?
CHRISTINE: Très sympa!
NATHALIE: Où est ton livre de maths? Je t'aide tout de suite!

L'art du dialogue

a) Jouez le dialogue entre Christine et Nathalie.
b) Maintenant imaginez que Christine a une sœur, **Émilie. Christine et Émilie** ont des problèmes avec les maths. Elles demandent à Nathalie de les aider. Composez un nouveau dialogue. Pour cela, remplacez Christine par **Christine et Émilie.** Faites les changements nécessaires. Jouez ce nouveau dialogue.
c) Maintenant, **Christine et Émilie** demandent à **Suzanne et Nathalie** de les aider. Composez un nouveau dialogue. Pour cela, remplacez Nathalie par **Suzanne et Nathalie.** Faites les changements nécessaires. Jouez ce nouveau dialogue.

In the first transformation Christine and Émilie use **nous** and **notre,** and Nathalie addresses them with **vous** and **votre.** In the second transformation Christine and Émilie use **vous** in addressing Suzanne and Nathalie, who refer to themselves as **nous.** Note also that **dis** becomes **dites** and **écoute** becomes **écoutez.**

Leçon 2　Un garçon génial

Élisabeth a des opinions très *particulières* *sur* ses amis.　　　　　*special; about*

FRANÇOIS: Est-ce que tu *connais* Alain?　　　　　*know*

ÉLISABETH: Oui, je le connais bien!

FRANÇOIS: Qu'est-ce que tu penses de lui?

ÉLISABETH: Il est mignon . . .

FRANÇOIS: Est-ce que tu le trouves intelligent?

ÉLISABETH: Non, pas *spécialement*.　　　　　*especially*

FRANÇOIS: Est-ce que tu connais son cousin Christophe?

ÉLISABETH: Je le connais aussi. Il est photographe, n'est-ce pas?

FRANÇOIS: C'est ça! Est-ce que tu le trouves intelligent?

ÉLISABETH: Bien sûr! Je le trouve très intelligent . . .
En fait, je le trouve génial!　　　　　*In fact*

FRANÇOIS: Mais il ne parle jamais!

ÉLISABETH: Voilà *justement* pourquoi je le trouve très intelligent!　　　　　*precisely*

Est-ce qu'Élisabeth connaît Alain?　Qu'est-ce qu'elle pense de lui?
Est-ce qu'Élisabeth connaît Christophe?　Qu'est-ce qu'elle pense de lui?
Pourquoi est-ce qu'elle trouve Christophe intelligent?

CONVERSATION

Let's talk about the people you generally invite to your home.

1. Est-ce que vous invitez **vos amis?**
   Oui, je **les** invite. (Non, je ne **les** invite pas.)
2. Est-ce que vous invitez **les garçons de la classe?**
3. Est-ce que vous invitez **les filles de la classe?**
4. Est-ce que vous invitez **les amis de vos amis?**

OBSERVATIONS   Str. B

The above questions have the same subject and the same verb.
- What is the *subject?* What is the *verb?*   vous/invitez

The nouns in heavy type are *directly* affected by the verb. These nouns are the *direct objects* of the verb. In general, a noun which is a direct object comes *immediately after* the verb.

Direct object nouns can be replaced by *direct object pronouns.*
- How do you say *"I invite them"* in French?   je les invite
- What direct object pronoun replaces **vos amis? les garçons de la classe?**   les/les
  les filles de la classe? les amis de vos amis?   les/les
- Does the direct object pronoun come
  before or *after* the verb?   before

NOTE CULTURELLE   For reading and listening practice.

Quelques° compliments

Quelle est la qualité que vous admirez le plus chez° vos amis? La sincérité, la générosité ou l'intelligence? Pour les Français, l'intelligence est une qualité très importante. Aussi,° si vous voulez° faire° un compliment à un ami français, dites-lui:° «Tu es génial!» ou «Tu es brillant!» ou «Tu es remarquablement° intelligent!» ou plus simplement° «Oh là là, tu n'es pas bête, toi!»

Quelques *A few* **chez** *in* **Aussi** *So* **voulez** *want* **faire** *to pay* **dites-lui** *tell him* **remarquablement** *remarkably* **simplement** *simply*

Vocabulaire spécialisé   Adjectifs

étrange	*strange*	**remarquable**	*remarkable*
génial	*bright, brilliant, very smart*	**ridicule**	*ridiculous*
(*pl.* **géniaux**)		**snob**	*stuck-up, snobbish*
idiot	*stupid*		
mignon	*cute*		
(**mignonne**)			

Note: The adjective **snob** does not take an **-e** in the feminine:
          Marie est **snob.**

Structure

A. Le verbe connaître   Savoir is presented in the next lesson.

Note the forms and uses of the irregular verb **connaître** *(to know)*.

Infinitive		**connaître**	Est-ce que vous désirez **connaître** mes parents?
Present	je tu il/elle	**connais** **connais** **connaît**	Je **connais** Émilie. Est-ce que tu **connais** Paul? Jacques ne **connaît** pas mes parents.
	nous vous ils/elles	**connaissons** **connaissez** **connaissent**	Nous ne **connaissons** pas Paris. Est-ce que vous **connaissez** bien Québec? Mes amis **connaissent** un bon restaurant.
Passé composé	j'ai	**connu**	Quand est-ce que tu **as connu** mon cousin?

Connaître means *to know* in the sense of *being acquainted with people and places.*

In the **passé composé** and future, **connaître** may also mean *to meet someone* (for the first time).   Students may know the word "connoisseur." A wine connoisseur is someone who knows and is well acquainted with wines.

ACTIVITÉ 1   Paul

Paul est un nouvel étudiant à l'école. Dites qui connaît et qui ne connaît pas Paul.

→ mes amis (non)   **Mes amis ne connaissent pas Paul.**

1. nous (oui)
2. toi (non)
3. Sylvie (oui)
4. Jacqueline et Suzanne (non)
5. le professeur d'anglais (oui)
6. le professeur de maths (non)
7. vous (oui)
8. moi (oui)

ACTIVITÉ 2   Questions personnelles   Remind students that in negative sentences un, une, des become de (d').

1. Connaissez-vous New York? Chicago? la Nouvelle-Orléans? San Antonio? Québec? Paris? le Mexique? le Canada?
2. Dans votre ville, connaissez-vous un bon restaurant? un restaurant français? un restaurant bon marché? des magasins intéressants? un magasin de disques? un magasin de vêtements?
3. Connaissez-vous les parents de votre meilleur(e) ami(e)? ses frères? ses sœurs? ses amis?
4. Connaissez-vous des Français? des Françaises? des Canadiens? des élèves étrangers *(foreign)*?
5. Connaissez-vous personnellement *(personally)* le directeur (la directrice) de votre école? le capitaine de l'équipe de football de l'école? un athlète professionnel? un acteur de cinéma? le président des États-Unis?

The purpose of this activity is to provide practice using **connaître** with people and places. You may wish to expand on the responses. **Connaissez-vous un restaurant français? Comment s'appelle ce restaurant? Est-ce qu'on mange bien là?** etc.

Point out that direct object pronouns, in French as in English, replace the entire noun group: article, noun, adjective.
Direct object pronouns are NOT used to replace nouns introduced by un, une, des, du, de la.

B. Les pronoms *le, la, les*

In the questions below, the nouns in heavy type are the *direct objects* of the
verb. Note the forms and position of the *direct object pronouns* which are
used to replace those nouns in the answers.

Tu connais **Charles?**	Oui, je **le** connais. Je **l'**invite souvent.
Tu connais **Jacqueline?**	Oui, je **la** connais. Je **l'**invite aussi.
Tu connais **mes cousins?**	Je **les** connais bien. Je **les** invite.
Tu connais **mes amies?**	Je **les** connais aussi. Je **les** invite souvent.

To make sure that the students understand these sentences, you may ask for translations.

The direct object pronouns which correspond to the subject pronouns
il, elle, ils, elles are:

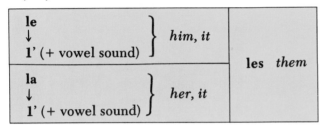

le ↓ **l'** (+ vowel sound)	*him, it*
la ↓ **l'** (+ vowel sound)	*her, it*
les	*them*

→ The direct object pronouns **le, la, l', les** can refer to either people or things.

Tu regardes Nicole?	Oui, je **la** regarde.	*I'm looking at her.*
Tu regardes la télé?	Oui, je **la** regarde.	*I'm watching it.*

→ The pronouns **le, la, l',** and **les** come before the verb. In negative sentences
they come between **ne** and the verb.

Tu connais Marc?	Non, je **ne le** connais pas.	
Vous regardez la télé?	Nous **ne la** regardons pas.	Nous **ne la** regardons jamais.

Direct objects are used with many of the verbs you have learned, such as:

acheter	Est-ce que tu **achètes** ces lunettes?	Non, je ne **les achète** pas.
aider	**Aides**-tu tes parents?	Bien sûr, je **les aide**.
aimer	**Aimes**-tu cette comédie?	Oui, je **l'aime** beaucoup.
attendre	Est-ce que Paul **attend** Marie?	Oui, il **l'attend**.
avoir	Est-ce que tu **as** mes disques?	Non, je ne **les ai** pas.
chercher	**Cherchez**-vous votre argent?	Oui, je **le cherche**.
connaître	**Connaissez**-vous mes cousines?	Non, je ne **les connais** pas.
écouter	Tu **écoutes** ce disque?	Oui, je **l'écoute**.
inviter	Est-ce que Marc **invite** Hélène?	Bien sûr, il **l'invite**.
mettre	Où **mets**-tu la voiture?	Je **la mets** dans le garage.
prendre	Vous **prenez** votre guitare?	Mais non, je ne **la prends** pas.
regarder	Quand **regardez**-vous la télé?	Nous **la regardons** à huit heures.
trouver	Comment **trouves**-tu Charles?	Je **le trouve** intelligent.
vendre	Henri **vend** ses cassettes?	Oui, il **les vend**.
voir	Quand **vois**-tu Pierre?	Je **le vois** samedi.

Students know many other verbs which take direct objects: amener, choisir, commander, comprendre, dépenser, détester, emprunter, entendre, étudier, finir, manger, perdre.

→ **Chercher, écouter,** and **regarder** are three verbs which take direct objects in French. Compare the French and English constructions.

chercher

Henri **cherche**	. . .	sa montre.		Il la **cherche.**
Henri looks	*for*	*his watch.*		*He looks for it.*

écouter

Jean-Paul **écoute**	. . .	ses amis.		Il les **écoute.**
Jean-Paul listens	*to*	*his friends.*		*He listens to them.*

regarder

Il **regarde**	. . .	Nicole.		Il la **regarde.**
He looks	*at*	*Nicole.*		*He looks at her.*

ACTIVITÉ 3 À la surprise-partie

Hélène connaît tous les invités (*guests*), mais Pierre ne les connaît pas.
Jouez les rôles d'Hélène et de Pierre. Utilisez le pronom complément qui
convient.

→ ces garçons français?   Hélène: **Moi, je les connais.**
                           Pierre: **Moi, je ne les connais pas.**

1. Paul?
2. Jacqueline?
3. Annie et Thérèse?
4. Marc et Philippe?
5. la fille là-bas?

6. cette étudiante?
7. Antoine?
8. les cousins d'Antoine?
9. la petite amie de Jacques?
10. ses frères?

VARIATIONS with voir, inviter, attendre, écouter, chercher, regarder.

ACTIVITÉ 4 Un choix difficile *(A difficult choice)*

Imaginez que vous allez passer le mois de juillet en France. Vous êtes
limité(e) à 20 kilos de bagages. Dites si oui ou non vous allez prendre les
choses suivantes. Utilisez le pronom complément qui convient.

→ la raquette de tennis   **Je la prends. (Je ne la prends pas.)**

1. les disques
2. le livre de français
3. la guitare
4. le transistor
5. le téléviseur

6. mon maillot de bain
7. ma bicyclette
8. mes chemises
9. mes chaussures de tennis
10. mes chaussures de ski

ACTIVITÉ 5 La télé et la radio

Pierre regarde les programmes suivants à la télé. Nicole les écoute à la radio. Jouez les deux rôles d'après le modèle.

→ le match de football Pierre: **Je le regarde à la télé.**
  Nicole: **Moi, je l'écoute à la radio.**

1. les matchs de tennis
2. le concert
3. la pièce de théâtre
4. le programme de musique

5. Mike Wallace
6. Barbara Walters
7. mes acteurs préférés (*favorite*)
8. mes actrices préférées

ACTIVITÉ 6 Zut alors! OPTIONAL

Les personnes suivantes cherchent certains objets, mais elles ne les trouvent pas. Exprimez cela d'après le modèle.

→ Paul (sa guitare) **Paul cherche sa guitare. Il ne la trouve pas.**

1. Sylvie (ses disques)
2. Henri (son vélo)
3. Jacques (Catherine)
4. Catherine (Antoine)
5. mes amis (leurs livres)
6. Robert (ses cousines)

ACTIVITÉ 7 Opinions personnelles OPTIONAL

Exprimez votre opinion personnelle au sujet des personnes suivantes. Pour cela, utilisez le pronom complément qui convient et l'adjectif entre parenthèses dans des phrases affirmatives ou négatives.

→ Barbara Walters (géniale?) **Oui, je la trouve géniale.**
  (Non, je ne la trouve pas géniale.)

1. Woody Allen (amusant?)
2. Charlie Brown (mignon?)
3. les Beatles (extraordinaires?)
4. Miss Piggy (snob?)
5. mes professeurs (remarquables?)
6. le président (génial?)
7. les Français (snobs?)
8. les gens (*people*) snobs (ridicules?)
9. Dracula (remarquable?)
10. Frankenstein (mignon?)
11. les Who (mignons?)
12. mes amis (idiots?)

VARIATIONS using **très, assez, un peu.**

WOODY ALLEN
UN GÉNIE COMIQUE ! TIME
MANHATTAN
United Artists

ACTIVITÉ 8   Questions personnelles   OPTIONAL

Répondez aux questions suivantes. Dans vos réponses, utilisez un pronom complément.

1. Est-ce que vous aimez le théâtre? la danse? les sports? le français? les sciences? les maths? la musique? la musique disco?
2. Est-ce que vous regardez souvent la télé? les filles? les garçons? vos photos?
3. À la télé, regardez-vous les films policiers? les comédies? les films de science-fiction? les programmes de sport?
4. Est-ce que vous écoutez la radio? vos amis? vos amies? vos professeurs? vos parents? le professeur de français? vos disques préférés (favorite)?
5. Aimez-vous le Coca-Cola? le lait? le café? l'eau minérale? le thé?
6. Invitez-vous souvent votre meilleur ami? votre meilleure amie? vos cousins?
7. Admirez-vous le président des États-Unis? Abraham Lincoln? Martin Luther King, Jr.? Jacqueline Kennedy Onassis? les journalistes? les médecins?
8. Aidez-vous votre père? votre mère? vos amis?
9. Voyez-vous souvent vos cousins? vos grands-parents? vos voisins (neighbors)?

UN JEU

Nos relations avec les autres (other) personnes dépendent souvent de l'opinion que nous avons de ces personnes. Exprimez cela dans des phrases logiques, affirmatives ou négatives. Utilisez les éléments des colonnes A, B, C, D et E. Combien de phrases pouvez-vous (can you) faire en 10 minutes?

A	B	C	D	E
je	aider	Paul	trouver	idiot
Hélène	écouter	Suzanne		étrange
Patrick	regarder	ces filles		mignon
nous	inviter	ces garçons		remarquable
mes cousins				snob
				intelligent

→ **Patrick écoute Suzanne parce qu'il la trouve remarquable.**

→ **Nous n'invitons pas ces garçons parce que nous les trouvons snobs.**

Prononciation

Le son /ɲ/

Mot clé: mi**gn**on

Répétez les mots: a**gn**eau, campa**gn**e, Allema**gn**e, Espa**gn**e

Répétez les phrases: La campa**gn**e en Allema**gn**e est ma**gn**ifique.

La petite A**gn**ès est mi**gn**onne.

The sound /ɲ/ is pronounced somewhat like the *ny* in the English word *canyon*.

Note: The letters **gn** usually represent the sound /ɲ/.

Entre nous

Expression pour la conversation

je parie que ... *I bet that ...*   Vous n'avez pas l'air content (*happy*).
Je parie que vous avez perdu votre match de tennis!

Mini-dialogue   Franc is pronounced /frɑ̃/.

Marc est *franc*, mais il n'est pas toujours très *diplomate*!   *frank; diplomatic*

JANINE: Dis Marc, est-ce que tu connais Nicole?
MARC: Bien sûr, je la connais très bien. Je la trouve très sympathique.
JANINE: Et son frère Édouard? Je parie que tu le trouves sympathique aussi!
MARC: Non! Je le trouve idiot et snob.
JANINE: Merci! C'est mon petit ami!

L'art du dialogue

a) Jouez le dialogue entre Janine et Marc.
b) Maintenant imaginez que les rôles sont renversés (*reversed*). **Marc** demande à **Janine** son opinion, d'abord (*first*) sur **Édouard**, et ensuite sur **Nicole**. Faites les changements nécessaires. Jouez ce nouveau dialogue.

Leçon 3

STRUCTURES TO OBSERVE
• the position of object pronouns in the imperative
• the construction **le voilà**

Florence est amoureuse.

Olivier et Florence organisent un pique-nique. Qui vont-ils inviter?

OLIVIER: Dis! Il fait très beau aujourd'hui. Allons à la
campagne et faisons un pique-nique.

FLORENCE: Excellente idée. Invitons des copains!

OLIVIER: Qui?

FLORENCE: Nicole . . .

OLIVIER: D'accord. Invite-la!

FLORENCE: François et Bernard?

OLIVIER: Invite-les aussi!

FLORENCE: Invitons aussi Charles!

OLIVIER: Lui! Pas question! Il est trop gourmand!

FLORENCE: C'est vrai, mais il a une guitare, *et puis* il est   *and (moreover)*
amusant, et puis c'est un bon copain, et puis . . .

OLIVIER: Et puis tu es amoureuse de lui, n'est-ce pas?

FLORENCE: Euh . . .

OLIVIER: Bon, bon, je comprends. Invite-le!

FLORENCE: Tiens, *le voilà*.   *here he comes*

OLIVIER: Dis, Florence, pourquoi est-ce que tu rougis?

Est-ce qu'Olivier invite Nicole? Est-ce qu'il invite François et Bernard? Pourquoi est-ce qu'il
n'invite pas Charles? Pourquoi est-ce que Florence désire inviter Charles?

CONVERSATION

Imagine that a friend is organizing a party and is asking you if he should invite the following people. Say *yes*.

1. J'invite ta sœur?
   Oui, invite-**la!**
2. J'invite ton meilleur ami?

3. J'invite ta meilleure amie?
4. J'invite le professeur?
5. J'invite les élèves?

OBSERVATIONS Str. B

When you tell your friend he should invite the above people, you are using the *imperative.* Note the position of the *object pronoun* in the answer to the first question.

- Does this pronoun come *before* or *after* the verb? What connects it to the
  verb? a hyphen

(annotations: "after" above the word; "a hyphen" below)

NOTE CULTURELLE For reading and listening practice.

Vive l'amour!

Un journal français a organisé un sondage° sur la vie° senti-mentale des jeunes Français et des jeunes Françaises âgés de 15 à 20 ans. Voici les questions . . . et les réponses.°

Question 1: Êtes-vous actuellement° amoureux (amoureuse)?
  oui: 40%   non: 60%

Question 2: Si vous êtes amoureux (amoureuse), est-ce que c'est la première fois?°
  oui: 36%   non: 64%

Question 3: Est-ce que vos parents connaissent votre vie sentimentale?
  oui: 67%   non: 28%   je ne sais pas: 5%

sondage *opinion poll*   **vie** *life*   **réponses** *answers*
actuellement *right now*   **fois** *time*

Vocabulaire pratique

NOMS:	**un copain**	*friend, pal*	**une copine**	*friend, pal*
	un pique-nique	*picnic*		

ADJECTIFS: **amoureux (amoureuse)** — *in love* — Est-ce que Florence est **amoureuse** de Charles?

gourmand — *who likes food* — Pierre aime la bonne cuisine. Il est très **gourmand.**

VERBES: **organiser** — *to organize* — Qui va **organiser** le pique-nique?

rougir — *to blush, turn red* — Est-ce que vous **rougissez** quand vous êtes furieux *(furious)*?

Structure

A. La construction: pronom + *voici, voilà*

You may point out that the words **voici** and **voilà** stand for verbs. Literally **voici** means **vois ici**! *(see over here!)* and **voilà** means **vois là**! *(see over there!)*.

Note the position of the object pronouns with **voici** and **voilà**.

Où est ton électrophone?	**Le** voilà.	*There it is.*
Où est Florence?	**La** voici.	*Here she is.*
Où sont mes photos?	**Les** voilà.	*There they are.*
Où êtes-vous?	**Nous** voici.	*Here we are.*

Direct object pronouns come *before* **voici** and **voilà**.

ACTIVITÉ 1   L'album de photos

Imaginez que vous regardez votre album de photos avec un ami français.
Il vous demande de lui montrer *(to show him)* certaines personnes ou
certaines choses. Répondez à votre ami d'après le modèle.

→ Où est ta sœur?   **La voici!**

1. Où est ton père?
2. Où est ta meilleure amie?
3. Où sont tes cousins?
4. Où sont tes cousines?
5. Où est ton chien?
6. Où sont tes chats?
7. Où est ta maison?
8. Où est ta moto?

B. La place des pronoms à l'impératif

Note the position of the object pronoun when the verb is in the imperative.

	AFFIRMATIVE COMMAND	NEGATIVE COMMAND
J'invite Pierre?	Oui, invite-**le**!	Non, ne l'invite pas!
Je prends la guitare?	Oui, prends-**la**!	Non, ne **la** prends pas!
J'achète les disques?	Oui, achète-**les**!	Non, ne **les** achète pas!

In *affirmative* commands the object pronoun comes *after* the verb and is joined
to it by a hyphen.

In *negative* commands the object pronoun comes *before* the verb.

→ When placed after the verb, **me** becomes **moi**:

Invite-**moi** ce soir!	*but:* Ne m'invite pas demain!
Téléphonez-**moi** demain!	*but:* Ne **me** téléphonez pas aujourd'hui!

ACTIVITÉ 2   Le pique-nique

Olivier demande à Florence s'il doit *(should)* prendre certaines choses pour
le pique-nique. Florence répond affirmativement. Jouez les rôles d'Olivier
et de Florence d'après le modèle.

→ ma guitare   Olivier: **Est-ce que je prends ma guitare?**
Florence: **Oui, prends-la.**

1. le coca
2. les sandwichs
3. la salade
4. le gâteau
5. mes lunettes de soleil
6. mon appareil- photo
7. ton sac
8. les maillots de bain

VARIATION: —Où est-ce que je mets ma guitare?
—Mets-la ici (dans la voiture, sur la table, là-bas. . .).

ACTIVITÉ 3 Invitations

Imaginez qu'avec un ami vous préparez une liste de personnes à inviter à un pique-nique. Vous êtes limité(e) à 4 des personnes suivantes. Faites vos suggestions d'après le modèle.

→ Paul est assez sympathique.   **Invitons-le! (Ne l'invitons pas!)**

1. Sylvie est très sympathique.
2. Mes cousins ont une voiture.
3. Jacques est gourmand.
4. Robert a une guitare.

5. Mes cousines sont mignonnes.
6. Henri est snob.
7. Philippe n'est pas mon ami.
8. Albert est pénible.

ACTIVITÉ 4 S'il te plaît

Imaginez que vous passez l'hiver chez un ami français. Demandez à votre ami de faire les choses suivantes pour vous.

→ présenter / au professeur   **S'il te plaît, présente-moi au professeur.**

1. présenter / à tes amis
2. prêter / ta bicyclette
3. prêter / 10 francs
4. aider / avec le problème de maths

5. donner / l'adresse d'un bon dentiste
6. attendre / après la classe
7. inviter / à la surprise-partie
8. donner / de l'aspirine

C. Le verbe *savoir*

Note the forms and uses of the irregular verb **savoir** *(to know)*.

Infinitive		**savoir**	Qu'est-ce que vous désirez **savoir?**
Present	je	**sais**	Je **sais** où est Philippe.
	tu	**sais**	**Sais**-tu à quelle heure est le pique-nique?
	il/elle	**sait**	Jacques **sait** où j'habite.
	nous	**savons**	Nous ne **savons** pas que tu es malade.
	vous	**savez**	**Savez**-vous si Paul a une voiture?
	ils/elles	**savent**	Les élèves **savent** la leçon.
Passé composé	j'ai	**su**	Je n'ai pas **su** pourquoi vous êtes venus.

ACTIVITÉ 5 Où habite Robert?

Certaines personnes savent où habite Robert. Les autres *(others)* ne savent pas. Exprimez cela en utilisant le verbe **savoir.**

→ le professeur (non)   **Le professeur ne sait pas.**

1. nous (oui)
2. vous (non)
3. mes amis (oui)
4. Jacqueline (non)

5. Suzanne et Paul (oui)
6. moi (oui)
7. toi (non)
8. l'ami de Charles (non)

Stress that **connaître** is used with nouns referring to people and places; **savoir** is used with clauses, even those referring to people. **Je connais Jacques. Je sais où il habite.**

D. *Savoir ou connaître?*

Although both **connaître** and **savoir** mean *to know*, their uses are very different.

➜ **Connaître** means *to know* or *be acquainted with.* It is used with nouns or pronouns referring to *people* and *places*.

Tu **connais** Jacqueline?	Oui, je la **connais.**
Vous **connaissez** ce café?	Non, nous ne le **connaissons** pas.

➜ **Savoir** means *to know information.* It is used in the following constructions:

savoir (alone)
Je **sais!** Tu ne **sais** pas?   *I know! You don't know?*

savoir que . . .
Je **sais que** tu es français.   *I know that you are French.*

savoir si . . .
Savez-vous **si** Paul a une moto?   *Do you know if Paul has a motorcycle?*

savoir + interrogative expression (**où, comment, pourquoi, quand** . . .)
Je ne **sais** pas **quand** tu viens.   *I don't know when you are coming.*

savoir + noun or pronoun referring to something one learns or information
Tu **sais** la leçon?   *Do you know the lesson?*
Tu **sais** la date du pique-nique?   *Do you know the date of the picnic?*

The construction **savoir** + infinitive means *to know how to* do something, *to be able to* do something.

Savez-vous parler espagnol?   *Can you (Do you know how to) speak Spanish?*

Connaître may often be used with nouns referring to information. **Je connais la date du pique-nique.** This is not presented at this time in order to avoid confusion.

ACTIVITÉ 6 Dialogue

Demandez à vos camarades s'ils savent faire les choses suivantes.

➜ nager   Élève 1: **Est-ce que tu sais nager?**
                Élève 2: **Oui, je sais nager. (Non, je ne sais pas nager.)**

1. skier	5. piloter un avion	9. jouer du piano
2. jouer au tennis	6. parler japonais	10. jouer de la clarinette
3. faire de la voile	7. faire de la poterie	11. prendre des photos
4. chanter	8. faire la cuisine	12. parler espagnol

ACTIVITÉ 7 Une fille bien informée

Dites que Florence connaît les personnes suivantes. Dites aussi ce qu'elle sait à leur sujet (*about them*).

➜ Jacques / où il habite   **Elle connaît Jacques. Elle sait où il habite.**

1. Hélène / où elle habite	6. Suzanne / pourquoi elle est malade
2. Monsieur Moreau / où il travaille	7. Thérèse / pourquoi elle ne prête pas son vélo
3. Paul / quand il joue au tennis	8. mes cousins / quand ils vont à Paris
4. Annie / avec qui elle étudie	9. cette fille / avec qui elle sort
5. Robert / à quelle heure il vient	10. ce garçon / quand il part au Canada

Prononciation

Révision: les sons /ø/ et /œ/

/ø/ y<u>eux</u>, d<u>eux</u>, chev<u>eux</u>, bl<u>eu</u>, amour<u>eux</u>, serv<u>euse</u>, jou<u>euse</u>
Matthi<u>eu</u> est amour<u>eux</u> de la serv<u>euse</u>.
Les d<u>eux</u> filles sont très génér<u>euses</u>.
Le vi<u>eux</u> monsi<u>eur</u> a les chev<u>eux</u> blancs.

/œ/ l<u>eur</u>, c<u>œur</u>, <u>œil</u>, doct<u>eur</u>, h<u>eure</u>, jou<u>eur</u>, s<u>œur</u>, profess<u>eur</u>
Le profess<u>eur</u> Lesi<u>eur</u> parle avec l'ingéni<u>eur</u>.
J'ai mal au c<u>œur</u>, Doct<u>eur</u>.
L<u>eur</u> s<u>œur</u> vient à n<u>euf</u> h<u>eures</u>.

Entre nous

Expression pour la conversation

To indicate that you are changing your mind, you may say:

dans ce cas... *in that case*... —Oh là là! Il fait mauvais aujourd'hui!
  —Bon... **Dans ce cas**, je ne vais pas au pique-nique!

Mini-dialogue

Hélène a beaucoup d'admiration pour son cousin Jean-Philippe.
Personne ne sait pourquoi! *No one*

HÉLÈNE: Tu connais Jean-Philippe?
MARTINE: Non, je ne le connais pas. Qui est-ce?
HÉLÈNE: C'est mon cousin. C'est un garçon vraiment génial!
MARTINE: Bon ... Alors, invitons-le à la piscine samedi!
HÉLÈNE: Euh ... il ne sait pas nager.
MARTINE: Ah bon. Alors, invitons-le à jouer au tennis avec nous dimanche prochain!
HÉLÈNE: Euh ... il ne sait pas jouer au tennis.
MARTINE: Dans ce cas, invitons-le à la surprise-partie?
HÉLÈNE: Euh ... il ne sait pas danser.
MARTINE: Dis, Hélène. Qu'est-ce qu'il sait faire, ton cousin génial?
HÉLÈNE: Euh ... je ne sais pas!

L'art du dialogue

a) Jouez le dialogue entre Hélène et Martine.
b) Maintenant Hélène parle de deux garçons: **Jean-Philippe et Vincent**. Composez le nouveau dialogue. (Note: C'est un garçon vraiment génial → **Ce sont des garçons vraiment géniaux**.) Jouez ce nouveau dialogue.

Leçon 4 Un système efficace?

STRUCTURES TO OBSERVE
• the indirect object pronouns **lui, leur**
• the negative construction **ne...rien**

Qu'est-ce qui compte dans la *vie*? La famille, les amis, les *études* ... et aussi l'argent! Parents et enfants discutent souvent de ce problème important.

What counts; life; studies

Scène 1. Monsieur Moreau, Madame Vernier

M. MOREAU: Combien d'argent de poche donnez-vous à votre fille Isabelle?

MME VERNIER: Je lui donne vingt francs par semaine. Et vous, combien d'argent donnez-vous à votre fils Georges?

M. MOREAU: Ça dépend! La semaine dernière, il a bien travaillé en classe et je lui ai donné trente francs.

MME VERNIER: Et quand il ne travaille pas?

M. MOREAU: Je *ne* lui donne *rien*.

MME VERNIER: C'est un système *efficace*?

M. MOREAU: Très efficace!

Combien d'argent est-ce que Madame Vernier donne à sa fille? Quand est-ce que Monsieur Moreau donne de l'argent à son fils?

not ... anything effective

Scène 2. Isabelle Vernier, Georges Moreau

ISABELLE: Tu as des parents généreux?

GEORGES: Non, ils sont très radins. Je ne leur demande jamais rien.

ISABELLE: Mais tu as toujours de l'argent.

GEORGES: J'ai des grands-parents très généreux! Quand je leur *rends visite*, ils me donnent dix ou vingt francs.

ISABELLE: Tu leur rends souvent visite?

GEORGES: Tous les dimanches!

Est-ce que Georges a des parents généreux? À qui est-ce qu'il rend visite?

visit

CONVERSATION

Are you generous? Do you lend the following things to your friends?

1. Est-ce que vous prêtez vos disques **à vos amis?**
   Oui, je prête (Non, je ne prête pas) mes disques **à mes amis.**
2. Est-ce que vous prêtez vos livres **à votre meilleur ami?**
3. Est-ce que vous prêtez vos magazines **à votre meilleure amie?**
4. Est-ce que vous prêtez vos notes de français **à vos camarades?**

OBSERVATIONS   Str. B

Reread the first question carefully.

- What is the *subject*? the *verb*? the *direct object*?

_{vous}   _{prêtez}   _{vos disques}

In each question the noun in heavy type is the *indirect object* of the verb. Note that the indirect objects are introduced by à.

Indirect object pronouns replace indirect object nouns. Reread "**Un système efficace?**"

- Which pronoun replaces **à votre fille Isabelle? à votre fils Georges?**   _{lui}
- Which pronoun does Georges use instead of saying **à mes parents? à mes grands-parents?**

_{lui}   _{leur}   _{leur}

NOTE CULTURELLE   For reading and listening comprehension.

L'argent de poche

Demandez-vous° de l'argent à vos parents? Les jeunes Français n'ont pas le choix.° Les parents sont la source principale, et souvent unique,° d'argent. Combien d'argent donnent-ils à leurs enfants? Ça dépend! À quatorze ans, un garçon dispose de° 40 francs par mois. À seize ans, il dispose de 100 francs. Les filles sont moins favorisées:° elles disposent de 80 francs. Quand les parents donnent de l'argent à leurs enfants, ils posent° souvent des conditions. Ils leur demandent, par exemple,° de dépenser « utilement » ° cet argent. Les livres, les disques de musique classique sont des dépenses «utiles».

Les jeunes ont d'autres° idées. Ils préfèrent aller au cinéma ou au café avec leurs amis, acheter des disques de musique pop, des magazines de bandes dessinées,° des gadgets, etc. Pour les jeunes Français, l'argent des parents n'est donc° pas uniquement° une source de revenus.° C'est aussi une source de conflit!

Demandez-vous *Do you ask for* **choix** *choice* **unique** *only* **dispose de** *has . . . to spend* **favorisées** *favored* **posent** *lay down* **par exemple** *for example* **utilement** *in a useful way* **d'autres** *other* **bandes dessinées** *comics* **donc** *therefore* **uniquement** *only* **revenus** *income*

Vocabulaire pratique

NOMS: **l'argent de poche**	*allowance, pocket money*	**une dépense** *expense*
ADJECTIFS: **radin ≠ généreux** **(généreuse)**	*stingy ≠ generous*	
VERBE: **discuter**	*to discuss, talk about*	
EXPRESSIONS: **par (semaine, mois, . . .)**	*per (week, month, . . .)*	
tous les (toutes les)	*every*	

Note: **Tous les** is always followed by a plural noun:

tous les mois *every month*   **toutes les** semaines *every week*

Structure

A. Les expressions *quelqu'un, quelque chose* et leurs contraires

In each set of sentences compare the affirmative and negative constructions in heavy type.

Tu parles à **quelqu'un?**	*Are you talking to **someone?***
Non, je **ne** parle à **personne.**	*No, I'm not talking to **anyone**. (I'm talking to **nobody**.)*
Vous faites **quelque chose** maintenant?	*Are you doing **something** now?*
Non, nous **ne** faisons **rien.**	*No, we're **not** doing **anything**. (We're doing **nothing**.)*

To refer to unspecified people or things, French speakers use the following expressions:

quelqu'un	*someone, somebody, anyone*	**ne (n')... personne**	*nobody, not anybody (not anyone)*
quelque chose	*something, anything*	**ne (n')... rien**	*nothing, not anything*

→ Like all negative expressions, **personne** and **rien** require **ne** before the verb.

→ The words **personne** and **rien** may be used as subjects, objects of the verb, or after prepositions.

Personne n'est ici.   **Rien** n'est impossible.

Je n'invite **personne.**   Je **ne** fais **rien.**

Je **ne** parle à **personne.**   Je **ne** pense à **rien.**

> In the passé composé, **rien** comes between avoir and the past participle and **personne** comes after the past participle.
> Je n'ai rien fait.   Je n'ai vu personne.

→ If an adjective is used after the above expressions, the construction is:

quelqu'un (quelque chose, rien, personne) + de + adjective

quelqu'un d'intéressant   *someone interesting*
rien de spécial   *nothing special*

ACTIVITÉ 1   Sylvie est malade.

Sylvie est malade. Elle ne fait pas ce que Paul fait aujourd'hui. Exprimez cela d'après le modèle.

→ Paul dîne avec quelqu'un.   **Sylvie ne dîne avec personne.**

1. Il invite quelqu'un.
2. Il téléphone à quelqu'un.
3. Il parle à quelqu'un d'intéressant.
4. Il fait quelque chose.
5. Il mange quelque chose de bon.
6. Il fait quelque chose d'amusant.

ACTIVITÉ 2   Questions personnelles   OPTIONAL

Répondez aux questions suivantes affirmativement ou négativement.

→ Connaissez-vous quelqu'un de très intelligent?

Oui, je connais quelqu'un de très intelligent.
(Non, je ne connais personne de très intelligent.)

1. Invitez-vous quelqu'un ce week-end?
2. Faites-vous quelque chose de spécial?
3. Téléphonez-vous à quelqu'un ce soir?
4. Allez-vous au cinéma avec quelqu'un?
5. Étudiez-vous quelque chose d'intéressant en classe?
6. Regardez-vous quelque chose d'amusant à la télé?

Ce Noël,
offrez-lui un diamant.

B. Les pronoms *lui, leur*

Indirect object pronouns replace nouns which are introduced by **à**.
Note the forms and position of these pronouns in the answers to the
questions below.

Tu téléphones **à Jacques?**	Oui, je **lui** téléphone.
Tu parles **à Catherine?**	Non, je ne **lui** parle pas.
Tu téléphones **à tes amis?**	Oui, je **leur** téléphone.
Tu prêtes ton vélo **à tes cousines?**	Non, je ne **leur** prête pas mon vélo.

To make sure that the students
understand these sentences, you
may ask for English equivalents.

The indirect object pronouns corresponding to **il, elle, ils,** and **elles** are:

lui *to him, to her*	**leur** *to them*

Be sure students realize that in English the
word "to" may be left out.
I give her the book. I give the book to her.

→ Like the other object pronouns, **lui** and **leur** come *before* the verb,
except in affirmative commands.

Voici Henri.   Parle-**lui**!   Prête-**lui** ton vélo!

→ In negative sentences **lui** and **leur** come between **ne** and the verb.

Je **lui** parle.   Je **ne lui** parle pas de mes problèmes.

Indirect objects are used with several of the verbs you have studied:

You may ask the students to identify the
direct and indirect objects in the sentences.

donner	Qu'est-ce que tu donnes **à ton frère?**	Je **lui** donne un disque.
obéir	Tu obéis **à tes parents?**	Non, je ne **leur** obéis pas toujours.
parler	Tu parles français **à tes parents?**	Non, je ne **leur** parle pas français.
prêter	Tu prêtes ta moto **à tes amis?**	Non, je ne **leur** prête pas ma moto.
promettre	Tu promets **à ton professeur** d'étudier?	Oui, je **lui** promets d'étudier.
téléphoner	Vous téléphonez **à André?**	Oui, je **lui** téléphone souvent.
vendre	Tu vends ta radio **à tes cousins?**	Non, je ne **leur** vends pas ma radio.

Note that some of the above sentences have both a *direct* and an *indirect* object:

donner, prêter, vendre **quelque chose** *(direct object)* **à quelqu'un** *(indirect object)*

Other known verbs which may take direct and indirect objects are: **acheter, emprunter, présenter.**
Double object pronouns are taught in **Tous ensemble,** the second book of this series.

ACTIVITÉ 3 Expression personnelle

Dites si oui ou non vous téléphonez aux personnes suivantes. Utilisez un pronom complément d'objet indirect.

→ à votre professeur de français? **Je lui téléphone (souvent).**
(Je ne lui téléphone jamais.)

You may remind students that in French *téléphoner à* takes an indirect object.

1. à votre meilleur ami?
2. à votre meilleure amie?
3. à vos grands-parents?
4. au docteur?
5. au directeur (à la directrice) de votre école?
6. au président des États-Unis?
7. à vos cousins?
8. à vos cousines?

VARIATION with **parler**: *Je lui parle souvent.*

ACTIVITÉ 4 Cadeaux *(Gifts)*

Pierre a acheté des cadeaux de Noël. Christine lui demande quel cadeau il va donner aux personnes suivantes. Pierre lui répond. Jouez les rôles de Christine et de Pierre d'après le modèle.

→ à ton frère / des disques   Christine: **Qu'est-ce que tu donnes à ton frère?**
Pierre: **Je lui donne des disques.**

1. à Charles / un livre
2. à Annie / ma photo
3. à ta mère / un pull
4. à ton père / une cravate
5. à tes cousins / un poisson rouge
6. à tes amies / des chocolats
7. à tes amis américains / un tee-shirt
8. à tes admiratrices *(female admirers)* / mon autographe

Vocabulaire spécialisé Verbes qui prennent un complément indirect

demander (à)	*to ask, ask for*	Tu **demandes** de l'argent à Paul?	Non, je ne **lui demande** rien.
montrer (à)	*to show*	Qu'est-ce que tu **montres** à Anne?	Je **lui montre** ma photo.
rendre visite (à)	*to visit*	Tu **rends visite** à tes amis?	Oui, je **leur rends** visite.
répondre (à)	*to answer*	Tu **réponds** à Georges?	Oui, je **lui réponds**.

Notes: 1. **Répondre** and **rendre** are regular -re verbs.

2. **Visiter** is used with places, and **rendre visite (à)** with people.

Je **visite** le musée.   Nous **rendons visite** à notre tante.

3. **Demander** means *to ask* or *to ask for;* it does not mean "to demand." Note the construction with **demander:**

Je demande	à	Paul	. . .	sa bicyclette.
I ask	. . .	*Paul*	*for*	*his bicycle.*

To demand is **exiger**.
The construction **demander à quelqu'un de faire quelque chose** is introduced in *Tous ensemble,* the second book of this series.

ACTIVITÉ 5 Visites

Jacques va passer les vacances au Canada. Avant son départ (*departure*), il n'a pas assez de temps pour rendre visite à tous ses amis. Il décide de rendre visite aux filles seulement (*only*). Dites si oui ou non il rend visite aux personnes suivantes. Utilisez un pronom complément d'objet indirect.

→ Paul   **Il ne lui rend pas visite.**   VARIATIONS with **téléphoner, répondre, parler.**

1. Annie
2. Hélène et Catherine
3. son cousin
4. Henri

5. Albert et François
6. ses cousines
7. son amie américaine
8. le frère de Jacqueline

ACTIVITÉ 6 Questions personnelles   OPTIONAL

Dans vos réponses, utilisez les pronoms **lui** ou **leur.**

1. Le week-end, rendez-vous visite à vos cousins? à votre meilleur ami? à vos grands-parents?
2. Prêtez-vous vos disques à vos amis? à votre meilleure amie? à votre frère? à votre sœur?
3. Demandez-vous de l'argent à votre père? à votre mère?
4. Demandez-vous des conseils (*advice*) à vos parents? à vos amis? à votre professeur?
5. Quand vous avez un problème, parlez-vous à votre père? à votre mère? à vos amis? à vos professeurs?
6. Montrez-vous vos photos à vos amis? à vos cousins? à votre frère? à votre sœur?
7. Répondez-vous en français au professeur?
8. Obéissez-vous à vos parents? à vos professeurs? à votre conscience?

C. La place des pronoms compléments au passé composé   OPTIONAL   For recognition.

Note the position of the object pronouns in the answers to the following questions.

As-tu parlé **à Jacques?**	Oui, je **lui** ai parlé.
As-tu téléphoné **à Thérèse?**	Non, je ne **lui** ai pas téléphoné.
As-tu parlé **à tes professeurs?**	Oui, je **leur** ai parlé.
As-tu téléphoné **à tes amies?**	Non, je ne **leur** ai pas téléphoné.
As-tu invité **Jacques?**	Oui, je l'ai invité.
As-tu pris **mes disques?**	Non, je ne **les** ai pas pris.

→ In the **passé composé,** as in the present tense, the object pronouns come *before* the verb. The word order is:

subject (+ **ne**) + object pronoun + present of **avoir** (+ **pas**) + past participle

The agreement of the past participle with a preceding direct object is presented in *Tous ensemble.* In the above examples and in Activité 9, this agreement has been "hidden" so as to avoid confusing the students at this point.

ACTIVITÉ 7 Le Jour de l'An (New Year's Day)

En France, le Jour de l'An est un jour où on rend visite à ses amis et à sa famille. C'est aussi le jour des cadeaux (gifts) et des bonnes résolutions. Dites ce que Jean-Marc a fait le Jour de l'An. Pour cela, utilisez le **passé composé** des verbes suggérés (suggested) et remplacez les noms entre parenthèses par les pronoms **lui** ou **leur**.

VARIATION: Jean-Marc forgot to do these things.
Il ne lui a pas téléphoné.

→ (à Florence) téléphoner   **Il lui a téléphoné.**

1. (à sa cousine Annie) téléphoner
2. (à ses grands-parents) téléphoner
3. (à sa mère) donner des chocolats
4. (à son père) donner une cravate
5. (à son chien) donner un os (bone)

6. (à Paul et Antoine) prêter son vélomoteur
7. (à ses parents) promettre d'obéir Il leur a promis d'obéir.
8. (à son professeur d'anglais) promettre d'étudier
9. (à sa petite amie) promettre d'être patient
10. (à son oncle) rendre visite

Pronounced /ɔs/.

ACTIVITÉ 8 Chez Madame Saint Florent

Madame Saint Florent est la directrice d'une compagnie d'exportation (export company). Elle demande à son secrétaire s'il a fait certaines choses. Il répond affirmativement ou négativement et utilise les pronoms **lui** ou **leur**. Jouez les rôles de Madame Saint Florent et de son secrétaire d'après le modèle.

→ téléphoner à Monsieur Carabin (non)

Madame Saint Florent: **Avez-vous téléphoné à Monsieur Carabin?**
Le secrétaire: **Non, je ne lui ai pas téléphoné.**

1. téléphoner à Mademoiselle Flanel (oui)
2. parler aux clients américains (non)
3. parler à la cliente italienne (oui)
4. répondre à Monsieur Rabane (oui)
5. répondre à nos clients belges (non)
6. rendre visite à Mademoiselle Neuville (non)

```
CARA MIA PRET A PORTER FEMININ          *236.21.94
   Galerie du Pont Neuf 2 r du Pont Neuf (1er)  543.96.50
Carabalona E 12 r Bardinet 14ᵉ                  267.50.42
Carabalona Jean 3Bis r Jadin 17ᵉ                636.14.65
Carabasse G 10 r Cour des Noues 20ᵉ             272.36.91
Carabassis S 21 r Meslay 3ᵉ                     824.89.04
Caraben JC 12 r Chaussée d'Antin 9ᵉ             322.35.54
Carabeuf 16 r Lalande 14ᵉ                       566.96.64
Carabeufs 36 av Suffren 15ᵉ                     224.46.68
Carabia A 19 bd Montmorency 16ᵉ                 033.39.74
Carabin (Le) 6 r Dupuytren 6ᵉ                   540.97.24
Carabin 10 r Leneveux 14ᵉ                       250.43.66
Carabin A 285 r Vaugirard 15ᵉ                   828.27.43
Carabin C 24 r Mademoiselle 15ᵉ                 636.70.53
Carabin H docteur 25 r étienne Dolet 20ᵉ        203.08.00
Carabin H 25 r Fêtes 19ᵉ                        201.65.19
Carabin Henry 16 r Joinville 19ᵉ
```

ACTIVITÉ 9 Avant le départ (Before leaving)

Pierre va partir en vacances. Avant son départ, Jacques lui demande s'il a fait certaines choses. Pierre lui répond affirmativement ou négativement en utilisant les pronoms compléments **l'** ou **les**. Jouez le rôle de Pierre.

→ Tu as invité Robert? (oui)   **Oui, je l'ai invité.**
   Tu as invité Paul? (non)   **Non, je ne l'ai pas invité.**

1. Tu as vu Thomas? (oui)
2. Tu as vu Antoine? (non)
3. Tu as acheté ce sac? (oui)
4. Tu as vendu ton vélo? (non)

5. Tu as pris tes disques? (oui)
6. Tu as pris tes livres? (non)
7. Tu as mis ton argent à la banque (bank)? (oui)
8. Tu as mis tes livres dans ta chambre? (non)

Prononciation

Le son /ɥ/

Mot clé: l<u>ui</u>

Répétez les mots: h<u>ui</u>t, c<u>ui</u>sine, s<u>ui</u>s, j<u>ui</u>n, j<u>ui</u>llet, n<u>ui</u>t, S<u>ui</u>sse

Répétez les phrases: Le h<u>ui</u>t juillet je s<u>ui</u>s en S<u>ui</u>sse.

The sound /ɥ/ is similar to the sound /y/, but it is pronounced very rapidly.
The sound /ɥ/ is always followed by a vowel.

Contrastez: su—s<u>ui</u>s; eu—h<u>ui</u>t; mi<u>n</u>ute—mi<u>n</u>uit

Comment écrire /ɥ/: **u** (+vowel)

Entre nous

Expression pour la conversation

Ça ne fait rien. *It doesn't matter.*

—Tu viens au cinéma avec moi?
—Je n'ai pas d'argent!
—**Ça ne fait rien!** Je t'invite!

Mini-dialogue

Qu'est-ce que Brigitte et Pierre vont acheter *à* leur père pour son *anniversaire?*   *for; birthday*

BRIGITTE: Demain c'est l'anniversaire de Papa!
PIERRE: Tu as quelque chose pour lui?
BRIGITTE: Non, je n'ai rien!
PIERRE: *Moi non plus* . . .   *Neither do I*
BRIGITTE: Qu'est-ce qu'on lui achète?
PIERRE: Achetons-lui quelque chose d'original.
BRIGITTE: Une cravate?
PIERRE: Ce n'est pas très original!
BRIGITTE: Achetons-lui un pull!
PIERRE: Mais nous lui avons acheté un pull l'année dernière.
BRIGITTE: Alors, achetons-lui une *boîte* de chocolats!   *box*
PIERRE: Mais tu sais bien que Papa est au régime . . .
BRIGITTE: Ça ne fait rien.
PIERRE: Pourquoi est-ce que ça ne fait rien?
BRIGITTE: Parce que moi, je ne suis pas au régime . . . et *toi non plus!*   *neither are you*

L'art du dialogue

a) Jouez le dialogue entre Brigitte et Pierre.
b) Maintenant imaginez que c'est l'anniversaire de la mère de Brigitte et de Pierre.
   Composez le nouveau dialogue. Remplacez Papa par **Maman,** et une cravate par **de l'eau de cologne.** Faites les changements nécessaires. Jouez le nouveau dialogue.

Have students note that the stress pronoun **lui** becomes **elle,** but the indirect object **lui** stays **lui.**

UNITÉ 7

Leçon 5

STRUCTURES TO OBSERVE
- **dire**
- review of object pronouns (direct vs. indirect)

Êtes-vous sociable?

La sociabilité est l'art des bonnes relations avec les gens. Avez-vous des bonnes relations avec les autres personnes? Voici un petit test très simple. Étudiez les huit situations et choisissez l'option A ou B *qui* correspond à votre attitude personnelle.

which

1. Il y a un nouvel élève dans votre classe.
   A. Vous le présentez à vos amis et vous l'invitez chez vous.
   B. Vous lui parlez . . . le jour où il vous invite chez lui.

2. Votre petit frère ne comprend pas le problème de maths.
   A. Vous l'aidez.
   B. Vous lui *dites* que vous aussi vous ne comprenez pas les maths . . . et vous ne l'aidez pas.

   tell

3. Votre meilleure amie a un problème avec sa famille.
   A. Vous lui donnez des conseils utiles.
   B. Vous lui dites que ce n'est pas votre problème.

4. Vous avez rendez-vous avec un camarade. Ce camarade arrive *avec vingt minutes de retard.*
   A. Vous ne lui *dites* rien.
   B. Vous ne lui dites rien, mais vous êtes de très mauvaise humeur pour le reste de la journée.

   20 minutes late

   say

5. Un ami prend votre disque favori . . . et le casse par accident.
   A. Vous lui dites que ce n'est pas *grave*.
   B. Vous lui demandez d'acheter un autre disque.

   serious

6. Vous êtes dans le bus. Une personne âgée monte dans le bus. Il n'y a pas de place pour elle.
   A. Vous lui donnez votre place.
   B. Vous la *regardez fixement*, mais vous ne lui donnez pas votre place.

   stare at

7. Votre oncle favori va célébrer son quarantième anniversaire.
   A. Vous lui *écrivez* une lettre de *félicitations.*   *write; congratulations*
   B. Vous ne lui écrivez pas.
8. Votre meilleur ami est malade.
   A. Vous lui téléphonez ou vous lui rendez visite.
   B. Vous lui demandez s'il est contagieux et vous ne lui rendez pas visite.

INTERPRÉTATION

Combien de *réponses* A avez-vous?   *answers.*

de 6 à 8   Bravo! Vous êtes une personne généreuse et bien élevée.
           Vous avez certainement beaucoup d'amis.

de 3 à 5   Vous *avez* assez *bon caractère*, mais vous n'êtes pas toujours   *are good-natured*
           très sociable.

1 ou 2   La générosité n'est pas votre qualité principale. Faites un effort!

0   *Sans commentaire!*   *No comment!*

Vocabulaire pratique

NOMS:	**un anniversaire**	*birthday*	**une journée**	*day, whole day*
	un conseil	*(piece of) advice*	**la place**	*room; seat*
	les gens	*people*		

ADJECTIFS:	**autre**	*other*	Où est l'**autre** magazine?
	bien élevé	*well-behaved, polite*	Anne est une fille **bien élevée.**
	favori (favorite)	*favorite*	Quelle est votre classe **favorite?**
	utile ≠ inutile	*useful ≠ useless*	Le français est **utile,** n'est-ce pas?
VERBES:	**casser**	*to break*	Qui **a cassé** le téléviseur?
	descendre de	*to get off (out of)*	Nous **descendons du** train ici.
	être de bonne humeur	*to be in a good mood*	Je **suis de bonne humeur** quand je sors avec mes amis.
	être de mauvaise humeur	*to be in a bad mood*	Je **suis de mauvaise humeur** quand je n'ai rien à faire.
	monter dans	*to get on (in)*	Est-ce que tu **montes dans** ma voiture?

Note: **Autre** is used in the following cases:

un autre (une autre)	*another*	Voici **une autre** camarade.
l'autre	*the other one*	Je connais ce garçon, mais je ne connais pas **l'autre.**
les autres	*the others*	**Les autres** ne sont pas ici.

CONVERSATION

Let's talk about your friends again.

1. Est-ce que vous invitez souvent **vos amis** chez vous?
2. Est-ce que vous téléphonez souvent **à vos amis?**
3. Est-ce que vous **les** écoutez?
4. Est-ce que vous **leur** demandez des conseils?
5. Est-ce que vous **les** aidez avec leurs problèmes?
6. Est-ce que vous **leur** parlez de vos problèmes?

OBSERVATIONS   Str. C

Reread the first two questions.

- Are the words in heavy type the *direct* or the *indirect* object in question 1?   direct
  in question 2?   indirect

Reread questions 3 to 6. These questions contain object pronouns.

- Which pronouns are *direct* objects? Which are *indirect* objects?
  les   leur

NOTE CULTURELLE   For reading and listening practice.

La bonne éducation

En France, les parents insistent sur la «bonne éducation». Ils désirent que leurs enfants soient° «bien élevés». Qu'est-ce que c'est qu'un° enfant bien élevé? Est-ce que c'est un enfant qui est très intelligent et qui connaît beaucoup de choses? Pas nécessairement!° En France, la bonne éducation consiste à respecter ses° parents et ses professeurs, à être poli° avec les grandes personnes,° à être généreux avec ses amis. En un mot,° quelqu'un de bien élevé est quelqu'un qui pense aux autres.

Êtes-vous une personne bien élevée?

soient *be* **Qu'est-ce que c'est qu'un** *What is a*
nécessairement *necessarily* **ses** *one's* **poli** *polite*
grandes personnes *adults* **mot** *word*

Structure

A. Les verbes *dire*, *lire* et *écrire*

The verbs **dire** *(to say, tell)*, **lire** *(to read)*, and **écrire** *(to write)* are irregular.
Here are the forms of these three verbs.

Infinitive		**dire**		**lire**		**écrire**
Present	je	**dis**	je	**lis**	j'	**écris**
	tu	**dis**	tu	**lis**	tu	**écris**
	il/elle	**dit**	il/elle	**lit**	il/elle	**écrit**
	nous	**disons**	nous	**lisons**	nous	**écrivons**
	vous	**dites**	vous	**lisez**	vous	**écrivez**
	ils/elles	**disent**	ils/elles	**lisent**	ils/elles	**écrivent**
Passé composé	j'ai	**dit**	j'ai	**lu**	j'ai	**écrit**

Note: **Décrire** *(to describe)* is conjugated like **écrire**.

There are 3 verbs which have a **-tes** ending in the **vous** form of the
present: **dire**, **être**, and **faire**. Can your students name them?

Hertz vous dit oui.
location de voitures

ACTIVITÉ 1 Le meeting

Les étudiants ont organisé un meeting d'information.
À ce meeting, chacun dit quelque chose qui reflète
(reflects) sa personnalité. Exprimez cela en utilisant le
présent de **dire**.

→ Jeanne est brillante.   **Elle dit quelque chose de brillant.**

VARIATION: Have the students do
this activity in the passé composé.
Elle a dit quelque chose de brillant.

1. Vous êtes intelligents.
2. Catherine est géniale.
3. Jacques et Henri sont idiots.
4. Nous sommes remarquables.
5. Je suis bête.
6. Tu es stupide.
7. Alain est amusant.
8. Paul est drôle.

Vocabulaire spécialisé On lit, on écrit, on dit

on lit . . .

un journal	*paper, newspaper*	**des bandes dessinées**	*comics*
(*pl.* **journaux**)		**une histoire**	*story; history*
un magazine	*magazine*	**une revue**	*magazine*
un roman	*novel*		

on écrit . . .

un poème	*poem*	**une carte**	*card*
		une carte postale	*postcard*
		une lettre	*letter*

on dit . . .

un mensonge	*lie*	**la vérité**	*truth*

ACTIVITÉ 2   À la bibliothèque

Les étudiants suivants sont à la bibliothèque. Dites ce que chacun lit et ce
que chacun écrit. Pour cela, utilisez le présent des verbes **lire** et **écrire**.

→ Jérôme (un magazine / une lettre)   **Jérôme lit un magazine.**
Après il écrit une lettre.

VARIATION in the passé composé:
Jérôme a lu un magazine.
Après, il a écrit une lettre.

1. nous (un magazine de sport / des lettres)
2. Antoine (un livre d'histoire / des notes)
3. Françoise et Adèle (un article scientifique / un poème)
4. toi (une lettre / à Jacques)
5. vous (un livre de français / un mémo)
6. moi (une carte / une lettre à Sylvie)

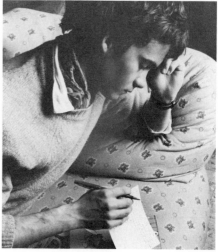

ACTIVITÉ 3   Questions personnelles   OPTIONAL

1. Aimez-vous lire?
2. Est-ce que vous préférez lire ou regarder la télé?
3. Quels livres lisez-vous en classe d'anglais?
4. Lisez-vous des magazines? Quels magazines?
5. Quel journal est-ce que vos parents lisent?
6. Aimez-vous les romans? les romans historiques?
les romans de science-fiction?
7. Quand vous lisez un journal, est-ce que vous lisez les bandes dessinées?
l'horoscope? la page des sports?
8. Quelles sont vos bandes dessinées favorites?
9. Aimez-vous écrire? Écrivez-vous des poèmes? des histoires drôles?
10. Écrivez-vous souvent à vos cousins? à vos grands-parents?

11. Quand vous êtes en vacances, est-ce que vous écrivez des cartes postales à vos amis?
12. À Noël, est-ce que vous écrivez des cartes de Noël? Combien?
13. Le 14 février, est-ce que vous écrivez des cartes de Saint-Valentin?
14. Est-ce que vous dites toujours la vérité à vos amis? à vos parents? à vos professeurs?
15. Selon vous *(In your opinion)*, est-ce que les journalistes disent la vérité?
16. Selon vous, est-ce que les personnalités politiques *(politicians)* disent souvent des mensonges?

ACTIVITÉ 4   Expression personnelle

Dites si vous avez fait récemment *(recently)* les choses suivantes.

→ lire un livre intéressant   **Oui, j'ai lu un livre intéressant.**
   (Non, je n'ai pas lu de livre intéressant.)

1. lire votre horoscope
2. lire des bandes dessinées
3. lire un magazine français
4. écrire une carte postale

5. écrire à un ami
6. écrire un poème
7. dire un mensonge
8. dire une plaisanterie *(joke)*

B. La conjonction *que*   OPTIONAL   For recognition.

Note the use of **que** *(that)* in the following sentences:

Il dit **que** vous parlez bien français.
Paul écrit **qu'**il a des amis suisses.
Je pense **que** tu vas être en retard.
Lucie sait **que** tu es souvent en retard.
Nous trouvons **que** Marc nage bien.

He says (that) you speak French well.
Paul writes (that) he has Swiss friends.
I think (that) you are going to be late.
Lucie knows (that) you are often late.
We find (that) Marc swims well.

The conjunction **que (qu')** is often used after verbs like **dire, écrire, penser, savoir,** and **trouver** to introduce a clause. In English, the equivalent word *that* is often left out.

ACTIVITÉ 5   Est-ce que les Américains sont sociables?

Est-ce que les Américains sont sympathiques? Des jeunes Français discutent de cette question. Exprimez l'opinion de chacun. Pour cela, utilisez l'expression **dire que.**

→ Robert / oui   **Robert dit que oui.**

1. Christine / non
2. Antoine et Charles / c'est vrai
3. moi / c'est vrai en général
4. toi / tu connais des Américains très sympathiques
5. nous / nous connaissons des Américains assez pénibles
6. vous / les Américains sont plus sociables que les Français

C. Récapitulation: les pronoms compléments

The direct and indirect object pronouns, together with their corresponding subject pronouns, are summarized in the chart below.

SUBJECT PRONOUNS	DIRECT OBJECT PRONOUNS	INDIRECT OBJECT PRONOUNS
je (j')	me (m')	me (m')
tu	te (t')	te (t')
il	le (l')	lui
elle	la (l')	lui
nous	nous	nous
vous	vous	vous
ils	les	leur
elles	les	leur

In affirmative commands, **me** becomes **moi**.

Téléphone-**moi** demain.

ACTIVITÉ 6   Une fille sociable

Stéphanie est une fille très sociable. Elle répond affirmativement aux questions d'Édouard. Jouez le rôle de Stéphanie, en utilisant le pronom complément d'objet direct ou indirect qui convient.

→ Tu invites tes amis américains?　**Bien sûr, je les invite.**

1. Tu téléphones à Jacques?
2. Tu parles à tes professeurs?
3. Tu écris à Jacqueline?
4. Tu écoutes tes parents?
5. Tu admires ta mère?

6. Tu comprends tes amis?
7. Tu rends visite à tes grands-parents?
8. Tu aimes tes cousins?
9. Tu aides ta sœur?
10. Tu connais Catherine?

ACTIVITÉ 7   Souvent?

Dites si oui ou non vous faites souvent les choses suivantes. Utilisez un pronom complément dans vos réponses.

→ acheter le journal?　**Je l'achète souvent.**
　　　　　　　　　　　　(Je ne l'achète pas souvent.)

1. lire le journal?
2. préparer les leçons?
3. regarder les programmes de sport?
4. parler au professeur?
5. parler français à vos camarades?
6. écrire à vos grands-parents?

7. lire les bandes dessinées?
8. dire la vérité?
9. aider votre mère?
10. aider vos frères?
11. perdre votre temps?
12. dépenser votre argent?

Avant de partir en vacances, Catherine a fait certaines choses pour ses amis.
Exprimez cela en utilisant le passé composé des verbes suivants et le
pronom complément d'objet indirect qui remplace l'expression entre
parenthèses.

VARIATION: As a warm-up
exercise, do the activity in the
present.

→ (à Pierre) donner son adresse   **Elle lui a donné son adresse.**

1. (à Suzanne) donner son numéro de téléphone
2. (à moi) donner ses magazines
3. (à Charles) vendre sa guitare
4. (à nous) vendre ses disques
5. (à ses grands-parents) écrire
6. (à vous) téléphoner
7. (à toi) dire au revoir
8. (à ses professeurs) dire au revoir aussi

ACTIVITÉ 9   **Pierre et Suzanne**   OPTIONAL

Pierre dit à Suzanne ce qu'il a fait le week-end dernier. Suzanne lui dit
qu'elle a fait les mêmes *(same)* choses. Jouez le rôle de Suzanne, en
utilisant le pronom complément d'objet direct ou indirect qui convient.

→ J'ai lu l'horoscope.   **Moi aussi, je l'ai lu.**

1. J'ai vu Jean-Paul.
2. J'ai acheté le journal.
3. J'ai téléphoné à Christine.
4. J'ai écrit à André.
5. J'ai mis mes disques.
6. J'ai parlé à mes amis.

Prononciation

Révision: les sons /ɔ/ et /o/

/ɔ/ b<u>o</u>nne, d<u>o</u>nne, b<u>o</u>tte, éc<u>o</u>le, r<u>o</u>man, <u>o</u>melette, s<u>o</u>rtir, p<u>o</u>che
  Nic<u>o</u>le a c<u>o</u>mmandé une b<u>o</u>nne <u>o</u>melette.
  Sim<u>o</u>ne, voilà deux d<u>o</u>llars c<u>o</u>mme argent de p<u>o</u>che.

Except at the end of a word, or when
followed by **se** as in **chose**, the letter **o**
represents the open sound /ɔ/.

/o/ b<u>eau</u>, <u>eau</u>, vél<u>o</u>, pian<u>o</u>, radi<u>o</u>, ch<u>o</u>se, nouv<u>eau</u>, idi<u>o</u>t
  Pierr<u>o</u>t a un nouv<u>eau</u> vél<u>o</u>.
  Le b<u>eau</u> Brun<u>o</u> joue du pian<u>o</u>.

Entre nous

Expression pour la conversation

Ça suffit! *That's enough!*

—Tu vas étudier après le dîner?
—Moi, non! J'ai étudié deux heures cet après-midi . . . et **ça suffit!**

Mini-dialogue

Pourquoi est-ce que Paul et Alain ne sont pas de bons amis?

ALAIN: Tu connais Paul?
SUZANNE: Oui, je le connais bien.
ALAIN: Tu lui parles souvent?
SUZANNE: Je lui parle assez souvent.
ALAIN: Alors, si tu le vois, demande-lui pourquoi il ne m'invite pas à sa surprise-partie samedi prochain.
SUZANNE: Tu *veux* savoir pourquoi Paul ne t'invite pas? *want*
Écoute, Alain, c'est très simple. En classe, tu ne lui parles pas. Tu ne l'aides jamais avec ses *devoirs*. Tu ne le présentes pas à tes amis. Et *homework*
quand il a besoin de quelque chose, tu ne lui prêtes jamais rien. Alors . . .
ALAIN: Ça suffit, Suzanne! Je ne te demande pas ton *avis!* *opinion*

L'art du dialogue

a) Jouez le dialogue entre Alain et Suzanne.
b) Maintenant imaginez qu'Alain veut *(wants)* savoir pourquoi **Hélène** ne l'invite pas. Composez un nouveau dialogue. Remplacez Paul par **Hélène.** Faites les changements nécessaires. Jouez le nouveau dialogue.

Le monde
des jeunes

SECTION MAGAZINE 4

Que dire?°

Imaginez que vous êtes en France.
Vous êtes dans les situations suivantes.°
Qu'est-ce que vous allez dire?

1. Quelqu'un téléphone. Vous
   répondez, mais vous ne comprenez
   pas très bien la personne qui parle.
   Vous dites:

   A. Zut!
   B. Pardon?
   C. Au revoir.

2. Vous êtes dans l'autobus. Vous
   marchez sur les pieds de quelqu'un.
   Vous dites:

   A. Après vous.
   B. Ce n'est pas moi.
   C. Excusez-moi.

3. Vous êtes à une surprise partie.
   Quelqu'un vous offre une cigarette,
   mais vous ne fumez° pas. Vous dites:

   A. Avec plaisir.°
   B. S'il vous plaît.
   C. Non, merci.

4. Vous êtes à la plage. Un ami vous
   présente à une autre personne. Vous
   dites:

   A. Enchanté(e).°
   B. Désolé(e).°
   C. Merci.

5. Un ami vient de recevoir° une
   mauvaise note° à un examen. Vous
   dites:

   A. Imbécile!
   B. Dommage!
   C. Félicitations!°

RÉPONSES: 1–B, 2–C, 3–C, 4–A, 5–B

---

350 **Que dire?** *What do you say?* **suivantes** *following* **fumez** *smoke* **plaisir** *pleasure* **Enchanté(e)**
Delighted **Désolé(e)** *Sorry* **vient de recevoir** *has just received* **note** *grade* **Félicitations!** *Congratulations!*

Soyez bon pour les PLANTES

Avez-vous une plante?
Les plantes ont beaucoup d'avantages.
    Elles décorent° votre chambre.
    Elles purifient l'air que vous respirez.°
    Elles demandent une attention minime.°
    Elles sont propres.°
Ce sont aussi des compagnons° idéals.
    Les plantes vous respectent.
    Les plantes ne vous insultent pas.
    Les plantes ne vous parlent pas
    continuellement de leurs problèmes.

Alors, si vous avez une plante:
    Soyez° bon pour elle.
Voici quelques° conseils élémentaires:

- Donnez-lui de l'eau quand elle a soif.
- Parlez-lui souvent.
- Dites-lui bonjour et bonsoir chaque° jour.
- Dites-lui qu'elle est belle.
- De temps en temps,° dites-lui «je t'aime».
- De temps en temps, mettez-lui un disque.
  (Les plantes adorent la musique classique,
  mais détestent la musique disco!)
- Ne l'insultez pas.
- Ne la maltraitez° pas!
- Soyez toujours poli et attentif avec elle.

Si vous observez ces conseils simples, votre plante vous aimera° éternellement.

LA MARGUERITE

Vous, les filles, voulez-vous° savoir s'ils vous aiment?
Et vous, les garçons, êtes-vous sûrs qu'elles vous aiment?
Allez consulter la marguerite.

Voici une marguerite:

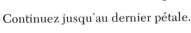

Enlevez° les pétales un à un.
Commençons par le premier pétale.

Il m'aime un peu . . .

beaucoup . . .

passionnément° . . .

à la folie° . . .

pas du tout!

Continuez jusqu'au dernier pétale.

---

décorent *decorate*   **respirez** *breathe*   **minime** *minimum*   **propres** *clean*   **compagnons** *companions*
Soyez *Be*   **quelques** *some*   **chaque** *every*   **De temps en temps** *From time to time*   **maltraitez** *mistreat*
aimera *will like*   **voulez-vous** *do you want*   **Enlevez** *Remove*   **passionnément** *passionately*
à la folie *madly*

Jeanne d'Arc

Qu'est-ce qu'ils ont fait?

Voici des Français et des Françaises célèbres° . . .
Savez-vous pourquoi ils sont célèbres?

Faites correspondre° les personnes (colonne A) avec ce
qu'elles° ont fait (colonne B).

A

1. Jeanne d'Arc (1412–1431)
2. Bougainville (1729–1811)
3. L'Enfant (1754–1825)
4. La Fayette (1757–1834)
5. Napoléon (1769–1821)
6. Niepce (1765–1833)
   et Daguerre (1789–1851)
7. Pasteur (1822–1895)
8. Blondin (1824–1897)
9. Pierre (1859–1906) et
   Marie (1867–1934) Curie
10. Cousteau (1910–)

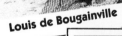
Louis de Bougainville

Pierre-Charles L'Enfant

Marquis de La Fayette

Napoléon Bonaparte

Jacques Cousteau

Pierre et Marie Curie

Charles Blondin

B

a. Ils ont inventé la photographie.
b. Il a aidé les patriotes américains pendant la guerre°
   d'Indépendance.
c. Ils ont découvert° le radium.
d. Il a été le premier homme à traverser° les chutes°
   du Niagara . . . sur une corde raide.°
e. Il a exploré les espaces sous-marins.°
f. Elle a libéré° la France de l'occupation anglaise.
g. Il a dessiné° les plans de Washington.
h. Il a visité Tahiti . . . et il a donné son nom à une
   fleur.°
i. Empereur des Français. Il a vendu la Louisiane
   aux États-Unis.
j. Il a inventé une méthode pour stéréliser le lait.

célèbres *famous*   **Faites correspondre** *Match*   **ce qu'elles** *what they*
guerre *war*   **ont découvert** *discovered*   **traverser** *to cross*   **chutes** *falls*
corde raide *tightrope*   **espaces sous-marins** *undersea world*
a libéré *liberated*   **a dessiné** *drew*   **fleur** *flower*

Louis Pasteur

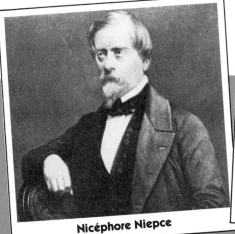

Nicéphore Niepce

Jacques Daguerre

RÉPONSES:
1–f, 2–h, 3–g, 4–b,
5–i, 6–a, 7–j, 8–d,
9–c, 10–e

353

Je rougis quand...

Est-ce que vous rougissez?
Tout le monde° rougit!
Nous avons demandé à six Français
pourquoi ils rougissaient.°

Voici leurs réponses:

Annie *(16 ans)*
Je rougis quand mes parents me posent
des questions indiscrètes.

Éric *(14 ans)*
Je rougis quand une fille me regarde.

Sylvie *(15 ans)*
Je rougis quand le professeur me pose°
une question en classe.

François *(13 ans)*
Je ne rougis jamais sauf° quand je suis
en colère°... Mais je ne suis jamais en
colère.

Thomas *(15 ans)*
Je rougis quand je dis un mensonge.

Isabelle *(15 ans)*
Je rougis quand quelqu'un me dit que
je suis jolie ... ou que je suis idiote.

Tout le monde *Everyone*   **rougissaient** *would blush*   **pose** *asks*   **sauf** *except*   **en colère** *angry*

Le Skate

Est-ce que le skate est un sport dangereux? Ça dépend où, comment et dans quelles conditions on le pratique.°
Un jeune professeur d'éducation physique, Monsieur Philippe Lebagny, a eu l'idée d'introduire° le skate dans sa classe de gymnastique. Il a commencé avec 24 filles et garçons. L'expérience° a eu un succès extraordinaire! Les 200 élèves de l'école ont acheté l'équipement nécessaire. Maintenant ils apprennent l'art et la technique du skate: contrôle de l'équipement, contrôle de l'équilibre,° slalom, figures libres,° etc.
La championne de l'école: une petite fille de 10 ans.

pratique *engages in* d'introduire *of introducing* expérience *experiment*
équilibre *balance* libres *free*

Une Française qui a tout fait

Dans sa vie,° **Marie Marvingt** a été pilote.
   (Elle a établi° le premier record de distance en avion.)
Elle a été alpiniste.
   (Elle a fait l'ascension de plusieurs° sommets dans les Alpes.)
Elle a conduit° un train.
Elle a piloté un bateau à vapeur.°
En mer,° elle a nagé pendant 20 kilomètres.
À cheval, elle a fait le saut périlleux° au galop.
À bicyclette, elle a fait le trajet° Nancy-Naples (1900 kilomètres).
En canoë, elle a fait le trajet Paris-Coblence (700 kilomètres).
En ski, elle a remporté° 20 premiers prix.°
Elle a appris six langues.°

Marie Marvingt est née en 1875. Elle est morte en 1963.

Dans sa vie, Marie Marvingt a tout fait . . . ou presque!°

---

vie *life* **a établi** *established* **plusieurs** *several* **a conduit** *drove* **bateau à vapeur** *steamboat*
En mer *At sea* **saut périlleux** *somersault* **trajet** *trip* **a remporté** *won* **prix** *prizes* **langues** *languages*
presque *almost*

LE SPORT,
c'est la santé°

Comment maigrir?
C'est simple! Faites du sport!
Quand vous faites du sport, vous perdez des calories inutiles.
Vous exercez° aussi vos muscles, vos réflexes et votre intelligence.
Le sport, c'est la santé physique et la santé de l'esprit!°

sport	avantages
la marche 	Quand vous marchez pendant une heure, vous perdez 300 calories. Vous exercez aussi les muscles de vos jambes.
le jogging 	Quand vous faites du jogging pendant une heure, vous perdez 700 calories. Le jogging est excellent pour le cœur et les poumons.°
la natation 	Quand vous nagez pendant une heure, vous perdez 600 calories. La natation est un sport complet, parce que vous exercez tous les muscles de votre corps.°
le tennis 	Quand vous jouez au tennis pendant une heure, vous perdez 500 calories. Vous exercez aussi vos réflexes.
le vélo 	Quand vous faites du vélo pendant une heure, vous perdez 600 calories. Le vélo est un sport excellent pour rester en bonne forme physique.
le ski 	Quand vous faites du ski pendant une heure, vous perdez 500 calories. Le ski est un sport fascinant° . . . mais dangereux. Attention aux accidents!

la santé *health*   **exercez** *exercise*   **esprit** *mind*   **poumons** *lungs*   **corps** *body*   **fascinant** *fascinating*

Les jeunes Français et l'argent

Est-ce que vos parents vous donnent de l'argent? Ou est-ce que vous travaillez pour gagner° votre argent?

Et qu'est-ce que vous faites avec votre argent? Est-ce que vous le dépensez ou est-ce que vous l'économisez?

L'argent est un problème pour les jeunes du monde entier.°

Nous avons interrogé° des jeunes Français sur° ce problème difficile. Voici comment ils ont répondu à nos questions:

1. Est-ce que vos parents vous donnent de l'argent?

   Oui, ils me donnent de l'argent régulièrement 54%
   Oui, ils me donnent de l'argent de temps en temps.° 40%
   Non, ils ne me donnent pas d'argent 6%

2. Est-ce que vous travaillez pour avoir de l'argent?

   Oui, je travaille régulièrement 12%
   Oui, je travaille de temps en temps 30%
   Non, je ne travaille pas 58%

3. Généralement, combien d'argent est-ce que vos parents vous donnent par mois?

   Moins de 50 francs 26%
   De 50 francs à 100 francs 50%
   De 100 francs à 200 francs 20%
   Plus de 200 francs 4%

4. Avec votre argent, est-ce que vous faites des économies?°
   Oui 72%
   Non 28%

5. Comment est-ce que vous dépensez votre argent?

   Je vais au cinéma 82%
   J'achète des magazines 60%
   J'achète des disques 50%
   J'achète des bonbons 40%
   J'achète des cadeaux° pour l'anniversaire
   de mes amis ou de mes parents 20%

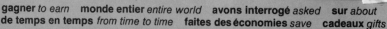

358   **gagner** *to earn*   **monde entier** *entire world*   **avons interrogé** *asked*   **sur** *about*
de temps en temps *from time to time*   **faites des économies** *save*   **cadeaux** *gifts*

Le budget d'ANNE-MARIE

Anne-Marie Pécoul a seize ans.
Combien d'argent est-ce qu'elle a?
Ça dépend! Ses parents lui donnent
  de l'argent assez régulièrement.
Quand elle a des bonnes notes en
  classe, elle reçoit° un supplément.
De temps en temps,° elle fait du
  «baby-sitting» pour les enfants de
  la voisine.°

Voici le budget d'Anne-Marie pour
  la semaine du 2 avril.

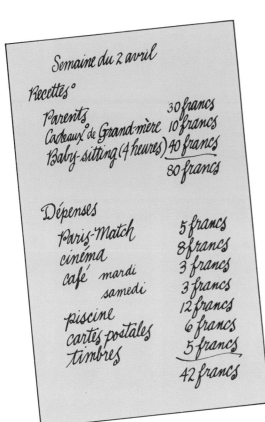

Semaine du 2 avril

Recettes°

Parents	30 francs
Cadeaux° de Grand-mère	10 francs
Baby-sitting (4 heures)	40 francs
	80 francs

Dépenses

Paris-Match	5 francs
cinéma	8 francs
café mardi	3 francs
samedi	3 francs
piscine	12 francs
cartes postales	6 francs
timbres	5 francs
	42 francs

PROJETS CULTURELS

Projets individuels

1. *Prepare a poster advertising one or several vacation areas of your choice in France or in French-speaking countries. Possibilities range from the Sahara to Tahiti, from the Alps to the Gaspé Peninsula in Québec. (Source: travel agencies, travel magazines)*
2. *The French played an important role in the exploration of the North American continent. Illustrate a map showing the explorations of one of the following men: Jacques Cartier, Champlain, La Salle, Marquette, Duluth, Jolliet. (Source: encyclopedia, history book)*

Projets de classe

1. *Using pictures from French magazines (Paris-Match, Jours de France, Elle), prepare a bulletin board display about French teenagers. List the differences you notice between French and American teenagers: ways of dressing, gestures, general expressions, attitudes, activities.*
2. *Using advertisements from French magazines (Paris-Match, Jours de France, Elle), prepare a bulletin board exhibit of French products: motorcycles, bicycles, stereo equipment, kitchen and house furnishings, etc. List the differences between French and American products: size, shape, price, etc.*
3. *The Americans won the Revolutionary War with considerable help from the French. Prepare a bulletin board exhibit illustrating the French role during the Revolution, using maps, diagrams, portraits of important people. You will want to include La Fayette, Rochambeau, Admiral de Grasse, as well as Benjamin Franklin. (Source: encyclopedia, history book)*

reçoit *receives*   De temps en temps *From time to time*
voisine *neighbor*   Recettes *Income*   cadeaux *gifts*

THEATRE

CHAILLOT
THEATRE NATIONAL

Création
9 mai - 1er juillet 1978
Grand Théâtre

Cyrano
ou les Soleils de la Raison

de Claude Bonnefoy
d'après la vie et l'œuvre de
Savinien de Cyrano de Bergerac
(1619-1655)

Mise en scène
André-Louis Périnetti
Scénographie et costumes
Michel Launay
Assistante pour les costumes
Emmanuelle Cotteau

Avec
Léonor Añaya
Claude Bolsone
Alain Chevallier
Jean-Pierre Ducos
Florence Giorgetti
Jacques Giraud
Marc Imbert
Renate Klett
Jean-Jacques Lagarde
Jean-Paul Lefcire
François Litondé
Patrick Lerille
Jim Adhi Limas
Jean-Claude Martin
Louis Merino
Patrick Masse
Robert Dhroguier
Joseph Dodd
Bernadette Rollin
Michel Ruhl
Monique Sunlay

Production audiovisuelle
Bernard Lolley
Direction technique
Patrick Pavillard
Régie générale
Simon Deshbalse
Alain Wandling
Déléguée à la production
Yvonne Maffre

C'est un
Spectacle
inter
France

**Ce spectacle est présenté
à la Salle Gémier (entrée par les jardins)**

Location aux caisses, place du Trocadéro, de 11 h à 19 h

CHAILLOT
THEATRE NATIONAL

27 mai - 1er juillet 1978   Création
Gémier

Les Baracos

De Jean-Jacques Varoujean
Compagnie Régis Santon

THEATRE NATIONAL   Direction : André-Louis Périnetti

LOCATION :
aux caisses, place du Trocadéro, de 11 h à 19 h
(sauf dimanches et fêtes légales)
pour les deux salles (Grand Théâtre et salle Gémier)

Pendant la demi-heure qui précède les représentations,
la vente des billets est assurée :
• aux caisses, place du Trocadéro, pour le Grand Théâtre
• aux caisses du hall d'accueil Gémier
(entrée par les jardins) pour la salle Gémier.

OBJECTIVES

This unit is a consolidation unit where the students are invited to develop their reading, writing, and speaking skills. Review is also stressed. The grammar and vocabulary contents have therefore been kept light.

Language
- **pouvoir, vouloir, devoir**
- the pronouns y and **en**
- adverbs in **-ment**
- expressions of quantity

Vocabulary
- the theater
- descriptions
- prepositions of place
- meals and food

Culture

The cultural information focuses on miscellaneous aspects of life in France—the café, French cooking, the theater.

Since reading is stressed, the *Presentation* texts are longer than in previous units. These texts form the five acts of a minidrama. The **Entre nous** sections, entitled **Rencontres**, contain simple readings about student life in France. These readings elicit responses from the students who are asked to describe their own environment, orally or in writing.

UNITÉ 8
« La Leçon »
(un drame en 5 actes)

361

This unit presents a story in five episodes. The story is a play . . .about
a play. The five acts have the following characters:

Isabelle: l'actrice principale   Nicole: une actrice
Jean-Claude: un ami d'Isabelle   M. Marsan: le père de Jean-Claude
Robert: un acteur   Mme Marsan: la mère de Jean-Claude

UNITÉ 8

Leçon 1

Acte 1.
Jean-Claude n'a pas de chance.

STRUCTURES TO OBSERVE
* vouloir, pouvoir, devoir

Personnages: Jean-Claude, Isabelle

Characters

Samedi, 4 avril

Dans deux semaines, le club dramatique du *lycée* Balzac va présenter une
pièce. Cette pièce s'appelle «La Leçon». *À cause des répétitions,* Isabelle,
l'actrice principale, est très *occupée en ce moment.* Jean-Claude, son
meilleur ami, *veut* l'inviter à aller au cinéma avec lui . . . mais sans succès!

high school
*Because of the
rehearsals
busy at present
wants*

JEAN-CLAUDE:	Tu veux venir au cinéma cet après-midi?	
ISABELLE:	Je suis *désolée*, mais je *ne peux pas*.	*sorry; can't*
JEAN-CLAUDE:	Tu ne peux pas . . . ou tu ne veux pas?	
ISABELLE:	Je te dis que je ne peux pas.	
JEAN-CLAUDE:	Et pourquoi est-ce que tu ne peux pas?	
ISABELLE:	Parce que je *dois* aller à une répétition.	*must*
JEAN-CLAUDE:	Quelle répétition?	
ISABELLE:	La répétition de «La Leçon».	
JEAN-CLAUDE:	Quelle leçon?	
ISABELLE:	«La Leçon»! Écoute, Jean-Claude! *Ne fais pas l'idiot!*	*Don't act dumb!*
JEAN-CLAUDE:	Bon, bon. Est-ce que je peux aller à cette répétition avec toi?	
ISABELLE:	Si tu veux.	
JEAN-CLAUDE:	Et ce soir, nous allons au cinéma, d'accord?	
ISABELLE:	Impossible! J'ai une autre répétition.	

CONVERSATION

Questions sur le texte:

1. Comment s'appelle l'actrice principale?
2. Qui est son meilleur ami?
3. Comment s'appelle la pièce?
4. Pourquoi est-ce qu'Isabelle est très occupée?
5. Où est-ce que Jean-Claude veut *(does ... want)* inviter Isabelle cet après-midi?
6. Où est-ce que Jean-Claude veut l'inviter ce soir?
7. Est-ce qu'Isabelle accepte l'invitation pour cet après-midi? Pourquoi pas?
8. Est-ce qu'elle accepte l'invitation pour ce soir? Pourquoi pas?

OBSERVATIONS   Str. C

Reread questions 5 and 6 carefully.
In question 6, **Isabelle** has been replaced by a
direct object pronoun.

- What is that pronoun?   l'
- Does that pronoun come *before* or *after* the
  infinitive **inviter**?   before

MINISTÈRE DE L'ÉDUCATION NATIONALE

ACADÉMIE DE VERSAILLES

LYCÉE HOCHE

73, avenue de Saint-Cloud
78002 VERSAILLES
Tél.: 950.58.21

CARTE D'ÉTUDIANT

NOTE CULTURELLE   For reading and listening practice.

Le lycée

Le lycée est l'école secondaire qui° correspond plus ou moins
à la «high school» américaine. Généralement,° le lycée d'une
ville porte° le nom° d'une personne célèbre de cette ville. Le
lycée Balzac, à Tours, porte le nom d'Honoré de Balzac, un
écrivain° célèbre, originaire de° la ville de Tours.

qui *that*   **Généralement** *Generally*   **porte** *bears*   **nom** *name*
écrivain *writer*   **originaire de** *native of*

You may locate Tours on the map on p.viii.

Vocabulaire spécialisé Le théâtre

NOMS:	**un acteur**	*actor*	**une actrice**	*actress*
	un auteur	*author*	**une pièce**	*play*
	un costume	*costume*	**une répétition**	*rehearsal*
	un metteur en scène	*director*	**une représentation**	*performance*
	un rôle	*role, part*	**la salle**	*hall, (theatrical) house*
			la scène	*stage; scene*

VOCABULARY EXPANSION: **répéter** *(to rehearse)*, **apprendre par cœur** *(to memorize, learn by heart)*, **les coulisses** *(wings)*, **le souffleur** *(prompter)*, **le maquillage** *(make-up)*, **le décor** *(scenery)*

Structure

A. Les verbes *pouvoir* et *vouloir*

Note the forms of the two irregular verbs **pouvoir** *(to be able)* and **vouloir** *(to want)*.

Infinitive	pouvoir		vouloir	
Present	je	**peux**	je	**veux**
	tu	**peux**	tu	**veux**
	il/elle	**peut**	il/elle	**veut**
	nous	**pouvons**	nous	**voulons**
	vous	**pouvez**	vous	**voulez**
	ils/elles	**peuvent**	ils/elles	**veulent**
Passé composé	j'ai	**pu**	j'ai	**voulu**

Uses of *pouvoir:*

Pouvoir has several English equivalents.

may	Est-ce que je **peux** jouer dans la pièce?	*May I act in the play?*
	Non, tu ne **peux** pas.	*No, you **may not**.*
can	À quelle heure **peux**-tu venir?	*At what time **can** you come?*
	Je **peux** venir à une heure.	*I **can** come at one.*
to be able	Jean n'a pas **pu** venir avec nous.	*Jean **was not able** to come with us.*

In general, **pouvoir** does not stand alone. It is usually followed by an infinitive or the negative word **pas**.

Peut-il sortir avec nous?	*Can he go out with us?*
Oui, il **peut** sortir avec nous.	*Yes, he **can** (go out with us).*
(Non, il **ne peut pas**.)	*(No, he **can't**).*

The English "can" meaning "to know how to do something" is expressed with **savoir**.
Savez-vous jouer? *Can you act?*

ADJECTIFS:	**célèbre**	*famous*	«La Leçon» est une pièce **célèbre**.
	occupé	*busy*	Le metteur en scène est très **occupé**.
VERBE:	**jouer**	*to act, play*	L'acteur principal **joue** très bien.
EXPRESSIONS:	**à cause de**	*because of*	Nous travaillons beaucoup **à cause de** la pièce.
	en ce moment	*at present, right now*	**En ce moment** nous avons une répétition.

Note: **à cause de** vs. **parce que**

À cause de means *because of:* it is followed by a noun or pronoun.
Parce que means *because:* it is followed by a clause (that is, a subject and a verb).

Isabelle ne vient pas **à cause de** la répétition.   (= *because of the rehearsal*)
Elle ne vient pas **parce qu'**elle a une répétition. (= *because she has a rehearsal*)

Uses of *vouloir:*

Vouloir can be followed by a noun or an infinitive.

Veux-tu ce livre?	*Do you want this book?*
Voulez-vous aller au théâtre?	*Do you want to go to the theater?*

When making a request, French people often use **je voudrais** (*I would like*), which is more polite than **je veux**.

Je voudrais vous parler.	*I would like to talk to you.*

Vouloir, like **pouvoir**, is rarely used alone. When accepting an offer, the French often use the expression **vouloir bien**.

Veux-tu venir avec moi?	*Do you want to come with me?*
Oui, je **veux bien**.	*Yes, I do (want to).*

To ask what something *means*, the French use the expression **vouloir dire**.

Qu'est-ce que cette expression **veut dire**?	*What does that expression mean?*
Qu'est-ce que vous **voulez dire**?	*What do you mean?*

ACTIVITÉ 1 Projets de week-end

Les amis suivants ont décidé de sortir ensemble ce week-end, mais chacun a une idée différente. Dites ce que chacun veut faire. Pour cela, utilisez le présent de **vouloir**.

→ Isabelle (aller au cinéma)   **Isabelle veut aller au cinéma.**

1. Jean-Claude (faire une promenade à la campagne)
2. nous (jouer aux cartes)
3. vous (aller en ville)
4. moi (faire du sport)
5. Sylvie et Thérèse (organiser un pique-nique)
6. toi (faire une promenade à bicyclette)
7. mes amis (aller au concert)
8. René et moi (voir une pièce)

ACTIVITÉ 2 Le coût de la vie *(The cost of living)*

You may first want to review the numbers in Appendix 2, p.401.

Dites ce que chaque personne veut acheter. Ensuite dites si oui ou non cette personne peut acheter cette chose avec l'argent qu'elle a. Étudiez le modèle attentivement!

→ Pierre (une guitare / 20 dollars)
    Pierre veut acheter une guitare. Avec vingt dollars il ne peut pas acheter une guitare.

1. Sylvie (un pull / 15 dollars)
2. moi (une cassette / 8 dollars)
3. Raphaël (des bonbons / un dollar)
4. mes cousines (des blue-jeans / 18 dollars)
5. toi (un téléviseur / 100 dollars)

6. vous (une caméra / 5 dollars)
7. mes parents (une voiture / 1.000 dollars)
8. Jean-Claude (un vélo / 10 dollars)
9. nous (un lit / 200 dollars)

ACTIVITÉ 3 Désolé! *(Sorry!)* OPTIONAL

You may first want to review the formation of the passé composé.

À cause de l'examen, les étudiants suivants n'ont pas pu faire certaines choses. Exprimez cela en utilisant le passé composé de **pouvoir**.

→ Jean-Claude n'a pas téléphoné.   **Il n'a pas pu téléphoner.**

1. Sylvie n'a pas fini le roman.
2. Antoine n'a pas écrit à ses amis.
3. Nous n'avons pas visité le musée.

4. Vous n'avez pas rendu visite à vos cousins.
5. Je n'ai pas pris de photos.
6. Tu n'as pas fait de sport.

B. Le verbe *devoir*

The verb **devoir** *(to have to)* is irregular. Note the forms in the chart below.

Infinitive	devoir	
Present	je **dois** tu **dois** il/elle **doit**	nous **devons** vous **devez** ils/elles **doivent**
Passé composé	j'ai **dû**	

Have students note the circumflex accent on the past participle. This mark distinguishes **dû** from **du (de + le)**.

The verb **devoir** has several English equivalents:

should
must   Est-ce que je **dois** étudier?
to have to

{ *Should I study?*
{ *Must I study?*
{ *Do I have to study?*

The verb **devoir** is usually followed by an infinitive. It is not used alone.

Bien sûr, tu **dois étudier!**

{ *Of course, you should (study).*
{ *Of course, you must (study).*
{ *Of course, you have to (study).*

When **devoir** is followed by a noun, it means *to owe*.
Je dois 10 francs à Bernard. *I owe Bernard 10 francs.*

ACTIVITÉ 4 Excuses!

Jean-Claude a proposé à ses amis de repeindre *(to repaint)* sa chambre avec lui, mais chacun trouve une excuse. Dites que les personnes suivantes ne peuvent pas aider Jean-Claude. Dites aussi ce qu'elles doivent faire.

→ Annette (étudier) **Annette ne peut pas. Elle doit étudier.**

1. Christophe (apprendre son rôle)
2. toi (faire les costumes)
3. Lucien (aller au théâtre)
4. moi (faire du piano)
5. Marie-Claire (rester à la maison)
6. Henri et Bernard (travailler)
7. Jacques et moi, nous (préparer l'examen)
8. Danièle et Nathalie (aller à une répétition)

ACTIVITÉ 5 Questions personnelles OPTIONAL

1. Devez-vous beaucoup étudier pour la classe de français? pour la classe de maths?
2. À la maison, devez-vous aider vos parents? vos frères et vos sœurs?
3. Pouvez-vous utiliser *(use)* la voiture de vos parents? les disques de vos amis?
4. À l'école, pouvez-vous apprendre l'allemand? étudier la physique? jouer au tennis? faire du théâtre?
5. Cet été, devez-vous travailler? Voulez-vous voyager?
6. Voulez-vous aller en France? travailler en France?
7. Voulez-vous aller à l'université? à quelle université?
8. Voulez-vous être professeur? médecin? ingénieur? journaliste?

C. La place des pronoms avec l'infinitif   OPTIONAL   For recognition.

Note the position of the object pronouns in the answers to the following questions:

| Vas-tu inviter tes cousins? | Oui, je vais
Non, je ne vais pas | } **les** inviter. |
| Veux-tu parler à Stéphanie? | Oui, je veux
Non, je ne veux pas | } **lui** parler. |

In French, a pronoun which is the object of an infinitive comes immediately *before* that infinitive.

ACTIVITÉ 6   La liste de Jean-Claude   Note that this exercise mixes direct and indirect object pronouns.

Jean-Claude a préparé une liste de choses à faire avant les vacances. Mélanie lui demande s'il va faire ces choses. Jean-Claude lui répond affirmativement et lui dit quand il va les faire. Jouez les rôles de Mélanie et de Jean-Claude d'après le modèle.

VARIATION with **vouloir**:
—Tu veux parler...
—Oui, je veux lui parler...

VARIATION with **devoir**:
—Tu dois parler...
—Oui, je dois lui parler...

→ parler à Raymond (demain)   Mélanie: **Tu vas parler à Raymond?**
                Jean-Claude: **Oui, je vais lui parler demain.**

1. téléphoner à Annette (ce soir)
2. écrire à Sylvie (mardi)
3. inviter tes cousins (samedi)
4. vendre ton vélo (ce week-end)
5. chercher ton passeport (dans deux jours)
6. chercher tes photos (ce soir)
7. rendre visite à ta tante (demain)
8. réserver ton billet (lundi)

ACTIVITÉ 7   Cadeaux d'anniversaire *(Birthday presents)*

Imaginez qu'un ami a acheté les cadeaux d'anniversaire suivants. Dites à qui il doit donner chacun de ces cadeaux. Utilisez un pronom complément d'objet indirect pour remplacer les personnes suivantes.

Les cadeaux: une cravate, des chocolats, un tee-shirt, Mad magazine, un roman de science-fiction, un poster des Beatles, un puzzle, une photo de toi

You may elicit different choices of presents from the class.

→ à ton meilleur ami   **Tu dois lui donner la cravate (le poster des Beatles ...).**

1. à ton père
2. à ta mère
3. à ta meilleure amie
4. à tes grands-parents
5. à tes cousins
6. au professeur

VARIATION with direct object pronouns. Use the presents as cues, and have the students say to whom he should give each one.
la cravate: **Tu dois la donner à ton père (au professeur...).**

Prononciation

Les terminaisons -*tion* et -*sion*

The ending -**tion** is pronounced /sjɔ̃/. Be sure to avoid the English *shun*.

attention, prononciation, répétition, présentation, représentation, ambition
Faites attention à la prononciation de cette section.

The ending -**sion** is pronounced /zjɔ̃/. Be sure to avoid the English *zhun*.

révision, télévision, occasion
J'ai eu l'occasion de parler à la télévision.

The ending -**stion** is pronounced /stjɔ̃/: **la question.**

Entre nous

Expressions pour la composition

cela	*that*	Comprends-tu **cela?**
pour cela	*because of that,*	Je veux voyager cet été. **Pour cela**, je dois
	for that reason	travailler maintenant.

In conversational French, **cela** is often replaced by **ça.**

Rencontres

Dans *Rencontres* vous allez *faire connaissance avec* Michèle, une jeune Française. Ensuite, dans À *votre tour*, vous allez lui parler de vos projets.

*Encounters;
to meet
Your turn*

Aujourd'hui Michèle va parler de ses projets. Écoutez-la.

Bonjour, je m'appelle Michèle Martinot. J'ai quinze ans et j'habite à Annecy. Je vais au <u>lycée</u>. Mon lycée s'appelle le lycée Berthollet. C'est un lycée excellent, mais on doit étudier beaucoup!

high school

Après le lycée, je veux aller à l'université, mais avant, je veux voyager un peu. Je voudrais visiter les États-Unis. Je voudrais, par exemple, passer un hiver dans le Colorado. J'adore faire du ski!

Plus tard, je veux être <u>ingénieur-chimiste</u>. Je voudrais travailler dans un laboratoire. Cela veut dire que je dois étudier les maths et la <u>chimie</u>. <u>Malheureusement</u>, je ne suis pas très bonne en maths. Je dois étudier <u>comme une brute</u>! Et vous, qu'est-ce que vous voulez faire dans la <u>vie</u>?

chemical engineer

*chemistry;
Unfortunately*

= beaucoup

life

À votre tour

Maintenant, *présentez-vous* et parlez de vos projets.

introduce yourself

Je m'appelle ... J'ai ...
Mon école s'appelle ... C'est une école ... On doit ...
Après l'université, je veux ...
Avant, je voudrais ...
Je voudrais aussi ...
Plus tard, je veux être ...
Je voudrais travailler ...
Pour cela, je dois ...

Claude Berthollet (1748–1822) was a French chemist. He discovered the properties of chlorine.

Leçon 2

Acte 2. «La Leçon»

Scène 1. Une répétition
Vendredi, 10 avril

«La Leçon» est une pièce d'Eugène Ionesco, un auteur célèbre. «La Leçon» est l'histoire d'un professeur qui *martyrise* son élève. Isabelle joue le rôle de cette élève. Pendant les répétitions, elle est toujours un peu nerveuse.

Le metteur en scène lui dit souvent:

   «Isabelle, tu ne parles pas *assez distinctement*. Parle plus distinctement!»

ou bien:

   «Isabelle, tu n'es pas assez naturelle. Joue plus naturellement . . .»

Isabelle *fait beaucoup d'efforts* . . . mais est-ce qu'elle va avoir le *trac* pendant la représentation?

makes suffer

distinctly enough

tries hard
stage fright

Scène 2. La représentation
Samedi, 25 avril

Finalement le jour de la représentation arrive. Il y a beaucoup de spectateurs dans la salle. Mais aujourd'hui Isabelle n'est pas nerveuse *du tout!* Elle parle distinctement et joue très naturellement. *En fait*, elle joue *brillamment!*

Les spectateurs aiment beaucoup la pièce et *applaudissent longuement.* C'est un très grand succès pour la jeune actrice.

at all

In fact;
brilliantly

applaud for a
long time

CONVERSATION

Questions sur le texte:

1. Qui est l'auteur de «La Leçon»?
2. Quel rôle joue Isabelle?
3. Pendant les répétitions, est-ce qu'elle parle **distinctement**? Est-ce qu'elle joue **naturellement**?
4. Pendant la représentation, est-ce qu'elle parle **distinctement**? Est-ce qu'elle joue **naturellement**?

OBSERVATIONS   Str. A

Reread carefully the questions in 3 and 4. These questions concern the manner in which Isabelle speaks and acts. The words in heavy type are called *adverbs of manner*.

- Which 4 letters do these adverbs end in? -ment
- Which 2 letters do the corresponding English adverbs end in? -ly

NOTES CULTURELLES   For reading and listening practice.

1. Le théâtre en France   La France a une longue tradition théâtrale. Aujourd'hui, le gouvernement encourage les jeunes acteurs et les jeunes actrices. Il donne aussi des subventions° aux grands théâtres nationaux. Voilà pourquoi le théâtre est un spectacle° très populaire . . . et bon marché.

2. Ionesco   Eugène Ionesco est né en Roumanie, mais il a écrit ses pièces en français. Son théâtre est un théâtre d'avant-garde. «La Leçon» est une de ses premières pièces.

subventions *subsidies*   **spectacle** *show*

Vocabulaire spécialisé   La description

NOMS:	**une façon**	*fashion, way, manner*		
	une manière	*manner, way*		
ADJECTIFS:	**attentif**	*attentive, alert*	**nerveux**	*nervous*
	(attentive)		**(nerveuse)**	
	brillant	*brilliant, bright*	**rapide**	*quick, rapid*
	calme	*calm*	**sérieux**	*serious*
	distinct	*distinct*	**(sérieuse)**	
	général	*general*	**stupide**	*stupid, dumb*
	(pl. généraux)		**timide**	*timid*
	naturel	*natural*		
	(naturelle)			
EXPRESSIONS:	**d'une façon** ⎱	*in a way*	Il parle **d'une façon** intelligente.	
	d'une manière ⎰		Vous répondez **d'une manière** brillante.	

Structure

A. Les adverbes en -ment

The words in heavy type are *adverbs of manner.* Compare the endings of these adverbs with the endings of the corresponding English adverbs.

> Isabelle parle **distinctement.**   *Isabelle speaks distinctly.*
> Je travaille **sérieusement.**   *I work seriously.*

Many French adverbs which end in **-ment** correspond to English adverbs which end in *-ly.* These adverbs are derived from adjectives according to the following pattern.

If the masculine form of the adjective ends in:	the adverb is formed:	
a vowel	masculine adjective + -ment	calme → calmement vrai → vraiment
a consonant	feminine adjective + -ment	général, générale → généralement naturel, naturelle → naturellement

Adjectives in -ant and -ent are exceptions to the above pattern.
patient patiemment   élégant élégamment
Note: The endings **-emment** and **-amment** are pronounced like "amant."

ACTIVITÉ 1   Tennis

Les personnes suivantes jouent au tennis d'une manière qui correspond à leur personnalité. Exprimez cela en utilisant un adverbe en **-ment.**

→ Paul est rapide.   **Il joue rapidement.**

1. Isabelle est naturelle.
2. Charles est timide.
3. Catherine est sérieuse.
4. André est stupide.
5. Jean-Marc est calme.
6. Sylvie est nerveuse.

ACTIVITÉ 2   D'une certaine manière

Le professeur dit aux élèves comment ils doivent faire certaines choses. Jouez le rôle du professeur et des étudiants d'après le modèle.

→ Travaillez d'une manière sérieuse.   Le professeur: **Travaillez d'une manière sérieuse.**
L'élève: **Je travaille sérieusement.**

1. Parlez d'une manière naturelle.
2. Parlez d'une manière distincte.
3. Jouez d'une manière calme.
4. Ne répondez pas d'une manière stupide.
5. Répondez d'une manière correcte.
6. Faites vos devoirs *(homework)* d'une manière rapide.
7. Écoutez-moi d'une manière attentive.
8. Dépensez votre argent d'une manière utile.

B. Les expressions de quantité avec les verbes

In the sentences below, the expressions of quantity in heavy type modify the verbs.

Est-ce que tu travailles **beaucoup?**   Non, je ne travaille pas **beaucoup.**
Vous n'étudiez pas **assez.**   Moi, j'étudie **trop.**

When an expression of quantity modifies a verb, it usually comes immediately after the verb. Contrast the word order in French and in English:

J'aime **beaucoup** le théâtre.   *I like theater a lot.*
Tu n'étudies pas **assez** la prononciation.   *You do not study pronunciation enough.*
Vous jouez **trop** au tennis.   *You play tennis too much.*

Vocabulaire spécialisé   Expressions de quantité

peu	little, not much	J'étudie **peu.**
assez	enough	Je travaille **assez.**
beaucoup	much, very much, a lot	Tu manges **beaucoup.**
trop	too much	Vous parlez **trop.**

Be sure that the students understand that in French *very much* and *too much* are expressed by single words (**beaucoup** and **trop**). Be careful that your students do not generate wrong expressions like "très beaucoup" or "trop beaucoup."

ACTIVITÉ 3   Pas d'accord!

Un professeur fait certaines remarques à ses élèves, mais ils ne sont pas d'accord avec lui. Jouez les deux rôles d'après le modèle.

→ Vous travaillez. (pas assez / trop)   Le professeur: **Vous ne travaillez pas assez.**
   L'élève: **Je travaille trop.**

1. Vous étudiez. (pas assez / beaucoup)
2. Vous parlez en classe. (trop / peu)
3. Vous jouez. (trop / pas beaucoup)
4. Vous regardez la télé. (trop / peu)
5. Vous pensez à vos amies. (beaucoup / pas assez)
6. Vous aimez vos classes. (pas assez / beaucoup)

ACTIVITÉ 4   Dialogue   OPTIONAL

Demandez à vos camarades s'ils font les choses suivantes. Dans leurs réponses, vos camarades doivent utiliser une expression de quantité du **Vocabulaire spécialisé.**

→ étudier?   —**Est-ce que tu étudies?**
   —**J'étudie peu (trop, assez, beaucoup).**
   (Je n'étudie pas assez [beaucoup].)

1. travailler?
2. voyager?
3. aller au cinéma?
4. aimer le théâtre?
5. aimer le français?
6. jouer au tennis?
7. sortir avec tes amis?
8. dormir?

C. Les expressions de quantité avec les noms

You may point out that after an expression of quantity, **de** is used instead of **du, de la, de l', des.**
Note: The partitive article is reviewed in Leçon 4.

In the answers to the questions below, the expressions of quantity introduce nouns. Note the forms of these expressions of quantity.

Tu as des vacances?	J'ai **peu de** vacances.
Vous avez de l'argent?	Nous n'avons pas **assez d'**argent.
Vous faites du sport?	Nous ne faisons pas **beaucoup de** sport.
Isabelle a des amis?	Elle a **beaucoup d'**amis.
Vous avez des examens?	Nous avons **trop d'**examens.

When an expression of quantity introduces a noun, the construction is:

expression of quantity + **de** + noun
↓
d' (+ vowel sound)

ACTIVITÉ 5 Beaucoup ou pas beaucoup?

Lisez la description des personnes suivantes. D'après cette description, dites si ces personnes ont beaucoup de ce qui est indiqué entre parenthèses. Vos phrases peuvent être affirmatives ou négatives.

→ Annette est très snob. (des amis?) **Elle n'a pas beaucoup d'amis.**
 (Elle a beaucoup d'amis.)

1. Paul est très sympathique. (des amis?)
2. Jacqueline est très intelligente. (des idées?)
3. Henri déteste la musique. (des disques?)
4. Philippe n'aime pas attendre. (de la patience?)
5. Catherine est très malade. (de la fièvre?)
6. Mélanie est une excellente actrice. (du talent?)
7. Thomas achète des vêtements très chers. (de l'argent?)
8. Antoine ne gagne jamais aux cartes. (de la chance?)

ACTIVITÉ 6 Questions personnelles OPTIONAL

Dans vos réponses, utilisez l'une des expressions de quantité suivantes: **assez de, peu de, beaucoup de, trop de.**

→ Avez-vous des examens? **Nous avons peu (beaucoup, trop) d'examens.**
 (Nous n'avons pas beaucoup [assez, trop] d'examens.)

1. Avez-vous des amis?
2. Avez-vous de l'argent?
3. Faites-vous du sport à l'école?
4. Faites-vous des progrès en français?
5. Avez-vous des amis intéressants?
6. Avez-vous des vacances?
7. Avez-vous des projets (plans) pour les vacances?
8. Avez-vous des professeurs sympathiques?

You may want to contrast **J'aime beaucoup le tennis** and **Je fais beaucoup de tennis.** In the first sentence, **beaucoup** modifies the verb (how much I like tennis). In the second sentence, **beaucoup de** introduces the noun (how much tennis I play).

Prononciation

Révision: les sons /ɑ̃/ **et** /an/, /am/, /ɛn/, /ɛm/

Contrastez: /ɑ̃/ brill**an**t, mom**en**t, pr**en**ds, **en**t**en**dre, dem**an**de, l**am**pe, p**en**d**an**t

/an/, /am/ **An**ne, **an**imal, **an**née, **am**i, **am**our, Mad**am**e

/ɛn/, /ɛm/ sc**èn**e, pr**en**nent, compr**en**nent, Hél**èn**e, m**êm**e

The letters **an** (**am**) and **en** (**em**) represent the nasal vowel /ɑ̃/, unless they are followed by a vowel or an **n** or **m**. When pronouncing /ɑ̃/, be sure not to pronounce an /n/ or /m/ after it.

Entre nous

Expressions pour la composition

heureusement	*fortunately*	J'ai beaucoup d'amis! **Heureusement!**
malheureusement	*unfortunately*	**Malheureusement**, je n'ai pas beaucoup d'argent.
par exemple	*for instance,*	Je fais du sport tous les week-ends. Samedi
	for example	dernier, **par exemple**, j'ai joué au tennis.

Rencontres

Aujourd'hui Michèle vous parle des sports qu'elle aime *pratiquer*. Écoutez-la!   *to engage in*

> Est-ce que vous aimez le sport? Moi, j'aime beaucoup le sport. Malheureusement, en France on ne fait pas beaucoup de sport. Au lycée, par exemple, nous faisons peu de sport. Heureusement, il y a les vacances!
> En hiver, je fais beaucoup de ski. Je skie assez bien! En été, je joue souvent au tennis. J'ai fait beaucoup de progrès l'été dernier, mais j'ai encore beaucoup de progrès à faire.   *still*
> J'ai fait aussi un peu de voile. C'est un sport très intéressant, mais hélas trop   *alas*
> cher pour moi.

À votre tour   You may want to review sports vocabulary on pp. 145, 237, 288.

Maintenant parlez des sports que vous aimez et que vous pratiquez.

J'aime . . .   Aux États-Unis on fait . . .

À l'école, je fais . . .   Au printemps, je . . .

En hiver, je . . .   En été, je . . .

L'été dernier, j'ai . . .

Leçon 3

Acte 3.
L'invitation de Jean-Claude

STRUCTURES TO OBSERVE
• the pronoun **y**
• the pronoun **en**

Personnages: Isabelle, Robert, Nicole, Jean-Claude

Samedi, 25 avril, onze heures et demie

La représentation est *finie.* Isabelle est dans la *salle de maquillage* avec
Robert et Nicole, les deux autres acteurs.

over; dressing room

ROBERT:	Félicitations, Isabelle! Tu as été extraordinaire!	
ISABELLE:	Merci! Toi aussi, tu as été formidable. Et toi aussi, Nicole.	
NICOLE:	Qu'est-ce qu'on fait maintenant?	
ROBERT:	J'ai un peu faim.	
ISABELLE:	Et moi, j'ai soif.	
NICOLE:	Allons au Café de la Renaissance.	
ROBERT:	Excellente idée! Allons-*y.*	*there*
JEAN-CLAUDE	*(qui vient d'arriver):* Vous ne pouvez pas y aller.	
	J'*en* viens . . . Il est fermé!	*from there*
ISABELLE:	Zut alors!	
JEAN-CLAUDE:	J'ai une idée. Venez chez moi!	
ROBERT:	Tes parents sont d'accord?	
JEAN-CLAUDE:	Ils sont toujours d'accord quand j'amène mes copains.	
ISABELLE:	Est-ce qu'ils nous attendent?	
JEAN-CLAUDE:	Mais non. Ils dorment à cette heure-ci. Alors, vous venez chez moi?	
ROBERT:	*On y va!*	*Let's go!*

CONVERSATION

Questions sur le texte:

1. Quelle heure est-il?
2. Où sont Isabelle et ses amis?
3. Qui félicite *(congratulates)* Isabelle?
4. Qui a faim?
5. Qui a soif?

6. Qui propose d'aller au Café de la Renaissance?
7. Est-ce que les amis y vont?
8. Qui y est allé?
9. Qui **en** vient?

OBSERVATIONS   Str. A, B

Reread questions 7 and 8.

These questions mean **Est-ce que les amis vont au café?** and **Qui est allé au café?**

• Which one-word pronoun is used to replace **au café** in these questions?   y

Reread question 9. This question means **Qui vient du café?**

• Which pronoun is used to replace **du café?**   en

NOTE CULTURELLE   For reading and listening practice.

Le café

Où rencontrez-vous vos amis? Chez vous? ou dans un autre endroit?° Généralement, quand un jeune Français veut rencontrer ses amis, il leur donne rendez-vous au café. Le café est l'endroit idéal pour passer un bon moment avec ses° amis. C'est aussi un endroit où l'on vient pour écouter de la musique, pour téléphoner, pour étudier, pour regarder les gens qui passent dans la rue°... et, bien sûr, pour commander un sandwich ou boire un jus de fruits.

endroit *place*   **ses** *one's*   **rue** *street*
On usually becomes **l'on** after a vowel sound: **où l'on vient**...

A L'OPÉRA le grand café
SES FRUITS DE MER, SES POISSONS
4 BdDESCAPUCINES·073 47 45
parking Paramount a 30 m

dans un décor Belle Epoque
LE CAFÉ FRANÇAIS
28 FÉVRIER
15 MAI
AUTOUR D'UN VIN
PÉCHARMANT 1976
Appellation contrôlée
SPÉCIALITÉS DU PÉRIGORD QUERCY
tout à discrétion
Buffet "FOU" 80 F
Menu "GOURMAND" 100 F
17 bd St-Jacques
PARIS 14° · Tél 589 89 80
DÎNER en MUSIQUE
avec pianiste
85 F/105 F

Vocabulaire pratique

| VERBE: | **fermer** | *to close, shut* | **Fermez** vos livres! |
| NOM: | **félicitations!** | *congratulations* | Vous avez gagné le match de foot? **Félicitations!** |

Structure

A. Le pronom y

You may point out that the expression il y a contains the pronoun y. The negative form is il n'y a pas.

Note the use of the pronoun y *(there)* in the answers to the following questions:

Allez-vous souvent **au théâtre?**	Oui, j'y vais souvent.	If the students have difficulty
Vas-tu **au cinéma** ce soir?	Non, je n'y vais pas.	understanding the pronoun y,
		you may want to translate
Est-ce que les amis vont **au café?**	Non, ils n'y vont pas.	these sentences.
Est-ce qu'ils vont **chez Jean-Claude?**	Oui, ils y vont.	
Es-tu allé **en France?**	Oui, j'y suis allé cet été.	
Habites-tu **à Paris?**	Non, je n'y habite pas.	

The pronoun y replaces names of places introduced by prepositions such as **à, en, dans, chez,** etc.

→ Like other object pronouns, y comes before the verb, except when the verb is in the affirmative imperative.

Have the students note the liaisons: vas-y allez-y allons-y

—Allons au café! —Bonne idée! Allons-y avec nos amis!

→ In negative sentences the word order is:

subject	+	n'y	+	verb	+	pas

ACTIVITÉ 1   Dialogue

Demandez à vos camarades si oui ou non ils vont souvent dans les endroits *(places)* suivants.

→ au cinéma?   —**Est-ce que tu vas souvent au cinéma?**
—**Oui, j'y vais souvent! (Non, je n'y vais pas souvent!)**

1. au concert?
2. à l'école?
3. en ville?
4. dans les magasins?
5. chez tes amis?
6. chez tes grands-parents?
7. en voyage?
8. chez le dentiste?
9. chez le pâtissier?
10. chez le marchand de disques?

ACTIVITÉ 2   Pas le week-end

Le week-end, les personnes suivantes ne font pas ce qu'elles font pendant la semaine. Exprimez cela en utilisant le pronom **y.**

→ Robert dîne au restaurant.   **Le week-end, il n'y dîne pas.**

1. Mes cousins dînent à la cafétéria.
2. Nous dînons en ville.
3. Vous êtes à l'université.
4. Les étudiants sont en classe.
5. Le médecin va à l'hôpital.
6. Nous allons à l'école.
7. Je vais à la bibliothèque.
8. Tu restes chez toi.
9. Suzanne reste chez son amie.
10. Vous restez chez vos parents.

ACTIVITÉ 3   **Questions personnelles**   OPTIONAL

Répondez affirmativement ou négativement aux questions suivantes, en
utilisant le pronom **y**.

Before doing questions 5–8, you may want to review the passé composé.

1. Maintenant, êtes-vous en classe?
2. Le samedi, allez-vous au cinéma?
3. Le dimanche, dînez-vous au restaurant?
4. Le week-end, restez-vous chez vous?

5. Êtes-vous allé(e) en France?
6. Êtes-vous allé(e) à San Francisco?
7. Êtes-vous allé(e) à la Nouvelle-Orléans?
8. Êtes-vous allé(e) au Canada?

Vocabulaire spécialisé   Où?

NOMS:	**une fenêtre**	*window*	
	une porte	*door*	
PRÉPOSITIONS:	**dans**	*in*	Suzanne est **dans** sa chambre.
	sur	*on*	Le chat noir est **sur** le lit.
	sous	*under*	Le chat blanc est **sous** le lit.
	devant	*in front of*	La table est **devant** la fenêtre.
	derrière	*behind*	Le chien est **derrière** la porte.
	entre	*between*	Le lit est **entre** la porte et la fenêtre.
	près de	*next to, near*	La chaise est **près de** la table.
	loin de	*far from*	Elle est **loin de** la porte.
	à droite de	*to the right of*	**À droite de** la fenêtre, il y a un oiseau.
	à gauche de	*to the left of*	**À gauche de** la fenêtre, il y a des poissons rouges.

ACTIVITÉ 4 **Rangement** *(Cleaning up)*

You may practice y by asking questions about the illustration.
—Est-ce que ses disques sont sur son lit?
—Non, ils n'y sont pas! Ils sont sous la table.

Jeannette aide Pierre à ranger *(to clean up)* sa chambre. Pierre demande où sont certaines choses. Jeannette lui répond. Jouez les deux rôles, mais avant regardez l'illustration attentivement!

➔ mes disques? (la table)   Pierre: **Où sont mes disques?**
Jeannette: **Ils sont sous la table.**

1. mon transistor? (la table)
2. mes chaussures? (le lit)
3. mon blue-jeans? (le lit)
4. mon vélo? (la porte)

5. ma raquette? (la porte)
6. mes livres? (le sac)
7. le sac? (la fenêtre)
8. ma guitare? (la fenêtre)

In many instances several answers are possible. **La guitare est près de la fenêtre, à gauche de la fenêtre.**

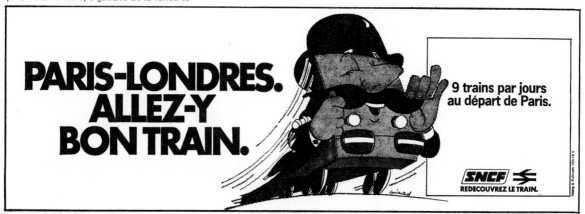

ACTIVITÉ 5   Questions personnelles

Savez-vous où sont les personnes et les choses suivantes en ce moment? Répondez affirmativement ou négativement aux questions. Utilisez le pronom **y**.

→   Est-ce que votre mère est chez vous?   **Oui, elle y est.**
                                              (Non, elle n'y est pas.)

1. Est-ce que le professeur est chez lui?
2. Est-ce que les élèves sont dans la classe?
3. Est-ce que le professeur est devant les élèves?
4. Est-ce que le directeur est derrière la porte?
5. Est-ce que vos livres sont dans votre sac?
6. Est-ce que votre sac est sous la table?

B. Le pronom *en* remplaçant *de* + nom

Make sure that the students do not confuse **en** the pronoun with **en** the preposition: **en France, en classe,** etc.

Note the use of the pronoun **en** in the answers to the following questions:

Tu viens **du théâtre?**	Oui, j'**en** viens.	*I am coming from there.*
Vous venez **de ce café?**	Non, nous n'**en** venons pas.	*We are not coming from there.*
Parles-tu **de tes amis?**	Oui, j'**en** parle.	*Yes, I speak about them.*
As-tu parlé **de la pièce?**	Non, je n'**en** ai pas parlé.	*No, I didn't talk about it.*

The pronoun **en** replaces **de** + noun or noun phrase.

→   Like other object pronouns, **en** comes before the verb, except when the verb is in the affirmative imperative.

Parlez de la pièce.   Parlez-en à vos amis.   Have the students note the liaison: **parlez-en.**

ACTIVITÉ 6   Bavardages *(Gossip)*

Isabelle ne parle jamais de ce qui concerne *(what is related to)* l'école, mais elle parle de tout le reste *(everything else)*. Dites si oui ou non elle parle des sujets suivants. Utilisez le pronom **en.**

→   des examens?   **Elle n'en parle pas.**
    des vacances?   **Elle en parle.**

VARIATION with the passé composé:
Elle n'en a pas parlé. Elle en a parlé.

1. de ses professeurs?
2. de ses amis?
3. de la pièce?
4. de sa nouvelle robe?
5. de son nouveau disque?
6. de la classe d'anglais?
7. de ses projets de vacances?
8. de son professeur de maths?

ACTIVITÉ 7 **Questions personnelles**

Répondez affirmativement ou négativement aux questions suivantes.
Utilisez le pronom **en**.

1. Avec vos amis, parlez-vous de vos professeurs? de vos parents? de vos
   problèmes? de vos projets? de musique? de sport?
2. Avec vos parents, parlez-vous de vos professeurs? de vos amis? de vos
   problèmes? de vos projets? de musique? de sport?
3. Jouez-vous du piano? de la flûte? du violon? de la clarinette?

Prononciation

Révision: les sons /u/ et /y/

/u/   v**ou**s, t**ou**t, **où**, s**ou**s, beauc**ou**p, j**ou**rnal, b**ou**che, n**ou**velle
     Avez-v**ou**s tr**ou**vé le n**ou**veau j**ou**rnal?
     Combien c**oû**te la s**ou**pe du j**ou**r?

/y/   v**u**, t**u**, **eu**, s**u**r, c**u**rieux, rev**u**e, b**u**s, men**u**
     As-t**u** entend**u** cette m**u**sique c**u**rieuse?
     Lucile a l**u** le men**u**.

Entre nous

Expression pour la composition

de temps en temps   *from time to time,*   Au printemps, je vais **de temps**
                                        once in a while   **en temps** à la campagne.

Rencontres

Aujourd'hui Michèle vous parle du week-end. Écoutez-la!

Qu'est-ce que vous faites le week-end?
Moi, j'aime aller au cinéma. En général, j'y vais le samedi avec mes
copains. De temps en temps, j'y vais
aussi le dimanche avec mes parents...
mais c'est rare.

J'aime aussi aller au café. J'y vais
quand j'ai rendez-vous avec un
ami. J'y vais après le cinéma. J'y
vais pour écouter des disques. J'y
vais aussi quand je n'ai rien de
spécial à faire.

J'aime aller à la campagne, mais
je n'y vais pas souvent parce que
je n'ai pas de voiture. Ce week-end
je vais aller à un concert de jazz
avec des copains. Et après? Je ne
sais pas.

À votre tour

Maintenant parlez de vos week-ends.

J'aime . . .
Je vais souvent . . .
J'y vais quand . . .
Je n'y vais pas quand . . .
J'aime aussi aller . . . J'y vais . . .
Ce week-end, je vais . . .

Leçon 4

Acte 4. Deux toasts

Personnages: Jean-Claude, Isabelle, Robert, Nicole

Dimanche, 26 avril, minuit et demi

Scène 1. Une bonne surprise

Les amis viennent d'arriver chez Jean-Claude. Jean-Claude va dans la cuisine.
Il *ouvre* le réfrigérateur et . . . *découvre* un repas froid.

opens;
discovers

JEAN-CLAUDE: Dites, ma mère a préparé une
surprise!

ISABELLE: Quelle surprise?

JEAN-CLAUDE: Un repas.

ROBERT *(qui a toujours faim): Pas possible!*
Qu'est-ce qu'il y a?

Not really!

JEAN-CLAUDE: Il y a du rosbif, du caviar, de la
salade de tomates, des *œufs en
gelée,* de la glace, un gâteau . . . Et
ce n'est pas tout! Il y a une autre
surprise!

jellied eggs

Œufs en gelée are
poached eggs
surrounded by
jellied consommé.

NICOLE: Quoi?

JEAN-CLAUDE: Il y a du champagne!

ROBERT: Du champagne? Nous allons vraiment célébrer le succès de la pièce.

Scène 2. Le festin

(Jean-Claude passe les plats à ses amis.)

festin *feast*

JEAN-CLAUDE: Est-ce que tu as du caviar?

ISABELLE: Oui, merci. J'*en* ai.

some

JEAN-CLAUDE: Ça ne fait rien. Reprends-en! Et
toi, Robert, tu as du rosbif?

ROBERT: Oui, j'en ai, mais je veux bien en reprendre!

JEAN-CLAUDE: Tu veux des œufs, Nicole?

NICOLE: Non, merci. J'en ai déjà pris. Je n'ai
plus faim . . . mais j'ai un peu soif.

JEAN-CLAUDE: Eh bien, nous allons boire le champagne.

(Jean-Claude va chercher le champagne . . .)

JEAN-CLAUDE: Maintenant, buvons le champagne!
Je propose un toast: «Au succès de la pièce!»

ROBERT: Et moi, je propose un toast à la mère de
Jean-Claude: «À Madame Marsan, excellente
cuisinière . . . et mère extraordinaire!»

CONVERSATION

Questions sur le texte:

1. Est-ce qu'il y a **du caviar?**
2. Est-ce qu'Isabelle **en** prend?
3. Est-ce qu'il y a **du rosbif?**
4. Est-ce que Robert **en** prend?

5. Est-ce qu'il y a **des œufs** (eggs)?
6. Est-ce que Nicole **en** a pris?
7. Est-ce qu'il y a **du champagne?**
8. Est-ce que les amis **en** boivent?

OBSERVATIONS Str. C

Reread questions 2, 4, 6, and 8.

• Which object pronoun replaces **du caviar** in question 2? en
  du rosbif in question 4? **des œufs** in question 6? en/en
  du champagne in question 8? en

NOTE CULTURELLE   For reading and listening practice.

La cuisine française

Avez-vous déjà° dîné dans un restaurant français?

Pour beaucoup de personnes, la cuisine française est la meilleure cuisine du monde.° C'est une cuisine fine et délicate où les sauces ont beaucoup d'importance.

Les Américains ont emprunté un grand nombre de mots au vocabulaire de la cuisine française. Connaissez-vous les mots suivants: **soufflé, filet mignon, tarte, mayonnaise, purée, mousse au chocolat?**

déjà ever   **du monde** in the world

Vocabulaire pratique

| NOMS: | **un plat** | dish, course (in a meal), platter | **la cuisine** | cooking; kitchen |
| | **un repas** | meal | **une cuisinière** | cook (female) |

VERBES: **célébrer** to celebrate   Ils **célèbrent** le succès de la pièce.
        reprendre to have more, take seconds   **Reprenez** du champagne!

EXPRESSIONS: **déjà** already   J'ai **déjà** bu du champagne. Et toi?
             vive ...! hurray for ...!   **Vive** les vacances!

Notes: 1. **Célébrer** is conjugated like **préférer** and **espérer.**
       2. **Reprendre** is conjugated like **prendre.**
       3. In the **passé composé,** the word **déjà** comes between the auxiliary verb (**être** or **avoir**) and the past participle:

   Nous sommes **déjà** allés en France. Et vous?

Vive is a verbal form which theoretically agrees with the noun subject which follows: **Vivent les vacances!** However, it is common practice to treat it as an invariable expression: **Vive les vacances!**
In interrogative sentences, **déjà** is the equivalent of *ever.* **Avez-vous déjà visité Paris?**

Structure

A. Le verbe *ouvrir*

Note the forms and uses of the irregular verb **ouvrir** *(to open).*

Infinitive		ouvrir	Je vais **ouvrir** la porte.
Present	j'	**ouvre**	J'**ouvre** une lettre.
	tu	**ouvres**	Tu **ouvres** une enveloppe.
	il/elle	**ouvre**	Il **ouvre** le livre.
	nous	**ouvrons**	Nous **ouvrons** le réfrigérateur.
	vous	**ouvrez**	Vous **ouvrez** la porte du garage.
	ils/elles	**ouvrent**	Ils **ouvrent** la fenêtre.
Passé composé	j'**ai**	**ouvert**	Qui a **ouvert** mon sac?

➔ Although **ouvrir** has an infinitive ending in **-ir**, the present tense forms have the endings of regular **-er** verbs.

➔ Other verbs conjugated like **ouvrir** are:

découvrir	*to discover*	Jacques **a découvert** la vérité.
offrir	*to give* (a present), *to offer*	Qu'est-ce que tu vas **offrir** à Isabelle pour son anniversaire?

Offrez des disques à écouter...

alain allanic

Disque FPLI 0091. RCA

ACTIVITÉ 1   L'anniversaire de Jean-Claude

Dites quels cadeaux *(gifts)* les personnes suivantes offrent à Jean-Claude pour son anniversaire.

➔ Paul: un disque   **Paul lui offre un disque.**

1. nous: des bonbons
2. Isabelle: un pull
3. ses parents: un vélo
4. toi: ta photo
5. vous: un livre
6. moi: une cassette

VARIATION with the passé composé: **Paul lui a offert un disque.**

B. Révision: *du, de la, des*

Note the use of **du, de la,** and **des** in the following sentences.

Veux-tu **de la** glace?	*Do you want (any) ice cream?*
Jean-Claude mange **du** rosbif.	*Jean-Claude is eating (some) roast beef.*
Charles achète **des** bananes.	*Charles is buying (some) bananas.*

→ To express *a certain quantity of* or *a certain amount of,* French speakers use:

du, de la (de l')	+	*singular* noun
des	+	*plural* noun

partitive article

plural indefinite article

→ In negative sentences, **du, de la,** and **des** become **de (d').**

—Tu veux **du** coca? —Non, merci. Je **ne** veux **pas de** coca.

→ Although *some* or *any* may be omitted in English, **du, de la,** and **des** must be expressed in French.

ACTIVITÉ 2 **Au restaurant** You may want to review foods on pp. 229, 232.

Nicole et ses amis vont commander ce qu'ils aiment. Dites ce que chacun prend d'après le modèle.

→ Isabelle aime le Coca-Cola.
Elle prend du Coca-Cola.

1. Nicole aime la salade.
2. J'aime le rosbif.
3. Tu aimes la glace.
4. Marie aime l'eau minérale.
5. Nous aimons le thé.
6. Henri et Bernard aiment le café.
7. Liliane et Sophie aiment le gâteau.
8. Vous aimez le jambon.

VARIATIONS with **commander, vouloir, manger**
or **boire. Elle commande du Coca-Cola. Elle
veut du Coca-Cola. Elle boit du Coca-Cola.**

Vocabulaire spécialisé Au supermarché

Les fruits *Fruits*

une banane **une orange** **une poire** **une pomme** **des fraises** **des cerises**
banana *orange* *pear* *apple* *strawberries* *cherries*

Les légumes *Vegetables*

une pomme de terre **des frites** **une carotte** **des petits pois** **des haricots**
potato *French fries* *carrot* *peas* *string beans*

une tomate **du riz**
tomato *rice*

Les autres produits *Other products*

du sel **de l'huile** **du vinaigre**
salt *oil* *vinegar*

un œuf **du beurre**
egg *butter*

de la confiture **du sucre**
jam *sugar*

There is no elision or liaison with **haricots**.

ACTIVITÉ 3 Le chef

Imaginez que c'est vous qui faites la cuisine. Vous voulez préparer les plats suivants. Demandez à un ami d'acheter les ingrédients nécessaires. Pour cela, utilisez les produits des vocabulaires de cette page et des pages 229 et 232.

→ une omelette au jambon **Achète des œufs, du sel, du beurre et du jambon.**

1. une omelette au fromage
2. une salade de fruits
3. une salade de légumes
4. une soupe de légumes
5. des frites
6. un «banana split»
7. un petit déjeuner américain (*American breakfast*)
8. un repas végétarien

VOCABULARY EXPANSION: fruits: **un ananas** (*pineapple*), **un melon**, **un pamplemousse** (*grapefruit*), **une framboise** (*raspberry*), **une pêche** (*peach*)

légumes: **un radis** (*radish*), **un champignon** (*mushroom*), **des épinards** (*spinach*)

produits: **le beurre de cacahuète** (*peanut butter*), **du poivre** (*pepper*), **de la mayonnaise**, **des céréales**

C. Le pronom *en* remplaçant *du, de la, des* + nom

Note the use of **en** in the answers to the following questions.

Veux-tu **du champagne?**	Oui, j'**en** veux. ⎫	*Yes, I want some.*
Veux-tu **de la glace?**	Oui, j'**en** veux. ⎭	
Veux-tu **de l'eau minérale?**	Non, je n'**en** veux pas. ⎫	*No, I don't want any.*
Veux-tu **des fruits?**	Non, je n'**en** veux pas. ⎭	
Est-ce qu'il y a **du pain?**	Oui, il y **en** a.	*Yes, there is some.*
Est-ce qu'il y a **des frites?**	Non, il n'y **en** a pas.	*No, there aren't any.*
As-tu mangé **du caviar?**	Oui, j'**en** ai mangé.	*Yes, I ate some.*
As-tu pris **des photos?**	Non, je n'**en** ai pas pris.	*No, I didn't take any.*

The pronoun **en** replaces direct object nouns introduced by **du, de la, de l',** or **des.**

→ Like other object pronouns, **en** comes before the verb, except when the verb is in the affirmative imperative.

Prends de la glace!   Prends-en!

→ **En** replaces both masculine and feminine, and singular and plural nouns.

→ In the above sentences, **en** corresponds to the English pronouns *some* and *any.*

→ There is liaison after **en** when the next word begins with a vowel sound.

—As-tu des amis français?   —Oui, j'en ai.

In an infinitive construction, **en** comes before the infinitive.
Il y a du champagne. Je vais en boire. Mes amis veulent en boire aussi.

ACTIVITÉ 4   Un repas végétarien

Nicole est végétarienne. Dites si oui ou non elle mange les choses suivantes.

VARIATIONS with **vouloir, prendre, acheter. Elle en veut.**

→ du rosbif?   **Elle n'en mange pas.** Elle en prend. Elle en achète.

des pommes de terre?   **Elle en mange.**

1. de la glace?	6. du melon?
2. de la viande?	7. du poulet?
3. des petits pois?	8. des spaghetti?
4. des carottes?	9. du jambon?
5. des oranges?	10. de la salade?

VARIATION as a dialog between Nicole and a waiter:
—Voulez-vous du rosbif?
—Non, merci. Je n'en veux pas.

ACTIVITÉ 5   Dialogue

Demandez à vos camarades s'ils font les choses suivantes.

→ le sport   **—Fais-tu du sport?**
         —Oui, j'en fais. (Non, je n'en fais pas.)

1. la gymnastique	4. le théâtre	7. le ski nautique *(water-skiing)*
2. le piano	5. le tennis	8. la poterie
3. la photo	6. le ski	9. la danse

LES MENUS DE LA SEMAINE

Jambon de pays
Couronne d'aubergines(*)
Fromage de chèvre
Compote de pommes

MARDI

Potage fermière
Escalopes de veau poêlées
Epinards à la crème
Yaourt

MERCREDI

Concombre en salade
Bœuf en boulettes
Pâtes au beurre
Mousse au chocolat

JEUDI

Velouté d'asperges
Poulet rôti
Fromage blanc à la crème

VARIATION with the passé composé for items 1, 2, and 3:
—Moi, j'ai fait du golf!
—Et alors? Moi aussi, j'en ai fait.

ACTIVITÉ 6   Moi aussi   OPTIONAL

Jean-Claude pense qu'il est absolument *(absolutely)* unique, mais Isabelle lui dit qu'elle fait les mêmes *(same)* choses. Jouez les deux rôles d'après le modèle.

→ Je fais du golf.   Jean-Claude: **Moi, je fais du golf!**
Isabelle: **Et alors?** *(So what?)* **Moi aussi, j'en fais.**

1. Je fais du judo.
2. Je prends des belles photos.
3. Je bois du champagne.
4. J'ai des amis intelligents.
5. J'ai des idées intéressantes.
6. J'ai de la patience.

ACTIVITÉ 7   Questions personnelles   OPTIONAL

Répondez affirmativement ou négativement aux questions suivantes. Utilisez le pronom **en** dans vos réponses.

1. À la cafétéria, mangez-vous des légumes? des fruits? du jambon?
2. Chez vous, mangez-vous de la viande? de la salade? du caviar?
3. À la cafétéria, buvez-vous du lait? du coca? du champagne?
4. Avez-vous des bons professeurs? des amis intéressants? des amis français? des amis en France?

ACTIVITÉ 8   Dialogue   OPTIONAL

Demandez à vos camarades s'ils ont fait les choses suivantes le week-end dernier. Utilisez le passé composé des verbes suivants. Vos camarades vont utiliser le pronom **en** dans leurs réponses.

→ manger des fraises?   —**As-tu mangé des fraises?**
—**Oui, j'en ai mangé. (Non, je n'en ai pas mangé.)**

1. manger du poisson
2. acheter du chewing-gum
3. acheter des bonbons
4. prendre de l'aspirine
5. prendre des photos
6. boire de l'eau minérale

Prononciation

Le son /p/

Mot clé: p̲eu

Répétez les mots: p̲oire, p̲omme, p̲lat, p̲etits p̲ois, p̲orte, p̲rès, p̲ièce

Répétez les phrases: P̲aul n'a p̲as p̲u p̲artir avec P̲ierre.
La p̲omme et la p̲oire sont sur le p̲lat.

The French consonant sound /p/, like the sounds /k/ and /t/, is pronounced without releasing a puff of air.

Entre nous

Expression pour la composition

hélas *unfortunately, alas*

—Vous avez de l'argent?
—**Hélas**, moi, je n'en ai pas.

Rencontres

Aujourd'hui Michèle va vous parler du repas de midi.
Écoutez-la!

Où déjeunez-vous? Moi, je déjeune à la cantine du lycée. Ce n'est pas toujours fameux ... mais, hélas, je n'ai pas le choix. Comme entrée, nous avons des radis, ou des carottes, ou des tomates, et quelquefois du jambon ou des sardines. Comme plat principal, nous avons de la viande avec des légumes ... pommes de terre, petits pois, haricots ... ou des macaronis. Mon plat préféré est le poulet avec des frites. Nous en avons le mercredi. Le vendredi, nous avons du poisson. Je n'en mange jamais, même quand j'ai faim. Je déteste le poisson. Quelle horreur!

Après le plat principal, nous avons de la salade et du fromage et finalement un dessert : banane, pomme, ou yogourt. Parfois nous avons de la glace, mais c'est assez rare.

Comme boissons, nous avons de la limonade, du cidre ou de l'eau. Et bien sûr, nous avons tout le pain que nous voulons ...

do you have lunch
cafeteria; great
choice; first course
radishes
sometimes
main course

even

How awful!

Sometimes

À votre tour

Maintenant décrivez votre repas de midi.
En général, je déjeune . . .
Comme entrée, il y a . . .
Comme plat principal, il y a . . .
Mon plat préféré est . . .
Nous en avons . . .
J'aime . . .
Je n'aime pas . . .
Comme dessert, il y a . . .

Leçon 5

Acte 5.
Une mauvaise surprise!

Personnages: Madame Marsan, Monsieur Marsan

Dimanche, 26 avril, 8 heures du matin

Madame Marsan va dans la cuisine. Là, elle a une très mauvaise surprise!
La cuisine *en effet* est dans un désordre inimaginable. *indeed*

Ce n'est pas tout! Quand elle ouvre le réfrigérateur, elle découvre
qu'il est . . . vide!

Les amis de Jean-Claude ont mangé le repas qu'elle *avait préparé* *had prepared*
spécialement pour ses invités, Monsieur et Madame Charron!

Monsieur Charron est le président de la *banque* où travaille son mari. *bank*
Quel désastre! Madame Marsan va chercher son mari. *What a disaster!*

M. MARSAN: Tu es malade?

MME MARSAN: Non, je ne suis pas malade. Je suis furieuse!

M. MARSAN: Qu'est-ce qu'il y a?

MME MARSAN: Hier, Jean-Claude a invité des amis et ils ont
mangé mon repas . . .

M. MARSAN: Est-ce qu'il reste du caviar?

MME MARSAN: Non, il n'en reste plus.

M. MARSAN: Et le rosbif?

MME MARSAN: Ils l'ont mangé aussi.

M. MARSAN: Et la glace?

MME MARSAN: Il en reste un peu, mais il n'en reste pas
assez pour nos invités.

M. MARSAN:	Et le champagne?	
MME MARSAN:	J'en ai acheté trois bouteilles, mais les amis de Jean-Claude en ont bu deux!	
M. MARSAN:	Cherchons une solution!	
MME MARSAN:	Il n'y en a pas!	
M. MARSAN:	*Mais si!* Allons faire les courses et . . .	*Yes there is!*
MME MARSAN:	Mais c'est dimanche aujourd'hui. Les magasins sont fermés.	
M. MARSAN:	C'est vrai!	
MME MARSAN:	Quelle catastrophe!	
M. MARSAN:	Tiens! Le téléphone.	
MME MARSAN:	Qui peut téléphoner à cette heure?	

(M. Marsan va répondre au téléphone. Il revient, content.)

MME MARSAN:	Qui est-ce?	
M. MARSAN:	C'est Monsieur Charron. Il a eu un accident hier soir! Rien de sérieux, mais il ne peut pas utiliser sa voiture . . . Il *s'excuse infiniment,* mais il ne peut pas venir.	*is terribly sorry*
MME MARSAN:	Cet accident, c'est un véritable miracle.	
M. MARSAN:	Et après tout, cette histoire, ce n'est pas un vrai drame!	

⌐ Vocabulaire pratique

NOMS:	**un drame**	*drama, tragedy*	**une bouteille**	*bottle*	
	un invité	*guest* (male)	**une invitée**	*guest* (female)	
ADJECTIFS:	**content ≠ triste**	*happy ≠ sad*		Quand mes amis ne sont pas **contents** je suis **triste**.	
	furieux (furieuse)	*mad, angry, furious*		Pierre est **furieux** parce que Sylvie n'a pas téléphoné.	
	véritable	*real, true*		Tu es un **véritable** ami!	
	vide ≠ plein	*empty ≠ full*		Le garage est **plein** de bouteilles **vides**.	
VERBE:	**utiliser**	*to use*		Je peux **utiliser** la voiture ce soir?	
EXPRESSIONS:	**il reste**	*there is/are . . . left*		**Il reste** une bouteille de champagne.	
	ne . . . plus	*no longer, no more*		Il **ne** reste **plus** de rosbif.	
	qu'est-ce qu'il y a?	*what's the matter?*		**Qu'est-ce qu'il y a?** Tu as l'air triste!	

Note: The expression **qu'est-ce qu'il y a?** has two different meanings:

What is there . . . ?	**Qu'est-ce qu'il y a** dans le réfrigérateur?
What's the matter?	Pourquoi pars-tu? **Qu'est-ce qu'il y a?**

CONVERSATION

Questions sur le texte:

Questions 6 and 7 present instances of agreement of the past participle with preceding direct objects. This grammar point is formally presented in **Tous ensemble** and does not need to be developed here.

1. Où va Madame Marsan dimanche matin?
2. Quelle est la mauvaise surprise?
3. Qui a mangé le repas?
4. Comment s'appellent les invités?
5. Qui est Monsieur Charron?
6. Combien de bouteilles de champagne est-ce que Madame Marsan a achetées?
7. Combien de bouteilles est-ce que les amis de Jean-Claude ont bues?
8. Pourquoi est-ce que Madame Marsan ne peut pas faire les courses?
9. Qui téléphone?
10. Pourquoi est-ce que Monsieur Charron ne peut pas utiliser sa voiture?
11. Pourquoi est-ce que l'accident est un miracle?

NOTE CULTURELLE

For reading and listening practice.

Le champagne

Le champagne est un vin d'origine française. Le vrai champagne vient de la Champagne, une région située° à l'est° de la France. Aujourd'hui les Américains ont imité les Français. On fait du champagne en Californie et dans l'état° de New York ... «Mais est-ce que c'est du vrai champagne?» se demandent° les Français.

située *situated* **est** *east* **état** *state* **se demandent** *wonder*

Vocabulaire spécialisé Les repas

NOMS:		VERBES:	
le petit déjeuner	*breakfast*	**prendre le petit déjeuner**	*to have (eat) breakfast*
le déjeuner	*lunch*	**déjeuner**	*to have (eat) lunch*
le dîner	*dinner, supper*	**dîner**	*to have (eat) supper, dinner*

un verre
une fourchette
une assiette
une tasse
un couteau (*pl.* couteaux)
une cuillère
une serviette

VOCABULARY EXPANSION: **une soucoupe** *(saucer)*, **un bol** *(bowl)*, **une cuillère à soupe**, **une cuillère à café** *(teaspoon)*

Before doing this activity, you may want to review times.

ACTIVITÉ 1 Questions personnelles

1. Quel est votre repas préféré? Pourquoi?
2. À quelle heure prenez-vous le petit déjeuner en semaine *(during the week)*?
3. À quelle heure prenez-vous le petit déjeuner le dimanche?
4. À quelle heure déjeunez-vous?
5. Où déjeunez-vous pendant la semaine?
6. À quelle heure dînez-vous?
7. En général, qu'est-ce que vous mangez au petit déjeuner?
8. Qu'est-ce que vous avez mangé au dîner hier?

Structure

A. Le pronom *en* avec les expressions de quantité

Note the use of the pronoun **en** in the answers to the following questions.

—As-tu beaucoup d'argent?
—Non, je n'**en** ai pas **beaucoup.**   *No, I don't have much (of it).*
 J'**en** ai **peu.**   *I have little (of it).*

—Mangez-vous assez de fruits?
—Oui, j'**en** mange **assez.**   *Yes, I eat enough (of them).*

With expressions of quantity, such as **beaucoup de, assez de, peu de, trop de,**
the pronoun **en** replaces **de** + noun or noun phrase.

→ Although the expressions *of it* and *of them* are usually left out in English,
  the pronoun **en** must be used in French.

Si vous ne buvez pas de lait, mangez-en.

ACTIVITÉ 2 Critiques

Jean-Claude et Isabelle critiquent *(are criticizing)* leur école. Isabelle est
d'accord avec ce que Jean-Claude dit. Jouez le rôle d'Isabelle.

→ Nous n'avons pas beaucoup de vacances.

  Isabelle: **C'est vrai! Nous n'en avons pas beaucoup.**

1. Nous avons beaucoup de préparations.
2. Nous avons trop d'examens.
3. Nous faisons peu de sport.
4. Nous faisons peu de progrès.
5. Nous lisons trop de livres.
6. Nous n'avons pas assez de vacances.

ACTIVITÉ 3   Questions personnelles   OPTIONAL

Répondez aux questions suivantes en utilisant une expression de quantité:
peu, beaucoup, assez, trop et le pronom **en.**

→ Faites-vous du sport?   **J'en fais peu (beaucoup, assez, trop).**
(Je n'en fais pas assez [beaucoup]).

1. Avez-vous des amis?
2. Avez-vous des disques?
3. Avez-vous des vacances?
4. Avez-vous des projets de vacances?
5. Achetez-vous des disques?
6. Achetez-vous des magazines?
7. Lisez-vous des livres?
8. Faites-vous des progrès en français?

B. Le pronom *en* avec *un, une* et les nombres

Note the use of **en** in the sentences on the right.

Jean-Claude a un électrophone.   Isabelle **en** a **un** aussi.
Jean-Claude a une guitare.   Isabelle **en** a **une** aussi.
Jean-Claude a douze disques.   Isabelle **en** a **vingt.**

The pronoun **en** replaces nouns or noun phrases introduced by **un, une,** or a number.
Contrast the French and the English sentences below.

As-tu des frères?   J'en ai **un.**   *I have one (of them).*
As-tu des cousines?   J'en ai **cinq.**   *I have five (of them).*
Combien d'élèves est-ce qu'il y a?   Il y **en** a **25.**   *There are 25 (of them).*

→ Whereas the expression *of them* is usually left out in English, **en** must be
used in French.

→ In a negative sentence with **en,** the numbers **un** and **une** are not used after **pas.**

Tu as un vélo?   Oui, j'**en** ai **un.**   *Yes, I have one.*
Tu as un électrophone?   Non, je **n'en** ai **pas.**   *No, I don't have one.*

You may indicate that in the above sentence, the entire negative answer would be:
Je n'ai pas d'électrophone. En replaces **d'électrophone.**

ACTIVITÉ 4   Dialogue

Demandez à vos camarades s'ils ont les choses suivantes.

→ une guitare?   —**As-tu une guitare?**
                    —**Oui, j'en ai une. (Non, je n'en ai pas.)**

1. un vélo?   4. une radio?   7. un chien?
2. une montre?   5. un livre de français?   8. un chat?
3. un électrophone?   6. un appareil-photo?   9. un oiseau?

396   Unité huit

ACTIVITÉ 5   Les billets de théâtre *(Theater tickets)*

Imaginez que vous vendez des billets pour la représentation théâtrale de votre école. Dites combien de billets les personnes suivantes veulent. Utilisez le pronom **en**.

→ Isabelle: 1   **Isabelle en veut un.**

1. Jean-Pierre: 2
2. Marc: 3
3. Annette: 6
4. Jean-Louis: 5
5. Sylvie: 4
6. Sophie: 10
7. Bernard: 12
8. Christine: 7

ACTIVITÉ 6   Questions personnelles   OPTIONAL

→ Combien de frères avez-vous?   **J'en ai un (deux, trois, etc.).**
(Je n'en ai pas.)

1. Combien de sœurs avez-vous?
2. Combien de disques avez-vous?
3. Combien de cousins avez-vous?
4. Combien de cousines avez-vous?
5. Combien de professeurs différents avez-vous?
6. Combien de mois de vacances avez-vous?

ACTIVITÉ 7   Vrai ou faux?   OPTIONAL

Lisez les phrases suivantes et déterminez si elles sont vraies ou fausses. Si elles sont vraies, confirmez-les. Si elles sont fausses, rectifiez-les *(correct them)*. Utilisez le pronom **en** d'après le modèle.

→ Il y a soixante minutes dans une heure.   **Oui, il y en a soixante.**

Il y a quarante états *(states)* aux États-Unis.   **Non, il y en a cinquante.**

1. Il y a vingt-trois élèves dans cette classe.
2. Il y a dix garçons dans cette classe.
3. Il y a neuf filles dans cette classe.
4. Il y a sept jours dans une semaine.
5. Il y a vingt-six jours en février.
6. Il y a douze mois dans l'année.

Prononciation

Révision: les sons /ə/, /ɛ/, /e/

/ə/ le, ce, me, petit, repas, cerises, revenir, devant
Je trouve ce petit repas remarquable.

/ɛ/ elle, belle, veste, verre, reste, terre, pièce, manière
Elle achète cette belle veste.

/e/ les, ces, mes, dîner, déjeuner, invité, célébrer, général, assez, et
Les invités vont assister à un dîner élégant.

The letter **e** followed by one consonant and a vowel is often not pronounced.
The letter **e** at the end of a word is a "mute **e**" and is usually not pronounced.
The letter **e** followed by two consonants is almost always pronounced /ɛ/.
Usually **è** and **ê** are pronounced /ɛ/, and **é** is pronounced /e/.
The letters **es** in words like **les** and **des**, and the letters **er, et,** and **ez** at the end of the word are usually pronounced /e/.

An e followed by a consonant + r or l is mute: **reprendre.**

Entre nous

Expression pour la composition

donc *therefore*   Je dois travailler cet été.
                       Donc, je ne vais pas voyager!

Rencontres

Michèle parle de ses vacances. Écoutez-la.

En France, nous avons relativement beaucoup de vacances. J'ai compté le *(counted)* nombre de jours de vacances que nous avons. Au total, nous en avons 180.

À Noël nous avons quinze jours de vacances. Nous en avons aussi quinze à Pâques. Les grandes vacances *(Easter; Summer vacation)* commencent le 30 juin et finissent le 15 septembre.

J'ai beaucoup de projets de vacances. Cette année je voudrais aller en Grèce avec des copains. Hélas, pour voyager, j'ai besoin d'argent. Moi, je n'en ai pas assez. Je n'ai pas de job et mes parents ne sont pas généreux. Donc, cette année je vais faire comme les autres années. Je vais passer mes vacances en Normandie chez mes grands-parents.

À votre tour

Maintenant parlez de vos vacances.

Aux États-Unis, nous . . .
À Noël, nous avons . . .
Au printemps, nous . . .
Les grandes vacances . . .
J'ai . . . (Je n'ai pas . . .)
Cette année, je voudrais . . .

Je voudrais aussi . . .
Mais pour faire cela, on doit avoir . . .
Moi, j'en ai . . . (Moi, je n'en ai pas.)
Mes parents . . .
Donc, cette année, je vais . . .

French students also get a week vacation in February and five or six days at Toussaint (Nov. 1).

Appendix 1 Sound–spelling Correspondences

SOUND	SPELLING	EXAMPLES

Vowels

SOUND	SPELLING	EXAMPLES
/a/	**a, à, â**	M<u>a</u>d<u>a</u>me, l<u>à</u>-b<u>a</u>s, thé<u>â</u>tre
/i/	**i, î**	v<u>i</u>site, N<u>i</u>ce, d<u>î</u>ne
	y (initial, final, or between consonants)	<u>Y</u>ves, Gu<u>y</u>, st<u>y</u>le
/u/	**ou, où, oû**	T<u>ou</u>louse, <u>où</u>, a<u>oû</u>t
/y/	**u, û**	t<u>u</u>, L<u>u</u>c, s<u>û</u>r
/o/	**o** (final or before silent consonant)	pian<u>o</u>, idi<u>o</u>t, Marg<u>o</u>t
	au, eau	j<u>au</u>ne, Cl<u>au</u>de, b<u>eau</u>
	ô	h<u>ô</u>tel, dr<u>ô</u>le, C<u>ô</u>te-d'Ivoire
/ɔ/	**o**	M<u>o</u>nique, N<u>o</u>ël, j<u>o</u>lie
	au	P<u>au</u>l, rest<u>au</u>rant, L<u>au</u>re
/e/	**é**	D<u>é</u>d<u>é</u>, Qu<u>é</u>bec, t<u>é</u>l<u>é</u>
	e (before silent final **z, t, r**)	ch<u>e</u>z, <u>e</u>t, Rog<u>e</u>r
	ai (final or before final silent consonant)	j'<u>ai</u>, m<u>ai</u>, japon<u>ai</u>s
/ɛ/	**è**	Mich<u>è</u>le, <u>È</u>ve, p<u>è</u>re
	ei	s<u>ei</u>ze, n<u>ei</u>ge, tour <u>Ei</u>ffel
	ê	t<u>ê</u>te, <u>ê</u>tre, Vi<u>ê</u>t-nam
	e (before two consonants)	<u>e</u>lle, Pi<u>e</u>rre, Ann<u>e</u>tte
	e (before pronounced final consonant)	Mich<u>e</u>l, av<u>e</u>c, ch<u>e</u>r
	ai (before pronounced final consonant)	fr<u>ai</u>nçaise, <u>ai</u>me, M<u>ai</u>ne
/ə/	**e** (final or before single consonant)	j<u>e</u>, D<u>e</u>nise, v<u>e</u>nir
/ø/	**eu, œu**	d<u>eu</u>x, Mathi<u>eu</u>, <u>œu</u>fs
	eu (before final **se**)	nerv<u>eu</u>se, génér<u>eu</u>se, séri<u>eu</u>se
/œ/	**eu** (before final pronounced consonant except /z/)	h<u>eu</u>re, n<u>eu</u>f, Lesi<u>eu</u>r

Nasal vowels

SOUND	SPELLING	EXAMPLES
/ã/	**an, am**	Fr<u>an</u>ce, qu<u>an</u>d, l<u>am</u>pe
	en, em	H<u>en</u>ri, p<u>en</u>dant, déc<u>em</u>bre
/ɔ̃/	**on, om**	n<u>on</u>, Sim<u>on</u>, b<u>om</u>be
/ɛ̃/	**in, im**	Mart<u>in</u>, <u>in</u>vite, <u>im</u>possible
	yn, ym	s<u>yn</u>dicat, s<u>ym</u>pathique, Ol<u>ym</u>pique
	ain, aim	Al<u>ain</u>, améric<u>ain</u>, f<u>aim</u>
	(o) + in	l<u>oin</u>, m<u>oin</u>s, p<u>oin</u>t
	(i) + en	b<u>ien</u>, Juli<u>en</u>, vi<u>en</u>s
/œ̃/	**un, um**	<u>un</u>, Lebr<u>un</u>, parf<u>um</u>

SOUND	SPELLING	EXAMPLES

Semi-vowels

/j/	**i, y** (before vowel sound)	bien, piano, Lyon
	-il, -ill (after vowel sound)	œil, travaille, Marseille
/ɥ/	**u** (before vowel sound)	lui, Suisse, juillet
/w/	**ou** (before vowel sound)	oui, Louis, jouer
/wa/	**oi, oî, oy** (before vowel)	voici, Benoît, voyage

Consonants

/b/	**b**	Barbara, banane, Belgique
/k/	**c** (before **a, o, u,** or consonant)	Coca-Cola, cuisine, classe
	ch(r)	Christine, Christian, Christophe
	qu, q (final)	Québec, qu'est-ce que, cinq
	k	kilo, Kiki, ketchup
/ʃ/	**ch**	Charles, blanche, chez
/d/	**d**	Didier, dans, médecin
/f/	**f**	Félix, franc, neuf
	ph	Philippe, téléphone, photo
/g/	**g** (before **a, o, u,** or consonant)	Gabriel, gorge, légumes, gris
	gu (before **e, i, y**)	vague, Guillaume, Guy
/ɲ/	**gn**	mignon, champagne, Allemagne
/ʒ/	**j**	je, Jérôme, jaune
	g (before **e, i, y**)	rouge, Gigi, gymnastique
	ge (before **a, o, u**)	orangeade, Georges, nageur
/l/	**l**	Lise, elle, cheval
/m/	**m**	Maman, moi, tomate
/n/	**n**	banane, Nancy, nous
/p/	**p**	peu, Papa, Pierre
/r/	**r**	arrive, rentre, Paris
/s/	**c** (before **e, i, y**)	ce, Cécile, Nancy
	ç (before **a, o, u**)	ça, garçon, déçu
	s (initial or before consonant)	sac, Sophie, reste
	ss (between vowels)	boisson, dessert, Suisse
	t (before **i** + vowel)	attention, Nations Unies, natation
	x	dix, six, soixante
/t/	**t**	trop, télé, Tours
	th	Thérèse, thé, Marthe
/v/	**v**	Viviane, vous, nouveau
/gz/	**x**	examen, exemple, exact
/ks/	**x**	Max, Mexique, excellent
/z/	**s** (between vowels)	désert, télévision, Louise
	z	Suzanne, zut, zéro

400

Appendix 2 Numbers

A. Cardinal numbers

0	zéro	18	dix-huit	82	quatre-vingt-deux
1	un (une)	19	dix-neuf	90	quatre-vingt-dix
2	deux	20	vingt	91	quatre-vingt-onze
3	trois	21	vingt et un (une)	100	cent
4	quatre	22	vingt-deux	101	cent un (une)
5	cinq	23	vingt-trois	102	cent deux
6	six	30	trente	200	deux cents
7	sept	31	trente et un (une)	201	deux cent un
8	huit	32	trente-deux	300	trois cents
9	neuf	40	quarante	400	quatre cents
10	dix	41	quarante et un (une)	500	cinq cents
11	onze	50	cinquante	600	six cents
12	douze	60	soixante	700	sept cents
13	treize	70	soixante-dix	800	huit cents
14	quatorze	71	soixante et onze	900	neuf cents
15	quinze	72	soixante-douze	1.000	mille
16	seize	80	quatre-vingts	2.000	deux mille
17	dix-sept	81	quatre-vingt-un (une)	1.000.000	un million

Notes:
1. The word **et** occurs only in the numbers 21, 31, 41, 51, and 61: vingt et un
2. **Un** becomes **une** before a feminine noun: trente et une filles
3. **Quatre-vingts** becomes **quatre-vingt** before another number: quatre-vingt-cinq
4. **Cents** becomes **cent** before another number: trois cent vingt
5. **Mille** never adds an -s: quatre mille

B. Ordinal numbers

1$^{er\ (ère)}$	premier (première)	5^e	cinquième	9^e	neuvième
2^e	deuxième	6^e	sixième	10^e	dixième
3^e	troisième	7^e	septième	11^e	onzième
4^e	quatrième	8^e	huitième	12^e	douzième

Note: **Premier** becomes **première** before a feminine noun: **la première histoire**

Appendix 3 Verbs

A. Regular verbs

INFINITIVE	PRESENT		PASSÉ COMPOSÉ	
parler (*to talk, speak*)	je **parle**	nous **parlons**	j'ai **parlé**	nous avons **parlé**
	tu **parles**	vous **parlez**	tu as **parlé**	vous avez **parlé**
	il **parle**	ils **parlent**	il a **parlé**	ils ont **parlé**
IMPERATIVE: **parle, parlons, parlez**				
finir (*to finish*)	je **finis**	nous **finissons**	j'ai **fini**	nous avons **fini**
	tu **finis**	vous **finissez**	tu as **fini**	vous avez **fini**
	il **finit**	ils **finissent**	il a **fini**	ils ont **fini**
IMPERATIVE: **finis, finissons, finissez**				
vendre (*to sell*)	je **vends**	nous **vendons**	j'ai **vendu**	nous avons **vendu**
	tu **vends**	vous **vendez**	tu as **vendu**	vous avez **vendu**
	il **vend**	ils **vendent**	il a **vendu**	ils ont **vendu**
IMPERATIVE: **vends, vendons, vendez**				

B. *-er* verbs with spelling changes

INFINITIVE	PRESENT		PASSÉ COMPOSÉ
acheter (*to buy*)	j'**achète**	nous **achetons**	j'ai **acheté**
	tu **achètes**	vous **achetez**	
	il **achète**	ils **achètent**	
Verb like **acheter:** amener (*to bring, take along*)			
espérer (*to hope*)	j'**espère**	nous **espérons**	j'ai **espéré**
	tu **espères**	vous **espérez**	
	il **espère**	ils **espèrent**	
Verbs like **espérer:** célébrer (*to celebrate*), préférer (*to prefer*)			
commencer (*to begin, start*)	je **commence**	nous **commençons**	j'ai **commencé**
	tu **commences**	vous **commencez**	
	il **commence**	ils **commencent**	
manger (*to eat*)	je **mange**	nous **mangeons**	j'ai **mangé**
	tu **manges**	vous **mangez**	
	il **mange**	ils **mangent**	
Verbs like **manger:** nager (*to swim*), voyager (*to travel*)			
payer (*to pay, pay for*)	je **paie**	nous **payons**	j'ai **payé**
	tu **paies**	vous **payez**	
	il **paie**	ils **paient**	

C. Irregular verbs

INFINITIVE	PRESENT		PASSÉ COMPOSÉ
avoir	j'**ai**	nous **avons**	j'**ai eu**
(*to have,*	tu **as**	vous **avez**	
own)	il **a**	ils **ont**	
IMPERATIVE: **aie, ayons, ayez**			
être	je **suis**	nous **sommes**	j'**ai été**
(*to be*)	tu **es**	vous **êtes**	
	il **est**	ils **sont**	
IMPERATIVE: **sois, soyons, soyez**			

INFINITIVE	PRESENT		PASSÉ COMPOSÉ
aller	je **vais**	nous **allons**	je **suis allé(e)**
(*to go*)	tu **vas**	vous **allez**	
	il **va**	ils **vont**	
boire	je **bois**	nous **buvons**	j'**ai bu**
(*to drink*)	tu **bois**	vous **buvez**	
	il **boit**	ils **boivent**	
connaître	je **connais**	nous **connaissons**	j'**ai connu**
(*to know*)	tu **connais**	vous **connaissez**	
	il **connaît**	ils **connaissent**	
devoir	je **dois**	nous **devons**	j'**ai dû**
(*to have to,*	tu **dois**	vous **devez**	
should, must)	il **doit**	ils **doivent**	
dire	je **dis**	nous **disons**	j'**ai dit**
(*to say, tell*)	tu **dis**	vous **dites**	
	il **dit**	ils **disent**	
dormir	je **dors**	nous **dormons**	j'**ai dormi**
(*to sleep*)	tu **dors**	vous **dormez**	
	il **dort**	ils **dorment**	
écrire	j'**écris**	nous **écrivons**	j'**ai écrit**
(*to write*)	tu **écris**	vous **écrivez**	
	il **écrit**	ils **écrivent**	
Verb like **écrire:** décrire (*to describe*)			
faire	je **fais**	nous **faisons**	j'**ai fait**
(*to make, do*)	tu **fais**	vous **faites**	
	il **fait**	ils **font**	
lire	je **lis**	nous **lisons**	j'**ai lu**
(*to read*)	tu **lis**	vous **lisez**	
	il **lit**	ils **lisent**	
mettre	je **mets**	nous **mettons**	j'**ai mis**
(*to put,*	tu **mets**	vous **mettez**	
place)	il **met**	ils **mettent**	
Verb like **mettre:** promettre (*to promise*)			

INFINITIVE	PRESENT		PASSÉ COMPOSÉ
ouvrir (to open)	j'ouvre tu ouvres il ouvre	nous ouvrons vous ouvrez ils ouvrent	j'ai ouvert
Verbs like ouvrir: découvrir (to discover), offrir (to offer)			
partir (to leave)	je pars tu pars il part	nous partons vous partez ils partent	je suis parti(e)
pouvoir (to be able, can)	je peux tu peux il peut	nous pouvons vous pouvez ils peuvent	j'ai pu
prendre (to take)	je prends tu prends il prend	nous prenons vous prenez ils prennent	j'ai pris
Verbs like prendre: apprendre (to learn), comprendre (to understand), reprendre (to have more, take seconds)			
savoir (to know)	je sais tu sais il sait	nous savons vous savez ils savent	j'ai su
sortir (to go out, get out)	je sors tu sors il sort	nous sortons vous sortez ils sortent	je suis sorti(e)
venir (to come)	je viens tu viens il vient	nous venons vous venez ils viennent	je suis venu(e)
Verb like venir: revenir (to come back)			
voir (to see)	je vois tu vois il voit	nous voyons vous voyez ils voient	j'ai vu
vouloir (to want)	je veux tu veux il veut	nous voulons vous voulez ils veulent	j'ai voulu

D. Verbs with *être* in the passé composé

aller (to go)	je suis allé(e)	passer (to go by, through)	je suis passé(e)
arriver (to arrive, come)	je suis arrivé(e)	rentrer (to go home)	je suis rentré(e)
descendre (to go down)	je suis descendu(e)	rester (to stay)	je suis resté(e)
entrer (to enter, go in)	je suis entré(e)	revenir (to come back)	je suis revenu(e)
monter (to go up)	je suis monté(e)	sortir (to go out, get out)	je suis sorti(e)
mourir (to die)	je suis mort(e)	tomber (to fall)	je suis tombé(e)
naître (to be born)	je suis né(e)	venir (to come)	je suis venu(e)
partir (to leave)	je suis parti(e)		

FRENCH-ENGLISH VOCABULARY

The French-English Vocabulary contains active and passive words from the text, as well as the important words of the illustrations used within the units. Obvious passive cognates have not been listed. Illustrations in the Sections Magazines are glossed where used.

The numbers following an entry indicate the unit and lesson in which the word or phrase is activated. (**P** stands for **Prélude.**) Passive meanings are separated from active meanings by a semicolon.

Nouns: If the article of a noun does not indicate gender, the noun is followed by *m.* (*masculine*) or *f.* (*feminine*). If the plural (*pl.*) is irregular, it is given in parentheses.

Adjectives: Adjectives are listed in the masculine form. If the feminine form is irregular, it is given in parentheses. Irregular plural (*pl.*) forms are also given in parentheses.

Verbs: Verbs are listed in the infinitive form. An asterisk (✶) in front of an active verb means that it is irregular. (For forms, see the verb charts in Appendix 3C.) Irregular present tense forms are listed when they are used before the verb has been activated. Irregular past participle (*p. part.*) forms are listed separately.

Words beginning with an **h** are preceded by a bullet (•) if the **h** is aspirate; that is, if the word is treated as if it begins with a consonant sound.

a

a: il y a there is, there are (**2.4**)

à at, to, in (**1.1**); from, for, by **à cause de** because of (**8.1**) **à...heure(s)** at . . . (o'clock) (**P.4**) **à quelle heure?** (at) what time? (**P.4**) **à qui est/sont...?** whose . . . is it/are they?, to whom does/do . . . belong? (**3.5**)

un **abonnement** season ticket **abord: d'abord** first **absolument** absolutely

un **accent** accent mark, accent, stress **accomplir** to accomplish

un **accord** agreement **d'accord** okay, all right (**2.1**) **être d'accord** to agree (**2.1**)

un **achat** purchase **acheter** to buy (**4.2**)

un **acteur** actor (**5.1**)

une **activité** activity

une **actrice** actress (**5.1**) **actuellement** right now **adéquat** adequate

un **adjectif** adjective

un **admirateur, une admiratrice** admirer **admirer** to admire **adorer** to love, adore (**1.4**)

une **adresse** address

un **adverbe** adverb

un **aéroport** airport

une **affaire** business, concern **des affaires** things, personal belongings **affirmatif (affirmative)** affirmative, "yes" **affirmativement** in the affirmative, saying "yes"

l' **Afrique** *f.* Africa (**2.4**)

un **âge** age **quel âge as-tu (avez-vous)?** how old are you? (**3.3**) **âgé** old (**3.3**)

une **agence** agency **une agence de tourisme** tourist agency **une agence de voyages** travel agency

l' **agneau** *m.* lamb (**5.2**) **ah!** ah! oh! (**2.1**) **ah bon!** all right! (**3.4**) **ai: j'ai** I have **aider (à)** to help (**7.1**)

un **ailier (gauche, droit)** (*soccer*) (left, right) wing **aimable** friendly **aimer** to like (**1.4**)

l' **air** *m.* air **avoir l'air** to seem, look (**6.1**) **aise: mal à l'aise** uncomfortable, ill at ease

un **album** album (**3.3**)

l' **Algérie** *f.* Algeria (*country in North Africa*) **algérien (algérienne)** Algerian

l' **Allemagne** *f.* Germany (**2.4**) **allemand** German (**2.4**)

l' **allemand** *m.* German (*language*)

✶ **aller** to go (**3.1**) **aller à pied** to walk, go on foot (**5.5**) **aller à vélo (bicyclette)** to go by bicycle (**5.5**) **aller bon train** to go at a good pace **aller en auto (en train)** to go by car (by train) (**5.5**) **allez: comment allez-vous?** how are you? (**P.2**) **allô** hello (*used to answer the telephone*) **allons!** let's go (**3.1**) **allons...!** let's go (*somewhere*)! (**3.1**) **alors** then, well then, so (**1.5**) **et alors?** so what? (**1.5**) **zut alors!** darn (it)! rats! (**P.4**)

un **alpiniste, une alpiniste** alpinist, mountain climber **amener** to bring, take along (**6.5**) **américain** American (**2.4**)

un **Américain, une Américaine** American (**2.4**)

l' **américanisation** *f.* americanization

l' **Amérique** *f.* America (**2.4**)

un **ami, une amie** (close) friend (**2.1**) **un petit ami** boyfriend (**2.3**) **une petite amie** girlfriend (**2.3**) **amicalement** love (*at the end of a letter*) (**6.5**)

405

amitiés best regards (*at the end of a letter*) (**6.5**)

amoureux (amoureuse) in love (**7.3**)

amusant amusing (**2.1**)

amuser to amuse **amusez-vous bien** have a good time

un **an** year **avoir... ans** to be . . . (years old) (**3.3**) **le Jour de l'An** New Year's Day

analyser to analyze

ancien (ancienne) former

un **âne** donkey

un **ange** angel

anglais English (**2.4**)

l' **anglais** *m.* English (*language*)

un **Anglais, une Anglaise** English person (**2.4**)

l' **Angleterre** *f.* England (**2.4**)

un **animal** (*pl.* **animaux**) animal (**3.4**)

animé: un dessin animé cartoon (**5.1**)

l' **année** *f.* year (**P.5**)

un **anniversaire** birthday (**7.5**) **l'anniversaire de (Marc) est** (Marc's) birthday is (**P.5**) **mon anniversaire est...** my birthday is . . . (**P.5**)

un **anorak** (ski) jacket, parka (**4.2**)

août August (**P.5**)

un **appareil-photo** (*pl.* **appareils-photo**) (still) camera (**2.2**)

une **apparence** appearance

un **appartement** apartment

appelez: vous vous appelez your name is

appelle: comment s'appelle...? what's . . .'s name? (**2.1**) **comment s'appelle-t-il/elle?** what's his/her name? (**2.1**) **comment t'appelles-tu?** what's your name? (**P.2**) **je m'appelle** my name is (**P.2**) **...s'appelle** . . . is called, . . .'s name is

l' **appendicite** *f.* appendicitis

un **appétit** appetite

applaudir to applaud

apporter to bring

* **apprendre** to learn (**5.5**) **apprendre à** + *inf.* to learn how to (**5.5**) **appris** (*p. part. of* **apprendre**) (**6.4**)

approximatif (approximative) approximate

après afterwards, after (**6.5**) **après tout** after all (**5.1**) **d'après** according to

un **après-midi** afternoon (**4.2**) **de l'après-midi** in the afternoon, P.M. (**P.4**)

l' **arabe** *m.* Arabic (*language*)

l' **Arc de Triomphe** *m. triumphal arch in Paris, commemorating Napoleon's victories*

un **archéologue** archaeologist

l' **argent** *m.* money (**4.1**) **l'argent de poche** pocket money, allowance (**7.4**)

un **arrière (gauche, droit)** (*soccer*) (left, right) fullback **un arrière central** (*soccer*) center half back

une **arrivée** arrival

arriver to arrive, come (**1.1**)

l' **art** *m.* art

un **artiste, une artiste** artist **artistique** artistic

une **ascension** ascent

l' **Asie** *f.* Asia (**2.4**) **assez** rather (**2.1**) enough (**8.2**)

une **assiette** plate, dish (**8.5**) **assister (à)** to attend, be present at, go to (**6.4**)

un **athlète, une athlète** athlete

l' **athlétisme** *m.* track and field

l' **Atlantique** *m.* Atlantic Ocean **attaquer** to attack **attendre** to wait, wait for (**4.5**) **attentif (attentive)** attentive (**8.2**)

une **attention** attention **attention!** careful! **faire attention** to pay attention, be careful (**5.4**) **attentivement** attentively **au** at (the), to (the), in (the) (**3.1**) **au contraire** on the contrary (**1.2**) **au moins** at least (**3.2**) **au printemps** in (the) spring (**P.6**) **au revoir** good-by (**P.1**) **aujourd'hui** today (**P.5**) **aussi** also, too (**1.1**); so **aussi...que** as . . . as (**4.3**) **moi aussi** me too (**P.2**)

un **auteur** author (**8.1**)

une **auto** car, automobile (**2.2**)

un **autobus** bus (**5.5**)

l' **automne** *m.* fall, autumn (**4.2**) **en automne** in (the) fall, autumn (**P.6**)

l' **autorisation** *f.* permission **autre** other (**7.5**) **d'autre** other **d'autres** other people, others **l'autre** the other one (**7.5**) **les autres** the others (**7.5**) **un autre** another (**7.5**)

une **autruche** ostrich **aux** at (the), to (the), in (the) (**3.1**) **avance: d'avance** ahead **avant** before (**6.5**)

un **avant centre** (*soccer*) center forward **avant-garde** avant-garde (*relating to new and experimental methods in the arts*) **avec** with (**1.1**)

l' **avenir** *m.* future

une **aventure** adventure

un **avion** airplane (**5.5**)

un **avis** opinion

un **avocat, une avocate** lawyer (**7.1**)

* **avoir** to have, own (**2.2**) **avoir...ans** to be . . . (years old) (**3.3**) **avoir besoin de** to need (**4.4**) **avoir chaud** to be (feel) warm (**4.4**) **avoir de la chance** to be lucky (**4.4**) **avoir envie de** to want, feel like (having) (**4.4**) **avoir faim** to be hungry (**4.4**) **avoir froid** to be (feel) cold (**4.4**) **avoir l'air** to seem, look (**6.1**) **avoir mal (à)** to be in pain, have a sore . . . (**6.1**) **avoir raison** to be right (**4.4**) **avoir soif** to be thirsty (**4.4**) **avoir tort** to be wrong (**4.4**) **avril** April (**P.5**) **poisson d'avril** April fools'

b

le **bac, baccalauréat** *diploma given at the end of secondary school*

bain: un bain de soleil sun-bath   une salle de bains bathroom (6.2)

un bal dance, ball

un ballon ball

une banane banana (8.4)

une bande dessinée comic strip   des bandes dessinées comics (7.5)

une banque bank

des bas stockings (4.3)   bas sur pattes short-legged

le basket, basketball basketball (3.2)

un basset basset-hound

un bateau (pl. bateaux) boat (5.5)

le bavardage gossip

beau (bel, belle; beaux) good-looking, beautiful (2.1) (4.3)   il fait beau it's nice (weather) (P.6)

beaucoup (de) much, very much, a lot (1.3) (8.2)

bel (see beau) good-looking, beautiful (4.3)

belge Belgian (2.4)

la Belgique Belgium (2.4)

belle (see beau) good-looking, beautiful (2.1) (4.3)

besoin: avoir besoin de to need (4.4)

bête silly, stupid (2.3)

le beurre butter (8.4)

une bibliothèque library (3.1)

une bicyclette bicycle (2.2)   aller à bicyclette to go by bicycle (5.5)

bien well (1.1)   bien sûr sure, of course (1.2)   ça va (très) bien I'm/everything's (very) well (P.2)   c'est bien that's good (fine) (2.5)   eh bien! well! (2.3)   être bien to be well, feel good (6.1)

la bière beer (5.2)

le bifteck steak

un billet bill, bank note (4.1) ticket (6.4)

bizarre bizarre, strange

blanc (blanche) white (2.2)

bleu blue (2.2)

blond blond (2.1)

un blue-jeans (pair of) jeans (4.2)

∗ boire to drink (5.2)

une boisson drink, beverage (5.2)

une boîte box   une boîte aux lettres mailbox

une bombe bomb

bon (bonne) good (2.3)   ah bon! all right! (3.4)   bon marché inexpensive (4.1)   bon voyage! have a good trip!   il fait bon it's fine (pleasant) (weather) (P.6)

des bonbons m. candy (4.5)

le bonheur happiness

bônjour hello, good morning, good afternoon (P.1)

bonsoir good evening

une botte boot (4.2)

une bouche mouth (6.1)

un boucher, une bouchère butcher

un boulanger, une boulangère baker

les boules f. bowling

une bouteille bottle (8.5)

une boutique boutique, shop

un bras arm (6.1)

brésilien (brésilienne) Brazilian

bricoler to build and fix things

brillamment brilliantly

brillant brilliant, bright (8.2)

brun dark-haired (2.1)

une brute brute   comme des brutes like mad

bu (p. part. of boire) (6.3)

un buffet buffet spread

buissonnière: l'école buissonnière playing hooky

un bureau desk (6.2)   un bureau de tabac tobacco shop

un bus bus (5.5)

un but goal   un gardien de but goalie   une ligne de but goal line

buvez drink

c

c' (see ce)

ça that, it   ça dépend it depends (4.1)   ça n'a pas d'importance it doesn't matter (3.1)   ça ne fait rien it doesn't matter (7.4)   ça suffit! that's enough! (7.5)   ça va? how are you? how's everything? (P.2)   ça va everything's fine (going well); fine, I'm OK, everything's all right (P.2); good   c'est ça! that's it! that's right! (2.1)   comme ci, comme ça so-so (P.2)

un cadeau (pl. cadeaux) gift, present

le café coffee (5.2)

un café café (French coffee shop) (3.1)

une cafétéria cafeteria (3.1)

une calculatrice calculator

un calendrier date book

calme calm (8.2)

calmement calmly (8.2)

un camarade, une camarade classmate, school friend (2.1)

une caméra movie camera (2.2)

la campagne country, countryside (3.1)

le Canada Canada (2.4)   canadien (canadienne) Canadian (2.4)

un canard duck

un canari canary

un caniche poodle

un canoë canoe

la Cantatrice chauve The Bald Soprano (play by Eugène Ionesco)

une cantine cafeteria, school cafeteria

une capitale capital

capricieux (capricieuse) capricious

un caractère character

un cardiologue cardiologist

le Carnaval winter carnival celebration in Nice and other French-speaking cities, held at Mardi Gras

un carnet notebook

une carotte carrot (8.4)

carré square   le Vieux Carré the French Quarter in New Orleans

une carte map; card (7.5)   jouer aux cartes to play cards (3.2)   une carte postale postcard (7.5)

un cas case   dans ce cas in that case (7.3)

un casque helmet

un casse-pieds "pain (in the neck)"

casser to break (7.5)

une **cassette** cassette (**2.2**)
cause: à cause de because of (**8.1**)
ce (c') this, that, it **ce que** that **ce sont** these are, those are, they are (**2.4**)
c'est that's, it's (**P.1**) he's, she's (**2.3**) **c'est-à-dire** that is to say **c'est ça!** that's it! that's right! (**2.1**) **c'est combien?** how much is it? (**P.3**) **c'est...francs** it's . . . francs (**P.3**) **c'est le (10 septembre)** it's (September 10th) (**P.5**) **qu'est-ce que c'est?** what is it? what's this? (**4.1**)
ce (cet, cette; ces) this, that, these, those (**4.2**) **ce...-ci** this (over here) (**4.2**) **ce...-là** that (over there) (**4.2**) **ce soir** tonight, this evening (**4.2**)
cela that (**8.1**) **pour cela** because of that, for that reason (**8.1**)
célèbre famous (**8.1**)
célébrer to celebrate (**8.4**)
le **céleri** celery
cent one hundred (**4.1**) **pour cent** percent
un **centime** centime (*1/100 of a franc*)
central center **un arrière central** (*soccer*) center halfback
un **centre** center **un avant centre** (*soccer*) center forward
cependant nevertheless
une **cerise** cherry (**8.4**)
certain certain **certains** some, some people
certainement certainly (**5.5**)
ces these, those (**4.2**)
c'est (*see* ce)
c'est-à-dire that is to say
cet this, that (**4.2**)
cette this, that (**4.2**)
chacun each one, every one
une **chaise** chair (**6.2**)
une **chambre** room; bedroom (**6.2**)
un **champion, une championne** champion
un **championnat** championship
les **Champs-Élysées** m. *avenue in Paris*

chance: avoir de la chance to be lucky (**4.4**)
un **changement** change **changer** to change
une **chanson** song
le **chantage** blackmail **chanter** to sing (**1.4**)
un **chanteur, une chanteuse** singer
un **chapeau** (*pl.* **chapeaux**) hat (**4.3**)
chaque each, every
la **chasse** hunting
un **chat** cat (**3.4**)
chaud warm, hot (**4.2**) **avoir chaud** to be (feel) warm (**4.4**) **il fait chaud** it's hot (weather) (**P.6**)
une **chaussette** sock (**4.2**)
une **chaussure** shoe (**4.2**) **des chaussures de ski** ski boots
un **chef** head, chef
une **chemise** shirt (**4.3**)
un **chemisier** blouse (**4.3**)
cher (chère) expensive (**4.1**) dear (**4.4**)
chercher to look for, pick up, get (**7.1**)
un **cheval** (*pl.* **chevaux**) horse (**3.4**)
les **cheveux** m. hair (**6.1**)
chez at/to . . .'s (house) (**3.2**); in **chez (le pharmacien)** at/to (the pharmacist's) (**4.5**) **chez moi (toi, lui...)** (at) home (**3.2**)
chic nice; elegant, in style (**4.2**)
un **chien** dog (**3.4**)
la **chimie** chemistry
un **chimiste** chemist
la **Chine** China (**2.4**)
chinois Chinese (**2.4**)
un **chirurgien** surgeon
un **chocolat** chocolate, cocoa
choisir to choose (**4.1**)
un **choix** choice
une **chose** thing (**6.3**) **quelque chose** something, anything (**7.4**)
ci: ce...-ci this . . . (over here) (**4.2**) **ce mois-ci** this month (**4.2**) **ci-dessus** above
le **cidre** cider
le **cinéma** movies (**5.1**)
un **cinéma** movie theater (**3.1**)

cinq five (**P.3**)
cinquante fifty (**P.3**)
cinquième fifth (**3.4**)
une **clarinette** clarinet (**3.2**)
une **classe** class **en classe** in class (**1.5**) to class (**3.1**) **classique** classical
une **clé** key **un mot clé** key word, practice word
un **client, une cliente** client, customer
une **cloche** bell
un **coca** Coke (**5.2**)
un **Coca-Cola** Coca-Cola (**5.2**)
un **cochon** pig
un **cœur** heart (**6.1**)
une **coïncidence** coincidence **colère: en colère** angry **collectionner** to collect
un **collège** (un **Collège d'Enseignement Secondaire**) junior high school
une **colonne** column
combien how much (**P.3**) **c'est combien?** how much is it? (**P.3**) **combien de** how much, how many (**4.1**)
une **comédie** comedy (**5.1**) une **comédie musicale** musical comedy (**5.1**)
un **comédien, une comédienne** comedian
commander to command; to order (**5.2**)
comme like, as (**4.4**) **comme ci, comme ça** so-so (**P.2**)
commencer to begin, start (**6.3**)
comment how (**1.3**) what (**2.1**) **comment allez-vous?** how are you? (**P.2**) **comment dit-on?** how do you say? (**4.5**) **comment est-il/elle?** what's he/she like? what does he/she look like? (**2.1**) **comment s'appelle...?** what's . . .'s name? (**2.1**) **comment s'appelle-t-il/elle?** what's his/her name? (**2.1**) **comment t'appelles-tu?** what's your name? (**P.2**) **comment vas-tu?** how are you? (**P.2**)
un **commentaire** comment
un **commerçant, une commerçante** shopkeeper

commet: on commet un excès one overdoes things

commun: en commun in common

une **compagnie** company

un **compagnon** companion

une **comparaison** comparison

comparer to compare

un **complément** object

complet (complète) complete

complétant: en complétant by completing

compléter to complete

un **compliment** compliment **faire un compliment** to pay a compliment

compliqué complicated (4.5)

composer to compose

* **comprendre** to understand (5.5)

compris included

compris (*p. part. of* **comprendre**) (6.4)

compter to count

un **concert** concert (3.1)

conduit: elle a conduit she drove

la **confiture** jam (8.4)

un **conflit** conflict

le **confort** comfort

confortable comfortable

conjugué conjugated

une **connaissance** acquaintance **faire connaissance avec** to meet **faire la connaissance de** to meet

connaissent: ils connaissent they know

connaissez: vous connaissez you know

* **connaître** to know, be acquainted with (7.2)

connu (*p. part. of* **connaître**) (7.2)

un **conseil** (piece of) advice (7.5) **des conseils** advice

conservateur (conservatrice) conservative (4.3)

consister to consist

constamment constantly

consulter to consult

contagieux (contagieuse) contagious

content happy (8.5)

contiennent: ils contiennent they contain

continuellement continually

continuer to continue

contradiction: l'esprit *m.* **de contradiction** disagreeing

le **contraire** opposite **au contraire** on the contrary (1.2)

contre against, in exchange for

un **contrôle** control

convient: qui convient (that is) appropriate

un **copain, une copine** friend, pal (7.3)

le **corps** body

une **correspondance** correspondence

correspondant that corresponds

correspondre to correspond, match

un **costume** suit (4.3) costume (8.1)

la **côte** coast

la **Côte d'Azur** Riviera (*southern coast of France on the Mediterranean*)

la **Côte-d'Ivoire** Ivory Coast (*French-speaking country in West Africa*)

côté: à côté de next to

une **couleur** color **de quelle couleur?** what color? (2.2)

une **coupe** cup

courant everyday

un **cours** street, drive, parkway

une **course** race, errand **faire les courses** to go shopping (5.4)

court short (4.3)

un **court de tennis** tennis court

un **cousin, une cousine** cousin (3.2)

le **coût** cost

un **couteau** (*pl.* **couteaux**) knife (8.5)

coûter to cost (4.1)

un **couturier** fashion designer

une **couverture** cover

une **cravate** tie (4.3)

un **crémier, une crémière** dairy person

le **créole** Creole (*French dialect spoken in Louisiana and the Caribbean*)

un **crétin, une crétine** cretin, idiot

un **critique** critic

critiquer to criticize

croisé: un mot croisé crossword puzzle

un **croissant** crescent roll

une **cuillère** spoon (8.5)

la **cuisine** cooking (5.3)

une **cuisine** kitchen (6.2)

une **cuisinière** cook (*female*) (8.4)

culturel (culturelle) cultural

curieux (curieuse) curious

la **curiosité** curiosity

d

d' (*see* **de**) (1.1)

d'abord first

d'accord okay, all right (2.1) **être d'accord** to agree (2.1)

une **dame** lady, woman (*polite term*) (2.1)

dangereux (dangereuse) dangerous (5.3)

dans in (3.3)

la **danse** dance (5.3)

danser to dance (1.2)

la **date** date (P.5)

d'avance ahead

de from, of, about (1.1) **de l'après-midi** in the afternoon, P.M. (P.4) **pas de** not a, not any, no (2.2)

décembre December (P.5)

décider to decide (6.4)

décorer to decorate

découvert (*p. part. of* **découvrir**) (8.4)

* **découvrir** to discover (8.4)

* **décrire** to describe (7.5)

décrivant describing

un **défaut** shortcoming

défini definite

un **degré** degree **il fait...degrés** it's . . . degrees (P.6)

la **dégustation** tasting

dehors outside

déjà ever; already (8.4)

déjeuner to have (eat) lunch (8.5)

le **déjeuner** lunch (8.5) **le petit déjeuner** breakfast (8.5)

délicat delicate

demain tomorrow (P.5)

demander to ask (3.5) ask for (7.4) **se demander** to wonder

demi: ...heure(s) et demie half past . . . (P.4) **midi et demi** half past twelve (*noon*) **minuit et demi** half past twelve (*midnight*)

un **demi (gauche, droit)** (*soccer*) (left, right) halfback
une **démocratie** democracy
un **démon** devil
démonstratif (démonstrative) demonstrative
une **dent** tooth (**6.1**)
un **dentiste, une dentiste** dentist
un **départ** departure, leaving
dépend: ça dépend it depends (**4.1**)
dépendre to depend
une **dépense** expense (**7.4**)
dépenser to spend (**4.1**)
dernier (dernière) last (**6.2**)
derrière behind (**8.3**)
des some, any (**2.4**) of (the), from (the), about (the) (**3.2**)
un **désastre** disaster
descendre to go down (**6.5**)
descendre de to get off, out of (**7.5**)
désirer to wish, want (**1.4**)
désobéir to disobey (**6.4**)
désolé sorry
un **désordre** disorder
un **dessert** dessert (**5.2**)
le **dessin** art, drawing (**5.3**)
un dessin animé cartoon (**5.1**)
dessinée: une bande dessinée comic strip **des bandes dessinées** comics (**7.5**)
dessiner to draw
déterminer to determine
détester to dislike, hate (**1.4**)
deux two (**P.3**)
deuxième second (**3.4**)
devant in front of (**8.3**)
développé developed
deviennent: ils/elles deviennent they become
* **devoir** to have to, should, must (**8.1**)
les **devoirs** *m.* homework
d'habitude usually
un **diamant** diamond
un **dictionnaire** dictionary
Dieu *m.* God **mon Dieu!** my goodness!
difficile hard, difficult (**2.5**)
dimanche *m.* Sunday (**P.5**)
dîner to have (eat) dinner (**1.1**) to have (eat) supper (**8.5**)
le **dîner** dinner, supper (**8.5**)

diplomate diplomatic
* **dire** to say, tell (**7.5**)
c'est-à-dire that is to say
vouloir dire to mean (**8.1**)
directement directly
un **directeur, une directrice** director, principal
dis (donc)! say! hey! (**1.4**)
discuter to argue; to discuss, talk about (**7.4**)
disposer (de) to have to spend
une **dispute** dispute, quarrel
un **disque** record (**2.2**)
distinct distinct (**8.2**)
distinctement distinctly (**8.2**)
une **distraction** leisure activity
dit (*p. part. of* **dire**) (**7.5**)
dit: comment dit-on? how do you say? (**4.5**) **il/elle dit** he/she says **on dit** people say
dites: vous dites you say, tell **dites (donc)!** say! hey! (**1.4**)
divers diverse, different
dix ten (**P.3**)
dix-huit eighteen (**P.3**)
dixième tenth (**3.4**)
dix-neuf nineteen (**P.3**)
dix-sept seventeen (**P.3**)
un **docteur** doctor (**6.1**)
doit: il doit he should **on doit** one must
un **domaine** domain, area
domestique domestic
dommage too bad (**1.1**) **c'est dommage** that's too bad (**1.1**)
donc therefore (**8.5**) **dis (dites) donc!** say! hey! (**1.4**)
donner to give (**7.1**) **donne-moi, donnez-moi** give me (**P.3**)
* **dormir** to sleep (**6.5**)
un **dos** back (**6.1**)
doublé dubbed
douze twelve (**P.3**)
douzième twelfth (**3.4**)
un **drame** drama (**5.1**) tragedy (**8.5**)
droit: un ailier droit (*soccer*) right wing **un arrière droit** (*soccer*) right fullback **un demi droit** (*soccer*) right halfback **un inter droit** (*soccer*) right inside

droite: à droite de to the right of (**8.3**)
drôle funny (**2.3**)
du of (the), from (the), about (the) (**3.2**) some, any (**5.2**) **du matin** in the morning, A.M. (**P.4**) **du soir** in the evening, P.M. (**P.4**)
dû (*p. part. of* **devoir**) (**8.1**)
dynamique energetic

e

l' **eau** *f.* water (**5.2**) **l'eau de cologne** cologne **l'eau minérale** mineral water (**5.2**)
un **échange** trade, exchange
échanger to trade, exchange
les **échecs** *m.* chess (**3.2**)
un **éclair** eclair (*pastry*)
une **école** school (**3.1**) **l'école buissonnière** playing hooky
économies: faire des économies to save money
économique economical
économiser to save, economize
un **économiste, une économiste** economist
écossais Scottish
écouter to listen (to) (**1.4**)
écoute! écoutez! listen! (**2.5**)
* **écrire** to write (**7.5**)
écrit written
écrit (*p. part. of* **écrire**) (**7.5**)
écrit: il/elle écrit he/she writes
un **écrivain** writer
l' **éducation** *f.* education, manners **l'éducation physique** physical education
effet: en effet in effect, indeed
efficace effective
un **effort** effort **faire beaucoup d'efforts** to try hard
égaler to equal
une **église** church (**3.1**)
l' **Égypte** *f.* Egypt (**2.4**)
égyptien (égyptienne) Egyptian (**2.4**)
eh! hey! (**1.4**) **eh bien!** well! (**2.3**)
l' **électronique** *f.* electronics
un **électrophone** record player (**2.2**)

l' **élégance** f. elegance, style
élégant well-dressed; elegant (**4.3**)
élémentaire elementary
un **élève**, une **élève** (high school) student (**2.1**)
élevé: bien élevé well-behaved, polite (**7.5**)
l' **élision** f. elision (*in French, the dropping of a final vowel*)
elle she (**1.2**) it (**2.2**) her (**2.5**)
elles they (**1.2**) them (**2.5**)
éloignée: la famille éloignée distant family (**3.3**)
embêtant annoying
un **empereur** emperor
un **employé**, une **employée** employee, salesperson
emprunter to borrow (**3.2**)
en in, to (**4.5**); by **en automne (hiver, été)** in (the) fall (winter, summer) (**P.6**) **en classe** in class (**1.5**) to class (**3.1**) **en vacances** on vacation (**1.5**) **en ville** downtown, in town (**1.5**)
en from there, of (about) it/them (**8.3**) some, any (**8.4**)
enchanté delighted
encore still
un **endroit** place
l' **énergie** f. energy
des **enfants** m. children (**3.3**)
enfin finally, at last (**6.3**)
une **énigme** enigma, mystery
enlever to remove
un **ennemi**, une **ennemie** enemy
une **enquête** survey
l' **enseignement** m. teaching
enseigner to teach
ensemble together, at the same time (**6.1**)
ensuite then, after (**6.2**); afterward(s)
entendre to hear (**4.5**)
entier (entière) entire
entraider: s'entraider to help one another
entre between (**8.3**)
une **entrée** first course (*of a meal*)
entrer (dans) to enter, go in (**6.5**)
l' **envie** f. desire **avoir envie de** to want, feel like (having) (**4.4**)

épais thick
une **épicerie** grocery (**4.5**)
un **épicier**, une **épicière** grocer (**4.5**)
une **épidémie** epidemic
l' **équilibre** m. balance
une **équipe** team (**6.3**)
un **équipement** equipment
équitable fair
une **erreur** error
un **esclave** slave
l' **espace** m. space **les espaces sous-marins** undersea world
l' **Espagne** f. Spain (**2.4**)
espagnol Spanish (**2.4**)
l' **espagnol** m. Spanish (*language*)
une **espèce** kind
espérer to hope (**5.1**)
l' **esprit** m. spirit, mind **l'esprit de contradiction** disagreeing
l' **essentiel** m. important thing
est: il/elle est he/she/it is **est-ce que** *phrase used to introduce a question* (**1.2**) **quel jour est-ce?** what day is it? (**P.5**) **qui est-ce?** who's that? who is it? (**P.1**)
l' **est** m. east
un **estomac** stomach
et and (**P.3**) **et alors?** so what? (**1.5**)
établir to establish
un **étage** floor
un **état** state
les **États-Unis** m. United States (**2.4**)
été (*p. part. of* **être**) (**6.2**)
l' **été** m. summer (**4.2**) **en été** in (the) summer (**P.6**)
éternellement eternally
étrange strange (**7.2**)
étranger (étrangère) foreign **à l'étranger** abroad
un **étranger**, une **étrangère** foreigner
* **être** to be (**1.5**) **être à** to belong to (**3.5**) **être bien** to be well, feel good (**6.1**) **être d'accord** to agree (**2.1**)
une **étude** study
un **étudiant**, une **étudiante** (college) student (**2.1**)
étudier to study (**1.2**)
eu (*p. part. of* **avoir**) (**6.3**)
euh... er . . . , uh . . . (**P.6**)
l' **Europe** f. Europe (**2.4**)

européen (européenne) European
eux them (**2.5**)
un **événement** event (**6.3**)
évidemment of course (**4.3**)
exactement exactly
un **examen** exam, test
excellent excellent (**5.3**)
exceptionnel (exceptionnelle) exceptional
excès: on commet un excès one overdoes things
excuser: s'excuser to excuse oneself, be sorry **excusez-moi** excuse me
un **exemple** example **par exemple** for example, for instance (**8.2**)
exercer to exercise
explique: tout s'explique everything is clear
un **explorateur**, une **exploratrice** explorer
explorer to explore
exportation: une compagnie d'exportation export company
une **exposition** exhibit
exprimer to express
extérieur exterior, outside
extra, extraordinaire extraordinary, great
extrêmement extremely

f

facile easy (**2.5**)
une **façon** fashion, way, manner (**8.2**) **d'une façon** in a way (**8.2**)
la **faim** hunger **avoir faim** to be hungry (**4.4**)
* **faire** to do, make (**5.4**) **faire attention** to pay attention, be careful (**5.4**) **faire de** + *activity* to do, play, study, participate in (**5.4**) **faire des progrès** to make progress (**5.4**) **faire des projets** to make plans (**5.4**) **faire les courses** to go shopping (**5.4**) **faire un match** to play a game, match (**5.4**) **faire un voyage** to take a trip (**5.4**)

411

faire une promenade (à pied, en voiture) to take a walk, drive (**5.5**)   **se faire** to make

fait (*p. part. of* **faire**) (**6.2**)

fait: en fait in fact

fait: ça ne fait rien it doesn't matter (**7.4**)   **il fait (beau, bon, chaud, frais, froid, mauvais)** it's (nice, fine, hot, cool, cold, bad) weather (**P.6**)   **il fait...degrés** it's . . . degrees (**P.6**)   **il fait moins...** it's . . . (degrees) below (zero) (**P.6**)   **il fait zéro** it's 0° (**P.6**)   **quel temps fait-il?** how (what) is the weather? (**P.6**)   **quelle température fait-il?** what's the temperature? (**P.6**)

fameux (fameuse) famous, great

familial (of the) family

une **famille** family (**3.3**)   **en famille** at home   **la famille éloignée** distant family (**3.3**)   **la famille proche** immediate family (**3.3**)

un **fana,** une **fana** fan

fantastique fantastic; great, terrific (**2.2**)

fascinant fascinating

fatigué tired (**4.4**)

un **fauteuil** armchair (**6.2**)

faux (fausse) false, wrong (**2.5**)

favori (favorite) favorite (**7.5**)

favorisé favored

félicitations! congratulations! (**8.3**)

féliciter to congratulate

féminin feminine

une **femme** woman (**2.1**); wife

une **fenêtre** window (**8.3**)

fermer to close, shut (**8.3**)

la **ferveur** fervor

un **festin** feast

une **fête** holiday, feast, party

février February (**P.5**)

la **fièvre** fever, temperature (**6.1**)

une **figure** face (**6.1**); figure

une **fille** girl (**2.1**) daughter (**3.3**)

un **film** movie (**5.1**)   **un film d'aventures** adventure movie (**5.1**)   **un film policier** detective movie (**5.1**)

un **fils** son (**3.3**)

fin fine

la **fin** end

finalement finally (**6.3**)

fini over, finished

finir to finish (**4.1**)

fixement: regarder fixement to stare at

flambé flaming

flatter to flatter

une **fleur** flower

une **flûte** flute (**3.2**)

fois times

une **fois** time

folie: à la folie madly

le **foot, football** soccer (**3.2**)   **jouer au football** to play soccer (**3.2**)

le **footing** jogging (**5.3**)

une **forme** form   **en forme** in shape

formidable great, terrific (**2.2**)

fort strong

fou (folle) crazy

un **foulard** scarf

une **fourchette** fork (**8.5**)

frais: il fait frais it's cool (weather) (**P.6**)

une **fraise** strawberry (**8.4**)

franc (franche) frank

un **franc** franc (*monetary unit of France, Belgium, and Switzerland*)

français French (**2.4**)

le **français** *m.* French (*language*)

un **Français,** une **Française** French person (**2.4**)

la **France** France (**2.4**)

francophone French-speaking

un **frère** brother (**3.2**)

des **frites** *f.* French fries (**8.4**)

froid cold   **avoir froid** to be (feel) cold (**4.4**)   **il fait froid** it's cold (weather) (**P.6**)

le **fromage** cheese (**5.2**)

un **fruit** fruit (**8.4**)

fumer to smoke

furieux (furieuse) furious, mad, angry (**8.5**)

g

gagner to win (**6.3**); to earn

une **galerie** gallery

le **galop** gallop

un **garçon** boy (**2.1**)   waiter (**7.1**)

un **gardien de but** goalie

une **gare** train station

un **gâteau** (*pl.* **gâteaux**) cake (**4.4**)

gauche left   **à gauche de** to the left of (**8.3**)   **un ailier gauche** (*soccer*) left wing   **un arrière gauche** (*soccer*) left fullback   **un demi gauche** (*soccer*) halfback   **un inter gauche** (*soccer*) left inside

géant giant

gelée: en gelée jellied

général (*pl.* **généraux**) general (**8.2**)   **en général** in general

généralement generally (**8.2**)

généraliste: un médecin généraliste general practitioner

généreux (généreuse) generous (**4.3**)

la **générosité** generosity

génial (*pl.* **géniaux**) bright, brilliant, very smart (**7.2**)

un **génie** genius

le **genre** gender

les **gens** *m.* people (**7.5**)

la **géographie** geography

géographique geographic

une **glace** mirror; ice cream (**5.2**)

une **gorge** throat (**6.1**)   **avoir mal à la gorge** to have a sore throat (**6.1**)

gourmand who likes food (**7.3**)

un **gourmand,** une **gourmande** person who likes to eat

grâce à thanks to

grand tall, big (**2.1**)   **des grandes personnes** *f.* adults   **un grand magasin** department store (**4.1**)

une **grand-mère** grandmother (**3.3**)

un **grand-père** grandfather (**3.3**)

les **grands-parents** grandparents (**3.3**)

gratuit free

grave serious

la **Grèce** Greece

un **grenier** attic

une **griffe** label

la grippe flu (6.1)
gris gray (2.2)
gros (grosse) fat (4.4); big (4.4)
grossir to get fat, gain weight (4.1)
la Guadeloupe Guadeloupe (*a French island in the West Indies*)
une guerre war
une guitare guitar (2.2)
la gymnastique gymnastics (5.3)

h

h. =heure(s) (P.4)
habillé dressed
habiter to live (1.1)
une habitude habit d'habitude usually
haïtien (haïtienne) Haitian
des•haricots *m.* string beans (8.4)
•hasard: par hasard by any chance
hélas too bad; unfortunately, alas (8.4)
un hélicoptère helicopter
un•héros hero
l' heure *f.* time, hour à...heure(s) at . . . (o'clock) (P.4) à quelle heure? (at) what time? (P.4) ...heure(s) (dix) (ten) past . . . (P.4) ...heure(s) et demie half past . . . (P.4) ...heure(s) et quart quarter past . . . (P.4) ...heure(s) moins (dix) (ten) of . . . (P.4) ...heure(s) moins le quart quarter of . . . (P.4) il est...heure(s) it is . . . (o'clock) (P.4) quelle heure est-il? what time is it? (P.4)
heureusement fortunately (8.2)
hier yesterday (6.2)
une histoire story, history (7.5)
historique historical
l' hiver *m.* winter (4.2) en hiver in (the) winter (P.6)
•hm! *used to show you hear what is said, but you do not want to answer* (4.4)
le•hockey hockey jouer au hockey to play hockey

un homme man (2.1)
un hôpital (*pl.* hôpitaux) hospital (3.1)
l' horreur *f.* horror quelle horreur! how awful!
l' huile *f.* oil (8.4)
•huit eight (P.3)
•huitième eighth (3.4)
l' humeur *f.* mood être de bonne (mauvaise) humeur to be in a good (bad) mood (7.5)
un hypermarché shopping center
hypocrite hypocritical

i

ici here (1.5)
l' idéalisme *m.* idealism
une idée idea (4.4) changer d'idée to change one's mind (4.4)
idiot stupid (7.2) faire l'idiot to act dumb
une idole idol
il he (1.2) it (2.2) il y a there is, there are (2.4)
une île island
illustre well-known
ils they (1.2)
imaginer to imagine
imiter to imitate
immédiatement immediately
un immeuble apartment house
l' impératif *m.* imperative (command) tense
l' importance *f.* importance ça n'a pas d'importance it doesn't matter (3.1)
impossible impossible
incomplet (incomplète) incomplete
indéfini indefinite
indiqué indicated
indiscret (indiscrète) indiscreet
indispensable necessary
indisposé indisposed, uncomfortable
individuel (individuelle) individual
infiniment terribly
un infinitif infinitive
influencer to influence
l' information *f.* information
informé informed
un ingénieur engineer (7.1)
inimaginable unimaginable
l' injustice *f.* injustice

inscrit registered
insister to insist
un instrument instrument (3.2)
insulter to insult
intellectuel (intellectuelle) intellectual
intelligent intelligent (2.1)
un inter (gauche, droit) (*soccer*) (left, right) inside
interdit prohibited, forbidden
intéressant interesting (2.1)
international (*pl.* internationaux) international
un interprète, une interprète interpreter, translator (7.1)
interrogatif (interrogative) interrogative
l' interrogation *f.* interrogation, asking questions
interroger to ask
introduire to introduce
inutile useless (7.5)
les Invalides *m.* monument in Paris, Napoleon's tomb
inventer to invent
un inventeur, une inventrice inventor
une inversion inversion, turning around
invité invited
un invité, une invitée guest (8.5)
inviter to invite (1.1)
irlandais Irish
l' Italie *f.* Italy (2.4)
italien (italienne) Italian (2.4)
l' italien *m.* Italian (*language*)

j

j' (*see* je) (1.1)
jamais never ne...jamais never (7.1)
une jambe leg (6.1)
le jambon ham (5.2)
janvier January (P.5)
le Japon Japan (2.4)
japonais Japanese (2.4)
le japonais Japanese (*language*)
jaune yellow (2.2)
je I (1.1)
un jeu (*pl.* jeux) game (3.2) les Jeux Olympiques Olympic Games
jeudi *m.* Thursday (P.5)
jeune young (3.3)
les jeunes *m.* young people (4.2)

413

le jogging jogging (5.3)
joli pretty (2.3)
joué played
jouer to play (1.1) to act (8.1) **jouer à** + *sport, game* to play (3.2) **jouer de** + *instrument* to play (3.2)
un joueur, une joueuse player (6.3)
un jour day (P.5) **au jour le jour** from day to day **le Jour de l'An** New Year's Day **quel jour est-ce?** what day is it? (P.5) **tous les jours** every day
un journal (*pl.* **journaux**) paper, newspaper (4.5); diary **chez le marchand de journaux** at the newsstand
un journaliste, une journaliste journalist (7.1)
une journée day, whole day (7.5)
joyeux (joyeuse) happy
juger to judge
juillet July (P.5)
juin June (P.5)
un jumeau, une jumelle twin
une jupe skirt (4.3)
le jus d'orange orange juice (5.2)
jusqu'à until (6.5)
juste fair
justement in fact, precisely

k

un kilo kilogram
un kilomètre kilometer

l

l' (*see* **le, la**) (2.1)
la the (2.1) her, it (7.2)
là there (1.5); here **ce...là** that . . . (over there) (4.2) **oh là là!** oh dear! wow! whew! (P.3)
là-bas over there (1.5)
la laine wool
le lait milk (5.2)
une lampe lamp (6.2)
le langage language
une langue language, tongue
une larme tear

le the (2.1) him, it (7.2)
le (lundi) on (Mondays) (5.1)
une leçon lesson
légendaire legendary
un légume vegetable (8.4)
les the (2.4) them (7.2)
une lettre letter (7.5)
leur, leurs their (3.4)
leur (to) them (7.4)
la liaison *linking of two words*
libéral (*pl.* **libéraux**) liberal
libérer to liberate, free
la liberté liberty
un libraire, une libraire bookseller, bookstore owner (4.5)
une librairie bookstore (4.5)
libre free
un lieu (*pl.* **lieux**) place
une ligne line **une ligne de touche** (*soccer*) touch line, side line
une limite limit
limité limited
la limonade lemon soda (5.2)
✱ **lire** to read (7.5)
lis: je lis I read
lisez read
une liste list
un lit bed (6.2) **au lit** in bed
un livre book (2.2)
logique logical
logiquement logically
loin de far from (8.3)
un loisir leisure activity
long (longue) long (4.3)
longtemps for a long time (6.3)
longuement a long time
une loterie raffle
le loto lotto, lottery, bingo
un loup wolf
le Louvre *museum in Paris*
lu (*p. part. of* **lire**) (7.5)
lui him (2.5) (to) him, (to) her (7.4)
lundi *m.* Monday (P.5)
la lune moon
des lunettes *f.* glasses (4.2) **des lunettes de soleil** sunglasses (3.1)
un lycée high school

m

M. Mr. (P.1)
m' (*see* **me**) (7.1)

ma my (3.3)
Madame (Mme) Mrs. (P.1)
Mademoiselle (Mlle) Miss (P.1)
un magasin store, shop (4.1) **un grand magasin** department store (4.1)
un magazine magazine (7.5)
magnifique great (1.1) **c'est magnifique** that's great (1.1)
mai May (P.5)
maigrir to get thin, lose weight (4.1)
un maillot (sports) jersey
un maillot de bain bathing suit, swimsuit (4.2)
une main hand (6.1)
maintenant now (1.3)
mais but (1.1) **mais non** of course not (1.2) **mais oui** all right; certainly (1.2)
une maison house (3.1) **à la maison** at home, home (1.5) **la Maison des Jeunes** Youth Center
mal badly, poorly (1.1) **avoir mal (à)** to be in pain, have a sore . . . (6.1) **ça va (très) mal** I'm/everything's (very) bad (P.2) **c'est mal** that's bad (2.5) **mal à l'aise** uncomfortable (ill at ease) **pas mal** not bad (3.3)
malade sick (3.1)
un malade, une malade sick person
malheureusement unfortunately (8.2)
manger to eat (5.2) **une salle à manger** dining room (6.2)
une manière manner, way (8.2) **d'une manière** in a way (8.2)
un manteau (*pl.* **manteaux**) coat (4.3)
m'appelle: je m'appelle my name is (P.2)
un marchand, une marchande merchant, storekeeper, dealer (4.5) **chez le marchand de journaux** at the newsstand
la marche walking

un **marché** market
bon marché inexpensive
(**4.1**) **Au Bon Marché** *department store in Paris* un
marché aux puces flea
market
marcher to work (*function*),
walk (**2.2**); to step on
mardi *m.* Tuesday (**P.5**)
Mardi Gras *m.* Shrove
Tuesday
une **marguerite** daisy
un **mari** husband
le **Maroc** Morocco (*country in
North Africa*)
marquer to mark
mars March (**P.5**)
un **Martiniquais, une Martiniquaise** *person from Martinique*
la **Martinique** Martinique
(*French island in the West
Indies*)
martyriser to make suffer
masculin masculine
un **match** game, (sports) match
(**6.3**) **faire un match** to
play a game, match (**5.4**)
les **maths** *f.* math
un **matin** morning (**4.2**) **du
matin** in the morning, A.M.
(**P.4**) **le matin** in the
morning
mauvais bad (**2.3**) **il fait
mauvais** it's bad (weather)
(**P.6**)
me (to) me (**7.1**)
une **médaille** medal
un **médecin** doctor (**6.1**)
les **médicaments** *m.* medicine
meilleur better (**4.3**) **le
meilleur** best (**4.4**) **un
meilleur ami, une meilleure
amie** best friend (**3.3**)
la **mélancolie** melancholy
un **membre** member
même same, even
un **mensonge** lie (**7.5**)
une **mer** sea **en mer** at sea
les fruits de mer seafood
merci thank you (**P.3**) no
thank you (**5.2**)
mercredi *m.* Wednesday (**P.5**)
une **mère** mother (**3.3**)
mes my (**3.3**)
messieurs gentlemen
une **mesure** measurement

la **météo** weather report
une **méthode** method
un **mètre** meter
métrique metric
un **métro** subway (**5.5**)
un **metteur en scène** director (*of
a play, movie*) (**8.1**)
mettez put
* **mettre** to put, place, put on,
turn on, set, take (*time*) (**6.4**)
un **meuble** piece of furniture
(**6.2**) **les meubles** furniture (**6.2**)
mexicain Mexican (**2.4**)
le **Mexique** Mexico (**2.4**)
midi noon (**P.4**)
mieux better **tant mieux**
so much the better
mignon (mignonne) cute (**7.2**)
mille one thousand (**4.2**)
des **milliers** *m.* thousands
un **million** one million (**4.2**)
un **millionnaire, une millionnaire**
millionaire
mince slim, slender, thin (**4.4**)
minérale: l'eau minérale *f.*
mineral water (**5.2**)
une **mini-cassette** cassette recorder (**2.2**)
minime minimum
minuit midnight (**P.4**)
une **minute** minute **une minute!** just a minute! (**5.4**)
mis (*p. part. of* **mettre**) (**6.4**)
Mlle Miss (**P.1**)
Mme Mrs. (**P.1**)
la **mode** fashion (**4.3**); style
à la mode popular; in fashion, fashionable (**4.3**)
moi me (**2.5**) **moi aussi**
me too (**P.2**)
moins less (**4.3**) **au moins**
at least (**3.2**) **...heure(s)
moins (dix)** (ten) of . . .
(**P.4**) **...heure(s) moins le
quart** quarter of . . .
(**P.4**) **il fait moins...** it's
. . . (degrees) below (zero)
(**P.6**) **le moins** the least
(**4.4**) **moins...que** less . . .
than (**4.3**)
un **mois** month (**P.5**) **ce mois-ci** this month (**4.2**)
un **moment** moment **en ce
moment** at present, right
now (**8.1**)
mon (ma; mes) my (**3.3**)

le **monde** world **tout le
monde** everyone
Monsieur (M.) Mr. (**P.1**)
un **monsieur** (*pl.* **messieurs**) gentleman, man (*polite term*)
(**2.1**)
monter to go up (**6.5**)
monter dans to get on, in
(**7.5**)
une **montre** watch (**2.2**)
montrer to show (**7.4**)
mort (*p. part. of* **mourir**) (**6.5**)
un **mot** word **un mot clé** key
word, practice word
un **mot croisé** crossword puzzle
un **moteur** motor
une **moto** motorcycle (**2.2**)
* **mourir** to die (**6.5**)
la **moutarde** mustard
moyenne: en moyenne on the
average
muet (muette) silent
musclé muscular
un **musée** museum (**3.1**)
musical (*pl.* **musicaux**) musical
un **musicien, une musicienne**
musician
la **musique** music
myope nearsighted
le **mystère** mystery

n

n' (*see* **ne**) (**1.1**)
nager to swim (**1.4**)
la **naissance** birth
* **naître** to be born (**6.5**)
la **natation** swimming (**5.3**)
national (*pl.* **nationaux**) national
une **nationalité** nationality (**2.4**)
les **Nations Unies** *f.* United Nations
naturel (naturelle) natural
(**8.2**)
naturellement naturally (**8.2**)
nautique: le ski nautique
water-skiing
ne...jamais never (**7.1**)
ne...pas not (**1.1**) **n'est-ce
pas?** no? isn't it (so)? right?
(**1.3**)
ne...personne nobody, not anybody (**7.4**)
ne...plus no longer, no more
(**8.5**)

ne...rien nothing, not anything (**7.4**) **ça ne fait rien** it doesn't matter (**7.4**)

né (*p. part. of* **naître**) (**6.5**)

nécessaire necessary

nécessairement necessarily

négatif (négative) negative, "no"

négativement in the negative, saying "no"

neige: il neige it's snowing (**P.6**)

la **neige** snow

nerveux (nerveuse) nervous (**8.2**)

n'est-ce pas? no? isn't it (so)? right? (**1.3**)

neuf nine (**P.3**)

neuvième ninth (**3.4**)

un **nez** nose (**6.1**)

un **niveau** (*pl.* **niveaux**) level

Noël *m.* Christmas

noir black (**2.2**)

un **nom** name, noun

un **nombre** number

nombreux (nombreuse) numerous, many

non no (**P.3**) **mais non** of course not (**1.2**) **non compris** not included **non plus** neither

normal (*pl.* **normaux**) logical **c'est normal** that's logical (normal)

la **Normandie** Normandy (*province in northwestern France*)

nos our (**3.5**)

une **note** note, grade

notre (*pl.* **nos**) our (**3.5**)

nous we (**1.3**) us (**2.5**) (to) us (**7.1**)

nouveau (nouvel, nouvelle; nouveaux) new (**4.3**) **de nouveau** again

nouvelle (*see* nouveau) new (**4.3**)

une **nouvelle** (piece of) news (**6.3**)

la **Nouvelle-Angleterre** New England

novembre November (**P.5**)

un **nuage** cloud

une **nuit** night (**4.2**) **cette nuit** tonight (**4.2**)

un **numéro** number

o

obéir to obey (**6.4**)

un **objectif** objective

un **objet** object, thing

obligatoire required

observer to observe

obstiné obstinate, stubborn

une **occasion** occasion **d'occasion** secondhand

occupé busy (**8.1**)

un **océan** ocean

octobre October (**P.5**)

un **œil** (*pl.* **yeux**) eye (**6.1**)

un **œuf** egg (**8.4**)

offert (*p. part. of* **offrir**) (**8.4**)

* **offrir** to give (*a present*), to offer (**8.4**)

oh là là! oh dear! wow! whew! (**P.3**)

un **oiseau** (*pl.* **oiseaux**) bird (**3.4**)

une **omelette** omelet (**5.2**)

on one, you, they, people, we (**4.5**) **on y va!** let's go!

un **oncle** uncle (**3.3**)

onze eleven (**P.3**)

onzième eleventh (**3.4**)

opposer to match up

l' **optimisme** *m.* optimism

optimiste optimistic

l' **or** *m.* gold

une **orange** orange (*fruit*) (**8.4**)

une **orangeade** orange drink, orange soda

ordinal (*pl.* **ordinaux**) ordinal

un **ordinateur** computer

un **ordre** order

une **oreille** ear (**6.1**)

organisé organized

organiser to organize (**7.3**)

originaire de native of

original (*pl.* **originaux**) original

une **origine** origin

un **os** bone

ou or (**1.1**)

où where (**1.3**)

l' **ouest** *m.* west

oui yes (**P.3**) **mais oui** all right; certainly (**1.2**)

ouvert (*p. part. of* **ouvrir**) (**8.4**)

* **ouvrir** to open (**8.4**)

p

le **Pacifique** Pacific Ocean

le **pain** bread (**5.2**)

une **paire** pair

une **panne** breakdown

un **pantalon** (pair of) pants (**4.2**)

le **papier** paper

Pâques *f.* Easter

par per (**7.4**) **par exemple** for example, for instance (**8.2**) **par hasard** by any chance

un **parc** park (**3.1**)

parce que because (**1.3**)

pardon excuse me (**P.3**)

un **parent** parent, relative (**3.3**)

une **parenthèse** parenthesis

paresseux (paresseuse) lazy

parfait perfect (**4.2**)

parfois sometimes

un **parfum** perfume

parier to bet **je parie que** I bet that (**7.2**)

parisien (parisienne) Parisian

parlant talking

parler to speak, talk (**1.1**)

un **participe** participle

participer à to participate in

particulier (particulière) special

une **partie** part

* **partir** to leave (**6.5**) **partir à** to leave for (*a place*) (**6.5**) **partir de** to leave (*a place*) (**6.5**)

partitif (partitive) partitive

partout everywhere

pas not **ne...pas** not (**1.1**) **pas de** not a, no, not any (**2.2**) **pas du tout** not at all (**1.2**) **pas mal** not bad (**3.3**) **pas question!** nothing doing! no way! (**3.3**)

passé past

le **passé composé** compound past tense

passer to spend (*time*) (**4.5**); to take (*a test*) **passer par** to go by, through (**6.5**)

un **passe-temps** hobby

passionnant exciting (**5.3**)

un **passionné, une passionnée** enthusiast

passionnément passionately

un **patient, une patiente** patient

le **patin à roulettes** roller-skating

le **patinage** skating (5.3)

une **pâtisserie** pastry, pastry shop (4.4)

un **pâtissier, une pâtissière** pastry cook, baker (4.5)

pattes: bas sur pattes short-legged

pauvre poor (3.1)

payer to pay, pay for (4.4)

un **pays** country (2.4)

une **pêche** peach

une **pédale** pedal

un **pédiatre** pediatrician

pendant for (+ *time*), during (6.1) **pendant combien de temps** for how long (6.1)

pénible annoying (2.3)

penser to think (3.5)

perdre to lose, waste (4.5) **perdre son temps** to waste one's time (6.3)

un **père** father (3.3)

un **permis** license

un **perroquet** parrot

un **personnage** character

une **personnalité** personality **personne de** nobody (7.4) **ne...personne** nobody, not any (7.4)

une **personne** person (2.1) **des grandes personnes** adults **des personnes** people **personnel (personnelle)** personal

le **personnel** personnel

personnellement personally

petit short, little (2.1)

un **petit ami** boyfriend (2.3) **une petite amie** girlfriend (2.3)

le **petit déjeuner** breakfast (8.5) **prendre le petit déjeuner** to have (eat) breakfast (8.5)

des **petits pois** *m.* peas (8.4)

peu (de) little, not much (8.2) **un peu** a little, a little bit (1.3)

peut-être maybe, perhaps (2.4)

peux: je peux I may, can **tu peux** you can

une **pharmacie** pharmacy, drug-store (4.5)

un **pharmacien, une pharma-cienne** pharmacist (4.5)

un **philosophe** philosopher

la **photo** photography (5.3)

une **photo** photograph, picture (3.3)

un **photographe, une photographe** photographer

la **photographie** photography

une **phrase** sentence

physique physical

la **physique** physics

un **piano** piano (3.2)

une **pièce** coin (4.1) room (6.2) play (8.1) **une pièce de théâtre** play (5.1)

un **pied** foot (6.1) **à pied** on foot **aller à pied** to walk, go on foot (5.5) **faire une promenade à pied** to take a walk (5.5)

piloter to fly (a plane), pilot

un **pique-nique** picnic (7.3)

une **piscine** swimming pool (3.1)

une **place** (town) square, place; seat (6.4) room (7.5)

une **plage** beach (3.1)

une **plaisanterie** joke

un **plaisir** pleasure

plaît: s'il te (vous) plaît please (P.3)

la **planche à voile** wind-surfing

une **planète** planet

une **plante** plant

un **plat** dish, course (*of a meal*), platter (8.4)

plein full (8.5)

pleut: il pleut it's raining (P.6)

la **pluie** rain

le **pluriel** plural form

plus more (4.3) **le plus** the most (4.4) **moi non plus** me neither **ne...plus** no longer, no more (8.5) **non plus** neither **plus...que** more than, . . .-er than (4.3)

plusieurs several

poche: l'argent *m.* **de poche** pocket money, allowance (7.4)

un **poème** poem (7.5)

un **poil** hair

une **poire** pear (8.4)

un **poisson** fish (3.4) **poisson d'avril** April fools'

un **poisson rouge** goldfish (3.4)

poli polite

policier: un film policier de-tective movie (5.1)

politique political

une **pomme** apple (8.4)

une **pomme de terre** potato (8.4)

ponctuel (ponctuelle) punc-tual, on time

un **pont** bridge

populaire popular

une **porte** door (8.3)

porter to wear (4.2); to bear

poser to ask (*a question*), lay down

possessif (possessive) possessive

des **possessions** *f.* possessions, be-longings

la **poterie** pottery (5.3)

une **poule** hen

le **poulet** chicken (5.2)

un **poumon** lung

pour for (1.5) in order to (6.2) **pour cela** because of that, for that reason (8.1) **pour cent** percent **pour rien** no reason

pourquoi why (1.3)

poursuit: il poursuit he pur-sues

pouvez: vous pouvez you can

* **pouvoir** to be able, can, may (8.1)

pratique practical

pratiquer to practice, play

préféré favorite

préférer to prefer (5.1)

premier (première) first (P.5) (3.4)

la **première** *eleventh school year in France*

* **prendre** to take, have (5.5) **prendre le petit déjeuner** to have (eat) breakfast (8.5)

préparer to prepare

près de next to, near (8.3)

le **présent** present (tense)

une **présentation** introduction

présenté introduced

présenter to introduce, pres-ent (7.1)

presque almost

prêter to lend, loan (7.1)

principal (pl. principaux) prin-cipal, main

le **printemps** spring (4.2) **au printemps** in (the) spring (P.6)

pris (*p. part. of* **prendre**) (6.4)

privé private

417

privé: être privé de to be deprived of

un **privilège** privilege

un **prix** price (4.2); prize

probablement probably

un **problème** problem (4.4)

prochain next (6.2)

proche: la famille proche immediate family (3.3)

un **produit** product (8.4)

un **professeur** teacher (2.1) professor (7.1)

professionnel (professionnelle) professional

un **programmateur, une programmatrice** (computer) programmer

un **programme** program

progrès: faire des progrès to make progress (5.4)

un **projet** plan **faire des projets** to make plans (5.4)

une **promenade** walk, drive **faire une promenade** to take a walk, a drive (5.5) **faire une promenade à pied** to take a walk (5.5) **faire une promenade en voiture** to take a drive (5.5)

* **promettre** to promise (6.4)

promis (*p. part. of* **promettre**) (6.4)

un **pronom** pronoun

proposer to propose; to suggest, offer (6.5)

propre clean

prudent prudent, careful

psychologique psychological

pu (*p. part. of* **pouvoir**) (8.1)

une **puce** flea **un marché aux puces** flea market

puis then, besides, moreover

un **pull, pull-over** sweater, pull-over (4.2)

puni punished

une **punition** punishment

purifier to purify

q

qu' (*see* **que**) (1.2)

une **qualité** quality

quand when (1.3)

une **quantité** quantity

quarante forty (P.3)

quart: ...heure(s) et quart quarter past ... (P.4) **...heure(s) moins le quart** quarter of ... (P.4)

quatorze fourteen (P.3)

quatre four (P.3)

quatre-vingt-dix ninety (4.1)

quatre-vingts eighty (4.1)

quatrième fourth (3.4)

que that (3.5) than, as (4.3); whom **est-ce que** *phrase used to introduce a question* (1.2) **qu'est-ce que** what (4.1) **qu'est-ce que c'est?** what is it? what's this? (4.1) **qu'est-ce qu'il y a?** what's the matter? what is there? (8.5)

quel (quelle) what, which (4.2) **à quelle heure?** (at) what time? (P.4) **quel...!** what a . . .! (6.3) **quel âge as-tu (avez-vous)?** how old are you? (3.3) **quel jour est-ce?** what day is it? (P.5) **quel temps fait-il?** how (what) is the weather? (P.6) **quelle heure est-il?** what time is it? (P.4) **quelle température fait-il?** what's the temperature? (P.6)

quelque some, a few

quelque chose (de) something, anything (7.4)

quelquefois sometimes

quelqu'un (de) someone, somebody, anyone (7.4)

une **question** question **pas question!** nothing doing! no way! (3.5)

qui who, whom (1.5); that **qui est-ce?** who's that? who is it? (P.1)

quinze fifteen (P.3)

quitter to leave

quoi? what? (2.1)

r

raconter to tell (about) (6.3)

radin stingy (7.4)

une **radio** radio (2.2)

un **radis** radish

une **raison** reason **avoir raison** to be right (4.4)

le **rangement** cleaning up

ranger to clean up

rapide quick, rapid (8.2); fast

rapidement rapidly, quickly (8.2)

une **raquette** racket (2.2)

rarement rarely, seldom (1.3)

raté unsuccessful

réaliste realistic

un **réaliste, une réaliste** realist

une **récapitulation** review, summary

récemment recently

les **recettes** *f.* income

recevoir to receive

reçoit: il/elle reçoit he/she receives

une **recommandation** recommendation

reconnaissez: vous reconnaissez you recognize

rectifier to correct

réel (réelle) real

un **réflexe** reflex

un **réfrigérateur** refrigerator

regarder to watch, look at (1.4)

un **régime** diet (4.1) **être au régime** to be on a diet (4.1)

regretter to be sorry

régulier (régulière) regular

régulièrement regularly

relativement relatively

relisez reread

remarquable remarkable (7.2)

remarquablement remarkably

une **remarque** remark

remplacer to replace

remporter to win

une **rencontre** encounter

rencontrer to meet (6.5)

un **rendez-vous** date, appointment (3.1) **j'ai rendez-vous avec** I have a date with (P.5)

rendre to render **rendre visite à** to visit (*people*) (7.4)

les **renseignements** *m.* information

rentrer to come back, go back, go home (1.2)

renversé reversed

un **repas** meal (8.4)

une **répétition** rehearsal (**8.1**)
répondre to answer (**6.3**)
une **réponse** answer
* **reprendre** to have more, take seconds (**8.4**)
une **représentation** performance (**8.1**)
représenter to represent
réservé reserved
réserver to reserve
respecter to respect
respirer to breathe
une **responsabilité** responsibility
un **restaurant** restaurant (**3.1**)
au restaurant at the restaurant (**1.5**)
le **reste** rest **tout le reste** everything else
rester to stay (**3.1**) **il reste** there is (are) . . . left (**8.5**)
retard: de retard behind, late **en retard** late
un **retour** return
une **retraite** retreat
réussir to succeed, pass (*a test*) (**4.1**) to be successful (with) (**6.1**) **ne réussir pas** to fail, flunk (*a test*) (**4.1**)
* **revenir** to come back (**5.4**)
revenu (*p. part. of* **revenir**) (**6.5**)
le **revenu** revenue, income
une **révision** review
revoir: au revoir good-by (**P.1**)
une **revue** magazine (**7.5**)
riche rich (**3.1**)
ridicule ridiculous (**7.2**)
rien de nothing (**7.4**) **ça ne fait rien** it doesn't matter (**7.4**) **ne...rien** nothing, not anything (**7.4**) **pour rien** no reason
une **rivière** river
le **riz** rice (**8.4**)
une **robe** dress (**4.3**)
un **rôle** role, part (**8.1**)
un **roman** novel (**7.5**)
romantique romantic
le **romantisme** romanticism
rond round
le **rosbif** roast beef (**5.2**)
une **roue** wheel
rouge red (**2.2**)

rougir to blush, turn red (**7.3**)
roulettes: le patin à roulettes roller-skating
la **Roumanie** Romania
une **rue** street, road
russe Russian

S

sa his, her, its (**3.4**)
le **sable** sand
un **sac** bag, handbag (**2.2**)
le **Sagittaire** Sagittarius
sais: je ne sais pas I don't know (**P.1**) **je sais** I know (**P.1**)
une **saison** season
une **salade** salad (**5.2**)
la **salle** *inside section of a café;* hall, (theatrical) house (**8.1**) **une salle à manger** dining room (**6.2**) **une salle de bains** bathroom (**6.2**) **une salle de maquillage** dressing room
un **salon** living room (**6.2**) **le salon de la voiture** car show
salut hi (**P.1**)
une **salutation** greeting
samedi *m.* Saturday (**P.5**)
une **sandale** sandal (**4.2**)
sans without (**6.4**)
la **santé** health
s'appelle: comment s'appelle...? what's . . .'s name? (**2.1**) **comment s'appelle-t-il/elle?** what's his/her name? (**2.1**)
sauf except
* **savoir** to know (**7.3**) **savoir + inf.** to know how to, be able to (**7.3**)
un **saxo(phone)** saxophone (**3.2**)
la **scène** scene, stage (**8.1**)
scientifique scientific
un **sculpteur** sculptor
secondaire secondary
une **seconde** second **une seconde!** just a second! (**5.4**)
un **secrétaire, une secrétaire** secretary
seize sixteen (**P.3**)
un **séjour** living room
le **sel** salt (**8.4**)
selon vous in your opinion
une **semaine** week (**P.5**) **en semaine** during the week

semblable similar
le **Sénégal** Senegal (*French-speaking country in West Africa*)
sénégalais Senegalese
un **sens** sense
sensationnel sensational; great, terrific (**2.2**)
sensible aware
sentimental (*pl.* **sentimentaux**) sentimental
s'entraider to help one another
sept seven (**P.3**)
septembre September (**P.5**)
septième seventh (**3.4**)
une **série** series
sérieusement seriously (**8.2**)
sérieux (sérieuse) serious (**8.2**)
sert: on sert they serve
une **serveuse** waitress (**7.1**)
une **serviette** napkin (**8.5**)
ses his, her, its (**3.4**)
seul alone, by oneself (**6.5**)
seulement only
s'excuser to excuse oneself, be sorry
s'expliquer to be clear
un **shampooing** shampoo
un **short** (pair of) shorts (**4.2**)
si if (**3.5**) **si oui ou non** whether or not **s'il te (vous) plaît** please (**P.3**)
si so; yes (*to a negative question*) (**5.2**)
un **signe orthographique** spelling mark
une **signification** significance, meaning
signifier to mean
s'il te (vous) plaît please (**P.3**)
une **silhouette** figure
une **similarité** similarity, likeness
simple simple (**4.5**)
simplement simply
sincère sincere (**2.1**)
la **sincérité** sincerity
situé situated
six six (**P.3**)
sixième sixth (**3.4**)
le **skate, skate-board** skateboarding
un **skate-board** skateboard
le **ski** skiing (**5.3**) **le ski nautique** water-skiing

skier to ski (**1.1**)
snob snobbish, stuck-up (**7.2**)
la **sociabilité** sociability
la **sociologie** sociology
un **sociologue, une sociologue** so-
ciologist
une **sœur** sister (**3.2**)
soif: avoir soif to be thirsty
(**4.4**)
un **soir** evening (**4.2**) **ce soir**
tonight, this evening (**4.2**)
du soir in the evening,
P.M. (**P.4**)
une **soirée** evening
soixante sixty (**P.3**)
soixante-dix seventy (**4.1**)
un **solde** (clearance) sale
le **soleil** sun
un **sommet** summit
son (sa; ses) his, her, its
(**3.4**); one's
un **son** sound
un **sondage** poll **un sondage
d'opinion** opinion poll
sont: ils/elles sont they are
sors: je sors I go out
* **sortir** to go out, get out (**6.5**)
sortir de to get out of (*a
place*) (**6.5**)
la **soupe** soup (**5.2**)
sous under (**8.3**)
sous-marins: les espaces *m.*
sous-marins undersea world
souvent often (**1.3**)
souviens: je me souviens I
remember
soyeux (soyeuse) silky
soyez...! be . . . !
spécial (*pl.* **spéciaux**) special
spécialement especially
spécialisé specialized
un **spécialiste, une spécialiste**
specialist
un **spectacle** show
un **spectateur, une spectatrice**
spectator
un **sport** sport (**3.2**)
sportif (sportive) sportive, who
likes sports, athletic
un **stade** stadium (**3.1**)
un **stage** course of instruction
un **standard** switchboard
une **station de ski** ski resort
stériliser to sterilize
la **structure** structure
stupide stupid (**8.2**)

le **style** style (**4.3**)
su (*p. part. of* **savoir**) (**7.3**)
une **subvention** subsidy
un **succès** success **avoir du
succès** to be successful
le **sucre** sugar (**8.4**)
suffit: ça suffit! that's enough!
(**7.5**)
suggéré suggested
suisse Swiss (**2.4**)
la **Suisse** Switzerland (**2.4**)
suite: tout de suite right away,
right now (**7.1**)
suivant following
sujet subject
super great, terrific
le **superlatif** superlative
un **supermarché** supermarket
superstitieux (superstitieuse)
superstitious
un **supplément** supplement
supposer to suppose
sur on (**3.5**); about
sûr sure, certain **bien sûr**
sure, of course (**1.2**)
une **surboum** party
sûrement surely (**5.5**)
une **surprise-partie** (informal)
party (**2.1**)
surtout especially
sympa, sympathique nice,
pleasant (**2.1**)
une **symphonie** symphony
un **système** system

t

t' (*see* **te**) (**7.1**)
ta your (**3.3**)
tabac: un bureau de tabac tobacco shop
une **table** table (**6.2**)
Tahiti Tahiti (*French island in
the South Pacific*)
le **tahitien** Tahitian (*language*)
tant mieux so much the better
une **tante** aunt (**3.3**)
un **tapeur** leech
**t'appelles: comment t'appelles-
tu?** what's your name? (**P.2**)
tard late (**6.5**)
une **tarte** tart, pie
une **tasse** cup (**8.5**)
te (to) you (**7.1**)
un **tee-shirt** tee shirt (**4.2**)
la **télé** TV (**2.2**)

le **télégraphe** telegraph
un **téléphone** telephone (**6.2**)
téléphoner to call, phone
(**1.1**)
un **téléviseur** TV set (**2.2**)
la **télévision** television, TV
la **température** temperature
quelle température fait-il?
what's the temperature?
(**P.6**)
le **temps** time, weather **de
temps en temps** from time
to time, once in a while
(**8.3**) **pendant combien de
temps** for how long (**6.1**)
perdre son temps to
waste one's time (**6.3**)
quel temps fait-il? how
(what) is the weather?
(**P.6**) **tout le temps** all
the time **trouver le temps
long** to be bored (**6.3**)
tenez! look!
le **tennis** tennis **jouer au
tennis** to play tennis
la **terminale** *twelfth school year
in France, last year of lycée*
la **terrasse** *sidewalk section of a
café*
tes your (**3.3**)
une **tête** head (**6.1**) **avoir mal à
la tête** to have a headache
(**6.1**)
le **thé** tea (**5.2**)
théâtral theatrical
un **théâtre** theater (**3.1**)
un **thermomètre** thermometer
tiens! look! hey! (**1.2**)
un **timbre** stamp (**3.5**)
timide timid (**8.2**)
un **tirage** drawing
un **titre** title
toi you (**2.5**) **et toi?** and
you? (**P.2**)
la **toilette** toilet
une **tomate** tomato (**8.4**)
tomber to fall (**6.5**)
ton (ta; tes) your (**3.3**)
tort: avoir tort to be wrong
(**4.4**)
toujours always (**1.3**)
un **tour** tour, trip, trick **à votre
tour** your turn **jouer un
tour** to play a trick
une **tour** tower **la tour Eiffel**
Eiffel Tower

420

le **tourisme** tourism, travel
un **touriste, une touriste** tourist
tous all **tous (toutes) les** every (**6.4**) **tous les jours** every day
la **Toussaint** All Saints' Day (*November 1*)
tout everything, all (**3.2**) **après tout** after all (**5.1**) **pas du tout** not at all (**1.2**) **tout de suite** right away, right now (**7.1**) **tout le monde** everyone **tout le temps** all the time **tout s'explique** everything is clear
le **trac** stage fright
traditionnellement traditionally
un **train** train (**5.5**) **aller bon train** to go at a good pace
un **trajet** trip
un **transistor** transistor radio (**2.2**)
un **transport** means of transportation
travailler to work (**1.4**)
traverser to cross
treize thirteen (**P.3**)
trente thirty (**P.3**)
très very (**1.1**)
triangulaire triangular
un **tricot** sweater
triste sad (**6.1**)
trois three (**P.3**)
troisième third (**3.4**)
une **trompette** trumpet
trop (de) too, too much (**3.3**) (**8.2**)
un **trophée** trophy
trouver to think; to find (**3.5**) **trouver le temps long** to be bored (**6.3**)
tu you (**1.3**)
la **Tunisie** Tunisia (*country in North Africa*)
tunisien (tunisienne) Tunisian
turc (turque) Turkish

un, une one (**P.3**) a, an (**2.1**)
uni united **les États-Unis** *m.* United States (**2.4**) **les Nations Unies** *f.* United Nations

unique only
uniquement only
une **unité** unit
une **université** university
un **usage** use
utile useful (**7.5**); valuable
utilement in a useful way
utilisant: en utilisant using
utiliser to use (**8.5**)

va: ça va? how are you? how's everything? (**P.2**) **ça va** everything's fine (going well); fine, I'm OK, everything's all right (**P.2**); good
les **vacances** *f.* vacation (**3.3**) **en vacances** on vacation (**1.5**) **les grandes vacances** summer vacation
une **vache** cow
un **vainqueur** winner
vais: je vais I am going
la **vanille** vanilla
vapeur: un bateau à vapeur steamboat
vas: comment vas-tu? how are you? (**P.2**)
le **veau** veal
un **végétarien, une végétarienne** vegetarian
un **véhicule** vehicle
le **vélo** bicycling (**5.3**)
un **vélo** bicycle (**2.2**) **aller à vélo** to go by bicycle (**5.5**)
un **vélomoteur** motorbike (**2.2**)
un **vendeur, une vendeuse** salesperson (**7.1**)
vendre to sell (**4.5**)
vendredi *m.* Friday (**P.5**)
* **venir** to come (**5.4**) **venir de + *inf.*** to have just (**5.5**)
un **ventre** stomach (**6.1**) **avoir mal au ventre** to have a stomachache (**6.1**)
venu (*p. part. of* **venir**) (**6.5**)
un **verbe** verb
vérifier to verify
véritable real, true (**8.5**)
la **vérité** truth (**7.5**)
un **verre** glass (**8.5**)
vert green (**2.2**)
une **veste** jacket (**4.3**)
les **vêtements** *m.* clothing (**4.2**)

veulent: ils/elles veulent they want
veut: il/elle veut he/she wants
veux: je veux I want **tu veux** you want
la **viande** meat (**5.2**)
victorieux (victorieuse) victorious
vide empty (**8.5**)
la **vie** life **c'est la vie!** that's life!
vieil (*see* **vieux**) old (**4.3**)
vieille (*see* **vieux**) old (**4.3**)
vieux (vieil, vieille; vieux) old (**4.3**) **le Vieux Carré** *the French Quarter in New Orleans*
une **ville** city, town (**3.1**) **en ville** in town, downtown (**1.5**)
le **vin** wine (**5.2**)
le **vinaigre** vinegar (**8.4**)
vingt twenty (**P.3**)
violent violent (**5.3**)
un **violon** violin (**3.2**)
une **vipère** snake
le **visage** face
une **visite** visit **rendre visite à** to visit (*people*) (**7.4**)
visiter to visit (*a place*) (**1.1**)
vive...! hurray for . . . ! (**8.4**)
le **vocabulaire** vocabulary
voici this is, here's, here comes (**P.1**)
voilà that is, there's (**P.1**)
la **voile** sailing (**5.3**) **faire de la voile** to sail **la planche à voile** wind-surfing
* **voir** to see (**6.3**)
un **voisin, une voisine** neighbor
une **voiture** car (**2.2**) **aller en voiture** to go by car (**5.5**) **faire une promenade en voiture** to take a drive (**5.5**)
une **voix** voice
le **volley, volleyball** volleyball (**3.2**) **jouer au volleyball** to play volleyball (**3.2**)
vos your (**3.5**)
votre (*pl.* **vos**) your (**3.5**)
voudrais: je voudrais I would like (**8.1**)
voulez: vous voulez you want
* **vouloir** to want (**8.1**) **vouloir bien** to want to (**8.1**) **vouloir dire** to mean (**8.1**)

voulu (*p. part. of* vouloir) (**8.1**)
vous you (**1.3**) (**2.5**) (to) you (**7.1**)
un voyage trip **bon voyage!** have a good trip! **faire un voyage** to take a trip (**5.4**) **une agence de voyages** travel agency
voyager to travel (**1.4**)
une voyelle vowel
voyons! come on! come now! (**4.2**)

vrai true, right (**2.5**)
vraiment really (**P.5**)
vu (*p. part of* voir) (**6.3**)
une vue view

w

les W.C. (water–closets) toilet, bathroom
un week-end weekend (**4.2**)

y

y there (**8.3**) **il y a** there is, there are (**2.4**) **on y va!** let's go!
des yeux *m.* eyes (**6.1**)
le yogourt yogurt

z

zéro zero (**P.3**) **il fait zéro** it's 0° (**P.6**)
zut (alors)! darn (it)! rats! (**P.4**)

ENGLISH-FRENCH VOCABULARY

The English-French Vocabulary contains only active vocabulary.

a

a, an un, une (**2.1**) **a little (bit)** un peu (**1.3**) **a lot** beaucoup (**1.3**)
able: to be able (to) *savoir + *inf.* (**7.3**) *pouvoir (**8.1**)
about de (**1.1**) **about whom** de qui (**1.5**) **to talk about** discuter (**7.4**)
acquainted: to be acquainted with *connaître (**7.2**)
to act jouer (**8.1**)
active: to be active in *faire de + *activity* (**5.4**)
actor un acteur (**5.1**)
actress une actrice (**5.1**)
to adore adorer (**1.4**)
adventure movie un film d'aventures (**5.1**)
advice: (piece of) advice un conseil (**7.5**)
Africa l'Afrique *f.* (**2.4**)
after ensuite (**6.2**) après (**6.5**) **after all** après tout (**5.1**)
afternoon un après-midi (**4.2**) **good afternoon** bonjour (**P.1**) **in the afternoon** de l'après-midi (**P.4**) **this afternoon** cet après-midi (**4.2**) **tomorrow afternoon** demain après-midi (**4.2**)
afterwards après (**6.5**)
to agree être d'accord (**2.1**)
ah! ah! (**2.1**)

airplane un avion (**5.5**)
alas hélas (**8.4**)
album un album (**3.3**)
alert attentif (attentive) (**8.2**)
all tout (**3.2**) **after all** après tout (**5.1**) **all right** d'accord (**2.1**) **all right!** ah bon! (**3.4**) **everything's all right** ça va (**P.2**) **not at all** pas du tout (**1.2**)
allowance l'argent *m.* de poche (**7.4**)
alone seul (**6.5**)
along: to take along amener (**6.5**)
already déjà (**8.4**)
also aussi (**1.1**)
always toujours (**1.3**)
am (*see* to be)
A.M. du matin (**P.4**)
America l'Amérique *f.* (**2.4**)
American américain (**2.4**)
amusing amusant (**2.1**)
an un, une (**2.1**)
and et (**P.3**) **and you?** et toi? (**P.2**)
angry furieux (furieuse) (**8.5**)
animal un animal (*pl.* animaux) (**3.4**)
annoying pénible (**2.3**)
another un (une) autre (**7.5**)
to answer répondre (à) (**6.3**)
any des (**2.4**) du, de la, de l', de (**5.2**) en (**8.4**) **not any** pas de (**2.2**)

anybody: not anybody ne...personne (**7.4**)
anyone quelqu'un (de) (**7.4**)
anything quelque chose (de) (**7.4**) **not anything** ne...rien (**7.4**)
apple une pomme (**8.4**)
appointment un rendez-vous (**3.1**)
April avril (**P.5**)
are (*see* to be) **there are** il y a (**2.4**) **these/those/they are** ce sont (**2.4**)
arm un bras (**6.1**)
armchair un fauteuil (**6.2**)
to arrive arriver (**1.1**)
art le dessin (**5.3**)
as comme (**4.4**) **as . . . as** aussi...que (**4.3**)
Asia l'Asie *f.* (**2.4**)
to ask demander (à) (**3.5**) **to ask for** demander (**7.4**)
at à (**1.1**) chez (**3.2**) **at . . .'s (house)** chez... (**3.2**) **at home** à la maison (**1.5**) chez (moi, toi...) (**3.2**) **at last** enfin (**6.3**) **at least** au moins (**3.2**) **at . . . (o'clock)** à...heure(s) (**P.4**) **at present** en ce moment (**8.1**) **at (the pharmacist's)** chez (le pharmacien) (**4.5**) **at the restaurant** au restaurant (**1.5**) **at what time?** à quelle heure? (**P.4**)

to attend assister (à) (6.4)

attention: to pay attention faire attention (5.4)

attentive attentif (attentive) (8.2)

August août (P.5)

aunt une tante (3.3)

author un auteur (8.1)

automobile une auto, une voiture (2.2)

autumn: in (the) autumn en automne (P.6) this autumn cet automne (4.2)

away: right away tout de suite (7.1)

b

back un dos (6.1)

back: to come back rentrer (1.2) *revenir (5.4)

to go back rentrer (1.2)

bad mauvais (2.3)

I'm/everything's (very) bad ça va (très) mal (P.2)

it's bad (weather) il fait mauvais (P.6) not bad pas mal (3.3) that's bad c'est mal (2.5) (that's) too bad! (c'est) dommage! (1.1)

badly mal (1.1)

bag un sac (2.2)

baker un pâtissier, une pâtissière (4.5)

banana une banane (8.4)

banknote un billet (4.1)

basketball le basket(ball) (3.2)

bathing suit un maillot de bain (4.2)

bathroom une salle de bains (6.2)

to be *être (1.5) to be . . . (years old) avoir... ans (3.3)

to be able (to) *savoir + inf. (7.3) *pouvoir (8.1)

to be acquainted with *connaître (7.2) to be active in *faire de + activity (5.4) to be bored trouver le temps long (6.3) to be born *naître (6.5) to be careful faire attention (5.4) to be cold avoir froid (4.4) to be hungry avoir faim (4.4) to be in a good (bad) mood être de bonne (mauvaise) humeur (7.5) to be in

pain avoir mal (6.1) to be lucky avoir de la chance (4.4) to be present at assister à (6.4) to be right avoir raison (4.4) to be thirsty avoir soif (4.4) to be warm avoir chaud (4.4) to be well être bien (6.1) to be wrong avoir tort (4.4)

beach une plage (3.1)

beans, string beans des •haricots m. (8.4)

beautiful beau (bel, belle; beaux) (2.1) (4.3)

because parce que (1.3) because of à cause de (8.1) because of that pour cela (8.1)

bed un lit (6.2)

bedroom une chambre (6.2)

beer la bière (5.2)

before avant (6.5)

to begin commencer (6.3)

behind derrière (8.3)

Belgian belge (2.4)

Belgium la Belgique (2.4)

to belong to *être à (3.5) to whom does/do . . . belong à qui est/sont... (3.5) which belongs to de (3.2)

below: it's (five) below il fait moins (cinq) (P.6)

best: the best . . . (in) le meilleur...(de) (4.4) best friend un meilleur ami, une meilleure amie (3.3) best regards amitiés (6.5)

bet: I bet that je parie que (7.2)

better meilleur (4.3)

between entre (8.3)

beverage une boisson (5.2)

bicycle un vélo, une bicyclette (2.2) to go by bicycle aller à vélo (bicyclette) (5.5)

bicycling le vélo (5.3)

big grand (2.1)

bill (money) un billet (4.1)

bird un oiseau (pl. oiseaux) (3.4)

birthday un anniversaire (7.5) (Marc's) birthday is (May 3rd) l'anniversaire de (Marc) est le (3 mai) (P.5) my birthday is (March 2nd) mon anniversaire est le (2 mars) (P.5)

bit: a little bit un peu (1.3)

black noir (2.2)

blond blond (2.1)

blouse un chemisier (4.3)

blue bleu (2.2)

to blush rougir (7.3)

boat un bateau (pl. bateaux) (5.5)

book un livre (2.2)

bookseller un (une) libraire (4.5)

bookstore une librairie (4.5) bookstore owner un (une) libraire (4.5)

boots des bottes f. (4.2)

bored: to be bored trouver le temps long (6.3)

born: to be born *naître (6.5)

to borrow emprunter (3.2)

bottle une bouteille (8.5)

boy un garçon (2.1)

boyfriend un petit ami (2.3)

bread le pain (5.2)

to break casser (7.5)

breakfast le petit déjeuner (8.5) to have (eat) breakfast prendre le petit déjeuner (8.5)

bright génial (pl. géniaux) (7.2) brillant (8.2)

brilliant génial (pl. géniaux) (7.2) brillant (8.2)

to bring amener (6.5)

brother un frère (3.2)

brunet(te) brun (2.1)

bus un autobus, un bus (5.5)

busy occupé (8.1)

but mais (1.1)

butter le beurre (8.4)

to buy acheter (4.2)

by: by oneself seul (6.5) to go by passer par (6.5) to go by bicycle aller à vélo (bicyclette) (5.5) to go by car, by train . . . aller en auto, en train... (5.5)

c

café un café (3.1)

cafeteria une cafétéria (3.1)

cake un gâteau (pl. gâteaux) (4.4)

to call téléphoner (1.1)

calm calme (8.2)

calmly calmement (8.2)

camera un appareil-photo (*pl.* appareils-photo) (**2.2**) **movie camera** une caméra (**2.2**)

can * pouvoir (**8.1**)

Canada le Canada (**2.4**)

Canadian canadien (canadienne) (**2.4**)

candy des bonbons *m.* (**4.5**)

car une auto, une voiture (**2.2**) **to go by car** aller en auto (voiture) (**5.5**)

card une carte (**7.5**) **(playing) cards** des cartes (**3.2**)

careful: to be careful faire attention (**5.4**)

carrot une carotte (**8.4**)

cartoon un dessin animé (**5.1**)

case: in that case dans ce cas (**7.3**)

cassette une cassette (**2.2**) **cassette recorder** une mini-cassette (**2.2**)

cat un chat (**3.4**)

celebrate célébrer (**8.4**)

certainly mais oui (**1.2**) certainement (**5.5**)

chair une chaise (**6.2**) **armchair** un fauteuil (**6.2**)

cheese le fromage (**5.2**)

cherries des cerises *f.* (**8.4**)

chess les échecs *m.* (**3.2**)

chicken le poulet (**5.2**)

children les enfants *m.* (**3.3**)

China la Chine (**2.4**)

Chinese chinois (**2.4**)

to **choose** choisir (**4.1**)

church une église (**3.1**)

city une ville (**3.1**)

clarinet une clarinette (**3.2**)

class: in class en classe (**1.5**) **to class** en classe (**3.1**)

classmate un (une) camarade (**2.1**)

to **close** fermer (**8.3**)

close friend un ami, une amie (**2.1**)

clothing les vêtements *m.* (**4.2**)

coat un manteau (*pl.* manteaux) (**4.3**)

Coca-Cola un Coca-Cola (**5.2**)

coed une étudiante (**2.1**)

coffee le café (**5.2**)

coin une pièce (**4.1**)

Coke un coca (**5.2**)

cold: it's cold (weather) il fait froid (**P.6**) **to be (feel) cold** avoir froid (**4.4**)

college student un étudiant, une étudiante (**2.1**)

color: what color? de quelle couleur? (**2.2**)

to **come** arriver (**1.1**) * venir (**5.4**) **come on! come now!** voyons! (**4.2**) **here comes** voici (**P.1**) **to come back** rentrer (**1.2**) * revenir (**5.4**)

comedy une comédie (**5.1**) **musical comedy** une comédie musicale (**5.1**)

comics des bandes dessinées *f.* (**7.5**)

complicated compliqué (**4.5**)

concert un concert (**3.1**)

congratulations! félicitations! (**8.3**)

conservative conservateur (conservatrice) (**4.3**)

contrary: on the contrary au contraire (**1.2**)

cook une cuisinière (*female*) (**8.4**)

cooking la cuisine (**5.3**)

cool: it's cool (weather) il fait frais (**P.6**)

to **cost** coûter (**4.1**)

costume un costume (**8.1**)

country un pays (**2.4**)

country(side) la campagne (**3.1**)

course (*of a meal*) un plat (**8.4**)

course: of course bien sûr (**1.2**) évidemment (**4.3**) **of course not** mais non (**1.2**)

cousin un cousin, une cousine (**3.2**)

cup une tasse (**8.5**)

cute mignon (mignonne) (**7.2**)

d

to **dance** danser (**1.2**)

dancing la danse (**5.3**)

dangerous dangereux (dangereuse) (**5.3**)

dark-haired brun (**2.1**)

darn (it)! zut! zut alors! (**P.4**)

date (*on the calendar*) la date (**P.5**) un rendez-vous (**3.1**) **I have a date with** j'ai rendez-vous avec (**P.5**)

daughter une fille (**3.3**)

day un jour (**P.5**) une journée (**7.5**) **what day is it?** quel jour est-ce? (**P.5**)

whole day une journée (**7.5**)

dealer un marchand, une marchande (**4.5**)

dear cher (chère) (**4.4**) **oh dear!** oh là là! (**P.3**)

December décembre (**P.5**)

to **decide** décider (de) (**6.4**)

degrees: it's . . . degrees il fait...degrés (**P.6**)

department store un grand magasin (**4.1**)

depends: it depends ça dépend (**4.1**)

to **describe** * décrire (**7.5**)

desk un bureau (**6.2**)

dessert un dessert (**5.2**)

detective movie un film policier (**5.1**)

to **die** * mourir (**6.5**)

diet un régime (**4.1**) **to be on a diet** être au régime (**4.1**)

difficult difficile (**2.5**)

dining room une salle à manger (**6.2**)

dinner le dîner (**8.5**) **to have (eat) dinner** dîner (**1.1**)

director un metteur en scène (**8.1**)

to **discover** * découvrir (**8.4**)

to **discuss** discuter (**7.4**)

dish un plat (**8.4**) une assiette (**8.5**)

to **dislike** détester (**1.4**)

to **disobey** désobéir (à) (**6.4**)

distant family la famille éloignée (**3.3**)

distinct distinct (**8.2**)

distinctly distinctement (**8.2**)

to **do** * faire (**5.4**) **to do + pastime** * faire de + pastime (**5.4**)

doctor un médecin, le docteur (**6.1**)

dog un chien (**3.4**)

doing: nothing doing! pas question! (**3.5**)

door une porte (**8.3**)

down: to go down descendre (**6.5**)

downtown en ville (**1.5**)

drama un drame (**5.1**)

drawing le dessin (**5.3**)

dress une robe (**4.3**)

drink une boisson (**5.2**)

to **drink** * boire (**5.2**)

drive: to take a drive faire une promenade (en voiture) (5.5)
drugstore une pharmacie (4.5)
dumb stupide (8.2)
during pendant (6.1)

e

ear une oreille (6.1)
easy facile (2.5)
to **eat** manger (5.2) **to eat breakfast** prendre le petit déjeuner (8.5) **to eat dinner** dîner (1.1) **to eat lunch** déjeuner (8.5) **to eat supper** dîner (8.5)
egg un œuf (8.4)
Egypt l'Égypte f. (2.4)
Egyptian égyptien (égyptienne) (2.4)
eight •huit (P.3)
eighteen dix-huit (P.3)
eighth •huitième (3.4)
eighty quatre-vingts (4.1) **eighty-one** quatre-vingt-un (4.1)
elegant chic (4.2) élégant (4.3)
eleven onze (P.3)
eleventh onzième (3.4)
empty vide (8.5)
engineer un ingénieur (7.1)
England l'Angleterre f. (2.4)
English anglais (2.4)
enough assez (de) (8.2) **that's enough!** ça suffit! (7.5)
to **enter** entrer (dans) (6.5)
er . . . euh... (P.6)
Europe l'Europe f. (2.4)
evening un soir (4.2) **in the evening** du soir (P.4) **this evening** ce soir (4.2) **tomorrow evening** demain soir (4.2)
event un événement (6.3)
every tous (toutes) les (6.4)
everything tout (3.2) **everything's all right** ça va (P.2) **how's everything?** ça va? (P.2)
example: for example par exemple (8.2)
excellent excellent (5.3)
exciting passionnant (5.3)
excuse me pardon (P.3)
expense une dépense (7.4)
expensive cher (chère) (4.1)

eye un œil (pl. yeux) (6.1)

f

face la figure (6.1)
to **fail** ne réussir pas (4.1)
fall: in (the) fall en automne (P.6) **this fall** cet automne (4.2)
to **fall** tomber (6.5)
false faux (fausse) (2.5)
family la famille (3.3) **distant family** la famille éloignée (3.3) **immediate family** la famille proche (3.3)
famous célèbre (8.1)
far from loin de (8.3)
fashion la mode (4.3) une façon (8.2) **to be in fashion (fashionable)** être à la mode (4.3)
fat gros (grosse) (4.4) **to get fat** grossir (4.1)
father un père (3.3)
favorite favori (favorite) (7.5)
February février (P.5)
to **feel: to feel good** être bien (6.1) **to feel like (having)** avoir envie de (4.4)
fever la fièvre (6.1)
fifteen quinze (P.3) **3:15** trois heures et quart (P.4)
fifth cinquième (3.4)
fifty cinquante (P.3)
finally enfin, finalement (6.3)
to **find** trouver (3.5)
fine ça va (P.2) **fine!** d'accord! (2.1) **it's fine (weather)** il fait beau (P.6) **that's fine** c'est bien (2.5)
to **finish** finir (4.1)
first premier (première) (3.4) **(June) first** le premier (juin) (P.5)
fish un poisson (3.4)
five cinq (P.3)
flu la grippe (6.1)
to **flunk** (a test) ne réussir pas (4.1)
flute une flûte (3.2)
food: who likes food gourmand (7.3)
foot un pied (6.1) **to go on foot** aller à pied (5.5)
for pour (1.5) **for + time** pendant (6.1) **for a long time** longtemps (6.3)

for example (instance) par exemple (8.2) **for how long** pendant combien de temps (6.1) **for whom** pour qui (1.5)
fork une fourchette (8.5)
fortunately heureusement (8.2)
forty quarante (P.3)
four quatre (P.3)
fourteen quatorze (P.3)
fourth quatrième (3.4)
France la France (2.4)
French français (2.4)
French fries des frites f. (8.4)
Friday vendredi m. (P.5)
friend un ami, une amie (2.1) un copain, une copine (7.3) **best friend** un meilleur ami, une meilleure amie (3.2) **school friend** un (une) camarade (2.1)
from de (1.1) **from time to time** de temps en temps (8.3)
front: in front of devant (8.3)
fruit(s) les fruits m. (8.4)
full plein (8.5)
funny drôle (2.3)
furious furieux (furieuse) (8.5)
furniture les meubles m. (6.2) **piece of furniture** un meuble (6.2)

g

to **gain weight** grossir (4.1)
game un jeu (pl. jeux) (3.2) (sports) un match (6.3) **to play a game** (sports) faire un match (5.4)
general général (pl. généraux) (8.2)
generally généralement (8.2)
generous généreux (généreuse) (4.3)
gentleman un monsieur (pl. messieurs) (2.1)
German allemand (2.4)
Germany l'Allemagne f. (2.4)
to **get** chercher (7.1) **to get fat** grossir (4.1) **to get off/out (of)** descendre (de) (7.5) **to get on/in** monter dans (7.5) **to get out (of)** *sortir (de) (6.5) **to get thin** maigrir (4.1)
girl une fille (2.1)

girlfriend une petite amie (2.3)

to give donner (7.1) (*a present*) *offrir (8.4) **give me** donne-moi (*familiar*), donnez-moi (*formal*) (P.3)

glass un verre (8.5)

glasses des lunettes *f.* (4.2)

to go *aller (3.1) **let's go!** allons! (3.1) **to be going (to do something)** aller + *inf.* (3.1) **to go back** rentrer (1.2) **to go by/through** passer par (6.5) **to go by bicycle** aller à vélo (bicyclette) (5.5) **to go by car, by train . . .** aller en auto, en train... (5.5) **to go down** descendre (6.5) **to go home** rentrer (1.2) **to go in** entrer (dans) (6.5) **to go on foot** aller à pied (5.5) **to go out** *sortir (6.5) **to go shopping** faire les courses (5.4) **to go to** assister à (6.4) **to go up** monter (6.5)

goldfish un poisson rouge (3.4)

good bon (bonne) (2.3) **good morning (afternoon)** bonjour (P.1) **that's good** c'est bien (2.5) **to feel good** être bien (6.1)

good-by au revoir (P.1)

good-looking beau (bel, belle; beaux) (2.1) (4.3)

grandfather un grand-père (3.3)

grandmother une grand-mère (3.3)

grandparents les grands-parents *m.* (3.3)

gray gris (2.2)

great magnifique (1.1) fantastique, formidable, sensationnel (2.2) **that's great** c'est magnifique (1.1)

green vert (2.2)

grocer un épicier, une épicière (4.5)

grocery une épicerie (4.5)

guest un invité, une invitée (8.5)

guitar une guitare (2.2)

gymnastics la gymnastique (5.3)

h

hair les cheveux *m.* (6.1)

half past (two) (deux) heures et demie (P.4)

hall la salle (8.1)

ham le jambon (5.2)

hand une main (6.1)

handbag un sac (2.2)

happy content (8.5)

hard difficile (2.5)

hat un chapeau (*pl.* chapeaux) (4.3)

to hate détester (1.4)

to have *avoir (2.2) (*food or drink*) prendre (5.5) **to have a (headache, sore throat, stomachache)** avoir mal (à la tete, à la gorge, au ventre) (6.1) **to have breakfast** prendre le petit déjeuner (8.5) **to have dinner** dîner (1.1) **to have just** *venir de + *inf.* (5.5) **to have lunch** déjeuner (8.5) **to have more** *reprendre (8.4) **to have supper** dîner (8.5) **to have to** *devoir (8.1)

he il (1.2)

head une tête (6.1)

headache: to have a headache avoir mal à la tête (6.1)

to hear entendre (4.5)

heart un cœur (6.1)

hello bonjour (P.1)

to help aider (à) (7.1)

her elle (2.5) son, sa, ses (3.4) la (7.2) **(to) her** lui (7.4) **what's her name?** comment s'appelle-t-elle? (2.1)

here ici (1.5) **here comes, here's** voici (P.1) **this . . . over here** ce...-ci (4.2)

hey! tiens! (1.2) eh! dis (donc)! dites (donc)! (1.4)

hi salut (P.1)

high school student un (une) élève (2.1)

him lui (2.5) le (7.2) **(to) him** lui (7.4)

his son, sa, ses (3.4) **what's his name?** comment s'appelle-t-il? (2.1)

history une histoire (7.5)

home, at home à la maison (1.5) chez (moi, toi...) (3.2) **to go home** rentrer (1.2)

to hope espérer (5.1)

horse un cheval (*pl.* chevaux) (3.4)

hospital un hôpital (*pl.* hôpitaux) (3.1)

hot chaud (4.2) **it's hot (weather)** il fait chaud (P.6)

house une maison (3.1) **at/to . . .'s house** chez... (3.2) **(theatrical) house** la salle (8.1)

how comment (1.3) **how are you?** ça va? comment vas-tu? comment allez-vous? (P.2) **how do you say . . . ?** comment dit-on...? (4.5) **how many** combien (de) (4.1) **how much** combien (P.3) combien de (4.1) **how much is it?** c'est combien? (P.3) **how old are you?** quel âge as-tu (avez-vous)? (3.3) **how's everything?** ça va? (P.2) **how's the weather?** quel temps fait-il? (P.6) **to know how to** *savoir + *inf.* (7.3) **to learn how to** *apprendre à + *inf.* (5.5)

hundred cent (4.1)

hungry: to be hungry avoir faim (4.4)

hurray for . . . ! vive...! (8.4)

i

I je (1.1) moi (2.5) **I don't know** je ne sais pas (P.1) **I have a date with** j'ai rendez-vous avec (P.5) **I know** je sais (P.1) **I'm okay** ça va (P.2) **I'm (very well; well; so-so; bad; very bad)** ça va (très bien; bien; comme ci, comme ça; mal; très mal) (P.2)

ice cream une glace (5.2)

idea une idée (4.4)

if si (3.5)

immediate family la famille proche (3.3)

in à (1.1) dans (3.3) (*a country*) au, aux, en (4.5) **in a way** d'une façon, d'une manière (8.2) **in class** en classe (1.5) **in front of** devant (8.3)

in love amoureux (amoureuse) (7.3)
in order to pour (6.2) in style chic (4.2) in that case dans ce cas (7.3) in the afternoon de l'après-midi (P.4) in the morning (evening) du matin (soir) (P.4) in town en ville (1.5)
inexpensive bon marché (4.1)
instance: for instance par exemple (8.2)
instrument un instrument (3.2)
intelligent intelligent (2.1)
interesting intéressant (2.1)
interpreter un (une) interprète (7.1)
to introduce présenter (7.1)
to invite inviter (1.1)
is (see to be) isn't it (so)? n'est-ce pas? (1.3) there is il y a (2.4)
it il, elle (1.2) le, la (7.2) it depends ça dépend (4.1) it doesn't matter ça n'a pas d'importance (3.1) ça ne fait rien (7.4) it's c'est (P.1) it's . . . francs c'est...francs (P.3) it's . . . (o'clock) il est...heure(s) (P.4) it's (fine, nice, hot, cool, cold, bad) (weather) il fait (beau, bon, chaud, frais, froid, mauvais) (P.6) it's (September 10th) c'est le (10 septembre) (P.5) it's raining (snowing) il pleut (neige) (P.6) that's it c'est ça (2.1) what time is it? quelle heure est-il? (P.4) who is it? qui est-ce? (P.1)
Italian italien (italienne) (2.4)
Italy l'Italie f. (2.4)
its son, sa, ses (3.4)

j

jacket une veste (4.2) ski (down) jacket un anorak (4.2)
jam la confiture (8.4)
January janvier (P.5)
Japan le Japon (2.4)
Japanese japonais (2.4)
jeans un blue-jeans (4.2)
jogging le footing, le jogging (5.3)

journalist un (une) journaliste (7.1)
juice: orange juice le jus d'orange (5.2)
July juillet (P.5)
June juin (P.5)
just: to have just *venir de + inf. (5.5) just a second (minute)! une seconde (minute)! (5.4)

k

kitchen une cuisine (6.2)
knife un couteau (pl. couteaux) (8.5)
to know *connaître (7.2) *savoir (7.3) I don't know je ne sais pas (P.1) I know je sais (P.1) to know how to *savoir + inf. (7.3)

l

lady une dame (2.1)
lamb l'agneau m. (5.2)
lamp une lampe (6.2)
last dernier (dernière) (6.2) at last enfin (6.3)
late tard (6.5)
lawyer un (une) avocat (7.1)
to learn *apprendre (5.5) to learn + subject *faire de + subject (5.4) to learn how to *apprendre à + inf. (5.5) to learn to play + instrument *faire de + instrument (5.4)
least: at least au moins (3.2) the least . . . (in) le moins... (de) (4.4)
to leave *partir (6.5) to leave (a place) partir de (6.5) to leave for (a place) partir à (6.5)
left: there is/are . . . left il reste (8.5)
left: to the left of à gauche de (8.3)
leg une jambe (6.1)
lemon soda la limonade (5.2)
to lend prêter (7.1)
less moins (4.3) less . . . than moins...que (4.3)
let's . . . nous form of any verb (5.5) let's go! allons! (3.1)

letter une lettre (7.5)
library une bibliothèque (3.1)
lie un mensonge (7.5)
like comme (4.4) what does he/she look like? comment est-il/elle? (2.1) what's he/she like? comment est-il/elle? (2.1)
to like aimer (1.4) I would like je voudrais (8.1) who likes food gourmand (7.3)
to listen (to) écouter (1.4) listen! écoute! écoutez! (2.5)
little petit (2.1) peu (de) (8.2) a little (bit) un peu (1.3)
to live habiter (1.1) living room un salon (6.2)
to loan prêter (7.1)
long long (longue) (4.3) for a long time longtemps (6.3) for how long pendant combien de temps (6.1) longer: no longer ne...plus (8.5)
to look avoir l'air (6.1) look! tiens! (1.2) to look at regarder (1.4) to look for chercher (7.1) what does he/she look like? comment est-il/elle? (2.1)
to lose perdre (4.5) to lose weight maigrir (4.1)
lot: a lot beaucoup (1.3)
love (at the end of a letter) amicalement (6.5) in love amoureux (amoureuse) (7.3)
to love adorer (1.4)
lucky: to be lucky avoir de la chance (4.4)
lunch le déjeuner (8.5) to have (eat) lunch déjeuner (8.5)

m

mad furieux (furieuse) (8.5)
magazine un magazine, une revue (7.5)
to make *faire (5.4) to make plans faire des projets (5.4) to make progress faire des progrès (5.4)
man un homme, un monsieur (polite term) (2.1)
manner une façon, une manière (8.2)

many: how many combien de (4.1)

March mars (P.5)

match un match (6.3) **to play a match** faire un match (5.4)

matter: it doesn't matter ça n'a pas d'importance (3.1) ça ne fait rien (7.4) **what's the matter?** qu'est-ce qu'il y a? (8.5)

may *pouvoir (8.1)

May mai (P.5)

maybe peut-être (2.4)

me moi (2.5) me (7.1) **excuse me** pardon (P.3) **me too** moi aussi (P.2) **to me** me (7.1)

meal un repas (8.5)

to mean *vouloir dire (8.1)

meat la viande (5.2)

to meet rencontrer (6.5)

merchant un marchand, une marchande (4.5)

Mexican mexicain (2.4)

Mexico le Mexique (2.4)

midnight minuit (P.4)

milk le lait (5.2)

million million (4.2)

mineral water l'eau minérale f. (5.2)

minute: just a minute! une minute! (5.4)

Miss Mademoiselle (Mlle) (P.1)

Monday lundi m. (P.5)

money l'argent m. (4.1) **pocket money** l'argent de poche (7.4)

month un mois (P.5) **this month** ce mois-ci (4.2)

mood: to be in a good (bad) mood être de bonne (mauvaise) humeur (7.5)

more plus (4.3) **more ... than** plus...que (4.3) **no more** ne...plus (8.5) **to have more** *reprendre (8.4)

morning un matin (4.2) **good morning** bonjour (P.1) **in the morning** du matin (P.4) **this morning** ce matin (4.2) **tomorrow morning** demain matin (4.2)

most: the most ... (in) le plus...(de) (4.4)

mother une mère (3.3)

motorbike un vélomoteur (2.2)

motorcycle une moto (2.2)

mouth une bouche (6.1)

movie un film (5.1) **adventure movie** un film d'aventures (5.1) **detective movie** un film policier (5.1) **movie camera** une caméra (2.2) **movie theater** un cinéma (3.1)

movies le cinéma (5.1)

Mr. Monsieur (M.) (P.1)

Mrs. Madame (Mme) (P.1)

much, very much beaucoup (1.3) beaucoup de (8.2) **how much?** combien? (P.3) **how much is it?** c'est combien? (P.3) **not much** peu (de) (8.2) **too much** trop (3.3) trop de (8.2)

museum un musée (3.1)

musical comedy une comédie musicale (5.1)

must *devoir (8.1)

my mon, ma, mes (3.3) **my birthday is (March 2nd)** mon anniversaire est le (2 mars) (P.5) **my name is** je m'appelle (P.2)

n

name: my name is je m'appelle (P.2) **what's ...'s name?** comment s'appelle...? (2.1) **what's his/her name?** comment s'appelle-t-il/elle? (2.1) **what's your name?** comment t'appelles-tu? (P.2)

napkin une serviette (8.5)

nationality une nationalité (2.4)

natural naturel (naturelle) (8.2)

naturally naturellement (8.2)

near près de (8.3)

to need avoir besoin de (4.4)

nervous nerveux (nerveuse) (8.2)

never ne...jamais (7.1)

new nouveau (nouvel, nouvelle; nouveaux) (4.3)

news: (piece of) news une nouvelle (6.3)

newspaper un journal (pl. journaux) (4.5)

next prochain (6.2) **next to** près de (8.3)

nice sympathique (2.1) **it's nice (weather)** il fait bon (P.6)

night une nuit (4.2)

nine neuf (P.3)

nineteen dix-neuf (P.3)

ninety quatre-vingt-dix (4.1)

ninth neuvième (3.4)

no non (P.3) pas de de (5.2) **no?** n'est-ce pas? (1.3) **no longer (more)** ne...plus (8.5) **no thank you** non merci, merci (5.2) **no way!** pas question! (3.5)

nobody ne...personne, personne de (7.4)

noon midi (P.4)

nose un nez (6.1)

not ne...pas (1.1) **not a, not any** pas de (2.2) **not anybody** ne...personne (7.4) **not anything** ne...rien (7.4) **not at all** pas du tout (1.2) **not bad** pas mal (3.3) **not much** peu (de) (8.2) **of course not** mais non (1.2)

nothing ne...rien, rien de (7.4) **nothing doing!** pas question! (3.5)

novel un roman (7.5)

November novembre (P.5)

now maintenant (1.3) **come now!** voyons! (4.2) **right now** tout de suite (7.1) en ce moment (8.1)

o

to obey obéir (à) (6.4)

o'clock heure(s) (P.4) **at ... o'clock** à...heure(s) (P.4) **it is ... o'clock** il est...heure(s) (P.4)

October octobre (P.5)

of de (1.1) **because of** à cause de (8.1) **of course** bien sûr (1.2) évidemment (4.3) **of course not** mais non (1.2) **of whom** de qui (1.5)

off: to get off (of) descendre (de) (7.5)

to offer proposer (6.5) *offrir (8.4)

often souvent (1.3)

oh! ah! (2.1) **oh dear!** oh là là! (P.3)

oil l'huile f. (8.4)

okay d'accord (2.1) **I'm okay** ça va (P.2)

428

old âgé (3.3) vieux (viel, vieille; vieux) (4.3) **how old are you?** quel âge as-tu (avez-vous)? (3.3) **to be . . . years old** avoir...ans (3.3)
omelette une omelette *f.* (5.2)
on sur (3.5) **come on!** voyons! (4.2) **on Monday** lundi (5.1) **on Mondays** le lundi (5.1) **on the contrary** au contraire (1.2) **on vacation** en vacances (1.5)
once in a while de temps en temps (8.3)
one un, une (P.3)
one (*you, they, people*) on (4.5)
oneself: by oneself seul (6.5)
to open *ouvrir (8.4)
or ou (1.1)
orange une orange (8.4)
orange juice le jus d'orange (5.2)
order: in order to pour (6.2)
to order commander (5.2)
to organize organiser (7.3)
other autre (7.5) **the other one** l'autre (7.5) **the others** les autres (7.5)
our notre, nos (3.5)
out: to go (get) out *sortir (6.5) **to get out of** descendre de (7.5)
over . . .'s (house) chez... (3.2) **over there** là-bas (1.5) **that . . . over there** ce ...-là (4.2) **this . . . over here** ce ...-ci (4.2)
to own *avoir (2.2)

p

pain: to be in pain avoir mal (6.1)
pal un copain, une copine (7.3)
pants un pantalon (4.2)
paper un journal (*pl.* journaux) (4.5)
parents les parents...*m.* (3.3)
park un parc (3.1)
parka un anorak (4.2)
part un rôle (8.1)
to participate in *faire de + *activity* (5.4)
party une surprise-partie (2.1)
to pass (*a test*) réussir (4.1)
past: half past (two) (deux) heures et demie (P.4)

quarter past (two) (deux) heures et quart (P.4)
pastry une pâtisserie (4.4) **pastry cook** un pâtissier, une pâtissière (4.5) **pastry shop** une pâtisserie (4.4)
to pay (for) payer (4.4) **to pay attention** faire attention (5.4)
pear une poire (8.4)
peas des petits pois *m.* (8.4)
people on (4.5) les gens *m.* (7.5) **young people** les jeunes *m.* (4.2)
per par (7.4)
perfect parfait (4.2)
performance une représentation (8.1)
perhaps peut-être (2.4)
person une personne (2.1)
pharmacist un pharmacien, une pharmacienne (4.5)
pharmacy une pharmacie (4.5)
phone un téléphone (6.2)
to phone téléphoner (1.1)
photograph une photo (3.3)
photography la photo (5.3)
piano un piano (3.2)
to pick up chercher (7.1)
picnic un pique-nique (7.3)
picture une photo (3.3)
to place *mettre (6.4)
plane un avion (5.5)
plans: to make plans faire des projets (5.4)
plate une assiette (8.5)
platter un plat (8.4)
play une pièce (de théâtre) (5.1)
to play jouer (1.1) **to play +** *instrument* jouer de (3.2) *faire de (5.4) **to play +** *sport* jouer à (3.2) *faire de (5.4) **to play a game, match** (*sports*) faire un match (5.4)
player un joueur, une joueuse (6.3)
pleasant sympathique (2.1) **it's pleasant (weather)** il fait bon (P.6)
please s'il te plaît (*familiar*), s'il vous plaît (*formal*) (P.3)
P.M. de l'après-midi, du soir (P.4)
pocket money l'argent *m.* de poche (7.4)
poem un poème (7.5)
polite bien élevé (7.5)

pool: swimming pool une piscine (3.1)
poor pauvre (3.1)
poorly mal (1.1)
postcard une carte postale (7.5)
potato une pomme de terre (8.4)
pottery la poterie (5.3)
to prefer préférer (5.1)
present: at present en ce moment (8.1) **to be present at** assister à (6.4)
to present présenter (7.1)
pretty joli (2.3)
price un prix (4.2)
problem un problème (4.4)
products des produits *m.* (8.4)
professor un professeur (7.1)
progress: to make progress faire des progrès (5.4)
to promise *promettre (6.4)
pullover un pull (pull-over) (4.2)
to put *mettre (6.4) **to put on** mettre (6.4)

q

quarter of (two) (deux) heures moins le quart (P.4) **quarter past (two)** (deux) heures et quart (P.4)
quick rapide (8.2)
quickly rapidement (8.2)

r

racket une raquette (2.2)
radio une radio (2.2) **transistor radio** un transistor (2.2)
raining: it's raining il pleut (P.6)
rapid rapide (8.2)
rapidly rapidement (8.2)
rarely rarement (1.3)
rather assez (2.1)
rats! zut! zut alors! (P.4)
to read *lire (7.5)
real véritable (8.5)
really vraiment (P.5)
reason: for that reason pour cela (8.1)
record un disque (2.2)
record player un électrophone (2.2)
recorder: cassette recorder une mini-cassette (2.2)
red rouge (2.2) **to turn red** rougir (7.3)

regards: best regards amitiés (6.5)

rehearsal une répétition (8.1)

relatives les parents *m.* (3.3)

remarkable remarquable (7.2)

restaurant un restaurant (3.1) **at the restaurant** au restaurant (1.5)

rice le riz (8.4)

rich riche (3.1)

ridiculous ridicule (7.2)

right vrai (2.5) **all right** d'accord (2.1) **all right!** ah bon! (3.4) **right?** n'est-ce pas? (1.3) **right away** tout de suite (7.1) **right now** tout de suite (7.1) en ce moment (8.1) **that's right** c'est ça (2.1) **to be right** avoir raison (4.4) **to the right of** à droite de (8.3)

roast beef le rosbif (5.2)

role un rôle (8.1)

room une pièce (6.2) la place (7.5)

S

sad triste (6.1)

sailing la voile (5.3)

salad une salade (5.2)

salesperson un vendeur, une vendeuse (7.1)

salt le sel (8.4)

same: at the same time ensemble (6.1)

sandals des sandales *f.* (4.2)

Saturday samedi *m.* (P.5)

saxophone un saxo(phone) (3.2)

to **say** *dire (7.5) **how do you say . . . ?** comment dit-on...? (4.5) **say!** dis (donc)! dites (donc)! (1.4)

scene la scène (8.1)

school une école (3.1) **school friend** un (une) camarade (2.1)

seat une place (6.4)

second deuxième (3.4) **just a second!** une seconde! (5.4)

seconds: to take seconds *reprendre (8.4)

to **see** *voir (6.3)

to **seem** avoir l'air (6.1)

seldom rarement (1.3)

to **sell** vendre (4.5)

September septembre (P.5)

serious sérieux (sérieuse) (8.2)

seriously sérieusement (8.2)

to **set** *mettre (6.4)

seven sept (P.3)

seventeen dix-sept (P.3)

seventh septième (3.4)

seventy soixante-dix (4.1)

she elle (1.2)

shirt une chemise (4.3)

shoes des chaussures *f.* (4.2)

shop un magasin (4.1)

shopping: to go shopping faire les courses (5.4)

short petit (2.1) court (4.3)

shorts un short (4.2)

should *devoir (8.1)

to **show** montrer (7.4)

to **shut** fermer (8.3)

sick malade (3.1)

silly bête (2.3)

simple simple (4.5)

sincere sincère (2.1)

to **sing** chanter (1.4)

sister une sœur (3.2)

six six (P.3)

sixteen seize (P.3)

sixth sixième (3.4)

sixty soixante (P.3)

skating le patinage (5.3)

to **ski** skier (1.1) **ski jacket** un anorak (4.2)

skiing le ski (5.3)

skirt une jupe (4.3)

to **sleep** *dormir (6.5)

slender mince (4.4)

slim mince (4.4)

smart: very smart génial (*pl.* géniaux) (7.2)

snobbish snob (7.2)

snowing: it's snowing il neige (P.6)

so alors (1.5) **so what?** et alors? (1.5) **so-so** comme ci, comme ça (P.2)

soccer le foot(ball) (3.2)

socks des chaussettes *f.* (4.2)

soda: lemon soda la limonade (5.2)

some des (2.4) du, de la, de l' (5.2) en (8.4)

somebody quelqu'un (de) (7.4)

someone quelqu'un (de) (7.4)

something quelque chose (de) (7.4)

son un fils (3.3)

sore throat: to have a sore throat avoir mal à la gorge (6.1)

soup la soupe (5.2)

Spain l'Espagne *f.* (2.4)

Spanish espagnol (2.4)

to **speak** parler (1.1)

to **spend** dépenser (4.1) (*time*) passer (4.5)

spoon une cuillère (8.5)

sport un sport (3.2)

spring: in the spring au printemps (P.6) **this spring** ce printemps (4.2)

stadium un stade (3.1)

stage la scène (8.1)

stamp un timbre (3.5)

to **start** commencer (6.3)

to **stay** rester (3.1)

stingy radin (7.4)

stockings des bas *m.* (4.3)

stomach un ventre (6.1)

stomachache: to have a stomachache avoir mal au ventre (6.1)

store un magasin (4.1) **department store** un grand magasin (4.1)

storekeeper un marchand, une marchande (4.5)

story une histoire (7.5)

strange étrange (7.2)

strawberries des fraises *f.* (8.4)

string beans des •haricots *m.* (8.4)

student (*high school*) un (une) élève, (*college*) un étudiant, une étudiante (2.1)

to **study** étudier (1.2) **to study + *subject*** *faire de + *subject* (5.4)

stupid bête (2.3) idiot (7.2) stupide (8.2)

style le style (4.3) **in style** chic (4.2)

subway un métro (5.5)

to **succeed** réussir (4.1)

successful: to be successful (with) réussir (6.4)

sugar le sucre (8.4)

to **suggest** proposer (6.5)

suit un costume (4.3)

summer: in (the) summer en été (P.6) **this summer** cet été (4.2)

Sunday dimanche *m.* (P.5)

sunglasses des lunettes *f.* de soleil (3.1)

supper le dîner (8.5)   **to have (eat) supper** dîner (8.5)
sure bien sûr (1.2)
surely sûrement (5.5)
sweater un pull (pull-over) (4.2)
to swim nager (1.4)
swimming la natation (5.3)
swimming pool une piscine (3.1)
swimsuit un maillot de bain (4.2)
Swiss suisse (2.4)
Switzerland la Suisse (2.4)

t

table une table (6.2)
to take *prendre (5.5)   **to take + *time*** *mettre (6.4)   **to take a drive** faire une promenade (en voiture) (5.5)   **to take a trip** faire un voyage (5.4)   **to take a walk** faire une promenade (à pied) (5.5)   **to take along** amener (6.5)   **to take seconds** *reprendre (8.4)   **to take the bus, the subway** . . . prendre le bus, le métro... (5.5)
to talk parler (1.1)   **to talk about** discuter (7.4)
tall grand (2.1)
tea le thé (5.2)
teacher un professeur (2.1)
team une équipe (6.3)
tee shirt un tee-shirt (4.2)
teeth les dents *f.* (6.1)
telephone un téléphone (6.2)
television set un téléviseur (2.2)
to tell *dire (7.5)   **to tell (about)** raconter (6.3)
temperature la température (P.6) la fièvre (6.1)   **what's the temperature?** quelle température fait-il? (P.6)
ten dix (P.3)
tenth dixième (3.4)
terrific fantastique, formidable, sensationnel (2.2)
than que (4.3)
thank you merci (P.3)
that que (3.5) ce, cet, cette; ces (4.2) cela (8.1)   **because of that** pour cela (8.1)   **for that reason** pour cela (8.1)

that is voilà, c'est (P.1)   **that's bad** c'est mal (2.5)   **that's enough!** ça suffit! (7.5)   **that's good (fine)** c'est bien (2.5)   **that's great!** c'est magnifique! (1.1)   **that's it (right)** c'est ça (2.1)   **that's too bad!** c'est dommage! (1.1)   **who is that?** qui est-ce? (P.1)
the le, la, l' (2.1) les (2.4)
theater un théâtre (3.1)   **movie theater** un cinéma (3.1)
theatrical house la salle (8.1)
their leur, leurs (3.4)
them eux, elles (2.5) les (7.2)   **(to) them** leur (7.4)
then alors (1.5) ensuite (6.2)   **well then** alors (1.5)
there là (1.5) y (8.3)   **over there** là-bas (1.5)   **that . . . over there** ce . . .-là (4.2)
there is (are) il y a (2.4)
there is (are) . . . left il reste (8.5)   **there's** voilà (P.1)   **what is there?** qu'est-ce qu'il y a? (8.5)
therefore donc (8.5)
these ces (4.2)   **these are** ce sont (2.4)
they ils, elles (1.2) on (4.5)   **they are** ce sont (2.4)
thin mince (4.4)   **to get thin** maigrir (4.1)
thing une chose (6.3)
to think penser (3.5)
third troisième (3.4)
thirsty: to be thirsty avoir soif (4.4)
thirteen treize (P.3)
thirty trente (P.3)   **3:30** trois heures et demie (P.4)
this ce, cet, cette; ces (4.2)   **this is** voici (P.1)
those ces (4.2)   **those are** ce sont (2.4)
thousand mille (4.2)
three trois (P.3)
throat la gorge (6.1)   **to have a sore throat** avoir mal à la gorge (6.1)
through: to go through passer par (6.5)
Thursday jeudi *m.* (P.5)
ticket un billet (6.4)

tie une cravate (4.3)
time: at the same time ensemble (6.1)   **at what time?** à quelle heure? (P.4)   **for a long time** longtemps (6.3)   **from time to time** de temps en temps (8.3)   **to waste one's time** perdre son temps (6.3)   **what time is it?** quelle heure est-il? (P.4)
timid timide (8.2)
tired fatigué (4.4)
to à (1.1) chez (3.2) (*a country*) au, aux, en (4.5)   **to, in order to** pour (6.2)   **to . . .'s (house)** chez... (3.2)   **to class** en classe (3.1)   **to (the pharmacist's)** chez (le pharmacien) (4.5)   **to whom** à qui (1.5)
today aujourd'hui (P.5)
together ensemble (6.1)
tomato une tomate (8.4)
tomorrow demain (P.5)   **tomorrow (morning, afternoon, evening)** demain (matin, après-midi, soir) (4.2)
tonight ce soir, cette nuit (4.2)
too aussi (1.1) trop (3.3) trop de (8.2)   **me too** moi aussi (P.2)   **(that's) too bad!** (c'est) dommage! (1.1)   **too much** trop (3.3) trop de (8.2)
tooth une dent (6.1)
town une ville (3.1)   **in town** en ville (1.5)
tragedy un drame (8.5)
train un train (5.5)   **to go by train** aller en train (5.5)
transistor radio un transistor (2.2)
translator un (une) interprète (7.1)
to travel voyager (1.4)
trip: to take a trip faire un voyage (5.4)
true vrai (2.5) véritable (8.5)
truth la vérité (7.5)
Tuesday mardi *m.* (P.5)
turn: to turn on *mettre (6.4)   **to turn red** rougir (7.3)
TV set un téléviseur (2.2)
twelfth douzième (3.4)
twelve douze (P.3)
twenty vingt (P.3)
two deux (P.3)

u

uh . . . euh... **(P.6)**
uncle un oncle **(3.3)**
under sous **(8.3)**
to **understand** *comprendre **(5.5)**
unfortunately malheureuse-
    ment **(8.2)** hélas **(8.4)**
United States les États-Unis *m.*
    (2.4)
until jusqu'à **(6.5)**
up: to go up monter **(6.5)**
us nous **(2.5)** **(to) us** nous
    (7.1)
to **use** utiliser **(8.5)**
useful utile **(7.5)**
useless inutile **(7.5)**

v

vacation les vacances *f.* **(3.3)**
    on vacation en vacances **(1.5)**
vegetables les légumes *m.* **(8.4)**
very très **(1.1)** **very much**
    beaucoup **(1.3)** beaucoup
    de **(8.2)**
vinegar le vinaigre **(8.4)**
violent violent **(5.3)**
violin un violon **(3.2)**
to **visit** (*place*) visiter **(1.1)** (*peo-
    ple*) rendre visite à **(7.4)**
volleyball le volley(ball) **(3.2)**

w

to **wait (for)** attendre **(4.5)**
waiter un garçon **(7.1)**
waitress une serveuse **(7.1)**
to **walk** marcher **(2.2)** aller à
    pied **(5.5)** **to take a walk**
    faire une promenade (à pied)
    (5.5)
to **want** désirer **(1.4)** avoir envie
    de **(4.4)** *vouloir **(8.1)**
    to want to vouloir bien **(8.1)**
warm chaud **(4.2)** **to be
    (feel) warm** avoir chaud **(4.4)**
to **waste** perdre **(4.5)** **to waste
    one's time** perdre son temps
    (6.3)
watch une montre **(2.2)**
to **watch** regarder **(1.4)**
water l'eau *f.* **(5.2)** **mineral
    water** l'eau minérale **(5.2)**
way une façon, une manière
    (8.2) **in a way** d'une façon,
    d'une manière **(8.2)**

no way! pas question! **(3.5)**
we nous **(1.3)** on **(4.5)**
to **wear** porter **(4.2)**
**weather: how (what) is the
    weather?** quel temps fait-il?
    (P.6) **it's . . . weather** il
    fait... **(P.6)**
Wednesday mercredi *m.* **(P.5)**
week une semaine **(P.5)** **this
    week** cette semaine **(4.2)**
weekend: this weekend ce
    week-end **(4.2)**
weight: to gain weight grossir
    (4.1) **to lose weight**
    maigrir **(4.1)**
well bien **(1.1)** **I'm/every-
    thing's (very) well** ça va (très)
    bien **(P.2)** **to be well** être
    bien **(6.1)** **well!** eh bien!
    (2.3) **well then** alors **(1.5)**
well-behaved bien élevé **(7.5)**
what comment? quoi? **(2.1)**
    qu'est-ce que **(4.1)** quel
    (quelle) **(4.2)** **at what
    time?** à quelle heure?
    (P.4) **so what?** et alors?
    (1.5) **what a . . . !** quel
    (quelle)...! **(6.3)** **what
    color?** de quelle couleur?
    (2.2) **what day is it?** quel
    jour est-ce? **(P.5)** **what
    does he/she look like?** com-
    ment est il/elle? **(2.1)**
    what is it? qu'est-ce que
    c'est? **(4.1)** **what is there?**
    qu'est-ce qu'il y a? **(8.5)**
    what time is it? quelle heure
    est-il? **(P.4)** **what's . . .'s
    name?** comment s'appelle...?
    (2.1) **what's he/she like?**
    comment est-il/elle? **(2.1)**
    what's his/her name? com-
    ment s'appelle-t-il/elle?
    (2.1) **what's the matter?**
    qu'est-ce qu'il y a? **(8.5)**
    what's the temperature?
    quelle température fait-il?
    (P.6) **what's the weather?**
    quel temps fait-il? **(P.6)**
    what's this? qu'est-ce que
    c'est? **(4.1)** **what's your
    name?** comment t'appelles-
    tu? **(P.2)**
when quand **(1.3)**
where où **(1.3)**
whew! oh là là **(P.3)**
which quel (quelle) **(4.2)**

while: once in a while de temps
    en temps **(8.3)**
white blanc (blanche) **(2.2)**
who qui **(1.5)** **who is that
    (it)?** qui est-ce? **(P.1)** **who
    likes food** gourmand **(7.3)**
whole day une journée **(7.5)**
whom qui **(1.5)**
whose . . . is it/are they? à qui
    est/sont...? **(3.5)**
why pourquoi **(1.3)**
to **win** gagner **(6.3)**
window une fenêtre **(8.3)**
wine le vin **(5.2)**
winter: in (the) winter en hiver
    (P.6) **this winter** cet hiver
    (4.2)
to **wish** désirer **(1.4)**
with avec **(1.1)** **with whom**
    avec qui **(1.5)**
without sans **(6.4)**
woman une femme, une dame
    (*polite term*) **(2.1)**
to **work** travailler **(1.4)** (*func-
    tion*) marcher **(2.2)**
would: I would like je voudrais
    (8.1)
wow! oh là là **(P.3)**
to **write** *écrire **(7.5)**
wrong faux (fausse) **(2.5)** **to
    be wrong** avoir tort **(4.4)**

y

year l'année *f.* **(P.5)** **this
    year** cette année **(4.2)** **to
    be . . . years old** avoir...ans
    (3.3)
yellow jaune **(2.2)**
yes oui **(P.3)** (*to a negative
    question*) si **(5.2)**
yesterday hier **(6.2)**
you tu, vous **(1.3)** toi **(2.5)**
    on **(4.5)** te, vous **(7.1)**
    and you? et toi? **(P.2)**
    to you te, vous **(7.1)**
young jeune **(3.3)** **young
    people** les jeunes *m.* **(4.2)**
your ton, ta, tes **(3.3)** votre,
    vos **(3.5)** **what's your
    name?** comment t'appelles-tu?
    (P.2)

z

zero zéro **(P.3)** **it's 0°** il
    fait zéro **(P.6)**